*new dictionary of the* history of ideas

# EDITORIAL BOARD

# *new dictionary of the* history of ideas

maryanne cline horowitz, editor in chief

volume 6

Taste to Zionism, Index

**CHARLES SCRIBNER'S SONS**
*An imprint of Thomson Gale, a part of The Thomson Corporation*

Detroit • New York • San Francisco • San Diego • New Haven, Conn. • Waterville, Maine • London • Munich

**New Dictionary of the History of Ideas**
**Maryanne Cline Horowitz, Editor in Chief**

**LIBRARY OF CONGRESS CATALOGING-IN-PUBLICATION DATA**

New dictionary of the history of ideas / edited by Maryanne Cline Horowitz.
    p. cm.
    Includes bibliographical references and index.
    ISBN 0-684-31377-4 (set hardcover : alk. paper) — ISBN 0-684-31378-2 (v. 1) — ISBN 0-684-31379-0 (v. 2) — ISBN 0-684-31380-4 (v. 3) — ISBN 0-684-31381-2 (v. 4) — ISBN 0-684-31382-0 (v. 5) — ISBN 0-684-31383-9 (v. 6) — ISBN 0-684-31452-5 (e-book)
    1. Civilization—History—Dictionaries. 2. Intellectual life—History—Dictionaries.
    I. Horowitz, Maryanne Cline, 1945–

CB9.N49 2005
903—dc22                                                    2004014731

This title is also available as an e-book.
ISBN 0-684-31452-5
Contact your Thomson Gale sales representative for ordering information.

Printed in the United States of America
10 9 8 7 6 5 4 3 2

# CONTENTS

# EDITORIAL AND PRODUCTION STAFF

**Project Editors**
Mark LaFlaur, Scot Peacock, Jennifer Wisinski

**Editorial Support**
Kelly Baiseley, Andrew Claps, Alja Collar, Mark Drouillard,
Kenneth Mondschein, Sarah Turner, Ken Wachsberger,
Rachel Widawsky, Christopher Verdesi

**Art Editor**
Scot Peacock

**Chief Manuscript Editor**
Georgia S. Maas

**Manuscript Editors**
Jonathan G. Aretakis, John Barclay, Sylvia Cannizzaro,
Melissa A. Dobson, Ted Gilley, Gretchen Gordon,
Ellen Hawley, Archibald Hobson, Elizabeth B. Inserra,
Jean Fortune Kaplan, Christine Kelley, John Krol,
Julia Penelope, Richard Rothschild, David E. Salamie,
Linda Sanders, Alan Thwaits, Jane Marie Todd

**Proofreaders**
Beth Fhaner, Carol Holmes, Melodie Monahan,
Laura Specht Patchkofsky, Hilary White

**Cartographer**
XNR Productions, Madison, Wisconsin

**Caption Writer**
Shannon Kelly

**Indexer**
Cynthia Crippen, AEIOU, Inc.

**Design**
Jennifer Wahi

**Imaging**
Dean Dauphinais, Lezlie Light, Mary Grimes

**Permissions**
Margaret Abendroth, Peggie Ashlevitz, Lori Hines

**Compositor**
GGS Information Services, York, Pennsylvania

**Manager, Composition**
Mary Beth Trimper

**Assistant Manager, Composition**
Evi Seoud

**Manufacturing**
Wendy Blurton

**Senior Development Editor**
Nathalie Duval

**Editorial Director**
John Fitzpatrick

**Publisher**
Frank Menchaca

# READER'S GUIDE

*This Reader's Guide was compiled by the editors to provide a systematic outline of the contents of the* New Dictionary of the History of Ideas, *thereby offering teachers, scholars, and the general reader a way to organize their reading according to their preferences. The Reader's Guide is divided into four sections: Communication of Ideas, Geographical Areas, Chronological Periods, and Liberal Arts Disciplines and Professions, as indicated in the outline below.*

## COMMUNICATION OF IDEAS

**Introduction to History of Communication of Ideas**

**Communication Media**

## GEOGRAPHICAL AREAS

**Global Entries**

**Africa**

**Asia**

**Europe**

**Middle East**

**North America**

**Latin and South America**

## CHRONOLOGICAL PERIODS

**Ancient**

**Dynastic (400 C.E.–1400 C.E.)**

**Early Modern (1400–1800 C.E.)**

**Modern (1800–1945)**

**Contemporary**

## LIBERAL ARTS DISCIPLINES AND PROFESSIONS

**Fine Arts**

**Humanities**

**Social Sciences**

**Sciences**

**Professions**

**Multidisciplinary Practices**

**Especially Interdisciplinary Entries**

## COMMUNICATION OF IDEAS

This category is the newest aspect of the *New Dictionary of the History of Ideas*; cultural studies, communications studies, and cultural history are moving the disciplines in this direction.

**Introduction to History of Communication of Ideas**

The following entries focus on the media humans have used to communicate with one another.

Absolute Music
Aesthetics: Asia
Architecture: Overview
Architecture: Asia
Arts: Overview
Astronomy, Pre-Columbian and Latin American
Bilingualism and Multilingualism
Borders, Borderlands, and Frontiers, Global
Calendar
Cinema
City, The: The City as a Cultural Center
City, The: The City as Political Center
Communication of Ideas: Africa and Its Influence
Communication of Ideas: Asia and Its Influence
Communication of Ideas: Europe and Its Influence
Communication of Ideas: Middle East and Abroad
Communication of Ideas: Orality and Advent of Writing
Communication of Ideas: Southeast Asia
Communication of Ideas: The Americas and Their Influence
Consumerism
Cultural Revivals
Cultural Studies
Dance
Diffusion, Cultural
Dress
Dualism
Education: Asia, Traditional and Modern
Education: Global Education
Emotions
Experiment
Garden
Gesture
Humor
Iconography
Images, Icons, and Idols
Japanese Philosophy, Japanese Thought
Language and Linguistics
Language, Linguistics, and Literacy
Learning and Memory, Contemporary Views
Mathematics
Media, History of
Metaphor
Migration: United States
Modernity: Africa
Museums
Music, Anthropology of

## Communication Media

This is a listing of the types of historical evidence the author used in writing the entry. While entries in the original Dictionary of the History of Ideas were to a great extent the history of texts, the entries in the New Dictionary of the History of Ideas are generally the cultural history of ideas, making use of the records of oral communication, visual communication, and communication through practices, as well as the history of texts, in order to show the impact of the idea on a wide variety of people.

### ORAL

The selective list below contains the entries that give the most coverage to historical examples of the oral transmission and transformation of ideas.

COMMUNICATION THROUGH HIGH TECHNOL-
OGY MEDIA (radio, television, film, computer, etc.)

## VISUAL

Each of the following entries in the *NDHI* either evocatively describes ideas, includes a visual image of an idea, or provides historical examples of societies visually transmitting and transforming ideas.

Scientific Revolution
Sexuality: Overview
Sexuality: Sexual Orientation
Shinto
Slavery
Social History, U.S.
Sophists, The
Sport
Subjectivism
Superstition
Surrealism
Symbolism
Syncretism
Taste
Terror
Text/Textuality
Theater and Performance
Theodicy
Third Cinema
Third World Literature
Toleration
Totalitarianism
Totems
Trade
Tragedy and Comedy
Treaty
Untouchability: Menstrual Taboos
Utilitarianism
Utopia
Victorianism
Virtual Reality
Visual Culture
Visual Order to Organizing Collections
Volunteerism, U.S.
War
War and Peace in the Arts
Westernization: Southeast Asia
Witchcraft
Witchcraft, African Studies of
Women and Femininity in U.S. Popular Culture
Women's History: Africa
World Systems Theory, Latin America
Yin and Yang

## PRACTICES

Most of the entries in the *NDHI* discuss how specific societies habituated people to specific ideas. This selective list includes the entries on schools of thought and practice, religions, and political movements, as well as the entries on distinctive practices.

Abolitionism
Afropessimism
Agnosticism
Alchemy: China
Alchemy: Europe and the Middle East
Anarchism
Ancestor Worship
Animism
Anticolonialism: Africa
Anticolonialism: Latin America
Anticolonialism: Middle East
Anticolonialism: Southeast Asia
Anticommunism: Latin America
Antifeminism

Anti-Semitism: Overview
Anti-Semitism: Islamic Anti-Semitism
Apartheid
Aristotelianism
Asceticism: Hindu and Buddhist Asceticism
Asceticism: Western Asceticism
Astrology: Overview
Astrology: China
Atheism
Avant-Garde: Militancy
Behaviorism
Black Consciousness
Buddhism
Bureaucracy
Bushido
Cannibalism
Capitalism: Overview
Capitalism: Africa
Cartesianism
Character
Chicano Movement
Chinese Thought
Christianity: Overview
Christianity: Asia
Cinema
Citizenship: Naturalization
Civil Disobedience
Classicism
Classification of Arts and Sciences, Early Modern
Colonialism: Africa
Colonialism: Latin America
Colonialism: Southeast Asia
Communication of Ideas: Orality and Advent of Writing
Communism: Europe
Communism: Latin America
Communitarianism in African Thought
Computer Science
Confucianism
Conservatism
Constitutionalism
Cosmopolitanism
Creationism
Critical Theory
Cultural Capital
Cultural Studies
Cynicism
Dance
Daoism
Deism
Dialogue and Dialectics: Socratic
Dialogue and Dialectics: Talmudic
Discrimination
Diversity
Eclecticism
Ecumenism
Empire and Imperialism: Overview
Empire and Imperialism: Americas
Empire and Imperialism: Asia
Empire and Imperialism: Europe
Empire and Imperialism: Middle East
Empire and Imperialism: United States
Empiricism
Epicureanism
Equality: Overview
Etiquette

## TEXTUAL

Every entry in the *New Dictionary of the History of Ideas* used texts. The following is a list of entries that focused mainly on the history of a succession of texts. Each academic discipline has a succession of major authors with whom later practitioners of the discipline build upon and respond to creatively. The historian of a discipline—such as the history of political philosophy, literary history, or the history of science—considers the responses of thinkers and practitioners of a discipline to the major earlier texts in the discipline. In tracing the origin, development, and transformation of an idea, the historian of ideas considers thinkers' responses to texts from a variety of disciplines.

## GEOGRAPHICAL AREAS

### Global Entries

**New Dictionary of the History of Ideas**

**New Dictionary of the History of Ideas**

## CHRONOLOGICAL PERIODS

This section is divided according to five periods in world history: Ancient, Dynastic, Early Modern, Modern, and Contemporary. Use this section together with the section on Geographical Areas.

### Ancient (before 400 C.E.)

ENTRIES FOCUSED ON THE PERIOD

ENTRIES WITH EXAMPLES FROM BEFORE 400 C.E.

Generally the examples in this category are from the ancient Middle East, Europe, or Asia.

New Dictionary of the History of Ideas

## Modern (1800–1945)
### ENTRIES FOCUSED ON THE PERIOD

ENTRIES WITH EXAMPLES FROM THE PERIOD
1800–1945

**Contemporary**

Jihad
Liberation Theology
Liberty
Life
Linguistic Turn
Literary History
Logic and Philosophy of Mathematics, Modern
Maoism
Marxism: Overview
Marxism: Asia
Marxism: Latin America
Media, History of
Modernization
Modernization Theory
Nationalism: Overview
Nationalism: Africa
Nationalism: Cultural Nationalism
Nationalism: Middle East
Neocolonialism
Neoliberalism
Nuclear Age
Orientalism: African and Black Orientalism
Pan-Africanism
Pan-Arabism
Pan-Asianism
Pan-Islamism
Pan-Turkism
Paradigm
Parties, Political
Personhood in African Thought
Phenomenology
Philosophies: Feminist, Twentieth-Century
Poetry and Poetics
Populism: Latin America
Populism: United States
Positivism
Postcolonial Studies
Postcolonial Theory and Literature
Postmodernism
Pragmatism
Presentism
Privatization
Protest, Political
Psychoanalysis
Psychology and Psychiatry
Quantum
Queer Theory
Realism: Africa
Relativism
Relativity
Science Fiction
Segregation
Sexual Harassment
Sexuality: Sexual Orientation
Sociability in African Thought
Social Darwinism
Socialisms, African
Structuralism and Poststructuralism: Overview
Structuralism and Poststructuralism: Anthropology
Subjectivism
Technology
Terrorism, Middle East
Text/Textuality
Theater and Performance
Third Cinema

Third World
Totalitarianism
Virtual Reality
Virtue Ethics
War
Westernization: Africa
Westernization: Southeast Asia
Witchcraft
Womanism
Women and Femininity in U.S. Popular Culture
Women's Studies
Zionism

ENTRIES WITH EXAMPLES FROM THE PERIOD
SINCE 1945 (especially since the 1970s)
Absolute Music
Aesthetics: Africa
Aesthetics: Asia
Aesthetics: Europe and the Americas
Africa, Idea of
Afrocentricity
Afropessimism
Agnosticism
Algebras
Alienation
Altruism
Ambiguity
America
Analytical Philosophy
Anarchism
Animism
Anthropology
Antifeminism
Anti-Semitism: Overview
Architecture: Overview
Architecture: Africa
Arts: Overview
Arts: Africa
Asceticism: Western Asceticism
Asian-American Ideas (Cultural Migration)
Assimilation
Atheism
Authenticity: Africa
Authoritarianism: Overview
Authoritarianism: East Asia
Authoritarianism: Latin America
Authority
Autobiography
Autonomy
Avant-Garde: Overview
Aztlán
Barbarism and Civilization
Beauty and Ugliness
Behaviorism
Bilingualism and Multilingualism
Biography
Biology
Body, The
Bushido
Calculation and Computation
Cannibalism
Capitalism: Overview
Cartesianism
Casuistry
Causality
Causation

## LIBERAL ARTS DISCIPLINES AND PROFESSIONS

This section is in accord with the university divisions of the Liberal Arts into Fine Arts, Humanities, Social Sciences, and Sciences and the graduate programs of the professions of Law, Medicine, and Engineering. The sample of Interdisciplinary Programs are listed under their most common university grouping. For example, Fine Arts includes Performance Arts; Social Sciences includes Women's Studies and Gender Studies, as well as Ethnic Studies; Sciences includes Ecology and Geology, as well as Computer Sciences; Humanities includes programs of Communication, Language, and Linguistics. Meanwhile, the growth of interdisciplinary programs reflects the increasing overlap between studies listed under the labels of Fine Arts, Humanities, Social Sciences, and Sciences. A discipline or interdisciplinary program only appears once, but an entry may appear under the several disciplines and interdisciplinary programs that influenced the scholarship of the article. Titles that appear in bold indicate entries that are especially suited as a introduction to the discipline.

Under the category Multidisciplinary Practices, there are entries on the many methods, techniques, theories, and approaches that have spread across the disciplines. The Multidisciplinary Practices help explain the contemporary trend of interdisciplinarity for which the history of ideas has long been known. At the end of this Reader's Guide is a listing of a number of entries that overlap three of the four divisions and a listing of entries that overlap all four divisions.

Utilitarianism
Victorianism
Virtual Reality
Volunteerism, U.S.
Westernization: Middle East
Westernization: Southeast Asia
Wisdom, Human
Witchcraft
Witchcraft, African Studies of
Yin and Yang
Yoga

**Humanities**
  COMMUNICATION, LANGUAGE, AND LINGUISTICS
    Aesthetics: Africa
    Aesthetics: Asia
    Africa, Idea of
    Afrocentricity
    Agnosticism
    Algebras
    Americanization, U.S.
    Analytical Philosophy
    Anthropology
    Anticolonialism: Africa
    Asceticism: Hindu and Buddhist Asceticism
    Asceticism: Western Asceticism
    Astronomy, Pre-Columbian and Latin American
    Authenticity: Africa
    Avant-Garde: Overview
    Avant-Garde: Militancy
    Aztlán
    Barbarism and Civilization
    Beauty and Ugliness
    Behaviorism
    Bilingualism and Multilingualism
    Body, The
    Borders, Borderlands, and Frontiers, Global
    Buddhism
    Calculation and Computation
    Calendar
    Cannibalism
    Casuistry
    Censorship
    Chinese Thought
    Cinema
    Civil Disobedience
    **Classification of Arts and Sciences, Early Modern**
    Colonialism: Southeast Asia
    Communication of Ideas: Africa and Its Influence
    Communication of Ideas: The Americas and Their Influence
    Communication of Ideas: Asia and Its Influence
    Communication of Ideas: Europe and Its Influence
    Communication of Ideas: Middle East and Abroad
    Communication of Ideas: Orality and Advent of Writing
    Communication of Ideas: Southeast Asia
    Computer Science
    Consumerism
    Context
    Continental Philosophy
    Cosmopolitanism
    Creolization, Caribbean
    Critical Theory
    Cultural Capital

    Cultural History
    Cultural Revivals
    Cultural Studies
    Cynicism
    Dance
    Democracy
    Determinism
    Dialogue and Dialectics: Socratic
    Diasporas: Jewish Diaspora
    Dictatorship in Latin America
    Diffusion, Cultural
    Discrimination
    Diversity
    Dream
    Dress
    Ecumenism
    Education: Asia, Traditional and Modern
    Empire and Imperialism: Asia
    Empire and Imperialism: Europe
    Empire and Imperialism: United States
    Empiricism
    Encyclopedism
    Epistemology: Ancient
    Epistemology: Early Modern
    Epistemology: Modern
    Ethnicity and Race: Africa
    Ethnicity and Race: Anthropology
    Ethnicity and Race: Islamic Views
    Etiquette
    Eurocentrism
    Everyday Life
    Examination Systems, China
    Extirpation
    Fallacy, Logical
    Feminism: Overview
    Feminism: Chicana Feminisms
    Fetishism: Overview
    Fetishism: Fetishism in Literature and Cultural Studies
    Feudalism, European
    Formalism
    Gender: Gender in the Middle East
    Gender in Art
    Geometry
    **Gesture**
    Globalization: Asia
    Globalization: General
    Greek Science
    Harmony
    Hegemony
    Hermeneutics
    Hinduism
    History, Economic
    History, Idea of
    Humanism: Africa
    Humanism: Chinese Conception of
    Humanism: Europe and the Middle East
    Humanism: Renaissance
    Humanity: African Thought
    Human Rights: Overview
    Idealism
    Ideas, History of
    Identity: Identity of Persons
    Identity, Multiple: Overview
    Identity, Multiple: Jewish Multiple Identity
    Indigenismo

READER'S GUIDE

## Social Sciences

**New Dictionary of the History of Ideas**

**New Dictionary of the History of Ideas**

## Multidisciplinary Practices

The *New Dictionary of the History of Ideas* has many entries that discuss the methods by which scholars and researchers pursue knowledge. The entries below discuss approaches, methods, and practices that have influenced many disciplines.

**Especially Interdisciplinary Entries**

The most interdisciplinary entries synthesized knowledge by using the methods and focusing on the topics of practitioners of several disciplines. Very few entries listed below are in only one division. Common pairs for the history of ideas are social sciences and humanities, social sciences and sciences, and humanities and sciences. In the early twenty-first century there is generally a recognition of the common overlap of the social sciences with the humanities; social scientists may take ethical and literary factors into consideration and humanists may incorporate societal contexts into their work. The presence of psychology in the sciences, as well as the quantitative nature of some social sciences work, creates an overlap of social sciences with sciences. Another interesting overlap is between humanities and sciences—topics that in antiquity were treated as philosophy or religion are now investigated by those following scientific methods.

# T

**TASTE.** We tend to use the word *taste* in two different ways. First, to refer to the ability to judge a thing correctly, usually (but not always) a work of art from an aesthetic point of view. Second, we use the word to refer to a particular set of aesthetic preferences, and given the most popular sense of this second usage, we understand that one person's set of preferences may differ from another person's set. In this article, *taste* refers to taste in the first sense, and *personal taste* refers to it in the second. "Personal taste" does not imply that one person's set of aesthetic preferences cannot be shared by others.

## Taste

Taste in this first sense, by which we mean the ability to correctly judge aesthetic objects and events, has a long history, but happily that history is fairly easy to trace and fairly easy to contextualize. We will start in ancient Greece. In those philosophic traditions that begin with Greece, Aristotle (384–322 B.C.E.) is the first person who offers us a formula for beauty. If a thing possesses a certain set of properties—objective properties that anyone with working senses and a passing familiarity with those properties can easily pick out—then that thing is beautiful. Aristotle said that an object is beautiful if it is ordered, symmetrical, and definite, and if it demonstrates each of these virtues to a high degree. This analysis we call "formal," because it focuses on the presence in the object of certain aesthetic properties that have to do with the form (as distinguished from the content) of the object. If a set of criteria can be discovered, the presence of which will ensure that an object is beautiful, and the absence of which will ensure that it is not, then through this the correctness of aesthetic judgments can be established.

Formalism, as an objective approach to aesthetic judgment, has been very popular. We find in St. Augustine of Hippo (354–430) a formalist account of beauty: for an object to be beautiful is for it to exhibit unity, number, equality, proportion, and order, with unity as the most basic notion. And in the work of St. Thomas Aquinas (1224–1274), we find a formal account of beauty, which rests on three conditions: integrity or perfection, due proportion or harmony, and brightness or clarity. We find examples of formalists in eighteenth-century Britain. The third earl of Shaftesbury (Anthony Ashley Cooper, 1671–1713) believed that so long as one was disinterested in attitude, one's judgment that an object was beautiful was correct as long as the object exhibits "unity in multiplicity." Francis Hutcheson (1694–1746) believed that, given a disinterested attitude, if an object exhibits "uniformity amongst variety," that object is beautiful. The essayist and statesman Joseph Addison (1672–1719) believed that an

object was worthy of positive aesthetic judgment if it exhibited greatness and uncommonness. And jumping to the twentieth century, we find formalist accounts of aesthetic merit (though not explicitly about beauty per se) in the work of G. E. Moore (1873–1958) ("organic unity") and Clive Bell (1881–1964) ("significant form").

While theorists such as Shaftesbury and Hutcheson include clear formalist elements in their theories of aesthetic merit, they also stand at the beginning of a tradition of philosophers of aesthetics sometimes referred to as "taste theorists." The taste theorists are found, generally, in eighteenth-century Britain, and they begin as a bridge between objective formalist and subjective accounts of beauty. Although individual subjectivity now begins to appear in accounts of aesthetic judgment, it is important to note that these accounts were not antirealist (antirealism being the position that judgments about aesthetic objects are neither true nor false). Quite to the contrary, theorists like Shaftesbury and Hutcheson were still aesthetic realists (realism being the position that there are real answers to questions of aesthetic merit, that judgments about aesthetic objects really are true or false). In order to access the formal conditions of beauty, Shaftesbury and Hutcheson said that the attender must put himself or herself into a proper frame of mind. From this proper perspective—from the proper exercise of one's faculty of taste—one could judge correctly whether a thing is beautiful or not. The inclusion in their theories of the formal elements of "unity in multiplicity" and "uniformity amongst variety" were meant as explanations for why the exercise of one's taste would result in aesthetic enjoyment and correct judgment, but it is the exercise of taste that, in their theories, is logically prior: one exercises taste; one enjoys and judges positively; and notes subsequently that this enjoyment and positive judgment are occasioned by the presence of certain objective, formal features. Shaftesbury and Hutcheson are joined in their theories—which mix objective features of objects with subjective features of judgment—by others, most notably Joseph Addison (1672–1719), Archibald Alison (1757–1839), Lord Kames (Henry Home, 1696–1782), and Alexander Gerard (1728–1795).

The eighteenth-century British taste theorists are, in some sense, a product of their times. There are three items that motivate them. First, they rejected as insufficient pure formalist, objectivist theories of beauty. Second, they were inspired by empiricism, and they sought to connect knowledge with the focus on the senses as the medium through which reality was taken in. In aesthetic theory, this can been seen in the move from the Platonism apparent in theories like Shaftesbury's to

*Les Demoiselles d'Avignon* (1907) by Pablo Picasso. **Oil on canvas.** Theories of taste have had a long history. In ancient Greece Aristotle claimed that order and proportion contributed to beauty. Twentieth-century theorists found distinctly asymmetrical works such as those of Picasso to have visual merit as well.  AP/WIDE WORLD PHOTOS

the almost physiological tone of theories such as those of Hutcheson and Edmund Burke (1729–1797). Third, with political theorists in Britain like Thomas Hobbes (1588–1679) and John Locke (1632–1704) came a new focus on the authority and autonomy of the individual. This celebration of the individual, his rights, and the dominion and prerogative of his judgments, can be seen in the fundamental premises

upon which David Hume (1711–1776) and Immanuel Kant (1724–1804) build their theories of aesthetic judgment.

Although formalist accounts persist into the twentieth century, they reach a point of diminished popularity at the end of the eighteenth century when mixed objective-subjective accounts, such as those offered by Shaftesbury and Hutcheson, are replaced in popularity by more purely subjective accounts offered by, to name the two most influential, Hume and Kant. Instead of focusing on the aesthetic object, both of these theorists focus on the aesthetic attender. Instead of offering objective-criteria formulae for what makes an object aesthetically good or beautiful, they focus exclusively on the qualities of the attender that make him or her a good judge.

Hume believed in the indisputability of particular taste and the sovereignty of the individual judge, but he also believed that "amidst all the variety and caprice of tastes, there are certain general principles of approbation and blame." For Hume, an object is beautiful if and only if it provokes aesthetic sentiment in appropriately disposed competent critics, which he calls "true judges." True judges have the following traits: (1) serenity of mind (mentioned earlier than the other five), (2) delicacy of taste, (3) they are well practiced, (4) they are versed in comparison between objects, (5) they are free from prejudice, and (6) they have good sense (i.e., their senses work very well).

Kant's focus was similar, although the theoretical details are rather different. Kant's means of establishing the worthiness of aesthetic judgment focuses somewhat less on the individual than Hume's, and more on what is common about judgment. It is from the dual vantage point of the authority of the subject's judgment and the call to universality of judgment—that we expect and even demand commonality in judgment—that Kant develops his view. Kant thought that the key to securing this universality was twofold: first, we recognize that each person has basically the same "common sense" for recognizing beauty in objects, and that aesthetic judgment is not merely a matter of sentiment but a matter of free play between the understanding and the imagination. Second, it is important for the judge to be properly disposed to making a correct judgment, and the proper disposition is for the judge to be disinterested—to consider the object/event for its own sake alone, without regard for any relation it bears to anything else, including personal interests. Given disinterest on the part of the judge, and given that we all have similar faculties for understanding the world—particularly, the formal structures and purposefulness of the phenomenal world—we would all judge similarly, at least with regard to individual, particular aesthetic judgments.

Hume and Kant opened the door for other subjective accounts of aesthetic goodness, but the real investment in subjective accounts came in the twentieth century and was provided by an assortment of aestheticians, Frank Sibley (1923–1996) being perhaps the most famous, who argue that reductions of evaluative aesthetic claims will never result in arrangements of objective properties. Sibley first identified aesthetic concepts and aesthetic terms as ones that necessarily include taste in their application. In justifying the use of aesthetic terms, however, we naturally seek out a basis that does not refer to taste. We look for the objective basis for our use of such terms, and we commonly expect to find such bases. Unfortunately, this only flows in one direction. While we may naturally look to non-aesthetic features to ground our ascriptions of aesthetic ones,

we cannot, no matter how full an account we offer, ever say that, due to the presence of given nonaesthetic features an aesthetic feature must certainly be present. We would, says Sibley, be suspicious of anyone who says that we can create a rule that states that a certain aesthetic feature can be created by inserting certain nonaesthetic ones. We would say that such a person is not exercising taste and, moreover, did not really understand the aesthetic term at issue unless he could correctly apply it in instances where citing the rule was not an option.

This movement, first begun in the latter eighteenth century, but really brought to bloom in the twentieth—twentieth-century formalists notwithstanding—through the work of Sibley and others, is a movement from objective accounts of beauty to subjective ones. The subjective accounts focus on taste, on the attenders or audience members (1) exercising their ability to judge correctly from an aesthetic point of view and (2) finding enjoyment in attending to those aesthetic qualities that properly should ground such enjoyment.

## Personal Taste

The second sense in which the word *taste* is used, what we are calling "personal taste," focuses on particular sets of aesthetic preferences. There is certainly a relationship between taste and personal taste, and we want to explore that a bit later on. For now, consider the nature of the preference that one may exhibit for vanilla ice cream over chocolate, for chicken over fish, for saturated colors over muted ones, and for action-adventure films over romantic comedies. In these matters, it is the rare observer who will assert that there is clearly a correct decision to be made, that one of each pair is clearly to be preferred over the other. Most observers are content to say that these are all simply matters of personal preference. Moreover, there are now many who say that all aesthetic judgments are on a continuum with such exemplars of personal preference. As mentioned earlier, antirealism is the position that there is nothing right or wrong about an aesthetic judgment that refers to anything beyond that judge's preference—that all aesthetic judgment is a matter of personal preference. If one takes such phrases as "beauty is in the eye of the beholder" and "there's no disputing individual taste" out of the realist contexts that the taste theorists had originally envisioned for them, one may understand taste as merely a set of personal preferences, over which external adjudication—or perhaps any adjudication—is inappropriate.

One challenge to this move toward antirealism as a theoretical platform for talking about personal taste is the widespread agreement in judgment forthcoming from certain aesthetic comparisons. Almost no one, on a "blind hearing," prefers Salieri to Mozart, and it is easy to develop a list of such comparisons, each instance of agreement serving as one more bit of inductive evidence in support of aesthetic realism. There is an explanation for this, and it turns on the fact that there are purposes to our aesthetic choices. We mean to invest our attention in those aesthetic experiences that we predict we will find more enjoyable, satisfying, rich, and rewarding. There are few museum or gallery patrons who will spend minutes upon minutes staring at Andy Warhol's *Campbell's Soup Can* or a Marcel Duchamp ready-made. These conceptual works can be taken in quickly, and perhaps fully so. But it is not uncommon to see patrons spend a good deal of time in front of a mature Joseph Mallord William Turner, Paul Cézanne, or Henri Matisse. If the experience one seeks is deep visual satisfaction, one will tend to invest attention in objects that most likely will provide this.

One's personal taste can be understood, then, as a series of past choices and resulting experiences that provide a basis upon which one will make future investment predictions and choices. If one has a rewarding experience listening to a Billie Holiday song, one will most likely seek out more Billie Holiday songs, and it is likely that one will also seek out blues in general. If one has a less than rewarding experience looking at a Jackson Pollock work, then one will probably avoid Pollock in the future, and it may be expected that one may avoid modern art altogether. If one has a good experience with works by Mark Rothko, one may reasonably expect to enjoy the work of Agnes Martin. All of this is based on induction. We find patterns in the world that serve us, that promote survival, flourishing, or simple enjoyment. It is only reasonable that we will follow those patterns and that, to some degree, groups of people who are similar will find similar patterns.

A second challenge, perhaps more intriguing than the first, is the regular phenomenon that with exposure, time, and information, aesthetic preferences tend to grow and develop in fairly predictable ways. The film preferences of freshman students tend to be for very recent works that provide immediate, easy reward. The preferences of students who have taken a few film courses tend to be informed by a much broader temporal span of the film world and tend to focus on films that require some subject-initiated investment of attention, both cognitive and psychological. The preferences of senior level film studies majors (and perhaps their professors) may be seen as bizarre by the aforementioned freshmen, as such preferences may well include silent films, nonnarrative films, and directors like Sergei Eisenstein, Ingmar Bergman, and Federico Fellini. College students commonly move in their musical preferences from rock to jazz and classical, if not giving up the former, at least adding to it the latter. The best explanation for this is that taste grows in regular ways, and once these regularities are identified, taste can be educated: personal taste can grow in sophistication.

We need to be careful here to distinguish between the effects of education as a tool for social or cultural indoctrination and education as a means of facilitating experience, furthering horizons, and encouraging genuine aesthetic enjoyment. It would be a shame and a loss to move a student, through the education of taste, to less aesthetic enjoyment, and there is a danger in declaring that a person's aesthetic preferences are wrong if they do not match some standard or other. This returns us to the authority and autonomy of individual judgment with which the taste theorists wrestled.

One bit of support for the appropriate plurality of personal taste comes from the diversity of aesthetic preferences that follows geographical, ethnic, and even gender identities. The patterns of bright, colorful dress that one may see in the Maya,

the Masai, and the Mongolians are very different from the patterns one sees in mainstream Europe and mainstream North America. Visually, traditional Asian artwork is easily separated from mainstream European and American artwork. One can take this to an even more basic level: the traditional Asian conception (or definition) of the aesthetic property of balance appears to be different from the mainstream European or American definition. If our very definitions of aesthetic properties diverge, yet in both contexts there is a general valuing of, in this case, balance, then the preferences that follow from this will diverge, as well.

Similar sorts of cases of diversity will manifest themselves in comparisons among ethnicities even within a geographical region. Public-space ambient music tends to follow these preferences; the music one hears in shopping centers in one part of the country may differ radically from the music one hears in another part. This is most likely more than simply the management's preferences. The choice in ambient music more likely follows the management's best judgments concerning the sort of music that the likely clientele will enjoy and that will keep them shopping. This is partly a geographical phenomenon, but in many places, can involve ethnic and subcultural considerations, as well.

## The Relationship between Taste and Personal Taste

The recent understanding of taste (as closer to personal taste and away from the more traditional, realist sense of the word) can still be seen as pointing toward greater authority of the judgment of the individual that was one of the motivators of the original taste theorists. If there is ultimately no way to reasonably, authoritatively, or meaningfully adjudicate among divergent particular judgments or among divergent personal tastes as sets of matters of choice, then the eighteenth-century move toward a fuller respect for individual autonomy in aesthetic judgment has brought us to a point where taste gives way to personal taste. If one believes that Hume failed in his attempt to render consistent the authority of the individual with the call to commonality in judgment, and if one rejects Kant's attempt to solve the antinomy of taste ("taste is at the same time subjective and individual yet also universal") and save aesthetic realism where perhaps Hume was unable to, one may believe that, in these failures, the realist version of a singular, correct definition of taste is rightly abandoned. We may see as continuous with the decision between vanilla and chocolate ice cream a preference for Pink Floyd over Beethoven, Albee over Shakespeare, and Pollock over Rembrandt. Still, the recognition of this continuity is not a cause for surrender to the philosophy of "anything goes." As individuals may reasonably be expected to pursue those experiences that they find rewarding, and to make their investments of aesthetic attention based on predictions derived from patterns of past reward, we will continue to see some degree of commonality in personal judgment. The degree to which we see this—however modestly or subtly—will continue to advance culture positively.

*See also* **Aesthetics; Arts; Beauty and Ugliness; Cultural Studies; Objectivity; Subjectivism.**

BIBLIOGRAPHY

Addison, Joseph, and Richard Steele. "On the Pleasures of the Imagination." In *Selections from The Tatler and The Spectator.* Edited by Robert Allen. New York: Holt, Rinehart and Winston, 1957.

Dickie, George. *Evaluating Art.* Philadelphia: Temple University Press, 1988.

Goldman, Alan. "The Education of Taste." *British Journal of Aesthetics* 30 (1990): 105–116.

Hume, David. *Of the Standard of Taste and Other Essays.* Edited by J. W. Lenz. New York: Bobbs-Merrill, 1965.

Hutcheson, Francis. *An Inquiry into the Original of Our Ideas of Beauty and Virtue.* New York: Garland, 1971.

Kant, Immanuel. *Critique of Judgment.* Translated by Werner S. Pluhar. Foreword by Mary J. Gregor. Indianapolis: Hackett, 1987.

Kivy, Peter. "Recent Scholarship and the British Tradition: A Logic of Taste, The First Fifty Years." In *Aesthetics: A Critical Anthology,* edited by G. Dickie, R. Sclafani, and R. Roblin. 2nd ed. New York: St. Martin's, 1989.

Shaftesbury, Anthony Ashley Cooper. *Characteristics of Men, Manners, Opinions, Times.* New York: Bobbs-Merrill, 1964.

Sibley, Frank. "Aesthetic Concepts." *Philosophical Review* 68 (Oct. 1959): 421–450.

*David E. W. Fenner*

**TECHNOLOGY.** Introduced in the first decades of the nineteenth century, the word *technology* signified the pursuit of a science to encompass all the *industrial arts. Mechanical arts,* a term used in medieval and early modern Europe, indicated something different because it included, for example, painting and sculpture. The introduction of the term *technology* corresponded somewhat contemporaneously with the introduction of other key terms for modernity, including *scientist, class, capitalism,* and *socialism.* They all come from a time troubled by the "machinery question," a fundamental topic for both political economists and Romantic authors during the same period. This question was posed as a response to the installation of an endless series of novel machines in newly built textile factories, which seemed to have nurtured a class differentiation between those who were amassing fortunes by owning the machines and those who were barely paid at subsistence level to work in them. Having won a decisive battle against those who defended the old order by crediting land rather than labor as being the source of value, classical political economists were unprepared to challenge the popular assumption of machinery being the source of value. The dramatic change similarly confused the best of the future critics of these economists. A young Karl Marx (1818–1883) assumed that the new machinery, despite the hardships that it imposed on many, inevitably paved the way to a better future society.

The denaturalization of the landscape ensuing from the spread of steam engines overwhelmed the Romantics, who lamented the loss of a better (past) society. Despite their unheard objections, for decades England had used previous "atmospheric" engines for draining mines, with pistons that moved up by the pressure of the steam and down by the

pressure of the atmosphere, in the pattern of the engine that Thomas Newcomen introduced early in the eighteenth century. By the last two decades of the same century, following James Watt's series of modifications, there were also engines with pistons moving in both directions only by the pressure of the steam. Like the electronic computer of the last decades of the twentieth century and the electric generator of the last decades of the nineteenth, Watt's steam engine was heralded as a universal (global, general purpose) machine, that is, a machine that could be automatically used in all places and at all times.

A technological progressive in comparison to Newcomen, Watt turned out to be conservative next to those who configured the successor models to his engine, namely, high-pressure steam engines versus his low-pressure model. A myriad of local reconfigurations were needed before the supposedly global steam engine could produce mechanical motion, first, strong enough to pull a train or propel a ship, and second, uniform enough to spin a fine textile or generate electricity. The need for reconfiguring a universal machine was repeated in the history of the supposedly universal electric generator and, more recently, regarding the supposedly universal electronic computer. The safety of low-pressure versus the efficiency of high-pressure engines has also been a perpetual issue, reproduced in the "battle of the currents" (direct versus alternating) between Thomas Edison and George Westinghouse during the 1880s and 1890s and the analog versus digital battle between engineers and mathematicians during the 1950s and 1960s. A symbol of progress in the 1880s, Edison in more recent times is viewed as exhibiting a puzzling conservatism. Biographers of the Massachusetts Institute of Technology electrical engineering professor Vannevar Bush are equally puzzled by how the preferences of this champion of mechanized analysis of the interwar period appear to be so incompatible with the prevalent post–World War II computing orientation.

### Technocracy

The work of a generation of historians sensitive to the symmetrical study of technological success and failure suggests that animated debates concerning choice between competing technologies have been the rule, not the exception. In the case of the automobile—another technology assumed to be globally preeminent—early-twentieth-century battery-run and internal-combustion-powered vehicles competed hard in various local contexts against each other (as well as against those moved by steam pressure). Now a technical hope of the future, the electric car did not lose in the past because of an internal technical inferiority; the gasoline-driven internal combustion engine prevailed because of an abstracted over a socially situated conception of technical efficiency. Unsurprisingly, the term *technology* became widely used only after the early-twentieth-century rise of "technocracy," a movement that promoted an abstracted conception of technical superiority by seeking to replace the acknowledged subjectivity of politics by the assumed objectivity of engineering.

The technocracy movement was propelled by the establishment of Fordism, a mode of mass production of automobiles with internal combustion engines. The technical efficiency of the automobile assembly line of the factories of Henry Ford was unquestionable in the 1910s. Things changed in the following decade when competitors chose production flexibility over efficiency by challenging the Fordist reliance on a combination of increasingly specialized machines and degraded skills; rather than producing a more affordable car but one offered only in a single model—the infamous black Model T—Ford's competitors elected the option of producing a variety of car models.

Taylorism was the other side of Fordism because it started from changes in labor efficiency that were to match changes in machine efficiency. Interested in increasing the efficiency of low-skill work and then returning a portion of the extra value to be produced to the workers in the form of better wages, Frederick W. Taylor, through what became known as "scientific management," proposed a scheme for a decisive advance in industrialization regardless of the availability and the wills of skilled workers, by relying on the unskilled labor of destitute urbanite and/or peasant masses. Varying mixes of the Taylorist-Fordist combination appealed to societies as different as that of the Germany and the USSR of the interwar period. Organic components of Stalinism, Taylorism, and Fordism also puzzled the most critical spirits of interwar Europe, including Antonio Gramsci, the imprisoned leader of the Italian Communist Party. In the pursuit of a worker who ought to abandon all preindustrial attitudes that were incompatible with the uniformity expected by the Taylorist-Fordist mode of production, Gramsci saw the potential for moral and material improvement of the working class, which he considered prerequisite to its emancipation.

Ford was not the only one concerned with creating a massive demand for his product to match its mass supply by his factories. Samuel Insull—who had started as Edison's secretary before he controlled, through dubious financial schemes, an empire of electrical utilities—had clearly realized the need for around-the-clock demand for electricity to take advantage of mass-production-capacity installations. Whatever technology might have been, it has been shaped both in production and in consumption, by invention and in use. The study of the history of the experience of technology vis-à-vis consumption, such as in a First World household or a Third World farmstead, has managed a decisive blow for the commonplace assumption of technology's universalism. It has shown that technology's easy mix with time-honored ideologies such as sexism or racism has increased the household work of a First World woman and decreased the resources of a Third World habitant.

Unregulated overproduction across the whole of industry accumulated the forces that were unleashed with the 1929 stock market crash. Herbert Hoover, the engineer-president was replaced by the iron politics of Franklin D. Roosevelt. The state-driven civilian rural electrification of the 1930s, which matched demand to supply, the Manhattan Project, and the rest of the state-driven military-technological projects of World War II shaped the emergence of "technology policy" as a key issue for the post–World War II state. Success in what is now called technology policy has in fact been a prerequisite for the

constitution of the modern state as such on both sides of the Atlantic. The end of the *ancient régime* in France and of the democracy of artisans, farmers, and merchants in the United States was marked by the state's pursuit of a technology for the mass manufacturing of guns with as uniform (or "interchangeable") parts as possible. The transfer of this technology to the rest of U.S. manufacturing over the course of the nineteenth century resulted in the so-called American system of manufactures, which took the millions visiting the world's fairs by surprise.

**Technological Determinism**

A visit to a world's fair after the mid-nineteenth century proved that the "machinery question" had been practically answered by the tremendous increase in the number and kinds of new machines. With the interconnection of machines into networks (of transportation, energy, communication, and so on), the term *technology* started to obtain a new meaning. In doubt by then about machinery inexorably dictating a better society, Marx liked the new term enough to correct his earlier editions of *Das Kapital* by carefully distinguishing between the "technical" and the "technological," according to whether the same process was experienced as an objective, product-making process or a subjective, value-forming one, respectively. Unlike the technical, the technological was subjective in that the revelation of the surplus value produced depended on political prerequisites. Technology, like surplus value, was a concept that pointed to an unspecified agency. Technology has since been recognized by its effects, whereas the issue of agency has remained conveniently abstract. In surveying the subsequent history of the use of the concept, Leo Marx, a distinguished historian of technology, finds that its abstractness has sustained the hegemony of the ideology of "technological determinism," the assumption that technology is autonomous from society.

Technological determinism matches well with the canonical presentation of the archetypal engine of Watt as being self-regulated because of the inclusion of a mechanism known as the "governor" (the foundational circuit of "cybernetics"). It was this ideological canon that was displayed at world's fairs, not, for instance, a diorama of the lethal steam boiler explosions that killed thousands. Historians have found that the dominance of technological determinism explains the many waves of technological utopianism and technological enthusiasm of the recent centuries. It explains why the late-nineteenth-century crash of the utopian hope that the telegraph would bring world peace was not taken into account in the enthusiasm that surrounded the initial emergence of the telephone, the radio, the television, and, more recently, the Internet. It also explains why the dramatic revelation of the destructive power of the atomic energy in Hiroshima was quickly followed by the hope that a nuclear reactor to run everybody's automobile was just around the corner. It finally explains why Leo Marx finds that technology has emerged as a "hazardous concept."

*See also* **Computer Science; Nuclear Age; Science; Science, History of.**

**BIBLIOGRAPHY**

Adler, Ken. *Engineering the Revolution: Arms and Enlightenment in France, 1763–1815.* Princeton, N.J.: Princeton University Press, 1997.

Berg, Maxine. *The Machinery Question and the Making of Political Economy, 1815–1848.* Cambridge, U.K.: Cambridge University Press, 1980.

Corn, Joseph J., ed. *Imagining Tomorrow: History, Technology, and the American Future.* Cambridge, Mass.: MIT Press, 1986.

Cowan, Ruth Schwartz. *More Work for Mother: The Ironies of Household Technology from the Open Hearth to the Microwave.* New York: Basic, 1983.

Frison, Guido. "Some German and Austrian Ideas on *Technologie* and *Technik* between the End of the Eighteenth Century and the Beginning of the Twentieth." *History of Economic Ideas* 6, no. 1 (1998): 107–133.

Hounshell, David A. *From the American System to Mass Production, 1800–1932: The Development of Manufacturing Technology in the United States.* Baltimore: Johns Hopkins University Press, 1984.

Kline, Ronald. "Construing 'Technology' as 'Applied Science': Public Rhetoric of Scientists and Engineers in the United States, 1880–1945." *Isis* 86, no. 2 (1995): 194–221.

Marx, Leo. "Technology: The Emergence of a Hazardous Concept." *Social Research* 64, no. 3 (1997): 965–988.

Sinclair, Bruce, ed. *Technology and the African-American Experience: Needs and Opportunities for Study.* Cambridge, Mass.: MIT Press, 2004.

Smith, Merritt Roe, and Leo Marx, eds. *Does Technology Drive History? The Dilemma of Technological Determinism.* Cambridge, Mass.: MIT Press, 1994.

*Aristotle Tympas*

**TEMPERANCE.** In classical and medieval thought, temperance, or *sōphrosynē,* could signify one or more of a congeries of traits, such as moderation, self-knowledge, self-restraint, or independence. These virtues were to be cultivated by the individual. In modern history, however, the meaning of temperance has become narrowed to refer only to limits on the consumption of alcoholic beverages, whether those restrictions are placed by an individual upon his or her personal consumption or by the state upon the habits of those subject to its jurisdiction. The principal agency in accomplishing this change in meaning has been a set of social movements whose origins lie in the sixteenth-century Protestant Reformation, but whose full flowering occurred in the nineteenth and twentieth centuries. Temperance movements have appeared in many societies, drawn upon diverse sources of support, pursued a variety of goals, and enjoyed widely varying degrees of success. In general, however, the temperance impulse in the modern world has been successful, whether its progress is measured by average levels of consumption or by preferences for less intoxicating forms of alcohol.

### Temperance as Ideal and Issue

Most of the world's religions embrace temperance from alcoholic beverages as a virtue. For Hindu Brahmins, Buddhists,

Jews, Roman Catholic Christians, and especially for Muslims and Protestant Christians, temperance and, for some, abstinence is valued. Tantra Hinduism, Daoism, and Roman Catholicism incorporate alcohol into ritual, among others, but only a few mystical sects, such as Islamic Sufism, celebrate intoxication. As a result, the worth of temperance itself has rarely been at issue in any society, even when social conflict over drinking has been most bitter. Nearly all drinkers regard their own behavior as temperate. Rather, discord over temperance typically arises when one segment of society attempts to impose restrictions upon another's drinking—that is, when interpretations of the meaning of temperance clash. Temperance can also become involved in a struggle over other issues.

Colonial regimes, for example, have often imposed controls on the drinking of indigenous peoples, even when the introduction of alcohol into native cultures has undermined traditional ways and left native societies vulnerable to imperial domination. The European colonial powers in central Africa sought to compartmentalize the drinking of native laborers in space and time so as to safeguard productivity, and mine owners in South Africa went even further in the same direction when they forced prohibition on their workforces.

As early as the dawn of the nineteenth century, the United States federal government mandated prohibition for Native Americans. But embattled indigenous peoples have also sought to use temperance for their own purposes, as a buttress of anticolonial resistance, as was the case for South African kings, leaders of Native American revitalization movements such as the Seneca Handsome Lake and the Shawnee Tenskwatawa (1775–1836), and the Indian nationalist movement led by M. K. Gandhi (1869–1948). In such cases, the hypocrisy of colonial authorities in preaching temperance while allowing, or even fostering, alcohol consumption has given a weapon to those seeking to overthrow or reject their dominion.

In industrial societies, employers have often found it expedient to support controls on workers' alcohol consumption in the hope of habituating their workforce to the discipline of machine production. But militant workers' movements, such as the English Chartists, the Knights of Labor in the United States and Canada, Austrian Socialists, and Spanish anarchists, have realized the value of temperance in mobilizing sober opposition to capital or to capitalist governments. Furthermore, successful revolutionary movements have sometimes included liquor control among their tools for reshaping society, as was the case for the Mexican government in the 1930s and the early Soviet regime.

Temperance has been a subtler instrument in inter-group struggles when classes or professions have deployed it as a means of self-definition or as a vehicle for claims of expertise. In many industrializing English-speaking societies, middle classes have adopted sobriety as a badge of respectability, distinguishing themselves at least rhetorically from allegedly profligate elites on one hand and from purportedly dissolute workers on the other. Among professionalizing groups, physicians in particular have often taken leadership roles in temperance advocacy in societies as diverse as the United States,

Britain, Denmark, France, Australia, Imperial Russia, and the Soviet Union. In such cases, as sociologist Joseph Gusfield shows, temperance serves both as a badge of personal rectitude and as an assertion of the fitness of a class or profession to set society's direction.

## Temperance Movements

The first temperance campaign in modern history was mounted by Martin Luther (1483–1546) and his followers as part of the Protestant Reformation, and was directed at the episodic drunkenness of traditional German drinking bouts. It failed, however, and German intellectuals instead came to view unconstrained drinking as a positive, indeed defining, Germanic trait.

Organized temperance societies next appeared in Britain and the United States in the early nineteenth century. Although the appearance of such societies derived critical impetus from evangelical Protestantism in both countries, temperance advocacy was by no means limited to evangelicals or to Protestants. By the 1870s, the Church of England had created its own temperance society, and during the same decade in the United States the founding of the Catholic Total Abstinence Union (CTAU) demonstrated Roman Catholic concern with the issue. The CTAU's definition of "temperance" as total abstinence also indicated how far temperance reform had traveled during its first half-century, since early American temperance reformers had first defined only moderation in the use of alcoholic beverages and later abstinence only from distilled spirits as their goal. Many reformers, however, soon moved to appeals for abstinence from all intoxicating beverages and then to a demand for state action to stop liquor sales, or prohibition. By the early twentieth century, movements for prohibition had appeared as well in Britain, in other British settler societies—Canada, Australia, and New Zealand—and in Nordic countries. The prohibition cause peaked during the 1910s and 1920s, when various forms of large-scale prohibition were adopted in Iceland (1915–1922), Finland (1919–1932), Norway (1916–1927), Russia and the Soviet Union (1914–1925), Canadian provinces (varying periods between 1901 and 1948) and by the Canadian federal government (1918–1919), and in the United States (1918–1933). In addition, a majority of voters in New Zealand twice supported prohibition (in 1911 and 1919), but the measure was never enacted. For those nations involved, World War I furnished a crucial stimulus for new restrictions on alcohol sales, such as the Carlisle system, a British scheme for government ownership and management of the liquor industry, and the French government's ban on absinthe.

Although temperance reform is commonly thought to have declined following the death of prohibition, new movements have simply taken on novel guises. American National Prohibition had been repealed only two years when a new self-help movement for habitual drunkards, Alcoholics Anonymous (AA), grew from the chance meeting of two drunks in Akron, Ohio. AA has since become a worldwide movement, with popular manifestations or imitations in countries such as Mexico and Japan, and its twelve-step method has found application to a variety of habits and afflictions. Since the 1940s,

academics following in the footsteps of E. M. Jellinek at the former Yale (University) Center of Alcohol Studies have taken a leading part in alcohol research and policy advice. Employers have continued to offer intervention in their workers' personal habits through "employee assistance programs." Both government policies and new organizations such as Mothers against Drunk Driving and Students against Destructive Decisions have focused on preventing or punishing drunken driving.

Women have often played key roles in temperance reform. In the United States, although women made up a large proportion of the membership of early temperance societies, they generally worked under male leadership. This began to change during the 1850s with the founding of the Independent Order of Good Templars, which soon became an international organization in which women in theory, and sometimes in practice, held equal status with male members. Women definitely seized the initiative in American temperance reform, however, in 1873–1874, when tens of thousands of women undertook nonviolent direct action against retail liquor dealers, using mass marches and public prayer and song. In the aftermath of the Women's Temperance Crusade, the national Woman's Christian Temperance Union (WCTU) was founded, and it soon became the largest organization of American women. Through the visit of an American activist from the Crusade the British Women's Temperance Association, Britain's first national women's temperance society, was established in 1876.

American and British women temperance activists soon began to extend their movement across the world, leading to the establishment in 1884 of the World's Woman's Christian Temperance Union (WWCTU). Although it was always controlled by American and British women, the WWCTU made temperance for the first time an international movement. Through this vehicle advocacy of other issues, such as peace and women's enfranchisement, was also spread.

Despite the common belief that failure of the various national prohibition schemes ended its impact, in fact temperance reform has exerted far-reaching influence upon consumption patterns, in large part because of its protean character and ability to adapt to diverse national cultures. Examples of its adaptability include AA in Roman Catholic Mexico, which in 1997 held the world's second largest number of local chapters; the Pioneer Total Abstinence Association of the Sacred Heart, an Irish Catholic society that at its peak in 1960 enrolled one-sixth of the Irish population and also attracted members in other countries; and the Danshukai societies in Japan, which have altered AA practices to fit Japanese culture. In the older industrialized countries at the outset of the twenty-first century, overall per capita consumption of alcohol was declining from peaks reached during the late twentieth century, and spirits and sometimes wine were being replaced in public preference by less potent beers, even in societies with long traditions of wine drinking. Nevertheless, rising consumption in the developing world, especially in China and India, presents new challenges to one of the world's historically most influential social movements.

See also **Religion and the State.**

BIBLIOGRAPHY

Barrows, Susanna, and Robin Room, eds. *Drinking: Behavior and Belief in Modern History.* Berkeley: University of California Press, 1991.

Blocker, Jack S., Jr. *American Temperance Movements: Cycles of Reform.* Boston: Twayne, 1989.

Blocker, Jack S., Jr., David M. Fahey, and Ian R. Tyrrell, eds. *Alcohol and Temperance in Modern History: An International Encyclopedia.* 2 vols. Santa Barbara, Calif.: ABC-Clio, 2003.

Blocker, Jack S., Jr., and Cheryl Krasnick Warsh, eds. *The Changing Face of Drink: Substance, Imagery, and Behaviour.* Ottawa, Canada: Histoire sociale/Social History, 1997.

Gusfield, Joseph R. *Symbolic Crusade: Status Politics and the American Temperance Movement.* Rev. ed. Urbana: University of Illinois Press, 1986.

Heron, Craig. *Booze: A Distilled History.* Toronto: Between the Lines, 2003.

Kurtz, Ernest. *Not-God: A History of Alcoholics Anonymous.* Rev. ed. Center City, Minn.: Hazelden, 1991.

Tyrrell, Ian R. *Woman's World/Woman's Empire: The Woman's Christian Temperance Union in International Perspective.* Chapel Hill: University of North Carolina Press, 1991.

*Jack S. Blocker Jr.*

**TERROR.** An apprehension of danger or impending violence, terror is akin to fear in an accentuated or distilled form and is often accompanied by trembling. It underpins many aspects of existence, especially the cut-and-thrust of the evolutionary drive and the predatory nature of the food chain. Lacking the "blood and sawdust" element associated with "horror," it has nevertheless become allied with atrocities and outrages, from the emperors of Rome down to the massacring armies of Genghis Khan, Attila the Hun, and the later purges of dictators such as Stalin, Hitler, and Pol Pot.

## The Politics of Oppression

In Europe, terror was employed as a tool by the church and state, often to suppress dissent and maintain the status quo. Campaigns like the Albigensian Crusade, in which the soldiers of Pope Innocent tortured, burned, and butchered the heretical sect of the Cathars, are examples of the extremes to which a religious body was prepared to go in order to maintain its authority, and the same might be said of the witch trials and the Spanish Inquisition. Many philosophers and statesmen have viewed such brutalities in terms of the degeneration of a cause. The German philosopher Georg Wilhelm Friedrich Hegel (1770–1794) considered the "Reign of Terror" of the French Revolution (April 1793 to July 1794) as a crisis of the human spirit: a vast abstract notion of freedom had arisen that annulled all moral and humanitarian considerations. Others saw it as a brutal mob avenging themselves on their enemies. During this period around seventeen thousand people were put to death, and the republican leader Maximilien de Robespierre (1758–1794) observed "in times of peace the springs of popular government are in virtue, but in times of revolution, they are both in virtue and terror."

Under ruthless regimes, people tend to adopt a docile attitude toward those in authority. It is not uncommon for families, neighbors, and friends to betray each other. Trust and the communal patterns of daily life inevitably suffer—during Stalin's pogroms, for instance, hundreds of thousands of children were orphaned and left to roam the country, living rough, often starving, and many of these eventually became soldiers who were notably brutal and insensitive. In order to pursue his policies—particularly the collectivization of Soviet agriculture and the removal of all rival left-wing factions—Stalin institutionalized terror, creating government mechanisms that were extensions of his will, oiled by bureaucrats and fueled by propaganda. So many thousands were put to death on a daily basis that the appalling became indistinguishable from the ordinary.

From a despot's point of view, the advantage gained from terror tactics is that he has under him a cowed, servile population; the disadvantage is that, having dispatched so many to camps or firing squads, he may start to anticipate revenge from every quarter and extend his field of killing until his situation becomes more isolated and absurd.

## The Culture of Terror

But terror need not imply persecution or a life-threatening situation. It has another strand, a religious, aesthetic aspect that implies awe or reverence before a universe whose many mysteries—including those of religion—have never been fully grasped. William Wordsworth (1770–1850), in his poem *The Prelude* (published 1850), spoke of the "ministry of fear" and evoked the brooding silence of a huge mountain peak hemming him in as he rowed across Esthwaite Lake. The British

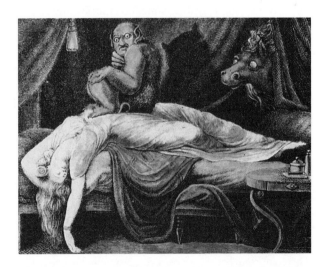

***The Nightmare,* engraving after 1790 painting by Henry Fuseli.** The popularity of horror-themed books, films, and works of art suggests that on some level people are drawn to the concept of terror—or at least that of fabricated terror that can be easily banished. © HENRY FUSELI/FORTEAN PICTURE LIBRARY

---

## GODS OF TERROR

The black Hindu goddess Kali was depicted with three eyes and four arms, bloated with the blood of her victims; Seth, the dark god of Egypt, as a monster or crocodile; and Satan, the adversary of Jehovah, as a scaly dragon devouring the souls of the dead. The Russians envisaged a figure of legendary dread in the "Pest Maiden," whose billowing skirts unloosed plague and famine.

In ancient Greece, Pan the goat-god was associated with surges of panic and terror, such as a flocks bursting into a stampede or men overcome with fear and trembling in the depths of the forest. Apart from being a musician and flock-keeper, Pan was a god of the hunt. Undoubtedly a primal terror is that of the hunted creature pursued by an avenging pack. The phrase "thrill of the chase" may be counterbalanced by "terror of the quarry." Frightened cries or pleas for clemency may have featured in the early articulation of speech.

---

## NICCOLÒ MACHIAVELLI

Niccolò Machiavelli's (1469–1527) manual of Renaissance statesmanship, *The Prince,* is a classic treatise on leadership utilizing terror or fear. It urges the ideal prince not to put "the reproach of cruelty" before such overwhelming issues as political unity and that "it is much safer to be feared than to be loved when one of the two must be lacking." While seldom quoting or approving Machiavelli—unjustly his name became synonymous with conspiracy and deceit—many subsequent leaders and dictators have taken his strictures to heart.

---

politician and thinker Edmund Burke (1729–1797), in his *Philosophical Enquiry into the Origin of Our Ideas of the Sublime and Beautiful* (1757), saw terror as an elevating, thrilling sensation deriving from the "sublime" and accompanying the observation of soaring, stupendous scenery. In the *Duino Elegies* (1923), the Austrian poet Rainer Maria Rilke (1875–1926) perceived "beauty" as "nothing but the beginning of terror," implying that, in the act of emotional surrender or identification, man lays himself open to a force over which he can exercise little control. Buildings, too, can produce such an effect. There are churches whose massive, solemn architecture, like those of the London architect Nicholas Hawksmoor (c. 1661–1736), induce a dread concomitant with an all-powerful deity.

Contemporary evangelists emphasize the "love of God," but men like Martin Luther feared God just as much. The latter

was literally a "terrible" power capable of visiting plague, famine, and earthquake. During the Middle Ages and the early modern period, numerous "panic" and "God-fearing" cults sprang up—from the flagellants to the Anabaptists—that exploited mass credulity, drawing upon the end of the world or "day of judgment" theme and the glorious, terrifying visions of the Book of Revelation—a favorite text, significantly, of the deranged, self-appointed messiah David Koresh (1959–1993), who died amid the blood and flames of his apocalyptic vision at Waco, Texas, taking his followers with him.

During the early Romantic period, the classic terror image *The Nightmare* (1782) was painted by Henry Fuseli (1741–1825), showing a young woman sprawled out sleeping and the head of a phantom horse rising above the bed. Perched on the woman's breast is a small hairy incubus. The popularity of such works gives rise to the question: Do people enjoy being terrified? The answer is that, in comfortable surroundings, they may enjoy the vicarious thrill of a mental journey through terrains littered with ruined castles, skulls, vampires, and apparitions: hence the enduring appeal of Gothic novels like *The Castle of Otranto, Dracula, Frankenstein,* and, more recently, the horror film and works of popular authors like Stephen King. Furthermore, the terrors banished at the climaxes of books and films are reassuring compared with the spectacular diseases and potential nuclear catastrophes filling much contemporary reality. Ghosts and ghouls, for all their menacing antics, hint at a startling extension of existence rather than the terminal facts of modern warfare. The effect of such works is to reassure more than terrify, for usually the fears are objectified and framed in the neutral environment of the page or screen.

### The Amygdala
Since the 1990s, terror has been localized in tiny pathways between nerve cells in a small, almond-shaped clump of tissue called the amygdala. Joseph LeDoux—an authority on

the emotional brain—observed, "We have shown that the amygdala is like the hub in the centre of a wheel of fear. If we understand the pathways of fear, it will ultimately lead to better control." Part of the primitive brain, the amygdala seems to have developed early, steering organisms away from poisons and predators. Some researchers associate it with conditions like depression and autism. Specific fears can be "burned" into it and stimulate a trigger reaction or recurrent terror. Through research into the amygdala and neurocircuitry, some hope that terror, man's oldest adversary, will be conquered, provoking the question: Will there be such a thing as a hero in the future?

*See also* **Heresy and Apostasy; Machiavellism; Mind; Terrorism, Middle East; War.**

BIBLIOGRAPHY

Burke, Edmund. *Philosophical Enquiry into the Origin of Our Ideas of the Sublime and Beautiful.* Edited by David P. Womersley. New York: Penguin, 1999. Primary source dealing with "terror" as an incarnation of what is sublime in nature.

Carter, Rita. *Mapping the Mind.* London: Weidenfeld and Nicolson, 1998. Cogent, popular study of how the brain works, with sections on the amygdala or "fear center."

Cohn, Norman Rufus Colin. *The Pursuit of the Millennium.* London: Secker and Warburg, 1957. An authoritative look at the "panic cults" and apocalyptic terrors of the Middle Ages and early modern periods.

Conquest, Robert. *The Great Terror: Stalin's Purge of the Thirties.* New York: Macmillan, 1968. A gripping account of Stalin's purges.

Fumagalli, Vito. *Landscapes of Fear: Perceptions of Nature and the City in the Middle Ages.* Translated by Shayne Mitchell. Cambridge, U.K.: Polity, 1994. Enlightening psychogeography of the medieval world.

Machiavelli, Niccolò. *The Prince.* Translated by Peter Bondanella and Mark Musa. Oxford: Oxford University Press, 1998. Treatise on realpolitik in the sixteenth century.

Newman, Paul. *A History of Terror.* Stroud, U.K.: Sutton, 2001. Accessible survey of the various manifestations of terror and panic against a historical backdrop.

Schmitt, Jean-Claude. *Ghosts of the Middle Ages.* Chicago: University Press of Chicago, 1998. Shows how "ghosts" were harnessed to the chariot of religion.

*Paul Newman*

**TERRORISM, MIDDLE EAST.** While terrorism has arisen in a variety of cultures and historical periods, much of the world's attention on this phenomenon in the late twentieth and early twenty-first centuries has centered on the Middle East. Middle Eastern terrorism emerged in Western consciousness during the 1970s, primarily through the rise of secular leftist and nationalist groups among Palestinian exiles, which targeted Israelis and their supporters both within and outside of Israel. Some (such as Yasir Arafat's Fatah movement and George Habash's Popular Front for the Liberation of Palestine) were part of broader political movements within the umbrella of the Palestine Liberation Organization, while others (such as Abu Nidal's Fatah faction) operated outside the

PLO. Palestinian nationalists were inspired in part by the success of the Algerian revolution, which used terror as a tactic to free that North African nation from French colonialism in 1962, and by the case of Israel, which won independence from Britain in 1948 in part through the efforts of terrorist groups led by future prime ministers Menachem Begin and Yitzhak Shamir. Without a recognized government or territory, terrorism appeared to many Palestinians to be a more realistic option than conventional or guerrilla warfare.

The rise of Palestinian terrorism was concomitant with the rise of Palestinian nationalism, where successive betrayals and defeats by Arab governments had led Palestinians to take leadership in their own national struggle. The use of such high-profile tactics as airline hijackings and embassy takeovers helped call attention to the plight of the Palestinian people, most of whom were living under Israeli military occupation or in forced exile in refugee camps in neighboring Arab states. Though such tactics led the West to belatedly recognize the Palestinians as a distinct people with national aspirations, it also gave Israel and the United States the excuse to thwart these goals on the grounds that the nationalist movement was led by terrorists.

The fratricidal Lebanese civil war (1975–1990) brought to the fore a number of ethnic-based militias that utilized terror, including the right-wing Phalangists, based in the Maronite Christian community, and—following the 1982 Israeli invasion and subsequent U.S. intervention—Shiite Islamic groups, some of which coalesced into the Hizbollah movement.

Turkey has been subjected to widespread terrorism by extreme leftist and extreme rightist groups, particularly during the late 1970s and early 1980s. Also during this period, Armenian terrorists would periodically assassinate Turkish diplomats in retaliation for the 1915 genocide and the refusal of Turkey's government to acknowledge their culpability. Kurdish nationalists, under the leadership of the Kurdish Workers Party (PKK), engaged in a series of terrorist attacks in Turkey through the 1990s in an effort to secure greater autonomy.

Leftist and Islamic groups used terror on a limited scale against the shah's repressive regime in Iran during the 1970s. During the early 1980s, following the shah's ouster in a largely nonviolent revolution and the subsequent consolidation of power by hardline Islamists, there was an upswing in terrorism that included assassinations of top officials of the revolutionary government.

In recent decades, the failure of secular nationalist and leftist movements in the Middle East has given rise to Islamic groupings, some of which have engaged in terrorism. Many were Arab veterans of U.S.- and Pakistani-backed mujahideen groups fighting the Communist Afghan government and its Soviet backers during the 1980s. This period saw the beginning of a tactic (which had previously been utilized primarily by Hindu Sri Lankan Tamils) where assailants, carrying explosives in a vehicle or strapped to themselves, would blow themselves up along with their targets, a phenomenon that became known as suicide bombings.

Several autocratic Arab regimes, long accused of corruption and abandonment of Islamic values, have become targets of Islamic radicals. Egypt was a hotbed of such movements throughout the 1980s and into the 1990s, with terrorists targeting government officials (including President Anwar Sadat), wealthy Egyptian elites, and foreign tourists. Conservative monarchies in Saudi Arabia, Kuwait, and Bahrain, along with their Western supporters, became targets of radical Islamists during this period as well. Algeria became the site of the most deadly acts of terrorism in the region beginning in the early 1990s, when the radical Armed Islamic Group (GIA) arose following a military coup that short-circuited scheduled national elections. During the 1990s, when the PLO's renunciation of terrorism and peace talks with Israel failed to end the occupation, Palestinian Islamic groups such as Hamas and Islamic Jihad, later joined by a renegade Fatah faction known as the Al-Aqsa Martyrs Brigade, commenced a suicide bombing campaign against Israel.

The ouster of Saddam Hussein's regime by invading U.S. forces in 2003 has resulted in Iraq's becoming a major center of terrorism. Though most of the Iraqi resistance to the U.S. occupation has targeted occupation forces, there has also been a series of bombings against civilians by both Iraqi and foreign terrorists.

The late 1990s saw the emergence of the Islamist Al Qaeda network, led primarily by Saudi exiles such as Osama bin Laden, who have targeted a number of Arab and Western targets, particularly the United States. Chief among their grievances have been U.S. support for Arab dictatorships; the American-led sanctions, bombings, and invasion of Iraq; U.S. support for Israel; and the ongoing U.S. military presence in the heart of the Islamic world. Al Qaeda's financial resources and sophisticated organization has taken terrorism to unprecedented levels, most dramatically illustrated by the devastating September 11, 2001, terrorist attacks on the United States that killed over three thousand people.

**State-Sponsored Terrorism**
Most governments and peoples of the Middle East categorically oppose terrorism. The taking of innocent human life is proscribed under Islam just as it is under Christianity and Judaism. However, a number of radical Middle Eastern states—such as the Islamist military government in Sudan, the Libyan regime of Muammar Qaddafi, the Baathist government of Syria, the former Taliban regime in Afghanistan, the Islamic Republic of Iran, and Saddam Hussein's former regime in Iraq—have provided or continue to provide funding and logistical support for terrorist groups.

Such activities have contributed to these governments' international isolation, although the United States has at times exaggerated the extent of support these regimes have provided terrorists in order to further advance other policy goals. U.S. forces bombed Libya in 1985, Iraq in 1993, and Sudan and Afghanistan in 1998 because of their governments' alleged support for terrorism, although some of these air strikes resulted in widespread civilian casualties themselves. In 2001, the U.S.-led air strikes played a decisive role in the ouster of the Taliban

**Poster celebrating Palestinian suicide bomber, Jenin, 2002.** Palestinian desire for Israeli withdrawal from occupied territories such as the West Bank has led to the formation of several terrorist organizations who utilize violent methods of coercion such as kidnapping, hijackings, and bombings. AP/WIDE WORLD PHOTOS

government in Afghanistan, which had provided sanctuary for Al Qaeda. Some intelligence and military officers and other officials in Saudi Arabia and Pakistan are believed to have quietly supported Islamist terrorists, although top government leaders largely support antiterrorism efforts.

Far more consequential, however, both politically and in terms of civilian lives, have been acts of state terror stemming directly from armed forces of governments themselves. For example, the Kurdish minorities in Iraq (particularly during the 1980s) and in Turkey (particularly during the 1990s) were subjected to widespread massacres, destruction of villages, and forced relocation, with civilian death tolls in the tens of thousands. In the former case, the United Nations Security Council set up a safe haven for Kurds in the northern part of Iraq following a devastating 1991 Iraqi offensive, the first time the UN had restricted the right of the armed forces of a sovereign country to operate within its internationally recognized borders on human rights grounds. During the Turkish invasion of Cyprus in 1974, hundreds of ethnic Greek civilians were killed, and ethnic cleansing uprooted the majority of the population in the northern one-third of the island; killings and forced relocations on a lesser scale occurred in other parts of Cyprus during this period against ethnic Turks. Successive Arab-dominated Sudanese governments contributed to the deaths of hundreds of thousands of Christian and animist blacks in the southern part of the country through massacre and forced starvation, more recently targeting black Muslims in the Dafur region in the west. Algerian forces killed thousands of civilians in counter-insurgency operations in the early to mid-1990s. In southern Iraq, Saddam Hussein's armed forces were responsible for the deaths of thousands of civilians following an uprising by Shiite Arabs in 1991. In Iran, too, under both the U.S.-backed shah and the Islamic regime that replaced it, thousands of Iranians have been killed by secret police and other government forces. The U.S. bombing of Afghanistan during the fall of 2001 appears to have killed more civilians than the September 11, 2001, attacks against the United States that prompted it.

Decades of Israeli bombing and shelling of civilian areas in Lebanon are believed to have resulted in the deaths of more than twenty thousand people. The number of Palestinian civilians killed in Israeli assaults in the occupied West Bank and Gaza Strip far surpasses the number of Israeli deaths from Palestinian terrorists. Israeli maltreatment of Palestinians under occupation, which has included widespread violations of the Fourth Geneva Convention, has been the subject of a series of UN Security Council resolutions demanding that such practices be halted, although the United States has blocked their enforcement and vetoed dozens of similar resolutions. Reports from reputable human rights organizations have also accused Moroccan occupation forces in Western Sahara of widespread abuses, particularly during the initial conquest of the former Spanish colony in 1975.

## The Function of Terrorist Groups

In general, terrorism by non-state actors arises from those who are too weak to engage in more conventional forms of armed struggle or are motivated by the sheer frustration of their situation. Some individuals who enlist with radical Islamist groups may also be promoted in part by the perceived glory of martyrdom. Supporters of such terrorism justify such actions as a means of inflicting damage on political entities and societies as a whole that are seen as carrying out mass violence through government forces too strong to confront directly.

For example, Israel's occupation and colonization of Palestinian territory seized in the Six-Day War in 1967, the ongoing repression, and rejection of demands for a full withdrawal in return for security guarantees—combined with Israel's overwhelming military power and the large-scale military, financial, and diplomatic support from the world's only remaining superpower—have led some Palestinians to support suicide bombing as a means of convincing Israel that the costs of holding on to the occupied West Bank and Gaza Strip are higher than withdrawal. Such violence has actually hardened the attitudes of Israelis and their American backers, as it appears to reinforce their assumption that the Palestinians' actual goal is not just ending the Israeli occupation of the West Bank and Gaza Strip, but the destruction of Israel itself.

The terrorism of previous decades in the Middle East, like terrorism practiced by leftist and nationalist movements elsewhere, was based upon the idea of "propaganda of the deed"—inspiring popular struggle and demoralizing their opponents. In this regard, it was almost uniformly unsuccessful, particularly as enhanced security measures made successful terrorist operations more difficult.

Suicide bombing not only was easier to carry out, since the terrorists were willing to kill themselves in the process, but Islamist groups were able—despite Islamic prohibitions against suicide and killing innocent people—to take advantage of the exalted role of martyrdom among Muslims to gain recruits and popular support. Such terrorist operations, with their poten-

tial for inflicting enormous casualties, appear to also be designed to provoke a disproportionate reaction from governments with superior armed forces, resulting in large-scale civilian casualties and thereby increasing support for their extreme anti-Western ideology. A number of strategic analysts have argued that the U.S. response to September 11, particularly the invasion of Iraq, have actually strengthened Al Qaeda by leading increasing numbers of alienated young Muslims to adopt bin Laden's view of a holy war between Islam and the West.

Some groups, such as Al Qaeda, function primarily to promote their causes through terrorism. Others, like Hamas, carry out civilian functions—such as running health clinics and schools and providing social services—as well as supporting an armed wing involved in terrorism. Some have evolved into political parties: for example, since the mid-1990s, Hizbollah has refrained from attacks against civilians, has largely restricted its armed activities to Israeli occupation forces, and has competed in Lebanese parliamentary elections.

Most contemporary Middle Eastern terrorist groups have emerged out of situations where there has been widespread social dislocation through war or uneven economic development. Virtually all have emerged in situations where legal nonviolent means of political change have been suppressed. The disproportionate level of terrorism in the Middle East appears to be less a result of anything inherent within Arab culture or within Islam than a consequence of the systematic denial by governments to allow for the manifestation of basic rights, including the right of self-determination. Given that the primary supporters and arms providers of most of these repressive Middle Eastern governments are Western powers such as the United States, the threat from terrorism is unlikely to be suppressed through military means alone.

*See also* **Jihad; Terror; War.**

**BIBLIOGRAPHY**

Esposito, John L. *Unholy War: Terror in the Name of Islam.* New York: Oxford University Press, 2002.

Fisk, Robert. *Pity the Nation: The Abduction of Lebanon.* New York: Nation Books, 2002.

Halliday, Fred. *Two Hours That Shook the World—September 11, 2001: Causes and Consequences.* London: Saqi Books, 2002.

Sayagh, Yezid. *Armed Struggle and the Search for State: The Palestinian National Movement, 1949–1993.* New York: Oxford University Press, 1997.

Telhami, Shibley. *The Stakes: America and the Middle East.* Boulder, Colo.: Westview Press, 2002.

Zunes, Stephen. *Tinderbox: U.S. Middle East Policy and the Roots of Terrorism.* Monroe, Maine: Common Courage Press, 2003.

*Stephen Zunes*

**TEXT/TEXTUALITY.** This is not a definition. Well, of course it is—after all, it is appearing in a dictionary—and yet, in a certain and actually rather important way, it is not. Or, put differently, precisely to the extent that the text is not an idea, this is not a definition. Of course, the text can be treated as an idea, perhaps even one whose time has come, but doing so misses something important about what the text is. In fact, what one misses in treating the text as an idea is its resistance to both idealism and the history of ideas, a resistance marked—however obliquely—by the necessarily digressive form of this definition that is not one.

## Etymology

*Text* derives from the Latin *textus* (a tissue), which is in turn derived from *texere* (to weave). It belongs to a field of associated linguistic values that includes weaving, that which is woven, spinning, and that which is spun, indeed even web and webbing. *Textus* entered European vernaculars through Old French, where it appears as *texte* and where it assumes its important relation with *tissu* (a tissue or fabric) and *tisser* (to weave). All of these resonant associations are relevant to understanding how "the text" is used in contemporary scholarship, especially the interplay between its nominal and verbal forms, an interplay that registers the quality of what Julia Kristeva has called the text's "productivity," that is, its capacity to enable and exceed the producing, the materialization, of products.

The emergence of the text as an important concept in humanistic scholarship has taken many twists and turns. When Walter Benjamin, in his essay "The Image in Proust," described Proust's writing as a *textum,* a weaving not unlike the raveling and unraveling carried out by Penelope in the *Odyssey,* he was bringing to closure a tradition that dates back at least to Quintilian (c. 35–100 C.E.), a tradition of associating the literary work with a tissue woven of many threads. If it makes sense to associate Benjamin with the closure of this tradition, it is because in his insistence on the dialectic of raveling and unraveling, he foregrounds a key preoccupation of what came to be known as textual criticism. Textual criticism—a distinctive fusion of the practices of biblical exegesis, paleography, and philology linked now with the figure of the German philologist Karl Lachmann (1793–1851)—was an institutionally and largely theologically organized emphasis on the text as an empirical object. This expressed itself during the fourteenth century in the works of William Langland, Geoffrey Chaucer, and John Wycliffe (among others) as a concern for the original and therefore true words contained in any writing—in effect, what God actually said. The text was defined either in opposition to commentary and annotation or in opposition to all that is supplemental: introductions, appendices, etc. This was a text understood as a thing, as a specific and precise configuration of words toward which one was then authorized to turn his or her hermeneutical attentions.

## Text and Semiological Text

When in 1972 Oswald Ducrot and Tzvetan Todorov published *The Encyclopedic Dictionary of the Sciences of Language,* it was the text as thing, the text of textual criticism, that oriented the first of their two entries on "the text," which focused on the way the text fills a gap in linguistics, rhetoric, and stylistics by providing them with a concept of the autonomous and closed unit that arises through the individuated use of a language sys-

tem. In effect, "the text" answers the question: what thing is produced when a linguistic code is used to generate a message? In this it substitutes for either discourse or speech act. Significantly, though the *Encyclopedic Dictionary* contains a second entry on the text, it appears in an appendix, the very sort of supplementary material typically distinguished from the text of textual criticism. This text is dubbed "semiological" by the authors, a characterization meant to note the rather different way this second text engages the traditions and practices of humanistic scholarship.

In his contribution to the *Encyclopaedia Universalis* of the following year, Roland Barthes repeats this division of the concept of the text, suggesting that—despite the centrality of his contribution to the theorization of the semiological text—he found the division, if not compelling, then certainly useful. Framing his discussion in terms of the "crisis of the sign," Barthes reminds us that the second text has a rather different genealogy than the text of textual criticism. For one thing, its emergence is considerably more recent. Although many of the writers who mattered to the theorists of the semiological text—Stéphane Mallarmé, Honoré de Balzac, Edgar Allan Poe, the Comte de Lautréamont, and others—wrote during the nineteenth century, the theorization of the text their work enabled unfolded during the postwar period in France. Nineteen-sixty is the date typically given for the emergence of the second text, and this is because it was in 1960 that the first issue of the influential journal *Tel Quel* appeared. While it is certainly the case that the text and *Tel Quel* are intimately related, the intellectual insights that converged in the concept of the text are discernible already in the 1940s. This becomes evident if one compares Maurice Blanchot's 1948 essay "Literature and the Right to Death" with his "Reflections on Nihilism" from part two of *The Infinite Conversation* (1969). In "Reflections" Blanchot makes explicit how his earlier meditation on literature, the book, the work, and death—framed largely in terms of the Hegelian principle of negativity—converts almost effortlessly into the properly textual concerns of Barthes and Jacques Derrida. Indeed, Blanchot appears to trace here precisely the movement from work to text that was to be thematized so fruitfully by Barthes in 1971. Perhaps because Derrida has made his debt to Blanchot explicit, it is difficult not to read in the title of the opening section of *Of Grammatology* (1966), "The End of the Book and the Beginning of Writing," the palimpsestic presence of Blanchot's conception of the disappearance of literature and the absence of the book. While it is true that Blanchot holds the very term "text" in abeyance (systematically preferring "work"), it is clear that his profoundly philosophical engagement with the literary object opened what Barthes was later to call the "methodological field" of the semiological text.

## Tel Quel

While it might be argued that the appearance of Michel Foucault's "Language to Infinity" (an essay openly in dialogue with Blanchot) in an early issue of *Tel Quel* is what destined the encounter between the journal and the concept of the text, this presupposes rather than establishes the relevance of Blanchot. What clearly makes *Tel Quel* so pertinent to the emergence of the text is the fact that its longtime senior editor, Philippe Sollers, sought explicitly to devote the resources of the journal to the dissemination of the concept. Indeed, it is largely through the intellectual debates stirred by the journal that the text and textuality came to belong together. Although it ceased publication in the 1980s (morphing into *L'infini* in 1982), the journal not only brought together all of the major theorists of the text—Barthes, Derrida, Kristeva, and Sollers—but, by virtue of its role in the French institutions of intellectual power, it allowed the text both to materialize and to do so in a manner that left it marked by the conditions of its emergence. Despite its heady and deeply theoretical character, the text was always in some ways a "pop" phenomenon. With the creation of the *Tel Quel* series at Editions du Seuil in 1962 (which eventually included major works by Barthes, Derrida, and Kristeva), not only was the text being widely disseminated (many titles in the series were translated), it became the topic of discussion at seminars, colloquia, and, thanks to Bernard Pivot's *Apostrophes,* nationally televised debates. Those eager to dismiss the importance of the text typically point to this as evidence of its degraded character, but in thereby hiding the commodity character of virtually all academic concepts they overlook the distinctly textual character of the text. The heterogeneous threads woven into the concept always included unruly, indeed compromising, material elements; indeed, this was part of its purchase on the concept of materialism, a purchase that might be said to culminate in the displacement of context (whether social or historical) by contextuality.

## Jacques Derrida: Writing

Philosophically, the semiological or second text was given its earliest and perhaps most enduring formulation in the work of Jacques Derrida. Although it is true that Barthes had a longer, much more intimate, affiliation with *Tel Quel* (first publishing there in 1961), he would have been the first to admit that most of the heavy theoretical lifting was done by those around him, certainly by Derrida (and earlier Roman Jakobson, Claude Lévi-Strauss, and Jacques Lacan), but also by his protégée, and later master, Julia Kristeva. Certainly, *Tel Quel's* tenacious defense of the politics of writing (both phonetic and grammatological or *arché*) is unthinkable in the absence of Derrida. Indeed, Derrida's attack on idealism provided Sollers and others affiliated with the journal with rigorous means by which to link their early commitment to literature with a post-engagement leftism. Derrida's first sustained presentation of the concept of the text appears in *Of Grammatology,* although one finds important strands of the insight it crystallizes in his earlier reading of Edmund Husserl. There, the text is used in a way consistent with its use in textual criticism, except that it is linked to a meditation on the relation between what makes science scientific and writing, a link forged by making consistent appeal to Maurice Merleau-Ponty's use of the Husserlian concept of "interweaving" in the former's lectures on "The Origins of Geometry" from the 1950s. Invoked both by Husserl and by Merleau-Ponty to designate the encounter between language and thought, interweaving is taken up by Derrida as a way to introduce the rhetoric of textuality within a theorization of writing and its place in the dispute between science and philosophy. For example, in "Form and Meaning"

(another early essay on Husserl) Derrida explicitly translates interweaving (given in German as *Verwebung*) as the Latin *texere,* and does so in anticipation of a formulation in which linguistic and prelinguistic strata are shown to interact in accord with "the controlled system of a sort of text." "Sort of" here marks the advent of the semiological text—that is, the concept through which Derrida seeks to challenge phenomenology's account of the being of meaning.

## The Text as Philosophical Paradigm

*Of Grammatology* draws out the relation between this text and a critique of the philosophical ethnocentrism expressed in the subordination of writing to speech. Although Derrida frames the issue in terms of a critique of Ferdinand de Saussure's account of the linguistic sign, it is clear that the problems raised regarding Husserl's figure of interweaving are not far away. Indeed, Saussure's subordination of writing to speech is read as an expression of his tacit agreement with Husserl's phenomenological construal of language. To challenge this subordination and the ethnocentrism sustaining it, Derrida uses the logic of the text, that is, the argument that the interweaving that confounds the distinction between different levels of consciousness and dimensions of reality also confounds not just the distinction between speech and writing but the distinction between thought and signs. Here, the semiological text comes to designate the unstable process whereby experience and representation (whether linguistic or not) engage one another in a radically undecidable manner. The oft-cited formulation "there is nothing outside the text," which appears in the discussion of Jean-Jacques Rousseau, thus asks, at one level, to be taken this way: there is no experience that can be absolutely separated from the systems of representations developed for its expression. The text then is less a thing than a philosophical paradigm, that is, a way of representing—within the protocols and procedures of a certain discourse—the undecidable limits of representation. It is not that there is nothing but representation. Rather, if there is nothing outside the text, it is because there is nothing but the enduring missed encounter between experience and representation.

Because of the intimacy that defines the relation between *Of Grammatology* and *Writing and Difference* (from the same year), it is important here to acknowledge the way Derrida mobilizes Sigmund Freud to extend his critique of experience, a critique that might otherwise appear to leave both the personal and the ineffable unthematized. In "Freud and the Scene of Writing" Derrida, by tracing Freud's ambivalent relation to the metaphors of writing as they appear in various discourses, shows how a textual logic is at work both in Freud's account of neurophysiology (the thematics of *Bahnung,* "pathmaking") and in his account of the psychical interaction of memory and perception, whether in waking life or in the dream. Thus, the semiological text, by representing the undecidable interweaving at work in the different operations of the psychical apparatus, is shown to have yet another relation to the systemic mediation of experience. If, as Derrida argues, the signifier and the signified are interwoven—in effect, structured by the differing deferral of *différance* (Derrida's well-known neologism)—then, strictly speaking, there are no ideas. Idealism is then thrown into crisis, and while Derrida's materialism has consistently defied philosophical categorization, it is clear that the text paradigm, in foregrounding the interminable labor of differentiation, exhibits an unmistakable materiality.

## Julia Kristeva: Textual Productivity and Intertextuality

Perhaps because Julia Kristeva's earliest articulations of the theory of textuality are framed within the context of a more intimate dialogue with Marxism than Derrida's, the text's materiality receives more direct attention. Specifically, in several of the essays that comprise *Séméiotiké* (1969) Kristeva links the text with the concept of productivity. This term derives from her effort to rethink Marx's concept of the "mode of production" from the vantage points of linguistics and psychoanalysis, with the aim of capturing both how values (economic, linguistic, etc.) are effects of a system of relations, and how this system is defined by a heterogeneity of relations (social, psychic, etc.) that sustain themselves in a permanent state of crisis. In the essay "The Productivity Called the Text," Kristeva shows how the text, again as paradigm rather than as thing, allows one to think about how language is deployed in ways that undercut its communicative function, at once revealing and confounding the codes that organize the production of linguistic messages. Although it is impossible to designate the product of the productivity called the text, it is clear that what is at stake here is the subject in process/on trial (Kristeva's original formulation invites both). The text provides one with the conceptual means by which to theorize and thus analyze the formation and deformation of the human being that takes place in the circuits of symbolic exchange.

Crucial to her point about the systemic articulation of heterogeneous relations is the conceptual innovation of intertextuality. Derived from the semiological concept of substance (used by Louis Hjelmslev to track the plane of content from one sign system to another), intertextuality describes the transpositions that allow different semiological registers to engage one another. Kristeva's earliest characterizations of intertextuality—for example, "in the space of a text several utterances, taken from other texts, intersect and neutralize each other"— associate it with the process of literary allusion. In *Revolution of Poetic Language* (1974), however, a much stronger accent falls on the dynamics of transposition—that is, the unstable process whereby differently realized texts collide in, say, a novel—and she goes out of her way to disassociate intertextuality from the "study of sources." Because intertextuality is identified in *Revolution* as a third primary process (primary processes were Freud's list of psychic activities that effect the form and content of dreams), it is equally clear that transposition is designed to give the analyst access to the permutation of subject positions undergone in the production of a work. Kristeva's emphasis on textual interactivity underscores the interdisciplinary character of the text paradigm. No doubt because her mentor, Barthes, drew heavily on Hjelmslev's substance in his influential studies of fashion, where clothing is photographed, written about, and worn, Kristeva's use of intertexuality deliberately engages the forms of textuality that arise both in different sign systems and in different disciplines. Not

surprisingly, therefore, music and painting have mattered deeply to Kristeva's thinking about literature.

A final conceptual innovation must be mentioned. Throughout the late 1960s and early 1970s Kristeva appealed to a distinction between the "pheno-text" and the "geno-text." Obviously modeled on the discourse of genetics (such as phenotype and genotype), this distinction was not about restoring the work's "organic" character. Instead, it sought to stress the continuum of effects that passed between the formation of the speaking subject and the works produced by him or her. In *Revolution,* this distinction is tied to one between the semiotic and the symbolic, and Kristeva uses it to analyze how the subject's relation to the maternal body and the social order manifests itself in the form and content of a poem. In designating different levels of the text, the pheno-text and geno-text serve to give the textual paradigm access to a field of literary production that reaches well beyond the poem without, however, renouncing any claim on its formal detail. In providing the analyst with the conceptual means by which to track the transposition of the semiotic into the symbolic, the pheno-text/geno-text distinction gives intertexuality its deep structure. In doing so it makes the process of transposition central to Kristeva's theory of the text, a theory that, among other things, calls the concept of the literary tradition deeply into question.

## Roland Barthes: Pleasure of the Text

As *Tel Quel*'s "spiritual advisor," Roland Barthes (1915–1980) had enormous influence on the fate of the text. Although he often deferred to the theoretical rigor of others, he was unquestionably the text's most articulate and tenacious cultural ambassador. Like Kristeva he was keen to extrapolate the literary implications of the semiological text, and for this reason—not to mention the largely literary cast of the American reception of textuality—his studies *S/Z* and *The Pleasure of the Text* still define for many in the Anglophone world what the second text is. This reputation is by no means undeserved. It does, however, tend to obscure the permutations undergone by Barthes's text. In *S/Z* (a textual analysis of Balzac's *Sarrazine* [1830]), for example, Barthes deploys a straightforwardly etymological notion of the text by identifying five codes that, in his account of the story, are "woven together" in its narration. Although the strong suggestion made by the study is that this approach is warranted by its pedagogical value (and Barthes's skills here are legendary), it is clear that Barthes is reading the narrative in a deliberately textual manner. That is, he is constructing the means by which the story produces the possibility of its meanings, including, it should be added, the intensely queer motif of the sexual undecidability around which the narration winds and unwinds. This approach, also exemplified in numerous essays of the period, does at a certain point succumb to the affective charge it channels, resulting in the publication of *The Pleasure of the Text* (1973), where the figure of weaving, while not giving way entirely, recedes in importance. In its place appears a theme first programmatically identified in his groundbreaking essay from 1971, "From Work to Text": the theme of pleasure, later set off against its more strictly Lacanian double, *jouissance.*

As part of Barthes's professional trajectory from semiotics to semioclasm ("sign breaking" or the defiling of the sacred status of signs), this shift clearly registers the impact of Kristeva (and to a lesser extent, Derrida) on his writing. Indeed, in engaging the theme of pleasure Barthes openly weaves into his text the problem of the body and its drives. Although struck by Kristeva's semiotics, Barthes rechannels pleasure toward the practice of the reader, that is, the highly mediated encounter between the absent body of the writer and the present, indeed attentive, body of the critic/theorist. Drawing on Blanchot's neutered account of literary space, Barthes reframes this encounter in the distinctly queer mood of promiscuous anonymity, making the textual paradigm accommodate a distinctly sexual, indeed homo-textual, relationality.

This attention to the reader's body and its practices (what the body does when it reads) finds perhaps its highest expression in Barthes's critique of the literary object, the work. Not content to stress the existential aspect of one's practice, Barthes links such practice to the social reproduction of the literary institution, arguing that its organizing conceit, the concept of a commodity laden with values deposited there by a genius, in short the literary work, is not only an ideological confection of that institution, but one being deployed in a rear-guard action against challenges being mounted against it from within a heterogeneous field of writings. Here, the methodological field of the text serves both to frame the literary institution, to account for its reproductivity, while also establishing how one might read from the inside out, that is, with an eye toward grasping how reading is also always an engagement with its social and psychic conditions. In thus calling for a paradigm shift from the work to the text, Barthes is not only echoing Derrida's call for the end of the book in historical terms, but is situating the text itself as the context for a transformation of intellectual power in the West, one that in demythologizing some of its most cherished ideas, challenges the West's ability to define and thereby legitimate its cultural values. In this sense the text is not itself an idea.

## Textual Analysis outside Literary Studies

The specific terms in which the integrity of the literary object was questioned by the semiological text helped to catalyze discussion about objects in other disciplines. Kristeva's interest in painting and music has already been remarked. The most concerted effort to make the textual paradigm matter outside literary studies, however, was in cinema studies, where in the course of the 1970s "textual analysis" came to be synonymous with a rigorous psychoanalytically and/or philosophically inflected neo-formalism. This development had strong immediate repercussions outside France, notably in Britain, where many of the writers affiliated with the journal *Screen* saw themselves as contributing to the "textual analysis" initiative. In France, the figures typically associated with elaborating the cinematic text would include Christian Metz, Marie-Claire Ropars-Wuilleumier, Raymond Bellour, Michel Marie, and Thierry Kuntzel. That each is quite distinctive does not deny that, taken as a whole, they represent a concerted effort to displace the filmographic or humanistic object of cinema studies by bringing to bear upon the institutional consensus sustaining it all the questions animated in the works of Derrida, Kristeva, and Barthes.

Because the sound track figured centrally as one of the "codes" to weave into the textual analysis of film, music (one of several components of the sound track), and more specifically musicology, also became a site for the elaboration of the semiological text. Pitched against musicological structuralism (of the sort embodied in the work of Jean-Jacques Nattiez), the textual analysis of music sought to push away from the concerns of compositional syntax, and toward music's performativity, especially its interaction with the array of practices legitimated by post-Cagean aesthetics, notably of course dance and experimental theater. While it is certainly true that the textual analysis of music has never had the sort of impact enjoyed by cinema studies, the writings of Daniel Charles and Ivanka Stoïanova have had influence. Moreover, precisely because of its emergence in musicology the textual paradigm has in significant ways secured its status as a uniquely powerful model of interdisciplinary and inter-media critical analysis. Indeed, textuality as a quality attributable to a wide variety of cultural practices derives its analytical force from the disciplinary dissemination both latent within the paradigm and materialized in its historical development.

## The Global Social Text

Derrida, Kristeva, and Sollers were all still writing. Barthes died in 1980. Of the "textual survivors," none has assumed Barthes's ambassadorial responsibilities. In that sense the hour of the text may have passed. However, precisely because the semiological text posed the question of the literary, indeed the cultural, institution, thereby challenging the very logic of disciplinary reason and the ethnocentrism supporting it, the text retains what Benjamin called a "weak Messianic charge." This utopian and necessarily metacritical residue is nowhere more evident than in Gayatri Spivak's concept of "text-ility." Deftly picking up the etymological thread of the semiological text as a weaving, Spivak, in the controversial *A Critique of Post-Colonial Reason* (1999), deploys "text-ility" as the conceptual means by which to think the making and unmaking of the global social text. Specifically, she attempts to articulate the geopolitics of textile production in "the South," the multicultural fashion system supported in sectors of postcolonialism, and the "traveling theories" (a term derived from Edward Said's essay by that name) of largely Western academic intellectuals. Unashamed of her debts to Barthes and especially Derrida, Spivak makes it clear that in important ways the theory of the text, especially as it supplements itself, remains unfinished. At the very least she reminds us emphatically of what the text has always asked that we make of it: the theoretical and practical loom of the not there, the not yet—perhaps even the undefinable.

*See also* **Literary Criticism; Literary History; Literature.**

BIBLIOGRAPHY

Barthes, Roland. *Image, Music, Text.* Edited and translated by Stephen Heath. New York: Hill and Wang, 1977.
———. *The Pleasure of the Text.* Translated by Richard Miller. New York: Hill and Wang, 1975. Originally published in French, 1973.
———. *S/Z.* Translated by Richard Miller. New York: Hill and Wang, 1974. Originally published in French, 1970.

Benjamin, Walter. "On the Image of Proust." In *Walter Benjamin: Selected Writings*, 4 vols., edited by Marcus Bullock et al. Cambridge, Mass.: Harvard University Press (Belknap), 1996–2003. Vol 2 (1999), 237–247. Originally published in German, 1929.

Blanchot, Maurice. *The Book To Come.* Translated by Charlotte Mendell. Stanford, Calif.: Stanford University Press, 2003. Originally published in French, 1959.

Charles, Daniel. "La musique et l'écriture." *Musique en jeu* 13 (1973): 3–13.

Derrida, Jacques. *Of Grammatology.* Translated by Gayatri Chakravorty Spivak. Baltimore: Johns Hopkins University Press, 1976. Originally published in French, 1967.

———. *Writing and Difference.* Translated by Alan Bass. Chicago: University of Chicago Press, 1978. Originally published in French, 1967.

Ducrot, Oswald and Tzvetan Todorov. *Encyclopedic Dictionary of the Sciences of Language.* Translated by Carolyn Porter. Baltimore: Johns Hopkins University Press, 1979. Originally published in French, 1972.

Jameson, Fredric. "The Ideology of the Text." In *The Ideologies of Theory: Essays 1971–86.* Minneapolis: University of Minnesota Press, 1988. Vol. 1, 17–71.

Kristeva, Julia. *Desire in Language: A Semiotic Approach to Literature and Art.* Edited by Leon Roudiez. New York: Columbia University Press, 1980. Originally published in French, 1969–1979.

———. *Revolution in Poetic Language.* Translated by Margaret Waller. New York: Columbia University Press, 1984. Originally published in French, 1974.

Metz, Christian. *Language and Cinema.* Translated by Donna Jean Umiker-Sebeok. The Hague: Mouton, 1974. Originally published in French, 1971.

Mowitt, John. *Text: The Genealogy of an Antidisciplinary Object.* Durham, N.C.: Duke University Press, 1992.

Ropars-Wuilleumier, Marie-Claire. *Le texte divisée.* Paris: Presses Universitaires de France, 1981.

Said, Edward. "The Problem of Textuality: Two Exemplary Positions." *Critical Inquiry* 4, no. 4 (summer 1978): 673–714.

Sollers, Philippe. *Logiques.* Paris: Editions du Seuil, 1968.

Spivak, Gayatri Chakravorty. *A Critique of Postcolonial Reason: Toward a History of the Vanishing Present.* Cambridge, Mass.: Harvard University Press, 1999.

Stoïanova, Ivanka. *Geste, Texte, Musique.* Paris: Union Générale d'Éditions, 1978.

*The Tel Quel Reader.* Edited by Patrick ffrench and Roland-François Lack. London: Routledge, 1998.

*John Mowitt*

## TEXTILES AND FIBER ARTS AS CATALYSTS FOR IDEAS.

Working with fiber has generated many seminal ideas in the course of human history, including the first notions of rotary motion, machines, and computers. The fiber arts also have provided an important means of expression of the human condition.

### String

At some unknown time before 25,000 B.C.E. (when we get our first direct evidence), humans figured out that you could make long, strong flexible strings by twisting together thin, easily bro-

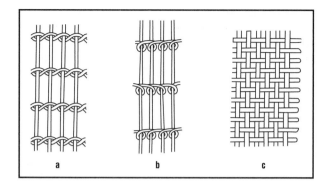

**Figure 1.** Earliest weaves: (a) twining with paired wefts; (b) warp-wrap twining; (c) plain-weave. COURTESY OF THE AUTHOR

ken plant fibers. Twist adds great strength, as one learns by twisting together a handful of fibers from a dead vine after the winter weather has rotted away (retted) the woody parts. The resulting string can be used in numerous ways to make life easier and more convenient: for tying things together (increasing one's power to carry, to store, and to make compound tools) or tying things down, and for crafting snares and nets (making hunting and fishing far more efficient). String is probably the special tool—almost unseen in the material record—that allowed the human race to move, during the Upper Paleolithic, into many ecological niches they otherwise could not have handled. All human cultures have string. Actual impressions of twisted plant fiber string and twined netting were found at Pavlov, Czech Republic, from 25,000 B.C.E., the middle of the Upper Paleolithic (Fig. 1a). These remains are already so sophisticated that string- and net-making must have been practiced for some time, possibly since the start of the era of cave art, c. 40,000 B.C.E. Other evidence of Paleolithic string and its uses has been found across Europe from 20,000 B.C.E., including increasing numbers of bone needles and fine-holed beads.

Once the domestication of plants and animals began in the Near East at the beginning of the Neolithic, c. 9000 B.C.E., evidence for fiber arts increases dramatically (partly because the newly permanent settlements make it easier to find human artifacts at all), allowing us to see new ideas in fiber and string technology.

Flax, still today an important fiber plant, was one of the first plants domesticated, and one of the first animals domesticated was the sheep (specifically *Ovis orientalis*). But sheep were domesticated for meat, not wool, as most people assume. Their coats were not soft and woolly, but coarse and bristly like a deer's, and it evidently took some four thousand years of inbreeding and selection to develop usably woolly sheep. Before that, domestic sheep and cattle were raised to be killed for food, but around 4000 B.C.E. people conceived the radical idea that they did better by keeping the sheep alive. Instead of providing one feast and one hide, each animal could provide a continuing supply of wool for clothing and of milk for food (preservable as yogurt and cheese). This change, as revolutionary as domestication itself, came to be known as the "secondary products revolution." Wool, from ever woollier sheep, is still one of the most important fibers worldwide.

**Figure 2.** Women weighing and preparing wool, spinning with drop-spindle, weaving on warp-weighted loom. From Greek wedding vase, 560 B.C.E. THE METROPOLITAN MUSEUM OF ART, FLETCHER FUND, 1931 (31.11.10) PHOTOGRAPH, ALL RIGHTS RESERVED, THE METROPOLITAN MUSEUM OF ART

Another key Neolithic invention was the spindle. Plant fibers are often long, making them easy to twist by hand into a single length of string. But for longer pieces, or if the fibers are short, one encounters a problem, for the string, once twisted, becomes quite ornery the moment you let go of one end to add more fiber to the other. It either untwists or gnarls up in a tangle, both effects being counterproductive. The solution is to wind it up on something, say a stick, which both stores it and keeps it from tangling or untwisting. But then the easiest way to twist more fiber onto the free end is to turn the stick itself. That's what a spindle is: a rod for holding the finished thread while adding twist to the newly forming part. The spindle can be twirled in the hand (hand-held), or with one end in a dish (supported), or hanging in the air from the newly forming thread (dropped) (Figs. 2 and 10). The speed and steady inertia of its spin can be increased by adding a little flywheel to the rod: an apple or potato will do, but we start finding small clay disks or wheels for the purpose, called spindle whorls, early in the Neolithic, by 6000 B.C.E. Spinning with a whorl-weighted spindle is many times faster (and easier) than twisting without a spindle.

So from the notion of twist to the notion of twirling a stick to the addition of the spindle whorl, humans came up with their first ideas of rotary motion, translated only much later, c. 3000 B.C.E., to the idea of the load-bearing wheel—a key idea that seems now to have been thought up only once, and in the area where spindles were invented.

Spindle technology was so easy, efficient, and portable that it remained essentially unchanged for seven thousand years, until the invention of the foot-powered spinning wheel in the Middle Ages, a design that quadrupled the speed of spinning and that was apparently jump-started by ideas from China, and finally, the spinning jenny—a hand-powered multiple spinning machine—during the industrial revolution. Hand spindles are still used in rural areas, however, where women make thread from fiber while doing other chores.

**Textiles**

Toward the end of the Paleolithic, people developed the idea of interlacing string or other long thin elements in a regular way to form a broad fabric: impressions of twined net or cloth

were found at Pavlov (see above) from 25,000 B.C.E., and fragments of mats and baskets are often found in the Near East from 7000 B.C.E. onwards. In a sense, the idea of interlacing is far older, since other large primates, such as chimps, will loosely "weave" together a few branches in a treetop to make a comfortable place to nap. (One can still see pleached [plaited] fences woven of the live branches of hedge plants in rural Wales [Fig. 3], and house walls woven of dead branches [wattle] were common in earlier times.) But interlacing in a *regular* way to make a *portable* object was a much newer idea.

Cloth differs from mats and baskets in one important respect. Mats and baskets, which hold their shape, are made principally from stiff materials, whereas cloth (whose prime quality is floppiness) is made entirely from pliable string or thread. A little experimentation will convince the reader that one cannot compactly interlace several pieces of string that are simply lying about: one set of string must be held under tension—a substitute for stiffness. This "foundation" set of threads is called the warp, and the frame that holds it is the loom (Fig. 4). Then it's easy to lace in crossways a second set—the weft or woof (both from the same ancient linguistic root as *weave*). There are also ways of holding several sets of material taut, as in braiding and other forms of plaiting and netting; but tension is basic to all of these.

**Heddles**

Most cloth today is true weave, in which the weft simply goes over and under successive warp threads (Fig. 1c; possibly in a pattern) rather than twisting around the warp or around other weft (twining; Fig. 1a–b). Because of the twist, twined fabrics are inherently more stable than those in true weave (consider how easily a torn edge of modern cloth frays out). Early cloth-like fabrics were therefore twined, as at Pavlov and in the earliest known cloth in the Western Hemisphere (from at least 8000 B.C.E.). The only advantage to true weave is that, unlike twining, the weaving process is mechanizable, making the production of true-weave cloth many times faster than that of twined cloth. When you can make so much so fast, the problem of unraveling becomes less important (and one can prevent raveling by binding the raw edges). Our first proof of true weaving occurs at Çatal Höyük, in central Turkey, around 6000 B.C.E., where we find a large amount of plain-weave

**Figure 3.** Freshly "pleached" hedge: thin, live branches have been bent obliquely to the right and woven across upright stakes. Powys, Wales, 1989. E. J. W. BARBER

**Figure 4.** Earliest extant depiction of loom. At bottom: horizontal ground loom with warp stretched between two beams pegged to the ground. At top: either weft-preparation or a mat loom. Painted dish, Badari, Egypt, c. 4200 B.C.E. © PETRIE MUSEUM OF ARCHAEOLOGY, UNIVERSITY COLLEGE LONDON

linen—coarse and fine; tight and open; hemmed, fringed, and with reinforced woven selvedges of three sorts—and a very small amount of twined linen. The sheer statistics, as well as the fine and even weaving, tell us that these people knew and used the heddle—the invention that mechanized the loom.

Heddles are difficult to explain abstractly (although easy to use) and must have been very difficult to think up. The evidence suggests that the heddle was invented only once in human history and spread across the world from there. In 1900, when extensive ethnographic work was being done in remote parts of the earth, it was clear that many human cultures had never got the idea of weaving with heddles, or even, in a few cases, of any kind of weaving.

Let's imagine a loom in which the warp lies horizontally. The problem is to separate the warp threads so that one half—every second thread—is lifted. When the weft passes through the resulting "tunnel" (called the shed, from an old word for "divide"), it leaves its trail under one (lifted) thread, over the next (unlifted) thread, under the next, and so on. This can be accomplished easily by shoving a rod, called a shed bar, through the warp in exactly this way: then lift the rod, and you open the shed.

But the problem of lifting the other half of the warp, for what is called the countershed, is not so easy. You could stick a second rod into the opposite shed, but you will find your two rods interfere with each other hopelessly: one prevents the other from being raised. What you need is a discontinuous rod. Impossible.

The solution is to lay the second rod on *top* of the warp (not the obvious place), where it won't interfere with the shed rod, then make a series of string nooses (heddles), each of which is attached to this rod (the heddle bar) and to one warp thread. Among them, they catch up all the intervening warp threads that still need to be raised. Now raise the heddle bar, and you open the countershed.

The solution of this difficult three-dimensional problem produced the world's first complex machine, one with multiple moving parts, before 7000 B.C.E., more than a millennium before the invention of fired pottery and nearly four thousand years before the hot-working of metals.

## Looms

Once heddles were invented, loom weaving spread rapidly, spawning different types of looms. Narrow band-looms must have come first, then wider ones, with the warp stretched horizontally (as in Mesopotamia, Egypt, China, and Southeast Asia), vertically (Syria), or aslant (Europe and Central and South America), and tensioned with twin beams (Mesopotamia, Egypt, and Syria), weights (Europe), or the body (China, Southeast Asia, and Central and South America) (see Figs. 2, 4, 5, and 10). On all these early looms, the heddle bars—of which there might be several, for patterning—had to be shifted by hand to change the sheds.

The next conceptual development was to rig up pulley-linked treadles to use the feet for changing sheds, thereby freeing the hands to manipulate the weft more efficiently. Our first evidence for treadled looms comes in a manuscript of 1200. It shows the weft carried in a true shuttle (Fig. 6) rather than on a simple stick bobbin (as in Figs. 2 and 10). With the flick of one hand, this boat-shaped device can be shot rapidly through the wide-open shed—lightly supported on the horizontal warp as it passes across—and caught with the other hand, ready for the return shot a moment later when the stomp of one foot changes the shed. Again the new ideas, possibly inspired by information about Chinese practices, helped speed the work enormously.

To produce the elaborate silk brocades Chinese customers wanted, weavers eventually developed a system of pulling ("drawing") the pattern heddles up by means of strings attached to special heddle bars that caught up the requisite threads for each row of the pattern. Called the draw-loom, this extremely complicated

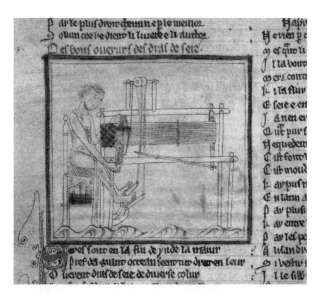

**Figure 6.** Earliest depiction of horizontal treadle loom, c. 1200. COURTESY OF THE MASTER AND FELLOWS OF TRINITY COLLEGE, CAMBRIDGE

device required both a weaver to insert the variously colored wefts and a "draw-boy" (or -girl) perched above the loom to pull the strings. At the beginning of the nineteenth century, with fancy brocades in high demand in Europe, a French inventor from Lyon (center of the European silk industry), J. M. Jacquard, figured out how to mechanize the draw-loom process by punching onto cards the information about which heddles to raise for each successive row of the pattern (Fig. 7). The information was picked up mechanically, since the needles that slid through holes in a given card caused iron bars to lift hooks attached to the heddles. This idea of punch-hole patterns to encode and store information, already used in Lyon for simpler textile mechanization by 1730, facilitated the development of data storage and control mechanisms in the later nineteenth century, leading ultimately to the twentieth-century computer.

## Clothing

Why was textile production such a catalyst for new ideas? Presumably because textiles had such important uses that people were pushed hard to improve the technology. But what were these uses, and how did we become so dependent on them?

Cloth is so perishable that until the advent of writing we have very little direct evidence of how textiles were used in early eras. (Writing began in the Near East shortly before 3000 B.C.E., by which time humans had been speaking for more than 100,000 years.) But we have a few interesting hints.

As already discussed, string alone enabled people to catch and hold more; nets did likewise. But cloth enabled people to cover and wrap things, and especially, because of its extreme flexibility, things of odd or lumpy shape—like the human body.

Already at 20,000 B.C.E., still in the Upper Paleolithic, we have a few representations of people wearing clothing clearly made from twisted fiber string. For example, a carved "Venus" (or fertility) figure from Lespugue, France, depicts a plump

**Figure 5.** Woman weaving on a foot-tensioned backstrap loom. From a figurine on top of bronze Chinese vessel, Han Dynasty (206 B.C.E.–220 C.E.).

**Figure 7.** Jacquard loom. © BETTMANN/CORBIS

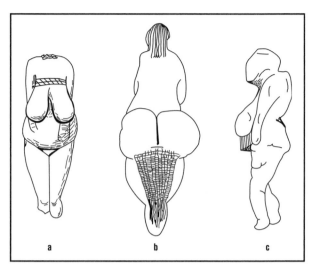

**Figure 8.** Paleolithic "Venus" figures of c. 20,000 B.C.E. wearing string clothing: (a) cords across chest (Kostenki, Russia); (b) string skirt in rear (Lespugue, France); (c) string skirt in front (Gagarino, Russia). The string skirt apparently signaled child-bearing status. COURTESY OF THE AUTHOR

woman wearing a so-called string skirt, a belt-band supporting a row of strings that hang down like a skirt or apron (Fig. 8b). (The carver marked not only the twists on the strings but even how the strings are coming untwisted at the bottom.) Other Venuses of the same era from Russia (Figs. 8a and c) are shown wearing string skirts or twisted bands worn across the chest, while the Venus of Willendorf (Austria) wears a spirally worked cap on her head.

All this clothing, clearly, was fashioned from string. Yet none is of any use for either warmth or what we would call modesty. So why did Paleolithic people trouble to make such clothing?

Apparently to communicate messages. String skirts continue to appear on European figurines through the Neolithic and Bronze Ages, by which time we begin to find actual string skirts preserved on buried women (in Denmark, where woolen garments often survive), and we see them occasionally in Iron Age Greece (in literature, and on figurines and vases). These women—both those buried and those represented and talked about—are clearly not children, but full-grown. In recent centuries such skirts still turn up as a key part of women's folk costumes (rural dress) throughout eastern Europe, from the Adriatic to the Urals and from southern Greece to Latvia.

Wherever we find representations or physical remains, the woman has reached child-bearing age; wherever we find direct information about the skirt's meaning, from Homer to the

modern ethnographers, it invariably indicates something about the ability or willingness to bear children. In eastern Europe, in fact, we learn that girls are not *allowed* to wear them until they reach puberty, at which point they *must* do so. In short, the string skirt (or its surrogate) gives the viewer crucial biosocial information about both the females who wear it and those who do not.

A quite different piece of clothing, in these societies, signals that the woman is also married and therefore no longer available: a headdress completely covering the hair. (It was, and in some places still is, widely believed that a woman's fertility resides in her hair.) In modern Western societies, this message is conveyed by a piece of jewelry, the wedding ring.

What we see, then, is that humans started to devise clothing as a means of communication, and not, as is generally supposed, for warmth. We tend to forget that prolonged exposure to less-than-extreme cold inures the body to frigid weather (and, in fact, the humans in most depictions prior to the Bronze Age, which begins about 3000 B.C.E. in the Near East, are naked). Although not so flexible as language, clothing signals have the advantage that they do not die away instantly, but rather persist over time. If a woman wears a wedding ring, she doesn't have to keep saying "I'm taken" every time a man looks at her. The earliest signals sent by clothing that we can detect thus concern marital status. Such signals gradually formed a vital communication system parallel to but independent of language.

Although harder to pin down, early uses also include marking special events, particularly religious rites, and along with this, marking people central to those events. For instance, Upper Paleolithic cave art includes a depiction of what appears to be a dancing man clad in what look like a deerskin and antlers (Trois Frères, France), presumably involved in a ritual.

One of the earliest clear depictions we have of a religious scene is on a tall alabaster vase from the great Mesopotamian

**Figure 9.** Naked workers (middle) and clothed elite (above) involved in agricultural ritual. Adapted from stone vase, Uruk (Warka), c. 3200 B.C.E.

city of Uruk, shortly before 3000 B.C.E. (Fig. 9). The bottom registers depict the key domestic plants and animals (wheat and sheep); above them, lines of naked workmen carry baskets laden with agricultural produce. In the top register we see people wearing kilts or long robes presenting some of this produce to a long-robed woman who, judging from the banners hung next to her, is either the goddess Inanna or her priestess. So people already "dressed up" for religious ceremonies, and the textiles sometimes marked the religious space itself.

We still tend to dress more specially for church, synagogue, mosque, or temple; special shawls, robes, or hats usually mark key participants; and the place of worship is generally set off or "dressed" with special textiles, from altar cloths to prayer rugs to screens and pavilions. In fact, in many cultures (for example, Indonesia or classical Greece), the laying out or hanging of special textiles serves to make that space sacred for the moment, in order to carry out a wedding, funeral, judgment, or other rite. Anyone of that culture, seeing that textile, recognizes its significance, although others probably will not.

The Uruk vase shows us something beyond religious status, however. While the peasants are naked, the elite are coming to be distinguished by their clothing. This idea of social status as economic and political, rather than solely marital or religious, seems to begin with the concentration of masses of people into cities in the fourth millennium B.C.E. and to spread with the quest for metals that ensued.

Metals were the first important commodity that people could neither grow nor find in their backyards; obtaining them required organizing resources to support expeditions to mine ore or to trade for finished metal. This meant increasingly permanent stratification into leaders and followers (instead of temporary stratification for local warfare) and quickly led to the differentiation between those who had power—and easy access to imported goods—and those who did not. The ancient

monuments show us that soon everyone in "civilized" areas took up clothing. Wearing clothes even came to be viewed as a mark of being civilized, to the Chinese and to many other cultures.

## Clothing Design

Belts, cloaks, kilts—the earliest garments depicted—are mere wraparounds. The Egyptians are the first on record to think of sewing up cloth into a permanently formed dress, in their case a tube for the torso, held up by a strap over one or both shoulders and forming a sort of jumper (Figs. 10 and 11a). The earliest preserved body garment we possess is a First Dynasty linen shirt (c. 3100 B.C.E.) in which the idea of tubes has already been taken further to include sleeves (Figs. 11b and 12). Where one would expect the narrow supporting straps, two long rectangles of cloth were added, sewn up along the edges to form tube sleeves.

In the Near East, on the other hand, people seem to have worked from the concept of a garment hung from the shoulders. When they began sewing up clothes, rather than draping them anew with each wearing, they cut a neck hole in the middle of the cloth and sewed up the sides, eventually adding two tubes for sleeves (Fig. 11c). Our first extant example of this garment type was found in Tutankhamen's (c. 1370–1352 B.C.E.) tomb (though details show it to be a Syrian import). This general design, improved by opening the front for easy donning (Fig. 11d), was destined to survive till today as our basic upper garment. Our oldest examples of this construction occur on magnificently preserved Caucasoid mummies from the deserts of central Asia from 1000 B.C.E.

These same immigrants also preserve our first examples of another clever use of cloth tubes: trousers, invented shortly before 1000 B.C.E. by Eurasian horsemen for protection while riding horseback (Fig. 13). Again, this clothing design has come down to us as one of our basic garments.

As textile technology progressed, who wore what often became strictly codified. In Egypt, only the pharaoh folded his kilt with the left lappet on top; in Rome, only the emperor could wear a garment entirely of purple, and only noble citizens a purple stripe. This meant the viewer could read rank and station from another's costume, even, in some cases, down to the last degree. In China, for example, officials of all types sewed onto their robes fair-sized rectangular emblem-patches, known as rank badges, that specified their exact rank and position in the governmental hierarchy. (The highest emblem was the dragon, which only the emperor could wear.) Aztec warriors, for their part, displayed their degree of prowess in battle as special emblems on their cloaks. Less formally, but just as rigidly, European folk dress evolved in such a way that the knowledgeable viewer could look at a village woman's garb and determine that, for example, the wearer had reached puberty, was a Christian rather than Muslim or Jewish, was not particularly wealthy, came from a certain village or locality, and was a skilled and diligent worker. The elements that conveyed this information accrued one by one over twenty thousand years, to the point that the costume represents multiple layers of walking history.

**Figure 10.** Egyptian textile workers (right to left: spinner, flax-splicer, overseer, two weavers squatting beside horizontal ground loom). Mural in tomb of Khnumhotep, Beni Hassan; Twelfth Dynasty (early 2nd millennium B.C.E.). THE METROPOLITAN MUSEUM OF ART, ROGERS FUND, 1933 (33.8.16) PHOTOGRAPH, ALL RIGHTS RESERVED, THE METROPOLITAN MUSEUM OF ART

Although much of this kind of information could be read from nineteenth-century traditional dress throughout Eurasia, the same could not be said in England, for an interesting reason. There the nobility habitually gave its cast-off clothing to the servants and tenant farmers, a practice that increasingly obscured an observer's ability to determine someone's standing by clothing alone, although poor fit, fraying edges, and outmoded fashion would give clues. Consequently there is no English "peasant costume" as in other parts of Europe. In this way, although court dress at the top of the scale was highly controlled, dress in the lower classes became more democratic, a trait that, to some extent, moved to North America with the colonists. In the early twenty-first century, the farther west you go across the United States, the less dress and its potential signals of status matter to many people. On West Coast college campuses it can be hard to tell students from professors, and at the Los Angeles Opera you may see everything from tuxedos and jeweled evening gowns to blue jeans—and running shoes on both sexes. For the middle class, at least, what you wear during leisure time is more a function of how you feel that day than of how you wish others to perceive you. If anything, the Bronze Age idea of telling people your social rank through dress has been emphatically rejected, and westerners will complain about easterners' "class consciousness."

The same people, however, still send messages through the textiles they choose to wear by selecting them according to their personalities—within, of course, the general mores of their culture. Pluck them out of Los Angeles and drop them into, say, Ankara or Turfan, and their clothing readily signals their cultural origin.

Handmade textiles, too, have always had a personal element. Those who wove, embroidered, or knotted pile for home use are repeatedly documented as taking the attitude, "If I'm going to put this much work in, and use it all my life, I want it to look the way *I* want it to look." Hence no two rugs or aprons or blouses looked alike: the traditional was simultaneously personal.

**Furnishings**

Since about the third millennium, messages similar to those given by clothing have been transmitted by the textiles we use to dress our surroundings. We mentioned using cloth to set apart and adorn religious or sacred space, but textiles also adorned the home, as bedcovers, curtains, cushions, and so forth. Evidence from Çatal Höyük, Turkey, whence some of our earliest textile fragments (6000 B.C.E.), indicates that people slept and sat on low clay platforms covered with padding (dried grass? rushes?) topped with mats or textiles. The ancient Egyptians manufactured only plain white linen for normal household use—sheets, bedspreads, towels, and clothing—but from at least 2000 B.C.E., they were importing fancily patterned woolen cloth from the Aegean to make into

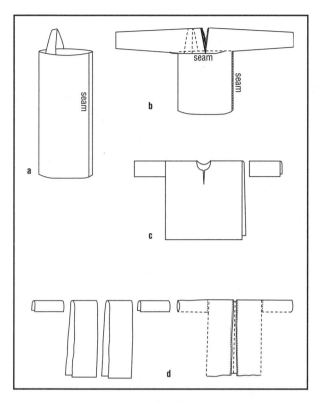

**Figure 11.** Construction of early clothing types: (a) Egyptian dress made of tube with shoulder strap; (b) Egyptian shirt, in which shoulder-straps were elongated into sleeves; (c) Syrian shirt with neck-hole in cloth hung from shoulders; (d) Eurasian nomad shirt, hung from shoulders but with front opening. COURTESY OF THE AUTHOR

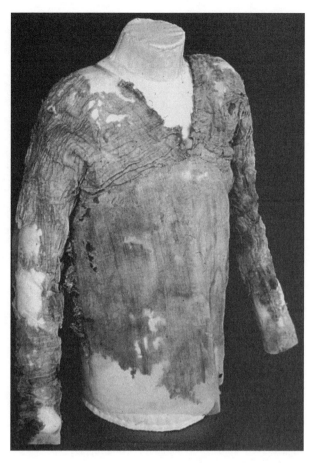

**Figure 12.** Earliest preserved body-garment: linen shirt with sleeves finely pleated for trim fit. Tarkhan, Egypt, First Dynasty, c. 3000 B.C.E. COPYRIGHT: PETRIE MUSEUM OF ARCHAEOLOGY, UNIVERSITY COLLEGE LONDON

ostentatiously colorful canopies, apparently to advertise their social status. Around 1370 B.C.E. we also glimpse colorful rugs and cushions, again probably of imported fabric.

We read in classical Greek literature that cloth tents were set up temporarily on temple grounds for celebrations. These pavilions were constructed from textiles decorated with elaborately woven scenes—rare and expensive textiles dedicated to the deities as votive gifts and stored in temple storehouses. Temples served as the treasuries, and indeed, museums, of the ancient world, just as cathedrals did in medieval times, and the rarer the gift, the higher the giver in people's estimation.

Among nomadic peoples of Eurasia, cloth furnishings were even more important than among their sedentary neighbors, since cloth was highly utilitarian yet portable. They made their houses out of collapsible wicker frames covered with felt (densely matted wool) and fastened with colorful woven straps that signaled to visitors whose yurt (felt tent) it was (Fig. 14). Their possessions were stored in chests covered with brightly patterned felt padding, and their precious china teacups were carried in padded felt pouches. Pile carpets formed the (movable) floors, and colorful interior hangings further insulated and adorned the walls. Even the plates for dry foods were often made of felt. Because textiles were so central, they were an

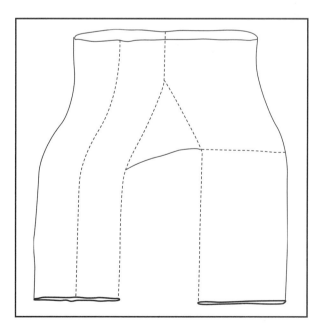

**Figure 13.** Construction of a pair of woolen trousers found with the mummies at Cherchen, 1000 B.C.E. COURTESY OF THE AUTHOR

**New Dictionary of the History of Ideas**

**Figure 14.** Nomadic Kazakh family setting up yurt (portable felt house), Nan Shan, Uyghur Autonomous Region, 1995.  E. J. W. BARBER

important form of gift exchange: in frozen burial sites of the fourth century B.C.E., in the Altai Mountains, excavators found saddle cloths of Chinese embroidered silk from far to the east, and of Persian woolen tapestry from far to the west, as well as of local polychrome felt cutwork.

As the world became more interconnected, trade in textiles became increasingly important. We hear of such trade already between Mesopotamia and Syria before 2000 B.C.E. and between Assyria and Anatolia (roughly modern Turkey) in 1800 B.C.E.; between China and India in the second century B.C.E., and between China and Rome in the early centuries C.E. (along the newly opened, so-called Silk Road). Long voyages of discovery were undertaken by Europeans in the fifteenth and sixteenth centuries to open up more trade with the Orient in textiles, as well as in spices and other commodities, leading to the accidental opening of routes to the New World. As such trade became serious international business, textile wars also broke out—the struggles among the Spanish, British, and Dutch over the wool trade among them—for, as the middle class rose after the breakdown of feudalism, more and more people wanted to display their status by means of elegant textiles for the furnishings of their parlors as well as their clothing. Imported fabrics spelled luxury, and their display announced those ever-crucial social messages.

*See also* **Class; Communication of Ideas; Dress; Life Cycle; Trade.**

**BIBLIOGRAPHY**

Adovasio, J. M., Olga Soffer, and B. Klima. "Palaeolithic Fibre Technology: Interlaced Woven Finds from Pavlov I, Czech Republic, c. 26,000 year, B.P." *Antiquity* 70 (1996): 526–534. Earliest preserved textile remains yet found.

Anawalt, Patricia Reiff. "A Comparative Analysis of the Costumes and Accoutrements of the Codex Mendoza." In *The Codex Mendoza,* edited by Frances Berdan and Patricia Anawalt, vol. 1, 103–150. Berkeley: University of California Press, 1992. Aztec clothing described and analyzed.

Barber, E. J. W. *The Mummies of Ürümchi.* New York: Norton, 1999. Superbly preserved textile finds from prehistoric Central Asia.

———. "On the Antiquity of East European Bridal Clothing." In *Folk Dress in Europe* and *Anatolia: Beliefs about Protection and Fertility,* edited by Linda Welters, 13–31. Oxford: Berg, 1999. History of the string skirt and its relatives.

———. *Prehistoric Textiles: The Development of Cloth in the Neolithic and Bronze Ages.* Princeton: Princeton University Press, 1991. The majority of the data in this entry is documented in this compendium of archaeological textile data from 20,000 B.C.E. to about 400 B.C.E., from Iran to Britain. Includes massive bibliography and index.

———. *Women's Work: The First 20,000 Years: Women, Cloth, and Society in Early Times.* New York: Norton, 1994.

Broudy, Eric. *The Book of Looms.* New York: Van Nostrand Reinhold, 1979. Lavishly illustrated, with well-selected bibliography.

Emery, Irene. *The Primary Structures of Fabrics: An Illustrated Classification.* Washington, D.C.: Textile Museum, 1966.

Geijer, Agnes. *A History of Textile Art.* Translated by R. Tanner. London: Pasold Research Fund, 1979. Classic general history of textiles.

Rudenko, S. I. *Frozen Tombs of Siberia: The Pazyryk Burials of Iron Age Horsemen.* Translated by M. W. Thompson. Berkeley: University of California Press, 1970. Superbly preserved textiles from prehistoric Siberia.

Sherratt, Andrew. "Plough and Pastoralism: Aspects of the Secondary Products Revolution." In *Patterns of the Past: Studies in Honour of David Clark,* edited by I. Hodder, G. Isaac, and N. Hammond, 261–305. Cambridge, U.K.: Cambridge University Press, 1981.

*E. J. W. Barber*

# THEATER AND PERFORMANCE.

"Performance" is an influential theoretical paradigm in the arts and humanities, with adherents in disciplines as diverse as anthropology, linguistic philosophy, and theater. Since the early 1980s, thinking about performance has been fostered in "performance studies" programs, disciplinary hybrids with widely variant intellectual genealogies, united by their commitment to performance as their central object and method of research.

## Performance Studies' Interdisciplinary Genealogy

Histories of performance studies most frequently cite its formation in the convergence of experimental theater and structuralist anthropology in the late 1960s. Avant-garde theater practitioners in the United States such as Richard Schechner were exploring cultural traditions of performance that fell outside entrenched disciplinary traditions of Western theatrical practice and theater studies. Their work drew on research into archaic ritual and non-Western performance forms, unsettling representational conventions of illusionism and distinctions between artistic disciplines, exploring the significance of neglected parts of the performance process, such as audience response, rehearsal, and training, and blurring the boundaries between art and everyday life. Their investigations coincided with the structural anthropologist Victor Turner's interest in ritual, festival, and other forms of symbolic, collective action. Turner's dramatically inflected analysis of public culture and social events saw performance as the site of a given culture's fullest and most self-conscious expression of its unique values and categories, and the engine of its perpetuation and transformation. Schechner and Turner's research collaboration spurred the formation of New York University's Performance Studies Department in 1980.

The contemporary field of performance studies as a whole owes its genesis to a still broader range of disciplinary interests.

The Department of Performance Studies at Northwestern University, for example, grew from the tradition of oral interpretation of literature dating back to the late nineteenth century. Attuned to the rhetorical power of acts of verbal and embodied performance, the Northwestern school's interest is still primarily in performance as a mode of human communication that is "creative, constructed, collaborative, and contingent." Influential currents in the sociology and psychology of the 1960s and 1970s also informed the development of performance studies. These included the theorization of play, social dramaturgy, and the presentation of self in everyday life developed in the work of Johan Huizinga, Roger Caillois, Erving Goffman, and others, and the interpretive or symbolic anthropology of Clifford Geertz. At its broadest level, performance studies probably owes most to the linguistic turn in the arts and humanities, and its development has been closely aligned with poststructuralist or postmodernist innovation in philosophy, linguistics, anthropology, feminism, area studies, cultural studies, folklore, postcolonial studies, and queer studies.

## Performance as Object

As an "interdiscipline," performance studies prides itself on its open, multivocal, and fluid character, refusing to dictate either a core methodology or canonical body of knowledge and resisting a fixed or exclusive definition of performance itself. That said, scholarship that goes under the banner of performance studies has in common a focus on process, action, events, and behaviors, be they physical, verbal, artistic, or technological, and claims performance—the execution or carrying out of things—as both its object and its method of study. This focus entails abandoning static, object-oriented, or textual approaches to cultural analysis, inclining instead toward processual, interactional, and experiential perspectives. An art historian or archaeologist working in performance studies, for example, might examine how a given object has functioned or been understood over time and in particular material and social contexts; a performance historian might concentrate on situating a historical document in the contexts and moments of its enunciation; an idea or political principle would not be approached in the abstract but through an analysis of its embodied enactment in ceremony, debate, or communal events. In the words of one of its more famous exponents, Dwight Conquergood, performance studies means understanding "culture" as a verb rather than a noun.

Among the basic premises shared by scholars in performance studies is the conviction that performance is one of the most powerful means that humans have for constructing reality, forging and sustaining collectivities, social relationships, and individual identities, and for questioning or imagining them otherwise. Performance is also a means for accomplishing agendas and forwarding arguments, for learning and persuading through the agency of narrative, semiotic communication, corporeal style and training, pleasure, and participation. While performance studies retains close ties to the study of Western theatrical practice, it regards illusionistic, representational theater as but one category in a broad spectrum of performance

**Outdoor performance of Euripedes'** *Iphigenia in Taurus,* **Brad-field College, Berkshire, England, 1912.** The field of performance studies has its roots in the mid-nineteenth century, when experimental and avant-garde theater met structuralist anthropology. Performance was seen as a means to build new realities and stimulate the mind. © HULTON-DEUTSCH COLLECTION/CORBIS

practices, the majority of which are more concerned with *poesis* than mimesis, with making (of realities and meanings) rather than faking. Performance studies resists drawing hard and fast lines between aesthetic modes of performance and deliberative or habitual forms of action, arguing instead that analytical models used for either can be productively applied to both. However, the bulk of performance studies scholarship is still drawn to those actions along what Richard Schechner has called the "performance continuum" between everyday enactments and the performing arts, actions that are framed or designated in specific social contexts as performance.

## Performance as Method
While performance studies scholars espouse a range of often innovative methodologies, the ephemeral, subjective nature of performance as its subject matter poses unique challenges. For a majority of those in the field, understanding performance as a way of knowing entails a commitment to participant-observer ethnography as the principal research methodology. Dwight Conquergood, who has written extensively on this issue, sees the performance ethnographer and her "informant" (or the teacher and student, performer and audience) as engaged in reciprocal, collaborative performances. Studying performance in this way foregrounds cultural knowledge as contingent, socially located, embodied, and contested, and implies that the ethnographer is directly implicated in and responsible to the community in which he or she studies. Following from this assumption, performance studies scholars frequently vaunt an open, politicized commitment to a position within their field and understand their performance scholarship as a mode of advocacy as much as analysis. Furthermore, they are frequently practitioners or artists themselves, confusing traditional anthropological distinctions between the subject and object of research.

## Performance, Performativity, and Theatricality
The performance concept has since the late 1980s enjoyed a reach beyond this interdisciplinary constellation of performance studies through the elaboration of theories of performativity. Judith Butler's famous formulation draws on continental philosophy and the work of the linguist J. L. Austin to argue that, through processes of forcible iteration, discourse has the power to enact or materialize (to "perform") that which it names. Adherents of performativity use these theories, in the place of earlier theories of "representation," to explain the ways in which norms of gender and sexuality are produced, reproduced, and modulated in cultural production. Thanks to this work, the performance concept has a life throughout the arts and humanities, even as current debates in performance studies seek to reconcile their field's orientation around acts of performance (the tactical and interpretive agency of the performer and audience, and the subversive or deconstructive nature of theatrical traditions) with performativity's emphasis on the power of textual systems.

## The State of the Field
Performance studies has been most notable for work that examines the politics and poetics of identity (gender, race, ethnicity, and sexuality) in ways that are both responsive to the claims of human creativity and criticality and cognizant of the normative forces that constrain such expressions. This work avoids the Enlightenment distinctions between mind and body that have proved an obstacle to similar critique from other disciplines. Significant areas of interest in the field in the early twenty-first century include tourism, urban festivity, historical ethnography, pedagogy, and the performance of space and place. True to the origins of performance studies, much work examines contemporary performance art and experimental theater from a perspective that provocatively mixes criticism and practice. In a field that has historically privileged the localized study of live, embodied action and interaction, interest in globalization, diaspora, cyber-communities, and virtual, technological, and "mediatized" performance has proved theoretically fertile. Some prominent scholars have made broad claims that performance is the predominant paradigm of a globalized age, comparable to the colonial era's orientation around models of "discipline."

Performance studies is flourishing both within and outside the United States. Its flagship journals, *The Drama Review* (TDR) and *Text and Performance Quarterly* have been joined by publications such as *Performance Research;* performance research centers have been established in Cardiff, Wales, and Christchurch, New Zealand; and conferences have been held in Japan, Germany, and Singapore. The doctoral programs at New York University and Northwestern University, and the performance studies focus areas of numerous communications programs, have been joined by a world theater and dance program at UCLA, and formerly traditional theater programs (at the University of California at Berkeley, for example) are adopting the performance studies moniker as they increasingly embrace research interests and theoretical paradigms from outside the bounds of Western institutionalized theater.

Whether performance studies can sustain itself as an "interdisciplinary" formation, given the claims made on the performance concept by a range of disciplinary competitors, has been a matter for debate since the earliest inception of performance studies institutions. As a powerful tool for thinking about cultural process from the point of view of human action and expression, however, the performance concept will doubtless be a significant feature in the landscape of cultural criticism for some time to come.

*See also* **Avant-Garde; Musical Performance and Audiences; Structuralism and Poststructuralism.**

**BIBLIOGRAPHY**
Butler, Judith. *Bodies That Matter: On the Discursive Limits of "Sex."* New York and London: Routledge, 1993.
Carlson, Marvin. *Performance: A Critical Introduction.* 2nd ed. New York: Routledge, 2004.
Conquergood, Dwight. "Performance Studies: Interventions and Radical Research." *TDR: The Drama Review* 46, no. 2 (2002): 145–156.
Dailey, Sheron J., ed. *The Future of Performance Studies: Visions and Revisions.* Annandale, Va.: National Communication Association, 1998.
McKenzie, Jon. *Perform or Else: From Discipline to Performance.* London and New York: Routledge, 2001.
Schechner, Richard. *Performance Studies: An Introduction.* New York and London: Routledge, 2002.

*Margaret Werry*

**THEODICY.** Gottfried Wilhelm Leibniz's (1646–1716) neologism *théodicée* (from Greek *theos*, God + *dike*, justice) means divine justice, but the term has long been conflated with John Milton's (1608–1674) promise to "justify the ways of God to men." In 1791 Immanuel Kant (1724–1804) defined theodicy as "the defense of the highest wisdom of the creator against the charge which reason brings against it for whatever is counterpurposive in the world" (p. 24).

Many intellectual historians see theodicy as a specifically modern, perhaps even a more specifically eighteenth-century phenomenon, but the term has come to have broader meanings. Auguste Comte (1798–1857) described all natural and philosophical theology as theodicy. Scholars of religion call all efforts to answer a problem of evil thought to be universal theodicies. The Book of Job, the Indian doctrine of karma, and even capitalist faith in the market have all been seen as theodicies.

There is good reason to restrict the meaning of the term, however, if not to post-Leibnizian thought then at least to philosophical discussions of a certain sort. Works like the Book of Job do not offer philosophical justifications of God, or even accounts of his justice; slamming the door in the face of human demands for intelligibility simply cuts the knot. Much can be learned from examining the presuppositions that make the door-slam inadmissable in the modern age.

## Early Modern Theodicy

Pierre Bayle (1647–1706) forced the problem of evil in his 1697 *Dictionnaire historique et critique*. He may have been inspired by Nicolas de Malebranche's (1638–1715) insistence on the world's imperfections—albeit in the context of an argument for the supremacy of God. For Malebranche, evils prove that God sought not to create the best of all possible worlds but only the most perfect in relation to God's ways. He could have created a better world, but this world, the work of "general" rather than "particular volition," better expresses his nature.

Leibniz's *Essais de théodicée* (1710) responded to Bayle's challenge, but offers little that was really new. Leibniz himself traced its most famous claim—that this is "the best of all possible worlds"—back to Plato. The related idea that a perfect world is not possible because not all possible things are "compossible" with each other has a Stoic pedigree. Both claims had come close to the surface of Martin Luther's polemic with Desiderius Erasmus and were explicitly made by Spanish Jesuits and by the Cambridge Platonists.

While Leibniz thought that we would do well to be more attentive to the good in our lives, his argument was a priori. A God infinite in goodness, power, and wisdom would not create a world unless it were good, and, if several worlds were possible, would create none but the best. "It is true that one may imagine possible worlds without sin and without unhappiness," Leibniz conceded. Yet, "these same worlds again would be very inferior to ours in goodness. I cannot show you this in detail. For can I know and can I present infinities to you and compare them together? But you must judge with me ab effectu, since God has chosen this world as it is" (*Theodicy* §10).

*Optimism.* Christian Freiherr von Wolff (1679–1754), Leibniz's most influential disciple, thought that Leibniz had unnecessarily abandoned the best argument against atheism—the argument from design, known in Germany as teleology or physico-theology. Much early-eighteenth-century thought offered teleological arguments that this was the best possible world. The word *optimism* (from *optimum*, the best), coined in the 1730s, lumped together decidedly different arguments. Wolff's Leibnizian arguments are quite different from Alexander Pope's assertion, in his best-selling *Essay on Man* (1733), that "Whatever IS, is RIGHT."

The hollowness of optimistic claims was shown by Samuel Johnson's *Rasselas* (1759), Voltaire's *Candide* (1759), and most decisively by David Hume's posthumously published *Dialogues Concerning Natural Religion* (1779). Hume's character Philo declares "Epicurus' old questions" concerning the compatibility of belief in God with evil "yet unanswered." Immanuel Kant tried to show that they could never be answered.

*Kant.* Although he was originally a defender of optimism and remained impressed by the evidences of physico-theology, Kant pulled the rug out from under the project of theodicy. As an endeavor fusing theoretical and practical reason, philosophical theodicy for Kant represented a particularly dangerous form of pretension: it threatened to blunt the sense that

---

### THEODICIES OF SUFFERING AND GOOD FORTUNE

Max Weber thought that the problem of theodicy was the stimulus for the "rationalization of religious ideas" in all—not just monotheistic—religious traditions. Alongside "theodicies of suffering," accounts of the nature and distribution of misfortune in the world that console those who suffer, Weber discerned another kind of view that reassures those who do not suffer that it is just and right that they be spared. He deems this the "theodicy of good fortune" (ch. 6).

The idea seems to have roots in Marx, but Weber adds the idea that those theodicies that last are those that speak both to the fortunate and to the unfortunate. He thought only three have ever done so: Zoroastrian dualism, the Calvinist understanding of the hidden God (*deus absconditus*), and the Indian doctrine of karma, "the most complete formal solution of the problem of theodicy (ch. 8).

Weber's is the most impressive effort to expand the meaning of theodicy beyond its monotheistic origins. No longer a problem only for theists, theodicy arises in response to the general problem of the "the incongruity between destiny and merit" (a Kantian problematic), which challenges all human efforts at making theoretical and practical sense of the world. Weber's understanding of theodicy as a species of the problem of meaning has shaped important theories of religion by Clifford Geertz and Peter Berger.

---

defined the human ethical vocation—that the world of our experience is not as it ought to be. In his mature philosophy of religion, Kant was particularly attentive to insincerity and saw philosophical theodicies as a key example.

In his essay "On the Failure of All Philosophical Efforts in Theodicy" (1791), Kant likened theodicists to Job's comforters. By contrast, Job, whose faith in God was firmly rooted in the moral law rather than in the claim to be able to understand God's ways, was able to stand fast in his piety despite his "counterpurposive" experiences. In the place of the hypocrisy of "doctrinal" theodicy Kant recommended Job's "authentic theodicy": "honesty in openly admitting one's doubts; repugnance to pretending conviction where one feels none" (p. 33).

### Progress and Pessimism

Theodicy was not yet dead, however. Georg Wilhelm Friedrich Hegel (1770–1831) thought philosophical efforts at theodicy had failed only because they did not see history philosophically. Properly understood, history is "the true theodicy." Like other nineteenth-century accounts of necessary progress, he did not deny the reality of evil. Evil qua evil is a necessary moment in the unfolding of spirit. For Karl Marx (1818–1883) and Friedrich Engels (1820–1895) feudalism was a necessary stage in human history. For Herbert Spencer (1820–1903) the competition that led to the "survival of the fittest" was the best promise for a bright future.

In response, Arthur Schopenhauer (1788–1860) developed his philosophical "pessimism," a deliberate reversal of optimism. This is not the best of all possible worlds, but the worst, a mindless machine of self-inflicted suffering, among whose cleverest devices are precisely the philosophical theories of teleology and progress. All efforts to make life bearable only make things worse. The only hope is to deny the will to live. Schopenhauer claimed that his pessimism made it like Buddhism, a mistaken equation that persists to this day.

In turn, thinkers as varied as Friedrich Nietzsche, William James, and Karl Barth argued for views that acknowledged the impossibility of canceling out the evils of the world and yet affirmed the world. But these views are no longer theodicies—or at least do not claim to be. What makes it possible for us to resist pessimism is not reflection on the experienced order of the world but will (Nietzsche), temperament (James), or grace (Barth).

***Contemporary debates.*** Debate on theodicy has come to be dominated by two very different tendencies. There has been a revival of philosophical theodicy among analytic philosophers of religion, who have moved from attention to the "logical problem of evil" to the "evidential problem of evil." Alvin Plantinga has revived the important distinction between the "defense" of a view against objections and the far more demanding philosophical establishment of that view, which he calls "theodicy," and which he thinks we can do without. On the other hand, the very desire to do theodicy has been condemned as irreligious or ideological. "The disproportion between suffering and every theodicy was shown at Auschwitz with a glaring, obvious clarity," wrote Emmanuel Levinas (p. 162).

*See also* **Evil; Philosophy of Religion.**

**BIBLIOGRAPHY**
Adams, Marilyn McCord, and Robert Merrihew Adams, eds. *The Problem of Evil.* Oxford and New York: Oxford University Press, 1990.
Bayle, Pierre. "Manichees." In *Historical and Critical Dictionary: Selections.* Translated by Richard H. Popkin, 144–153. Indianapolis: Hackett, 1991.
Kant, Immanuel. "On the Miscarriage of All Philosophical Trials in Theodicy." Translated by George di Giovanni. In *Religion and Rational Theology,* edited by Allen W. Wood and George di Giovanni, 19–37. Cambridge, U.K.: Cambridge University Press, 1996.
Leibniz, Gottfried W. *Theodicy: Essays on the Goodness of God, the Freedom of Man, and the Origin of Evil.* Translated by E. M. Huggard. La Salle, Ill.: Open Court, 1985.
Levinas, Emmanuel. "Useless Suffering." Translated by Richard Cohen. In *The Provocation of Levinas: Rethinking the Other,* edited by Robert Bernasconi and David Wood, 156–167. London and New York: Routledge, 1988.
Weber, Max. "The Sociology of Religion." Translated by Ephraim Fischoff. In *Economy, and Society: An Outline of Interpretive Sociology,* edited by Guenther Roth and Claus Wittich. Berkeley: University of California Press, 1978.

*Mark Larrimore*

**THEOLOGY.** *See* **Religion.**

**THIRD CINEMA.** "The anti-imperialist struggle of the peoples of the Third World and of their equivalents inside the imperialist countries constitutes today the axis of the world revolution. Third cinema is, in our opinion, the cinema that recognizes in that struggle the most gigantic cultural, scientific and artistic manifestation of our time, the great possibility of constructing a liberated personality with each people as the starting point—in a word, the decolonization of culture." These sentences were penned in 1969 by the revolutionary Argentine filmmakers Fernando Solanas and Octavio Getino in an essay titled "Towards a Third Cinema: Notes and Experiences for the Development of a Cinema of Liberation in the Third World."

This essay, along with several other manifestos, including the Brazilian Glauber Rocha's "Aesthetics of Hunger" and the Cuban Julio Garcia Espinosa's "For an Imperfect Cinema," placed questions regarding the interpenetration of political struggle, cultural struggle, and mass media squarely at the center of a global struggle against the intensification of Western imperialism. Other such proclamations, including Fernando

Birri's "Cinema and Underdevelopment" and Tomás Gutierrez Alea's "The Viewer's Dialectic," underscored and elaborated the concerns of Latin American revolutionaries with media and mass movements. What Solanas and Getino called "third cinema" was imagined, in short, as a cinema of liberation. Third cinema was to be filmmaking that would aid nationalist movements in creating a new sociocultural solidarity in the struggle against Western imperialism and for national self-determination.

**Third Cinema and the Third World**

Roy Armes, in his important work *Third World Film Making and the West,* suggests that during the 1960s "the steady development of industrialization combined with growing national awareness led almost imperceptibly to a belief, which came to be widely held, that an era of socialist revolution was dawning throughout the Third World." This belief was based in part upon Cuban resistance during an invasion orchestrated by the U.S. Central Intelligence Agency at the Bay of Pigs in 1961, and the success of Algerian nationalists after eight years of armed struggle against French rule in 1962. Armes notes that there gradually emerged what Gérard Chaliand called "a sort of third world euphoria" over the potential for genuine political change. This euphoria was connected to a host of factors including widespread "anti-colonial struggle, opposition to the Vietnam war, student revolt, a new consciousness on the part of American blacks, the emergence of armed guerilla groups in Latin America," and a reconceptualization of revolutionary strategies from the ferment of China and the Soviet Union. From so many uprisings and changes of consciousness there emerged the distinct possibility of what was to be a tricontinental revolution imagined via figures such as Frantz Fanon, Che Guevara, and Ho Chi Minh.

This possiblity of a tricontinental revolution informed the work of many third world revolutionaries and filmmakers. The people aided by their leaders and artists would reinvent the terms of a new social order free from domination by outsiders, or indeed by anyone. To put an end to the systematic, violent, and continuous exploitation of the third world by first world economies, militaries, and persons, it was necessary to invent revolutionary strategy on several levels and, moreover, revolutionary culture. Filmmakers from Africa, Asia, Latin America, and even Europe bent themselves to this task. The ideas of strategy and culture are important here because the category of "thirdness," as it turns out for many theorists of third cinema, was to be assigned *according to a film's aesthetic and political strategy* as much as by either its geographical provenance or its thematic content. In many cases, the operative question both for film commentators and filmmakers was, What can a cinema of liberation accomplish in bringing about the overthrow of Western imperialist domination and creating revolutionary culture? Given the ways in which colonized nations are dominated by their colonizers at economic, geographical, cultural, intellectual, and psychological levels, this cinema of liberation was understood to be, necessarily then, a cinema of subversion. Revolutionary cultural politics needed to subvert the dominant paradigms of social organization and interpersonal relations. As the filmmaker Glauber Rocha, whose masterfully subversive works including *Deus e o diabo na terra do sol* (1963; *Black God, White Devil*) and *Antonio das Mortes* (1969) remain staples of film-history courses, put it, "When one talks of cinema, one talks of American cinema. The influence of the cinema is the influence of *American cinema,* which is the most aggressive and widespread aspect of American culture throughout the world. . . . For this reason, every discussion of cinema made outside Hollywood must begin with Hollywood" (cited in Armes, p. 35).

## Formal Dimensions

The inception of third cinema brought together participants in a variety of anticolonial revolutions during a period in which the world was understood to be fundamentally polarized along lines of nation and class. Beginning in the late 1950s and early 1960s, many third world writers and filmmakers saw themselves working in their own national contexts but connected intimately to a global uprising against worldwide racist and capitalist colonization. These uprisings extended from the Cuban and Algerian revolutions to political upheavals in Brazil, Argentina, Chile, Senegal, and Vietnam. Many of these films appear crude and characterized by low production values but revolutionary filmmakers found it necessary to work on very small budgets with whatever materials were available. Most of the films are black and white and made with few takes. However, Espinosa's idea of "imperfect cinema" is central here because the practical and economic challenges to film production have formal consequences that speak to and of the problems faced by emergent nations.

Third cinema often uses a realistic style associated with cinema verité or sometimes with Italian neorealism. At times it uses nonprofessional actors or even workers and ordinary people doing their everyday tasks (as in the Chilean director Patricio Guzmán's three-part documentary *The Battle of Chile* [1975–1978]). Some of the films are forms of social realism that take a typical figure or situation and create an archetypical narrative that shows how the prevailing social order limits and often destroys individual possibilities. Filmmakers such as Lino Brocka (Philippines), Hector Babenco (Brazil), and Dariush Mehrjui (Iran) have worked in this manner. At the same time, figures such as Rocha, Djibril Diop Mambety (Senegal), and Gutierrez Alea (Cuba) use mythic elements and modernist devices of fragmentation. In almost every case, films that are considered to be part of the third cinema corpus make difficult demands on their viewers, who are addressed such that they must not only understand the films' nontraditional portrayals of the world but act upon that portrayal in order to change the world.

## Periodizing Third Cinema

The third cinema movement, which emerged as a corollary to the worldwide decolonization movement, exploded in the late 1960s and thereafter went through several incarnations. In particular, one could discern three breaks. The inaugural moment of third cinema, which carried the movement through the 1970s, was followed by an academic and institutional revitalization during the mid-1980s that focused on reception and interpretation as well as the practice of filmmaking. This mid-1980s resurgence of interest in third cinema occurred in part because it was felt that both national and perhaps more pointedly festival audiences did not easily fit into a standard differentiation between colonizer and colonized.

The uneasy fit of spectators into opposing first and third worlds, colonizers and colonized, which were formerly imagined as polar opposites, was exacerbated by the relative failure of revolutionary uprisings in the colonies to bring about the liberation of colonized peoples despite the fact that the colonies themselves had achieved nominal independence. It was further complicated by the growing numbers of third-world diasporic populations who faced difficult and vexing questions of existence and identity in the Western metropoles. Claiming that the unequal economic exchange between the first and the third world had its analogue in the unequal symbolic exchange between the first and the third world, Teshome Gabriel suggested that one of the effects of third cinema was to displace the Western(ized) viewer from his accustomed position of the privileged interpreter of the image. In assigning the category of thirdness to cinema, the spectators' reception became part of that assignation and Gabriel proposed that it was also possible to read "first" or "second" cinema (cinema which registered the malaise or alienation of third world subjects but was not in itself revolutionary) in a third cinema way. However, despite the blurring of some polar distinctions between oppressive colonizer and oppressed colonial subject, many if not most of the intellectuals, organizers, and filmmakers involved with what was still, if with some reservations, called third cinema, worked in solidarity with ongoing revolutionary activity in places like Nicaragua, El Salvador, and the Philippines. Finally, in the opening years of the twenty-first century, there was a growing reassessment of third cinema practices, which took account of postcolonial theories, globalization, and the emergence of what might be called a world media system.

## Ideology: Racism and Identification

Third cinema set out to destroy various aspects of what has been called the colonial mentality and to replace it with various forms of cultural affirmation. Summing up the situation of the third world and its peoples in 1969, Solanas and Getino wrote, "Just as they are not masters of the land upon which they walk, the neo-colonized people are not masters of the ideas in their heads" (p. 48). In a situation in which colonial control was maintained not only by economic and police violence but by mind control, third cinema was given the status of a weapon in a war that was not only for land and for laboring bodies, but also for minds. Quoting from their landmark film *La Hora de los Hornos* (*The Hour of the Furnaces,* 1968), a scathing analysis of the structure of Argentine society that sought to at once explain the violence foisted upon Argentina by Western capitalism and to offer a revolutionary solution, Solanas and Getino write, "In order to impose itself, neo-colonialism needs to convince the people of a dependent country of their own inferiority. Sooner or later the inferior man recognizes Man with a capital M; this recognition meant the destruction of his defenses. If you want to be a man, says the oppressor, you have to be like me, speak my language, deny your own being, transform yourself into me."

The situation of colonial identification with the oppressor was forcefully formulated fifteen years earlier by one of the clear influences on this manifesto, Frantz Fanon, the philosopher, psychoanalyst, and expositor of negritude from Martinique. Fanon, after completing his education in Paris and painfully discovering that in spite of his colonial French education he was not seen to be French by the French colonizers of Martinique, lived and worked in Algeria. In *Black Skin, White Masks* (1952), Fanon wrote, "To speak a language is to take on a world, a culture. The Antilles Negro who wants to be white will be the whiter as he gains greater mastery of the cultural tool that language is. . . . Historically, it must be remembered that the Negro wants to speak French because it is the key that can open doors which were still barred to him fifty years ago." Thus in a film like *La noire de . . .* (*Black Girl*, 1966) by the Senegalese writer and director Ousmane Sembene, an impoverished Senegalese woman who works as a maid for a white expatriate French couple is persuaded to return with them to France to work in their home. Audiences see how her need to leave a life with no promising future in a Senegal recoiling under the destruction of colonization is coupled to her aspiration for the wealth and power of the Western metropole. Her desire for a better life in France becomes part of her oppression and eventual destruction. Although motivated by dreams of a better life in the colonial center, she finds instead utter isolation and virtual enslavement. Her tragedy, which Sembene handles with a devastating economy of means that requires from audiences an intense engagement with the experience of the Senegalese protagonist, is, at the end of the film, shown as reported by a French newspaper in two column inches. The contrast between what she has undergone in the house of the French and the official story told in the "objective" language of the press raises her tragedy to the level of outrage while showing how inadequate dominant media are to understand the colonial condition.

## Mass Communications as Weaponry

What Fanon identified as the cultural and psychological dimensions of a racist—that is, white supremacist, imperialistic—capitalism, Solanas and Getino saw as being extended and intensified through mass communications:

As early as the 17th Century, Jesuit missionaries proclaimed the aptitude of the [South American] native for copying European works of art. Copyists, translator, interpreter, at best a spectator, the neocolonized intellectual will always be encouraged to refuse to assume his creative possibilities. Inhibitions, uprootedness, escapism, cultural cosmopolitanism, artistic imitation, metaphysical exhaustion, betrayal of country all find fertile soil in which to grow. (p. 47)

In seeking an alternative to mass communication's co-optation and colonization of spectators, all of the cultural conditions noted above become themes for various third cinema filmmakers: The culture, politics, psychology, and metaphysics of colonialism are analyzed at great length. For example,

another of Sembene's films, *Xala* (1973), depicts a postcolonial high government official of Senegal replicating the same patterns of domination practiced by the colonial masters: he steals the people's rice and fills the radiator of his Mercedes Benz with imported Evian water—but eventually he pays the price for his betrayal. In Gutierrez Alea's *Memories of Underdevelopment* (1968), the bourgeois protagonist, unable to identify with the project of the Cuban revolution despite his nationalist inclinations, cannot tap his creative powers and wastes away into "metaphysical exhaustion" and irrelevance. In Filipino filmmaker Lino Brocka's great *Manila in the Claws of Light* (1975), a provincial couple is lured by the glitz of Manila to the metropole in search of a better life, only to meet with betrayal and destruction.

The three films mentioned above along with myriad others foreground the pitfalls of what has been referred to in shorthand as a colonial mentality. Solanas and Getino bring the question of colonial culture to the question of neocolonial media as follows: "Mass communications tend to complete the destruction of a national awareness and of a collective subjectivity on the way to enlightenment, a destruction which begins as soon as the child has access to these media, the educational culture of the ruling classes. . . . Mass communications are more effective for neocolonialism than napalm" (pp. 48–49). They are more effective than napalm, for Solanas and Getino, because first world, capitalist mass communication's industries structure the imagination and organize the desire of viewers in terms or patterns that run counter to their own individual and collective/nationalist best interests. In this view, aside from seducing viewing subjects away from the immediate materiality of their own problems and the potential, collective solutions that may be at hand, "mass communications" as they stand under capitalism effect the ongoing normalization of, in Solanas and Getino's words, "Violence, Crime and Destruction . . . [as] Peace, Order and Normality." For this reason, "*Truth then amounts to subversion. Any form of expression or communication that tries to show national reality is subversion*" (p. 49).

## First, Second, and Third Cinema and the Lie of Neutrality

To equate the "showing of reality" with "subversion" does not necessarily lead to a naive theory about a medium that can transparently represent reality. Rather, what passes for reality is inexorably tied to the forms by which it is rendered. It was understood that representational forms, from news formats to standard Hollywood narratives of individual heroism, were and are part of the functioning of institutions, as well as the functioning of cultural and economic power. Therefore, it was also understood that control of the spectator is central to the maintenance of power. Opposed to such hegemonic functionality, third cinema creates an activist relation to knowledge making; third cinema makers work with "a camera in one hand and a rock in the other." They tried to show that because all representation is shot through with power relations, the most pernicious representations are generally those in which the process—that is, the mode of representing—is naturalized and/ or made invisible. If representation appears larger than

> I make the revolution; therefore I exist. This is the starting point for the disappearance of fantasy and phantom to make way for living human beings. The cinema of the revolution is at the same time one of destruction and construction: destruction of the image that neocolonialism has created of itself and of us, and construction of a throbbing, living reality which recaptures truth in any of its expressions.
>
> SOURCE: Fernando Solanas and Octavio Getino, "Towards a Third Cinema."

life, as something like a second nature, human beings are simultaneously persuaded of their powerlessness. Third cinema endeavors, in one way or another, to show the world as being constructed in and through social relations.

In bourgeois cinema, write Solanas and Getino, "Man is accepted only as a passive and consuming object; rather than having his ability to make history recognized, he is only permitted to read history, contemplate it, listen to it, undergo it" (p. 51). This leads to another important set of distinctions impacting the term *third cinema*, for "thirdness" is to be distinguished from a "firstness" and "secondness" in the cinema. First cinema is the dominant Hollywood product, a "spectacle aimed at a digesting object." "The world, experience and historic process are enclosed within the frame of a painting, the same stage of a theater, and the movie screen; man is viewed as a consumer of ideology, not as the creator of ideology" (p. 51). Auteurist cinema, including the French new wave and Brazilian Cinema Novo, constitute second cinema. Here the filmmaker seeks a new film language and endeavors to challenge social constraints, but ultimately finds him or herself "'trapped inside the fortress' as [Jean Luc] Godard put it" (Solanas and Getino, p. 52). The second cinema often thematizes the situation of disaffected colonial subjects but can neither posit nor effect a social basis of transformation, caught up as it is in the ideology of bourgeois individualism. It thus remains closer to forms of existentialism but is not yet revolutionary. Third cinema sets out to fight "the system," and sees itself as a weapon in a collective struggle against racist, capitalist domination. It is defined as a cinema of liberation. It understands the collective character not only of history making but of historically individuated subjects.

## Significance of Art

It is important to draw out the implications of third cinema as a practical critique of third world populations within the first and second worlds. Third cinema is put forward by Solanas and Getino as "above all, a new conception of filmmaking and the significance of art in our times" (p. 54).

Their phrase "*I make the revolution; therefore I exist*," echoes Rocha's important formulation in his essay from the same period, "The Aesthetics of Hunger": "The moment of violence is the moment when the colonizer becomes aware of the colonized." In other words, within the regime of institutionalized violence, any claim to existence, any assertion of will by the colonized, is taken as an act of violence or revolution by the colonial regime—for it is the working conceit of colonial regimes that colonial populations do not have will, do not suffer pain, humiliation, starvation, torture, and death, have no legitimate claims on the placid, beneficent world of colonial domination; and indeed, do not exist.

From such claims regarding revolution and violence emerges a theory of knowledge: "There is no knowledge of a reality as long as that reality is not acted upon, as long as its transformation is not begun on all fronts of struggle." To emphasize this point, Solanas and Getino invoke Marx's eleventh thesis on Ludwig Feuerbach: "The philosophers have only *interpreted* the world in various ways; the point, however, is to *change* it." Connecting third cinema to Marxism indicates that the historical development of class consciousness must be linked to developments of race consciousness and nationalist consciousness in the process of knowledge making. The world is not given merely in its representations. Representations present an interested picture of the world; in short, a worldview. This point connects the decolonization movements with the history and theory of Marxist revolution, and these thematics as well as those that arose with the negritude movement inform to varying degrees the work of many third cinema filmmakers.

## Authors of History

According to Solanas and Getino, the connection of third cinema to revolutionary practice led to the discovery of "a new facet of cinema: the participation of people who . . . were [formerly] considered spectators" (p. 61). Thus, unlike in first and second cinema, film is seen not as a spectacle but as a "detonator or a pre-text." Third cinema is experimental, and impels its audience toward social change: spectators become actors, the authors of history. "The film act means an open-ended film; it is essentially a way of learning" (p. 62). Thus, as opposed to traditional cinema, third cinema is "*cinema fit for a new kind of human being, for what each one of us has the possibility of becoming*" (p. 63). The third cinema movement therefore represents a consciousness of the history-making and knowledge-making aspects of film and understands the historical role of cinema as creating a liberated society. The function of third cinema, while centrally concerned with the objective transformation of society, is not only extrinsic to viewing subjects but intrinsic as well. For all of the debates that have occurred over the tenability and fate of third cinema, the urgent call of Solanas and Getino may yet be heard: "The decolonization of the filmmaker and of films will be simultaneous acts to the extent that each contributes to collective decolonization. The battle begins without, against the enemy who attacks us, but also within, *against the ideas and models of the enemy to be found inside each one of us*" (p. 63).

See also **Anticolonialism: Latin America; Marxism; Nationalism: Cultural Nationalism; Negritude; Neocolonialism; Third World.**

## BIBLIOGRAPHY

Armes, Roy. *Third World Film Making and the West.* Berkeley: University of California Press, 1987.

Beller, Jonathan. *Acquiring Eyes: Philippine Visuality, Nationalism and the World-Media-System.* Manila, Philippines: Ateneo de Manila University Press, 2004.

Birri, Fernando. "Cinema and Underdevelopment." In *New Latin American Cinema,* edited by Michael T. Martin. Detroit: Wayne State University Press, 1997.

Chaliand, Gérard. *Revolution in the Third World.* Translated by Diana Johnstone. Harmondsworth, U.K., and New York: Penguin; 1978.

Espinosa, Julio Garcia. "For an Imperfect Cinema." In *New Latin American Cinema,* edited by Michael T. Martin. Detroit: Wayne State University Press, 1997.

Fanon, Frantz. *Black Skin, White Masks.* Translated by Charles Lam Markmann. 1952. New York: Grove, 1967.

Gabriel, Teshome H. "Towards a Critical Theory of Third World Films." In *Questions of Third Cinema,* edited by Jim Pines and Paul Willemen. London: BFI, 1989.

Gutierrez Alea, Tomás. "The Viewer's Dialectic." In *New Latin American Cinema,* edited by Michael T. Martin. Detroit: Wayne State University Press, 1997.

Pines, Jim, and Paul Willemen, eds. *Questions of Third Cinema.* London: BFI, 1989.

Rocha, Glauber. "Aesthetics of Hunger." In *New Latin American Cinema,* edited by Michael T. Martin. Detroit: Wayne State University Press, 1997.

Solanas, Fernando, and Octavio Getino. "Towards a Third Cinema: Notes and Experiences for the Development of a Cinema of Liberation in the Third World." In *Movies and Methods: An Anthology,* edited by Bill Nichols. Vol. 1. Berkeley: University of California Press, 1976.

Wayne, Michael. "The Critical Practice and Dialectics of Third Cinema." In *The Third Text Reader: On Art, Culture, and Theory,* edited by Rasheed Araeen, Sean Cubitt, and Ziauddin Sardar. London and New York: Continuum, 2002.

*Jonathan Beller*

**THIRD WORLD.** The term *Third World* has long served to describe countries of Africa, Asia, and Latin America that have been seen to share relatively low per-capita incomes, high rates of illiteracy, limited development of industry, agriculture-based economies, short life expectancies, low degrees of social mobility, and unstable political structures. The 120 countries of the Third World also share a history of unequal encounters with the West, mostly through colonialism and globalization.

During the Cold War (1945–1991), *Third World* referred to countries that were relatively minor players on the international stage, strategic though they sometimes were to the United States and the Soviet Union as these superpowers sought to maintain their balance of terror. The tendency was to essentialize, oversimplify, and homogenize complex identities and diversities in the political systems of the Third World by focusing too narrowly on the politics of bipolarity. Yet the so-called Third World countries always had many more divergences than similarities in their histories, cultures, demographies, climates, and geographies, and a great variation in capacities, attitudes, customs, living standards, and levels of underdevelopment or modernization.

Unilinear assumptions of modernization also encouraged pejorative connotations of the Third World as cultures and peoples trapped in tradition and custom, with a progressive few desperately seeking a "civilizing mission" in order to graduate into the rights and freedoms that capitalism and its modernity promise individuals and communities. Deaf to the diversities in the history, politics, and economics of the countries in question, and to the cultural and intersubjective rationalities that give contextual meanings to development, the concept has failed to inspire a meaningful comparative analysis of development.

## Origins

The term *Third World* is European in origin, but analysts have yet to agree on its genesis. Some believe it came about through the search for an explanatory "third way" to the dualism of capitalism and socialism as analytical frameworks among European political scientists in the 1920s. This challenge became even more urgent in the 1950s as colonies increasingly gained independence and sought legitimacy as states and international actors in their own right. Others situate its birth with the classification of the world by the industrialized West into First (Western Europe and Japan), Second (the Soviet Bloc and its satellites), and Third (the rest) worlds. Still others have traced the term to 1940s and 1950s France, linking it with the "Third Estate" in French politics—the rising but underrepresented bourgeoisie in the French Revolution of 1789—who capitalized on the quarrel between nobility and clergy. Similarly, the Cold War provided the political opportunity for the "third way" in international politics, under the guidance of the newly independent developing countries. Whatever its origin, the idea of the Third World rapidly became embedded in the discourse and diplomacy of international relations, and those claiming or claimed by it were able to make the concept synonymous with radical agendas in liberation struggles and the clamor for more participatory and just international relations through new world orders.

### Historical, intellectual, and ideological context. Despite various appropriations or attempts at domesticating the concept, Third World has always been an uneasy, controversial, and polemical concept, especially to the increasingly sensitive, critical, and rights-hungry intellectuals and elites of the postcolonies. Over the years, there have been efforts to coin new terms to replace "Third World." From a communist revolutionary perspective, Mao Zedong formulated a theory of three worlds in which the First World consisted of the then-superpowers (Soviet Union and United States), whose imperialistic policies, as he felt, posed the greatest threat to world peace. Mao placed the middle powers (Japan, Canada, and Europe) in the Second World. Africa, Latin America, and Asia (including China) formed the Third World. Others have dismissed the notion of three worlds as inadequate, and have asked

for four or more worlds. To some, the Fourth World should comprise currently underrecognized and underrepresented minorities, especially the indigenous "first" peoples of various states and continents. Still to others, only bipolar divisions along lines of physical geography and locality make sense, regardless of the differences and inequalities that may unite people across physical boundaries or divide those within the same borders.

To others, the whole notion of worlds is misleading for various reasons. First, it implies an essential degree of separation between different parts of the globe that is simply not realistic in a globalizing world marked by multiple encounters and influences. Second, despite the efforts to stimulate and sustain Third World unity in the struggles against various forms of subjection, current obsession with belonging and boundaries have fueled the conflicts undermining Third World solidarity and action. Third, the increased degree of polarization within a global economic geography, along with the collapse of state socialism, and the insertion of capitalist social relations even among the communist giants of the world (Russia and China), suggest not a reduction but a multiplication of worlds, including the production of material conditions characteristic of the Third World even within First World societies. Fourth, the emergence of newly industrializing countries represents a form of dependent development and a further differentiation of the global economic geography. If globalization is producing Third World realities in First World contexts, it is at the same time producing First World consumers in Third World societies. In certain contexts, globalization has generated levels of poverty and victimhood that best justify the qualification as Fourth World.

***Movements associated with the Third World.*** During the Cold War, the term *Third World* or *Thirdism* inspired what came to be known as the "non-aligned movement" (NAM) a counterweight to the two rival Cold War blocs, and a kind of international pressure group for the Third World. NAM was founded on five basic principles—peace and disarmament; self-determination, particularly for colonial peoples; economic equality; cultural equality; and multilateralism exercised through a strong support for the United Nations. From the 1960s through the 1980s the movement used its majority voting power within the United Nations to redirect the global political agenda away from East-West wrangles over the needs of the Third World. However, in practice, with the exception of NAM's anticolonialism, about which there could be strong agreement, the aim of creating an independent force in world politics quickly succumbed to the pressure of Cold War alliances. By the 1970s, NAM had largely become an advocate of Third World demands for a New International Economic Order (NIEO), a role it shared with the Group of 77, the caucusing group of Third World states within the United Nations. Through NIEO, the Third World argued in favor of a complete restructuring of the prevailing world order, which they perceived to be unjust, as the only enduring solution to the economic problems facing them. At the level of UNESCO, Third World scholars waged a war against unequal cultural exchange through calls for a New World Information and Communication Order (NWICO). In general, the Third World wanted a new order based on equity, sovereignty,

interdependence, common interest, and cooperation among all states. Given the economic weakness of the Soviet Union, these demands were essentially directed at the West.

## Theories of "Third World" Development

In their quest for a new world order, Third World governments found measured support among radical academics who elaborated and drew from dependency and center-periphery frameworks to critique the basic tenets of modernization paradigms of development and underdevelopment. To these scholars, largely inspired by Marxism, the price of the development of the First World was the subjection to exploitation and dependency (or underdevelopment) that First World states and actors had brought to bear on the Third World through imperialism, colonialism, and globalization. Under the global capitalist system, the Third World can only play second fiddle to the real global decision-makers. This perspective explains both Third World economic underdevelopment and stalling democracy essentially in terms of the assimilation and exclusion logic of global capitalism, according to which only the handful of powerful economic elites in the Third World stand to benefit from its internalization and reproduction.

## The Future of the Third World

Because the idea of the Third World was partly created and largely sustained by the logic of bipolarity that governed the Cold War era, some argue that in a unipolar world, in which the United States is the only global gendarme, to claim the same degree of existence for the Third World as in the past would be tantamount to a "fantasy" with little conceptual and analytical utility. Still, some factors persist to make the Third World still relevant as a concept. In analytical terms, the Third World idea identifies a group of states whose common history of colonialism has left them in a position of economic and political weakness in the global system. In this sense, the recent alignment in global politics neither undermines the coherence of the idea nor justifies its abandonment. The Third World may continue to exist in this sense, but the changing context confronts it with new challenges and opportunities.

*See also* ***Capitalism; Development; Economics; Empire and Imperialism; Globalization; International Order.***

BIBLIOGRAPHY
Amin, Samir. *Delinking: Towards a Polycentric World.* London: Zed, 1990.
———. "Reflections on the International System." In *Beyond Cultural Imperialism: Globalization, Communication, and the New International Order,* edited by Peter Golding and Phil Harris, 10–24. London: Sage, 1997.
Denoon, Donald. "Third World" In *The Social Science Encyclopedia.* Edited by Adam Kuper and Jessica Kuper. London and New York: Routledge, 1985.
Frank, G. *Dependent Capitalism and Development.* New York: Monthly Review, 1978.
Haynes, Jeffrey. *Third World Politics: A Concise Introduction.* Oxford: Blackwell, 1996.
Independent Commisson of the South on Development Issues. *The Challenge to the South.* Oxford: Oxford University Press, 1990.

McGrew, A. "The "Third World" in the New Global Order." In *Poverty and Development in the 1990s*, edited by Tim Allen and Alan Thomas. Oxford: Oxford University Press in association with The Open University, 1992.

Merriam, Allen H. "What Does 'Third World' Mean?" In *The Third World: States of Mind and Being*, edited by Jim Norwine and Alfonso Gonzalez. Boston: Unwin Hyman, 1988.

Parkins, Colin. "North-South Relations and Globalization after the Cold War." In *Global Politics: An Introduction*, edited by Charlotte Bretherton and Geoffrey Ponton. Oxford: Blackwell, 1996.

Rangel, Charles. *"Third World" Ideology and Western Reality: Manufacturing Political Myth*. New Brunswick, N.J., and Oxford: Transaction, 1986.

Rodney, Walter. *How Europe Underdeveloped Africa*. Washington, D.C.: Howard University Press, 1981.

Roy, Ash Narain. *The "Third World" in the Age of Globalisation: Requiem or New Agenda?* London and New York: Zed, 1999.

Toye, J. F. J. *Dilemmas of Development*. Oxford: Blackwell, 1987.

Tussie, Diana. "Introduction." In her *Latin America in the World Economy: New Perspectives*. Aldershot, U.K.: Gower, 1983.

Wallerstein, Immanuel. *The Politics of the World-Economy*. Cambridge, U.K.: Cambridge University Press, 1984.

Wells, Clark. *The UN, UNESCO, and the Politics of Knowledge*. New York: St. Martin's, 1987.

*Francis B. Nyamnjoh*

# THIRD WORLD LITERATURE.

As a term of standard usage, though still minus "literature," *Third World* dates from the 1950s. (The *Oxford English Dictionary*'s first listing for it—still in its French form of *Tiers Monde*—is dated 1956.) Supposedly coined by the French sociologist Alfred Sauvy (1898–1990) in 1952, it initially referred to the independent and soon-to-be-independent nations of Africa and Asia that claimed to maintain a militarily nonaligned stance vis-à-vis both "First" and "Second" worlds—for instance, respectively, the United States, and its allies in NATO and SEATO, and the Soviet Union together with the nations of the Warsaw Pact, with the People's Republic of China a kind of wild card. But as this exact historical point of origin fades more and more into an unremembered past, *Third World* nevertheless continues to evoke the defining moments of a still iridescent lineage of the present: the era of anticolonial and national liberation mass movements and wars, from India to Algeria to Vietnam, that produced the contemporary grid of national boundaries in most of Africa and in large parts of Asia. Hence, the unmistakably radical overtone that is still audible in the term itself. And hence, given the eventual disappointment of that radical aspiration to become a "third"—that is, still another *new* world—there often appears an impulse to shrug it off in favor of more neutral-sounding terms such as "postcolonial."

Following Aijaz Ahmad, this "pre-history of the present" can be more precisely identified as the "Bandung Era," stretching from the meeting of nonaligned heads of Asian and African states in Bandung, Indonesia, in 1955—with statesmen such as Jawaharlal Nehru (1918–1970), Gamel Abdel Nasser (1889–1964), and Chou En-lai (1898–1976) presiding—to the Iranian Revolution of 1979 and its embrace of an openly antisecularist path to national emancipation. Though events in the world since the attacks of September 11, 2001, and the launching of a second war in the Persian Gulf in 2003 may at times seem to have set the historical clock back to a "Third World" moment—prospective or real Vietnam-style defeat for the United States in Iraq—the sense of repetition is finally possible only from the perspective of a newly humbled U.S. imperial hubris. Outside the metropolitan world, the struggles to resist or even just simply withstand what is now—relative to, say, 1968—the enormously worsened global crisis of capital seem to evoke only the terrible suffering and martyrdom of the successful war of national liberation eventually won, on the ground, by Vietnam in 1975. Long past is the historical conjuncture that saw in Vietnam the emblem, along with Cuba, of what Robert J. C. Young rechristens, in 2001, as "tricontinentalism": the uniting, within a "third" world forcibly triangulated by Cold War dualisms, of Asia and Africa, joined now by a Latin America obliged by modern imperialism to accept that, like the former regions, but unlike the settler colony to its north, it was also far "south" of the West.

For these reasons, "Third World literature" is not the name for a well-defined literary corpus—the way, say, "South African" literature, or even "Southern African" or "Latin American" can or could be. This is not just because, as Ahmad has noted, "it is in the metropolitan country . . . that a literary text is first designated a Third World text" (p. 44). It is also because Third World literature names a historical aspiration to objectivity, rather than an object per se. *Cahiers du retour au pays natal* could not belong to a Third World literature had its author, Aimé Césaire (b. 1913), not been Martinican, and probably had he not been a black Martinican. But just being Martinican does not itself make this work Third World in any meaningful sense either. It sounds more plausible to call *Martín Fierro*, the best known of the Argentina's nineteenth-century gaucho sagas, Third World than it does to call Argentine Jorge Luis Borges's (1899–1986) short story collection *Ficciones* by that name, even though only the latter (first published in 1944) falls within the appropriate, historically demarcated zone.

One might define Third World literature as composing the literatures of Asia, Africa, and Latin America—perhaps together with their respective metropolitan diasporas. But this could only work if the category was effectively restricted to works written after the end of World War II. And that still leaves the question of whether Third World literature continues to be written, or whether in fact it extends only as far as the various ideological slippage points for embattled nationalliberationist energies: as early as the 1970s in West and South Asia and as late as the 1980s and 1990s in South Africa and Central America. Perhaps even so severely qualified a categorization remains technically defensible, since it does, after all, provide a means, however contentious, to refer collectively to the literature of a transnational but sub-global entity. As recently as the shutting down of the World Trade Organization meetings in Cancún in 2003 by an Indian-Chinese-Brazilianled "Third World" alliance, this entity, in its political form, made its real presence known.

But, of course, what the notion of a third conveys—especially after the disappearance of a second—is essentially the fact that it is *not* first. Third World literature is that literature that is most emphatically *not* of the First—that is, *not* of the European, the Europeanized American, and perhaps simply *not* of the white man's world. In this sense it is Third World literature that inherited, if anything can be said to have done so, the revolutionary, utopian aspiration once claimed by a class, rather than a racial or ethnic "other": Third World literature appears, at times, to replace but also to act as a kind of relay for the lost promise of a "proletarian" literature. It is the non- or antibourgeois literature of a world for which literature itself has seemed to become irredeemably bourgeois. So, for example, not only in the militancy of a Ngugi wa Thiong'o or the epic gravity of a Pramoedya Anta Toer but even in the largely parodic structure of Latin American "magical realism," the direct mediation of class by "oppressed nation," theorized by Fanon, is arguably at work.

It is, ironically, just this absence of any positive, precisely determined empirical reference, this aspiration to "other" worldliness, however mystified, that has made of Third World literature what is still a key, if somewhat devalued, term in literary and cultural theory. Although it cannot refer to just any literary work, when it does refer to actually existing literature there is always embedded in the term itself a reference to the falsely claimed universality of the "Western canon." Thus whatever it is that, say, Tomás Gutiérrez Alea's film *Memorias del subdesarrollo* (Memories of underdevelopment, 1968), means on a literary and narrative plane, its meaning, as "Third World literature," is understood to be one that could not have been produced "in" the "First World."

In this register, one critical work above all has stamped our way of speaking and thinking of Third World literature: Fredric Jameson's 1986 essay "Third World Literature in the Era of Multi-national Capitalism." "As western readers, whose tastes (and much else) have been formed by our own modernisms," wrote Jameson, "a popular or socially realistic third-world novel tends to come before us, not immediately, but as though already-read. We sense, between ourselves and this alien text, the presence of another reader, of the Other reader, for whom a narrative, which strikes us as conventional or naïve, has a freshness of information and a social interest we cannot share" (p. 66). Jameson's reference to a habitual impression of the "conventional or naïve" in Third World literature has now itself come to seem naïve, and the sense of the "already-read" may now be replaced by a sense of an (always already) "unread." But the relation that Jameson captures here of reader to "Other reader" in and through Third World literature could not be more actual.

The tendency, since about 1990, to substitute the term *postcolonial* for Third World, reflects, of course, the rise of postcolonial theory in the metropolitan academy, and, if nothing else, the sense of embarrassment, within that academy, at making even the most remotely uncritical allusion to supposedly obsolete doctrines of national liberation. But, *mutatis mutandis,* the strange logical slippages bequeathed by history to Third World literature resurface in the newer jargon. Meanwhile, to be sure, the literature itself—Third World, postcolonial, or however it is to be framed—occupies a central position in the metropolitan canons that once excluded it even as the presence of its Other reader, in ethical as much as in literary form, is felt just as strongly, if not more urgently than ever before.

*See also* **Literature; Postcolonial Theory and Literature; Third Cinema; Third World.**

**BIBLIOGRAPHY**

Ahmad, Aijaz. *In Theory: Classes, Nations, Literatures.* London: Verso, 1992.

Jameson, Fredric. "Third-World Literature in the Era of Multi-national Capitalism." *Social Text* 15 (1986): 65–88.

Young, Robert J. C. *Postcolonialism: An Historical Introduction.* Oxford and Malden, Mass.: Blackwell, 2001.

*Neil Larsen*

**THOMISM.** *See* **Aristotelianism; Humanity: European Thought.**

# TIME.

This entry includes three subentries:

*China*

*India*

*Traditional and Utilitarian*

## CHINA

As in other civilizations, China has delved into both the sensible and the abstract, analytical aspects of time. Social-political time traditionally used sixty-day and sixty-year cycles, and a ten-day "week" framed plans, or divinations, about the near future (these schemata are seen in 1200 B.C.E. oracle records and remained ubiquitous). Usually, Chinese days were broken into twelve "hours" and 100 subunits ("minutes"). Archaeology provides examples of early imperial (c. 250–100 B.C.E.) clocks used by officialdom: one type was a gnomon chronometer—a small disk notched for diurnal shadows, in one case with sixty-nine subunits. Cosmic boards of the Han period (206 B.C.E. to 220 C.E.) mechanically aligned an inner wheel indicating segmented slices of time (seasons and hours) with cosmological categories and ecliptic constellations appearing on a square background. Third-century B.C.E. texts preserved in the western deserts refer to regulations for local functionaries in assigning times for signaling, delivering documents, and scheduling projects. Finally, in all time periods court experts performed time-related functions: calendar ritualists assigned dates for sacrifices and ceremonies; astrologers interpreted astral and meteorological portents, often drawing on computations for eclipses; and scholar-officials not only interpreted and debated the findings of such experts but also worked on genealogies and on philological research to correct primordial calendars, both of which played a role in political legitimacy.

Chinese thinkers did not devise philosophies, pedagogies, or keys of the sort developed in the West concerning time, and the context was chiefly driven by the state's need for cosmological and ritual correctness, and in some cases by cosmological and apocalyptic notions conveyed in Buddhist and Daoist scriptures. Yet China also produced its own sophisticated metaphysics of time—more accurately, sociocosmic "timing." The 3,000-year tradition known as "the Changes," or *Yi jing* (Book of changes), employed a set of arrayed lines, classically three or six per set, which was called a *gua*. The lines were associated with numbers; they could change in character (yin and yang) and concomitantly in numeric value; and they moved in and through other, associated, *gua* by means of permutations. Like dates and times of birth in Western astrology, they were used to predict career and health and to establish an individual's place in a local social or political network. The *Yi jing* achieved a high place in China's pedagogical, scholarly, and even political life, as influential in its way as the West's Bible. We should approach the *gua* system as an essential part of Chinese natural philosophy, a locus of scholarly work that linked broad areas of inquiry like cosmic patterns and regularity, divination, alchemy, chronology, medicine, and numerical principles.

## *Gua* Time

China's most ancient, and deeply imprinted, conceptions of time developed through divination. Beginning around 1400 B.C.E., diviners at the Shang courts made auguries based on linelike cracks created by heating plastrons and bones, a practice that involved complex skills in recording and tracking time by means of astral, calendric, and proto-*gua* devices. *Yi jing* provided a way to examine individual and cosmic time frames, as well as the metaphysics of time. Its oldest textual layers (the *gua* line matrices and various divination formulas), which stemmed in some ways from the line cracking of the Shang era, date to 800–700 B.C.E.; the "Judgment" and "Images" commentaries date from about 500–350 B.C.E. Later commentaries ("Great Treatise" and "Words"; roughly 350–200 B.C.E.) connected these time matrices with unifying metaphysical concepts. The "Judgment" and "Image" layers refer often to time (*shi*) in the sense of "timeliness within a development," or "season(s)." A strong metaphysical sense is found, for example, in the Judgment commentary's section on "Gen" (*Yi jing* hexagram no. 52): "*Gen* means stopping. When the timeliness [of this specific *gua*] comes to a stop, then one stops; when it goes, then one goes." This is not about duration of motion or transitional states of being, but one's own "timeliness" in being part of the *gua*'s field of influence.

The "Great Treatise" expanded the notional sense of time. Several words there, taken as a set, explicate "change" and, indirectly, "time": *bian* ("alternation," movement from state to state in a matrix); *hua* ("transformation" as growth, maturation, influence); *tong* ("projection, development," inferring an entire system from one of its aspects); *fan* ("reversion," a deduced return point, or node, in a cycle).

By about 100 B.C.E., the most concrete sense of time (qua timing) in *Yi jing* was the notion carried in the fourth term, *fan*: astronomic reversal and return of solstices and diurnal and sidereal cycles. But, like all other concepts of time and change, this

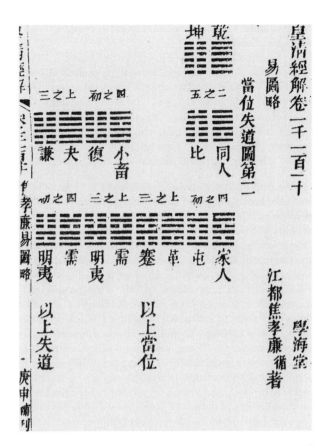

**Page showing the *Yi jing* system, from a Qing-era printing of the works of Jiao Xun.** Conceived some three thousand years ago, the *Yi jing* is a sociocosmic system of lines with numeric values. The interactions of the lines were studied by the Chinese in order to predict the future.

is analogized as yin-yang dualism; even in twelfth-century B.C.E. inscriptions, diviners had used the interplay of even and odd numbers in a *gua* and observed the way one *gua* reached out to a "changed" correspondent and functioned to bridge time in situations of prediction. During the Han dynasty, brilliant metaphysician-ritualists like Jing Fang and Yang Xiong worked to unify mathematics, musical theory, calendrics, and *gua* systematics. Beginning around 300 C.E., diviners increasingly used astral position timing and integrated various numerate techniques, spurring technical elaborations in personal astrology (death and important career-date predictions). The culture at large became attuned to the numerate and mechanized aspects of time as they sought to establish personal "timing."

Finally in the *Yi jing* system, "position" is a key component of time. The term *wei* refers not only to the situation surrounding a specific one of the six stacked lines of a *gua* but also to the line's interrelations. For example, a *gua*'s *wei* at the second line, traditionally a time of deference in a career, takes cues from its concurrent, yet future, partner *wei* at line five (career apogee, or seat of power). *Gua* time developed around the social appropriateness of one's *wei*, how much help one received from all entities acting in the matrix (the *wan-wu*), and, hermetically, the correctness of one's own union with the *gua* system.

## Manipulable Time and Social Time: Progress, Alchemy, Salvation

Some observers of China have thought that Chinese time was entirely cyclical. It is true that political life traditionally was based on dynastic rise and fall and the attendant appeals to astral cycles, and religious ideas and movements frequently were founded upon era cycles. But China was not much different from other civilizations. Linear chronology, unique cosmic moment, and social progress can be seen in various, albeit not always culturally dominant, contexts concerning time.

The pathbreaking historian Sima Qian (d. c. 90 B.C.E.), for example, honed the use of tables (time-linear in concept) to demonstrate the role of genealogies and blood lines in political history. Moreover, his remarks often suggest that a dynasty should not be a passive recipient of judgments derived from divination but should also be headed toward something—a socio-cosmic correctness and unity. Joseph Needham considered, perhaps too emphatically, that the technical and intellectual work of court experts to achieve that unity was scientific "progress," a way to understand linearity in Chinese time. But his observation prompts fruitful speculation. Chinese scholarship and bureaucratic institutions always recognized previous toilers and their goals. Scholar-officials occasionally sought to restore antique knowledge, in order to explain via commentaries rather technical matters or confront the influence of outside (foreign, in the case of Muslim and then Jesuit) court-appointed experts. Modern historians of Chinese sciences have fleshed out particular cases, and in them we see that "progress" often was ad hoc and piecemeal, or thwarted politically. Moreover, such "progress" was actually quite backward-looking, like sixteenth- and seventeenth-century European humanists who sought truths lodged in the biblical past—terms and keys to natural knowledge whose meanings had become obscured.

Another way to view Chinese ideas of time is through the cosmologies implied in computational astronomy. Early astronomers recognized what we term Metonic periods and Saros cycles, yet they were also attempting to reconcile the regularities of such cycles with all-important numerological constants. Unwieldy greatest common denominators resulted from factoring lunar, solar, and sidereal conjunctions, and such large numbers would represent a primordial cycle that could evidence new, or reformed, dynasties. Concomitantly, predictive astronomy often failed because of the need to fudge aesthetically desirable numerologies with data from incomplete, ad hoc observations of solstitial moments and tropical year lengths. Besides dyadic, "five phases," and other cycles, Chinese experts undertook to grasp enormous reaches of cosmic time and the way human society and politics fit into it.

Daoist cult scriptures applied similar sorts of calculated eras to their propaganda during dynastic strife—for instance, calculations that claimed when a judgment of the corrupt by the sage-god Laozi or the Dao itself would occur. One example is the fourth-century C.E. *Purple Texts Inscribed by the Spirits,* which influenced ideas of dynastic and millennial time, affecting legitimation ideologies as late as the reunification of China in the sixth and seventh centuries. Scriptures of this sort

utilized calendrical arts to provide yet other numerological bases for arguing the existence of ending-nodes in the large conjunction cycles. Daoist scriptural time-concepts frequently meshed with Buddhist ones. In the Buddho-Daoist mélange of scriptures and cult aims, tantric materials offered protection against apocalypse, as in the spells carried in the *Lotus Sutra,* which reached broad popular consumption from about 400 to 800 C.E. Such theologies reflect the cyclical nature of Chinese time but also furnish extremely important examples of unique (nonlinear, noncyclical) divine intervention into social time. Daoist scriptures speak of "seed people" planted by the Dao in order to renew the postapocalyptic world.

Chinese alchemy engaged in measurement and analysis. Although that in itself might imply notions of time, alchemy focused not on time but on the effort to "construct a model of the *Tao,* to reproduce in a limited space on a shortened time scale the cyclical energetics of the cosmos" (Sivin, 1976, p. 523). The early alchemical tradition known as *Zhouyi can tong qi* (originating in the second century and elaborated in Tang and Song times) was concerned with the progress of cosmogonic time and for that purpose used Han-era *gua* calendrics. Ultimately, such approaches to "timing" and "timeliness" carry with them elements of the timeless, namely, the Dao principle of numero-cosmogony as found in *Laozi, Huainanzi,* and *Zhuangzi,* and as made precise by the *Yi jing* system. Time as quantifiable durations of states and qualifiable modes of change was not a primary concern.

## Metaphysical Time: Terms and Philosophies

From about 500 to 200 B.C.E. several Chinese thinkers conceived time abstractly and without reference to *gua* systematics. Passages in *Zhuangzi, Huainanzi,* and *Shuowen jiezi* (a second-century C.E. lexicon) drew upon extant terms connoting "time," linking them with categories for space and motion: these terms included *shi* (season, historical moment), *yu* (spatial expanse, first delineated as the area of a roof's perimeter, later "the four directions plus up," and, for *Zhuangzi,* "reality without anything in it [the void-expanse]"), and *zhou* (the cyclic, expected return of any moving thing; for *Zhuangzi,* "what goes on extensively but has no beginning or end"); hence the binome *yuzhou*—limitless expanse conjoined with cyclical return. The oldest terms were not intentionally abstract, but pointed to social time, timeliness of action, and spatiality as products of motion and change.

When the oldest *Zhuangzi* passages were created (probably c. 300 B.C.E.), logico-analytic debates were popular, and we find statements of a certain Hui Shi, who states the paradox, "One sets out for Yue today, but arrives in the past." The authorial voice, Zhuangzi, ridicules Hui Shi's mode of knowledge, yet the much later (fourth century C.E.) commentary takes it seriously, arguing that the "setting out" and the "arriving" (abstractly analogized as "knowing" and its known "entity") are like facing mirrors, which make a continuum of reflection: thus the "knowing" about "setting out for Yue" engages simultaneously with its dyadic partner, the "arriving."

Equally striking was the Mohists' approach to time. Early Mohists (roughly 400–350 B.C.E.) were an influential community dedicated to knowledge, ethics, and supplying political-military services to regional courts. Their writings were poorly transmitted and taken up only rarely by later Chinese scholars. The brilliant reconstruction of the jumbled extant version of the Mohist *Canon* by A. C. Graham has shown that time was articulated with brief declarations of such notions as light, weight, speed, and geometric axioms. One logical premise concerns "Duration: what fills out different times. Extension: what fills different locations." The later Mohists (about 300 B.C.E.) blended their own thoughts into the *Canon* and distinguished between times with and without duration: "Of times in a movement some have duration, others do not have duration. The beginning does not have duration."

## Demands of Ritual Precision and the Impact of Western Learning

Since at least about 150 B.C.E. Chinese scholars, in the relatively rarefied contexts of court rites and projects, had perceived that space and time were quantifiable through measurement and notation of positions. But with the impact of Western learning after 1600, not only did the royal court become increasingly chronometric, so did urban and mercantile culture. In 1644 an important Jesuit, Adam Schall von Bell, proposed to the court that the one hundred minutes of the day be changed to ninety-six for purposes of meshing with the European twenty-four-hour clock. Gear-driven clocks introduced by Jesuits and other westerners made an enormous impact, and through much of the 1700s the court employed Jesuit clock technicians. Throughout urban China clock makers found a niche, and we even have writings on their arts that contain thoughts about time in a new, ontologically self-contained way, not part of traditional, relatively indirect, approaches to "time."

Many Chinese, familiar with Jesuit ideas, consciously isolated Western challenges to Chinese notions of time from the accompanying cosmological and theological arguments. Some, however, engaged the new theology. Zhuang Qiyuan (1559–1633), who was influenced by Jesuits, pondered integrating the Christian "god" into Confucianism: "People of our age all know there is a Heaven, but they do not all know the reason why Heaven is Heaven. If Heaven had no ruler, then there would only be the present moment, motionless and stagnant, dreamlike without the mysterious spirit." His descendant Zhuang Cunyu (1719–1788), not Jesuit-influenced in the same way, wrote that the "Great Ultimate" (an *Yi jing* schema for cosmic unity) is "Heaven. Nothing is prior to the beginning of Heaven." The latter Zhuang was arguing that Confucian (*Yi jing*) cosmology was temporally prior to all things, implicitly positing the Chinese view as favorable to a Christian heaven. The Zhuangs were influential in fostering the Han Learning movement. From about 1600 to 1825 quite a few leading scholars reconstructed Han-era masters of *Yi jing* systematics (like the aforementioned Jing Fang), purged their product of any Buddhist and Daoist taint, and reexamined China's own early mathematics. The movement developed tools for potentially taking astronomy and math back from the Jesuit grip. Yet the Western worldview would dominate, and after the 1949 Communist revolution, with its assaults on intellectual culture,

Chinese tradition—which had once accommodated a fine variety, including hermetic *gua* time, Daoist eschatology, and ad hoc technical progress in time-related arts like math, computational astronomy, and music—was replaced by modern science and physics and by reductionist interpretations of Western philosophy.

False dichotomies like "China the cyclical" versus "the West as progressive" do not work. Arnaldo Momigliano once demolished such caricatures about Jewish versus Greek "time," noting that even within one culture we must not automatically compare a historian's ideas about time with a philosopher's (given the latter's unbounded room for natural and metaphysical speculation). The same caveat applies to Chinese ideas of time. Educated officials, who wrote history, had to address the demands of political cycles, yet their classicist work could be "regressive"—seeking a perfect, primordial age of unity. Court ritualists perceived a certain progress in their arts, and alchemical writers and metaphysical philosophers used time-related ideas to pursue ontology and epistemology. The *gua* time presented here is just one possible, if important, way to approach a Chinese "concept" of time. The history of Chinese alchemy and medicine will in the future present other models, as will studies of scholar-ritualists.

*See also* **Alchemy: China; Astrology: China; Calendar; Chinese Thought; Cosmology: Asia; Daoism; Mohism.**

**BIBLIOGRAPHY**

Bokenkamp, Stephen R. "Time after Time: Daoist Apocalyptic History and the Founding of the T'ang Dynasty." *Asia Major*, 3rd ser., 7 (1994): 59–88.

Libbrecht, Ulrich. "Chinese Concepts of Time: *Yü-chou* as Space-Time." In *Time and Temporality in Intercultural Perspective*, edited by Douwe Tiemersma and H. A. F. Oosterling. Amsterdam: Rodopi, 1996. The first part is a critical review of Needham's piece.

Loewe, Michael. "The Cycle of Cathay: Concepts of Time in Han China and Their Problems." In *Time and Space in Chinese Culture*, edited by Chun-chieh Huang and Erik Zürcher. Leiden and New York: Brill, 1995.

Needham, Joseph. "Time and Knowledge in China and the West." In *The Voices of Time: A Cooperative Survey of Man's Views of Time as Expressed by the Sciences and by the Humanities*, edited by J. T. Fraser. 2nd ed. Amherst: University of Massachusetts Press, 1981. Nathan Sivin has convincingly demonstrated the unfeasibility of Needham's take on the "scientific" nature of Chinese Daoism.

Pregadio, Fabrizio. "The Representation of Time in the *Zhouyi cantong qi*." *Cahiers d'Extrême-Asie* 8 (1995): 155–173.

Sivin, Nathan. "Chinese Alchemy and the Manipulation of Time." *Isis* 67 (1976): 512–526. Closer analysis of Daoist-alchemical "time," to which Needham alluded briefly.

———. "Chinese Concepts of Time." *The Earlham Review* 1 (1966): 82–92.

———. "Cosmos and Computation in Early Chinese Mathematical Astronomy." in *T'oung Pao*, 2nd ser., 55 (1969): 1–73. A pathbreaking study of the historical and political implications of early seekers after precision in eclipse ephemerides, and their abilities (and failures) to perceive and apply cumulative achievements in mathematical astronomy.

Swanson, Gerald. "The Concept of Change in the *Great Treatise.*" In *Explorations in Early Chinese Cosmology,* edited by Henry Rosemont Jr. Chico, Calif.: Scholars, 1984.

*Howard L. Goodman*

## INDIA

In general, the conceptualization of time in Indian religious and philosophical thought is framed by a dichotomy between the phenomenal world and absolute transcendence—that is, the realms of time and the timeless. The former, the sphere of contingent temporality, is usually understood to be the world of suffering, of change and impermanence, of what is known in Sanskrit as *samsara.* The latter is the realm of God or the divine, the transcendental realm of changelessness and release from suffering (*moksha* or *nirvana*). While the Indian tradition does not, as was once thought by Westerners, entirely devalue the this-worldly (concerned with things in this world, as opposed to a future existence after death), the ultimate goal of all of the religious traditions that have sprung forth in India is indeed to overcome and transcend time and the death it entails.

As opposed to modern notions of the progressive nature of time, traditionally in Indian texts time is envisioned as degenerative and entropic. Such a viewpoint on the nature of cosmic time goes all the way back to the early Vedic cosmogonies where the universe is said to have been created by a god (Purusha, the Cosmic Man, or Prajapati, the "Lord of Creatures"). The work of creation, however, was defective. The creator "emits" from himself the creation, but in this cosmogonic move from primordial unity to multiplicity and diversity the product is characterized by disconnection, confusion, and disarray. The very parts of time are, in their original state, created in a "disjointed" manner: "When Prajapati had emitted the creatures, his joints became disjointed. Now Prajapati is the year, and his joints are the two junctures of day and night, of the waxing and waning lunar half-months, and of the beginnings of the seasons. He was unable to rise with his joints disjointed" (Shatapatha Brahmana 1.6.3.35).

The "natural state" of time is here mythically represented as discontinuous and chaotic. The point of such Vedic myths of origins is to represent God's cosmogonic activity as faulty—creation here is not cosmos. The universe, as it was in the beginning, is in need of repair. Vedic ritual activity was performed to continually "heal" a world that was created defective and perpetually tends toward its natural state of disjuncture. The ritual was conceived as a connective, reparative activity.

> With the Agnihotra [the twice-daily sacrifice performed at dawn and dusk] they healed that joint [which is] the two junctures of night and day, and joined it together. With the new and full moon sacrifices, they healed that joint [which is] between the waxing and waning lunar half-months, and joined it together. And with the Caturmasyas [performed quarterly at the beginning of the seasons] they healed that joint [which is] the beginning of the seasons, and joined it together. (Shatapatha Brahmana 1.6.3.36)

Such is the power of human ritual activity, but the natural tendency to entropy, to return to the "natural" state of discontinuity, requires that human's continually reinvigorate time through ritual.

This vision of time as perpetually degenerating, encoded in the earliest texts of the Indian tradition, continues in one form or another to the present. By more or less the turn of the Common Era, Hindu, Buddhist, and Jain traditions had all accepted the notion that time, now measured in incomprehensibly long cycles, is constantly replicating, at the macrocosmic level, the process of birth, aging, and death that characterize the life of humans. Furthermore, time (and everything in it) was also seen as indefinitely recycled. The conceptualization of the cyclical nature of time, together with the idea of entropy, characterizes the basic understanding of temporality in the Indian context.

The assumption of transmigration and rebirth, already appearing in the middle centuries of the first millennium B.C.E., had both micro- and macrocosmic applications. Just as souls were perpetually reborn, so was the universe and time itself. The Sanskrit name for this theory is *samsara,* a word that literally means, "to wander or pass through a series of states or conditions." *Samsara* describes the beginningless and endless cycle of cosmic or universal death and rebirth; all of phenomenal existence is thought to be transient, ever changing, and cyclical.

Cosmological time in the classical texts of Hinduism is measured in units ranging from the infinitesimally short (the "particle" or atom of time called the *truti,* the "moment" or kshana, and the "eye blink" or *nimesha*) to the unimaginably long (the life span of the god Brahma, reckoned at 4,320,000,000 human years, according to one method of calculation). Within this framework are large units of time called the "eons" or *yugas* (which further combined into even greater periods called "great eons" or *mahayugas*). The first of these is the "Golden Age" or *krita-yuga,* which lasts for about 4,000 divine years (each divine year is the equivalent of 360 human years), a period of happiness and great virtue. The next two eons, the *treta* and *dvapara,* are both shorter (3,000 and 2,000 divine years, respectively) and increasingly worse as all things, including life spans and the human's capacity for spirituality, decrease. The process culminates in the last and "dark" or *kali* yuga, which is identified always in these texts as the present age of utter degeneration. At the end of this final eon (which lasts 1,000 divine years), the world will end in a cataclysmic apocalypse. After a period of dormancy, the universe will be recreated and the process will begin again . . . endlessly.

In mythological terms, the cycle is said to involve the fall from a Golden Age of happiness and righteousness. Such a fall is sometimes attributed to the arising of greed and desire, which, together with hatred and ignorance, form the fundamental roots of negative karma, which keeps souls entrapped, and constantly circling in *samsara.* But it is, according to some theories, the simple "power of time" itself that results in the fall from grace in the "Golden Age":

> In the beginning, people lived in perfect happiness, without class distinctions or property; all their needs were

supplied by magic wishing-trees. Then because of the great power of time and the changes it wrought upon them, they were overcome by passion and greed. It was from the influence of time, and no other cause, that their perfection vanished. Because of their greed, the wishing-trees disappeared; the people suffered from heat and cold, built houses and wore clothes. (*Vayu Purana* 1.8.77)

The cyclical nature of time entails not just an inevitable degeneration of time, with the resulting decrepitude of moral sensibility and the increase in evil and suffering; it also implies an equally inevitable return to the Golden Age as the wheel of time turns once again. The righteous will survive as the seeds for a new and better cosmic era:

> In the Kali Age, men will be afflicted by old age, disease, and hunger and from sorrow there will arise depression, indifference, deep thought, enlightenment, and virtuous behavior. Then the Age will change, deluding their minds like a dream, by the force of fate, and when the Golden Age begins, those left over from the Kali Age will be the progenitors of the Golden Age. All four classes will survive as a seed, together with those born in the Golden Age, and the seven sages will teach them all dharma. Thus there is eternal continuity from Age to Age. (*Linga Purana* 1.40.72–83)

It is here the simple "force of fate" that impels the ever-changing world of samsara, characterized by an "eternal continuity" that links the circle of time. Evil and suffering are, from this point of view, the inexorable consequences of the eternal processes that guide the phenomenal universe.

Within this very large framework of ever-declining and infinitely repeated eons is found the divisions of calendrical time: the day (and its parts), fortnight, month, season, and year. The lunar calendar is divided into 360 days, each day divided into 30 units of 48 minutes called the *muhurta*s. The next unit traditionally was the fortnights of the waxing and waning moon. Together the two fortnights formed a month. The lunar year consists of twelve months divided into three four-month periods (the *caturmasya*s) or six seasons: spring, summer or the hot season, the rainy season, autumn, winter, and the cool season. The new year was reckoned to begin either with the full moon in the month of Tapasya (February–March) or with that of the month of Caitra (a.k.a. Madhu, March–April).

Also introduced already by the middle centuries B.C.E. in India and henceforth continuing in all Hindu, Buddhist, and Jain traditions was the notion that the world of *samsara* was fundamentally illusory. This doctrine, known as *maya* ("illusion"), held that it is because of our own ignorance that we perceive a world of differentiation and change; and it is through our own ignorance that we suffer and produce karma and thus circle through the cycle of perpetual rebirth. *Samsara* is contrasted to an unconditioned, eternal, and transcendent state that is equated with "freedom" or "liberation" from such transience, suffering, and rebirth, and the ultimate goal of all Indian religions is to attain such a state.

Whereas the monastic strains of Buddhism and Jainism tended to emphasize renunciation from the world of ordinary, worldly time and the suffering that accompanies it as soon as one had the inclination, in Hinduism a system of gradual withdrawal was recommended. At the level of the individual, a "lifetime" is ideally divided according to the Hindu theory of *ashrama*s or "stages of life," each with its own set of necessary and important religious duties. The first of these is the stage of the student who is charged with learning the sacred texts and rituals and serving the teacher. This is followed by the stage of life of the married householder who is to pursue worldly life (including pleasure and material gain) within the boundaries of proper religion or *dharma*. When the householder "sees his son's son," he should begin the process of retiring from worldly concerns and take up the life of the "forest-dweller." The final stage of life is that of the world-renouncer, the *samnyasi* who has given up worldly duties altogether and seeks the mystical knowledge whereby temporality itself is transcended and the eternal dimension of reality is fully realized. Such a person—and there are Buddhist and Jain equivalents—is thought to be permanently "released" from the bonds of time and forever is identified with the Absolute.

*See also* **Buddhism; Calendar; Hinduism; Jainism; Time: China; Time: Traditional and Utilitarian.**

**BIBLIOGRAPHY**
Gonda, Jan. *Prajapati and the Year*. Amsterdam and New York: North-Holland, 1984.
Lingat, Robert. "Time and the Dharma." *Contributions to Indian Sociology* 6 (1962): 7–16.
O'Flaherty, Wendy D. *Origins of Evil in Hindu Mythology*. Berkeley: University of California, 1976.
Panikkar, Raimon. "Toward a Typology of Time and Temporality in the Ancient Indian Tradition." *Quarterly of Asian and Contemporary Thought* 24, no. 2 (1974).
Reimann, Luis Gonzalez. *Tiempo Ciclico y eras del Mundo en la India*. Mexico City: El Colegio de México, 1988.
Samartha, Stanley J. *The Hindu View of History*. Bangalore: Christian Institute for the Study of Religion and Society, 1959.
Underhill, M. M. *The Hindu Religious Year*. London: Oxford University Press, 1921.

*Brian Smith*

## TRADITIONAL AND UTILITARIAN

A primary distinction separates sequential (or utilitarian) time, which has to do with the relations of before and after, from traditional time, which has to do with the relation of the present to both the past and the future. For Émile Durkheim (1858–1917), traditional societies were based on solidarities in traditional time, and they relegated to the margins of social life practical concerns emanating from sequential time, such as whether to do A before doing B. These latter (utilitarian) concerns typify, in Durkheim's view, magic on the peripheries of traditional societies and utilitarian thinking about means and ends, or causes and effects, central to the ordering of modern societies. For Max Weber (1864–1920), charismatic leaders introduced radical disruptions in social orders based on traditional times, but in order to survive, these movements had to become preoccupied with sequential or utilitarian time, with lines of success, and with logical or practical forms of thinking and action. Thus for Weber, charismatic authority, which is initially disdainful of practical concerns, defeats itself by its own successes, which dictate concern with means and ends, and causes and effects. Durkheim remains critical of such utilitarian concerns, even when they dominate the social order, because they are inadequate as bases for authority and social control. Thus in the disagreements between Weber and Durkheim one can find the roots of contemporary conflict in the field over whether utilitarian time is derived from, a side effect of, or opposed to traditional time and whether utilitarianism in various forms is typical of all social orders or primarily of modernity alone.

### The Origins of Utilitarian Modernity

Various attempts have been made to explain how the sense of time in modern societies has come to be dominated by the concerns of rationality, which relegates to the peripheries of social life such other sources of social order and allegiance as loyalty to kinship and ethnic groups, or commitment to mythical versions of the past and of the future. The move toward utilitarian time in Europe may be due to the marginalization of traditional time, in which the present is both embedded in the past and mortgaged to the future, from the social life of the nation. The causes of this development have been variously attributed to a number of sources, notably: the legacy of the church as a source of rational social control; the tendency of the Protestant Reformation to displace traditional time, in which the departed were still intimately linked with the ongoing life of the community and were a source of authority for kinship and ethnic groups; and the early dissolution of the feudal system and the resultant ordering of production and of relationships between employers and employees, even in late medieval agricultural communities, along rational lines.

Some scholars have focused on the monastic, highly rational ordering of temporal sequences as the source and model for the increasing regulation of the temporal sequences of public life in the Western city from the twelfth century onward. Others, following this line of argument, have traced the concern for the rational ordering of everyday life and the self-perfection of the individual to the attempt to turn Purgatory into a this-worldly state of mind, in which individuals have to take on a rational self-discipline in their use of time for the purpose of spiritual perfection. Max Weber credited the church in the Western city with breaking open the communities based on familial or ethnic ties and replacing them with the more inclusive ties among coreligionists. It is also widely understood that utilitarian time was advanced by the administrative rationality and control of the Christian Church in Europe as it took on a wide range of functions after the collapse of the Roman Empire from the fifth century onward.

When Latin was replaced, the newer vernaculars took on the function of providing the extended present for nations and a sense of sharing in a common time as well as space. They provided a common language that was exclusive of the dialects and other traditional sources of loyalty and solidarity. The vernacular, carried by the media and especially by the broadsheets, established a present and defined "the times" in which people were living, while relegating Latin to the past, to an old world that was passing away.

This strategy for relativizing and marginalizing is easily seen as utilitarian when it occurs under the auspices of the modern nation-state, as in the case of England under Henry VIII and Elizabeth, who replaced traditional religion with a more abstract or generalized form of ascetic belief and practice: from Scholasticism and systematic theology to science and public affairs. Here again, the broadsheet became the sacrament of a secular society.

If utilitarianism relegates traditional sources of solidarity, which rely on traditional time and its mediation of the past and the future to the present, utilitarian time construes an extended present, in which the various pasts of ethnic and kinship, racial or national groups are irrelevant to a discourse on precedents, conditions, and consequences of effective and legitimate action. Social processes are thus ordered in terms of sequences that link means to ends, causes to effects, and precedents to procedures: not in terms of priorities based on a wide range of collective memories and aspirations for the future. A major gulf thus opens up between discussions of social policy and the unsatisfied longings of minority or subordinate groups and communities, along with their aspirations for a redress of grievances in the future.

### Modern Societies

In modern societies, however, those who control public discourse have arrogated to themselves the kind of time that Durkheim regards as merely utilitarian, "temporal," and thus lacking in the bases of traditional solidarity that would have been available in more primitive societies, where temporal sequence was a matter of peripheral concern for individuals and those practicing magic: not for those on whom the duration of the society itself depended.

Thus, for Durkheim, modern societies represent an inversion of the traditional: a change in which type of time dominates public discourse, and a change in the sort of elites that control public discourse. Because of his antipathy to utilitarianism, Durkheim took as his preferred model traditional social systems that considered themselves to be part of time that runs from the past through the present into the future; thus the sort of time that is concerned with the logical and practical relation of means to ends and of causes to effects was relegated, in his view, to the social periphery. In modern societies, however, these oppositions were reversed, with the utilitarian engagement with time preoccupying the political and cultural center, and communities with their own traditional bases of solidarity (and their views of the present as being linked with the past and the future) being relegated to the periphery.

Sociologists and historians remain divided as to whether the new elites and their utilitarian view of time can provide the bases for solidarity and for personal identity, which had been mediated by powerful myths and rituals linking the self to the duration of the society from the past into the present and the future. Some regard this conflict as a contest for the "soul" of a nation such as America, while others regard the contest in more comparative terms as a problem faced by a wide variety of nations coping with indigenous and external sources of both threats and opportunities. Whether or not Durkheim is right about the inversion of time-sense between modern and traditional societies, a question remains as to whether any society, by its very formation, divides the flow of time into two separate streams, the one sequential or utilitarian, temporal and temporary, the other concerned with the long duration of peoples over many generations, and with the impact of both the past and the future upon the social present.

The question also remains whether, as Talal Asad argues, what is needed is an alternative to utilitarianism: a view of the world that "is not divided into significant binary features" (p. 15). In modern societies, of course, those opposites have been, at least since the Enlightenment, the modern and the premodern, and sometimes these oppositions have been arrayed in ideological discourse along lines separating the West from the East, or within the West between Europe and the United States. Other forms of binary opposition have arrayed the relatively educated, who have adapted well to living in a complex, highly differentiated society, in opposition to those who are looking for simpler formulations and more primitive forms of solidarity. For modern commentators working from within Weberian assumptions, utilitarianism has been accompanied by the emergence of a self with political rights and the freedom to make a variety of choices in the economy and the political system, as well as in the more intimate spheres of the family and local community. This freedom comes from the individuating consequences of complex societies, which keep individuals from being embedded in particular and highly limiting social contexts.

## Conclusion

It may well be that, as Durkheim argued, the division of the world into binary opposites begins with the formation of any social system, which pits its own times against those of other forms of social solidarity. Thus the tendency to divide time between the utilitarian and the traditional, between concern with means-ends or cause-effect relationships and the long extension of the present into the past and the future is typical of any social system. Pierre Bourdieu argues in this vein, and separates the two kinds of time into "field" and "habitus," their differences providing a potential source of tension within any social system.

Others, however, like Niklas Luhmann, argue that a binary opposition is typical of any social system. Luhmann uses the cybernetic model as an analogy for understanding the fluidity and complexity of relationships and practices in modern societies. On this view, the utilitarian tendency to divide time into two separate streams is not restricted to modern societies but is endemic to the formation of any social system.

*See also* **Enlightenment; Globalization; Modernity; Secularization and Secularism.**

### BIBLIOGRAPHY

Anderson, Benedict P. O'G. *Imagined Communities: Reflections on the Origin and Spread of Nationalism.* London: Verso, 1991.

Asad, Talal. *Formations of the Secular: Christianity, Islam, Modernity.* Stanford, Calif.: Stanford University Press, 2003.

Bourdieu, Pierre. *Outline of a Theory of Practice.* Translated by Richard Nice. New York: Cambridge University Press, 1977.

Bruce, Steve. *Politics and Religion.* Cambridge, U.K.: Polity, 2003.

Demerath, N. J. Cro*ssing the Gods: World Religions and Worldly Politics.* New Brunswick, N.J.: Rutgers University Press, 2001.

Durkheim, Émile. *The Elementary Forms of the Religious Life.* 1915. Translated by Joseph Ward Swain. New York: Free Press, 1965.

Fenn, Richard K. *Beyond Idols: The Shape of a Secular Society.* New York and Oxford: Oxford University Press, 2001.

Le Goff, Jacques. *The Birth of Purgatory.* Translated by Arthur Goldhammer. Chicago: University of Chicago Press, 1984.

Luhmann, Niklas. *The Differentiation of Society.* New York: Columbia University Press, 1982.

Martin, David. *Pentecostalism: The World Their Parish.* Oxford: Blackwell, 2002.

Norman, Edward. *Secularisation.* London: Continuum, 2002.

Sommerville, C. John. *The Secularization of Early Modern England: From Religious Culture to Religious Faith.* New York: Oxford University Press, 1992.

Weber, Max. *On Charisma and Institution Building: Selected Papers.* Edited by and with an Introduction by S. N. Eisenstadt. Chicago: University of Chicago Press, 1968.

Wilson, Bryan R. *Religion in Sociological Perspective.* Oxford and New York: Oxford University Press, 1982.

Wuthnow, Robert. *The Struggle for America's Soul: Evangelicals, Liberals, and Secularism.* Grand Rapids, Mich.: Eerdmans, 1989.

*Richard K. Fenn*

**TOLERATION.** Toleration is a policy or attitude toward something that is not approved and yet is not actively rejected. The word comes from the Latin *tolerare* (to bear or endure), suggesting a root meaning of putting up with something. There is no single and widely accepted definition of the term, and it is hardly an exaggeration to say that every author uses it in his or her own way. Therefore it may be best to understand the many uses of the word in terms of family resemblances.

It should be clear that each of the languages that uses a variant of the Latin term (German, *Toleranz;* Dutch, *tolerantie;* French, *tolérance;* Spanish, *tolerancia;* Italian, *tolleranza;* etc.) adds its own slightly different connotations to the word, based on historical experiences. Languages that do not derive the word from Latin have synonyms, each with some overlap and some difference in usage.

Throughout much of the history of the concept, *toleration* referred largely to a policy or attitude toward different religions. Intolerance could mean burning at the stake of heretics or apostates and forced conversions of adherents to different religions, and tolerance could mean anything short of that. By the late twentieth century, demands for toleration could also refer to other disputed behaviors such as sexual orientations, clothing and dress, drug use, vegetarianism versus meat-eating, and more (although religion was often not far behind these disputes). Ethnic and cultural behaviors and language usage could be the subject of tolerance and intolerance as well. In medicine, toleration refers to an organism's capacity to absorb or endure something without untoward consequences.

## Conceptual Nuances

Most uses of the word understand it as referring to a middle ground on a spectrum between rejection, intolerance, hate, and persecution on one end, and acceptance, approval, love, and respect on the other. They distinguish it from indifference because it only comes into play when something is disliked or disapproved and matters.

Who is doing the tolerating, who or what is being tolerated, and exactly what such toleration entails can vary enormously. Individuals can be said to tolerate their own personal foibles, not to tolerate fools, or to tolerate whole groups. Groups can be said to tolerate individuals within or without, or other groups. States and other political authorities can be said to tolerate individuals, groups, or other states. That which is tolerated can range from the very existence to the appearance, ideas, or activities of the tolerated entity. Toleration can range from providing only limited encouragement, to doing nothing, to applying limited sanctions short of persecution.

Some authors have tried to distinguish "toleration" from "tolerance," with the former referring to official policies and the latter to a personal attribute, but ordinary language does not seem to distinguish the two. For example, we can say that the behavior of tolerant persons shows that they tolerate others, or that all we are asking for from another person is toleration. We can also say that a government policy reflects tolerance of some activity.

Some authors have thought that toleration is only a second-best, half-way measure, and that we ought to go beyond toleration to embrace and respect others. This is certainly the right thing to do where whatever is being tolerated actually deserves to be embraced. But one can wonder if all human beings really are always doing things that deserve respect. What would the world be like if all people and all of their activities were worthy of embrace? Certainly unlike anything we have seen so far. Then, perhaps, there would be no need for a concept like toleration. But until that moment arrives, this is the term for the response to things that merit neither active persecution nor full acceptance.

Toleration may look weak and thin from the perspective of a possible acceptance and embrace, but it can look very good from the perspective of someone who is undergoing persecution. Many a victim of intolerance would just like to be left alone, and that is one of the modes of toleration. One of the paradoxes of toleration is that if one is tolerant of everything, then one is also tolerant of the intolerant. This may mean complicity with persecution, or at least failure to prevent it.

## Related Concepts

A large vocabulary of related concepts has been used to define and promote toleration. If, as mentioned above, religion created many of the disputes that lead to persecution, it also produced many concepts that can lead toward toleration. Irenicism

(the seeking of peace), the pursuit of concord, comprehension, latitudinarianism, and basic agreement on fundamentals have been policies of many theologians and churchmen. Where these policies recognize that we may never approve of everything the other thinks or does, they promote toleration. Where they imply that someday we will all agree, they go beyond it.

Other terms that have both religious and secular meanings are relevant. Mercy and charity may inspire one to tolerate. Patience is close to the root meaning of the Latin word, helping one endure what one disapproves. Humility, modesty, and skepticism about one's own knowledge of what is right may incline one to tolerate others even when one disagrees with them. Indulgence can mean allowing something that one could prevent. Compromise may mean conceding some points in order to gain others, tolerating the loss of the conceded points.

High-minded philosophical principles can lead toward toleration. Belief in the autonomy and independence of other people can justify leaving them alone even when one does not like what they are doing. Principles of impartiality and neutrality may make a state stay out of religious or other quarrels. Of course, not just any principle will do: most persecution is justified by principle as well.

Toleration has not always been the result of principle. It can come about for purely practical reasons because of exhaustion, impotence, or impasse. It can be the result of politique calculation that hostility does not pay. Swiss physician and theologian Thomas Erastus (1524–1583) gave his name to Erastianism, a term for state supremacy and policies that enforce toleration in order to maintain political stability and prevent religious fighting. Gag orders and decrees prohibiting further debate have often been used to silence contending parties in the hopes of reaching a modicum of mutual toleration.

Liberty of conscience and freedom of religion are policies that sometimes overlap with toleration and sometimes go beyond it. Liberty of conscience usually means that everyone may think what they like, and no one will inquire into what they think. But this is compatible with suppressing public expression of what one thinks. On the one hand, this may be better than regimes in which "thought police" are constantly monitoring people's ideas; on the other, it is not as free as forms of toleration that permit expression. Freedom of religion often means that one can choose among two or more established religions, but it sometimes also implies that one must choose one of the available religions. It may not tolerate rejection of all religion.

## Valence

In modern times and in liberal ideology, toleration has a positive valence, associated with open-mindedness and egalitarianism. It can be a valued character trait or a beneficial attribute of a group or state.

But toleration has also been considered a negative trait or attribute. It can be associated with laziness, carelessness, and slacking. While many moderns do not consider it lazy or careless to tolerate other religions, we can capture some of the force that this charge once had if we consider that doing nothing about cruelty or murder could be characterized as tolerating it. Then the tolerators would be tolerating something they should not, perhaps out of cowardice or carelessness.

Another negative valence of toleration can be found in the Marxist tradition, where tolerating something can be considered part of an oppressive regime. "Repressive tolerance" can include tolerating evil and oppressive people or activities. It can also mean tolerating a protesting group and thus depriving it of the importance it would have if it were taken seriously. In effect, this theory holds that in conditions of class inequality, both tolerance and intolerance are repressive.

Other modern groups have considered toleration condescending and ultimately affirmative of conditions of injustice. For example, T. S. Eliot (1888–1965) wrote that in the conditions of modern secularism "The Christian does not want to be tolerated" (Cranston, p. 101); rather, she wants to be respected. Similarly, spokespeople for ethnic groups, women, gays, and others have objected that simply being in a position of having to be tolerated is already unfair, reflecting power inequalities.

Perhaps because of its middle-way position, toleration is rarely likely to be stable over a long period. Rather, persons or states can become more or less tolerant or more or less tolerated as time goes by and opinions or conditions change. Since intolerance is often a response to a perceived threat, when the perception of threat increases or decreases, toleration may become less or more of an option. Individuals or groups that were once persecuted out of fear but are now perceived as harmless can become tolerated and eventually embraced. Vice versa, if people who were once considered innocuous become perceived as more of a threat, intolerance of them may increase.

## Toleration in the Ancient World

Cyrus the Great of Persia (r. c. 558–529 B.C.E.) is a key figure at the foundation of two traditions of toleration. He is praised in the Hebrew Bible for allowing the Jews to return to Jerusalem after Babylonian captivity. And Xenophon (c. 431–c. 352 B.C.E.) lauded him in *The Education of Cyrus* (after 394 B.C.E.) for his policy of religious toleration, placing him in the Greek tradition. Scholars have speculated that his toleration of Medes, Hyrcanians, and other religious and ethnic groups was largely an imperial political strategy. He needed to draw on the manpower of conquered kingdoms and knew it would be easier to defeat kings whose peoples believed they could thrive under his rule.

Aspects of Buddhist religious thought, which originated in India, also justified peacefulness and toleration. Ashoka (r. c. 273–232 B.C.E.), the last emperor of the Mauryan dynasty in India, renounced war and promoted Buddhism while remaining tolerant of other religions.

Throughout much of history, the ancient Chinese were tolerant of a variety of religions ranging from Confucianism to Buddhism and Taoism to animism. Manichaeans and Jews thrived at times. Scholars have speculated that it was precisely because they were tolerated and not persecuted that Jews in ancient China seem to have shed their identity and blended into the rest of the population.

The Koran contains passages about living in peace with peoples of other religions, especially "peoples of the book" (Jews and Christians). Therefore, Islamic cultures such as medieval Spain tolerated flourishing Christian and Jewish communities in what was known as *convivencia,* or living together in peace. The Ottoman Empire developed regimes of toleration of those religions that included the "millet" system, in which each religion had its own legal system and paid its own tax rate, even though only Muslims could hold higher offices.

The ancient Romans were generally tolerant of the existence of many cults because of polytheism, which implied that every hearth, city, and people could have its own gods. When they became an imperial power, they tolerated any religion that would also show signs of respect for Roman deities. They conceived of the Jewish War not as wars against that religion but against a rebellious subject people. Christians were persecuted for their refusal to take part in the imperial cult and for their disrespect for Roman rule, not merely for their religion.

## The Rise of Christian Persecution

Throughout world history, local practices of toleration have been interspersed with pogroms and persecution. Sometimes practices of toleration have come before ideas about it, and sometimes ideas have come before practices. Wherever toleration is practiced as a norm, there is not much need to think or write about it. By far the most elaborate discussion of the issue took place in the Christian West in the period from 1500 to 1800, precisely because a great deal of persecution was going on. To fully understand it, we must go back to the origins of Christian persecution.

The situation in the Roman Empire changed when the emperor Constantine (r. 306–337) legalized Christianity in 313 and promoted it as the public religion. Now it was implicated in state power and had to decide whether to tolerate or persecute others. In the following millennium there were wars against Muslims and persecution of pagans and Jews, as well as contentions within Christianity. With respect to the latter, one could justify intolerance if the people one disagreed with could be labeled as heretics or blasphemers.

The word *heresy* originally meant "choice," as in a choice of beliefs or sects, with no negative connotations. But various passages in the New Testament used it to mean sinful divisiveness. Early church fathers such as St. Irenaeus (c. 120 to 140–c. 200 to 203), Tertullian (c. 155 or 160–after 220), and Eusebius of Caesaria (c. 260–c. 339) refuted the chief early heresies. In 325 Constantine convened the Council of Nicaea to settle church doctrine and then issued an edict banning heresies. In 385 a Spanish bishop, Priscillian (c. 340–385), became the first person to be executed for heresy.

St. Augustine of Hippo (354–430) was the most influential theorist of persecution. After belonging to the Manichaean heresy in his youth, he joined the Catholic Church in 387 and eventually became a bishop. Facing Manichaean, Pelagian, and Donatist heresies, at first he advocated peaceful methods but by about 400 he began to endorse coercion. He interpreted the parable of the tares (Matt. 13:24–30) and the parable of the feast (Luke 14:21–23) to justify coercion of heretics. The latter was a particularly long stretch, because the parable merely has a rich man prepare a banquet and send his servant out into the streets to find people and "compel them to come in." Later, both Catholics and Protestants justified forced conversions on the basis of this invitation to a feast.

Further developments in the justification of persecution include the definitions of heresy in Gratian of Bologna's (d. before 1159) *Decretum* (c. 1140) and many further decrees. The persecution of heretics became the object of armed warfare in the bloody Albigensian Crusade (1209–1229). In 1233 Pope Gregory IX (ruled 1227–1241) assigned the persecution of heresy to the Dominican order, establishing the Inquisition.

***Medieval voices for tolerance.*** However, not everyone went along with the violent treatment of religious difference. The *Dialogue of a Philosopher with a Jew and a Christian* of Peter Abelard (1079–?1144) demonstrated that the pursuit of knowledge could not be detached from the inclusion of diverse standpoints. John of Salisbury (c. 1115–1180) and Marsilius of Padua (c. 1280–c. 1343) combined defenses of personal liberty with functionalist accounts of the organic unity of the political community to maintain that the health of the body politic requires freedom of thought, speech, and even action. John Wycliffe (1330–1384) developed a theory of toleration that derived from his theology of grace and his political theory of the king's responsibility to protect the welfare of both the graced and the ungraced.

Medieval times also included voices for toleration from the disempowered. Menachem Ha-Me'iri (1249–1316) developed a uniquely Jewish theory of toleration to justify cooperation with gentiles. Christine de Pisan (1364–1430) stressed the interdependence of the various parts of the body politic to justify tolerant treatment of differences of gender, class, and nationality.

In the late medieval or early Renaissance period, Nicholas of Cusa's *The Peace of the Faith* (1453) recognized that mankind was inherently and inescapably diverse in language, culture, and politics. If there will always be different customs and rites, toleration is justified because persecution is futile. Giovanni Pico della Mirandola (1463–1494) and others from this period also developed toleration for non-Christians from their interests in the Jewish Kabbalah and pagan philosophy.

## Early Modern Period

The Protestant Reformation created the most serious challenge to toleration in early modern Europe. Martin Luther (1483–1546), John Calvin (1509–1564), and Huldrych Zwingli (1484–1531) were the three most influential leaders of this movement, which permanently divided Christian Europe. Each demanded toleration for their own movement, but could be intolerant of other religions. Early Catholic responses included violent repression of the Protestants, but Humanists like Desiderius Erasmus (1466?–1536) called for a more irenic response of continuing dialogue and peaceful admonition.

Early Protestants soon justified being left alone based on their interpretations of the Bible. Spiritualists like Hans Denck (c. 1495–1527) and Sebastian Franck (c. 1499–c. 1542) and mystics like Jakob Böhme (1575–1624) felt that God is within every man, and religious individualism is God's purpose. Persecuted Anabaptists from Balthasar Hubmaier (1485–1528) and David Joris (c. 1501–1556) to Thomas Helwys (c. 1550–c. 1616) and Leonard Busher (dates unknown) argued that religious persecution is against the spirit of Jesus Christ and that judgment about matters of faith should be left to God. Menno Simons (1496–1561), founder of the Mennonites, argued for Christian pacifism, and Italian Protestants like Bernardino Ochino (1487–1564) and Celio Secondo Curione (1503–1569) defended their right to religious toleration on such grounds as faith is a gift from God, it is tyranny to punish an error of the soul, and God's church has room for great variety.

At first the Protestants could claim the high moral ground because they did not use violence like their Catholic opponents. Then, in 1553, Michael Servetus (1511–1553) was burned for antitrinitarian heresy in Calvin's Geneva. This provoked Sébastien Castellio (1515–1563) to write some of the first sustained defenses of toleration. *De haereticis* (1554; Concerning heretics) collected the irenic opinions of several writers and essays by the author under false names. "Heretic" is just the word we use to describe those with whom we disagree, he asserts. The suffering of persecution is actually the sign of a true Christian, and persecution of people who are acting in accord with their consciences promotes hypocrisy and is harmful to everybody. In later works Castellio drew on the ancient skeptics for their rejection of pretended certainty and argued for the separation of church and state. Other writers including Jacobus Acontius (1492–1566) and Mino Celsi (d. c. 1575) followed up on Castellio's thinking. Among these, Dutchman Dirck Coornhert (1522–1590) insisted that civil unity was more important than religious unity; he was one of the first to argue in favor of tolerating atheists.

Throughout the early modern period, the ideal of the primitive church as voluntary and nonviolent appealed to many people. It could be carried to the point where Pietist Gottfried Arnold's *Impartial History of Churches and Heretics* (1699–1700) redescribed most alleged heretics as pious, and most of the orthodox as the real heretics.

***Catholic toleration.*** In the Anglophone world there has long been a tendency to claim that most theories of toleration came from the Protestant side. But Father Joseph Lecler found a Catholic writer in favor of toleration for almost every Protestant toleration theorist. For example, Cardinal Reginald Pole (1500–1558) developed the thought that "Heretics be not in all Things Heretics" into a defense of toleration. In the France of the religious civil wars of the sixteenth century, Chancellor Michel de l'Hôpital (1505–1573) strove for compromise and toleration between the Calvinists and Catholics, partly on the basis of his own Catholic religious convictions. The great author Michel de Montaigne (1533–1592) never renounced Catholicism even as his *Essays* (1580–1595) contained many reasons for toleration drawn from individualism, skepticism, and a deep sense of the bodily nature of human beings. Such thinkers were sometimes called "politiques" because of their arguments for toleration on practical political grounds.

Jean Bodin (1530–1596) is an intriguing figure, ostensibly Catholic, but he could have been a Judaizer. In several works including *Colloquium of the Seven about the Secrets of the Sublime* (c. 1588) he argued for nonviolence, neutrality, and mutual agreement not to discuss differences that might lead to fighting.

The Spanish conquest of Latin America led to much abuse of the natives, partly on the ground that they were not good Christians. Writers like the bishop of Chiapas, Bartolomé de Las Casas (1474–1566), wrote in their defense. Half-Spanish half-natives like Felipe Guaman Poma (1532–1614) wrote to reconcile the two cultures, to little effect. Garcilaso de la Vega, known as "the Inca" (1539–1616), also spoke up for tolerance from the native side.

By the mid-eighteenth century active persecution of Protestants in France had died down, but in 1762 Jean Calas, a Protestant, was the victim of a judicial murder. The famous writer Voltaire (1694–1778) took up the cause, publishing *A Treatise on Toleration* (1763), which received European-wide circulation and discredited such persecution in public opinion. It may have been the last major *cri de coeur* against religious violence, because even contemporary and later Catholic treatments of heresy such as François Adrien Pluquet's *Dictionary of Heresies* of 1762 and Nicolas-Sylvestre Bergier's *Methodical Encyclopedia* of 1788–1832 took for granted that heresy did not justify violence.

### Antitrinitarianism (Socinianism).
Antitrinitarianism or unitarianism—the theory that Jesus and the Holy Spirit did not share God's nature—was a heresy considered as bad as atheism and persecuted all over Europe. But conditions close to anarchy have often been good for toleration. The absence of centralized power in Poland in the later sixteenth century meant that it became a haven for Lelio (1525–1562) and Fausto (1539–1604) Sozzini, founders of the antitrinitarian Socinians, and followers such as Samuel Przypkowski (1592–1670). They developed a battery of reasons why they should not be persecuted, most of them rooted in Scripture. Their much-anathematized writings were published in the Netherlands, which had one of the freest presses of the day. Later, many thinkers such as Isaac Newton (1642–1727) were clandestine sympathizers with antitrinitarianism under another of its variants, Arianism.

### The Netherlands out front.
The Dutch published a great deal of toleration theory and practiced toleration to a substantial degree from the later sixteenth to the eighteenth centuries. During early decades of the Revolt of the Netherlands (1568–1648) almost anything could be published because of the exhaustion of the political authorities, the myriad of decentralized jurisdictions, and appreciation of the economic value of the book market. William the Silent (1533–1584), leader of the Dutch Revolt, wrote that repression of worship leads to hypocrisy and that no false religion would last.

In the early seventeenth century a theological dispute in the Netherlands between Gomarists and Arminians led to suppression of the Arminians, but also to many writings against that suppression. Simon Episcopius (1583–1643) and Jan Uytenbogaert (1557–1644) wrote that Christian charity and reciprocity requires freedom of conscience, even for Catholics. Hugo Grotius (Huigh de Groot; 1583–1645) defended a limited tolerance as part of his theory of natural law, which was developed by later natural-law theorists like the German Samuel von Pufendorf (1632–1694). Pufendorf's *Of the Nature and Qualification of Religion* (1687) claimed that the genius of the Christian religion was nonviolence, that people's thoughts were not punishable, and that the civil authorities should control religion.

Benedict Baruch Spinoza (1632–1677), an excommunicated Jew, wrote one of the most robust defenses of freedom of thought while living in the Netherlands. In his *Theological-Political Treatise* (1670) he argued for arming the state for security against the mob, and then for reining in the state in matters of religion. Pierre Bayle (1647–1706), a Huguenot refugee in the Netherlands, developed the most sophisticated and most tolerant theory of the century. In *Letters on the Comet* (1682) he showed how atheists could indeed live in civil peace, and in *Philosophical Commentary on the Words "Compel Them to Come In"* (1685) he developed a wide-ranging theory of toleration based on the rights of conscience, even erring conscience, that would protect not only Protestant sects, but Catholics and virtually all others as well. In his last writings, he asserted that he would rather live under an atheist king because that king would have one less reason to persecute.

### The English Civil War and its aftermath.
The anarchy of the English Civil War was also fertile ground for toleration writings. John Dury (1595–1680), Samuel Hartlib (c. 1600–1662), and Johann Comenius (1592–1670) drew on millenarian hopes to justify reunion and peace among Protestants. Merchant and Leveller William Walwyn (1600–1680) wrote in favor of complete religious toleration on religious grounds. Leveller Richard Overton (fl. 1642–1663) argued for toleration of Jews and Catholics and made free use of humor to take down overserious persecuting pride, a method recommended in Anthony Ashley Cooper, Third Earl of Shaftesbury's *Characteristics* (1711). John Milton (1608–1674) made an impassioned case for toleration of divorce in several pamphlets, and then wrote the first major defense of that aspect of toleration known as freedom of the press in *Areopagitica* (1644). His work was followed up in the first substantial French and German defenses of freedom of the press by Elie Luzac (1749) and Karl Friedrich Bahrdt (1787).

Roger Williams (1603?–1683) founded the English colony of Rhode Island as a haven of freedom of religion, and published *The Bloudy Tenent of Persecution* (1644) in favor of separation of church and state and freedom of religion on Christian grounds. William Penn (1644–1718) founded the colony of Pennsylvania as a haven for persecuted Quakers and published *The Great Case of Liberty of Conscience* (1671).

Thomas Hobbes (1588–1679) wrote *Leviathan* (1651), one of the most influential theories of absolute power in the history of political philosophy, but he has also been credited with a theory of toleration in the ruler's own self-interest. Trying to control people's thoughts may provoke too much opposition and squanders power that can best be used elsewhere.

The English philosopher John Locke's (1632–1704) first work on toleration opposed it (1667). But after living for some years in the Netherlands, becoming friends with Dutch toleration theorist Philip van Limborch (1633–1712), and reading Pierre Bayle and Adriaan Paets (1631–1686) he developed a theory of toleration, which he published in *A Letter Concerning Toleration* (1689). He relied on the Calvinist point that everyone is responsible for his own salvation, skepticism about who really knew the truth, and the political benefits of toleration. Like Milton, however, he was unable to conceive of toleration of Catholics and atheists because of their alleged political unreliability, but later wrote for legal endenization of Muslims and against licensing of the press.

***Economic interests, travel writings, and belles lettres.***
Beyond religious and philosophical ideas, one source of toleration in theory and practice was economics. The Dutch found that wide toleration paid off in economic growth and provided a demonstration effect for the rest of Europe. Henry Robinson's (c. 1605–c. 1664) pamphlets of the 1640s and Daniel Defoe's (1660–1731) many writings of the beginning of the eighteenth century pointed out the commercial benefits of toleration of merchants and customers of differing religions.

Another source of tolerationist ideas was travel literature, which introduced Europeans to different customs and religions from around the world. This could include actual travel accounts; somewhat fanciful travel literature such as Fernão Mendes Pinto's *Travels* (1614); and imaginative works like Denis Veiras's *History of the Sevarites* (1675–1679), Defoe's *Robinson Crusoe* (1719), and Jonathan Swift's *Gulliver's Travels* (1726).

Other genres of literature could be important, too. Aphra Behn's play *Oroonoko* (1688) taught English audiences to tolerate Africans, Gotthold Ephraim Lessing's *Nathan the Wise* (1779) expressed the values of toleration for late-eighteenth-century Germany, and Karl Friedrich Bahrdt's play *The Edict of Religion* (1787) ridiculed Frederick William II's attempt to legislate religious conformity.

Despite all of the foregoing defenses of toleration, open admission of Socinianism or atheism remained dangerous throughout the early modern period. One recourse for Socinians, atheists, and libertines was the circulation of manuscripts and even clandestine printed works in the large underground literature of the time. Much of this literature, which included many pleas for toleration, has been explored in the French annual *La lettre clandestine* (1992–).

***Toleration of Jews.*** Jews and heretics were often subjects of popular and clerical intolerance in medieval and early modern Europe, but writers could counteract some of that sentiment. Millenarians favored toleration of Judaism because they believed that the Jews must voluntarily convert before the restoration of Christ. Histories such as Jacques Basnage's *History of the Jews* (1707–1716) and Ludvig Holberg's *History of the Jews* (1742) helped place this much-maligned people in a more favorable light. The Jewish writer Moses Mendelssohn's *Jerusalem* (1783) was an eloquent plea for religious tolerance.

## Nineteenth and Twentieth Centuries

It seems safe to say that although toleration of differing religions remains a political issue even into the twenty-first century, there have been few or no substantial novelties concerning the idea of toleration since the eighteenth century. Wilhelm von Humboldt's *The Limits of State Action* of 1852, his follower John Stuart Mill's *On Liberty* of 1859, and twentieth-century pleas for tolerance have largely debated, restated, and updated the theoretical ideas already in place from earlier times.

## Legal Acts and Declarations

In addition to political pamphlets and philosophical arguments, from the sixteenth century on toleration can be tracked by study of the legal provisions that were decreed to grant it. One form of toleration was settled by the Peace of Augsburg of 1555, which ended some of the wars between Lutherans and Catholics. Under the formula *cuius regio eius religio* (the ruler determines the religion) it held that each prince could decide which of the two religions would be established in his territories and permitted adherents to the other religion to emigrate. Although not much, this was an entering wedge for wider forms of toleration. The principle was reaffirmed, this time including Catholicism, Lutheranism, and Calvinism, in the Peace of Westphalia of 1648.

The Revolt of the Netherlands against Spain after 1560 eventually gave the once-persecuted victorious Protestants the dilemma of deciding how to deal with the large number of Catholics in their territories. Pacts of tolerance were published as early as the 1570s, and in some localities Catholics were forbidden to proselytize or engage in public processions but were allowed to worship in private homes.

In 1568 the Diet of Torda in Transylvania consolidated religious enactments of the previous decades into a decree that "no one should be abused by anyone for his religion" and further similar provisions. In the following decades Anabaptists, Unitarians, Jews, and Orthodox Christians were protected by various laws and patents. In 1573 the king of Poland was forced to accede to the Confederation of Warsaw, which granted Catholics, Lutherans, Calvinists, and even antitrinitarians some protection from persecution, leading to a golden age for Socinians there that lasted for several decades until Catholicism regained the ascendancy.

After decades of civil war between Calvinist Huguenots and Catholics in France, Henry IV enacted the Edict of Nantes in 1598, which guaranteed Protestant rights to worship in their churches and even to certain fortified cities. Several other edicts of the sixteenth century attempted to settle continuing religious rivalry, but Louis XIV ended efforts to make coexistence possible by his Revocation of the Edict of Nantes in 1685. As many as a hundred thousand Calvinists fled France.

Taking advantage of the outflow of these talented and hardworking Huguenots, Frederick William I, the Calvinist great elector of Lutheran Brandenburg, issued the Decree of Potsdam in 1685, announcing that he would provide refuge to them and respect their religion. Many came and settled in Berlin, helping the city prosper.

The Toleration Act of 1689 demonstrates what the word could mean in England in that period. It suspended penal laws against Protestants who refused to conform to the Church of England. It did not lift penalties against antitrinitarians and Catholics, who were only given equal rights in 1813 and 1829, respectively. It maintained privileges such as exclusive qualification for political office for members of the Church of England. Nevertheless, this could be considered toleration because it allowed some dissenting sects that had not previously been permitted to worship in public to do so. Its perhaps unintended consequence was to keep alive the idea that other sects could eventually be tolerated, too.

Many who emigrated to the English colonies in North America did so in pursuit of religious freedom. Maryland's Act Concerning Religion of 1649 was the first to spell out religious freedom. As mentioned above, Roger Williams founded the colony of Rhode Island in order to institute religious liberty. By the later eighteenth century, the ideal of religious toleration was often institutionalized by declarations of rights. The Virginia Declaration of Rights of 1776, several other state declarations, and the First Amendment to the United States Constitution (1791) provided for religious freedom. In France, the "Declaration of the Rights of Man and of the Citizen" of the National Assembly in 1789 provided that "No one shall be disquieted on account of his opinions, including his religious views, provided their manifestation does not disturb the public order established by law" (Article 10). The United States and France served as models for such ideals and declarations in many countries throughout the next century.

***Twentieth-century declarations.*** In the twentieth century, the United Nations internationalized the tradition of declarations of rights to toleration. In 1948 the General Assembly adopted the Universal Declaration of Human Rights, providing that "everyone has the right to freedom of thought, conscience and religion; this right includes freedom to change his religion or belief, and freedom, either alone or in community with others and in public or private, to manifest his religion or belief in teaching, practice, worship and observance" (Article 18).

In 1996 the United Nations Educational, Social, and Cultural Organization (UNESCO) issued a "Declaration of Principles of Tolerance." Ignoring the ordinary usage of *tolerance* as referring to the middle of the spectrum between persecution and warm embrace, UNESCO redefined it by fiat as "respect, acceptance and appreciation of the rich diversity of our world's cultures" (Article 1.1). This was surely well-intended as an effort to move people who are unjustifiably opposed to diversity toward more open-mindedness. But if warm embrace becomes the exclusive meaning of *toleration,* we will surely need another term for our attitude or policy toward the things we may justifiably not respect, accept, or appreciate, but also do not persecute.

*See also* **Christianity; Heresy and Apostasy; Liberalism; Liberty; Orthodoxy; Orthopraxy.**

## BIBLIOGRAPHY

PRIMARY SOURCES

Bahrdt, Karl Friedrich. *The Edict of Religion: A Comedy; and The Story and Diary of My Imprisonment.* 1789. Translated and edited by John Christian Laursen and Johan van der Zande. Lanham, Md.: Lexington, 2000.

Bayle, Pierre. *Pierre Bayle's Philosophical Commentary: A Modern Translation and Critical Interpretation.* 1685. Translated by Amie G. Tannenbaum. New York: Lang, 1987.

Castellion, Sébastien. *Concerning Heretics.* 1554. Translated by Roland H. Bainton. New York: Columbia University Press, 1935.

Locke, John. *A Letter Concerning Toleration, in Focus.* 1689. Edited by John Horton and Susan Mendus. London: Routledge, 1991.

Luzac, Elie. *Essay on Freedom of Expression.* 1749. In *Early French and German Defenses of Freedom of the Press,* edited by John Christian Laursen and Johan van der Zande. Leiden: Brill, 2003.

Milton, John. *Areopagitica.* 1643. In *Areopagitica and Other Political Writings by John Milton,* edited by John Alvis. Indianapolis: Liberty Fund, 1999.

Penn, William. *The Great Case for Liberty of Conscience.* 1670. In *The Political Writings of William Penn,* edited by Andrew R. Murphy. Indianapolis: Liberty Fund, 2002.

Pufendorf, Samuel. *Of the Nature and Qualification of Religion in Reference to Civil Society.* 1687. Edited by Simone Zurbuchen. Indianapolis: Liberty Fund, 2002.

Robinson, Henry. *Liberty of Conscience.* 1644. San Francisco: California State Library, 1940.

Spinoza, Benedictus de. *Theological-Political Treatise.* 1670. Translated by Samuel Shirley. Indianapolis: Hackett, 2001.

Williams, Roger. *The Bloudy Tenent of Persecution.* London: n.p., 1644.

SECONDARY SOURCES

Berkvens-Stevelinck, Christiane, Jonathan Israel, and G. H. M. Posthumus Meyjes, eds. *The Emergence of Tolerance in the Dutch Republic.* Leiden, Netherlands: Brill, 1997.

Cranston, Maurice. "John Locke and the Case for Toleration." In *On Toleration,* edited by Susan Mendus and David Edwards. Oxford: Clarendon, 1987.

Eijnatten, Joris van. *Liberty and Concord in the United Provinces: Religious Toleration and the Public in the Eighteenth-Century Netherlands.* Leiden, Netherlands: Brill, 2003.

Guggisberg, Hans R. *Sebastian Castellio, 1515–1563: Humanist and Defender of Religious Toleration in a Confessional Age.* Göttingen, Germany: Vandenhoeck and Ruprecht, 1997.

Jordan, W. K. *The Development of Religious Toleration in England.* 4 vols. London: Allen and Unwin, 1932.

Laursen, John Christian, ed. *Histories of Heresy in Early Modern Europe: For, against, and beyond Persecution and Toleration.* New York: Palgrave Macmillan, 2002.

———, ed. *Religious Toleration: "The Variety of Rites" from Cyrus to Defoe.* New York: St. Martin's, 1999.

Laursen, John Christian, and Cary J. Nederman, eds. *Beyond the Persecuting Society: Religious Toleration before the Enlightenment.* Philadelphia: University of Pennsylvania Press, 1998.

Lecler, Joseph. *Toleration and the Reformation.* 2 vols. London: Longmans, 1960.

Levine, Alan. *Sensual Philosophy: Toleration, Skepticism, and Montaigne's Politics of the Self.* Lanham, Md.: Lexington, 2001.

Murphy, Andrew R. *Conscience and Community: Revisiting Toleration and Religious Dissent in Early Modern England and America.* University Park: Pennsylvania State University Press, 2001.

Nederman, Cary J. *Worlds of Difference: European Discourses of Toleration, c. 1100–c. 1550.* University Park: Pennsylvania State University Press, 2000.

Nederman, Cary J., and John Christian Laursen, eds. *Difference and Dissent: Theories of Toleration in Medieval and Early Modern Europe.* Lanham, Md.: Rowman and Littlefield, 1996.

*John Christian Laursen*

## TOTALITARIANISM.

Totalitarianism is a concept rooted in the horror of modern war, revolution, terror, genocide, and, since 1945, the threat of nuclear annihilation. It is also among the most versatile and contested terms in the political lexicon. At its simplest, the idea suggests that despite Fascist/Nazi "particularism" (the centrality of the nation or the master race) and Bolshevist "universalism" (the aspiration toward a classless, international brotherhood of man), both regimes were basically alike—which, as Carl Friedrich noted early on, is not to claim that they were wholly alike. Extreme in its denial of liberty, totalitarianism conveys a regime type with truly radical ambitions. Its chief objectives are to rule unimpeded by legal restraint, civic pluralism, and party competition, and to refashion human nature itself.

Coined in May 1923 by Giovanni Amendola, *totalitarianism* began life as a condemnation of Fascist ambitions to monopolize power and to transform Italian society through the creation of a new political religion. The word then quickly mutated to encompass National Socialism, especially after the Nazi "seizure of power" in 1933. By the mid-1930s, invidious comparisons among the German, Italian, and Soviet systems as totalitarian were becoming common; they increased considerably once the Nazi-Soviet pact was signed in 1939. Meanwhile, recipients of the totalitarian label took different views of it. Although, in the mid 1920s, Benito Mussolini and his ideologues briefly embraced the expression as an apt characterization of their revolutionary élan, Nazi politicians and propagandists saw a disconcerting implication. Granted, Adolf Hitler and Joseph Goebbels, during the early 1930s, had a penchant for cognate expressions such as "total state"; so, too, did sympathetic writers such as Ernst Forsthoff and Carl Schmitt. At around the same time, Ernst Jünger was busy expounding his idea of "total mobilization." But "totalitarianism" was treated with greater circumspection. The *Volksgemeinschaft* (national community), Nazi spokesmen insisted, was unique: the vehicle of an inimitable German destiny based on a national, racially based, rebirth. *Totalitarianism* suggested that German aspirations were a mere variant on a theme; worse, a theme that current usage extrapolated to the Bolshevist foe.

Once Fascism and Nazism were defeated, a new global conflict soon emerged, and with it a reinvigorated role for "totalitarianism." Anxiety over Soviet ambitions in Europe prompted Churchill's use of the term twice in his "Iron Curtain" speech on March 5, 1946, at Fulton, Missouri. A year later, the Truman Doctrine entrenched the word in American foreign policy and security jargon. Then the Cold War took its course, punctuated by the Berlin Airlift, the building of the Berlin Wall, the Sino-Soviet treaties, the Korean War, the Cuban Missile Crisis, and the Hungarian, Czech, and Polish uprisings. At each turn, the language of totalitarianism received a further boost, though there were significant national variations in the credence it received. In the United States, the language of totalitarianism, despite dissenting voices, had wide appeal across the political spectrum. In France, by contrast, it had practically none until the decay of existentialism and the appearance of Solzhenitsyn's work on the Soviet Gulag triggered a major attitudinal shift. Postwar Germany represents an intermediate case: officially sanctioned by the Federal Republic, *totalitarianism* became the focus of major intellectual controversy from the late 1960s onward.

Even periods of engagement with the Soviet Union—notably détente and the Ronald Reagan–Mikhail Gorbachev dialogue—stimulated debate over totalitarianism. Some commentators optimistically announced its softening and demise, while others deplored collaborating with the totalitarian enemy. During the Soviet Union's last decade, Western academics and foreign policy experts argued over the distinction between two kinds of regime. Authoritarian regimes (sometimes also called "traditional" or "autocratic") typified the apartheid state in South Africa, Iran under the Pahlavis, and the South American military juntas. Though hierarchical, vicious, and unjust, they had limited goals, and they left large parts of society (religious practice, family, and work relations) untouched. Conceivably, they were capable of reformist evolution toward representative government. In contrast, totalitarian regimes were depicted as utopian, inherently expansionist, and indelibly tyrannical, an evil empire. Treating them as normal states was folly. Meanwhile, in central Europe, embattled oppositionists during the late 1970s and 1980s were coining terms that suggested novel permutations on the classical model. "Posttotalitarian" regimes, suggested Václav Havel in *The Power of the Powerless* (1978), retained a brutal apparatus of coercion but were no longer able to enthuse their populations with faith. Resistance required puncturing a hollow, mechanically recited ideology by everyday acts of noncompliance and by "living in truth" (that is, by speaking and acting honestly).

Following the collapse of the Soviet Union, twenty-first-century Islamism and the "war against terror" continued to keep the idea of totalitarianism salient. Yet if all these experiences are inseparable from the discourse of totalitarianism, its longevity has also been promoted by three rather different factors. One factor is the term's elasticity. It can be applied either to institutions or to ideologies, to governments or to movements, or to some combination of all of these. Additionally, it can be invoked to delineate an extant reality or a desire, myth, aim, tendency, experiment, and project. *Total* and its cognates (*totality, total war,* etc.) are commonplaces of the current age, so it is unsurprising that *totalitarianism* is also one. A second factor, more important still, is the role played by journalists, novelists, poets, playwrights, and filmmakers in publicly disseminating the images of totalitarian domination. Their role was to ensure that totalitarianism never became a recondite, academic term but one central to the vernacular of educated people. Totalitarianism was a buzzword of political journalism before it received, in the late 1940s and 1950s, searching treatment by social science and political theory. Its first literary masterpiece was Arthur Koestler's *Darkness at Noon* (1941) with its sinister portrayal of the Communist confessional. Many great works on a similar theme followed, making totalitarianism vivid and unforgettable to readers electrified by the pathos and terror such writing evoked.

Still, no novelist is more responsible for the notion that totalitarianism penetrates the entire human personality, dominating it from within, than George Orwell (Eric Arthur Blair, 1903–1950). That view appeared nothing less than prescient when stories later circulated in the 1950s about "brainwashing" of captured prisoners of war (POWs) during the Korean War. Orwell deserves a special place in any historical audit of totalitarianism for another reason. *Nineteen Eighty Four* (1949) introduced terms—"Thought Police," "Big Brother," "Doublethink"—that have since entered the English language as unobtrusively as those of Shakespeare and the King James Bible. So long as his work appears in the secondary school and university curricula, totalitarianism as an idea will survive. In a similar way, no one is more responsible for informing a general public about the Soviet Gulag than Aleksandr Solzhenitsyn (b. 1918). To his extraordinary novels, memoirs, and what he called "experiments in literary investigation," one may add the work of Osip Mandelstam, Nadezhda Mandelstam, Anna Akhmatova, Boris Souvarine, and Boris Pasternak. Each bequeathed a searing portrait of the depravity and recklessness of "totalitarian" systems.

Finally, totalitarianism's endurance as a term owes much to its capacity for provocative and counterintuitive application. It was not only heterodox Marxists such as Herbert Marcuse who indicted modern pluralist regimes for a systemically imbecilic, one-dimensional, and totalitarian mass culture. Liberals such as Friedrich Hayek also warned in 1944 of totalitarian developmental tendencies—particularly the fetish with state planning and intervention—that were paving the "road to serfdom." Many critics of the New Deal took a similar view; Herbert Hoover notoriously called Franklin Delano Roosevelt a "totalitarian liberal." Also disquieting was the sociologist Erving Goffman's contention in *Asylums* (1961) that Nazi death camps were broadly comparable to widely accepted "total institutions" such as the asylum, prison, barracks, and orphanage. The implication was that totalitarianism was not an exotic species of regime "over there" but a legitimized institution or trend deeply embedded within modernity as a whole.

## Origins, Trajectory, Causation

Theorists of totalitarianism take very different views of its origins. For some, Hannah Arendt foremost among them, totalitarianism is radically new, an unprecedented development that attended Europe's economic, political, and moral ruination during and after World War I. From this perspective, attempts to locate a long-established lineage of totalitarianism are fundamentally mistaken. So, too, are analogies of totalitarianism with Caesarist, Bonapartist, and other dictatorial regimes. Totalitarianism is conjunctural or unique, not an extreme version of something previously known. The point of using the term is precisely to show the novelty of the regime type and the crisis it denotes. Other writers, conversely, believe that totalitarianism has deeper roots. Hence it might be said that totalitarianism is

a perverted outgrowth of the Martin Luther–sanctioned authoritarian state, or an exaggerated legacy of tsarist intolerance. Or it might be agued that "totalitarian dictatorship" is ancient, prefigured in the Spartan state or the Roman imperial regime of Diocletian (r. 284–305). That was the judgment of Franz Neumann, who in addition claimed that National Socialism had revived the "fascist dictatorship" methods of the fourteenth-century Roman demagogue Cola di Rienzo. Nor, according to still others, should totalitarianism be understood as an exclusively occidental institution. Karl Wittfogel in *Oriental Despotism* (1957) found "total power" in the hydraulic governance of ancient China. And while sinologists have major reservations about describing Maoism as totalitarian, victims such as Harry Wu, imprisoned for nineteen years in the Chinese Laogai, exhibit no such compunction. Totalitarianism has also been located in Africa, for instance, in the rule of Shaka Zulu, while the Soviet Union itself was often depicted as a hybrid entity, more "Asian" than Western.

The search for the roots of totalitarian ideas, as distinct from institutions, has generated yet another fertile literature. Karl Popper found prototototalitarianism in Plato. Max Horkheimer and Theodor Adorno spied a totalitarian dialectic evolving out of an "Enlightenment" fixation on mathematical formalization, instrumental reason, and the love of the machine. J. L. Talmon discovered a creedal, "totalitarian democracy" arising from one tendency among eighteenth-century philosophies. Enunciated by Jean-Jacques Rousseau (1712–1778), Morelly (fl. mid-eighteenth century), and Gabriel Bonnot de Mably (1709–1785); radicalized by the French Revolution, especially during its Jacobin phase; reincarnated in the Babouvist conspiracy, "totalitarian democracy" amounted to a leftist "political messianism" that preached the arrival of a new order: homogenous, egalitarian, yet supervised by a virtuous revolutionary vanguard able to divine the general will. This reminds one of Alexis de Tocqueville's observation, in *The Ancien Regime and the French Revolution* (1856), that the Revolution's "ideal" was nothing less than "a regeneration of the whole human race. It created an atmosphere of missionary fervor and, indeed, assumed all the aspects of a religious revival." That "strange religion," he continued, "has, like Islam, overrun the whole world with its apostles, militants, and martyrs" (p. 44).

Tocqueville's reference to Islam was deliberately discomfiting. It reminded his audience of what a modern "enlightened" European revolution shared with a declining Oriental civilization. Less than a century later, Bertrand Russell augmented that idea when he suggested that Bolshevism was like Islam, while John Maynard Keynes, in lapidary mood, remarked that "Lenin [was] a Mahomet, and not a Bismarck." Yet since Al Qaeda's suicide attack on the World Trade Center and the Pentagon on September 11, 2001, a growing number of commentators have contended that it is *modern* Islam, or at least the current of Islamism associated with the legacy of the Egyptian Muslim Brotherhood and the Saudi Wahhabite movement, with which previous European revolutions are best compared. On this account, twenty-first century Islamist (and perhaps Baʿathi) ideology, practice, and organization bear many disquieting parallels with National Socialism and Bolshevism.

Modern Islamism is a radical movement in which pluralism is anathema, and in which politics itself is derided as a sphere of venality. To that extent it mirrors Islamic doctrine more generally since the suras of the Koran make no categorical or principled distinction between public and private spheres: every duty emanates from God alone. The state has no independent authority. Among Islamist militants, the substitute for political institutions is, above all, the fellow-feeling and camaraderie bestowed by membership of a secret society and the existential tests that confront the believer. "Muslim totalitarianism" reconfigures the capillary, decentralized organization of its Western precursors. Islamist militants combine the conspiratorial anti-Semitism of the Nazis (for whom they entertain a nostalgic admiration) with the pan-territorial ambitions of Bolshevik universalism. Islamist language is also replete with millenarian images of struggle, merciless destruction, and "sacred terror." Bent on purifying the world of Zionism, liberalism, feminism, and Crusader (U.S.) hegemony, Islamist ideology articulates a mausoleum culture of submission, nihilism, suicidal martyrdom for the cause, and mythological appeal to a world about to be reborn. That archaic demands for the reestablishment of the hallowed caliphate are pursued with all the means modern technology affords is consistent with the "reactionary modernism" of earlier totalitarian movements.

Such totalitarian parallels or intellectual lineages do not satisfy those who insist that family resemblance is no substitute for attributable historical causation. And since the early 1950s it has frequently been acknowledged that theorists of totalitarianism are much more adept at constructing morphologies than they are at establishing the precise relationship of totalitarian regimes to one another. François Furet argued this point eloquently, claiming too that Arendt's hodgepodge reconstruction of totalitarianism's career had failed to explain the "very different origins" of fascism and communism. Like Ernst Nolte, Furet was convinced that a "historico-genetic" approach to these movements was required to supplement the standard typological one. Like Nolte, as well, he believed that Bolshevism and National Socialism were historically linked, still a taboo contention among many leftists. Yet Furet disagreed with Nolte's contention that, essentially, National Socialism was a reaction to Bolshevism, a defensive if evil posture that gained credibility owing to the disproportionate influence of Jews in Marxist and socialist parties. According to Furet, the genealogical relationship between Bolshevism and National Socialism was not principally cause and effect. Each had its own endogenous history. The two movements' affinity derived instead from the fact that both of them (and Italian Fascism too—Mussolini was once a revolutionary socialist) emerged from the same "cultural" atmosphere: a late-nineteenth-, early-twentieth-century milieu suffused with "hatred of the bourgeois world." Deep and bitter loathing of that world was well established before World War I and thus also before the October Revolution. Equally, German anti-Semitism did not require Jews to be major spokesmen and leaders of the left to be an object of detestation. Anti-Semitism was already firmly established before Bolshevism erupted, because Jews were seen as a vanguard of democracy itself. Bourgeois democracy was the common enemy of totalitarian movements: the "communist sees it as the

breeding ground of fascism, while the fascist sees it as the antechamber of Bolshevism (Furet and Nolte, p. 33)."

## Totalitarian Characteristics

A conventional way of describing totalitarianism is to present a list of characteristics common to Italian Fascism, German National Socialism, and Soviet Bolshevism. (Other regimes may also be included—notably, Chinese Communism under the rule of Mao, the Democratic People's Republic of Korea (North Korea), and Pol Pot's "Democratic Cambodia.") But how capacious should that portmanteau be? In *Totalitarianism*, published in 1954, Carl Friedrich itemized five elements, which, in a subsequent collaboration with Zbigniew Brzezinski, he increased to six. Yet, before that, Arthur M. Hill concocted fifteen points that Norman Davies, in *Europe: A History* (1997), expanded to seventeen. Recurrently mentioned features of totalitarianism include the following:

- A revolutionary, exclusive, and apocalyptical ideology that announces the destruction of the old order—corrupt and compromised—and the birth of a radically new, purified, and muscular age. Antiliberal, anticonservative, and antipluralist, totalitarian ideology creates myths, catechisms, cults, festivities, and rituals designed to commemorate the destiny of the elect.

- A cellular, fluid, and hydralike political party structure that, particularly before the conquest of state power, devolves authority to local militants. As it gains recruits and fellow believers, the party takes on a mass character with a charismatic leader at its head claiming omniscience and infallibility, and demanding the unconditional personal devotion of the people.

- A regime in which offices are deliberately duplicated and personnel are continually shuffled, so as to ensure chronic collegial rivalry and dependence on the adjudication of the one true leader. To the extent that legal instruments function at all, they do so as a legitimizing sham rather than a real brake on the untrammeled use of executive power. Indeed, the very notion of "the executive" is redundant since it presupposes a separation of powers anathema to a totalitarian regime.

- Economic-bureaucratic collectivism (capitalist or state socialist) intended to orchestrate productive forces to the regime's predatory, autarchic, and militaristic goals.

- Monopolistic control of the mass media, "professional" organizations, and public art, and with it the formulation of a cliché-ridden language whose formulaic utterances are designed to impede ambivalence, nuance, and complexity.

- A culture of martial solidarity in which violence and danger (of the trenches, the street fight, etc.) are ritually celebrated in party uniforms, metaphors ("storm troopers," "labor brigades"), and modes of address ("comrade"). Youth are a special audience for such a culture, but are expected to admire and emulate the "old fighters" of the revolution.

- The pursuit and elimination not simply of active oppositionists but, and more distinctively, "objective enemies" or "enemies of the people"—that is, categories of people deemed guilty of wickedness in virtue of some ascribed quality such as race or descent. Crimes against the state need not have actually been committed by the person accused of them. Hence the "hereditary principle" in North Korea where punishment is extended to three generations (the original miscreants, their children, and their grandchildren). Under totalitarianism, it is what people are, more than what they do that marks them for punishment. As Stéphane Courtois observes, "the techniques of segregation and exclusion employed in a 'class-based' totalitarianism closely resemble the techniques of 'race-based' totalitarianism" (p. 16). Soviet and Chinese Marxism may have claimed to represent humanity as a whole, but only a humanity divested first of millions—classes, categories—who were beyond the pale of Marxist doctrine. Its universalism was thus always, like National Socialism, an exclusive affair.

- Continual mobilization of the whole population through war, ceaseless campaigns, "struggles," or purges. Moreover, and notwithstanding ideological obeisance to ineluctable laws of history and race, totalitarian domination insists on febrile activity. The mercurial will of the leader and the people as a whole must constantly be exercised to produce miracles, combat backsliding, and accelerate the direction of the world toward its cataclysmic culmination.

- The pervasive use of terror to isolate, intimidate, and regiment all whom the regime deems menacing. Charged with this task are the secret police rather than the army, which typically possesses significantly fewer powers and less status than it does under a nontotalitarian dictatorship or "authoritarian" regime.

- The laboratory of totalitarian domination is the concentration camp. The experiment it conducts aims to discover the conditions under which human subjects become fully docile and pliable. In addition, a slave labor system exists side by side with a racial and/or class-oriented policy of genocide. In Nazi Germany, Jews were the principal objective enemy—over six million were murdered—but there were others such as Slavs and Gypsies. In the Soviet Union, key targets of annihilation or mass deportation were Cossacks (from 1920), kulaks (especially between 1930–1932), Crimean Tartars (1943), Chechens, and Ingush (both in 1944). The Great Purge of 1937–1938 is estimated to have killed close to 690,000 people, but this is dwarfed by the systematically induced famine in Ukraine in 1932–1933,

thought to have killed around six million. Pol Pot's Cambodian Communist Party had a similar penchant for mass extermination, as did the Chinese Communist Party (CCP) under Mao: the Chairman boasted that 700,000 perished in the 1950–1952 campaign against "counterrevolutionaries." The CCP targeted landlords and intellectuals, and through a policy of accelerated modernization created the famine of the Great Leap Forward that claimed around 30 million victims.

It should be noted that there is widespread disagreement among commentators about whether Italian Fascism is properly classified as a totalitarian system. Hannah Arendt and George Kennan thought otherwise. Mussolini's regime, on such accounts, is best comprehended as an extreme form of dictatorship or, according to Juan Linz, a species of "authoritarianism." Though preeminent, it shared power with other collective actors such as the monarchy, the military, and the Catholic Church in a way that was utterly alien to National Socialism and Bolshevism. Official anti-Semitism was less intense and less vigorously policed. And Mussolini was domestically ousted in a way that indicates a far more precarious grip on power than either Hitler or Stalin evinced.

### The Coherence of Totalitarianism

Since the 1950s, the majority of academic commentators who favor the term have acknowledged that totalitarianism was never fully successful in its quest for complete domination. (Critics of the concept of totalitarianism are considered in the final section of this entry.) This was the key intuition of David Riesman in his correspondence with Hannah Arendt (he read in manuscript the last part of *The Origins of Totalitarianism* [1951]). It was also a theme of the Harvard Project on the Soviet Social System and its literary offspring—notably, Alex Inkeles and Raymond Bauer's *The Soviet Citizen: Daily Life in a Totalitarian Society* (1961). To that extent, as Daniel Bell remarked, totalitarianism was always a concept in search of reality. Unlike political philosophers, moreover, social scientists tend to see totalitarianism as an ideal-type, a one-sided model constructed for research purposes, which also suggests that totalitarianism in the flesh can be of greater or lesser virulence. Studies of inmate camp "culture" lend further credence to the oxymoronic concession that totalitarianism had its limits. Tsvetan Todorov and Anne Applebaum show that even under conditions expressly designed to expunge all traces of solidarity, acts of "ordinary virtue" persisted. Hence there were always people who maintained their dignity (by keeping as clean as they could), who cared for others (sharing food, tending the sick), and who exercised the life of the mind (by reciting poetry, playing music, or committing to memory camp life so as to allow the possibility of its being fully documented later). Michel Mazor's luminous, yet astonishingly objective, autobiographical account of the Warsaw Ghetto (*The Vanished City,* 1955) expresses a similar message of hope. Survivors of death camps and Gulags have typically conveyed a different message, however. Crushed by a merciless regime determined to exterminate not only an individual's life, but the concept of humanity itself, inmates endured a vertiginous "gray zone" of collaboration and compromise.

Any list of totalitarian features, such as the one itemized above, raises an obvious question: What gives the typology its coherence? Or, to put the matter differently, is there some property that furnishes the whole with its master logic or integral animation? Two frequently rehearsed, and related, answers are discernible. The first takes up the pronounced totalitarian attachment to the will, dynamism, and movement. As early as 1925, Amendola was struck by the "wild radicalism" and "possessed will" of the Italian Fascists. Mussolini himself spoke proudly of "la nostra feroce volonta totalitaria" ("our fierce totalitarian will"). And the virtue of "fanaticism," "will," and "the movement" for the nation's well-being was tirelessly rehearsed by Hitler and Goebbels, as it was later by Mao. *Yundong* (movement, campaign) was among the most salient ideas of the Chairman, who specifically emphasized the importance of chaos. Sinologist Michael Schoenhals observes that in its original Maoist sense (since disavowed by Deng Xiaoping and his successors, who prefer to speak of an incremental *fazhan* or "development"), *yundong* entails the deliberate "shattering of all regular standards," the suspension of all stabilizing rules, norms, and standards that may apply in ordinary times. The goals of this regularized suspension—there were sixteen major national "movements" between 1950 and 1976—were to orchestrate hatred against the Party's latest enemy (often previously hallowed figures within the Party), to arouse superhuman efforts in support of economic targets, and incessantly to combat "revisionism" and the emergence of new elites. The Soviet Union during the heyday of Stalinism exhibited similar characteristics, as Boris Pasternak's Dr. Zhivago explains:

The point is, Larissa Fyodorovna, that there are limits to everything. In all this time something definite should have been achieved. But it turns out that those who inspired the revolution aren't at home in anything except change and turmoil: that's their native element; they aren't happy with anything that's less than on a world scale. For them, transitional periods, worlds in the making, are an end in themselves.

The centrality of flux and activism to the idea of totalitarianism is integral to classical academic accounts of the phenomenon. It prompted Franz Neumann, in *Behemoth: The Structure and Practice of National Socialism* (1942), to call the Third Reich a "movement state," and Ernst Fraenkel to describe it as a "dual state" in which the "normal" functions of the legal and administrative apparatus were constantly undermined by Party "prerogative"—Fraenkel's term for the maelstrom of feverish Nazi initiatives that unleashed bedlam without respite. Similarly, Sigmund Neumann entitled his comparative study of the Nazi, Fascist, and Bolshevist hurricanes *Permanent Revolution: The Total State in a World at War* (1942).

Still, the most influential account along these lines was that proffered by Hannah Arendt. Totalitarianism, she argued, was a mode of domination characterized far less by centralized coordination than by unceasing turbulence. To confuse totalitarianism with dictatorship or to see it as a type of dictatorship (or even state) was to miss a fundamental distinction. Once consolidated, dictatorships—for instance, military juntas—typically

become routinized and predictable, domesticating and detaching themselves from the movements that were their original social basis. Totalitarian regimes, in contrast, rise to power on movements that, once installed in office, employ motion as their constitutive "principle" of domination. The volcanic will of the leader whose next decision could nullify all previous ones; rule by decree rather than law; the continual manufacture of new enemies; police institutions, Gulags, and death camps whose only purposes are to transform citizens into foes and transform individuals into an identical species and then into corpses: All these features characterize a regime-type of eternal transgression. "Terror," remarks Arendt, is itself "the realization of the law of movement; its chief aim is to make it possible for the force of nature or of history to race freely through mankind, unhindered by any spontaneous human action" (p. 465). Indeed, it is the grotesque destructiveness and futility of totalitarian systems, their attack on every norm that might anchor human life in something stable, that makes them so resistant to methodical analysis.

A second thread that runs through discussions about totalitarianism is the pagan ardor that Fascism, National Socialism, and Bolshevism were capable of generating. Once more, Amendola was a pioneer in this line of interpretation, calling Fascism a "war of religion" that demands total devotion. More sympathetically, the philosopher Giovanni Gentile, ghostwriter of Mussolini's "The Doctrine of Fascism" (1932), stressed the new movement's penetrative spirit. Of special significance was the myth of rebirth: the creation of a new nation or a world without classes, and the formation of a selfless New Man or Woman, untainted by decrepit habits. Fascism, Mussolini avowed, was the author of the Third Italian Civilization (the previous two being the Roman Empire and the Renaissance). Nazi ideology was also replete with notions of national redemption, the spirit of a rejuvenated people, and even the divine mission of the SS. World War I, and the community of front-line soldiers (*Frontsgemeinschaft*) or "trenchocracy" it witnessed, was typically identified as the crucible of this steely resurrection. Coup d'état strategizing, the battles to defeat the Whites during the civil war, and the perennial trumpeting of the class struggle, promoted a similar mentality among the Bolshevik leaders.

Commentators who stress the mythological component of totalitarianism—writing of "ersatz religions," "political religions," the "myth of the state," the "sacralization of politics," and "palingenesis"—include Raymond Aron, Albert Camus, Ernst Cassirer, Norman Cohn, Waldemar Gurian, Jacob Talmon, and Eric Voegelin. Worthy successors are Michael Burleigh, Roger Griffin, and Emilio Gentile. Gentile, while desisting from the view that political religion is the most important element of totalitarianism, nonetheless affirms that it is "the most dangerous and deadly weapon" in its ideological arsenal (p. 49). Civic religions, such as those found in the United States and France, are different from political religions because they celebrate a republican concept of freedom and law. Church and state are separated, but each has its legitimate sphere of activity. In contrast, the sacralization of politics under totalitarian rule, together with its liturgies, festivals, and cults, is marked by the deification of the leader; idolatrous worship of the state, which arrogates to itself the exclusive right to determine Good and Evil; marginalization or destruction of traditional religion; orgiastic mass rallies; immortalization of the party fallen; the appeal to sacrifice; and the cult of death. Interpretations of totalitarianism that emphasize political religion have one notable implication. They suggest that totalitarianism is best understood not as a singular event, or a unique set of institutions, but as a recurrent possibility of the modern world shorn of its customary restraints.

## Criticisms and Responses

At the risk of simplification, criticisms of the concept of totalitarianism may be divided into two main, though overlapping, types: moral-political and scientific. The first type of criticism takes different forms but often hinges on the argument that *totalitarianism* was employed during the Cold War as an ideological weapon of a particularly Manichaean, self-serving, and self-righteous kind. Starkly dividing the world into liberal democratic white-hats and communist black-hats, Abbott Gleason remarks, conveniently omitted the extent to which Western governments supported military and other regimes with bleak and bloody human-rights records. Describing military juntas as authoritarian rather than totalitarian made no difference to the people they murdered. A twist on this criticism, found among American disciples of the Frankfurt School, is that liberal democracy itself is not in principle the antithesis of totalitarianism, because both are disastrous permutations of "Enlightenment modernity." A rather different objection is that totalitarianism is an opportune way for former collaborators of Nazism, Bolshevism, and so forth, to dodge responsibility for their actions. Its exculpatory value turns on the claim that "resistance was impossible" or that "we were all brainwashed." Yet the charge of double standards is also made by those, such as Martin Malia, who vehemently defend the pertinence of *totalitarianism* as a label. Disavowing that term all too often means denying the evil symmetry of Nazism and Bolshevism. By recapitulating earlier leftist dogmas—that genuine antifascism required support for the Soviet Union, that comparisons with Nazi Germany are unacceptable because they play into the hands of U.S. imperialism—such denials can become an expedient means of rescuing Marxism from its real, sanguinary history. In a similar way, loose talk of the "dialectic of Enlightenment" is less a challenge to common sense than it is a meretricious affront to its very existence. In any case, the term *totalitarianism* preceded the Cold War by more than two decades.

Scientific objections to totalitarianism as an idea typically focus on a diverse set of issues. Critics argue that the notion is mistaken because:

- Totalitarianism is a fictive Orwellian dystopia instead of an empirical reality. The Soviet system, for instance, "did not exercise effective 'thought control,' let alone ensure 'thought conversion,' but in fact depoliticized the citizenry to an astonishing degree" (Hobsbawm, p. 394). Official Marxism was unspeakably dull and irrelevant to the lives of most people.

- *Totalitarianism* is a misnomer because in neither the Soviet Union nor Nazi Germany was terror total.

Instead it was always focused on particular groups. In the Soviet Union, terror formed a radius in which danger was greatest the nearer one was to power and purge. In Germany, once active domestic opposition to the Nazis was defeated, and Jews were deported to the camps, most citizens existed at peace with a regime they deemed legitimate. The majority would never have considered themselves as terrorized by it. Distinguishing between seasoned adversaries and pesky grumblers, the undermanned Gestapo rarely intruded into normal life. Denunciation by citizens of one another was a more effective means of garnering information than the prying eye of the security state.

- The theory of totalitarianism fails to specify a mechanism to explain the internal transition of the Soviet Union and China to nontotalitarian phases. Indeed, the very evolution of such regimes toward humdrum routinization flies in the face of the idea that totalitarianism is above all a movement that cannot be pacified, and is the antithesis of all forms of political normality.

- Totalitarian regimes are too heterogeneous for them to be classified under a single rubric. Under Mao, for instance, the People's Liberation Army was a more powerful organ of control than the security forces, while Mao's prestige was periodically checked, and occasionally deflated, by other CCP leaders. The contrasts between Hitler and Joseph Stalin are, Ian Kershaw suggests, even more telling. While Stalin was a committee man who ascended to rule within a recently established system, Hitler was a rank outsider, strongly averse to bureaucratic work of all kinds. Similarly, while Stalin was an interventionist micromanager, Hitler had little to do with the actual functioning of government. People did not so much directly follow his detailed orders, of which there were few, as second guess what he wanted them to achieve, thereby "working toward the Führer." Then again, Hitler was a spectacular and mesmerizing orator; Stalin's words were leaden by comparison. Mass party purges characterize one system, but not the other (the liquidation of the Röhm faction in 1934 was a singular event). And finally the systems over which the men prevailed had a different impetus. Stalin's goal of rapid modernization was, some say, a humanly understandable, if cruelly executed, objective; that the end justifies the means is a standard belief of all tyrants. Conversely, the mass slaughter of the Jews and others was, for Hitler, an end in itself, unquestionably irrational if not insane.

All these objections are themselves the targets of rebuttal. Modernization at the expense of the nation it is intended to benefit seems hardly rational. Its victims rarely thought so. And did not Hitler, too, think in terms of instrumental means and ends? The goal was a purified Aryan civilization, regenerate, martial, manly, and beautiful. To achieve it, putative nonhumans had to vanish from the face of the earth. Moreover, the transitions that Soviet and Chinese Communism witnessed by no means nullify the totalitarian model. They only appear to do so, Victor Zaslavsky argues, because of failure to distinguish between "system building" and "system maintenance" phases; the latter represents a more stable development, but one still mired in the militarization of society and mass surveillance. Where previous thinkers have erred is in identifying the "system building" stage with totalitarianism *tout court*. Finally, critics of the totalitarian model often object to it on spurious grounds. For to argue that totalitarianism was never systematic in its rule, never fully synchronized, but rather "chaotic," "wasteful," and "anarchic" is hardly a criticism of those such as Arendt who made such attributes pivotal to their theory. In good measure, her emphasis on movement is vindicated even by those who employ a different terminology. Examples include "regimes of continuous revolution" (enunciated by Michael Mann) and "cumulative radicalization" (preferred by Hans Mommsen).

## Conclusion

As a vehicle for condemnation as well as analysis, *totalitarianism* is likely to remain a vibrant idea long into the twenty-first century. Its extension to radical Islam is already evident. And as a potent reminder of the terrible deeds of which humans are capable, the concept has few conceptual rivals. Principled disagreements as well as polemics about its value continue to mark its career. Present dangers, and anxious debates about how they should best be characterized, suggest that the age of totalitarianism is not yet over.

*See also* **Authoritarianism; Communism; Fascism; Nationalism.**

**BIBLIOGRAPHY**

Applebaum, Anne. *Gulag: A History.* New York: Doubleday, 2003.

Arendt, Hannah. *The Origins of Totalitarianism.* 1951. Reprint, New York: Harcourt Brace, 1968. Rich, acute, idiosyncratic, puzzling, seminal.

Baehr, Peter, and Melvin Richter, eds. *Dictatorship in History and Theory: Bonapartism, Caesarism, and Totalitarianism.* Cambridge, U.K.: Cambridge University Press, 2004.

Berman, Paul. *Terror and Liberalism.* New York: Norton, 2003. On "Muslim totalitarianism."

Burleigh, Michael. *The Third Reich: A New History.* New York: Hill and Wang, 2001.

Canovan, Margaret. *Hannah Arendt: A Reinterpretation of Her Political Thought.* Cambridge, U.K.: Cambridge University Press, 1992. Unsurpassed analysis of Arendt's multilayered theory of totalitarianism.

Chandler, David. *Voices from S-21: Terror and History in Pol Pot's Secret Prison.* Berkeley: University of California Press, 1999.

Courtois, Stéphane, et al. *The Black Book of Communism: Crimes, Terror, Repression.* 1997. Reprint, Cambridge, Mass.: Harvard University Press, 1999. Foreword by Martin Malia. Contains chapters devoted to the Soviet Union, China, Cambodia, North Korea, Vietnam, Afghanistan, Central and Southeastern Europe, Latin America, and Africa.

Friedrich, Carl J., ed. *Totalitarianism: Proceedings of a Conference Held at the American Academy of Arts and Sciences, March 1953.*

Cambridge, Mass.: Harvard University Press, 1954. Contributors include Karl W. Deutsch, Erik H. Erikson, Waldemar Gurian, Alex Inkeles, George F. Kennan, Harold D. Lasswell, and Bertram D. Wolfe.

Friedrich, Carl J., and Zbigniew K. Brzezinski. *Totalitarian Dictatorship and Autocracy.* 2nd rev. ed. Cambridge, Mass.: Harvard University Press, 1965. Lucid and influential.

Furet, François, and Ernst Nolte. *Fascism and Communism.* Translated by Katherine Golsan. 1998. Reprint, Lincoln: University of Nebraska Press, 2001. A model of civilized debate by two of the twentieth century's foremost historians.

Gentile, Emilio. "The Sacralization of Politics: Definitions, Interpretations, and Reflections on the Question of Secular Religion and Totalitarianism." Translated by Robert Mallett. *Totalitarian Movements and Political Religions* 1, no. 1 (2000): 18–55.

Gleason, Abbott. *Totalitarianism: The Inner History of the Cold War.* New York: Oxford University Press, 1995. Excellent overall account which, despite its title, actually starts in the 1920s. My references to Giovanni Amendola come from this source.

Griffin, Roger, ed. *Fascism.* Oxford: Oxford University Press, 1995. Ably edited collection that stresses Fascism's ideological core in "palingenesis"—the myth of rebirth.

Hobsbawm, Eric. *Age of Extremes.* New York: Pantheon, 1994.

Kershaw, Ian, and Moshe Lewin, eds. *Stalinism and Nazism: Dictatorships in Comparison.* Cambridge, U.K.: Cambridge University Press, 1997. Includes essays by Michael Mann and Hans Mommsen.

Kirkpatrick, Jeane. *Dictatorships and Double Standards: Rationalism and Reason in Politics.* New York: Simon and Schuster, 1982.

Lifka, Thomas E. *The Concept "Totalitarianism" and American Foreign Policy, 1933–1949.* New York: Garland, 1988.

Lifton, Robert Jay. *Thought Reform and the Psychology of Totalism.* New York: Norton, 1961. Rich empirical study of Chinese Communist "brainwashing."

Linz, Juan J. *Totalitarian and Authoritarian Regimes.* Boulder, Colo.: Rienner, 2000. A rigorous analysis that distinguishes among a variety of authoritarian regimes.

Menze, Ernest A., ed. *Totalitarianism Reconsidered.* Port Washington, N.Y.: Kennikat, 1981. Contains two essays by Karl Dietrich Bracher.

Nathan, Andrew. *China's Transition.* New York: Columbia University Press, 1997.

Schapiro, Leonard. *Totalitarianism.* New York: Praeger, 1972.

Schoenhals, Michael, ed. *China's Cultural Revolution, 1966–1969: Not a Dinner Party.* Armonk, N.Y.: Sharpe, 1996.

Talmon, Jacob L. *The Origins of Totalitarian Democracy.* 1952. Reprint, Boulder, Colo.: Westview, 1985. A classic within the genre concerned with "political religion."

Todorov, Tsvetan. *Facing the Extreme: Moral Life in the Concentration Camps.* Translated by Arthur Denner and Abigail Pollak. New York: Owl, 1997.

Zaslavsky, Victor. "The Katyn Massacre: 'Class Cleansing' as Totalitarian Praxis." Translated by Joseph Cardinale. *Telos* 114 (1999): 67–107. Robust critique of the Frankfurt School's "dialectic of Enlightenment" approach; argues for two phases of totalitarian development.

*Peter Baehr*

**TOTEMS.**   The word *totem* is an anglicized rendering of the Ojibwa word *ninto:tem*. It refers to an animal or plant species emblematic of a specific group, notably a clan. While the term was originally applied only to practices of natives of northeastern North America, it was soon extended to refer to superficially similar phenomena around the globe, whose observances came to be known as "totemism."

## Evolutionary Theories

The concept of *totemism* as a form of religion was first formulated by John McLennan, one of the most prominent Victorian anthropologists, in an article entitled "The Worship of Animals and Plants" (1869–1870). McLennan based his concept on similarities between the beliefs and practices of native Australians on one hand, and native North Americans, especially from the northeastern United States, on the other. McLennan summarized his conclusions:

> There are tribes of men (called primitive) now existing on the earth in the totem stage, each named after some animal or plant, which is its symbol or ensign, and which by the tribesmen is religiously regarded; having kinship through mothers only, and exogamy as their marriage law. In several cases, we have seen, the tribesmen believe themselves to be descended from the totem, and in every case to be, nominally at least, of its breed or species. We have seen a relation existing between the tribesmen and their totem . . . that might well grow into that of worshipper and god, leading to the establishment of religious ceremonials to allay the totem's just anger, or secure his continued protection. (p. 518)

McLennan had earlier theorized that the earliest stages of human kinship and marriage, once humanity had evolved out of primeval hordes, were characterized by matrilineal descent and by exogamy—a term he coined and that was arguably his most lasting contribution to anthropology—the rule that states that one must marry outside one's own kin group. Totemism, he suggested, was the earliest stage of religion, the logical companion to matrilineal descent and exogamy. The rest of his essay attempted to demonstrate that the Greek and Roman deities were anthropomorphized versions of earlier totemic animal and plant spirits.

The thesis that the worship of animals and plants was the earliest form of religion was not original to McLennan. It had been formulated over one hundred years earlier in 1760 by the French Enlightenment thinker Charles de Brosses, in a book entitled *Du culte des dieux fétiches* (Of the cult of the fetish gods), in which he attempted to establish parallels between ancient Egyptian religion and the contemporary religious practices of sub-Saharan Africans. However, McLennan considered fetishism to be a more general concept than totemism, which he argued was its most primitive form.

***From Robertson Smith to Spencer and Gillen.***   In 1889 William Robertson Smith constructed a more elaborate scenario for the origin of religion around the idea of totemism. In *The Religion of the Semites,* he theorized that the original

form of Semitic religion (and by implication all religions) revolved around the notion of kinship between a human community, its totem species, and its god. Under normal circumstances, precisely because of such conceptions of kinship, men were forbidden to eat their totems. However, on specific ritual occasions, the totem animals were sacrificed and shared among members of the community and with their god, in an act where commensality—eating together—was literally a form of communion.

Robertson Smith's theories were a direct inspiration to those of Émile Durkheim and Sigmund Freud, but they were based on no concrete evidence and were entirely speculative. However, ten years later, the detailed ethnographic research of Baldwin Spencer and F. J. Gillen in *The Native Tribes of Central Australia* appeared to lend credence to his hypothesis. Spencer and Gillen described important ceremonies called Intichiuma, which members of the clan performed in order to ensure the natural increase of particular species of animal or plant. At the end of the ceremony, initiates (women and children were rigorously excluded) consumed small portions of the sacred species. Spencer and Gillen's work also included elaborate descriptions of initiation ceremonies and of the *churinga*—the sacred paraphernalia of totemic groups. They also contradicted McLennan's hypothesis that totems were associated with matrilineal descent. In fact, a child did not derive his totem directly from either his mother or father, but from the spot where his mother believed him to have been conceived.

***Frazer.***   Sir James Frazer's *Totemism and Exogamy* (1910) was a massive, four-volume compendium of instances of totemism throughout the world. Frazer rejected MacLennan's contention that totemism was the earliest form of religion: "If religion implies, as it seems to do, an acknowledgment of the part of the worshipper that the object of his worship is superior to himself, then pure totemism cannot properly be called a religion at all, since a man looks upon his totem as his equal and friend, not at all as his superior, still less as his god" (vol. 4, p. 5). Rather, he considered totemic practices to be a form of magic, historically prior to the emergence of religion per se. The title of his book notwithstanding, Frazer also disagreed with MacLennan's contention that totemism was necessarily associated with exogamy. Although Frazer conceded that this was frequently the case, he correctly noted that later ethnographers had amassed ample cases of cultures where totemism existed without exogamy, or vice versa, and he provided different speculative explanations for the origins of both phenomena.

## Durkheim and Freud

Émile Durkheim, in *The Elementary Forms of Religious Life* (1912), emphatically rejected Frazer's claim that totemism did not constitute a religion. On the contrary, he used totemism as a case of "the simplest and most primitive religion that observation can make known to us" (1995 ed., p. 21), basing his assertion on Australian ethnography (especially Spencer and Gillen) but resorting to examples from North America and elsewhere at critical junctures of his argument. Durkheim used his analysis of totemism to demonstrate the social origins of knowledge and the underlying unity of religious, philosophical, and

**Native American totem pole.** Totem poles served as memorials to deceased ancestors and representations of the lineage of the carver. © THE FIELD MUSEUM, #A108441

scientific thought. Australian social organization was quite complicated, with tribes divided and subdivided into exogamous moieties ("halves"), classes, and clans, each associated with different species, in a system that incorporated all natural phenomena. "[These] facts illuminate the manner in which the idea of genus or class took form among humans. . . . It was the phratries [i.e., moieties] that served as genera and the clans as species. It is because men formed groups that they were able to group things" (p. 145).

Totemism was not just a way of thinking but also of acting and feeling, organized around the separation of the domains of "sacred" and "profane" that, for Durkheim, constituted the essence of religion itself. More sacred than the totem animals themselves were the *churinga*, bull roarers of wood or stone with schematic representations of the totemic ancestors painted upon them. Uninitiated women and children were forbidden to see them on pain of death, and loss or destruction of one of them was considered catastrophic. But totemism was no more the literal worship of *churinga* than of animals and plants; rather, these were merely the symbolic representations of a force, which Durkheim called *mana*, that was simultaneously external and internal to the worshiper. For Durkheim, the totem was the flag of the clan, a concrete object on which the individual's allegiance was projected: ultimately, it was nothing other than society's representation of itself to its members. In this sense, religion in general and totemism in particular did not "rest upon error and falsehood" but was indeed "grounded in and express[ed] the real" (p. 2). Unlike his predecessors, Durkheim stressed the fundamental comparability of "primitive" and "modern" religious thought rather than their essential dissimilarity.

**Totem and Taboo.** A year later, Sigmund Freud was to suggest in *Totem and Taboo* (1913) that totemism was the expression of a psychological, rather than social, reality. His theory was predicated on the link between totemism and exogamy, which Freud took to be a manifestation of the horror of incest. He was also profoundly inspired by Robertson Smith's hypothesis of the ritual sacrifice and consumption of the totem animal. However, he incorporated these ideas into an original scenario of his own. Humanity, he suggested, once lived in primal hordes where the father monopolized all the women and exerted tyrannical authority over his children. His sons eventually conspired to kill him, eat him, and take his place. However, the guilt that they experienced not only prevented them from mating with their mother and sisters but ultimately caused them to institute a prohibition on incest.

> Psychoanalysis has revealed to us that the totem animal is really a substitute for the father, and this really explains the contradiction that it is usually forbidden to kill the totem animal, that the killing of it results in a holiday and that the animal is killed and yet mourned. The ambivalent emotional attitude which to-day still marks the father complex in our children and so often continues into adult life also extended to the father substitute of the totem animal. (p. 182)

For Freud, parallels between the behavior of "primitives" and "neurotics" led him to seek explanations of both phenomena in terms of his understanding of universal unconscious emotional processes.

## Critique and Elaboration

By the time Durkheim and Freud were writing, the very concept of totemism had already come under attack in a long article by American anthropologist A. A. Goldenweiser, "Totemism: An Analytical Study" (1910). Goldenweiser began by listing the main features believed to be symptomatic of totemism:

1. An exogamous clan.

2. A clan name derived from the totem.

3. A religious attitude towards the totem; as a "friend," "brother," "protector," etc.

4. Taboos, or restrictions against the killing, eating (sometimes touching and seeing), of the totem.

5. A belief in descent from the totem (pp. 182–183).

In a comparison of cases from around the world, he arrived at the devastating conclusion that "Each of these traits . . . displays more or less striking independence in its distribution; and most of them can be shown to be widely-spread ethnic phenomena, diverse in origin, not necessarily coordinated in development, and displaying a rich variability of psychological make-up" (p. 266). Goldenweiser was not quite prepared to give up the concept altogether and proposed a definition of the phenomenon in terms of the association between "definite social units" and "objects and symbols of emotional value" (p. 275). Arguably, such a definition was far too vague and general to be of any use. A few years later, in a highly influential synthesis of cultural anthropology, Robert Lowie was to summarize Goldenweiser's findings and draw an even more radical conclusion: "Why not abandon the vain effort to thrust into one Procrustean bed a system of naming, a system of heraldry, and a system of religious or magical observances?" (p. 143). In other words, he suggested that there was no such thing as totemism, that it was for all intents and purposes an invention of anthropologists.

### British functionalism and structural-functionalism.

British anthropologists were less ready to give up the concept of totemism than their American colleagues. Bronislaw Malinowski is often credited with an excessively utilitarian explanation of totemism: "The road from the wilderness to the savage's belly and consequently to his mind is very short, and for him the world is an indiscriminate background against which there stand out the useful, primarily the edible, species of animals or plants" (p. 44). Actually, Malinowski's position was slightly more complex, and he conceded that the "primitive" interest in nature, selective as it might be, was not limited to the edible, but included sentiments of admiration or fear. One way or the other, "the desire to control the species, dangerous, useful, or edible . . . must lead to a belief in special power over the species, affinity with it, a common essence between man and beast or plant" (p. 45).

A. R. Radcliffe-Brown, Malinowski's rival and contemporary, had a more sophisticated approach to the problem,

seeing it as part of "a much wider group of phenomena, namely the general relation between man and natural species in mythology and ritual. It may well be asked if 'totemism' as a technical term has not outlived its usefulness" (p. 117). More specifically, he suggested that totemism was a product of segmentary forms of social organization, the division of society into moieties, clans, or other similar institutions. He proposed a tentative analogy with sainthood in Roman Catholicism: saints are, at one level, universally recognized within the church, but also have particular relationships with specific congregations. In a similar manner, totem species do not simply stand for the clan, as Durkheim suggested, but also for the clan's place in a broader social scheme that includes all totemic species.

The students of Malinowski and Radcliffe-Brown tended to eschew general pronouncements on the nature of totemism. Instead, Raymond Firth, Meyer Fortes, and E. E. Evans-Pritchard, among others, wrote sophisticated ethnographic analyses of religion and social organization in specific societies, discussing totemism among the Tikopia, the Tallensi, or the Nuer in terms that could not readily be generalized. For example, Evans-Pritchard sought to understand totemism in terms of broader Nuer beliefs about *kwoth,* "God" or "Spirit." There were both higher and lower manifestations of "spirit," with totemic spirits definitely belonging to the realm of "spirits of the below." Nuer totems, he noted, were not symbols of lineages, since some lineages had none and other lineages shared the same totem but did not otherwise acknowledge kinship with one another. Nor did totems symbolize Spirit as such, but rather the relationship between God and a particular lineage. In short, such an analysis embedded totemism within the religious beliefs and practices of a particular society.

## The Structural Study of Totemism

Paradoxically, Claude Lévi-Strauss began his short book *Totemism* (1962) with the contention that totemism as such did not really exist, comparing it to the concept of hysteria that emerged in psychology at about the same period: "once we are persuaded to doubt that it is possible arbitrarily to isolate certain phenomena and to group them together as diagnostic signs of an illness, or of an objective institution, the symptoms themselves vanish or appear refractory to any unifying interpretation" (1963 ed., p. 1). Even more damning than Goldenweiser, he suggested that the very concept of "totemism" served as a mechanism for establishing a gulf between "primitive" and "civilized" humanity. Ostensibly, totemistic primitives were those who confused the boundaries between "nature" and "culture," if not worshiping animals and plants at least positing bonds of kinship between humans and nonhuman species.

In one sense, the book was an obituary, the history of an illusion. However, it ironically recouped the value of the very concept it pretended to dismiss, as can be seen in the book's most oft-cited phrase, a rejoinder to functionalist approaches: "natural species are chosen [as "totems"] not because they are 'good to eat' but because they are 'good to think'" (p. 89). Examples of so-called totemism were really instances of universal features of human thought, a theme to which Lévi-Strauss returned in *The Savage Mind* (1962), several chapters of which were also devoted to totems and totemism. Seen in this light, "totemism" was simply a variety of metaphorical thought—with the proviso that metaphor was an indispensable feature of human thought in general. What is more, the metaphor rested, not on the perception of intrinsic similarities, but rather on the recognition of systematic differences. In other words, if there were a Kangaroo clan and an Emu clan, this was not because members of the first clan considered themselves like kangaroos and the second clan like emus. Rather, the difference between species served as a metaphor for the difference between human groups, Nature as a metaphor for Culture.

***Animal symbolism and classificatory schemes.*** In a radical way, Lévi-Strauss changed the terms in which problems were phrased. (To the extent that his book sealed the death knell of the concept of "totemism," there ceased to be a single problem.) Whereas Lévi-Strauss's particular concerns were with uncovering the abstract properties of human thought lurking behind concrete instances of its application, British anthropologists were able to combine his approach with an enduring preoccupation with the dynamics of specific societies. In particular, they examined the social implications of the ways in which different cultures classified animals.

Undoubtedly the best-known example is Mary Douglas's analysis of the dietary prohibitions detailed in Leviticus Robertson Smith had suggested that the pig, along with the dog, the horse, the mouse, the dove, and some varieties of fish were offered as totemic sacrifices in early Semitic religion. Douglas suggested instead that the distinction between clean and unclean (and forbidden) animals was an artifact of a system of classification made very clear in the text, and that distinguished between the normal and the anomalous. Mammals that had cloven hooves and that chewed their cud were the typical food of pastoralists like the ancient Hebrews, a criterion that excluded the pig, just as the notion that creatures who live in the water should typically possess scales and fins excluded eels, sharks, or shrimp. But such concerns with alimentary purity accompanied a preoccupation with social purity, and especially with the maintenance of a clear boundary between Jews and Gentiles, expressed in terms of separation of the clean from the unclean.

Ralph Bulmer's analysis of the classification of the cassowary by the Karam of New Guinea took a similar approach. The cassowary, a relative of the ostrich and the emu, was not classed as a bird by the Karam. There were special rules for hunting cassowaries, who could not be shot with spear or arrow but had to be snared and bludgeoned. Live cassowaries had to be kept away from the village and fields, and usually they were cooked and eaten in the forest. Indeed, a person who killed a cassowary was ritually dangerous, and had to avoid the taro crops for a month. This attitude toward the cassowary simultaneously assimilated cassowaries to quasi-human status while highlighting the symbolic separation of the domains of the forest and the cultivated fields, a separation that in turn paralleled ambivalent relations between brother and sister. Sisters left the home village at marriage, but their children held residual rights in land; however, the brother's sons tended to view these rights ambivalently at best. This attitude was captured by the symbolism of the cassowary, which was equated with the father's sister's children.

Other work along similar lines included S. J. Tambiah's analysis of food prohibitions in Thailand and Edmund Leach's comparison of the sexual commutations of animal names in English and in highland Burma. Ultimately, such analyses represent the very antithesis of the aims of the early writing on totemism, which sought to demonstrate the illogical nature of "primitive" as opposed to modern European thought. Instead, modern anthropologists have insisted, not only on the logical nature of non-European thought, but on its deep affinities with our own modes of thinking and speaking.

*See also* **Myth; Religion; Symbolism; Untouchability: Taboos.**

BIBLIOGRAPHY
Bulmer, Ralph. "Why Is the Cassowary Not a Bird? A Problem of Zoological Taxonomy among the Karam of the New Guinea Highlands." *Man,* n.s., 2 (1967): 5–25.
Douglas, Mary. *Purity and Danger: An Analysis of Concepts of Pollution and Taboo.* London: Routledge and Kegan Paul, 1966.
Durkheim, Émile. *The Elementary Forms of Religious Life.* Translated by Karen E. Fields. New York: Free Press, 1995. Originally published in 1912.
Evans-Pritchard, E. E. *Nuer Religion.* Oxford: Clarendon, 1956.
Frazer, J. G. *Totemism and Exogamy: A Treatise on Certain Early Forms of Superstition and Society.* 4 vols. London: Macmillan, 1910.
Freud, Sigmund. *Totem and Taboo: Resemblances between the Psychic Lives of Savages and Neurotics.* Translated by A. A. Brill. New York: Vintage, 1946. Originally published in 1913.
Goldenweiser, A. A. "Totemism: An Analytical Study." *Journal of American Folk-lore* 23 (1910): 179–293.
Leach, Edmund R. "Anthropological Aspects of Language: Animal Categories and Verbal Abuse." In his *New Directions in the Study of Language,* edited by Eric H. Lenneberg. Cambridge, Mass.: MIT Press, 1964.
Lévi-Strauss, Claude. *The Savage Mind.* Chicago: University of Chicago Press. 1966.
———. *Totemism.* Translated by Rodney Needham. Boston: Beacon Press. 1963.
Lowie, Robert. *Primitive Society.* New York: Boni and Liveright, 1920.
Malinowski, Bronislaw. *Magic, Science and Religion and Other Essays.* Boston: Beacon Press, 1948.
McLennan, John. "The Worship of Animals and Plants." Reprinted in his *Studies in Ancient History. The Second Series: Comprising an Inquiry into the Origin of Exogamy.* London and New York: Macmillan, 1896. Originally published in 1869–1870.
Radcliffe-Brown, A. R. *Structure and Function in Primitive Society.* Glencoe, Ill.: Free Press, 1952.
Smith, W. Robertson. *The Religion of the Semites: The Fundamental Institutions.* Reprint, New York: Schocken Books, 1972. Originally published in 1889.
Spencer, Baldwin, and F. J. Gillen. *The Native Tribes of Central Australia.* Reprint, New York: Dover, 1968. Originally published in 1899.
Tambiah, S. J. "Animals Are Good to Think and Good to Prohibit." *Ethnology* 8 (1969): 424–459.

*Robert Launay*

# TRADE.

Trade is one of the basic processes that link individuals and groups. Trade binds people to one another through the expectations of reciprocal giving, through the formal calculus of wages and markets, and through the desires or needs to obtain items not locally available. In this way, trade is a fundamental element of human culture.

Trade and exchange are often used synonymously, but there is a basic difference. Trade refers to the movement of goods between individuals or groups where there is a general expectation of reciprocity and where the purpose is basically utilitarian. Exchange has a broader meaning, encompassing all movements of goods. The general expectation of reciprocity need not be a part of exchange, nor does exchange have to be utilitarian in nature. In contrast, both are central to trade.

## Approaches to the Study of Trade

Various perspectives can be applied to understanding trade. Here it is discussed as reciprocity, exploitation, and adaptation, and in the context of globalization.

*Trade as reciprocity.* The earliest anthropological approaches to trade focused on reciprocity and how the expectations of reciprocity shaped social relations. In the classic ethnography *Argonauts of the Western Pacific* (1922), for example, Bronislaw Malinowski described and interpreted a complex system of reciprocal trade in the Trobriand Islands known as the *kula*. The items traded in the *kula* were of two kinds: shell beads and armbands. The value of these items was determined by their age and renown—some were heirloom pieces and even had names. The goal of participants in the *kula* was to gain prestige by obtaining, and then giving away, large amounts of *kula* goods and particularly highly valued heirloom pieces. Participants could lose prestige if they gave away valued items but did not receive equivalents in return. Malinowski described individuals carefully planning *kula* expeditions to other islands and scheming ways to bring particular *kula* goods into their possession. In this way, *kula* was a system of reciprocal trade through which the Trobrianders created and maintained social status.

But what about less formal systems of reciprocal trade, like the giving of Christmas presents? If we give a Christmas present to our neighbors, we generally expect one in return. And, if we give a nice present, we expect a similarly nice one in return. There is no formal system like the *kula* in place, so how is reciprocity maintained? These more sophisticated questions about trade were asked by anthropologists after Malinowski, and many significant contributions were made. Among the most influential was the work of Marcel Mauss, whose essay *The Gift* (1954) posited a universal reciprocal structure for gift giving. Mauss argued that gifts symbolize the giver, and the act of giving symbolizes the relationship between the giver and the receiver. The act of giving a gift necessitates a reciprocal gift if a social relationship is to be maintained. If a reciprocal gift is not given, it signals the end of the relationship. Gift giving, then, often takes on a cyclical form (as is the case with Christmas presents) and is a fundamental way that humans maintain social relationships.

Anthropological work on trade as reciprocity was pulled together in a concise form by Marshall Sahlins. In *Stone Age Economics* (1972), Sahlins defined three forms of reciprocal trade: balanced reciprocity, generalized reciprocity, and negative reciprocity. Balanced reciprocity describes the forms of trade examined by Malinowski and Mauss, where there is an expected balance between what is given and what is received through trade. Generalized reciprocity is a less structured form of trade and takes place mainly within families and kin groups. For example, families often share an evening meal. Parents provide and prepare the food, and both parents and children share it. Children are expected to reciprocate by clearing the dishes, taking out the garbage, and loving and obeying their parents. Through these actions children maintain a general balance in the trade between family members, but no formal accounting is kept and no expectation of formal balance is ever made. This is the basic nature of generalized reciprocity. Negative reciprocity essentially refers to forms of cheating or stealing. Negative reciprocity occurs when one party in a trade relationship receives less than they give. Sahlins posited that negative reciprocity is most common when dealing with people from other societies for, as both Malinowski and Mauss imply, negative reciprocity within one's own society would seriously disrupt social relationships.

*Trade as exploitation.* Sahlins's definition of negative reciprocity illustrates the idea that not all trade takes place on an even footing. Some forms of trade are unequal, even exploitive. In the 1970s and 1980s a number of anthropologists began examining trade as an element of larger systems of production and consumption, often employing Marxist modes of production models. Eric Wolf's *Europe and the People without History* (1982) is illustrative of this type of research. Wolf explored three "modes of production": kin-based, which is characterized by generalized and balanced reciprocity; tributary, where tribute or taxes are provided to a centralized political authority that manages and maintains the society; and capitalist. For Wolf (and many others), the capitalist mode of production is rooted in exploitation. Workers sell their labor for wages but they must, by the very nature of capitalism, be paid less than their labor is actually worth—if not, then no profit would be possible. Wolf explains that capitalists in Europe were able to find a way around this problem by obtaining raw materials (and even labor in the form of slaves) for next to nothing by taking them from colonial areas. In the process, they actively exploited and essentially dehumanized the people living in those regions by creating a formal structure of negative reciprocity—one in which social relations cannot be maintained.

*Trade as adaptation.* The idea that trade is generally utilitarian in nature was seemingly ignored by anthropologists until the 1960s. At this time, theories of human behavior based on ecology began to be employed by anthropologists, and trade came to be seen as fundamental to the creation and maintenance of an ecosystem. Trade provided a mechanism through which matter, energy, and information moved through human-dominated ecosystems. For example, Stuart Piddocke (1965) argued that a reciprocal trade system known as the potlatch (and similar in nature to the *kula*) was essential to the survival of the Kwakiutl peoples of British Columbia. Piddocke demonstrated that the environment in which the Kwakiutl lived was subject to fluctuations that, in the same year, would

---

### THE FORMALIST/SUBSTANTIVIST DEBATE

In the 1950s a group of social scientists, the most prominent among them being Karl Polanyi, proposed that trade was a social construction like the rest of culture and could not be usefully examined outside of its unique social setting. This perspective came to be known as "substantivism." The substantivists argued that economic analyses of noncapitalist trade employing concepts like supply and demand, rational choice, profit, and other ideas linked to capitalist market economics was misguided, because these concepts were either meaningless or had different meanings in noncapitalist social settings. Other scholars, and archaeologists in particular, countered that markets and market-like economies were present for millennia before capitalism, and that many noncapitalist economies appear to be usefully analyzed with concepts and methods drawn from the study of capitalism. This perspective came to be known as "formalism." The "formalist/substantivist" debate consumed economic anthropology throughout much of the 1960s, with no clear winner emerging. In the early twenty-first century, most anthropologists see the benefits of both perspectives in understanding trade.

---

cause some populations to lack resources while others had excess resources. The potlatch, Piddocke argued, was a formal system in which populations redistributed resources from areas with excess to areas of scarcity. For the Kwakiutl, then, trade was part of their adaptation to a highly variable and unstable environment.

***Trade, globalization, and meaning.*** With increasingly global markets and the introduction of Western capitalism into all corners of the world, anthropologists have become increasingly concerned with the effects of trade on the cultures they study. As Wolf pointed out, initial trade relations in many of these areas were highly exploitive, and they essentially prevented the formation of social relationships between indigenous populations and Western capitalists. In most ways, the situation did not change much in the twentieth century, and many anthropologists are working at the turn of the twenty-first with indigenous populations to help them gain equity in trade relationships.

As Western products enter non-Western cultures, anthropologists have also become increasingly interested in the meanings people attach to things. How are new products integrated into society? What is the effect of the loss of indigenous products? Arjun Appadurai (1986) suggested that objects themselves are socially created, that their circulation through a society gives them meaning and purpose, and that they are recontexualized as they move through different social contexts. In this sense, the distinction between foreign and local goods becomes blurred, as "foreignness" and "localness" are attributes that are socially assigned and that can change as the context of their use changes, just as attributes such as "desirability," "utility," and "value" change in different contexts.

Trade not only brings Western products into non-Western cultures, but also many aspects of Western culture. Many anthropologists think that the adoption of capitalist modes of trade also promotes Western ideas such as profit, modernization, and individualism, pushing aside indigenous ideas of tradition and responsibility for the care of social relations. This process of Western ideas pushing out non-Western ones is called "Westernization," and is seen by many anthropologists as a major problem facing the non-Western cultures of the world. In a larger sense, Westernization is part of "globalization," the process through which international trade is increasingly binding the nations of the world together into a single, global economy. Again, many anthropologists view globalization as a major force acting to eliminate non-Western ideas and cultures from the global economy.

While Westernization and globalization may be forcing contemporary non-Western cultures to become more Western and global in their orientation, capitalist trade has had a much more profound effect on many historic non-Western cultures. In North America, for example, colonization by Europeans and the introduction of the fur trade in the 1600s led to competition between local groups, an increase in warfare, and dramatic population movements that transformed the social landscape of the Great Lakes and Plains regions. Trade brought with it not only Western goods (including guns, one of the items that fostered increased warfare), but also Western biota. European diseases such as smallpox and measles may have killed 80 percent of the indigenous peoples of North America. European plants and animals have dramatically changed ecosystems throughout the Americas. The point here is that trade brings with it many things in addition to the items

## WORLD SYSTEMS THEORY

Immanuel Wallerstein developed world systems theory in the early 1970s as a new way of looking at the rapid expansion of capitalism. Wallerstein posited that in capitalism a clear geographical hierarchy of trade evolved. Europe was the core, the area where raw materials were converted into finished products. The rest of the world was the periphery, the area where raw materials were obtained and finished products consumed. Capitalism expanded rapidly because it needed raw materials to create goods and markets to consume them. Nineteenth-century colonialism was the political actualization of these capitalist needs. However, finished products always cost more than the value of the raw materials needed to make them, so the periphery, in providing raw materials and consuming finished products, was actively exploited by the core, a process world systems theorists came to refer to as "underdevelopment." World systems theory provided social scientists a means to understand why and how the "developing" world was never able to actually "develop" despite many attempts to aid them in doing so—because they were being actively "underdeveloped" by the capitalist core. World systems theory continues to be one of the primary means that anthropologists and other social scientists use to examine and understand trade relations and their effects.

being traded—ideas, diseases, plants and animals—and all these have an effect on the peoples involved in trade.

## Trade and the Development of Civilization

With trade being such an important concept for anthropologists and other social scientists attempting to understand the historic and contemporary cultures of the world, it is not surprising that trade has been an important concept to scholars attempting to understand the evolution of cultures and, in particular, the development of civilization.

*Trade as redistribution.* Elman Service (1962) saw trade as a basic element in the evolution of chiefdoms out of tribal societies. Chiefs, Service argued, functioned as the operators of centralized redistribution networks, which took in surplus goods from all populations in a society and redistributed them back to those populations, but spread them evenly so that no single population lacked goods they needed, and no single population could acquire an ongoing surplus. This system of redistribution only evolved among sedentary agriculturalists, because it was among these societies that redistribution was needed. Redistribution allowed regional fluctuations in agricultural production (due to variation in rainfall, for example) to be evened out. More importantly, however, Service argued that redistribution both required and fostered the centralization of political authority, and thus was essential to the evolution of chiefs. It was only with the creation of a formal position of redistributor—a chief—that the smooth functioning of a system of redistribution could be ensured. And once the position had evolved, chiefs quickly learned to use their authority to provide or withhold goods to increase their authority in other areas of social life.

*Trade as legitimation.* But there are problems with Service's ideas. Not all chiefs function as redistributors, and not all societies with chiefs have resource bases that vary significantly. It is clear, however, that trade seems to be important in the evolution of many chiefdoms, and Mary Helms (1979) suggested that one reason might be that trade can serve as a mechanism for legitimating power. Helms studied the late prehistoric and early historic chiefdoms of Panama, where chiefs actively participated in and controlled trade in exotic goods such as gold ornaments, but had little to do with trade in basic, utilitarian goods of daily life. Helms argued that Panamanian chiefs used trade as a symbol of their ties to distant people and places and, through those ties, to exotic and even supernatural knowledge. Trade was not used as a means of controlling resources, but rather, of controlling knowledge and, through that control, of legitimating the chief's authority. The chief was the legitimate leader because, through trade, he had formed social relationships with neighboring and distant chiefs. He also gained knowledge of distant people and things through these relationships, and, in some cases, even knowledge of supernatural powers unknown to the society he governed but well understood by distant people with whom he was in contact through trade.

*Trade as finance.* One of the key aspects of the evolution of civilization is the creation of surpluses to finance the support of individuals who are removed from production to become political leaders, priests, artisans, soldiers, and the like. Elizabeth Brumfiel and Timothy Earle (1987) suggested that trade, in the form of mobilization of surpluses, is a process through which this key aspect of civilization is played out.

They argue that political leaders evolve as individuals who are able to mobilize surpluses in order to finance their own support and, later, support for other political personnel. Over time, mobilization increases, and political leaders are able to finance support for larger numbers of people. Brumfiel and Earle suggest that this form of "staple finance" is often transformed into "wealth finance" as polities become larger and more complex. Political leaders employing wealth finance use trade to mobilize wealth, often in the form of exotic goods from distant locales, to finance support for political personnel. Wealth finance is less cumbersome than staple finance, as bulk goods such as food are not involved, and often provides political leaders with new avenues for social control. For example, complex administrative structures may be needed to maintain access to and control over trade in wealth items, and a market system may be required in order to provide political personnel a means to transform wealth items into staples. In this way, the mobilization of wealth through trade is seen as a driving force in the evolution of civilization.

## Conclusions

Trade is the movement of goods between individuals or groups where there is a general expectation of reciprocity and where the purpose is basically utilitarian. Anthropologists have long been interested in trade because it is an important factor in shaping social relations. The earliest anthropological approaches to trade focused on reciprocity and how the expectations of reciprocity shaped social relations. But it was soon recognized that many forms of trade are unequal, even exploitive. Capitalism seems particularly exploitive, and with increasingly global markets and the introduction of Western capitalism into all corners of the world, anthropologists have become more and more concerned with the effects of trade on the cultures they study. Trade not only introduces Western products but also many aspects of Western culture, both good and bad, as well as Western plants, animals, and diseases. These have had a devastating effect on non-Western cultures and have profoundly impacted world history. Trade has also been important prehistorically and is an important concept to scholars attempting to understand the evolution of civilization. Trade has been seen as essential to the evolution of centralized polities, as trade provides means to both legitimate and finance positions of authority. With trade being such an important concept for understanding both contemporary and past cultures of the world, it is likely that research on trade will remain a central concern in anthropology and the other social sciences.

See also **Capitalism; Gift, The; Globalization; World Systems Theory, Latin America.**

BIBLIOGRAPHY

Appadurai, Arjun, ed. *The Social Life of Things: Commodities in Cultural Perspective.* Cambridge, U.K., and New York: Cambridge University Press, 1986.

Belshaw, Cyril S. *Traditional Exchange and Modern Markets.* Englewood Cliffs, N.J.: Prentice Hall, 1965.

Brumfiel, Elizabeth M., and Timothy E. Earle. "Specialization, Exchange, and Complex Societies: An Introduction." In *Specialization, Exchange, and Complex Societies,* edited by Elizabeth M. Brumfiel and Timothy E. Earle. Cambridge, U.K., and New York: Cambridge University Press, 1987.

Curtin, Philip D. *Cross-Cultural Trade in World History.* Cambridge, U.K., and New York: Cambridge University Press, 1984.

Hall, Thomas, ed. *A World-Systems Reader: New Perspectives on Gender, Urbanism, Indigenous Peoples, and Ecology.* Lanham, Md.: Rowman and Littlefield, 2000.

Helms, Mary W. *Ancient Panama: Chiefs in Search of Power.* Austin: University of Texas Press, 1979.

Humphrey, Caroline, and Stephen Hugh-Jones, eds. *Barter, Exchange, and Value: An Anthropological Approach.* Cambridge, U.K., and New York: Cambridge University Press, 1992.

Malinowski, Bronislaw. *Argonauts of the Western Pacific.* London: G. Routledge and Sons, 1922.

Mauss, Marcel. *The Gift: Forms and Functions of Exchange in Archaic Societies.* Glencoe, Ill.: Free Press, 1954.

Piddocke, Stuart. "The Potlatch System of the Southern Kwakiutl: A New Perspective." *Southwestern Journal of Anthropology* 21, no. 2 (1965): 244–264.

Plattner, Stuart, ed. *Economic Anthropology.* Stanford, Calif.: Stanford University Press, 1989.

Polanyi, Karl K., Conrad Arensberg, and Harry Pearson, eds. *Trade and Markets in the Early Empires.* New York: Free Press, 1957.

Sahlins, Marshall. *Stone Age Economics.* New York: Aldine, 1972. Reprint, London and New York: Routledge, 2004.

Service, Elman. *Primitive Social Organization.* New York: Random House, 1962.

Wallerstein, Immanuel. *The Modern World System.* New York: Academic Press, 1974.

Wolf, Eric. *Europe and the People without History.* Berkeley: University of California Press, 1982.

*Peter N. Peregrine*

**TRADITION.** The basic sense of the term *tradition* remains quite close to its etymological roots. The Latin noun *traditio* describes the handing over of an item or an idea, while the English *tradition* refers to a social or cultural institution that is handed down from the past. This much seems straightforward. Sacrificing cattle, singing at graduation, celebrating the New Year with fireworks: all these appear quite plainly to be traditions for their practitioners. For all its seeming simplicity, though, *tradition* is indeed the "particularly difficult word" that Raymond Williams called it in his account of its changing meanings over the centuries. Its intellectual usage is especially fraught with argument, and since the 1970s, the term has been subjected to so many debates and revisions that few scholars use it nowadays with any confidence in its transparency.

Let us first consider how tradition has acquired its specific ideological and academic meanings. Often these formal uses have expanded on, intensified, and arguably distorted the minimal sense of traditions as institutions passed on through historical eras.

For a start, the idea that tradition derives from the past has often involved a subtle shift in emphasis, from the process of transmission to the fact of repetition. In this view, deeming a cultural form a tradition implies that all its instances are identical, that it does not change over time. This is not necessarily the case, however. Think of how we refer to traditions like Greco-Roman sculpture or Renaissance painting. No one assumes these styles remained the same throughout the time they endured, only that their later manifestations were in some way shaped by precedents. Nor does derivation from the past exclude the idea that traditions embody active historical processes. A dynamic view of traditions as developing and changing continuities is intrinsic to the way we trace, say, a line from the Romanesque to the Gothic in the tradition of medieval European architecture. Nonetheless, the trend is to equate tradition with replication, to judge institutions traditions insofar as they reiterate past performance. Consider how we tend to think inauthentic any tradition that has been altered by contemporary practice. In this view we cannot adapt or reinvigorate real traditions, let alone create them. At best, we preserve them.

A closely related extension of the idea of tradition opposes it to modernity. If modernity is a state of ceaseless change, tradition, as unchanging repetition, is its antithesis. This notion is so well established it seems self-evident now, but it also subtly inflates the basic sense of the term. Its origins lie in the ideological conflicts surrounding the intellectual, political, and economic revolutions, starting in eighteenth-century Europe, that shaped what we now regard as modern society. On the one hand, the proponents of Enlightenment and their heirs have called for a world based on reason, not on what they regard as baseless custom. On the other hand, various strands of conservative and Romantic thought have celebrated tradition as the treasure chest of accumulated experience, collective cultural genius, and authentic human sentiment, all threatened by the totalitarian visions of social reformers. But the most important point here is that both camps see modern developments, like democracy or mechanization, as absolute departures from the past. The premodern or traditional past is not just what precedes these particular changes, then; instead, it becomes the opposite of historical change itself.

Once tradition acquires this extended sense as the opposite of modernity, it assumes quite a curious temporality too. It comes to be identified with the past from which it is passively handed down and not with the expanse of time through which it is transmitted, up to and including the present. But even while we insist that traditions are part of the past, we also thereby deny that they have real historical lives (except insofar as history has diluted them) precisely because we think they are unchanging. We think traditions persist across the passing of time, but we only think they are *in* it when we talk about their destruction. Modernity, on the other hand, exists in time inasmuch as it is constant change but precisely because it is change it has no past.

Another important effect of turning tradition into the opposite of modernity is that these problems with the concept seem to intensify the farther its objects lie from what we take to be modernity. Within societies felt to be mainly modern, for instance, an emphasis on static rather than changing continuity is much more pronounced in talk about folk art and custom than it is in high cultural criticism. An electronic composer can move the classical chamber music tradition forward, but a hip-hop artist who samples the blues is untrue to its authentic agrarian roots. Elite traditions can change and still be traditions, but folk traditions cannot.

The greatest confusions come, though, from describing non-Western peoples and their societies as traditional in contrast to a West conceived as modern. This idea has global reach now, and non-Western intellectuals use it if anything more often than their Western peers at present. But it first appeared in the West, and it found its strongest expression there in the theories of specialist anthropological disciplines and discourses (Kuper; Stocking, 1968, 1996).

Anthropology began life as the study of non-Western peoples, and it kept this orientation until the late twentieth century because of the idea that these peoples' communities somehow embodied the human past. In the nineteenth through to the early twentieth centuries, this idea informed evolutionary theories that pictured human communities climbing a ladder of cultural progress. Topmost was the industrial West, with its bureaucratic states, nuclear families, and monotheistic faiths; at the bottom were stateless foragers with extensive notions of kinship and beliefs in natural spirits. Anthropology was tasked, then, with discovering where in this evolutionary hierarchy to place the many communities known to the ethnological record. But it was largely taken for granted that all peoples evolved in one and the same direction. And if some were less advanced at present than others, this had to be because they had developed more slowly. Some communities ambled along the course of human historical development, whereas others raced ahead. Traditional peoples were still living in the same evolutionary past that modern societies had already left behind them.

The catastrophes of the first half of the twentieth century made it hard to sustain such sanguine faith that Western history represented the course of progress for all humanity. Also, by the 1940s, the claim that Western societies were more advanced than others suffered the taint of associations with discredited racist and fascist thought. Anthropology turned away from evolutionary comparisons in this period, instead cultivating a relativist attention to the differences among cultural systems in terms of their *internal* patterns. This did not weaken the tendency to contrast types of societies as traditional or modern, however. If anything, ironically, it strengthened it. This is because the idea that some communities changed more slowly than others was now understood as a function, not of their place on the ladder of progress, but of their own internal resistance to change. Instead of being considered still traditional inasmuch as they were not yet modern, communities like these were now imagined to be traditional by nature. The structuralists of the 1960s thus distinguished "hot" from "cold" societies: those that changed dynamically from those that tried to conserve old institutions. While some peoples therefore had histories proper, others experienced change as an entropic force in the face of which traditions only survived if they imposed their older structures on new events. Insofar as they succeeded at this, traditions actually swallowed up all trace of the fact that change had ever happened (Levi-Strauss).

In other words, anthropology gave a cultural cast to the schisms of time already implied in the contrast of tradition with modernity. Traditional peoples derived their ways from the past but had no histories. They lived across time but not in it. Modern people had histories, but the burden of the past was far behind them. They lived in time but did not straddle its passing.

Despite this confusion, the notion that some communities are traditional, and therefore the antithesis of the dynamic, changing West, has proven very resilient and influential. Advocates of modernization often assert how peoples need to leave traditional ways behind them—not just because traditions are part of the past in this view but also because they are held to be antithetical to change. The model of a contrast between the West and the Rest is also used quite widely to explain social inequalities and differences *within* the so-called developing nations that used to be grouped as the Third World. In this view developing nations have both modern and traditional sectors inside them, as if time ran on unrelated tracks not just for the world as a whole but even within some societies. Nor are such beliefs only held by self-described opponents of tradition. Multiculturalists and cultural conservatives often cherish traditions because they see them as islands of stability, in a modern world they judge to be unmoored and inauthentic. These sentiments usually add a mid-twentieth century anthropological perspective to the doubts about modernity and nostalgia for the past derived from older forms of anti-Enlightenment thinking.

Ironically, however, anthropology itself has mostly abandoned these ideas. In part this shift is due to a growing awareness of the conceptual problems presented by older anthropological usages. But the impetus to question older usage in the academy has itself arisen from broader intellectual and political developments in the decades after World War II.

By far the most important of these developments is the wave of European decolonization that took place in the 1950s and 1960s, creating a host of new independent nations out of the formerly colonized territories of Africa and Asia. Once these nations' political representatives took their places on the international stage, it became increasingly difficult to describe them in terms that made them seem less modern or developed than their peers from the states of the West. And even amidst the divisions of the Cold War era, the rise of a set of global institutions like the United Nations fostered a new sense of planetary civilization. The notion of a shared human fate, demanding respectful dialogue, became more widespread than ever during these decades.

In this changed political climate, many intellectuals became concerned with what it meant to call non-Western peoples traditional. Since tradition was so strongly imbued with the sense of being the antithesis of modernity, it seemed less and less appropriate to apply the idea to societies that now had the very same sets of institutions and ambitions that were identified with modernity in the West. In fact, as many thinkers came to insist, the use of terms like *tradition* did much more than impose anachronistic mistakes about the contemporary social lives and institutions of peoples outside the West. For in so doing it also demeaned and diminished them. In the first place it belittled their modern achievements, such as their struggles for liberation

and their quests to achieve economic and political equality with European and other Western nations. In this way it, if anything, distorted these societies' actual histories. This seemed all the more discordant in the context of the 1960s and 1970s, when the former colonies witnessed new waves of social and cultural dynamism while Western nations mostly seemed to stagnate. But secondly and even more insidiously, to call these peoples traditional seemed to deny that they possessed even the capacities to have such histories at all. The strong distinction this usage drew between those who were tradition-bound on the one hand and the dynamic West on the other now seemed offensive to the new international ethos of equality among peoples. Most important, it also echoed the sorts of colonial stereotypes about non-Western peoples that anticolonial movements had resisted in their struggles for freedom from Western domination. To say that people were ruled by the past began to sound suspiciously like an excuse for ruling over them in the present.

In the postcolonial era, therefore, many politically minded intellectuals found ideas about tradition versus modernity inseparable from the history of colonial rule over non-European societies. By the early 1970s, this judgment had also penetrated critical discussions within universities. Inspired by the radical social movements of the 1960s, a young generation of scholars had already started questioning the idea that the academy and its products were politically disinterested. Instead, they argued, the mainstream human or social sciences had tended toward complicity in modern structures of power (Foucault and Gordon). In the case of anthropology, its relationship with European colonialism was the form of guilt provoking most critiques it faced (Asad; Mafeje). In their harshest forms, these discussions even saw anthropology mocked for having been the willing "handmaiden" of colonialism. And if anthropology found itself accused of being the intellectual servant of the West's colonial projects, this criticism was largely due to the images of non-Western peoples the discipline had developed under the rubric of tradition.

To critical scholars who sympathized with anticolonial movements, then, the use of the term *tradition* became problematic. Influenced by critiques of colonial discourse in the humanities, such as Edward Said's *Orientalism* (1979), some began to see anthropology's emphasis on traditions as part of a broader set of misrepresentations of non-Western peoples in Western thought. In this view, the portrayal of people in terms of their traditions made them appear to be mysterious, accepting of authority, immersed in collective cultural and spiritual life—in other words, not at all like the rational, pragmatic individuals who had earned the rights and freedoms of modernity. In one such commentary, Johannes Fabian (1983) showed how many anthropologists had exoticized the peoples whom they studied. Even though they shared so much time with their subjects during field research, he pointed out, their writing tended to represent these people as if they lived in other epochs. Not only did this make them look as if they lived in the past, but it also made it possible to overlook the conditions of colonial domination they faced in the present.

Critiques like these are widely accepted by scholars now, and few would think it tenable to assert today that some peoples have traditions while others have histories. But this was not the only effect of the conversations that took place in this vein in the 1970s. By showing that there was a politics to the concept of tradition, these commentaries also opened up another kind of critical discussion about tradition in the 1980s and afterward. This second wave of studies has focused less on the ideological meanings implicit in the idea of tradition and more on the contested social contexts in which various parties refer to traditions in order to advance their own agendas.

The most important step in this direction was Eric Hobsbawm and Terence Ranger's collection of historical essays that showed how several institutions generally thought traditional, from chieftaincy in Africa to tartan-wearing in Scotland, were actually of recent historical vintage. In each case, these historians argued, an institution was made to seem as if it came from the age-old past, in order to grant legitimacy to a social group and its projects in the present. The real task of scholarship, then, was to study not the transmission or replication but the *invention* of traditions.

This argument is radically unsettling, of course. Traditions are supposed to be the stable, enduring antitheses of invention, not its new, ephemeral products. So the claim that they are the latter has inspired an enormous body of literature by way of response in the late twentieth and early twenty-first centuries.

Some have used this concept of invented traditions in order to revisit the relationship of ideas about tradition to colonialism. Instead of seeing tradition as a figment of the Western colonial mind alone, this kind of work examines the use of terms like *tradition* or *custom* by a range of social actors in colonial and postcolonial settings: by colonizers and colonized, urban elites and peasant villagers, nationalists and compradors, conservatives and modernizers, and even the scholars who study them all (Briggs; Foster; Jolly and Thomas; Keesing; Keesing and Tonkinson; Spiegel and Boonzaier). As these studies show, while Westerners may have used the idea of tradition to make non-Western peoples appear exotic and backward, non-Western peoples have used this concept to portray themselves as special communities, worthy of distinctive rights, entitlements, and identities. From this perspective tradition is less like an argument, true or false, about the lack of change in society and more like a language or idiom in which ever-changing arguments about social life are conducted. This treatment mitigates some of the most odious associations that critics of colonial discourse attached to the concept. It does not rescue the term itself for renewed academic use, however. Instead it demotes tradition to the status of a folk category—an excellent object of study just like any idea one finds in such wide social circulation, but hardly a viable tool of social analysis.

The convergence of the postcolonial moment with the critical turn in scholarship has thus made it very difficult for scholars to speak of traditions without embarrassment. One quite common response to this situation is to use the term as if in its naive sense, while hedging it in heavy layers of irony. While true to the uncertainties that now surround the label, this is a less than helpful strategy for conceptual clarification. Another more considered and productive response is to bite the bullet and try to understand the relations among society, culture, and

history with more rigor, self-reflection, and complexity than contrasts between tradition and modernity allow (Axel; Bauman and Briggs; Comaroff and Comaroff; Sahlins; Trouillot). But here there is also an irony of sorts. Although it may not use the term *tradition* with any innocence, what all such work affirms is that there are few more worthy tasks for the humanities and social sciences than helping us appreciate and understand the changing continuities in our social lives: the institutions that all of us keep handing down through time.

*See also* **Anthropology; Cultural Revivals; Ritual.**

**BIBLIOGRAPHY**

Asad, Talal, ed. *Anthropology and the Colonial Encounter.* London: Ithaca Press, 1973.

Axel, Brian Keith. *From the Margins: Historical Anthropology and Its Futures.* Durham, N.C.: Duke University Press, 2002.

Bauman, Richard, and Charles L. Briggs. *Voices of Modernity: Language Ideologies and the Politics of Inequality.* Cambridge, U.K., and New York: Cambridge University Press, 2003.

Briggs, Charles L. "The Politics of Discursive Authority in Research on the 'Invention of Tradition.'" *Cultural Anthropology* 11, no. 4 (1996): 435–469.

Comaroff, John Lionel, and Jean Comaroff. *Ethnography and the Historical Imagination.* Boulder, Colo.: Westview Press, 1992.

Fabian, Johannes. *Time and the Other: How Anthropology Makes Its Object.* New York: Columbia University Press, 1983.

Foster, Robert John. *Nation Making: Emergent Identities in Postcolonial Melanesia.* Ann Arbor: University of Michigan Press, 1995.

Foucault, Michel, and Colin Gordon. *Power/Knowledge: Selected Interviews and Other Writings, 1972–1977.* New York: Pantheon Books, 1980.

Hobsbawm, Eric, and Terence Ranger, eds. *The Invention of Tradition.* Cambridge, U.K., and New York: Cambridge University Press, 1983.

Jolly, Margaret, and Nicholas Thomas, eds. "The Politics of Tradition in the Pacific." Special issue of *Oceania* 62, no. 4 (1992).

Keesing, Roger M. *Custom and Confrontation: The Kwaio Struggle for Cultural Autonomy.* Chicago: University of Chicago Press, 1992.

Keesing, Roger M., and Robert Tonkinson, eds. "Reinventing Traditional Culture: The Politics of Kastom in Island Melanesia." Special issue of *Mankind* 13, no. 4 (1982).

Kuper, Adam. *Anthropology and Anthropologists: The Modern British School.* London and Boston: Routledge and Kegan Paul, 1983.

Levi-Strauss, Claude. *The Savage Mind.* Chicago: University of Chicago Press, 1966.

Mafeje, Archie. "The Ideology of Tribalism." *Journal of Modern African Studies* 9 (1971): 253–262.

Sahlins, Marshall David. *Islands of History.* Chicago: University of Chicago Press, 1985.

Said, Edward. *Orientalism.* New York: Vintage Books, 1979.

Spiegel, Andrew, and Emile Boonzaier. "Promoting Tradition: Images of the South African Past." In *South African Keywords: The Uses and Abuses of Political Concepts,* edited by Emile Boonzaier and John Sharp. Cape Town and Johannesburg, South Africa: David Philip, 1988.

Stocking, George W. *Race, Culture, and Evolution: Essays in the History of Anthropology.* New York: Free Press, 1968.

———. *Volksgeist as Method and Ethic: Essays on Boasian Ethnography and the German Anthropological Tradition.* Madison: University of Wisconsin Press, 1996.

Trouillot, Michel-Rolph. *Silencing the Past: Power and the Production of History.* Boston: Beacon Press, 1995.

Williams, Raymond. *Keywords: A Vocabulary of Culture and Society.* New York: Oxford University Press, 1983.

*Hylton White*

## TRAGEDY AND COMEDY.

Various ideas have been associated with the term *tragedy* and the term *comedy* over the centuries, including tragedy that is not tragic, in the sense of "sad" or "disastrous," and comedy that is not comic, in the modern prevalent meaning of "amusing." The modern English meaning of comedy as a synonym for *humor* is largely a twentieth-century development.

### Greek Origins

Tragedies are first heard of, as stage plays, in the Dionysiac celebrations in Athens at the turn of the fifth century B.C.E., and comedies appear as a contrasting type of play a century later. Aristotle (384–322 B.C.E.) said that tragedies dealt with *spoudaia* (serious matters) and comedies with *phaulika* (trivial subjects). Tragedies aimed at arousing and then purging emotions such as pity and fear. Effective tragedies need not end in disaster; he gives highest praise to the happily resolved *Iphigenia among the Taurians* of Sophocles, and, among narrative poems (since staging is not essential to tragedy), he considers the *Odyssey* to have a tragic story as well as the *Iliad,* though he notes at one point that the effects of such a double-plotted story (good end for the good, bad for the bad) are more appropriate to comedy.

Aristotle's treatment of comedy has not survived, and his analysis of tragedy was not cited in antiquity. His chief disciple, Theophrastus (c. 372–c. 287 B.C.E.) also dealt with tragedy and comedy, and his definitions were cited by the Latin grammarian Diomedes (4th century C.E.). They can be rendered as follows: "Tragedy deals with the fortunes of heroes in adversity," and "Comedy treats of private deeds with no threat to life." Diomedes adds that tragedies usually move from joy to sadness, comedies the opposite.

Meanwhile, Horace (65–8 B.C.E.) had discussed the genres in his *Ars poetica.* He explains the meaning of "tragedy" as "goat-song," so called because the winning players were rewarded with a cheap goat. He does not define the forms and deals mainly with questions of style, that is, tone and diction. The complaints of tragedy should not readily be mixed with the *privata carmina* (domestic verse) of comedy. Ovid (43 B.C.E.–17 C.E.), too, has style in mind when he says that tragedy is the gravest form of writing (*Tristia* 2.381). It consists of sublime verse, as opposed to the lighter forms of elegy (used for love poems) (*Amores* 3.1.39–42).

Another influential grammarian of the fourth century, Aelius Donatus, considers Homer the father of tragedy in the *Iliad* and the father of comedy in the *Odyssey.* He attributes

**Scene from *Electra* by Sophocles, 1908.** Sophocles was one of the three most important authors of tragedies in ancient Greece. He wrote more than one hundred plays, but only seven have survived in their entirety. © HULTON-DEUTSCH COLLECTION/ CORBIS

to Cicero (106–43 B.C.E.) a definition of comedy as "the imitation of life, the mirror of custom, the image of truth," which is later reflected in Hamlet's discourse to the players.

The chief Greek authors of tragedies were Aeschylus (525–456 B.C.E.), Sophocles (c. 496–406 B.C.E.), and Euripides (c. 484–406 B.C.E.). Comedy was divided into old, middle, and new. Aristophanes (c. 450–c. 388 B.C.E.) straddled the old and the middle periods, while Menander (342–292 B.C.E.) represented the new. The Latin playwrights Plautus (c. 254–184 B.C.E.) and Terence (186 or 185–?159 B.C.E.) specialized in adapting Greek comedies from Menander's period. As for tragedy, Lucius Annaeus Seneca (c. 4 B.C.E.?–65 C.E.) is the only known playwright whose works are extant. Plautus claimed that one of his plays, the *Amphitruo,* was a combination of comedy and tragedy, not because it used an elevated style, but rather because it introduced characters proper to both genres, kings and gods on the one hand and slaves on the other.

### The Latin World

By Seneca's time, plays may have largely or entirely ceased to be performed by actors and, at most, been presented only by public recitations. The term *tragedy* was also used for pantomime productions, *tragoediae saltatae,* and also for *citharoediae,* in which a tragic protagonist sang and accompanied himself on the lyre.

The most important treatment of tragedy and comedy in the early Middle Ages was that of St. Isidore of Seville (c. 560–636).

In book 8 of his *Etymologies,* he cites Horace's etymology for tragedy, taking it to mean that the poets were originally held in low esteem, but that later they became highly regarded for the skill of their very realistic stories. Tragic poets deal with public affairs, the histories of kings, and sorrowful matters, whereas comic poets recite the deeds of private persons and emphasize joyful things. However, the new comic poets, like Persius (34–62 C.E.) and Juvenal (c. 55 or 60–in or after 127 C.E.), are called satirists, and they expose vice. Both tragic and comic poems consist entirely of the dialogue of characters.

In book 18 of his encyclopedia, Isidore takes up tragedy and comedy again, this time as theatrical pieces. Comic and tragic (or comedic and tragedic) poets sang their poems on the stage, while actors and mines danced and made gestures. Thanks largely to this account, classical dramas were regarded in the Middle Ages and early Renaissance as having been recited by the poet himself, that is, Seneca, Plautus, or Terence (except that in Terence's case a stand-in was used); while he declaimed the lines of all of the characters himself, actors would mime their words and actions.

In addition to "theatricizing" tragedy and comedy in book 18, Isidore now gives a darker account of the subject matter of the two forms (there was some hint of this with regard to comedies in the account of the satirists in book 8). Here he says that the comedians sang not only of private men, but specifically of "the defilements of virgins and the loves of whores," and tragedians sang of the "sorrowful crimes of wicked kings" (18.45–46).

Just as influential as Isidore's accounts was a passage written a century before him by Boethius (c. 480–c. 524). In the *Consolation of Philosophy,* he portrays Lady Philosophy as inviting Lady Fortune to give an account of herself, and at one point she says, "What does the cry of tragedies bewail but Fortune's overthrow of happy kingdoms with a sudden blow?" (2 pr. 2). Subsequent commentators on the *Consolation* offered definitions of both tragedy and comedy. Notably, William of Conches, writing around the year 1125, says that tragedy begins in prosperity and ends in adversity, whereas in comedy the situations are reversed.

## Medieval Contributions

The most important medieval writer of comedy was Dante (1265–1321), and Geoffrey Chaucer (c. 1342–1400) was the most important author of tragedy. Dante does not seem to have known either the comedies of Terence and Plautus or the tragedies of Seneca. The latter had recently been discovered and were being studied in Padua during Dante's time, notably by Albertino Mussato, who considered tragedy to be a genre of elevated subject matter, consisting of two subgenres: those dealing with disasters (like Seneca's works and his own *Ecerinis*) used iambic verse, and those dealing with triumphs, like the works of Virgil (70–19 B.C.E.) and Publius Papinius Statius (c. 45–96 C.E.), used dactylic hexameters.

Dante's own definitions of comedy and tragedy in *De vulgari eloquentia* are not connected to ideas of misery or felicity. He agrees with Mussato in considering tragedy to use elevated subjects. It also uses the best syntax, verse forms, and diction.

Comedy on the other hand is a style inferior to that of tragedy, using both middling and humble forms. He cites lyric poems, including some of his own, as examples of tragedy. In *Inferno* (20.113) he has Virgil refer to the *Aeneid* as "my high tragedy." He may have based his ideas on Papias's definition of comedy in his *Elementarium* (c. 1045), repeated in the *Catholicon* of John Balbus of Genoa (1286): comedy deals with the affairs of common and humble men, not in the high style of tragedy, but rather in a middling and sweet style, and it also often deals with historical facts and important persons.

Dante's commentators did not know of the *De vulgari eloquentia,* and most of them, including Guido da Pisa and the author of the *Epistle to Cangrande* (which purports to be by Dante himself), follow definitions similar to those of the Boethian commentators; thus they explain Dante's choice of title by the fact that the work begins in misery (hell) and ends in felicity (heaven). They hold that Terence's comedies follow the same pattern, and that Seneca's tragedies trace the reverse movement (hardly true in either case). Some readers, like Dante's son Piero, followed the rubrical tradition that designated *Inferno, Purgatorio,* and *Paradiso* as three comedies, and found an upbeat conclusion to all of them: each ends with a reference to the stars.

Chaucer, for his part, like Dante's commentators, was influenced by the Boethian tradition. He translated the *Consolation* and used glosses derived from the commentary of Nicholas Trivet (1258?–?1328). But whereas Trivet repeated Conches's definition of tragedy and added to its iniquitous subject by repeating Isidore's statement about the crimes of the wicked kings, the gloss that Chaucer received and translated removed all such reference: "Tragedy is to say a dite [literary composition] of a prosperity for a time that endeth in wretchedness" (pp. 409–410). He thus restored the concept to its Boethian context by removing the suggestion that all tragic falls are deserved and punitive. Chaucer wrote tragedies of this sort himself, on the model of the narratives of Giovanni Boccaccio's (1313–1375) *De casibus virorum illustrium* (Boccaccio himself did not consider these stories to be tragedies) and later assigned them to the Monk in the *Canterbury Tales.* In the meantime, he wrote an extended tragedy, *Troilus and Criseyde.* John Lydgate (c. 1370–c. 1450) subsequently applied Chaucer's idea of tragedy to *The Fall of Princes,* his translation of the *De casibus,* and it was adopted in its sixteenth-century continuation, *A Mirror for Magistrates.* Thus Chaucerian tragedy was transmitted to the age of Shakespeare.

## The Renaissance

Shakespeare (1564–1616) himself does not say what he means by comedy and tragedy, but one can deduce from his characters that comedy has the general meaning of a pleasant or mirthful play, and that tragedy more often refers to an event than to a play, and more often concerns the downfall of an innocent than a guilty person. This is in contrast to formal discussions—like Sir Philip Sidney's (1554–1586) *Apology for Poetry*—that tend to restrict the subject of tragedy to bad men coming to bad ends, thereby "making kings fear to be tyrants." This is a kind of plot that received very low marks from Aristotle.

**Scene from Shakespeare's *As You Like It*, starring Cloris Leachman (left) and Katherine Hepburn (right).** Shakespeare, arguably the most famous dramatist in history, wrote numerous comedic plays, although he did not specifically explain what his criteria was for a play to be considered a comedy. © JOHN SPRINGER COLLECTION/CORBIS

By Sidney's time, Aristotle's *Poetics* was available in an accurate form (before the sixteenth century it was chiefly known from the commentary of Averroës [1126–1198], who understood comedy to refer to poems reprehending vice and tragedy to poems praising virtue). But it was mainly cited on minor points, or distorted through assimilation to Horatian concerns. Aristotle's insistence on unity of action was made equal to the newly invented unities of time and space.

Tragedy became an elite genre, in which only the best tragedies were thought worthy of the name of tragedy. In England this concept can be seen in Thomas Rymer's *Short View of Tragedy* (1692), when he speaks of "the sacred name of tragedy." Such an understanding is widely accepted and practiced in modern times, allegedly with the backing of Aristotle: the criterion that Aristotle gives for the most effective tragedy (the fall of a good man through a flaw) has been smuggled into the definition of and made a sine qua non for tragedy. Now there is no such thing as a bad or mediocre tragedy. For Aristotle, on the contrary, everything that was called a tragedy

or fitted general criteria was a tragedy, but some were better than others.

**Problems of Definition**

There have been dozens of attempts to define tragedy, understood as supreme tragedy, radical tragedy, pure tragedy, and the like. Most of these understandings are intuitive and personal to the definers and are based on a favorite example of tragedy (or a small cluster of favorite tragedies). To give a recent example, George Steiner defines tragedy as "the dramatic testing of a view of reality in which man is taken to be an unwelcome guest in the world"; and the plays that communicate "this metaphysic of desperation" are very few, "and would include *The Seven against Thebes, King Oedipus, Antigone,* the *Hippolytus,* and, supremely, the *Bacchae*" (1980 Foreword to *The Death of Tragedy,* 1961).

Because of the elevated status of the idea of tragedy, actual tragedies have become a thing of the past, represented by the classical plays, Shakespeare and his contemporary English dramatists and, in France, Jean Racine and Pierre Corneille sometimes extending to Lope de Vega in Spain. The only more recent work that is named a tragedy by its author and acknowledged to be a great work is Johann Wolfgang von Goethe's (1749–1832) *Faust: A Tragedy* (1808), but it is not usually considered to be a great tragedy or even a tragedy at all. (Whether Goethe himself meant to call Part 2 a tragedy is not clear; but it was published as such, posthumously, in 1832.)

Comedy, in contrast to tragedy, remained a general and amorphous genre, encompassing ineffective as well as effective examples. No comic masterpieces have been singled out as supreme comedies (though Shakespeare's plays are given high ranking), and plays that do not measure up to some classical standard have not in general been drummed out of the genre, though occasionally this sort of qualifying spirit can be seen when a dud is denigrated as "mere farce."

In England in Shakespeare's time, when the action of a play was not amusing but simply avoided the usual final disasters of tragedy, it was given the name of "tragicomedy," which Sidney referred to as a mongrel form. When Plautus invented the term to describe his *Amphitruo*, it was for a different reason: because it had the characters proper to tragedy (kings and gods) as well as those proper to comedy (slaves, etc.). The term was revived in Spain for yet another reason, by what might well be called a comedy of errors. When Fernando de Rojas (c. 1465–1541) adapted the twelfth-century Latin "comedy" *Pamphilus* and published it under the title of *The Comedy of Calisto and Melibea* (1500), readers complained that its action was not that of comedy but rather of tragedy, and he thought to satisfy them by calling it a tragicomedy. This work, usually called *Celestina*, gave rise to several sequels, among them *Segunda Comedia de Celestina* (1534), *Tragicomedia de Lisandro y Roselia* (1542), *Tragedia Policiana* (1547), *Comedia Florinea* (1554), and *Comedia Selvagia* (1554). During this time, *comedy* came to mean "any stage play," and the most celebrated adaptation of the *Celestina* was Lope de Vega's (1562–1635) great tragedy, *El Caballero de Olmedo*, which appeared in Part 24 of Vega's *Comedias* (1641). *Comedia* also became the general name for theater, a practice found in France, as in the Comédie Française in Paris.

In Italy in the sixteenth century, Dante's *Comedy* was given the title of *The Divine Comedy,* seemingly to make the point that it has nothing to do with any of the usual senses of comedy. In France in the 1840s Honoré de Balzac (1799–1850) gave to his collected works the retrospective title of *The Human Comedy,* not because of any theory of comedy, but to contrast the mundane world of his novels with the otherworldly actions and interests of Dante's work. The designation of "art comedy," commedia dell'arte, was given to plays performed by professional actors on stereotyped plots with much improvisation. In the eighteenth century in both France and Italy sentimental or "tearful" comedy and "musical" comedy came into vogue.

In the late twentieth century "musical comedy" was shortened to "musical," which was contrasted with "comedy," both being contrasted with "drama" (as in the Golden Globe Awards). The latter category includes all revived tragedies and also modern plays or films that are perceived to have a sense of the tragic.

*See also* **Theater and Performance.**

**BIBLIOGRAPHY**

Aristotle. *Poetics.* Edited and translated by Stephen Halliwell. Loeb Classical Library 199. Cambridge, Mass.: Harvard University Press, 1995.

Bayley, John. *Shakespeare and Tragedy.* London: Routledge and Kegan Paul, 1981

Boethius. *The Theological Tractates.* Edited and translated by S. J. Tester. Loeb Classical Library 74. Cambridge, Mass.: Harvard University Press, 1973.

Bradley, A. C. *Shakespearean Tragedy: Lectures on Hamlet, Othello, King Lear, Macbeth.* London: Macmillan 1904. The second edition appeared in 1905, with uncounted reprintings since.

Chaucer, Geoffrey. *The Riverside Chaucer.* Edited by Larry D. Benson. Boston: Houghton Mifflin, 1987.

Eagleton, Terry. *Sweet Violence: The Idea of the Tragic.* Malden, Mass.: Blackwell, 2003.

Isidore of Seville. *Etymologiae.* 1911. 2 vols. Edited by W. M. Lindsay. Reprint, Oxford: Clarendon, 1985. For English translations of pertinent passages, see Kelly, *Ideas and Forms,* chap. 3, sec. 1, 36-50.

Janko, Richard. *Aristotle on Comedy: Towards a Reconstruction of Poetics II.* Berkeley: University of California Press, 1984.

Kelly, Henry Ansgar. *Ideas and Forms of Tragedy from Aristotle to the Middle Ages.* Cambridge, U.K.: Cambridge University Press, 1993.

———. *Tragedy and Comedy from Dante to Pseudo-Dante.* Berkeley: University of California Press, 1989.

Nelson, T. G. A. *Comedy: An Introduction to the Theory of Comedy in Literature, Drama, and Cinema.* New York: Oxford University Press, 1990.

Segal, Erich. *The Death of Comedy.* Cambridge, Mass.: Harvard University Press, 2001.

Steiner, George. *The Death of Tragedy.* New York: Knopf, 1961. Reprint, with new foreword, New York: Oxford University Press, 1980.

Williams, Raymond. *Modern Tragedy.* London: Chatto and Windus, 1966. Reprint, with new afterword, London: Verso, 1979.

*Henry Ansgar Kelly*

**TRANSLATION.** What may summarily be called *translation* has been practiced in many parts of the world for centuries and even millennia. The rendering of Buddhist texts into literary Chinese and the Latinization of the Bible in the first millennium are two instances of celebrated achievements in the long history of translation. There are countless cases where translations are known to have played a decisive role in the development of literary cultures, pedagogical institutions, ecclesiastic reformations, and the global spread of the nation-state and capitalism, particularly since the Renaissance and the European conquest of the Americas. Yet, until the 1970s or 1980s, translation did not attract much academic attention and consequently had not been studied systematically, though such diverse writers as John Dryden (1631–1700), Motoori Norinaga (1730–1801), and Walter Benjamin (1892–1940) offered insightful speculations on their own practice of translation.

In the early twenty-first century a number of scholars became aware of both the conceptual complexity and the politico-ethical significance of translation. Simultaneously, they came to realize that translations not only in the fields of literature and religion must be problematized but also those in the spheres of commercial advertisement, popular entertainment, public administration, international diplomacy, scientific research and publication, judiciary procedure, immigration, education, and family livelihood.

The conceptual complexity of the term *translation* and the difficulty in any attempt to define it make it necessary to historicize the particular ways translation has been understood and practiced in modern societies. The politico-ethical significance of translation is always complicit with the construction, transformation, or disruption of power relations. Translation involves moral imperatives on the part of both the addresser and the addressee and can always be viewed, to a greater or lesser degree, as a political maneuver of social antagonism. In addition, the representation of translation produces sociopolitical effects and serves as a technology by which individuals imagine their relation to the national or ethnic community.

The particular way translation is represented is conditioned by the essentially "modern" *schema of co-figuration*—most typically, the communication model according to which translation is represented as a transfer of signification between two clearly demarcated unities of ethnic or national languages—by means of which one comprehends natural language as an ethno-linguistic unity. In other words, the commonsensical notion of translation is delimited by the schematism of the world (that is, by the act of representing the world according to the schema of co-figuration). Conversely, the modern image of the world as "inter-national" (that is, as consisting of basic units called *nations*) is prescribed by a representation of translation as a communicative and international transfer of a message between a pair of ethno-linguistic unities.

## The Concept of Translation and Its Complexity

The network of connotations associated with the term *translation* leads to notions of transferring, conveying, or moving from one place to another, of linking one word, phrase, or text to another. These connotations are shared among the words for translation in many modern languages: *fanyi* in Chinese, *translation* in English, *traduction* in French, *honyaku* in Japanese, *Übersetzung* in German, and so forth. It may therefore appear justified to postulate the following definition: "Translation is a transfer of the message from one language to another." Even before one specifies what sort of transfer this may be, it is hard to refrain from asking about the message. Is not the message in this definition a product or consequence of the transfer called translation rather than an entity that precedes the action of transfer, something that remains invariant in the process of translation? Is the message supposedly transferred in this process determinable in and of itself before it has been operated on? And what is the status of the language from which or into which the message is transferred? Is it justifiable to assume that the source language in which the original text makes sense is different and distinct from the target language into which the translator renders the text as faithfully as possible?

Are these languages countable? In other words, is it possible to isolate and juxtapose them as individual units, such as apples, for example, and unlike water? By what measures is it possible to distinguish one from the other and endow each with a unity? But for the sake of facilitating the representation of translation, however, is it not necessary to posit the organic unity of language rather than see it as a random assemblage of words, phrases, and utterances if one is to speak of translation in accordance with the definition?

Accordingly, the presumed invariance of the message transmitted through translation is confirmed only retroactively, after it has been translated. What kind of definition is it, then, that includes the term in need of explanation in the definition itself? Is it not a circular definition? Similarly, the unity of the source language and of the target language is also a supposition in whose absence the definition would make little sense. What might translation be if it were supposed that a language is not countable or that one language cannot be easily distinguished from another?

It is difficult to evade this problem when attempting to comprehend the terms *meaning* and *language*. At the least, it may be said that, logically, translation is not derivative or secondary to meaning or language; it is just as fundamental or foundational in any attempt to elucidate those concepts. Translation suggests contact with the incomprehensible, the unknowable, or the unfamiliar—that is, with the foreign—and there is no awareness of language until the foreign is encountered. The problematic of translation is concerned in the first place with the allocation of the foreign.

If the foreign is unambiguously incomprehensible, unknowable, and unfamiliar, then translation simply cannot be done. If, conversely, the foreign is comprehensible, knowable, and familiar, translation is unnecessary. Thus, the status of the foreign is ambiguous in translation. The foreign is incomprehensible and comprehensible, unknowable and knowable, unfamiliar and familiar at the same time. This foundational ambiguity of translation is derived from the position occupied by the translator. The translator is summoned only when two kinds of audiences are postulated with regard to the source text, one for whom the text is comprehensible at least to some degree, and the other for whom it is incomprehensible. The translator's work consists in dealing with difference between the two audiences. The translator encroaches on both and stands in the midst of this difference. In other words, for the first audience the source language is comprehensible while for the second it is incomprehensible. It is important to note that the term *language* in this instance is figurative: it need not refer to the natural language of an ethnic or national community—German or Tagalog, for example. It is equally possible to have two kinds of audiences when the source text is a technical document or an avant-garde work of art. In such cases *language* may well refer to a vocabulary or set of expressions associated with a professional field or discipline—for example, law; it may imply a style of graphic inscription or an unusual setting in which an artwork is displayed. This loose use of the term *language* invariably renders the task of determining the meaning of the term *translation* difficult, because all the acts of projecting, exchanging, linking, matching, and mapping could then be considered kinds of translation, even if not a single word is involved. Here the discernability of the linguistic and the nonlinguistic is at stake.

Roman Jakobson's famous taxonomy of translation attempts to restrict the instability inherent in the figurative use of the word *language*. Jakobson divides translation into three classes: "1) Intralingual translation or *rewording* is an interpretation of verbal signs by means of other signs of the same language. 2) Interlingual translation or *translation proper* is an interpretation of verbal signs by means of some other language. 3) Intersemiotic translation or *transmutation* is an interpretation of verbal signs by means of signs of nonverbal sign systems" (p. 261). According to the Jakobsonian taxonomy, one who translates "legal language" into common parlance would be performing an intralingual translation, while one who offers a commentary on an obscure artwork would be engaged in an intersemiotic translation. Neither can be said to be a translator strictly speaking. Only someone who translates a text from one language to another would be doing translation proper.

Jakobson's taxonomy neither elucidates nor responds to the supposition concerning the countability and organic unity of the source and target languages. It does not empirically validate the supposition; it merely repeats and confirms it. Nevertheless, it discloses that "translation proper" depends on a supposed discernibility between the interlingual and the intralingual, between a translation from one language to another and a rewording within the same language. It thereby prescribes and demarcates the locus of difference between two presumably ethnic or national language communities by virtue of the fact that Jakobson presupposes that translation proper can take place only between two unequivocally circumscribed languages. It therefore eradicates the various differences within such a linguistic community and locates the foreign exclusively outside the unity of a language.

No doubt this conception of translation is a schematization of the globally shared and abstractly idealized common-sensical vision of the *international* world as basic units—nations—segmented by national borders into territories. It is not simply Jakobson's idiosyncratic view. In this schematization, "translation proper" not only claims to be a description or representation of what happens in the process of translation; that description also prescribes and directs how to represent and apprehend what one does when one translates. In this respect, "translation proper" is a *discursive* construct: it is part of what may be called the regime of translation, an institutionalized assemblage of protocols, rules of conduct, canons of accuracy, and ways of viewing. The *discursive* regime of translation is *poietic*, or productive, in that it foregrounds what speech acts theorists call the "perlocutionary" effect. Just as a perlocutionary act of persuading might well happen in a speech act of arguing but persuasion does not always result from argument, "translation proper" need not be postulated whenever one acts to translate. Yet, in the regime of translation, it is as if there were a casual relationship between the co-figurative schematization of translation and the process of translation. Collapsing the process of translation onto its co-figurative schematization, the representation of translation repeatedly discerns the domestic language co-figuratively—one unity is

figured out, represented, and comprehended as a spatial figure, in contrast to another—as if the two unities were already present in actuality.

As long as one remains captive to the regime of translation, one can construe the ambiguity inherent in the translator's positionality only as the dual position a translator occupies between a native language and a foreign tongue. Hence the presumption persists that one either speaks one's mother tongue or a foreigner's. The translator's task would be to discern the differences between the two languages. And the difference one deals with in translation is always determined as that between two linguistic communities. Despite countless potential differences within one linguistic community, the regime of translation obliges one to speak from within a binary opposition, either to the same or to the other. Thus, in the regime of translation the translator becomes invisible. This attitude in which one is constantly solicited to identify oneself may be called "monolingual address," whereby the addresser adopts the position representative of a putatively homogeneous language community and enunciates to addressees who are also representative of a homogeneous language community. The term *monolingual address,* however, does not imply a social situation in which both the addresser and the addressee in a conversation belong to the same language; they believe they belong to different languages yet can still address each other monolingually.

**Translator: The Subject in Transit**
Is it possible to understand the act of translation outside monolingual address? To respond to this question, it may be helpful to consider the translator's position of address. When engaged in the task of translation, can she perform a speech act such as making a promise? Is the translator responsible for what she says while translating? Because of the translator's unavoidably ambiguous position, the answer too is ambiguous. Yes, she can make a promise, but only on behalf of someone else. She "herself" cannot make a promise. The translator is responsible for her translation but she cannot be held responsible for the pledges expressed in it, because she is not allowed to say what she means; she is required to say what she says without meaning it. In essence, the translator is someone who cannot say "I." Here the problem of the invariant message returns as the question of meaning, of what the translator "means" to say.

In relation to the source text, the translator seems to occupy the position of the addressee. She listens or reads what the original addresser enunciates. At the same time, however, there is no supposition that the addresser is speaking or writing to her. The addressee of the enunciation is not located where the translator is; in translation, the addressee is always located elsewhere. Here again the translator's positionality is inherently ambiguous: she is both an addressee and not an addressee. She cannot be the "you" to whom the addresser refers.

A similar disjunction can be observed in the enunciation of the target text—that is, in the translation. In relation to the audience of the target text, the translator seems to occupy the position of the addresser. The translator speaks or writes to the audience. But it is seemingly not the translator herself who speaks or writes to the addressee. The *I* uttered by the translator does not designate the translator herself but rather the subject of the original enunciation. And if the translator does indicate the subject of the translated enunciation by saying *I*—in a "translator's note," for example—she will then have to designate the original addresser as *he* or *she*.

In other words, in translation, the subject of the enunciation and the subject of the enunciated—the speaking I and the I that is signified—are not expected to coincide. The translator's desire is at least displaced, if not entirely dissipated, in the translated enunciation, if by *desire* one understands that what is signified by *I* in "my" utterance, ought to coincide with the supposedly concrete and unique—but imagined—existence of "me" (the desire expressed as "I want to be myself"). This is why the translator cannot be designated straightforwardly either as *I* or *you*: she disrupts the attempt to appropriate the relation of addresser and addressee as a *personal* relation between the first person and the second person. According to Émile Benveniste, only those directly addressing and those directly addressed can be called persons, whereas *he, she,* and *they* cannot be so designated (Benveniste, p. 224). Hence, the addresser, the translator, and the addressee cannot be persons simultaneously. The translator cannot be the first or second person, or even the third "person" undisruptively. Ineluctably, translation introduces an instability into the putatively *personal* relations among the agents of speech, writing, listening, and reading. The translator is internally split and multiple, devoid of a stable position. At best, she is *a subject in transit*.

In the first place, this is because the translator cannot be an "individual" in the sense of *individuum,* the undividable unit. In the second, it is because she is a *singular* that marks an elusive point of discontinuity in the social, even though translation is the practice of creating continuity from discontinuity. Translation is a *poietic* social practice that institutes a relation at the site of incommensurability. This is why the discontinuity inherent in translation would be completely repressed if one were to determine translation as the communication of information; the *ambiguity inherent in the translator's positionality* would have to be entirely overlooked as translation is grasped as the transfer of information.

The internal split within the translator demonstrates how the subject constitutes itself. In a sense, this internal split is homologous to what is known as the "fractured I." The temporality of "I speak" necessarily introduces an irreparable distance between the speaking I and the I signified, between the subject of the enunciation and the subject of the enunciated. The subject in the sense that I am here and now speaking designates the subject of the enunciation, but it does not signify it because every signifier of the subject of the enunciation may be lacking in the enunciated or the statement. In the case of translation, however, an ambiguity in the translator's personality marks the instability of the *we* as subject rather than the *I*, since the translator cannot be a unified and coherent personality in translation. This suggests a different attitude of address, namely, "heterolingual address" (Sakai, pp. i–xii)—that is, a situation in which one addresses oneself as a foreigner to another foreigner. Held captive in the regime of translation, however, the translator is supposed to assume the role of the

transcendent arbitrator, not only between the addresser and the addressee but also between their linguistic communities. As monolingual address, translation, as a process of creating continuity in discontinuity, is often replaced by the representation of translation in which translation is schematized according to the co-figurative communication model.

## Modernity and the Schema of Co-Figuration: A Genealogy of the Modern

Consider how translation is displaced by its representation and how collective subjectivity, such as national and ethnic subjectivity, is constituted in the representation of translation. Through the translator's labor, the incommensurable differences that call for the translator's service in the first place are negotiated. In other words, the work of translation is a practice by which the initial discontinuity between the addresser and the addressee is made continuous. In this respect translation is like other social practices; translation makes something representable out of an unrepresentable difference. Only retrospectively, therefore, can one recognize the initial incommensurability as a gap, crevice, or border between fully constituted entities, spheres, or domains. But when so represented, it is no longer an incommensurability. It is mapped onto a striated space, which may be segmented by national borders and other markers of collective (national, ethnic, racial, or "cultural") identification.

Incommensurable difference is more like a feeling prior to the explanation of how incommensurability occurred, and cannot be represented as a specific difference (in schemas of genera and species, for example) between two terms or entities. What makes it possible to represent the initial difference between one language unity and another as already determined is the work of translation itself. Hence the untranslatable, or what appears to be so, cannot exist prior to the enunciation of translation. It is translation that gives birth to the untranslatable. The untranslatable is as much a testimony to the sociality of the translator, whose elusive positionality reveals the presence of an aggregate community of foreigners between the addresser and the addressee, as the translatable itself. We fail to communicate because we are in common with one another. Community itself does not mean we share common ground. On the contrary, we are in community precisely because we are exposed to a forum where our differences and failure in communication can be manifest. Nevertheless, the translator's essential sociality with respect to the untranslatable is disregarded in monolingual address, and with the repression of this insight, monolingual address equates translation with the representation of translation.

When the temporality of translation by which the translator's disjunctive positionality manifests itself is erased, translation is displaced by the representation of translation. Because the disruptive and dynamic processes of translation are leveled out, the representation of translation makes possible the representation of ethnic or national subjects and, despite the presence of the translator, who is always ambiguous and disjunctive, translation as representation posits one language unity against another and one "cultural" unity against another. In this sense, the representation of translation transforms *difference in repetition* (Deleuze) into a *specific difference* between two particularities and serves to constitute the putative unities of national languages, thereby reinscribing the initial difference and incommensurability as a specific, or commensurate and conceptual, difference between two particular languages within the continuity of languages. As a result of this displacement, translation is represented as a form of communication between two fully circumscribed, different but comparable, language communities in which social antagonism and the various loci of difference are expunged.

The particular representation of translation as communication between two particular languages is no doubt a historical construct. Given the politico-social significance of translation, it is no accident that, historically, the regime of translation became widely accepted in many regions of the world, after the feudal order and its passive vassal subject gave way to the disciplinary order of the active citizen subject in the modern nation-state, to an order consisting of disciplinary regiments that Michel Foucault describes brilliantly. The regime of translation serves to reify national sovereignty. As Michael Hardt and Antonio Negri have argued, it makes "the *relation* of sovereignty into a *thing* (often by naturalizing it) and thus weed out every residue of social antagonism. The nation is a kind of ideological shortcut that attempts to free the concepts of sovereignty and modernity from the antagonism and crisis that define them" (Hardt and Negri, p. 95, italics in the original).

Kant thought of the schema as a "third thing" heterogeneous to either sensibility or understanding, in which an intuition (in sensibility) is subsumed under a concept (in understanding), and attributed it to the general faculty of imagination, a faculty to give a concept its figure or *Bild.* He called this operation of schema *schematism.* Following the Kantian schematism, the *poietic* technology embedded in the regime of translation that renders translation representable may be called "the schema of co-figuration." Since the practice of translation remains radically heterogeneous to the representation of translation, translation cannot always be represented as a communication between two clearly delineated ethno-linguistic unities. Rather, it was this particular representation of translation that gave rise to the possibility of figuring out the unity of ethnic or national language together with another language unity. Thanks to this co-figurative schematism, there emerges an ethno-linguistic unity as if it were a sensuous and unified thing hidden and dormant behind the surface of extensive variety. In other words, the schema of co-figuration is a technology by means of which an ethno-linguistic community is rendered representable, thereby constituting itself as a substratum upon which national sovereignty can be built. "People" is nothing but an idealization of this substratum.

This self-constitution of the nation does not proceed unitarily, but on the contrary, its figure constitutes itself only by making visible the figure of an other with which it engages in a relationship of translation. Precisely because the two nations are represented as equivalent and alike, however, it is possible to determine them as *conceptually different,* and their difference is construed as a *specific difference (diaphora)* between separate identities. Nevertheless, cultural difference, which calls for the work of a translator, is not a conceptual difference but an incommensurability. The relationship of the two terms as

equivalent and alike gives rise to the possibility of extracting an infinite number of distinctions between the two. Just as in the co-figuration of "the West and the Rest" by which the West represents itself, constituting itself by positing everything else as "the Rest," conceptual difference allows one term to be evaluated as superior to the other. This co-figurative comparison enables typical binary oppositions—such as the presence of scientific rationality versus its absence, the future-oriented spirit of progress versus the tradition-bound sense of social obligation, and internalization of religious faith and its accompanying secularism versus the inseparableness of the private and the public—to characterize the West and the Rest.

The "modern" is marked by the introduction of the schema of co-figuration, without which it is difficult to imagine a nation or ethnicity as a homogeneous sphere. The economy of the foreign—that is, how the foreign must be allocated in the production of the domestic and non-universal language—has played a decisive role in the *poietic*—and poetic—identification of national languages (Berman). Most conspicuously in eighteenth-century movements such as Romanticism in western Europe and *Kokugaku* (National Studies) in Japan, intellectual and literary maneuvers to invent, mythically and poetically, a national language were closely associated with a spiritual construction of a new identity that later naturalized national sovereignty. This substratum for the legitimization of national and popular sovereignty was put forward as a "natural" language specific to the "people," supposedly spoken by them in their everyday lives. Literary historians generally call this historical development "the emergence of the vernacular." With the irruption of the sphere of nearness—extensive obsessions with things of everydayness and experimental immediacy—in which the ordinary and the colloquial were celebrated, the status of "universal" languages such as Latin, literary Chinese, and Sanskrit was drastically and decisively altered. In their stead, languages emerged whose markers were ethnic and national—English, German, Japanese, Spanish and so forth—and the ancient canons were translated into these languages. For this reason, Martin Luther's German translation of the Bible and Motoori's Japanese phonetic translation of the *Kojiki* (Records of ancient matters) can be said to mark crucial steps in modernity. This emphasis on ordinary and colloquial languages was correlated with the reconception of translation and the schema of co-figuration.

Historically, how one represents translation does not only prescribe how we collectively imagine national communities and ethnic identities and how we relate individually to national sovereignty. It is also complicit with the discourse of the West and the Rest through which the colonial power relationship is continually fantasized and reproduced.

*See also* **Interpretation; Language and Linguistics; Language, Linguistics, and Literacy; Other, The, European Views of; Representation.**

**BIBLIOGRAPHY**
Benjamin, Walter. "The Task of The Translator." Translated by Harry Zohn, with a note by Steven Rendall. In *The Translation Studies Reader,* edited by Lawrence Venuti, 15–24. London: Routledge, 2000.

Benveniste, Émile. *Problems in General Linguistics.* Translated by Mary Elizabeth Meck. Coral Gables: University of Miami Press, 1971.

Berman, Antoine. *The Experience of the Foreign: Culture and Translation in Romantic Germany.* Translated by S. Heyvaert. Albany: State University of New York Press, 1992.

Deleuze, Gilles. *Difference and Repetition.* Translated by Paul Patton. New York: Columbia University Press, 1994.

Foucault, Michel. *Discipline and Punish.* Translated by Aln Sheridan. New York: Vintage Books, 1979.

Hardt, Michael, and Antonio Negri. *Empire.* Cambridge, Mass.: Harvard University Press, 2000.

Jakobson, Roman. "On Linguistic Aspects of Translation." In his *Selected Writings.* Vol. 2, 260–66. The Hague: Mouton, 1971.

Laca, Jacques. *Écrits.* Translated by Alan Sheridan. New York: W. W. Norton and Company, 1977.

Motoori, Norinaga. *The Kojiki-den.* Book 1. Translated by Ann Wehmeyer. Ithaca, N.Y.: East Asia Program, Cornell University, 1997.

Sakai, Naoki. *Translation and Subjectivity: On "Japan" and Cultural Nationalism.* Minneapolis: University of Minnesota Press, 1997.
———. *Voices of the Past: The Status of Language in Eighteenth-century Japanese Discourse.* Ithaca, N.Y.: Cornell University Press, 1992.

Venuti, Lawrence. *The Translator's Invisibility: A History of Translation.* London: Routledge, 1995.

*Naoki Sakai*

## TRANSNATIONALISM. *See* **Globalization.**

## TRAVEL FROM EUROPE AND THE MIDDLE EAST.

Travel, as a human activity, predates language. It should be no surprise, then, that some of the first ancient literary expressions from the European and African continents should use travel as a motif. Certainly the ancient Hebrew biblical narratives of Abraham, Isaac, Jacob, and Moses structure the lives of their subjects through travel. Greek and Roman epics—*The Odyssey* and *The Aeneid*—as well as the history of Thucydides, use travel as an important thematic element, connecting it with various aspects of conflict. Similarly, Herodotus (c. 484–c. 424 B.C.E.), in his historical, ethnographic, and geographic compendium, uses travel in part as his method of research. The Islamic tradition begins with epic travel—flight and return—continuing with pilgrimage, educational, and diplomatic travel. In the millennium and a half since, the motif of travel has attracted a number of images that structure our view of this basic human activity, images that appear in both fiction and nonfiction.

### Ancient and Medieval Travel: Epic Heroes, Pilgrims, and Merchants

The genre of epic structures the oldest European travel narratives extant, from the voyages of Ulysses to that of Beowulf. The epic as a form connects travel to conflict and cultural threat, as well as to the landscape of fantasy and to the epic hero. Just as the epic hero is larger and more marvelous than life, so the epic landscape is both marvelous and dangerous. The epic hero and those who accompany him are often engaged in activities that either preserve or extend the culture of which he is the ideal. Such an image of travel has little room for reflection or satiric treatment; the mood is one of high seriousness. The epic form is modified in the oldest Hebrew writings; there, the culture-creating protagonists become sometimes the focal point of narrative but always the recipients of divine directives regarding travel. Biblical travel is conceived in three ways: first, as travel toward a land of divine promise; second, as wandering to or in the land; and third, as exodus or flight. In the Islamic tradition, the travel of the prophet Muhammad contains the same elements of divine directive, flight, and return.

The rise of Christianity and Islam activates a second image associated with travel, that of pilgrimage. One could classify the ancient Hebrew narratives as pilgrimage, but the concept, which gains importance in the period from 800 to 1400 C.E. in Europe and Africa, involves other elements. Pilgrimage is conceived as reenactment; the pilgrim undertakes a sacred journey, the significance of which is primarily spiritual, as he or she visits sites important to sacred history. In the Christian and Islamic traditions, this sacred journey is conditioned by devotion and obedience. Medieval Christian tradition adds the element of veneration and indulgence: the idea that acts of veneration for holy relics and places could provide spiritual benefit can be traced back to the late classical period. But the explicit linking of acts of devotion with the remission of temporal punishment for sin only began with the First Crusade in 1095, when Pope Urban II announced the granting of indulgences to those who fought to regain the Christian holy shrines. Such a view, conditioned by conflict, both renders ambiguous the spiritual aspects of the journey and historically allows the symbolizing of acts of devotion. The act of pilgrimage also allows travelers to escape being accused of the sin of curiosity; travel for sightseeing is problematic in the Middle Ages, but travel for at least ostensibly spiritual reasons can sometimes escape this censure.

In medieval Europe, a mode of pilgrimage writing develops, in which certain items of information and structures of narration become standardized. This tradition approaches landscape and the journey in the following ways: first, the journey is conceived as outgoing; narratives focus on the hardships of the journey out and the travels between the holy places, instead of on the journey out and back. Second, the journey within the holy destination is organized in terms of "stations" or stopping places, often connected with specifically significant sites. These significant sites usually become connected allegorically with a variety of biblical significances. The twelfth-century pilgrimage guide writer Fetellus, for example, localizes a number of biblical references in one spot. When he describes the traditional hill of Christ's crucifixion in his narrative, he names this spot as the site on which Abraham sacrificed Isaac and as the place where Adam was buried (and resurrected by Christ's blood falling upon him). Furthermore, this site has significance for the future, being the place upon which Christ will return at the end of history. Specific physical characteristics of the site are used to bolster these allegorical accretions: the crack running through the rocks of the crucifixion hill is there because of the earth-rending strain of holding the cross. Other sites, from the city of Hebron to the Dead Sea, gain a number of allegorical significances based on their associations with the biblical narrative.

The third important type of travel, for the purposes of trade, had almost certainly been occurring concurrently with other forms of travel since the earliest human cultures. In Europe, commercial travel was seldom documented until well into the Middle Ages. By far the most important Continental writing about commercial travel was the narrative of Marco Polo, a Venetian who traveled to China and back during a twenty-four-year period, between 1271 and 1295. His writings were both widely publicized and widely ridiculed, as his European readers refused to believe the apparently miraculous accounts of the wealth, geographical wonders, and population of the Far East, as well as his account of offices he had held while in China. His ultimate nickname, Il Milione (The million), reflected the European public's sense that he had exaggerated the information that he brought back. The reaction to Marco Polo's narrative also points to the general reaction that hearers and readers in the Middle Ages expected from information derived through travel: generally they wanted to react with a sense of wonder and calculated disbelief to the tales brought back by far-flung narrators. This appetite for wonders can also be seen by the popularity of the information in the compendia of geographical and other lore compiled by such people as Vincent of Beauvais, the medieval encyclopedist (c. 1190–c. 1264).

### Renaissance Travel: Exploration and Empire
With the beginning of the early modern period, the primary image of travel gradually transforms from the traditional images of epic and pilgrimage into something new—exploration. There is a sense in which exploration retains the heroic character of epic travel: it often highlights conflict, whether conflict with the elements and a hostile landscape or conflict with the other cultures encountered. But explorers, while at some level imperialists, are, during the early period of exploration at least, not really larger-than-life figures. The curiosity about geographic features and other cultures ceases to be a minor sin and becomes the animating reason for travel. The explorer travels expressly to find new lands and peoples, desiring to trade with other cultures or to exploit the riches of new lands. In the initial European encounter with America, Christopher Columbus was very much the medieval man, looking during his voyage for the lost earthly paradise, said to be located in the west. The Spanish conquistadors saw themselves as feudal overlords of subject peoples, and conducted their conquests accordingly. Narrators of their voyages over the ocean and over land contributed to a perspective on the native civilizations they found there, a perspective that inherited the sense of wonder found in medieval travel narratives but also a less benign questioning of the humanity of the others who were encountered. Seeing the native civilizations as strange and wondrous tended to dehumanize the people encountered. But the New World yielded another, more tangible, reward to the explorers—the gold and silver of the Americas. Ultimately all the European exploratory ventures took part in a quest for resources, either precious metals or the natural resources of the lands discovered.

Exploration narratives were writings in search of a genre. It was important, for the first time, that each explorer "answere for himselfe, justifie his owne reportes, and stand accountable for his owne doings," according to England's greatest Renaissance collector and travel narrative editor, Richard Hakluyt, because these reports were becoming the guidebooks for colonists and pioneers. Curiosity about people, languages, and geography became a virtue, and truthfulness became important.

### Fact and Fiction in Travel Narratives
Travel narratives allowed ancient and medieval audiences to escape through literary fantasy and compare their culture to different ones. But the wondrous living denizens of these narratives—people whose heads grew beneath their shoulders, people who lived on odors, tribes of Amazon women—would be proven nonexistent. In their place, exploration narratives would put the actual wonders of spices, gold, silver, canoes, and differing customs. Before the early modern period, the veracity of travel narratives was not a serious issue because travel was a rare event and large-scale cross-cultural contacts relatively few. The few medieval narratives that realistically recounted diplomatic missions to the invading Mongol hordes during the thirteenth and fourteenth centuries were not widely known.

Thus, though medieval travelers were not generally believed, veracity was trivial. The situation changed in the fifteenth century with the first seaborne expeditions around the African continent and to the Americas. Though the earliest sea voyagers carried medieval descriptions of the places for which they searched, it soon became apparent that these descriptions were untrustworthy. Columbus carried on his first American voyage a copy of the fourteenth-century *Travels of Sir John Mandeville,* one of the most popular pilgrimage and travel narratives of the time, hoping to use its description to find the scriptural earthly paradise. Richard Hakluyt reprinted a Latin version of Mandeville's *Travels* in the first edition of his collection *The Principall Navigations* (1589). He most probably dropped it from the second edition of the collection because of its falsehoods.

Travel as exploration demanded a different set of criteria; instead of wonder and the imaginative, the requirements of the new travel narratives involved reliability and exactness of detail. This demand for descriptive exactness contributed to an extension of the exploratory image in travel writing into the twentieth century. Though exploration as an image of travel connotes objectivity and exactness, it is clear that this image is affected by the historical concommitants of conquest and imperialism. Certainly the information the explorers recount is conditioned by their Eurocentric perspective.

As representatives of the ascendant European culture and its political hegemony spread out across the globe, the amount of travel writing greatly expanded. Women undertook journeys in support of spouses or independently and related their experiences exploring and encountering other cultures, often in epistolary form. Lady Mary Wortley Montagu traveled to Turkey with her husband, a diplomat, between 1716 and 1718. Her letters closely observe the cultures through which she passed. It is clear, as well, that she is familiar with the male

## ISLAMIC TRAVELERS

Islamic travelers voyaged through Africa and into the Far East using established overland and sea routes from northern Africa and the Mideast. Routes were established in the Mediterranean to Spain and indirectly to the rest of Europe; overland, the great Silk Road reached into China; by sea, Arab traders reached India.

Of two important early Muslim travelers, Ibn Fadlan (Ahmad ibn Fadlan ibn al-'Abbas ibn Rashid ibn Hammad) and Ibn Jubayr (Abu al-Husayn Muhammad ibn Ahmad Jubayr), little is known. Ibn Fadlan includes little description of himself in his *risala*, or epistle, describing a diplomatic mission from the caliph of Baghdad in 921 to the Bulgarians of the Volga. Ibn Jubayr, a Spanish Arab traveler during the twelfth century, voyaged around the Mediterranean basin and through Mecca and Medina on a journey that he recorded in *rihla* form; it is the only journey for which he wrote a narrative of three that he made. What is known of his second journey is that he composed a poem celebrating Saladin's victory at Hittin.

The *rihla*, a genre of travel description in Arabic developed by various Islamic authors, encompassed various sorts of journey: pilgrimage, travel for learning, or travel for discovery. One of the greatest of the travelers of the Middle Ages, Shams al-Din ibn Battuta (1304–c. 1368), composed a *rihla* called *Tuhfat al-nuzzar fi ghara'ib al-amsar wa 'aja'ib al-asfar* (A feast for the eyes [presenting] exotic places and marvelous travels). This work so epitomized the genre of *rihla* that Ibn Battuta's work is often simply known by that name—the *Rihla*. Like Marco Polo, Ibn Battuta

and his account were greeted with skepticism by his contemporaries, including the great Islamic historian Ibn Khaldun. Also like Marco Polo, contemporary scholarship indicates that he was essentially truthful in most of his account. All in all, Ibn Battuta's account is a compendious store of information about the Muslim world of his day.

Leo Africanus (al-Hasan ibn Muhammad al-Wassan az-Zayyati), born in Islamic Spain, is one of the most important European writers about Africa between 1500 and 1800. His description of sub-Saharan and northern Africa, *Descrittione dell'Africa* (Description of Africa), was completed in 1529, after he had been captured by pirates and had converted to Christianity. His writing falls into the Arabic tradition of geography rather than into the tradition of the *rihla* account. Since, as a stranger in a different culture, he had no access to the traditional works of Arabic geography, he needed primarily to rely upon his memory to write his work. This necessity has led many readers to identify his *Description* more with genres of travel writing than geography.

One of the masters of *rihla* writing was the seventeenth-century Sufi scholar and poet Abu Salim Abd Allah ibn Muhammad al-Ayyashi, who left a detailed account of a journey that includes elements of pilgrimage and exploration. After a journey overland from his native Morocco to Cairo, al-Ayyashi continued his pilgrimage to Mecca and Medina. He was as interested in the people and customs that he saw as he was in the holy sites that he visited. His narrative makes clear the interconnected world of North African Islam and that of the Mideast.

tradition of travel writing, because she often provides a contrasting female perspective on her travel experiences, as do many female travel authors of the fifteenth through the eighteenth centuries. Mary Wollstonecraft's epistolary journal of her travels to Scandinavia in 1795, in the company of only her maid and infant daughter, was influenced (like Lady Wortley Montagu's) by the earlier letters of the French Madame de Sévigné. In general, the specifically female mode of travel writing has much in common with the parallel tradition of women's autobiography.

Men, meanwhile, continued the exploratory movement, this time under the aegis of scientific and sociological investigation. The narrative of David Livingstone in Africa in the mid-nineteenth century was constructed as an exploratory and imperialistic epic, while Mungo Park's narratives of Africa in the 1790s and Alexander von Humboldt's narratives of scientific discovery on the American continent from 1799 to 1804 combine both epic hardships and reports of important scientific investigations. Sir Richard Burton, one of the Victorian era's most intrepid travelers, hazarded his life in journeys

---

### EARLY MODERN EUROPEAN TRAVEL COLLECTIONS

The early modern period in Europe (roughly 1450–1700) was not only a time of intense exploratory activity but also a time in which a number of editors and collectors strove to collect, organize, and distribute overviews of nonfictional writing about travel. Nationalistic impulses as well as the need for information drove a number of editors between 1550 and 1650 to collect narratives.

Giovanni Ramusio (1485–1557) collected and translated the works in *Delle navigationi et viaggi* (On navigations and travels) between 1550 and 1559. In this work, he intended to produce a new kind of compendium, an overall survey of important geographical treatises, organized by global region. It contains writing by Leo Africanus, Antonio Pigafetta (who took part in Magellan's circumnavigation), and Amerigo Vespucci, among others.

Richard Hakluyt (c. 1552–1616) compiled, edited, and translated *The Principal Navigations, Voyages, Traffiques, and Discoveries of the English Nation* in two editions: 1589 and 1598–1600. Though both editions concentrated on English discoveries, the second edition especially had a larger scope, to provide information for English explorers and traders about all the areas in which they might have interest. Organized both chronologically and regionally, the collection provides a comprehensive look at the history of exploration and trade to the point of publication, insofar as Hakluyt was able to obtain information.

Samuel Purchas, a clergyman originally interested in a universal history of religions told through travel narratives, purchased Richard Hakluyt's literary effects around 1620. From it and his own collecting, Purchas compiled a collection called *Hakluytus Posthumous, or Purchas his Pilgrimes,* in 1625. Though organized in much the same way as Hakluyt's collection, Purchas's editorial methods and aims are quite different. He is interested as much in the edification and educational benefits of travel as he is in accurate information about exotic locations.

The *Collectiones peregrinationum in Indiam orientalem et Indiam occidentalem,* produced by the de Bry family at Frankfurt (begun by Théodor de Bry, but brought to conclusion by his sons; 1590–1634), enhanced narratives of travel with high-quality engravings.

---

through the Islamic world, including making a disguised pilgrimage to Mecca, bringing back the first eyewitness European description of that great journey (*Personal Narrative of a Pilgrimage to El-Medinah and Meccah;* 1855–1856). Travel writing of the exploratory type thus takes on a more personal and literary character as time goes on.

### Modern Images of Travel: Tourist or Ironist

Tourism began in the early modern period as travel for education. At this time, travel was seen as an important pedagogical capstone. In England, such important social and literary figures as Sir Philip Sidney (1554–1586) took the "grand tour" (an extended visit to important cities and courts of continental Europe) as an appropriate way to conclude their education in the arts of politics and culture. Ideally, the grand tour introduced its practitioner to the languages and polite societies of the Continent; practically, a number of English critics of this type of travel complained that it led to students coming back with French affectations and fashions, German manners, and Italian diseases. The playwright Thomas Nashe penned an ingenious satiric journey for his picaresque traveler Jack Wilton in *The Unfortunate Traveler* (1594). In the realm of nonfiction, the Oxford-educated eccentric Thomas Coryate penned his voluminous *Crudities* (1611), in which he paints himself as the innocent abroad, coming into contact with various kinds of picaresque adventures while undertaking a perhaps not-so-grand tour through the Continent. That Coryate had elements of the explorer in himself as well is evident from his death in India while on a more far-flung journey. George Sandys's *Relation of a Journey Begun Anno Domini 1610* combines the structures of pilgrimage narrative with the motivations of the practitioner of the grand tour.

During the eighteenth and early nineteenth centuries, travel became more consciously literary. Such figures as Samuel Johnson and James Boswell melded the tour of the countryside with autobiography, biography, and the essay, while Romantic period authors in Britain and on the Continent celebrated the imaginative potential of journeys through the natural world. This sort of travel often allied itself to the emerging genre of the novel, in which the physical journeys of various protagonists were paralleled by their interior development, sometimes with comic results.

However, travel could never fully become tourism until the level of danger inherent in the activity had diminished. One could say that tourism was born in Europe with the guides of Baedecker during the Victorian period and in America with the closing of the frontier in the late 1800s. But there had always been a sense of conflict between the "true" traveler and the mob of others; as early as the fourteenth century, Margery Kempe, the English mystic and pilgrim, lamented the motivations (curiosity and good fellowship) of her fellow pilgrims, to the point that her traveling companions attempted to strand her in Rome because of her constant moral hectoring. But with the advent of technology, one of the cachets of travel, its attendant dangers, had been removed. Thus, with the rise of tourism, a new tension arose in the image of travel: that between the true traveler and the tourist. While tourists stick to the instructions of Baedecker and travel in herds, the true traveler takes the road untraveled (at least by Europeans).

For literary travelers, this tension between tourism and other forms of travel produced much fruit. It would probably be a mistake to count various tourist guides as literary productions, but traveling authors have gained much ironic material by their appropriation of and resistance to the activities and material of tourism. During the early to mid-twentieth century, as well, there were still substantial portions of the globe generally off limits to tourists for political or other reasons. Modern authors tended to seek out just those sorts of marginal journeys.

Between the world wars, literary travelers often took the pose of ironists or reporters, sometimes espousing specific ideological points of view and sometimes using the profits gained by writing travel volumes to finance more "serious" literary pursuits. The English authors Graham Greene and Evelyn Waugh traveled extensively: Waugh used his journeys in the Mediterranean and South America as well as his stint as a reporter in Africa to provide material for some of his satiric novels. André Gide's travels in Africa and the Mideast animated his sense of the ideal artistic life: to construct a careful equilibrium between the exotic and the familiar.

The contemporary literary traveler becomes a complexly folded narrator, taking an ironic stance, not just toward other cultures but often toward other travelers and even to him- or herself. Contemporary travel writing partakes of many genres and modes: novelistic, picaresque, satiric, and contemplative. Even the ancient motif of flight and return is explored as a means of self-discovery. For postmodernity, travel becomes a means of self-discovery or self-exploration.

*See also* **Empire and Imperialism; Eurocentrism; Orientalism; Other, The, European Views of.**

**BIBLIOGRAPHY**

PRIMARY SOURCES

Casas, Bartolomé de las. *De unico vocationis.* Edited by Helen R. Parish and translated by Francis Sullivan. New York: Paulist Press, 1992.

Cortés, Hernán. *Letters from Mexico.* Edited and translated by A. R. Pagden. New York: Grossman, 1971.

Gide, André. *Amyntas.* Translated by Richard Howard. New York: Ecco, 1988.

Ibn Battuta. *Ibn Battuta in Black Africa.* Edited and translated by Said Hamdun and Noël King. 2nd ed. Princeton, N.J.: M. Weiner, 1994.

Ibn Jubayr. *The Travels of Ibn Jubayr.* Translated by R. J. C. Broadhurst. London: J. Cape, 1952.

Montagu, Mary Wortley. *Embassy to Constantinople: The Travels of Lady Mary Wortley Montagu.* Edited by Christopher Pick, with an introduction by Dervla Murphy. London: Century, 1988.

Polo, Marco. *The Travels of Marco Polo.* Edited by Ronald Latham. New York: Viking, 1958.

Pratt, Mary Louise. *Imperial Eyes: Travel Writing and Transculturation.* London and New York: Routledge, 1992.

Waugh, Evelyn. *When the Going Was Good.* Boston: Little, Brown, 1947.

Wollstonecraft, Mary. *Letters Written during a Short Residence in Sweden, Norway, and Denmark.* Edited by Carol H. Poston. Lincoln: University of Nebraska Press, 1976.

SECONDARY SOURCES

Campbell, Mary B. *The Witness and the Other World: Exotic European Travel Writing, 400–1600.* Ithaca, N.Y.: Cornell University Press, 1988.

Fussell, Paul. *Abroad: British Literary Traveling between the Wars.* Oxford: Oxford University Press, 1980.

Howard, Donald R. *Writers and Pilgrims: Medieval Pilgrimage Narratives and their Posterity.* Berkeley: University of California Press, 1980.

Speake, Jennifer, ed. *Literature of Travel and Exploration: An Encyclopedia.* 3 vols. New York: Fitzroy Dearborn, 2003.

*James P. Helfers*

**TREATY.** In modern diplomatic practice, a treaty is a formal written agreement between states (though recently also designating agreements with and between international organizations), which is legally binding under international law. Treaties differ from a variety of other international agreements like declarations, memorandums of understanding, and gentlemen's agreements, which only create moral and political obligations, nonbinding commitments, or what has been branded as "soft law." The Helsinki Final Act of the Conference on Security and Cooperation in Europe (1975) is an example of an important international agreement that was deliberately drafted in a way that was legally nonbinding to the parties at the time, circulated at the United Nations but deliberately not registered with the Secretariat. In legal jargon, and as codified in the preamble as well as Article 26 of the Vienna Convention on the Law of Treaties (1969), a treaty, unlike other international agreements, comes under "the fundamental principle" of *pacta sunt servanta.* This Latin phrase means that "agreements must be observed," unless forced upon or concluded in bad faith. *Pacta sunt servanta* is a Ciceronian principle that has been selectively and problematically appropriated by modern treaty law. In *De officiis* (3.24), Cicero (106–43 B.C.E.) speaks extensively of ethical conduct and makes no distinction between agreements and promises (*pacta et promissa*) in his meditation on the matter. By contrast, international legal discourse allows for agreements that do not follow the *pacta sunt servanta* rule, in turn providing for diplomatic flexibility and a bypassing of ethics. This makes it possible to daily exchange agreements and promises that have shades of legality, publicly simulating commitment, but in practice retaining opt-outs and remaining legally unenforceable.

## Linguistic Issues

Although the word *treaty* can be etymologically traced back to the Latin *tractus,* meaning treatment, handling, discussion, and management, there was no Latin word with that root having the notion of an (international) agreement. If anything, *tractus* sometimes had the sense of a disagreement, of a violent handling of affairs, such as the dragging by the hair of the priestess of Apollo. A common Latin word for treaty is *foedus*—interestingly a word that also meant the unseemly, horrible, and detestable, probably depicting in the mind of the users the forced circumstances and unholy power deals that led to the conclusion of some. Another Latin word for treaty is *conventio,* from which the English word *convention* derives, a term currently used as a synonym for *treaty,* especially when following long multilateral negotiations. *Conventio* has in addition the meaning of an assembly and is a word that literally translates *sumbasis,* an ancient Greek word for treaty. *Sumbainō* had the meaning of coming to an agreement but also of walking together, just like in the Latin *convenio.* Walking together along the same path or in the same direction is a good metaphor for agreement, though in practice it was also meant literally, like the walking together of comrades to the assembly, battlefield, or exile. There were other words for treaty in ancient Greek, such as *sumphōnia,* the harmony of speaking with a "common voice" about an issue, depicting people in great solidarity and symphony, or *sunthēkē,* which meant literally the composition of words, emphasizing the textual or synthetic sense of an agreement. But the most formal and solemn treaty was called *spondē,* meaning literally "libation," which included the calling of the gods to witness the treaty and the taking of the oaths that sanctified it. Unlike other agreements, the breaking of a *spondē* was not just an illegal or immoral act, but a sacrilege.

The move to the term *treaty* signifies a change from the usual metaphors of agreement but also a turn toward secularization in international relations and law. In the sense of a contract between states the first recorded use of *treete* is in 1430. But as a technical term of international law the word is commonly employed from the end of the seventeenth century onward (*Oxford English Dictionary*). Interestingly, the introduction of the term follows the end of the Thirty Years' War and the conclusion of the Treaty of Westphalia (1648), which is supposed to have secularized international norms and practice and provided the foundation of the modern (European) interstate system.

Typically, the only state that made and still makes the point of not using the name *treaty* for its legally binding international agreements is the Holy See. In diplomatic practice, bilateral treaties signed with the Vatican are called *concordats,* and canonists have gone to great pains to show that the "nature of concordats" bears practical similarities—but is not identical—to that of treaties. A concordat refers to a cordial agreement, a union of wills, the successful meeting of hearts and minds in Christian harmony. The concordat is supposed to pass its provisions spiritually, requires no diplomatic "handling," and its conclusion is avoided by the Holy See if it foresees complications in the ratification process from the other side. It is a euphemism through which papal treaty practice is rendered sui generis, supposed always to operate in concord, thus rhetorically separating itself from the worldly bargaining and crude pursuit of national interest associated with conventional treatymaking. Note also that in concordat practice, the Holy See emulates the discourse of the new covenant, which in Christian cosmology constitutes "the treaty of treaties," rendering all other sacred or secular agreements false or insignificant by comparison. It was the messianic advent of Jesus Christ that brought forth the "new covenant," bypassing and superceding the collective oath of the faithful to keep the "old covenant." As taken up in the Epistle to the Hebrews—which is precisely a call to reject the old and accept the new covenant—the old covenant requires command ethics and rabbinic enforcement, whereas the new one inscribes the divine laws in the minds and hearts of the people in concordat style (see sidebar).

The story of rendering the old covenant obsolete following the declaration of a momentous happening or new revelation has ironically established a pattern in secular treaty law, and specifically in the employment of the principle of *clausula rebus sic stantibus,* the "clause of things standing thus." This clause renders a treaty obsolete if there is a significant change in the conditions under which it was first concluded. The principle is a late-sixteenth-century invention coined by Alberico Gentili (1552–1608), a Protestant theologian and international jurist, in *De iure belli libri tres.* By mixing religious and legal discourse, oath-taking and treaty (*foedus*) ratification, Gentili suggests that there is in every treaty a silent assumption, an understanding (*intelligitur*) or mental reservation (*subintelligi*) of a *clausula rebus sic stantibus* (pp. 244–245, 599). This is only the case among Christian rulers, for Gentili doubts the legal durability of treaties concluded with untrustworthy infidel rulers (*nec fidere infidelibus potes*) on scriptural qua moral grounds: "For although the impious oath of an infidel may be accepted, yet what trust can be put in an unbeliever" (p. 660). That a tacit understanding of termination exists when circumstances fundamentally change reinforces the privilege of "mortal gods," but highly complicates the binding status of treaties between them. Not surprisingly, in actual diplomatic practice, statesmen from Otto von Bismarck (1815–1898) to Woodrow Wilson (1856–1924) considered the denouncement of or abrogation from a treaty as the solemn and inalienable right of state sovereignty. Taken to its logical conclusion, *clausula rebus sic standibus* poses a fundamental challenge to the principle of *pacta sunt servanta,* the treaty's defining characteristic. Still, the *rebus sic standibus* principle became part of customary international law and was codified—albeit in a more restrictive form because of its common abuse—in the Vienna Convention on the Law of Treaties (Article 62).

## Contexts

Examining how the concept of treaty developed as a basic form of inter- and cross-cultural handling requires consideration of

---

## COVENANTS OLD AND NEW

Had that first covenant been faultless, there would have been no occasion to look for a second to replace it. But God finds fault with his people when he says, "The time is coming, says the Lord, when I shall conclude a new covenant with the house of Israel and the house of Judah. It will not be like the covenant I made with their forefathers when I took them by the hand to lead them out of Egypt; because they did not abide by the terms of that covenant, and so I abandoned them, says the Lord. For this is the covenant I shall make with Israel after those days, says the Lord: I shall set my laws in their understanding and write them on their hearts; I shall be their God, and they will be my people. They will not teach one another, each saying to his fellow-citizen and his brother, "Know the Lord!" For all of them will know me, high and low alike; I shall pardon their wicked deeds, and their sins I shall remember no more." By speaking of a new covenant, he has pronounced the first one obsolete; and anything that is becoming obsolete and growing old will shortly disappear.

SOURCE: Hebrews 8:7–13, in *The Revised English Bible with the Apocrypha.*

---

its ideological affinities to the concept of trade. These affinities are lexically quite striking, more so in the French words for treaty and trade, *traité* and *traite,* respectively. This is not surprising when one recalls how the conclusion of treaties was an important means through which Western trade expanded, initially in the East and then globally. During this period we saw the development of the terms "treaty port" and "treaty national." Treaty ports were established all over the coasts of East Asia and along navigable waterways too, through treaties between Western nations and the rulers of China, Japan, Korea, and Siam. The treaty ports regime allowed for the establishment of self-administered foreign settlements for the purposes of trade, settlements that enjoyed varying degrees of autonomy. The main provision was that foreign or treaty nationals enjoyed extraterritoriality and were therefore deemed to be outside the jurisdiction of the country they actually resided in, thus being legally accountable only to their respective consular courts. Though treaty ports and nationals were not limited to the east coast of Asia, and could be found also in the Ottoman Empire and Morocco, it was in China that they reached unparalleled proportions to the bitterness of the local elite that was forced to capitulate. There was a time that up to eighteen countries, not only Western powers but also Mexico, Brazil, and Peru, signed such treaties with China, in the first instance for the promotion of trade, but in the longer term infiltrating the region culturally and politically through missionaries and consuls.

In the sense of "worldly handling," treaties were also used as an instrument for colonial expansion. Note, parenthetically, that formal treaties were not always employed, especially with regard to the colonization of Africa, or the Spanish conquests of America, which were "legalized" through the Papal Bull *Inter caetera* (1493). The latter gave the "illustrious sovereigns" of Castile the exclusive right to acquire all the land they had discovered or might discover in the future one hundred leagues west of the Azores and Cape Verde islands. In terms of local instruments, the Spanish morally and practically dispossessed indigenous peoples through a legal caricature, the *Requerimiento,* a Eurocentric and Christocentric document on the history and state of the world, read to the natives and asking them to accept it by submitting to Spanish sovereignty or be made to submit. Nonetheless, treaties with the natives were often employed by colonial powers when commercial, political, or military interests so demanded. Such treaties were textually very basic, written in paternalistic discourse, and indirectly legitimated colonial occupation and governance in exchange for vague promises of protection of native life, possession, and culture. Their current "anomalous" status in terms of legal claims and retrospective enforcement has become a hotly contested issue in, among other places, North America, Australia, and New Zealand.

Perhaps a paradigmatic treaty between a colonial power and an indigenous community is the Treaty of Waitangi (1840), concluded between Britain and the Maori chiefs of New Zealand (see sidebar). This treaty is interesting because it has been retrospectively enforced, albeit reluctantly and selectively, through a 1975 New Zealand Act of Parliament and currently forms the basis of a number of claims by Maori groups for partial restitution and nondiscrimination. Still, the treaty's terms and processes expose the catachrestic political environment within which colonial treaty-making was taking place. For a start, there are significant differences between the English and

## THE TREATY OF WAITANGI, 1840

Victoria, the Queen of England, in her concern to protect the chiefs and subtribes of New Zealand and in her desire to preserve their chieftainship and their lands to them and to maintain peace and good order considers it just to appoint an administrator one who will negotiate with the people of New Zealand to the end that their chiefs will agree to the Queen's Government being established over all parts of this land and (adjoining) islands and also because there are many of her subjects already living on this land and others yet to come. So the Queen desires to establish a government so that no evil will come to Maori and European living in a state of lawlessness. So the Queen has appointed me, William Hobson, a captain in the Royal Navy to be Governor for all parts of New Zealand (both those) shortly to be received by the Queen and (those) to be received hereafter and presents to the chiefs of the Confederation chiefs of the subtribes of New Zealand and other chiefs these laws set out here.

### The First

The chiefs of the Confederation and all the chiefs who have not joined that Confederation give absolutely to the Queen of England for ever the complete government over their land.

### The Second

The Queen of England agrees to protect the chiefs, the subtribes and all the people of New Zealand in the unqualified exercise of their chieftainship over their lands, villages and all their treasures. But on the other hand the Chiefs of the Confederation and all the Chiefs will sell land to the Queen at a price agreed to by the person owning it and by the person buying it (the latter being) appointed by the Queen as her purchase agent.

### The Third

For this agreed arrangement therefore concerning the Government of the Queen, the Queen of England will protect all the ordinary people of New Zealand and will give them the same rights and duties of citizenship as the people of England.

(Signed) W. HOBSON

Consul and Lieutenant-Governor

So we, the chiefs of the Confederation and of the subtribes of New Zealand meeting here at Waitangi having seen the shape of these words which we accept and agree to record our names and our marks thus.

Was done at Waitangi on the sixth of February in the year of our Lord 1840.

SOURCE: Literal translation of the Maori text of the Treaty as proposed by Sir Hugh Kawharu; quoted from Ian Brownlie, *Treaties and Indigenous Peoples*, pp. 6–7.

the Maori texts of the treaty as well as differences in the understanding of the concepts used within. The English text included a provision that the Maori chiefs were "claiming authority over the Tribes and Territories which are specified after our respective names," a passage that is missing from the Maori text. The Maori translations for "government" (*kawanatanga*) did not have the Western conception of the exercise of sovereignty, nor did "rights and duties" (*tikanga*) have the notion of the pursuit of individual claims and obligations outside the remit of local custom (see www.archives.govt.nz/holdings/treaty_frame.html). There are also variations between the original Maori text and the eight copies in Maori opened for signature. The more than five hundred signatures to the treaty were a "cumulative process," added by different chiefs on different copies at different locations in New Zealand. In addition, not all copies bear a government seal. Some chiefs signed on unknown dates and without any witnesses. Some signatories have not been identified. Others signed without any clarification on the text of what representative authority they had, if any. The "Confederation of the Chiefs" referred to in the treaty was instigated by the British Resident in 1835 and only covered the north of the country. What is more, some important chiefs and tribes rejected the treaty and refused to sign, yet found themselves bound by it. As a leading legal authority implies, even using the most "generous" and "creative" interpretation of the provisions of the treaty, the Maori people cannot overcome the biases of the initial colonial policy through which they were "legally" dispossessed of their lands and polities (Brownlie). Ironically, recent human rights treaties of which they are not a party may provide a better basis for recognition of their claims than the treaty they signed as "independent" and "sovereign" people. In practice, of course, indigenous groups use a combination of the original bilateral and recent multilateral treaties to support their claims.

## Jurisprudence

Such cases illustrate that the modern idea of treaty developed within but also beyond the parameters of international legal history. In global practice, and from a non-Western perspective, treaties of particular historical periods could be seen as instruments for the aggressive promotion of commercial and imperial interests. In this sense, their primary aim was less the creation of legally binding commitments and more the economic and political infiltration of territories whose population status was legally defined through the treaty in ways that made this possible. As unequal devices and cover-ups through which Western global hierarchy was legitimated and reinforced, such historical treaties provide an antinomy to their conventional legal purpose as currently understood. Yet there are specific conceptual and practical limitations that need to—and perhaps cannot—be overcome in transforming a treaty into a politically neutral instrument. For example, as the Vienna Convention on the Law of Treaties (Article 2.1a) and treaty specialists outline, the designation of an agreement as a "treaty" does not in itself render it into a treaty, if written in contrary spirit and terminology. Similarly, the designation of an agreement by a nontreaty name (including memorandum of understanding) does not mean that it is automatically not a treaty, if parties textually display intention to be bound, yet decide not to go through the usual legal motions. In short, almost anything is technically possible given that the status of international agreements, in the final analysis, always depends on the definition whims of sovereign agents. That is why legal attempts to progressively develop the concept of treaty by extending it to all kinds of agreements that create binding obligations, and thus challenging the devious uses of "soft law," may be important but can only go so far. Soft law is an expedient diplomatic practice that is likely to continue, exploiting the space between the "hard" obligations of treaty making and the dubious legality of nontreaty commitments, "creatively" mixing the two when politically necessary, establishing concomitant duties of varying degrees. This is not to belittle the usefulness and importance of treaties in creating contractual obligations that can be recognized if parties to a treaty agree (a current prerequisite under international law) to take disputes over validity and interpretation before an international tribunal or the International Court of Justice. It should be remembered, however, that treaties, like the one done in Waitangi, have also been an instrument to obliterate an international legal personality and deny an international *locus standi,* by creating internal rather than external treaty obligations, which can always be bypassed by new domestic law. From this perspective, as a means of both constituting and erasing international legal subjectivity, treaties have been essential in reproducing state sovereignty, through which humans invariably benefit or suffer.

*See also* **International Order; Peace; War.**

## BIBLIOGRAPHY

Aust, Anthony. *Modern Treaty Law and Practice.* Cambridge, U.K.: Cambridge University Press, 2000.

Brownlie, Ian. *Treaties and Indigenous Peoples.* Oxford: Clarendon, 1992.

Cicero. *De officiis.* Translated by Walter Miller. London: Heinemann, 1913.

Deloria, Vine, and David E. Wilkins. *Tribes, Treaties, and Constitutional Tribulations.* Austin: University of Texas Press, 1999.

Fairbank, John King. *Trade and Diplomacy on the China Coast: The Opening of Treaty Ports, 1842–1854.* Cambridge, Mass.: Harvard University Press, 1964.

Gentili, Alberico. *De iure belli libri tres.* Translated by John C. Rolfe. Oxford: Clarendon, 1933.

Herodotus. *Histories.* Rev. ed. Translated by Alfred Denis Godley. Cambridge, Mass.: Harvard University Press, 1938.

Hillgenberg, Hartmut. "A Fresh Look at Soft Law." *European Journal of International Law* 10, no. 3 (1999): 499–516.

Klabbers, Jan. *The Concept of Treaty in International Law.* Boston: Kluwer, 1996.

Ovid. *Metamorphoses.* Rev. ed. Translated by Frank Justus Miller. Cambridge, Mass.: Harvard University Press, 1984.

*The Revised English Bible with the Apocrypha,* Oxford: Oxford University Press, 1989.

Satow, Ernest. *A Guide to Diplomatic Practice.* London: Longmans, 1957.

Sinclair, I. M. *Vienna Convention on the Law of Treaties.* Manchester, U.K.: Manchester University Press, 1984.

*Costas M. Constantinou*

**TRIBALISM, MIDDLE EAST.** The term *tribe,* derived from the Latin *tribus,* refers to a group of persons forming a community and claiming descent from a common ancestor. In the Middle East and North Africa, unlike many other parts of the world, claiming tribal affiliation often positively affirms community, identity, and belonging. In the mid- to late twentieth century, nationalist leaders in some regions rejected claims to tribal identity as "primitive" or potentially divisive to national unity. In the early twenty-first century in Morocco, Yemen, and Jordan, tribal affiliations figure implicitly in electoral politics in many regions, although other aspects of personal and collective identity also come into play. In the Iraq ruled by Saddam Hussein (1979–2003), the mention in public of one's tribal identity, outlawed in the 1980s in an effort to forge national identity, crept back into common usage and regime practice by the mid-1990s. Tribal identities remain important in many regions of the Middle East. They provide the basis for many forms of communal and political solidarity, although never exclusive ones, in many parts of the Arabian peninsula, Iraq, Jordan, Syria, among Arabs in Israel, and in the Palestinian areas.

## Tribes in Seventh-Century Arabia

Tribal identities in the Middle East are best seen in the context of the wider social and economic networks in which they have played a part, from ancient empires to the present. Tribal, kinship, and genealogical identities also profoundly influenced religious and political formations in earlier periods of the Middle East. For example, studies of ancient Judaism now also take tribal relations more into account than did earlier accounts that relied primarily on textual exegesis. In all these cases, however, alternative forms of social and political identity were never entirely absent.

For example, in the Arabian peninsula at the time of the advent of Islam in 622 C.E., social position in both oasis towns and their hinterlands depended foremost on overlapping ties of family, kinship, and tribe. In this context, Islam offered a new form of belonging, the "firmest tie" in the language of the Koran (2: 256), binding believers to God and giving them a sense of individual responsibility. The Koran morally sanctions ties to family, kin, and tribe but the community of Muslims (Ar., *umma*), united in submission to the one God, takes precedence.

The sense of belonging as individuals to the community of Muslims as the principal social and religious identity broke with the primary loyalties of the pre-Islamic era, but in practice tribal structure and claimed descent remained essential to understanding political, social, and economic action from later historical periods to the present. Thus there are many early references to the prophet Muhammad as an arbitrator among feuding tribes, a role traditionally played by members of his descent group, the Quraysh, prior to the advent of Islam. Many tribal groups decided that their adherence to the community of Muslims ceased with Muhammad's death in 632 C.E., leaving them open to forge new alliances.

## Tribal Identity and Political Metaphor

Tribal genealogies and identities often employ metaphors such as the parts of the human body and the branches of a tree to symbolize stability, obligation, and belonging, but tribal and lineage identities in the Middle East are social constructs that change and are manipulated with shifting political and economic circumstances. Ibn Khaldun (1332–1406), the medieval North African historian and advisor to kings, recognized the flexible shape of tribal identities.

For Ibn Khaldun, "group feeling" (Ar., *'asabiyya*) exists when groups act cohesively, as if compelling ties of obligation hold them together to achieve common interests over extended periods of time. Thus belonging to a tribe does not depend on kinship or descent alone. In certain circumstances, individuals can change tribal, lineage, and clan affiliations. Dynasties and political domination were hard to sustain without such cohesiveness, especially present in tribal contexts. Group feeling is expressed in terms of presumed "blood" relationships, but in tribal contexts these are strong and compelling social metaphors for bonds of solidarity that take precedence over all other bonds of association. In Jordan, Iraq, Egypt, and elsewhere, tribal codes of responsibility and justice based on such cohesion often parallel the civil and criminal codes of state justice, and those of Islamic law, the *shari'a*.

## The Multiple Meanings of *Tribe*

The fact that one word, *tribe,* describes a range of ideas about society and social forms throughout the Middle East, as elsewhere in the world, does not make these meanings intrinsically related. For example, take the notion of tribe, still prevalent in many archaeological discussions, as an organizational level between "band" and "state." This formulation implies that tribes are on an evolutionary ladder and independent of states. Yet in earlier historical periods and in the present, tribes and states coexist and overlap. The problem of misrecognizing tribal identities is further compounded by the views of some Middle Eastern urban intellectuals who have adopted nineteenth-century evolutionary views and assume that tribes exist only at the fringes of states or are residues of pre-state formations. Both now and in the past, however, ideas of tribe share "family resemblances," possessing partial and overlapping similarities and a shared cultural logic. Far from being a relic of the past, "tribe" in the Arabian peninsula and the modern Middle East can even sustain modern national identity.

Tribal identity, like other bases of social cohesion, including kinship, citizenship, and nationalism, is something that people (and sometimes ethnographers and state officials) create, and it changes with historical and political context. The first form that the notion of tribe can take is the elaboration and use of explicit ethnopolitical ideologies by people themselves to explain their social and political organization. These locally held ideologies of tribal belonging in the Middle East are generally based on a concept of political identity formed through common patrilineal descent. A major exception is the Tuareg of the Sahara, where tribal identity is based on matrilineal descent—descent traced through the mother.

People in such tribes sometimes hold that how groups align themselves in time of dispute is explained by tribal and lineage identities alone, but other grounds for political action coexist and overlap. In precolonial Morocco as elsewhere, coalitions did not necessarily occur along the lines of tribe or lineage. This is demonstrated by the patterns of resistance in which people from various sections and tribes aligned themselves against the French in the early twentieth century. Precolonial accounts of disputes in western Morocco also suggest that alliances followed more flexible lines than those predicted by formal classification.

In general, tribal names and chains of patrilineal genealogies provide a range of potential identities rather than a basis for sustained collective action in itself. Often there is strong resistance to efforts to write down genealogies or claims to tribal descent because writing, by fixing the relationships among groups, distorts the ongoing process by which groups rework alliances and obligations and "re-imagine" the past in order to legitimate actions in the present.

For example, when Moroccan tribespeople discuss *tribe* (Ar., *qabila*), they elaborate the notion in different ways depending on their generation and social status. Socially and politically dominant individuals use ideas of tribe and lineage to fix political alliances with members of other tribal groups and to enhance their own position vis-à-vis state authorities and their followers. Ethnographers working in tribal societies have frequently based their accounts of kinship relations and tribal organization on information provided by such socially and politically dominant individuals. In contrast, the notions of tribal identity maintained by ordinary tribesmen, not to mention tribeswomen, often differ significantly from such formal ideologies of politically dominant tribal leaders.

A second notion of *tribe* is based on its use as an administrative device in contexts as varied as the Ottoman Empire, Morocco, Iran, and other countries prior to, during, and after colonial rule. Administrative assumptions concerning the nature of tribes are generally based, to some degree, on locally maintained conceptions modified for political purposes. Thus administrative concepts of tribe frequently assume a corporate identity and fixed territorial boundaries that many "tribes" do not possess and give privileges and authority to tribal leaders that are dependent on the existence of a state organization and not derived from leadership as understood by tribal people themselves. In cases such as Morocco and the Sudan, colonial authorities formally promoted "tribal" identities and developed tribal administration to a fine art in an attempt to retard nationalist movements. In reaction, the postcolonial governments of these and other countries signaled an ideological break with the colonial past by formally abolishing tribes as an administrative device, although such identities remain politically significant.

A third meaning of *tribe* refers to the practical notions that tribal people implicitly hold as a guide to everyday conduct in relating to their own and other social groups. These notions emerge primarily through social action. Tribal people do not always articulate such notions in ordinary situations because they are so taken for granted and because the social alignments based on these notions frequently shift. Practical notions of tribe and related concepts of social identity implicitly govern crucial areas of activity, including factional alignments over land rights, pastures, and other political claims, marriage strategies (themselves a form of political activity), and many aspects of patronage. In Jordan and among Palestinians in the occupied West Bank and in Israel, for example, Arabic newspapers are filled with announcements indicating the settlement of disputes among lineage and tribal groups precipitated by disputes or even automobile accidents resulting in personal injury in which tribal leaders mediate a settlement that is then publicly announced.

A fourth meaning of *tribe* relates to the analytical conceptions of the term held by anthropologists. Anthropological conceptions are intended primarily to make sociological sense of tribal social relations and often parallel those held by tribal people themselves. They are not more real than tribal people's conceptions of tribe or superior to them; they are a more explicit form of knowledge intended to explain how societies work. The anthropologist's objective is to achieve as adequate an understanding as possible of how people in a given society conceive of social forms, use this knowledge as a basis for social action, and modify these conceptions in practice and over time.

See also **City, The: The Islamic and Byzantine City; Identity: Personal and Social Identity; Nationalism: Middle East; Pan-Islamism.**

BIBLIOGRAPHY

Eickelman, Dale F. *The Middle East and Central Asia: An Anthropological Approach.* 4th ed. Upper Saddle River, N.J.: Prentice Hall, 2002. See chap. 5, "What is a Tribe?"

Khoury, Phillip S., and Joseph Kostiner, eds. *Tribes and State Formation in the Middle East.* Berkeley and Los Angeles: University of California Press, 1990. An indispensable review of the topic.

Peters, Emrys L. *The Bedouin of Cyrenaica: Studies in Personal and Corporate Power.* Edited by Jack Goody and Emanuel Marx. Cambridge, U.K., and New York: Cambridge University Press, 1990. A classic reference.

Shryock, Andrew. *Nationalism and the Genealogical Imagination: Oral History and Textual Authority in Tribal Jordan.* Berkeley and Los Angeles: University of California Press, 1997.

Varisco, Daniel Martin. "Metaphors and Sacred History: The Genealogy of Muhammad and the Arab 'Tribe.'" *Anthropological Quarterly* 68, no. 3 (July 1995): 139–156.

*Dale F. Eickelman*

**TROPE.** The trope concept, which is used increasingly in the social sciences to conceptualize the dynamics of definitions (and redefinitions) of social situations involved in communicative interaction, is derived from the Greek *tropos* (a turning), *tropë* (a turn), or *trepein* (to turn). It has long been used as a technical term in rhetoric to designate the use of a word or expression in a different sense than that which properly belongs to it in order to give liveliness, emphasis, perspective, coloration, or some other quality to an idea. The figures of speech (metaphor, metonym, synecdoche, and irony) are the four main categories of tropes, although tropes have been multitudinously identified in treatises on rhetoric.

## The Tropes in Classical Rhetoric

At issue here is the very human tendency when thinking about some difficult, banal, or obscure subject to think about something else that can enliven, offer perspective on, or cast light on the subject. Although a tropologist is anyone interested in the role figures of speech play in discourse, in the social sciences tropology is an interest in how such figurative expression can be used persuasively to affect the understanding of social situations and consequently effect social interaction. A basic question is what role figures of speech play in the figuring out and playing out of human life in society as, mainly, a playing out of categories of social belonging and social differentiation. As can be seen in the Greek root of the word, the use of tropes, these turnings of thought, raises the question of mutability in society and its susceptibility to persuasion and change of direction. Contemporary tropologists are particularly interested in the plotting of this dynamic.

The trope concept, and the rhetorical disciplines in general, have long been opposed by the exponents of clearly reasoned argument and of explicit syllogistic logic whose truth can be ascertained. These exponents dislike the volatility and obscurity that figures of speech bring into any argument. They have misgivings about the enthymemic quality—that is, the truncated syllogisms of rhetorical argument—caused by the use of the tropes. These objections were first raised by Plato

(c. 428–348 or 347 B.C.E.) in various dialogues with the Sophists, the professional rhetoricians of his time. Socrates (c. 470–399 B.C.E.) questioned the Sophists' practice of the arts of persuasion, in which belief and opinion were manipulated but what he considered true knowledge, obtained through the dialectic, was neglected. Nevertheless, Aristotle (384–322 B.C.E.), in both the *Poetics* and the *Rhetoric,* considers rhetoric the counterpart of logic and an offshoot of the dialectic, although he focuses on metaphor and not on the overarching concept of the trope as a whole. He holds rhetoric to be worthy of attention and study, particularly in the education of the young. Indeed, in the classical world, training in the rhetorical arts of speaking, persuading, and debating was the hallmark of elite education. This is seen both in Marcus Tullius Cicero (106–43 B.C.E.; *De Oratore*) and in the massive rhetorical treatise (essentially a schoolbook) *De Institutione Oratoria* or *On the Education of the Orator,* by Marcus Fabius Quintilian (c. 35–c. 100 C.E.). By "the orator," Quintilian meant scions of the patrician classes destined by birth to become persuasive in public affairs and naturally endowed to give shape and order to society. Important sections of this massive work are devoted to the various tropes and to the associated figures of speech that lie at the heart of rhetorical power and persuasion.

The idea of the trope and of studying the trope as affective and effective in public argument—that is, the idea of a science of tropology— was both appreciated and disliked by the ancients. The negative view of employing tropes in argument, which is that they confuse more than they enlighten, continues into the early modern period and is found in René Descartes (1596–1650), Thomas Hobbes (1588–1679), and John Locke (1632–1704), and can still be found in the present. Whereas the Cartesian, Hobbesian, and Lockian views first articulate early modern misgivings about the obfuscating role of the tropes and figures of speech in reasoned argument, other early moderns, such as Giambattista Vico (1668–1744) in the *New Science* (1725), argued that it was the tropes that enabled human understanding, or at least the escape from misunderstanding. Vico argued that a poetic logic existed in the creation and conduct of human life as it has evolved through the stages of civilization, and that studying the use and effect of the various tropes in discourse was central to understanding that logic and that evolution.

Vico devised an etymological method for discovering the tropes that were the source of our understanding of the world and of ourselves and whose evolutionary dynamic accounted for the cycle of civilization. His method is similar to the "genealogical method" developed by Friedrich Nietzsche (1844–1900) in *The Genealogy of Morals* (1897), through which he sought to discover the metaphors that lie behind the mummified concepts that we take as objective and direct representations of the world. For Nietzsche, all conceptualizing is willfully metaphoric, and it would follow that tropology is the only method through which to understand the springs of our thinking and its dynamic of power in human relations over time. His stark observations on the metaphoric basis of any supposedly secure metaphysical belief have become classics:

What then is truth? A movable host of metaphors, metonymies, and anthropomorphisms: in short, a sum

of human relations which have been poetically and rhetorically intensified, transferred, and embellished, and which, after long usage, seem to a people to be fixed, canonical, and binding. (1979, p. 23)

## The Tropes in Contemporary Thought

Nietzsche's tropological approach to human understanding is echoed in subsequent thought, and especially in such postmodern thinkers as Jacques Derrida and Michel Foucault and in postmodern deconstructionism. This late-twentieth-century work is co-occurrent with the revival of interest in Vico and his tropology in the 1960s and 1970s. The tropological theories of the historian Hayden White are notable here. White echoes Nietzsche's assertion in *The Use and Abuse of History* (1957) that historical writing is not a window enabling us to directly perceive historical reality but rather a perspectival screen always obstructing our view of the past in its particular way, according to the persona and preferences of the historian. In *Metahistory* (1973), White examines the great historians of the eighteenth and nineteenth centuries, Edward Gibbon (1737–1794), Alexis de Tocqueville (1805–1859), Thomas Babington Macaulay (1800–1859), Jules Michelet (1798–1874), Jacob Burckhardt (1818–1897), and Leopold von Ranke (1795–1886), showing how each had a particularly powerful poetic grasp of the part of the past that interested him and how this grasp was a function of the particular poetic tropes that he found evocative and helpful in organizing his thoughts. These tropological screens, or "governing metaphors," of historical writing acted in the particular historian to more or less self-consciously include or eliminate data from consideration. Historical understanding is thus anchored in the constraints exercised by the tropes the historian chooses.

White's work was accompanied in the seventies and eighties by tropological approaches to both anthropology and cognitive linguistics. Beginning in the collection *The Social Use of Metaphor* (1977) edited by David Sapir and Christopher Crocker, anthropologists gradually worked toward analyzing the role of the various tropes as they played off or interacted with each other in social life and culture. This interactive tropology, the authors in this collection argued, was useful in developing a more sensitive anthropological ethnography—that is, the study of the dynamics of "communicative interaction" in society and culture. Cognitive linguists, working over a twenty-year period that began in 1980, developed a linguistic theory of the logic behind the figuration of human understanding as anchored in bodily experience and projected out on the world. This is a theory sharply contesting the objectivist and rationalist paradigms in philosophy and in its way an actualization in cognitivist terms of Vico's efforts to identify the poetic logic of life in civilization. Cognitivists pay particular attention to the effect this logic has on the categorization processes in cognition, an emphasis that is congenial to anthropologists interested in the social categorization processes in culture and social relations.

The trope concept is an integral part of an enduring debate about the role of the figurative both in human communication and in bringing about social and cultural change. Cultures may vary in their stability over time, but all cultures are dynamic to one degree or another and can be persuaded to change the structure of their social relationships and turn in a new direction. The degree to which the tropes—themselves micro-turnings of thought—are influential in these macro-level social turnings has been a central question of tropology.

*See also* **Iconography; Ideas, History of; Postmodernism; Rhetoric.**

## BIBLIOGRAPHY

PRIMARY SOURCES

Nietzsche, Friedrich Wilhelm. *A Genealogy of Morals.* Translated by William A. Haussmann. New York: Macmillan, 1897.

————. *Philosophy and Truth: Selections from Nietzsche's Notebooks of the Early 1870's.* Translated by Daniel Breazeale. Atlantic Highlands, N.J.: Humanities, 1979.

————. *The Use and Abuse of History.* Translated by Adrian Collins. New York: Liberal Arts, 1957.

Quintilian, Marcus Fabius. *Quintilian's Institutes of Oratory; or, Education of an Orator.* 12 vols. Translated by John Selby Watson. London: H. G. Bohn. 1856.

Vico, Giambattista. *The New Science of Giambattista Vico.* 1744. Translated by Thomas Bergin and Max Fisch. Reprint, Ithaca, N.Y.: Cornell University Press, 1948.

SECONDARY SOURCES

Fernandez, James W., ed. *Beyond Metaphor: The Theory of Tropes in Anthropology.* Stanford, Calif.: Stanford University Press, 1991.

Fernandez, James W. *Persuasions and Performances: The Play of Tropes in Culture.* Bloomington: Indiana University Press, 1986.

Lakoff, George, and Mark Johnson. *Metaphors We Live By.* Chicago: University of Chicago Press, 1980.

————. *Philosophy in the Flesh. The Embodied Mind and Its Challenge to Western Thought.* New York: Basic, 1999.

Lakoff, George. *Women, Fires, and Dangerous Things: What Categories Reveal About the Mind.* Chicago: University of Chicago Press, 1987.

Sapir David, and Christopher Crocker, eds. *The Social Use of Metaphor: Essays on the Anthropology of Rhetoric.* Philadelphia: University of Pennsylvania Press, 1977.

White, Hayden V. "The Burden of History." In his *Tropics of Discourse: Essays in Cultural Criticism.* Baltimore, Md.: Johns Hopkins University Press, 1978.

————. *Metahistory: The Historical Imagination in Nineteenth-Century Europe.* Baltimore, Md.: Johns Hopkins University Press, 1973.

*James W. Fernandez*

**TRUTH.** The concept of truth is central to Western philosophical thought, especially to such branches of philosophy as metaphysics, epistemology, and the philosophy of language. In particular, the correspondence theory of truth has long been associated with a realist metaphysics, according to which objects exist independently of cognition by the human mind. Alternatives to the correspondence theory have, by contrast, been associated with antirealist metaphysics.

## The Correspondence Theory: Ancient and Modern

The correspondence theory of truth holds that a belief or proposition is true when it corresponds to the way the world is. The theory originated with Plato (c. 428–348 or 347 B.C.E.) and held the stage in Western theories of truth through the eighteenth century. At *Theaetetus* 188c–189b, Plato considered what is sometimes called the "existence" theory of truth: true opinion is thinking what is, while false opinion is thinking what is not (pp. 893–895). Plato dismissed this view of false opinion on the ground that to think what is not is to think nothing, and this is no more possible than to see nothing. At *Sophist* 240d–241a and 260c–263d, Plato proposed an alternative theory of truth designed to circumvent this difficulty: a thought resembles a sentence in consisting of a noun and a verb, and one's thought can be about something even though it is false because the noun refers to an object while the verb misdescribes this object (pp. 984, 1007–1011). This is a correspondence theory in the sense that truth requires that the truth bearer concatenate a noun and verb just as the object to which the noun refers has the property expressed by the verb.

At *De Interpretatione* 16a10–19, Aristotle (384–322 B.C.E.) endorsed Plato's *Sophist* point against the existence theory when he proposed that truth and falsity require names and verbs in combination or separation (p. 25). His definition of truth at *Metaphysics* Γ 7, 1011b26ff is committed to complex truth bearers: "To say of what is that it is not, or of what is not that it is, is false, while to say of what is that it is, and of what is not that it is not, is true . . . " (pp. 1597–1598).

The Stoics also offered a correspondence theory: "They [the Stoics] say that a true proposition [*axioma*] is that which is and is contradictory to something" (Sextus Empiricus, p. 203). However, the Stoics parted with Aristotle in defending the principle of bivalence, that there are only two truth values, true and false. St. Thomas Aquinas (c. 1224–1274) said that "truth is primarily in intellect; and secondarily in things, by virtue of a relation to intellect as to their origin" (p. 63).

Philosophers of the seventeenth and eighteenth centuries also accepted the correspondence definition of truth, but they differed from their ancient and medieval predecessors in emphasizing that the definition has no utility as a criterion of truth, that is, as a means to judge whether given propositions are true. René Descartes (1596–1650) conceded that "the word *truth,* in the strict sense, denotes the conformity of thought with its object" (p. 65). But he denied that this definition is useful for clarifying or explaining the concept: "it seems a notion so transcendentally clear that nobody can be ignorant of it" (p. 65); a definition can only cause confusion. He offered clear and distinct perception as a criterion of truth.

Baruch Spinoza (1632–1677) expressly applied *true* to ideas in *Ethics*: "A true idea must agree with its object" (p. 410). The axiom is used to show that reason regards things as necessary.

John Locke (1632–1704) endorsed the Platonic-Aristotelian view that *true* applies strictly to truth bearers of subject-predicate form—to propositions, in particular. He did not, however, formulate a correspondence definition of true proposition. Instead, he offered an account of the conditions in which truth is ascribed to ideas. Though ideas do not have a subject-predicate form and are thus not strictly true, one nevertheless ascribes truth to them in a manner that derives from one's "tacit supposition of their conformity to" their object (p. 514). When I ascribe truth to an idea belonging to another individual, I say that the idea is true when I suppose it conforms to my idea; and when I ascribe truth to my own idea, I suppose it is "conformable to some real existence" (Locke, p. 515). David Hume (1711–1776) loosely follows Locke in his account of the kinds of truth in the *Treatise*: "Truth is of two kinds, consisting either in the discovery of the proportions of ideas, consider'd as such, or in the conformity of our ideas of objects to their real existence" (p. 448). The second kind of truth, concerning matters of fact, echoes Locke's account of the ascription of truth to my own ideas and defines truth for matters of fact as conformity to the real existence of objects. Note that Hume endorses a correspondence theory only for matters of fact, not for matters of reason (or the discovery of proportions of ideas).

In the *Critique of Pure Reason,* Immanuel Kant (1724–1804) defined truth as correspondence: "The nominal definition of truth, namely that it is the agreement of cognition with its object, is here granted and presupposed; but one demands to know what is the general and certain criterion of the truth of any cognition" (p. 197). However, Kant denied that there is a universal material criterion of truth and observed that a universal formal criterion of truth, being nothing but logic, is sufficient only for consistency, not truth. Georg Wilhelm Friedrich Hegel (1770–1831) too accepted a correspondence definition of truth in his *Science of Logic*: "Objective truth is no doubt the Idea itself as the reality that corresponds to the Notion" (p. 784). But he did not see this as helping us with subjective truth.

## Pragmatist and Coherence Theories

In *Logic,* Kant noted that to judge whether a cognition is true, one must compare it with its object, and this requires another cognition of the object, which may be fallible—hence the judgment of truth is not sufficient for truth. Kant took this to show that the correspondence definition is useless as a criterion of truth. By contrast, followers of Kant took it to show that correspondence truth is unknowable or even unthinkable, since it requires comparing a cognition with its uncognized object, which is uncognizable. One can compare a cognition only with other cognitions. Moreover, a cognition cannot copy or resemble an object. This difficulty led many philosophers in the nineteenth century to seek an alternative to the correspondence definition, and they naturally sought to define truth in terms of the criterion of truth.

In "How to Make Our Ideas Clear," the American pragmatist Charles Sanders Peirce (1839–1914) proposed a method of clarifying our everyday conceptions: a conception is to be identified with the conception of the practical effects of its object. For example, "To say that a body is heavy means simply that, in the absence of opposing force, it will fall" (1992b, p. 48). Applying this to truth, to say that a belief is true is to say that it would permanently survive sustained inquiry conducted in a proper way. This is an epistemic definition of truth, since it defines truth in terms of proper inquiry. An epistemic definition runs into circularity if proper inquiry is in turn defined in terms of the aim of true belief. In "The Fixation of Belief," Peirce answered this threat of circularity by characterizing proper inquiry without employing the notion of truth—as inquiry that fixes belief by eliminating doubt.

Like Peirce, William James (1842–1910) applied a pragmatist theory of meaning to *true* and identified the notion of true belief with that of the consequences for experience of the belief's being true—"truth's cash-value in experiential terms" (p. 200). James differed from Peirce in characterizing a true belief as one that is eventually verifiable, rather than one that would be permanently fixed in sustained inquiry. This allows the possibility that a true belief will be permanently retracted after its eventual verification in sustained inquiry. James was more pragmatist than Peirce in attempting to use his pragmatist theory of true belief to explain the practical, and not merely cognitive, utility of true belief. A true belief is one that would fit my experience in a counterfactual circumstance. Because my true belief that the cowpath leads to a house would fit my experience were I to go down the path, it enables me to select the more useful course of action—going down the path that leads to food, as opposed to one that does not. Moreover, James, unlike Peirce, was guided in his choice of a definition of truth by the aim of finding a definition that explains the practical utility of true belief.

British idealists developed coherence theories of truth in the late nineteenth century. One motivation for these theories was epistemological: knowledge of whether a given judgment is true cannot result from comparing the target judgment with its object, as the correspondence theory requires; it must result from comparing judgments with other judgments. The available criterion here is coherence of the judgments with one another. This motivation for the coherence theory received its most extensive expression in the twentieth century in the American idealist Brand Blanshard (1892–1987) (pp. 225–237, 268). An alternative metaphysical motivation, to be found in the work of Francis Herbert Bradley (1846–1924) and Harold H. Joachim (1868–1938), appeals to the doctrine of internal relations. According to this doctrine, every relation is grounded in the natures of the relata. This is said by Bertrand Russell (1872–1970) to be equivalent to the monistic theory of truth, that judgments are not true one by one, but only abstracted from a concrete known whole (1906–1907, p. 37). From monism, it is supposed to follow that the truth of a judgment consists in its coherence with the whole, rather than in correspondence. Russell objects to the coherence theory on the ground that it does not rule out contrary propositions both being true: "coherence as the definition of truth fails because there is no proof that there can be only one coherent system" (1912, p. 122).

## The Correspondence Theory: Twentieth Century

The correspondence theory was revived at the beginning of the twentieth century by the founders of analytic philosophy, G. E. Moore (1873–1958) and Russell, in reaction to James, Bradley, and Joachim. The new correspondence theories addressed the worries of idealists and pragmatists about just what the correspondence relation is, if not the discredited copying relation, and what the terms of the relation are.

In lectures delivered in 1910 and 1911, Moore posed a problem like the one Plato urged against the existence theory of truth. On the one hand, if one believes that God exists, and this is true, one believes a fact (that God exists), and this fact is. On the other hand, one believes the same thing whether the belief is true or false; so there must be a fact even if one believes falsely that God exists; yet in this case there is no such fact (pp. 250–251). In "Beliefs and Propositions," Moore resolved this dilemma by denying that what one believes in a true or false belief is a fact. The clause "that $p$" in the description "the belief that $p$" does not name any fact or indeed anything at all. A belief, whether true or false, is not a relation between a believer and a fact, or even between a believer and a proposition. So one can believe the same thing in a false belief as in a true belief, even though for the false belief there is no fact. Moore nevertheless found it convenient to speak of beliefs as referring to facts: "To say that a belief is true is to say that the *fact to which it refers is* or has being; while to say that a belief is false is to say that the fact to which it refers is not—that there is no such fact" (p. 267). Moore was unable to analyze what is involved in referring (which amounts to correspondence when the fact referred to has being), but he was quite clear that, although "the belief that $p$ is true" is equivalent to "$p$" on the assumption that the belief $p$ exists, this is not a definition of truth precisely because "$p$" says nothing about the belief $p$ or a correspondence relation.

Russell tried to say what correspondence is in his work between 1906 and 1912. Othello's belief that Desdemona loves Cassio is a four-term relation between Othello, Desdemona, the relation of loving, and Cassio, while the corresponding fact (if there is one) is a two-term relation of loving between Desdemona and Cassio. Correspondence is then a certain match between the terms in the belief relation and the fact (1912, pp. 124–130). Later, Russell abandoned the idea that a false proposition is one that does not correspond to a fact, in favor of the view that it is one that bears a different correspondence relation to a pertinent fact (1956, p. 187). The latter view avoids a commitment to the idea that the clause "that $p$" in the description of a false belief names a fact, but it is encumbered with the burden of defining the two correspondence relations so that they cannot both obtain, on pain of allowing a proposition to be both true and false.

The British ordinary language philosopher John Langshaw Austin (1911–1960) proposed a correspondence theory in his article "Truth" (1950). His theory takes statements as truth bearers and states of affairs as truth makers, and it defines correspondence as a correlation that relies on conventions of two kinds: "demonstrative" conventions relating token states of affairs to statements, and "descriptive" conventions relating types of states of affairs to sentence types expressing those statements. A statement is true when the state of affairs to which it is correlated by demonstrative conventions is of a type with which the sentence used in making the statement is correlated by descriptive conventions. The British philosopher P. F. Strawson (b.1919) attacked Austin's theory, and correspondence theories more generally, on the ground that there are no bearers of truth values, there are no entities in the world amounting to facts, and there is no relation of correspondence (1950). Strawson

endorsed the opposing view that an assertion made by uttering "It is true that $p$" makes no assertion beyond one made by uttering "$p$," although it may be used to do things other than make this assertion (for example, confirm or grant the assertion that $p$).

The Polish-American logician Alfred Tarski (c. 1902–1983) offered a "semantic" conception of the truth of sentences in a given interpreted and unambiguous formalized language $L$. His account was intended to capture an Aristotelian notion of truth. Tarski set as a material adequacy condition on a theory of truth-in-$L$ what is called Convention T: that the theory entails all sentences of the form "$X$ is a true sentence if and only if $p$," where $X$ is a name of some sentence of $L$, and $p$ is the translation of this sentence into the metalanguage of the theory. Tarski then demonstrated that a recursive truth definition satisfies Convention T.

The basic idea of the truth definition is that a sentence such as "$a$ is $F$" (for a name "$a$" and a predicate "$F$") is true just in case $F$ applies to the object denoted by $a$, where application is defined case by case for each name in the language $L$. Now let us give a Tarski-like truth definition for a simple language $L$ with two names, "$a$" and "$b$," and one predicate "$F$." We may begin by defining truth separately for each atomic sentence of $L$ in semantic terms like "applies" and "denotes." (Tarski made central a notion of satisfaction related to application.) The basis clause is: "$a$ is $F$" is true just in case "$F$" applies to the object denoted by "$a$"; and similarly for "$b$ is $F$." We then define "denotes" for each name: "$a$" denotes $x$ just in case $x = a$; and similarly for "$b$." We define "applies": "$F$" applies to $y$ just in case ($y = a$ and $a$ is $F$) or ($y = b$ and $b$ is $F$). This has been called a disquotational definition of the semantic terms. Finally, we define truth for nonatomic sentences by exploiting the truth-functional properties of logical connectives like "or" and "not." Treating truth as involving subject-predicate form is mandated by the need to satisfy Convention T.

Tarski's theory formulated in terms of "denotes" and "applies" is plausibly regarded as a correspondence theory. However, Hartry H. Field (b. 1946) charged that Tarski's definition of truth does not reduce truth to a physicalistically acceptable property, as Tarski desired (1972). For Tarski's disquotational definitions of semantic terms do not provide an explanatory reduction of those terms to any general physical properties. This is shown by the fact that if we augment $L$ by adding a new name or predicate to form a language $L'$, the definition of truth-in-$L$ gives no hint of what truth-in-$L'$ amounts to. Field proposed that we remedy such difficulties by fitting Tarski's theory in terms of semantic concepts with a physicalistically acceptable causal theory of denotation and application, rather than a disquotational definition of these concepts.

## Deflationary Theories

Deflationary theories treat the truth predicate as having only a logical or grammatical function, rather than as ascribing a property or relation to a truth bearer, as on correspondence, pragmatist, and coherence theories. Frank Plumpton Ramsey (1903–1930) proposed, contrary to Moore, that *true* generally makes no substantive contribution to what is asserted in a statement: "'it is true that Caesar was murdered' means no more than that Caesar was murdered" (p. 157). "Whatever he says is true" comes out "For all $p$, if he says that $p$, then $p$." This is called the redundancy theory of truth. It is deflationary in denying that *true* expresses a property of truth bearers or a relation of correspondence between truth bearers and the way the world is.

In *Philosophical Investigations* (1958), Ludwig Wittgenstein (1889–1951) rejected his idea presented in the *Tractatus* (1961, originally published in 1922) that "This is how things are" expresses the general form of a proposition. This form of words does express a proposition, but "To say that this proposition agrees or does not agree with reality would be obvious nonsense." Rather, it is a propositional variable the value of which is fixed by an earlier statement, in the way the referent of a pronoun is fixed by an earlier use of a name. This proposal, known as the "prosentential" theory of truth because it treats "That is true" as a "prosentence," was subsequently developed by Dorothy Grover, Joseph L. Camp, Jr., and Nuel D. Belnap, Jr. (1975).

Willard Van Orman Quine (1908–2000) proposed that the truth predicate is used for semantic ascent, which in certain cases is indispensable for expressive purposes: "If we want to affirm some infinite lot of sentences that we can demarcate only by talking about sentences, then the truth predicate has its use" (p. 11). If we wish to say only that Tom is mortal, we can say "'Tom is mortal' is true," but we need not do so. But if we wish to affirm each of the sentences of Euclidean geometry, we have no option but to say "All the sentences of Euclidean geometry are true." We are saying no more than we would say by uttering each of the sentences, but since there are infinitely many of them, we cannot utter them all. For this reason, the truth predicate is practically indispensable. This suggests a disquotational theory of truth on which the content of *true* for a language is given by all the equivalences: "$p$" is true just in case $p$ (for all sentences "$p$" of the language). Presumably, occurrences of *true* in contexts like "What he said is true" or "That is true" would be either spelled out in the manner of Ramsey or implicitly defined by the T-equivalences in virtue of the fact that the subject of the sentence refers to a particular sentence. Paul Horwich developed a related minimalist theory of truth by taking as the axioms of the theory all the equivalences: the proposition that $p$ is true if and only if $p$ (1990). These deflationary theories have, in common with Moore's and Russell's correspondence theories, the disadvantage of entailing the principle of bivalence, which prohibits "truth-value gaps," as in borderline vague sentences or sentences with presuppositions that fail. A correspondence theory such as Field's can be formulated in a way that avoids bivalence (1972). Deflationary theories also differ from correspondence theories in making it impossible to ascribe truth to sentences in a language we can't understand. Field argued in a 1986 article that a deflationary notion of truth cannot be employed to account for how our tendency to believe truths explains our practical success in action.

Some have denied that truth is definable. Gottlob Frege (1848–1925) argued that if truth is definable as a property, then any judgment of whether an idea is true would involve judging whether the idea has the property, and the question would then arise whether it is true that the idea has the property, generating a circle (1956). The early Moore (1953, p. 262) and Donald Davidson (1917–2003) also denied that truth is definable. Since 1980, philosophers (e.g., Huw Price) have shown an interest in functionalist accounts of truth, which characterize truth in terms of its cognitive or social function, rather than define the concept in other terms.

*See also* **Logic; Philosophy; Platonism; Pragmatism.**

**BIBLIOGRAPHY**

Aquinas, St. Thomas. *Summa Theologiae.* 2 vols. Edited by Thomas Gilby. Garden City, N.Y.: Image Books, 1969.

Aristotle. *The Complete Works of Aristotle: The Revised Oxford Translation.* 2 vols. Edited by Jonathan Barnes. Princeton, N.J.: Princeton University Press, 1984.

Austin, J. L. "Truth." *Proceedings of the Aristotelian Society* 24 (1950): 111–128.

Blanshard, Brand. *The Nature of Thought.* 2 vols. New York: Allen and Unwin, 1939.

Bradley, F. H. *Essays on Truth and Reality.* Oxford: Clarendon, 1914.

Davidson, Donald. "The Folly of Trying to Define Truth." *Journal of Philosophy* 93 (1996): 263–278.

Descartes, René. "Letter to Marin Mersenne, 16 October 1639." In *Descartes: Philosophical Letters.* Translated and edited by Anthony Kenny. Minneapolis: University of Minnestoa Press, 1970.

Field, Hartry. "The Deflationary Conception of Truth." In *Fact, Science, and Morality: Essays on A. J. Ayer's Language, Truth, and Logic,* edited by Graham Macdonald and Crispin Wright. Oxford: Blackwell, 1986.

———. "Tarski's Theory of Truth." *Journal of Philosophy* 69 (1972): 347–375.

Frege, Gottlob. "The Thought: A Logical Inquiry." Translated by A. M. Quinton and Marcelle Quinton. *Mind* 65 (1956): 289–311.

Grover, Dorothy, Joseph L. Camp, Jr., and Nuel D. Belnap, Jr. "A Prosentential Theory of Truth." *Philosophical Studies* 27 (1975): 73–125.

Hegel, Georg Wilhelm Friedrich. *Hegel's Science of Logic.* Translated by A. V. Miller. Atlantic Highlands, N.J.: Humanities Press, 1989.

Horwich, Paul. *Truth.* Oxford: Blackwell, 1990.

Hume, David. *A Treatise of Human Nature.* 2nd ed., edited by L. A. Selby-Bigge. Oxford: Clarendon, 1978.

James, William. *Pragmatism: A New Name for Some Old Ways of Thinking, Together with Four Related Essays Selected from* The Meaning of Truth. New York: Longmans, Green, and Co., 1947.

Joachim, Harold H. *The Nature of Truth.* Oxford: Clarendon, 1906.

Kant, Immanuel. *Critique of Pure Reason.* Translated and edited by Paul Guyer and Allen W. Wood. Cambridge, U.K.: Cambridge University Press, 1997.

———. *Logic.* Translated by Robert S. Hartman and Wolfgang Schwarz. Indianapolis: Bobbs-Merrill, 1974.

Locke, John. *An Essay Concerning Human Understanding.* 2 vols. Edited by A. C. Fraser. New York: Dover Publications, 1959.

Moore, G. E. *Some Main Problems of Philosophy.* London: Allen and Unwin, 1953.

Peirce, Charles Sanders. *The Essential Peirce: Selected Philosophical Writings.* 2 vols. Edited by Nathan Houser and

Christian Kloesel. Bloomington: Indiana University Press, 1992–1998.

Plato. *The Collected Dialogues of Plato.* Edited by Edith Hamilton and Huntington Cairns. New York: Pantheon, 1961.

Price, Huw. *Facts and the Function of Truth.* Oxford: Blackwell, 1988.

Quine, W. V. *Philosophy of Logic.* Englewood Cliffs, N.J.: Prentice-Hall, 1970.

Ramsey, Frank P. "Facts and Propositions." *Proceedings of the Aristotelian Society* 7 (1927): 153–170.

Russell, Bertrand. *An Inquiry into Meaning and Truth.* London: Allen and Unwin, 1921.

———. *Logic and Knowledge, Essays 1901–1950.* Edited by R. C. Marsh. London: Allen and Unwin, 1956.

———. "On the Nature of Truth." *Proceedings of the Aristotelian Society* 7 (1906–1907): 28–49.

———. *The Problems of Philosophy.* New York: H. Holt, 1912.

Sextus Empiricus. *Against the Professors* 8.85–6. In *The Hellenistic Philosophers.* 2 vols. Edited and translated by A. A. Long and D. N. Sedley. Cambridge, U.K.: Cambridge University Press, 1987.

Spinoza, Baruch. *Ethics.* In *The Collected Works of Spinoza,* volume 1. Translated and edited by Edwin Curley. Princeton, N.J.: Princeton University Press, 1985.

Strawson, P. F. "Truth." *Proceedings of the Aristotelian Society* 24 (1950): 129–156.

Tarski, Alfred. "The Semantic Conception of Truth and the Foundations of Semantics." *Philosophy and Phenomenological Research* 4 (1944): 341–375.

Wittgenstein, Ludwig. *Philosophical Investigations.* Translated by G. E. M. Anscombe. New York: Macmillan, 1953.

———. *Tractatus Logico-Philosophicus.* Translated by D. F. Pears and B. F. McGuiness. London: Routledge and Paul, 1961.

*Frederick F. Schmitt*

# U

**UNIVERSALISM.** Since the late nineteenth century, the debate around issues concerning universalism and universalizability has intensified. Against the claims to universal knowledge made on behalf of Christianity, the West, rationality, and mankind, feminist, critical race, and postcolonial scholars and activists have shown that the issues are more complicated. Notwithstanding the validity of their criticism, universalism is not only compatible with the approaches that have condemned it, but is importantly in a sense presupposed by them.

First, we need to distinguish between different kinds of universalism. Universalism, in its most sophisticated form as it appears in the philosophy of science, defends the idea that thinking about any problem in science always leads to reasoning and that this reasoning will always seek the outermost limits through attempts to be universally valid, and to discover nonrelative truth. There are two forms of this simple and elegant idea about reason. One argues that this submission to an order of reason is a demand of reason itself. The other disagrees with the idea that we are ultimately submitting ourselves to an order of reason that is there for us to discover. Following Charles Peirce, this view argues that even as we try to think of this order of nature and of rationality, we are always doing so through a community of inquirers, so that this convergence of opinion about universally valid scientific laws always retains its ideal aspect. Here, Peirce sought to update Immanuel Kant's transcendental idealism, and show its relevance to the philosophy of science. For Kant, our scientific laws are valid for rational creatures such as us, and we can show their validity through transcendental deduction. But we cannot ultimately reach beyond the synthetic imagination and the categories of space and time that shape our world to reach into the world of things themselves. Convergence, for Peirce, means that divergent opinions can actually come to agreement on specific scientific laws and that unless there is a significant challenge to that agreement it will remain valid as true. But it is precisely because it is an agreement of a community of inquirers that also makes it open-ended, since such agreements can, at least in principle, always be challenged or re-elaborated by new paradigms of scientific truth. In some sense then, we are creating the order of reasons through the articulation of scientific laws. Simply put, there is always more to know, and as we know more, scientific laws that we previously thought of as unshakeable can either be criticized, extended, or in some cases, downright rejected. Peirce further argues that how well we think is ultimately dependent on the ethics of the scientific community to which we belong. Ethics then, as critiques of a community of knowledge, including scientific knowledge, can be fore grounded without necessarily losing the appeal to scientific laws as justifiable and as universally valid.

Feminists writing in the philosophy of science, such as Evelyn Fox Keller and Sandra Harding, have made important contributions in critiquing claims of universality for scientific law from at least two vantage points. The first and most important is that the community of knowledge is corrupt at the deepest level. It has adopted an ethics of scientific inquiry that, for the most part, has excluded women. Moreover, by so excluding women, it has in fact adopted notions of instrumental rationality that fail to achieve true objectivity because they relate to nature from a masculine or patriarchal viewpoint in which nature is reduced to something only valuable for its use to us. There is a rich and important literature in feminist epistemology and it is obviously impossible for me to be fair to the extent of the varieties of critique offered there. But even when such a feminist critique is allied with the searing analysis of the destructiveness of instrumental rationality as it takes over what we can even think of as reason—an analysis put forth by thinkers of the Frankfurt school such as Theodor Adorno and Max Horkheimer—it does not in itself necessarily lead to the rejection of a universality understood as always taking reason to its limit. This is true even if one allows, following Peirce, that that limit might always recede under the changing principles of scientific knowledge. Again, for Peirce, as for many feminists and other critical theorists, convergence remains always and still an ideal.

Indeed, we could argue that Peirce, following Kant, offers us a powerful critique of the pretensions of reason. This critique forces us to see how a thoroughgoing rationalism always is thrown back on the finitude of any actually given community of inquirers, humbled before their own historical position, even as they aspire to the scientific grandeur of ultimately trying to grasp the meaning of the universe. If Kant is right, we will never be able to think God's thoughts. But if Albert Einstein is also right, and the basic argument about reason is compelling, then any given community of inquirers will never stop trying.

Another central question in the debates surrounding universalism has been raised in ethics; precisely, the question is whether we need to rationalize ethical reasons into something more than a circular procedure for moral reasoning. In the famous case of John Rawls's proceduralism, he defends the hypothetical experiment of putting ourselves behind the veil of ignorance to imagine what Kant would have called our noumenal selves unbounded at least as imagined by the contingencies of our own history. Unlike Jürgen Habermas, Rawls does not want to defend his theory of justice or his own political liberalism through an overarching philosophical conception of reason and history that explains ethical and moral principles by an appeal to something outside of them.

Famously, Habermas argued against his predecessors, and indeed Kant himself, by trying to show us that reason can ground itself in universal principles of communicative action when combined with an empirically validated notion of evolutionary learning processes. This attempt to rationalize moral reason has been criticized extensively by theorists of language and of communication who have argued that first of all, no presuppositions can be found. Further, even if they could be found, they would not be strong enough to ground a normative theory, let along an overarching normative conception of modernity and of human moral learning leading to the one-way street of modern Europe. Habermas is adding an empirical dimension to the general and comprehensive worldview of strong universalism advocated by Hegel. For Hegel, the universal ideal of humanity unfolds in all its greatness and, despite its floundering, finally culminates in a grand unity of our particular historical expression and our universal moral selves in what some may have seen as a rather limited embodiment, i.e. the German state. Habermas, in other words, attempts a general and comprehensive theory, to use John Rawls's expression that justifies universalism through a connection of reason and an overarching concept of rationality. But, as mentioned earlier, Rawls himself rejects this as the basis of the universalizable ideals of what he calls political liberalism. Rawls, one of the greatest voices of this vision, argued that at least hypothetically, we should be able to imagine ourselves as noumenal beings that could idealize themselves so as to articulate and defend as reasonable certain universal principles of justice. Rawls certainly defends the universality of the principles of justice. But he refuses universalism understood as the attempt to ground moral reason in an order of reason outside of the procedure, such as in the case of Habermas, who seeks to ground morality and ethics in the presuppositions of language.

In her own work in moral philosophy, Martha Nussbaum has tried to defend universalism in the sense of defending an Aristotelian notion of a moral view of human nature. Her view too should be considered universalism in the sense that she argues that we can know what our nature is and derive from that knowledge a strong commitment to values, universalizable because they are true to the substance of our human nature. By universalizable, I mean to indicate ideals that purport to include all of humanity and therefore can be accepted by all of us. This way of thinking about what is universalizable emphasizes the idea of the scope of who should be included in the ideal of humanity, and the rights that are accorded to those so included. But universalism as defended by either Nussbaum or Habermas ultimately denies the central importance of the insight of the Kantian proceduralism of Rawls. That insight is for a norm to be truly universalizable, it cannot be based on a notion of the human that generalizes out of a particular experience. Again, the feminist critiques of man were not arguing against the aspiration to universalizability of the rights of man, but claiming instead that those rights were indeed only for men, in many instances being granted to men only, and thus fail the test of universalizability that they purported to meet. Feminists, of course, have been joined by postcolonial theorists who have reminded us that the identification of humanity as an ideal, including as a moral ideal, with European modernity, not only risks reducing the universal to the particular, but has also justified the worst forms of colonial cruelty.

A critique then, of European modernity as other than a particular form of history is crucial for the unmooring of the ideal of universality and even the ideal of humanity itself from its implications in a brutal imperialist history. Universalizable norms, in this sense, carry with them a specific kind of self-reflexivity in which universality as an ideal must always lead to critical analysis. The danger is not only of confusing generality with universality, but also of proclaiming a particular form of being human as if this were the last word on who and what we could be. Universality, in other words, as a claim to cover the scope even of rights to be protected is always open to the moral contest it protects.

When Hegel is removed from his presumptuous philosophy of history, the lingering truth of Hegel's insight is that the re-articulation of universality and universalizable norms always takes place through a struggle. Karl Marx saw that struggle, or at least the struggle that could ultimately bring us to our truest humanity, as the battle between classes. History in other words, had not stopped with the bourgeois German state, but would only reach its culmination when humanity realized itself in communism. The lingering importance of German idealism is that it teaches us that at the end of the day we are left with a struggle—the struggle to see that taking reason to its limit also takes us back to the limit of reason itself, as Kant so powerfully taught us. Therefore, Kant's critique itself is integral to what is understood as an ideal in which the procedures by which we seek to universalize a norm or an ideal are always themselves open to question and re-articulation.

This notion of universality, as an ideal whose meaning can be reinterpreted in order for it to be able to live up to its own claims, should not be confused with relativism. Relativism, which argues that norms, values, and ideals are always relative to culture, actually turns on a strong substantive claim about the nature of moral reality. Relativists have to become the strongest kinds of rationalists in order to defend their position. To defend relativism as a substantive truth about moral reality clearly has to appeal to a form of universal knowledge. After all, if the claim is that principles are always inevitably relative to culture, then that claim is one that must defend itself as a universal truth. In our globalized world, the remembrance and the commitment to universality demands nothing less of us than a commitment to the critique and the corresponding imaginative openness to the re-articulations of the ideal.

*See also* **Essentialism; Feminism; Human Rights; Humanity.**

**BIBLIOGRAPHY**

Adorno, Theodor, and Max Horkheimer. *Dialectic of Enlightenment.* New York: Continuum, 1999.

Appadurai, Arjun. *Modernity at Large: Cultural Dimensions of Globalization.* Minneapolis: University of Minnesota Press, 1996.

Butler, Judith. "Contingent Foundations." In *Feminist Contentions: A Philosophical Exchange,* edited by Seyla Benhabib et al. New York: Routledge, 1995.

Chakrabarty, Dipesh. *Provincializing Europe: Postcolonial Thought and Historical Difference.* Princeton, N.J.: Princeton University Press, 2000.

Habermas, Jürgen. *On the Pragmatics of Communication.* Cambridge: MIT Press, 1998.

———. *The Theory of Communicative Action.* Boston: Beacon Press, 1984.

Harding, Sandra. *Is Science Multicultural?: Postcolonialisms, Feminisms, and Epistemologies.* Bloomington: Indiana University, 1998.

Hegel, G. W. F. *Elements of the Philosophy of Right.* Cambridge, U.K.: Cambridge University Press, 1991.

———. *Phenomenology of Spirit.* Oxford: Oxford University Press, 1977.

Kant, Imannuel. *Critique of Pure Reason.* Cambridge, U.K.: Cambridge University Press, 1998.

Keller, Evelyn Fox, ed. *Feminism and Science.* Oxford: Oxford University Press, 1996.

Matustík, Martin Beck. *Jürgen Habermas: A Philosophical-Political Profile.* Oxford: Rowman and Littlefield, 2001.

Nagel, Thomas. *The Last Word.* New York: Oxford University Press, 1997.

Nussbaum, Martha. *Sex and Social Justice.* Oxford: Oxford University Press, 1999.

Peirce, Charles. *The Essential Peirce: Selected Philosophical Writings.* Bloomington: Indiana University Press, 1992.

Rawls, John. *Political Liberalism.* New York: Columbia University Press, 1993.

———. *A Theory of Justice.* Cambridge: Belknap Press, 1999.

Ruddick, Sara. *Maternal Thinking: Toward a Politics of Peace.* Boston: Beacon Press, 1995.

Spivak, Gayatri. *Critique of Postcolonial Reason: Toward a History of the Vanishing Present.* Cambridge, Mass.: Harvard University Press, 1999.

Williams, Patricia. *The Alchemy of Race and Rights.* Cambridge, Mass.: Harvard University Press, 1991.

*Drucilla Cornell*

## UNIVERSE, THEORIES OF. *See* **Cosmology.**

## UNIVERSITY.

This entry includes two subentries:

*Overview*
*Postcolonial*

### OVERVIEW

The university is a legal corporation empowered by civil or ecclesiastical authorities to award degrees certifying that the recipients have achieved significant levels of expertise in various disciplines. Teachers instruct students of various ages and preparation in higher learning in several subjects. Many, but not all, teachers are scholars who carry on original research in order to add to the body of knowledge available to all. The world outside the university expects it to contribute to society by creating new knowledge, by training learned professionals at an advanced level, and helping all students to develop intellectually and culturally. This is the idea of the university. It has not changed in substance in nine hundred years, even though ideas about how universities should fulfill their missions have changed and expanded.

### Precedents in the Ancient World and Islam

The ancient world did not have universities. But it did have several centers for research and study at an advanced level that provided the opportunity for a limited amount of informal education. Plato (427–348 B.C.E.) after 388 B.C.E. founded an Academy in Athens in which men gathered to discuss broad philosophical issues through interrogation and dialogue. The Academy lasted until 529 C.E., albeit with many changes. Aristotle (384–322 B.C.E.) had a circle of friends and pupils who gathered just outside Athens. After his death, Theophrastus (c. 372–c. 287 B.C.E.) made it into a center, usually known as the Peripatetic School, for the study of the subjects that interested Aristotle, which meant practically everything from natural science to poetry, but especially philosophy. Neither the Academy nor the Peripatetic School, which lasted until the third century C.E., offered structured education or awarded degrees.

The museum and its library in Alexandria, Egypt, was the most important center for advanced learning in the Greco-Roman world. *Museum* meant a place where learned men cultivated the muses, not a collection of artifacts. Founded in

**A student consults with Plato. Mural painting by Puvis de Chavannes.** While the ancient world did not have accredited universities, it did offer informal centers for education, such as the one founded in Athens, Greece, by Plato in the third century B.C.E. © BETTMANN/CORBIS

the third century B.C.E. by Ptolemy I Soter (r. 305–283 B.C.E.), the museum provided support for writers but soon attracted scholars in many other fields, especially astronomy, mathematics, and philosophy. Ptolemy I added a library that attempted to obtain, or make copies of, the works of all known Greek authors. Scholars corrected and edited the texts, an important form of advanced academic scholarship. The museum of Alexandria had numerous scholars, some of whom attracted followers, but it did not offer formal education or confer degrees. The persecutions of Ptolemy VIII (r. 145–116 B.C.E.) drove some scholars away and ended the museum's greatest days, although it lasted until 651. The idea motivating Plato's Academy, Aristotle's Peripatetic School, and the museum and library of Alexandria was the advancement of high-level scholarship in many fields through the gathering of scholars and texts.

Between the eighth and eleventh centuries the Islamic world created the college, called *masjid khan* and later *madrasa,* a place where mature scholars taught law based on the Koran to younger men. Teachers, advanced students who assisted the master in teaching, and beginning students lived together for several years in inns attached to important mosques. But Islamic law colleges did not develop the corporate structure and legal identity of the university, and they did not influence the Christian West. Nor did Islam have organized institutions for medical and philosophical higher education. Distinguished Islamic scholars such as the medical scholar Ibn Sina (or Avicenna, 980–1037) and the philosopher and commentator on Aristotle, Ibn Rusd (Averroës, 1126–1198), did not hold teaching positions but were court physicians most of their adult lives. In similar fashion, Jewish students came to learn from eminent Jewish interpreters of the Talmud, the basic source for Jewish law, in German and northern French towns, especially in the twelfth century. But the Talmudic schools did not evolve into universities.

## The Creation of the University

The Western European Middle Ages created the university, its most significant and enduring achievement after the Roman Catholic Church. No clear idea or plan lay behind the beginning of the university. Rather, the two original universities of Bologna and Paris arose spontaneously as practical responses to circumstances, desires, and needs. In the late eleventh century, law students began to gather in Bologna at the feet of senior jurists who looked to ancient Roman law as the guide for creating legal principles to sort out the conflicting claims

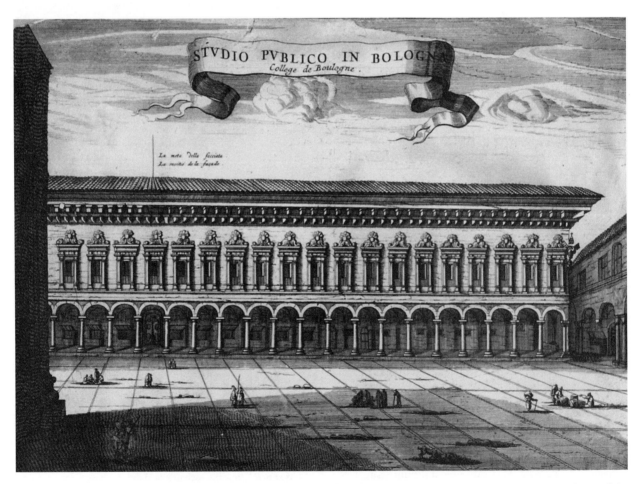

**Engraving of Bologna University, c. 1790.** Bologna University, established in the early thirteenth century, is considered one of the first two official universities. An important advancement in the history of the university occurred in Bologna in the 1220s when the government began taking responsibility for the teacher's salaries. HULTON GETTY/LIAISON AGENCY

and rights of empire, church, kingdoms, princedoms, towns, and individuals. In similar fashion students came to Paris to study arts, philosophy, and especially theology. In both cities enough teaching and organization regulating the teaching and the rights and obligations of teachers and students was in place by about 1150 that it could be said that universities were born.

Recognition that universities were new and unique institutions came after the fact. In the twelfth century *universitas* meant a group of people legally recognized as a collectivity. The corporation of masters and students at Paris first called itself a *universitas* in 1221. Hence, universities came into existence when society recognized that teachers and students as a collectivity had certain legal rights. Another term was *studium generale* (universal school), meaning an institution of higher learning that attracted students from a wide area and had the right to grant degrees authorizing the holder to teach anywhere in the world. A key event occurred in Bologna in the 1220s when the city government began to pay the salaries of teachers. This meant that professors would stay in one place and guaranteed the stability and continuity of the university. While pope and emperor played no role in their creation, civil governments, teachers, and students accepted that it was useful and orderly that popes and emperors should issue charters authorizing universities to award degrees recognized throughout Christendom.

These and other measures gave the university the basic shape that continues in the twenty-first century. The medieval university consisted of a corps of professors teaching arts (including logic, Latin literature, and mathematics), philosophy, medicine, surgery, science, canon law, civil law, and theology at an advanced level. Students of varying ages, from the early teens through men in their mid-twenties, heard lectures, studied texts required by university statutes, and participated in academic exercises for several years, sometimes for more than a decade. They submitted themselves to examinations for bachelor's, master's, and doctoral degrees. Upon obtaining degrees, they practiced or taught the disciplines that they had mastered. While sharing a basic structure, universities in northern and southern Europe differed. Many northern universities, including Paris and Oxford, taught mostly arts and theology to students studying for bachelors' degrees. Bologna and other Italian universities concentrated on law and medicine and awarded doctoral degrees.

European monarchs, princes, and towns founded and staffed at considerable expense a very large number of universities in the fourteenth, fifteenth, and sixteenth centuries. Historians frequently state that monarchs and cities founded universities in order to train civil servants to fill the expanding ranks of government offices, and certainly many law graduates did so. But contemporary documents do not mention this rationale for founding universities. Instead, university foundation charters offered as reasons the universal thirst for knowledge and the benefits to society of men learned in different subjects and full of mature counsel. There is no reason to doubt the sincerity of these lofty concepts. And reference to mature advice meant that university training would give those who later served ruler or town the scholarly perspective with which to approach complex issues.

## The University in the Renaissance and Reformation

In the Middle Ages and the Renaissance, universities enjoyed a nearly complete monopoly as educators of Europe's scholarly, civic, and ecclesiastical elites. Although no author or treatise articulated the idea that universities should train the intellectual and sometimes the political and ecclesiastical leaders of Europe, they did. In the sixteenth century European universities probably exerted the greatest influence on learning and society in their history. Professors at Italian universities made extraordinary, original, scholarly contributions in medicine, philosophy, mathematics, and astronomy. The original anatomical research of Andreas Vesalius (1514–1564) while at the University of Padua from 1537 to 1543 and the mathematical and scientific research of Galileo Galilei (1564–1642), who taught at the University of Pisa from 1589 to 1592 and the University of Padua from 1592 to 1610, were just the best known of many examples of innovative research with enduring consequences. Martin Luther (1483–1546) created a new theology while teaching at the University of Wittenberg from 1513 on. He and many other professors of theology led the Protestant Reformation through their teaching, writing, and advice to princes. The Reformation, in turn, changed Europe religiously, politically, and culturally.

As a result of the Protestant and Catholic Reformations, many European universities became closely allied with religious groups in ways that they never had been in the past. The Society of Jesus in particular dominated some older universities or played major roles in newly founded ones from the middle of the sixteenth century onward. On the other side of the religious divide, some universities became closely identified with Protestant churches, such as the University of Wittenberg with the Lutheran Church and several universities with Calvinism, especially in the Netherlands. The University of Leiden (founded in 1575) was the most important among the latter.

## Universities beyond Europe

When Europeans took their civilization to new continents, they quickly founded universities modeled on those of Europe. Catholic religious orders and Protestant churches founded most of the overseas universities, which trained indigenous clergy and produce educated lay leaders. The first universities founded in the New World were Santo Domingo (after 1538), Mexico (1551), and Lima (1571). A Catholic bishop of the Dominican Order founded the University of Santo Tomas in Manila, the Philippines, in 1611. The Congregational Church founded Harvard College in Cambridge, Massachusetts, in 1636 and named it for a minister who bestowed a considerable gift on the new college. These and many other universities across the world were based on European models. They were small in enrollment, faculty, and instruction at first, but grew over the centuries.

## Universities in Decline

By 1600 European universities were beginning a period of decline in accomplishments and influence that lasted about 250 years. Many new schools arose in both Catholic and Protestant Europe to take students away from universities and to offer employment for scholars. In the Catholic world the Society of Jesus or Jesuits and other new religious orders developed schools that taught part of the university curriculum. The Jesuits began by teaching Latin grammar, humanities, and rhetoric to boys aged ten to sixteen, then added a three-year program of logic, natural philosophy, and metaphysics at a higher level, as well as mathematics and occasionally other subjects. These were university subjects. The Jesuits had 578 schools, many with university-level instruction, across Europe in 1679. In Protestant Europe academies competed with universities. These were small schools offering higher instruction in a limited number of disciplines, especially arts and theology, without necessarily conferring degrees. The prototype was the Geneva Academy, founded by John Calvin in 1559. Academies hired excellent teachers and took students away from universities.

Learned societies, such as the Royal Society of London for the Advancement of Natural Knowledge, founded in 1662, offered more competition to universities by supporting scholars without requiring them to teach. Most learned societies on the Continent received funding from governments, which enabled them to offer salaries to members who carried on research in mathematics, astronomy, chemistry, and other subjects without teaching.

Enlightenment philosophes of the eighteenth century strongly criticized universities for not being useful to society because they held on to a traditional curriculum, a criticism often repeated in the next two centuries. The philosophes persuaded rulers to create nonuniversity institutions of higher learning to teach specialized practical subjects, such as agricultural technology, engineering, military science, surgery, even painting. They thought that such institutions would produce citizens capable of contributing useful knowledge to society and the state. Napoléon Bonaparte (who ruled France and much of Europe from 1799 to 1815) agreed. He abolished many universities in France and Germany and created technical schools in their place.

## The Nineteenth and Twentieth Centuries

Nineteenth-century German educational reformers revivified and gave new meaning to the idea of the university. Karl Wilhelm, baron von Humboldt (1767–1835), minister for education in Prussia, believed that universities should support *Wissenschaft*, faculty research and discovery in all fields, and should foster *Bildung*, or cultivation, meaning broad intellectual development and humanistic culture, in students. The new University of Berlin, founded in 1810, embodied Humboldt's vision. The renewed emphasis on research echoed the importance of innovative scholarship in theology, philosophy, law, and medicine by professors at medieval and Renaissance universities. The German research university of the second half of the nineteenth century realized the first goal and was widely copied by North American universities in the twentieth century. Many universities, especially those focusing on undergraduate education, in England, North America, and parts of the world influenced by England, emphasized a version of *Bildung* and called it *liberal education* in English and *culture générale* in French.

Beginning in the nineteenth century, governments assumed a greater role in higher education in Western Europe and the United States. National governments in France, Germany, Italy, and elsewhere founded new state universities and closed or took control of church-sponsored institutions. Governments provided funding for universities, but also brought them under the control of ministries of education and made professors into civil servants. This process continued in the twentieth century, especially in the former Soviet Union (1917–1991). In the United States, state governments founded land-grant colleges in the nineteenth century that often became the largest and most important universities in the state. Although the United States still has a large number of colleges and universities affiliated with religious denominations, the ties between churches and universities have weakened and sometimes been dissolved. Church-affiliated universities have become less insistent that professors be members of the affiliated church, and they increasingly attract students of many faiths or none at all.

Since World War II (1939–1945) the dominant ideas shaping the university are that it should create new learning, teach skills in all fields and especially science and medicine, help the economy create wealth, and support a knowledge-driven society. While not ignored, humanistic research and teaching are less central. The multi-university, as it is sometimes called, offers an astonishing range of institutes, centers, and schools to teach all manner of knowledge, much of it practical. Emblematic of the new conception of the university is the addition of business schools preparing students to be successful in the many areas of national and international commerce and finance.

The idea that universities should provide higher education for a much larger proportion of the population has also won wide support from the public and governments. Hence, beginning in the 1960s governments increased the number and enrollments of universities and eased or broadened admission requirements. In addition, many more older students attended universities than in the past. As a result, the number of university students in Europe, North America, and other parts of the world greatly increased in the last thirty years of the twentieth century. One or two percent, at most, of the university-age population (eighteen through twenty-four) attended European universities in the first half of the twentieth century. By contrast, about half of the university-age population received some university education in the United States at the end of the twentieth century. In Europe as well, an increasing number of young people are attending university. Also, the European Union is slowly moving toward cooperation between universities in different countries and greater mobility of professors and students.

## Women Students and Professors

Women were neither students nor professors in universities for many centuries. This was probably not the result of a conscious decision to exclude them, but the logical consequence of the view that universities prepared students for public careers and professions that women traditionally did not enter or from which they were barred. The path toward acceptance of women in universities was long and slow. The first woman to obtain a university degree was Elena Lucrezia Cornaro Piscopia (1646–1684), a Venetian noblewoman, who received a doctorate of philosophy from the University of Padua on 25 June 1678.

She did not attend lectures but obtained the degree through examination, an accepted practice in Italian universities. The second was Laura Bassi (1711–1778), a highborn Bolognese woman who obtained a doctorate of philosophy, again through examination, from the University of Bologna on 12 May 1732. She was the first female professor, as she taught experimental science at the University of Bologna from 1732 to 1738. The third was Maria Pellegrina Amoretti, who earned a doctorate in law from the University of Pavia on 25 June 1777.

From 1800 through 1945 more women, although still a small minority, attended university and earned degrees. Because many universities did not accept women as students, undergraduate colleges for women were founded, as well as new colleges and universities that admitted both men and women, especially in the United States. This changed greatly in the last thirty years of the twentieth century. Nearly all male-only colleges and universities in the United States accepted women as students, and a majority of women-only institutions enrolled men. But except for traditional female-dominated professions, such as nursing, only a few women were university professors in Europe and North America as late as the 1960s. Then, in response to larger societal moves to provide equal rights and opportunities for women, the barriers became lower or disappeared. By the twenty-first century women constituted the majority of undergraduates in American universities and about half of the students in law and medical schools. The number of women professors has increased greatly, although their distribution by fields varies. European universities also saw an expansion in the number of female students and professors, although the number of female faculty members varies considerably from country to country.

The idea of a university that offers education to students and supports advanced research by professors has proven to be one of the most enduring and influential ideas in Western civilization.

*See also* **Education.**

BIBLIOGRAPHY

Addy, George M. *The Enlightenment in the University of Salamanca.* Durham, N.C.: Duke University Press, 1966.

Bendall, Sarah, Christopher Brooke, and Patrick Collinson. *A History of Emmanuel College Cambridge.* Woodbridge, U. K.: Boydell Press, 1999. Has interesting intellectual, personal, and social detail.

Brockliss, L. W. B. *French Higher Education in the Seventeenth and Eighteenth Centuries: A Cultural History.* Oxford: Clarendon, 1987.

Clark, Burton R., and Gary R. Neave, eds. *The Encyclopedia of Higher Education.* 4 vols. Oxford and New York: Pergamon Press, 1992. Provides information on higher education in all parts of the world with a contemporary emphasis.

Grendler, Paul F. *The Universities of the Italian Renaissance.* Baltimore and London: Johns Hopkins University Press, 2002.

*History of Oxford University.* 8 vols. in 9 parts. Oxford: Oxford University Press, 1984–2000. Comprehensive history beginning with the earliest schools at Oxford through the twentieth century.

*History of Universities.* Avebury and Oxford, U.K.: Avebury Publishing Co. and Oxford University Press, 1981–. Annual volume covering universities in all centuries. Includes articles, comprehensive bibliography, and reviews.

Jarausch, Konrad H., ed. *The Transformation of Higher Learning 1860–1930: Expansion, Diversification, Social Opening, and Professionalization in England, Germany, Russia, and the United States.* Chicago: University of Chicago Press, 1983.

Jílek, Lubor, ed. *Historical Compendium of European Universities/Répertoire historique des universités européennes.* Geneva: CRE, 1984. Useful list with short historical summaries of European and overseas universities based on European models founded before 1800.

McClelland, Charles E. *State, Society, and University in Germany, 1700–1914.* Cambridge, U.K.: Cambridge University Press, 1980.

Ridder-Symoens, Hilde de, ed. *A History of the University in Europe.* Vol. 1, *Universities in the Middle Ages.* Cambridge, U.K.: Cambridge University Press, 1992. Vol. 2, *Universities in Early Modern Europe (1500–1800).* Cambridge, U.K.: Cambridge University Press, 1996.

Rothblatt, Sheldon, and Björn Wittrock, eds. *The European and American University since 1800: Historical and Sociological Essays.* Cambridge, U.K.: Cambridge University Press, 1993.

Seabury, Paul, ed. *Universities in the Western World.* New York and London: Free Press and Collier Macmillan, 1975.

*Paul F. Grendler*

## POSTCOLONIAL

The late twentieth century saw a renewed interest in the postcolonial development of higher education systems within broader literature on globalization and education policies. Particularly, efforts by international institutions, such as the World Bank, to prevent the global and local effects of the so-called knowledge divide, led to a number of policy documents and initiatives aimed at leveling the pace of changes and development in higher-education landscapes of rich and poor countries. Policy in this domain seemed largely influenced by studies that presented the gradual domination of managerialism in the organization of both teaching and research, the commercialization of research, and the outsourcing of many services to create leaner structures as inevitable consequences of globalization and the "knowledge explosion." As a result, most developing countries were restructuring their already inherited systems of higher education along similar patterns to those observed in the West and the Pacific Rim. How this process—sometimes described as the "recolonization" of education—translates into actual higher education landscapes around the world seems to depend on a number of contextual variables.

### A Contrasted Picture

A closer look at local and regional situations reveals persistent differences, in terms of institutional management, relations to the state, enrollments, and patterns of participation and academic careers. Beyond similar policy agendas, these realities signal contrasted histories and unequal states of development of higher education.

The fortune of universities and university education in countries that regained independence from waning European

---

### INDIAN HIGHER EDUCATION SYSTEM: THE CRIPPLED GIANT

When India achieved independence in 1947, only a few thousand students were enrolled in higher education. In 2004, with 250 universities and approximately 8 million students, India had the world's second-largest system of higher education and produced more Ph.D.s per capita than anywhere in the world. However, the gross enrollment ratio in tertiary education stagnated at 11 percent. This figure, although higher than the average of 4 percent in Africa, remained low as compared to the countries of North America (60 to 70 percent) and Europe (40 to 60 percent), or the recently developed Asian Tigers (33 to 55 percent).

---

colonial "empires" (e.g., France, Britain) in the mid-twentieth century have differed, following routes largely influenced by their regional environment. If university education in Jamaica, Malaysia, Nigeria, and India still bears the mark of a common colonial origin, the universities of the West Indies in Mona, of Ibadan, of Malaya, and the Jawaharlal Nehru University of Delhi have, by will or by happenstance, been permeable and responsive to the realities and needs of postcolonial societies they had, to a large extent, not been designed to serve.

With a few exceptions, these countries are located in low-income regions where university education was reluctantly established in the agonizing days of the colonial era. As part of the colonial educational edifice, universities contributed to the spreading of a knowledge base rooted in the Western episteme. But as training centers of a mid-ranked indigenous bureaucracy, they also turned out to be the breeding ground of two generations of postcolonial political elite who led their countries as politicians, public servants, professionals, and businessmen. Following independence, the mission of universities established under colonial rule or with Western universities as their models was everywhere challenged and replaced by much more ambitious agendas for the development of genuine postcolonial university education systems.

At the beginning of the twenty-first century, universities throughout the postcolonial world were still criticized for underachievement. The criticisms remained the same: it was said that the universities produced graduates who were unemployable; they inculcated alien values; they failed to serve the interests of the vast majority of the population through appropriate courses and research dealing with the problems of the common man; they engaged in pure research that adds little value to the economy; they lacked in innovation and perpetually copied in-

novations in the developed world that may not be suitable for local circumstances. Despite these criticisms, enrollment in higher education grew steadily over the period, and universities gradually emerged as protected spaces, promoting a unique gender- and minority-inclusive culture. From the 1980s, female enrollment grew considerably in the poorest countries while it remained fairly flat in Europe and America. However, in the case of sub-Saharan Africa, while significant progress was made, the troubles of history since the mid-twentieth century (unstable governments, supra- and international pressures, civil strife, pandemics) made it extremely difficult for universities to develop appropriate curricula or to adjust their research agendas to local needs and realities. Once the euphoria of the 1960s waned, universities fell victim to distrust from growing authoritarian regimes and were among the first victims in the 1980s of the structural

---

### Gross enrollment ratios (GER) in tertiary education, 2000–2001

| Country | GER M & F | GER Male | GER Female | Gender Parity Index for GER. Tertiary |
|---|---|---|---|---|
| Australia | 63 | 57 | 70 | 1.24 |
| Bangladesh | 7 | 8 | 5 | 0.55 |
| Belgium | 58 | 54 | 62 | 1.16 |
| Botswana | 5 | 5 | 4 | 0.89 |
| Brazil | 17 | 14 | 19 | 1.29 |
| Burundi | 1 | 2 | 1 | 0.36 |
| Cambodia | 3 | 4 | 2 | 0.38 |
| Canada | 59 | 51 | 68 | 1.34 |
| Chile | 38 | 39 | 36 | 0.92 |
| Czech Republic | 30 | 29 | 31 | 1.05 |
| Eritrea | 2 | 3 | - | 0.15 |
| Estonia | 58 | 45 | 70 | 1.55 |
| France | 54 | 48 | 59 | 1.23 |
| Ghana | 3 | 5 | 2 | 0.4 |
| Hong Kong | 25 | 24 | 25 | 1.06 |
| Hungary | 40 | 35 | 45 | 1.27 |
| Indonesia | 15 | 16 | 13 | 0.77 |
| Iran | 10 | 10 | 10 | 0.93 |
| Jamaica | 16 | (**) 11 | (**) 22 | 1.89 |
| Japan | 48 | 51 | 44 | 0.85 |
| Kenya | 3 | 3 | 3 | 0.77 |
| Lao | 3 | 4 | 2 | 0.59 |
| Lebanon | 42 | 40 | 44 | 1.09 |
| Lesotho | 3 | 2 | 3 | 1.76 |
| Libya | (**) 49 | (**) 50 | (**) 48 | 0.96 |
| Madagascar | 2 | 2 | 2 | 0.84 |
| Malaysia | 28 | 27 | 29 | 1.08 |
| Mauritania | 4 | 6 | 1 | 0.2 |
| Mexico | 21 | 21 | 20 | 0.96 |
| Morocco | 10 | 11 | 9 | 0.8 |
| Netherlands | 55 | 53 | 57 | 1.07 |
| Niger | 1 | 2 | 1 | 0.34 |
| Portugal | 50 | 43 | 58 | 1.37 |
| Russia | 64 | 56 | 72 | 1.29 |
| Rwanda | 2 | 2 | 1 | 0.5 |
| South Africa | 15 | 14 | 17 | 1.23 |
| Thailand | 35 | 33 | 37 | 1.11 |
| Trinidad and Tobago | 6 | 5 | 8 | 1.53 |
| Uganda | 3 | 4 | 2 | 0.52 |
| United Kingdom | 60 | 53 | 67 | 1.27 |
| United States | 73 | 63 | 83 | 1.32 |
| Vietnam | 10 | 11 | 8 | 0.74 |

SOURCE: UNESCO. 2003

---

---

THE EUPHORIA OF THE 1960S: UNIVERSITIES
AND POSTCOLONIAL DEVELOPMENT IN AFRICA

In 1962, UNESCO and the Economic Commission for Africa organized a conference on the Development of Higher Education in Africa in Tananarive, Madagascar, which highlighted many of the challenges of the African universities. The conference focused on problems related to staffing, financing, and content of higher education, with particular attention to the Africanization of staff and curriculum. The participants at Tananarive concluded that in addition to the role of teaching and of research, higher education was to contribute to the social, cultural, and economic development of Africa. Higher education was to do so by promoting national unity, prioritizing teaching and research on African concerns, and training human resources to meet "manpower" demand, while simultaneously maintaining international standards of academic quality. This focus on the role of universities in national development, marked the rise of the notion of the "developmental university."

---

adjustment policies imposed by the International Monetary Fund (IMF) and the World Bank on almost all African countries that qualified for loans.

Drastic cutbacks in research and infrastructure grants, along with the withdrawal of state support to student services and the rapid downfall of the standard of living of staff threw most developing world universities into a state of dereliction. The situation was condemned in the following terms by a task force convened by the World Bank in cooperation with UNESCO in 1999:

> Since the 1980s, many national governments and international donors have assigned higher education a relatively low priority. Narrow—and, in our view, misleading—economic analysis has contributed to the view that public investment in universities and colleges brings meager returns compared to investment in primary and secondary schools, and that higher education magnifies income inequality. As a result, higher education systems in developing countries are under great strain. They are chronically under-funded, but face escalating demand. (The Task Force on Higher Education and Society, 2000, p. 10)

**A Peripheral World of Learning**
The dilemma facing higher education worsened through the 1980s and 1990s due to a massive south-north intellectual migration flow. The movement illustrates in itself the role higher education plays in keeping up the tight and imbalanced links initiated in the colonial era.

Alongside the development of local elitist systems of higher education, and in reaction to the growing attractiveness of North American institutions among local "educated elites," colonial powers were keen to encourage the most promising graduates of secondary schools to further develop their training in the home institutions. This fact, added to the flow of students migrating as

a result of the higher education Malthusianism applied in the colonies, constituted the basis of a steady south-north study migration flow, which in many cases resulted in a "brain drain." Leaning on family networks or supported by external donors, and fostered by the ever-increasing economic gap between industrialized and developing countries, the flow was barely affected by the development of university education in newly independent countries. On the contrary, with local curricula largely untouched, postcolonial higher education offered excellent basic training to candidates for postgraduate programs in the developed world. This diversion of funding opportunities affected in return the quality of higher education in the developing countries. The earlier perspective of encouraging students from abroad to study in the United Kingdom or France as a form of colonial or postcolonial aid and encouragement of trade (in goods or ideas) was transformed; education came to be seen more as a directly saleable commodity. The concomitant abandonment of scholarship policies, which primarily affected students from low-income countries, impacted markedly on the origin of international students in host countries. However, as shown in Table 2, postcolonial study migration routes continued to reflect strong economic, cultural, and linguistic ties with the former home institutions, except where the United States and Australia (notably in Asia) took over leadership in the provision of higher education services.

**Mediating the Global and the Local**
The postcolonial era is marked in most countries by attempts to combine the quality of teaching inherited from highly elitist higher education systems and the necessity to widen access to higher education to "bridge the development gap" and to strengthen democratic institutions. However, political developments since the 1960s, economic choices, and global pressures show that higher education cannot be developed to the exclusion of broader policy initiatives, leaving out the sociocultural context. The unequal distribution of colonial universities generated con-

**The postcolonial routes to study abroad: main destinations in 2001**

| | Australia | Belgium | France | Germany | Japan | Netherlands | UK | USA |
|---|---|---|---|---|---|---|---|---|
| Algeria (F) | 36 | 613 | 24,040 | 346 | 32 | 38 | 586 | 381 |
| Cambodia (F) | 254 | 43 | 1,151 | 45 | 245 | 0 | 34 | 324 |
| Côte d'Ivoire (F) | 6 | 203 | 5,079 | 252 | 22 | 8 | 142 | 1,104 |
| D.R. Congo (B) | 2 | 3,482 | 1,516 | 206 | 0 | 38 | 39 | 0 |
| Djibouti (F) | 0 | 10 | 2,144 | 1 | 0 | 0 | 6 | 13 |
| Ghana (UK) | 90 | 51 | 118 | 374 | 112 | 82 | 2,015 | 4,282 |
| Hong Kong (UK) | 15,842 | 4 | 0 | 14 | 0 | 0 | 16,244 | 13,230 |
| India (UK) | 12,390 | 238 | 462 | 1,413 | 395 | 98 | 8,441 | 94,822 |
| Indonesia (NL) | 21,452 | 159 | 365 | 2,128 | 2,420 | 1,058 | 2,070 | 20,165 |
| Jamaica (UK) | 12 | 1 | 22 | 12 | 8 | 2 | 715 | 7,328 |
| Kenya (UK) | 1,054 | 113 | 228 | 202 | 105 | 34 | 4,788 | 10,805 |
| Madagascar (F) | 0 | 74 | 4,620 | 125 | 20 | 0 | 27 | 199 |
| Malaysia (UK) | 25,858 | 10 | 214 | 197 | 3,241 | 24 | 18,183 | 13,521 |
| Nigeria (UK) | 126 | 278 | 34 | 667 | 70 | 132 | 4,598 | 6,626 |
| Pakistan (UK) | 1,912 | 42 | 237 | 681 | 210 | 84 | 3,781 | 12,052 |
| Rwanda (B) | 8 | 574 | 36 | 100 | 2 | 29 | 93 | 452 |
| Senegal (F) | 6 | 202 | 243 | 247 | 48 | 4 | 52 | 1,269 |
| Singapore (UK) | 21,430 | 10 | 96 | 73 | 259 | 20 | 9,075 | 7,226 |
| Suriname (NL) | 4 | 34 | 22 | 2 | 0 | 1,737 | 12 | 209 |
| Trin. & Tob. (UK) | 20 | 0 | 48 | 13 | 4 | 2 | 883 | 5,032 |
| Vietnam (F) | 3,260 | 305 | 2,801 | 1,458 | 1,229 | 67 | 331 | 3,507 |
| Zambia (UK) | 164 | 18 | 10 | 35 | 26 | 10 | 799 | 1,063 |

Former colonial authorities in parentheses.

SOURCE: OECD statistics, 2001

trasting expectations from populations. National policies on education then endured enormous tensions from the multiple pressures of ever more exigent demands from an educated minority; of ever more dramatic educational, social, and regional discrepancies; and of ever more restrictive recommendations and conditions set by international organizations. The landscape of higher education that emerged from these contradictory tensions reflected both the peculiarities of national trajectories and the inequalities of the postcolonial world order.

*See also* **Colonialism; Education: Global Education; Education: India; Empire and Imperialism.**

BIBLIOGRAPHY

Ajayi, J. F. A., Lameck K. H. Goma, and G. Ampah Johnson. *The African Experience with Higher Education.* Athens: Ohio University Press, 1996.

Altbach, Philip G., and Suma Chitnis, eds. *Higher Education Reform in India: Experience and Perspectives.* New Delhi: Sage Publications, 1993.

Dunne, Mairead, and Yusuf Sayed. "Transformation and Equity: Women and Higher Eduation in Sub-Saharan Africa." *International Studies in Educational Administration* 30, no. 1 (2002): 50–66.

Federici, Silvia, George Caffentzis, and Ousseina Alidou, eds. *A Thousand Flowers: Social Struggles against Structural Adjustment in African Universities.* Trenton, N.J.: African World Press, 2000.

Hoogvelt, Ankie. *Globalisation and the Postcolonial World: The New Political Economy of Development.* Basingstoke, U.K.: Macmillan, 1997. 2nd ed., Baltimore: Johns Hopkins University Press, 2001.

Howe, Glenford D., ed. *Higher Education in the Caribbean: Past, Present and Future Directions.* Kingston, Jamaica: University of the West Indies Press, 2000.

Lebeau, Yann, and Mobolaji Ogunsanya, eds. *The Dilemma of Post-Colonial Universities: Elite Formation and the Restructuring of Higher Education in Sub-Saharan Africa.* Ibadan: IFRA/ABB, 2000.

Lee, W. O., and Mark Bray, eds. *Education and Political Transition: Perspectives and Dimensions in East Asia.* Hong Kong: CERC, University of Hong Kong, 1997.

Task Force on Higher Education and Society. *Higher Education in Developing Countries: Peril and Promise.* Washington, D.C.: World Bank, 2000.

Tikly, L. "Globalisation and Education in the Postcolonial World: Towards a Conceptual Framework." *Comparative Education* 37, no. 2 (2001): 151–171.

World Bank. *Constructing Knowledge Societies: New Challenges for Tertiary Education.* Washington, D.C.: World Bank, 2002.

*Yann Lebeau*

# UNTOUCHABILITY.

This entry includes three subentries:

*Overview*
*Menstrual Taboos*
*Taboos*

## OVERVIEW

A basic idea of social grouping emerged in one of the late poems in the earliest of the Hindu scriptures, the Rig Veda. In this mythic account, probably composed about three thousand years ago, the primeval man was sacrificed to make the *varnas* (castes): the Brahmans emerged from his head, the Kshatriyas from his arms, the Vaishyas from his thighs, and the Shudras from his feet. It is clear there is some ranking here, but the full-scale hierarchy based on degrees of purity and pollution emerged later, and untouchable castes became a category as *avarnas*, without *varna*, probably sometime after the fourth century C.E.

We find a development of this idea in the law books called *Dharmashastras* (300 B.C.E. to 500 C.E.). The first three *varnas* are known as the twice-born and are composed of Brahman priests and advisers, warriors and rulers, and merchants, all of whom undergo a ceremony in their youth admitting them into high status. Shudras, generally any caste that did manual work, were denied the privilege of studying the Vedas and were cast into a servant position. Untouchables were and are below the Shudras in any ranking, considered polluting to all and generally given the work in society that is filthy or demeaning.

In both law books and the epics, we find references to burning ghat workers, individuals who generally worked in the burning ghats with corpses and are considered unclean. A play from around the fifth century C.E., *Mrichcha katika* (The little clay cart) by Shudraka, includes two executioners who are actually quite intelligent and humorous but nevertheless untouchable. Burning ghat workers and executioners are two of the occupations still considered most polluting. The idea of persons who pollute was present early on, but the phenomenon of polluting castes developed later.

Parallel to the *varnas* and outside scripture were *jatis*, meaning "by birth" and also translated as *castes*. A *jati* is an endogamous group, sharing many customs and often an occupation, usually based in one language area. There were hundreds of *jatis* within each *varna*, and while untouchables were *avarna*, without *varna*, they were members of specific *jatis*.

## The Origin of Untouchability

There are many theories about the origin of caste and, subsequent to that, the origin of untouchable castes. The untouchable leader B. R. Ambedkar (1891–1956) held theories on both. He wrote that the caste system originated from the Brahman requirement of endogamy to preserve its purity and from that was spread to lower castes. Untouchables, he held, had been Buddhists isolated and despised when Brahmanism became dominant about the fourth century. His theory is important both because it led to his conversion to Buddhism and because it represents the need of all untouchables to explain their status. Most untouchable castes have a myth of origin usually relating to a cosmic mistake; almost none assume that a past karma of bad deeds has resulted in an untouchable status in this life. On the other hand, most caste Hindus think that sins or good deeds or the careful fulfillment of duty in a previous life produce the karma that determines the caste into which one is born.

Vivekananda Jha agrees on the time period of Ambedkar but disagrees with the idea of untouchables' Buddhist past, as do most caste Hindu writers. An influential book by Louis Dumont (1970) focuses exclusively on the concept of purity and pollution as determinants of the entire Hindu hierarchy. For Dumont, untouchables are necessary for the purity of Brahmans: "It is clear that the impurity of the Untouchable is conceptually inseparable from the purity of the Brahman. . . . In particular, untouchability will not truly disappear until the

purity of the Brahman is itself radically devalued" (p. 54). Other theorists limit the role of purity and pollution, holding chiefly that the purity needed for ritual spread to other occasions in life. A Marxist approach presumes tribal groups coming into the caste system found a ranking dependent on their economic opportunities. Many inside and outside of India hold that race is behind caste distinctions, especially that of Brahman and untouchable, and this belief is reflected in many untouchable belief systems, such as the supposition that untouchables were indigenous people ruling the land, forced to submit to invading Aryans (people speaking an Indo-European language and coming from outside India). Whatever their beginnings, untouchable groups were clearly delineated by the seventh century, when the Chinese traveler Xuanzang listed butchers, fishermen, public performers, executioners, and scavengers as marked castes living outside the city.

## The Voices of Untouchables

In the medieval period a few voices of untouchables emerged. In the fourteenth century in Maharashtra, Cokhamela and his family of the untouchable Mahar caste were part of a religious movement generally called bhakti devotional religion. Intensely personal, the movement included all castes, and their songs have come down through the ages. Cokhamela complained bitterly about the concept of purity, and one of his poems calls out, "We are born in impurity, we die in impurity, O God, who is pure?" (unpublished translation by Anne Murphy). He is saddened by his inability to enter the temple of his god. According to legend, he was born to a mother and father whose duty as Mahars was to take the village produce to the ruler, and he died while mending the village wall. Eknath, a Brahman *bhakta*, wrote two centuries later as if he were a Mahar, and more duties can be noted: caring for the horses of government officials, sweeping the village streets and hauling out the dead cattle, getting firewood for the village headman, and guarding the village.

Another poet-saint's voice is that of the Ravidas in the sixteenth century, who refers to his caste as an untouchable Chamar and his duties as working with leather: "O, people of the city! My notorious caste is Chamar! In my heart is the essence of all good qualities. . . . I carry cattle-hides all around Benaras." He believed in purity beyond caste: "Whether one's heart is Brahmin or Vashiya, Shudra or Kshatriya, Dom, Chandala, or Malech (a foreigner), through the worship of the Lord, one becomes pure" (unpublished translations by Anne Murphy). Ravidas is honored by both Sikhs and Hindus. Untouchables who convert to Sikhism from Chamar castes often take the name Ravidasi. It should be noted that anything to do with a dead cow or its hide is the work only of untouchables. A caste of drummers in the south known as the Parayan contributed the word *pariah* (outcaste) to English. In this case, the drumhead made of hide is polluting.

We do not hear from untouchables again until the nineteenth century. Then there are again direct voices: a plea from Mahars to be allowed to reenter the British army, closed to them after a century of employment; an adi-Hindu (first or pre-Hindu) movement in the north, an adi-Dravida (original Dravidians) movement in the south; a movement among toddy tappers to secure their economic base, become educated, and be considered no longer untouchable. Toward the end of the nineteenth century, the British began recording and codifying caste, and more untouchable castes based usually on occupation emerged: Bhangis or removers of human waste in the north; Doms, the caretakers of the extensive burning grounds in the holy city of Benaras (Varanasi); Dhobis, laundrymen who handle polluted clothing.

## The Beginnings of "Affirmative Action"

The British government had allowed separate electorates for "depressed classes" in the 1932 announcement of future government in India made after the Round Table Conferences in England. This provision was made at the insistence of the untouchable representatives, B. R. Ambedkar from the province of Bombay and Rao Bahadur Rettamalle Srinivasan of Madras—the two most active areas of reform—who felt, in the face of demands for separate constituencies from all other minorities, that proper elected representatives could only be elected by untouchables themselves. Mohandas K. Gandhi, then in prison for activities against the government in the interests of independence, thought separate electorates were too divisive and began a "fast unto death." Ambedkar gave in but bargained for reserved seats for untouchables in all elected bodies to be elected by the general electorate. Gandhi then began the Harijan Sevak Sangh (Organization for the Service of the People of God), which was intended to bring the issue of untouchability as an evil to the public mind and to bring change to the hearts of caste Hindus. *Harijan* became the most popular word for the general public, replacing *depressed classes, exterior castes, outcastes,* and *untouchables,* terms previously used. Ambedkar and other politically awakened untouchables rejected the word as patronizing and meaningless. The basic disagreement was between belief in a change of heart and belief in legal and political means of securing human rights.

By 1935 it had become clear that untouchable castes must be listed to determine who exactly would be eligible for the reserved seats and for educational and economic benefits. The criteria for listing stipulated specific castes in specific areas that were denied religious rights of entry into temples and civil rights of entry to public places and the use of wells. The word *specific* was necessary because the ways of identifying who is an untouchable can vary. Occupation is not always a reliable guide. Laundrymen (Dhobis) and barbers may be untouchables in certain areas of the north but not in the state of Maharashtra. The new term *scheduled castes,* those on a list or schedule, was applied to 429 castes. (By 1993 the number was given in a survey conducted by K. S. Singh as 4,635, using the same criteria but noting subcastes and small castes not previously identified.)

The background for these concessions, probably the first "affirmative action" in the world, was from movements among untouchables themselves, which were especially important in Madras and Bombay, provinces that in the early decades of the twentieth century decreed that "depressed classes" should be represented in government bodies and, in the case of Bombay, that public places should be open to all. There were a number of leaders in various movements for dignity and human rights in many areas, but the dominant figure since the

late 1920s was B. R. Ambedkar, who continued to be important in the early twenty-first century.

Ambedkar was born to a Mahar army schoolteacher and was urged to secure education both by his father and by caste Hindus interested in reform. He graduated from Elphinston College in Bombay, one of very few untouchables in western India to do so, and with the help of the reform-minded non-Brahman princes of the princely states of Baroda and Kolhapur was given a chance to secure an M.A. and a Ph.D. in economics from Columbia University in New York and a D.Sc. from the University of London. He also became a barrister in the course of his two periods overseas. He returned to India as one of the most highly educated men in western India and an instant source of pride to untouchables. From then on, Ambedkar tried to convince the British to give attention to untouchable needs and to awaken all untouchables to progress through conferences, newspapers (although the literacy rate was very low), and an occasional public demonstration for rights. He founded political parties as well as social organizations and an educational system, and in 1947 he was asked to serve as law minister in newly independent India's first cabinet. In that capacity, he was chair of the drafting committee of the Indian constitution.

## The Contemporary Period

Five phenomena mark the contemporary period: the reservation policy's results and disputes; the increased violence against untouchables; the growth of Dalit literature; the presence of a new and effective political party; and the image of Ambedkar all over India as a symbol of achievement and a claimant to all human rights. The reservation policy that provided a quota system for scheduled castes in all governmental political bodies and services and in educational institutions aided by the state was extended to "backward castes" in 1991 and produced a backlash from Brahman students who feared they would not be employed. Since that time higher castes have also claimed the right for reservation on economic grounds, but with the privatization of much government enterprise, the possibility of government positions for any caste is greatly lessened. Meanwhile, the years of reservation have created a large middle class among untouchables.

Increased violence, usually in the rural areas, when untouchables claim economic, religious, or social rights disputed by higher castes, is reported from all parts of India. The practice of untouchability was prohibited by law in the constitution, and there are many court cases, but much injustice is still handed out by police and higher castes, as detailed in the Human Rights Watch's publication *Broken People.*

A flowering of Dalit literature, "the literature of the oppressed," began in Marathi in the early 1970s with the poetry of the Dalit Panthers in Bombay and has now spread to almost every language area in India. *Dalit* means "ground down, broken up," as in the title *Broken People.* But like the African-American use of the word *black,* it is not a term indicative of victimization but a proud term indicating that an untouchable is not polluting but oppressed by others and that even a middle-class untouchable should identify with those still oppressed. The organization of young men who called themselves Dalit Panthers in imitation of the Black Panthers in the United States is no longer active, but *Dalit* has replaced the words *untouchable* and *harijan* in most public pronouncements and the press.

The name of the Bahujan Samaj Party (BSP) means the party of the majority, and in its founding by Kanshi Ram, an untouchable Sikh, in 1984 it was intended to include all nonelite groups, the majority in India. It has been very successful in the northern state of Uttar Pradesh, where Mayawati, a Chamar woman, served three terms as chief minister. Mayawati stressed the importance of Ambedkar and his liberal political philosophy but joined with the Bharatiya Janata Party (BJP), a conservative party led by Brahmins, in order to secure power to make changes in the state.

It is impossible to ignore the role of B. R. Ambedkar in any discussion of untouchables or Dalits in the early twenty-first century. His image is in every town and many villages, often represented by a statue of a man in suit and tie, the dress of most of the educated, holding a book that represents the constitution. He is a symbol of pride and revolt, an inspiration for continuing progress.

## Untouchability outside Hinduism

The caste system has permeated other religions in India, and untouchables exist in Christianity, Islam, and Sikhism, although without scriptural legitimacy. A movement among Dalit Christians for equal rights within the church is especially strong.

Many Dalits attended the 2001 United Nations conference on racism in Durban, contending that "descent-based" groups suffer the same discrimination as racial groups, a concept opposed by the government of India. Caste-like discrimination has been found in some other countries, with the Burakumin of Japan suffering in much the same way as Indian untouchables, although the rest of the caste hierarchy was not present.

*See also* **Hinduism; Untouchability: Menstrual Taboos; Untouchability: Taboos.**

**BIBLIOGRAPHY**
Ambedkar, B. R. "Castes in India." In *Dr. Babasaheb Ambedkar, Writings and Speeches,* edited by Vasant Moon, vol. 1. Bombay: Education Department, Government of Maharashtra, 1979.
———. "The Untouchables." In *Dr. Babasaheb Ambedkar, Writings and Speeches,* edited by Vasant Moon, vol. 7. Bombay: Education Department, Government of Maharashtra, 1990.
*Broken People: Caste Violence against India's Untouchables.* New York: Human Rights Watch, 1999.
Chokhamela. *On the Threshold: Songs of Chokhamela.* Translated by Rohini Mokashi-Punekar. Delhi: Book Review Literary Trust, 2002.
Deliège, Robert. *The Untouchables of India.* Translated by Nora Scott. Oxford: Berg, 1999.
Dumont, Louis. *Homo Hierarchicus: The Caste System and Its Implications.* Translated by Mark Sainsbury, Louis Dumont, and Basia Gulati. Rev. ed. Chicago: University of Chicago Press, 1980.
Jha, Vivekananda. "Stages in the History of Untouchables." *Indian Historical Review* 2 (1975): 14–31.
Mendelsohn, Oliver, and Marika Vicziany. *The Untouchables: Subordination, Poverty, and the State in Modern India.* Cambridge, U.K.: Cambridge University Press, 1998.
Moon, Vasant. *Growing Up Untouchable: A Dalit Autobiography.* Translated by Gail Omvedt. Lanham, Md.: Rowman and Littlefield, 2001.
Singh, K. S. *The Scheduled Castes.* Delhi: Oxford University Press, 1993.
Valmiki, Omprakash. *Joothan: An Untouchable's Life.* Translated by Arun Prabha Mukherjee. New York: Columbia University Press, 2003.
Zelliot, Eleanor. *From Untouchable to Dalit: Essays on the Ambedkar Movement.* 3rd ed. New Delhi: Manohar, 2001.
Zelliot, Eleanor, and Rohini Mokashi-Punekar, eds. *Untouchable Saints: An Indian Phenomenon.* New Delhi: Manohar, 2004.

*Eleanor Zelliot*

## MENSTRUAL TABOOS

Menstruation is a physiological process often imbued with powerful cultural and religious symbols. For men, it is a mysterious and sometimes frightening phenomenon—the shedding of blood without visible injury. For women, it has been a double-edged sword. Far too often, it has been used in misogynist ideologies as evidence of the defiling and ungodly nature of the female body, leading many societies to subject menstruating women to taboos that limit their autonomy and agency. However, not all societies have interpreted menstruation in the same way: in some cultures it has been perceived as relatively unimportant, subject to neither stigma nor taboo; in others, menstruation has been a sign of the magical power of the female body, in all its mysterious fecundity. Indeed many societies exhibit profound ambivalence where menstruation is concerned, imbuing it with both positive and negative meanings, making it difficult to arrive at a single interpretation of menstrual taboos.

## Menstrual Taboos in Tribal and Band Societies

The more positive or neutral associations of menstruation typically are found in small-scale, relatively egalitarian societies, where misogyny is in general less well developed. In many such societies, the menstruating woman was perceived as emitting a supernatural power, or mana; as anthropologists such as Mary Douglas have found, this sacred power is neither inherently good nor inherently bad. It is, however, extremely powerful, with a potential to be creative and energetic or destructive and even deadly. Thus menstruating women, like women who have recently given birth, had to observe strict taboos and to remain segregated from ordinary society, especially from men, who could be inadvertently hurt by a menstruating woman's mana.(It is noteworthy that males who had shed blood in war typically suffered similar proscriptions.)

Foragers such as the Eskimo feared the perceived danger of menstruating women on men's ability to hunt. The attitudes of Australian Aborigines, in contrast, are more complex and not altogether negative. Agricultural peoples too exhibit a variety of attitudes, with some making positive connections between agricultural fertility, the moon, and women's cycles, whereas others constructed symbolic oppositions between breast milk and menstrual blood as representations of birth and death and so found menstruating women to be a danger to crops and animals, and still others, such as Andean peoples, attached little significance to menstrual blood.

Menstrual taboos also serve to underline the gender segregation characteristic of many tribal societies, such as the Maori of New Zealand or the Arapesh of New Guinea. Sexual intercourse, in the case of the Mae Enga of the Central Highlands, was strictly limited in order to preserve male vitality, with menstrual blood, according to Mervyn Meggitt, perceived as especially corrupting to men's "vital juices."

Menstruating women, for the Lele of Africa, were prohibited from poking the fire or cooking for their husbands due to their polluting presence, while Bemba women feared pollution from the adulterous actions of men. These often rigid demarcations of sexual roles were thought to be necessary in upholding the foundation of community and preventing "sex pollution" from outside intermingling; the result, however, especially in the rigidly segregated societies of highland New Guinea, reflected and perpetuated a view that men and women belonged to two mutually distinct, hostile, and antagonistic spheres, both of which constituted a danger to the other.

Many such societies feature a special enclosed spaced, referred to in the anthropological literature as a "menstrual hut"—a nomenclature that reveals the unconscious biases of earlier scholars, who routinely referred to male ritual spaces as "men's houses," even when the "huts and "houses" were of similar size and construction. The retreat into sacred space protected the women themselves—as vulnerable carriers of a divine power—as well as other members of their society, who could be injured by a glance alone. Not all retreats to the hut constituted a punishment, however; for the Mbuti of Zaire, seclusion among women in the hut, or *elima,* gave rise to a spirit of community as younger and older women sang special songs to one another, sometimes to be joined by the musical replies of men who stood outside. Menstruation and isolation were also connected in rites of passage for young girls. Existing in a marginal state between childhood and adulthood, such girls could undergo seclusion followed by a ritual deflowerment, mortification, and beatings (as with the Uaupes of Brazil) or, in the case of the Deshast Brahmins of India, joyous celebrations, feasts, and the exchange of presents.

## Menstruation and Civilization

In general, however, the greater social inequalities and restrictions that accompany the rise of civilization brought with them an increase in negative attitudes toward women and their bodies and a greater attention to controlling female agency and reproductive powers. This can be seen in many of the great religions of the world and in the cultural traditions of the West. Among the ancient Greeks, for example, Pliny wrote that menstrual blood could "[turn] new wine sour," render crops barren, dull the "gleam of ivory," drive dogs mad, and even cause "very tiny creatures" such as ants to turn away in disgust from a grain of corn that had suffered contact with the offending woman. But what was an affliction—a curse—could also constitute a sacred gift or what the Romans called *sacra*; enclosed within male boundaries, woman were graced as well as burdened by the cyclical days of blood they had to bear.

The great religions that developed with the rise of civilization tended to further these ideas in religious texts and doctrines, especially when it came to delineating rules of sacred and ritual cleanliness and pollution. Zoroastrianism placed purity as one of the most important tenets in the upholding of the faith, with those deemed impure—including women during their menses but also priests with bleeding sores—prohibited from entering the fire temple. In Hinduism, where rules of untouchability could be vast and complex, bleeding women were expected to avoid worship, cooking, and members of their own family through restrictions that were precisely proscribed; according to the Vendidad (16.4), a woman in her menses "should keep fifteen paces from fire, fifteen from water . . . and three paces from a holy man." Visiting a consecrated holy place during menses was highly contaminating and therefore forbidden, as were women's involvement in ritualistic worship practices in general. Such a stigma was explained in part by the Bhagavata Purana, which described the menstrual cycle as constituting a partial karmic reaction to Indra's inadvertent killing of a brahmana; according to the text, after Indra killed the brahmana, he proceeded to negotiate with four groups who agreed to absorb one-quarter of the karmic reaction in exchange for a blessing. Women received the blessing of engaging in sex during pregnancy without endangering the embryo in exchange for accepting the monthly menstrual cycle.

In the Judeo-Christian tradition, the biblical Book of Leviticus was the most central and influential text in postulating rules having to do with cleanliness and uncleanness or what the anthropologist Mary Douglas called purity and danger. Leviticus stated that while menstruating, a woman would be considered unclean for seven days and anyone who touched her would also be unclean. The taboo continued to be recognized by Orthodox Jews, who relegated bleeding women to their own secluded sphere or enjoined them to abstain from sexual intercourse for seven days, followed by immersion in the *mikveh,* or ritual bath. Such isolation accorded with what was thought to be women's special burdens—or Eve's multiplying sorrows—as the prophet Micah enjoined them to "Be in pain, and labour to bring forth, O daughter of Zion, like a woman in travail" (Mic. 4:10). Such rites were also, however, continuous with other treatments in the Old Testament concerning the mundane and symbolic use of blood, which was seen as life-giving as well as defiling and all-important in the preparation of food or the act of sacrifice.

In the New Testament, Jesus encounters and cures a "woman with issue" who has been menstruating continuously for twelve years when she touches the hem of his garment—not his body—and is told, "Thy faith hath made thee whole" (Matt. 9:20–22). But Levitican notions of cleanliness and uncleanness, isolation and contamination, continued to pervade the early Christian world in such debates as the acceptability of menstruating women entering churches or receiving communion. In early Syrian Christian texts as well as the writing of Origen, women undergoing menses were prohibited, like their Jewish counterparts, from entering church or "mixing" reproductive blood with the sacrificial blood at the altar; it would therefore become a notable development when Pope Gregory I (590–604) informed Augustine, the monk and bishop of Canterbury, that menstruating women should not be forbidden from entering church or receiving communion, though "if [she] out of a sense of deep reverence does not presume to receive communion, she must be praised" (Bede, 1:27). Despite such leniency, penitential texts as well as a later archibishop of Canterbury, Theodore, chose to uphold the prohibition, which continued well into the Middle Ages.

## Medical Variations and Modern Interpretations

Ancient medical writers onward believed menstrual blood constituted a toxic substance that needed to purge itself from the body, with Hippocrates arguing that that fermentation in the blood precipitated menstruation because women were unable to rid themselves of their impurities in the blood through sweat alone. Aristotle for his part assumed that menstruation represented the excess blood not incorporated into the fetus, while Galen believed it to originate in part from residual blood in food that women were unable to digest. During the Middle Ages, menstruation continued to be regarded as malignant and unclean, emanating from the "imperfection" of women, though by the end of the sixteenth century, according to Ian Maclean, there was far less stress on the noxious nature of menses, and the majority of texts "stress their harmless excremental nature" (Maclean, p. 40). Still, sexual intercourse during the menstruation cycle, for example, continued to be a particularly charged subject for theologians and medical writers, with Thomas Aquinas in the thirteenth century rendering the deed a mortal sin, unless the woman's cycle was unusually prolonged and consummation was absolutely necessary. Such medical and theological ideas would decline only slightly in the early modern period, when Cardinal Cajetan demoted intercourse during menstruation to a "minor sin," though it remained, in Thomas Sanchez's words, "unseemly." Seventeenth-century writers continued to perpetuate the stigma that attached itself around the menstrual cycle, with the Englishman Helkiah Crooke questioning, "What pleasure of contentment could any man finde in a wife so lothsomely defiled, and that perpetually." The notion that a woman had to remain sexually untouchable, for her own sake as well as for her partner's, became especially pronounced in the nineteenth century, for example, when it was believed that gonorrhea could be transmitted to men through menstrual blood or that such emissions in general constituted a physiological as well as psychological threat. The new preoccupation with women's hysteria, and the frequent recommendation that such women be isolated in bed rest or asylum, was inexorably attached to the menstrual cycle, while a minority of physicians as late as 1920 could describe menstrual blood as containing highly toxic substances.

In the twentieth century anthropologists and psychoanalysts recognized the opportunity of examining culture through the prism of such a powerful taboo, which reflected a society's cosmological, symbolic, and social attitudes toward women, sex, blood, hygiene, and power. For Freud, the segregation of a woman during her menses might have served a hygienic purpose, though it above all reflected ambivalent notions and phobic fears about women as a whole; in the 1960s William Stephens continued the psychoanalytic treatment of the taboo, arguing that castration anxiety, from the sight of bleeding

genitals, resided behind the imposition of untouchability onto menstruating women across cultures. Bruno Bettelheim, on the other hand, argued that male envy had originally attached itself to the biologically powerful act of menstruation, with quarantine an attempt to level the playing field between the sexes. Feminist and matriarchalist theories would advance Bettelheim's relatively positive treatment of the powers inherent in menstruation, arguing for a more subtle approach in which the "forbidden" and the "holy" are conjoined and the very terms *taboo* and *defilement* contain more complex associations than those that cohere around *oppression* alone. Such ideas also harkened back to the interpretations of Émile Durkheim and Sir James Frazer, who argued that society's repulsion actually reflected the positive, or at least formidable and respected, "sacred," or "priestly," power inherent in menstruation, with women segregated not for their inferior status but rather their power. Still, negative vestiges of the taboo linger in euphemisms or "red humor" jokes, in the politicization and stigmatization of premenstrual syndrome, or even in continuing claims over menstruation's "toxicity"—evidence of the continuation of the myth of the bleeding woman who bears "Eve's curse" in silence and sorrow.

*See also* **Anthropology; Motherhood and Maternity; Untouchability: Overview; Untouchability: Taboos.**

### BIBLIOGRAPHY

Bede, the Venerable Saint. *Bede's Ecclesiastical History of the English People.* Edited by Bertram Colgrave and R. A. B. Mynors. Oxford: Clarendon, 1969.

Buckley, Thomas, and Alma Gottlieb. *Blood Magic: The Anthropology of Menstruation.* Berkeley: University of California Press, 1988.

Delaney, Janice, Mary Jane Lupton, and Emily Toth. *The Curse: A Cultural History of Menstruation.* New York: E. P. Dutton, 1976.

Grahn, Judy. *Blood, Bread, and Roses: How Menstruation Created the World.* Boston: Beacon Press, 1993.

Houppert, Karen. *The Curse: Confronting the Last Unmentionable Taboo; Menstruation.* New York: Farrar, Straus, and Giroux, 1999.

Knight, Chris. *Blood Relations: Menstruation and the Origins of Culture.* New Haven, Conn.: Yale University Press, 1991.

Lander, Louise. *Images of Bleeding: Menstruation as Ideology.* New York: Orlando Press, 1988.

Lupton, Mary Jane. *Menstruation and Psychoanalysis.* Urbana and Chicago: University of Illinois Press, 1993.

Maclean, Ian. *The Renaissance Notions of Woman: A Study in the Fortunes of Scholasticism and Medical Science in European Intellectual Life.* Cambridge, U.K.: Cambridge University Press, 1980.

Ruether, Rosemary Radford. "Women's Body and Blood: The Sacred and the Impure." In *Through the Devil's Gateway: Women, Religion, and Taboo,* edited by Alison Joseph. London: SPCK, 1990.

*Sarah Covington*

## TABOOS

The notion of *taboo* has a peculiar history : it was originally a Polynesian term referring to a ritual prohibition against contact with a thing, an animal, or a person. The term eventually became a widely discussed anthropological concept, and finally, in its last avatar, has been adopted by most languages to refer to something that is strictly and collectively forbidden. This wide recognition stems from the fact that every culture has things that are forbidden for religious reasons. Certain beings or objects are thought to possess a kind of substance that renders them untouchable or unapproachable. In some cases, they may be thought of as particularly pure; in other cases, on the contrary, it is their extreme impurity that entails the obligation to keep them apart. The violation of a taboo has different consequences: sometimes it leads only to some temporary defilement but, in other cases, it can be considered a crime. Finally, as far as people are concerned, the notion of *taboo* applies to persons at both ends of the social ladder: kings as well as untouchables, priests as well as hermits. But in some ritual circumstances, nearly everyone can be the object of some kind of taboo: in transitory states, for instance during the liminal stages of rites of passage, ordinary people are also considered to be taboo.

The word *taboo* was first used in the English language by Captain James Cook, who, as early as 1777, reported that some chiefs in Tonga were not allowed to behave like common people: they were *taboo,* Cook explained. The first European observers were not quite sure whether *taboo* meant "sacred" or "defiled." This uncertainty is probably due to the fact that the concept is ambivalent, and can mean both, depending on the case. Later scholars often pointed out this paradox: in his major study on the subject, Franz Steiner insisted that the Brahman was just as taboo as the untouchable. In the Polynesian context, the word *taboo* has largely been thought to be inseparable from the idea of *mana,* a term that refers to the religious power or force attached to some people or objects. A chief is said to possess *mana,* and is considered to be taboo by virtue of this power. The idea of *mana* was once given great importance in some anthropological writings: Marcel Mauss (1872–1950), for example, devotes a great deal of attention to the idea of *mana* in his studies of the gift and magic. Yet later observers noticed that *mana* was finally an empty concept that meant hardly more than a "thing" or a "thingamajig": and as it means nothing, it can be taken to mean anything.

The concept of *taboo* soon became part of the English language, but even before then it was widely discussed by early anthropologists. While it had fallen out of fashion by the end of the twentieth century and was hardly considered an essential anthropological concept, this was not the case in the nineteenth century, when it was seen as something that had to be explained by anthropologists. The "primitives," it was then thought, lived in a world dominated by taboo. James Frazer, for instance, regarded taboo as a symptom of irrationality: primitive man, he argued, believed he lived in a world full of supernatural dangers, and he protected himself by maintaining a distance between himself and those threats. Frazer's description of numerous cases of taboo and his interpretation of it were deeply influential and permeated Sigmund Freud's views on "primitive" societies. According to Freud (1856–1939), society derived from psychology, and this was particularly clear in "primitive" societies. In *Totem and Taboo* (1913),

Freud assimilates the primitive human to a neurotic, and the concept of *taboo* plays a significant role in supporting this equation. According to the father of psychoanalysis, the multitude of fears and prohibitions in which the "savage" lives parallels the world of the neurotic. Furthermore, people forbid only what they desire and are therefore always ambivalent toward their prohibitions. This is particularly true of the incest prohibition, which Freud labeled the *incest taboo*: the mother is a forbidden sexual partner because she is the object of an intense desire. All other taboos, such as food taboos, are only extensions of the fundamental incest taboo.

Like his contemporaries, Freud considerably exaggerated the importance of fear and prohibition in preindustrial societies. Modern anthropologists soon realized that the people they studied did not live in a world dominated by prohibitions of all kinds. It is interesting to note that Captain Cook had seen the Polynesians' taboos as more funny than frightening, and later, modernist anthropologists such as Bronislaw Malinowski (1884–1942) and native authors from tribal societies alike commented on the variability of attitudes toward taboos. At one extreme is the strict adherence of the religious to dietary restrictions, an attitude as likely to be found among urban sophisticates as isolated tribesmen, and at the other the relaxed and humorous attention noted by Cook. In the early 2000s anthropologists no longer considered *taboo* to be a unitary category. Malinowski opined that taboos are most strictly observed in arenas where technical competence is least likely to yield predictable results, an observation later extended to the study of contemporary professional athletes, who often observe personal rituals and taboos with great rigor before major games.

The term itself remains useful, as there is no other word to refer to what is both dangerous and forbidden. It resurfaced in the mid-twentieth century in the work of the anthropologist Marvin Harris, who considered that all prohibitions, and food taboos in particular, are not arbitrary but result from the material conditions in which people live: the taboo on eating cow or pig was dictated by the economic conditions in which Hindus and Arabs lived. On the whole, Harris's explanations are rather unconvincing and certainly fail to establish a true determination. In another vein, Mary Douglas notes that purity taboos cannot be explained by considerations of cleanliness. Dirtiness, she maintains, has first of all to be understood within a system of symbols and cannot be taken as an isolated phenomenon: what is pure exists only as the contrary of what is impure. Thus, taboos belong to a category or a system of classification.

As a general category, the concept of *taboo* illustrates the differences that divide contemporary anthropologists: those who seek a general understanding of humanity find some usefulness in broad concepts such as this. Others argue that it can be useful only at the cost of a serious impoverishment of social realities. Yet the fact remains that we have no other concept to describe socioreligious prohibitions.

*See also* **Anthropology; Untouchability: Overview; Untouchability: Menstrual Taboos.**

BIBLIOGRAPHY

Douglas, Mary. *Purity and Danger: An Analysis of Concepts of Pollution and Taboo.* London: Routledge and Kegan Paul, 1966.

Frazer, James G. *The Golden Bough: A Study in Comparative Religion.* London: Macmillan, 1894.

Freud, Sigmund. *Totem and Taboo: Some Points of Agreement between the Mental Lives of Savages and Neurotics.* Authorized translation by James Strachey. London: Routledge and Paul, 1950.

Harris, Marvin. *Cows, Pigs, Wars, and Witches: The Riddles of Culture.* New York: Vintage, 1974.

Steiner, Franz. *Taboo.* With a preface by E. E. Evans-Pritchard. London: Cohen and West, 1956.

*Robert Deliège*

## UPANISHADS. *See* **Communication of Ideas: Asia and Its Influence; Hinduism.**

## UTILITARIANISM.

*Utilitarianism* is the name of a group of ethical theories that judges the rightness of acts, choices, decisions, and policies by their consequences for human (and possibly animal) welfare. These theories have been widely influential among philosophers, economists, and political and social scientists, and, in the early twenty-first century, in the general area of applied or practical ethics. It would not be too much to say that utilitarian thinking undergirds one of the contending positions on virtually each of the issues in debate, whether to do with animal rights, euthanasia and physician-assisted suicide, health care coverage, or punishment. This is so, moreover, even as critics of utilitarianism as a normative ethical theory have become more numerous.

Classically, utilitarianism is the view that acts are right or wrong if they produce best consequences—that is, consequences with regard to human welfare that are at least as good as those of any alternative. This is the view normally associated with Jeremy Bentham (1748–1832), James Mill (1773–1836), and John Stuart Mill (1806–1873); with Henry Sidgwick (1838–1900) and G. E. (George Edward) Moore (1873–1958); more recently, with J. J. C. Smart (b. 1920) and Richard Mervyn Hare (1919–2002); and, more recently still, Peter Singer (b. 1946). It began, thus, in the nineteenth century in Britain, though traces of it can be found in earlier thinkers there, such as Francis Hutcheson (1694–1746), David Hume (1711–1776), and William Godwin (1756–1836). This classical version of the theory is also the view that contemporary critics, such as Amartya Sen (b. 1933), Bernard Williams (1929–2003), and Samuel Scheffler, attack. In fact, different versions of utilitarianism have been distinguished from classical- or act-utilitarianism, such as rule-utilitarianism, utilitarian generalization, motive utilitarianism, and so on, though it remains hotly debated how far these versions are ultimately distinct from the utilitarianism (and, to critics, from the objections directed against it).

Act-utilitarianism as it has come down to the present has three main components, and each has generated discussion in its own right. These are the consequence component, the value component, and the range component.

The consequence component maintains that rightness is tied to the production of good consequences (specifically, to consequences better than those of any alternative or best consequences). It may be argued that something in addition to consequences helps to determine an act's rightness, but consequentialism is the view that consequences alone determine this; act-utilitarians are consequentialists. Consequentialism in the early 2000s is the object of a good deal of criticism, though even in the nineteenth century it was sometimes controversial, as in the debates between Cardinal Newman (1801–1890) and Charles Kingsley (1801–1890). To some it is self-defeating, in that an effort to produce best consequences on each occasion may fail to produce best consequences overall. To others it seems inherently evil because it cannot exclude certain acts as intrinsically wrong or wrong independently of consequences (for example, lying). More recent criticisms have been equally strong. To John Rawls (b. 1921) impersonal accounts of rightness, such as best consequences, fail to take seriously the separateness of persons and so fail to treat people as autonomous individuals with their own individuality, plans, and worth. To Bernard Williams impersonal accounts of rightness run the risk of severing one from one's integrity, in the sense that pursuit of best consequences may not be compatible with pursuit of one's own projects, commitments, and relationships. Of course, some act-utilitarians, such as R. M. Hare (1919–2002), have resisted the Rawls-Williams objections, but others influenced by the theory, such as L. Wayne Sumner, have responded by trying to build a scheme of individual moral rights into the theory on the ground that doing so gives one the best chance of producing best consequences. (See indirect utilitarianism below.) Still more recent criticisms move in an epistemological direction. One cannot know at the time of acting, it is said, what (all) the consequences of one's proposed act will be. Some have seen this as demanding a role for rules as a guide; others, such as Peter Railton, have viewed it as a reason for not trying to act upon consequentialism in the first place and so for not using this account of rightness as if it were a decision procedure. He suggests a role for the concept of (good) character in determining how individuals shall act.

The value component has from Bentham onward spurred debate. It maintains that consequences are to be assessed by some standard of intrinsic goodness, the presence of which in the world is to be maximized. In the early twenty-first century this good in the case of act-utilitarianism is construed to be human welfare, but how "welfare" is to be understood is contentious. Thus, Bentham is a hedonist, maintaining that all and only pleasure (which his felicific calculus was supposed to be able to calculate) is intrinsically good; not surprisingly, Friedrich Nietzsche (1844–1900) referred to utilitarianism as a pig philosophy. John Stuart Mill spoke of happiness and pleasure and tried to introduce a distinction between higher and lower pleasures, and the mentor of the Bloomsbury Group, G. E. Moore, maintained that other things, such as beauty and friendship, as well as pleasure and/or happiness, were good in themselves. Most act-utilitarians have followed Moore in moving away from hedonism and from the emphasis upon happiness.

Three types of issues have dominated recent critical discussion of the value component. First, there has been a movement away from the old mental-state accounts of goodness (e.g., pleasure) to desire- or preference-satisfaction accounts. Economists have helped spur this development. It is unclear, however, upon which desires one is to focus. Problems to do with present or future desires have led theorists to an emphasis upon informed desires—that is, those desires one would have if one were fully informed, detached, free from bias and pressure, and so on. The thought seems to be that, in the appropriate circumstances, informed desires become actual, and so those desires upon which one (rightly) acts. (This thought, so construed, can then be wedded, in economics, to "revealed preference" accounts of goodness, which are widespread.) Second, there has been a movement away from agent-neutral values toward agent-relative ones. Values, it is said, are subjective, in the sense of being agent-relative; they are the values of agents. Utilitarianism, however, requires that desires be aggregated, weighed, and balanced in terms of, for example, agent-neutral concerns to do with the amount of desire-satisfaction produced, irrespective of which individual agents obtain that satisfaction. The question then arises whether any particular agent has reason to value pursuit of overall desire-satisfaction, in addition to or in place of his or her own. Third, if one focuses upon desires, then a question about moral filtering devices obviously arises. If one takes into account the desires of all those party to a situation, does one filter out the desires of evildoers? This seems contrary to the spirit of utilitarianism and its emphasis upon agent-neutral values. But if one does not filter out the desires of evildoers, does this mean that the utilitarian weighs and balances their desires, according to strength, with the desires of those against whom evildoers act?

The range component maintains that all those affected by the act are to have their desires taken into account. This has led notoriously, from the nineteenth century onward, to the problem of interpersonal comparisons of (pains and pleasures) or desire-satisfaction. One can only maximize desire-satisfaction across all those affected by the act if one can compare the effect of the act upon the desire sets of each individual involved, judge the strength and extent of that effect, and then compare the different results. How one does this, what measures or scales of comparison are used, is not obvious. Another problem with the range component that stirs debate in the early twenty-first century has been whether to include animals within the scope of utilitarianism. Bentham did, on the grounds that animals could suffer. But if informed desires are the focus of the value component, can animals have informed desires? The point is not obvious (just as it is not obvious that all humans can have informed desires). Some utilitarians want to keep a pain/pleasure standard of goodness for animals, but endorse desire-satisfaction accounts for humans. Still another problem for the range component has to do with the emphasis in utilitarianism upon maximization of what is deemed to be intrinsically good. Something short of this, of increasing the amount of good to some extent less than the greatest extent possible, is both possible and less problematic, at least if one treats Derek Parfit's "repugnant conclusion"—that one can increase the greatest total happiness (or desire-satisfaction) in the world by eliminating those at the bottom of the happiness

ladder—as tied to the general thrust of maximization of the good.

To a large extent, discussion of utilitarianism in the late twentieth to early twenty-first century has moved away from earlier concerns. It has centered around three developments. First, R. M. Hare and others have urged a kind of indirect utilitarianism, wherein one does not employ consequentialism at the level of practice, in order to decide what it would be right to do. Hare urges a two-level account of moral thinking, which is rule-utilitarian at the level of practice but act-utilitarian at the level of theory or rule/institutional design. In his hands, act-utilitarian thinking at the critical level will select as guides at the intuitive or practical level those rules whose general acceptance will give one the best chance of producing best consequences. In this way, it is only in exceptional circumstances that one's practical guides are exposed to consequentialist thinking. Thus, Hare hopes to avoid many of the problems that are held to beset the act-utilitarian, through the employment of consequentialism as a way of deciding what it would be right to do. Hare's two-level account of moral thinking can seem, then, a way of developing a further case for act-utilitarianism; other two-level theorists, it should be noted, do not see the split-level innovation as furthering this particular case. In fact, on Hare's account, since the focus of his theory is no longer acts, on a case-by-case basis, the name *act-utilitarianism* is something of a misnomer.

Second, because so many of the objections to act-utilitarianism (and consequentialism) have always centered around clashes with "ordinary moral convictions" or "commonsense morality," the question has arisen of whether our ordinary moral intuitions have probative force in ethics. To those who feel that they do have probative force, the problem has been to make it appear that certain of one's intuitions are more secure than others, so that they are believed to be more "true" or "correct" than the dictates of any normative ethical theory. Accordingly, one needs to identify which these crucial intuitions are. Different ways of doing this have been suggested, including Rawls's reflective equilibrium method. But it is clear, even in Rawls, that some intuitions survive intact, such as the wrongness of slavery. This intuition of his needs no revision. Other theorists privilege other of their intuitions about particular acts or classes of acts. Over privileging in this way, serious doubts can arise, no matter how secure one feels one's intuitions to be. Yet, it is from this very privileging that condemnations of act-utilitarianism typically begin. It is wrong to lie, and the act-utilitarian mounts a case for lying on this occasion; it is wrong to kill, but the act-utilitarian mounts a case in favor of active euthanasia or abortion or suicide. In this way, arguments about the probative force of certain of one's intuitions have taken on a life of their own and are often used in moral debate in the early twenty-first century. This is especially true in medical ethics, where some want to draw a distinction between killing and letting die and where act-utilitarians on the whole deny that such a distinction is morally significant or where some want to distinguish, say, between giving someone a pill which, if they take it, will kill them and giving someone an injection of a sufficiently large dose of morphine to hasten their death while intending only to relieve their pain.

Third, the enormous growth of applied or practical ethics, especially medical ethics, has brought act-utilitarianism and consequentialism into the public domain. Almost without exception, virtually every issue, whether to do with killing, the allocation of resources, or the case for animal experimentation, features a utilitarian line of argument, and this line of argument is also, typically, act-utilitarian in character. This in a way is odd: while theorists are developing more and different types of indirect utilitarianisms, most of the examples of applied ethics feature the direct application of consequentialism on a case-by-case basis, with, it is held, morally shocking results. To be sure, not everyone will be shocked any longer by a case in support of a doctor assisting a competent patient who voluntarily requests assistance in dying, but the case can be discussed from the level of rule or institutional design, as well as from the consequentialist realities of the situation in question. Moreover, there are more general questions that arise in the various areas of applied ethics, where act-utilitarians are taken to adopt a particular kind of stand. Thus, one can intentionally kill a patient or one can knowingly bring about or cause a patient's death: are these morally different? One can directly bring about a person's death or one can indirectly bring it about: are these morally different? One can bring about a person's death by action or one can bring it about by omission: are these morally different? One can bring about a person's death actively or passively: are these morally different? If the consequences appear the same or very similar, the act-utilitarian will be held to think there is no difference among these things. Because Hare and others favor an indirect form of utilitarianism, it is not uncommon in the early 2000s to treat these practical issues as if they involved direct consequentialists and leave until another occasion whether these consequentialists are also act-utilitarians. In this way, applied ethics has helped consequentialism to come to dwarf the other components of act-utilitarianism.

For Hare, moral education plays an important role in one's moral thinking. He rejects the employment of consequentialism on a case-by-case basis for deciding what to do and rejects as well the thought that consequentialism indicates the kind of thinking one should do at the intuitive or practical level. Instead, he emphasizes the role of character and character development: by education, individuals turn themselves into people whose actions flow from their character, in which the traits and dispositions that comprise character are inculcated in them overseen by the utilitarian goal of maximizing human welfare. This further reduces clashes with certain privileged moral intuitions, but it does not require that one treat those intuitions as having probative force. In this way, the moral thinking for Hare is much more intimately connected with one making one's self into the sort of creature who behaves out of certain dispositions than into the sort of creature who acts only out of consequentialist concerns.

Utilitarianism, then, has in latter years undergone a significant transformation at the hands of theorists. It is no longer the relatively simple, straightforward rubric that Bentham and John Stuart Mill took it to be; its statement, even by those who remain sympathetic to it, such as Hare and those influenced by him, is complicated and layered. An account of its historical development in terms of ideas, as can be seen here, shows that it has become sufficiently encumbered with distinctions and technicalities that it no longer really resembles the earlier view. Yet, in the twenty-first century, it is still common to find thinkers objecting to some particular view in moral, political, or social policy as "utilitarian," where the view they have in mind is the direct application of consequentialist thinking to decisions on how to behave. Thus, in modern medical ethics, there is little concern to get right the niceties of utilitarian theory; rather, the point is to protest about the "shocking" results that the direct application of consequentialist thinking can appear to produce in some instances.

*See also* **Happiness and Pleasure in European Thought; Hedonism in European Thought; Liberalism; Rational Choice; Virtue Ethics.**

## BIBLIOGRAPHY

Bentham, Jeremy. *An Introduction to the Principles of Morals and Legislation.* 1789. Reprint, New York: Hafner, 1948.

Hare, Richard Mervyn. *Moral Thinking: Its Levels, Method and Point.* Oxford: Clarendon, 1981.

Mill, John Stuart. *Utilitarianism.* 1861. Reprint, Englewood Cliffs, N.J.: Prentice-Hall, 1957.

Moore, George Edward. *Ethics.* 1912. Reprint, New York: Oxford University Press, 1961.

Nietzsche, Friedrich. *Beyond Good and Evil.* 1886. Reprint, Middlesex, U.K.: Penguin, 1990.

Parfit, Derek. *Reasons and Persons.* Oxford: Clarendon, 1984.

Railton, Peter. "Alienation, Consequentialism, and the Demands of Morality." *Philosophy and Public Affairs* 13 (1984): 134–171.

Rawls, John. *A Theory of Justice.* Cambridge, U.K.: Harvard University Press, 1971.

Scheffler, Samuel. *The Rejection of Consequentialism.* Oxford: Clarendon, 1982.

Sen, Amartya K. "Utilitarianism and Welfarism." *Journal of Philosophy* 76, no. 9 (September 1979): 463–489.

Sidgwick, Henry. *Methods of Ethics.* 7th ed. 1874. Reprint, London: Macmillan, 1907.

Singer, Peter. *Practical Ethics.* Cambridge, U.K.: Cambridge University Press, 1993.

Smart, John Jameison Carswell. "An Outline of a System of Utilitarian Ethics." In *Utilitarianism: For and Against,* by J. J. C. Smart and Bernard Williams. Cambridge, U.K.: Cambridge University Press, 1973.

Sumner, L. Wayne. *The Moral Foundations of Rights.* Oxford: Clarendon, 1987.

Williams, Bernard. "A Critique of Utilitarianism." In *Utilitarianism: For and Against,* by J. J. C. Smart and Bernard Williams. Cambridge, U.K.: Cambridge University Press, 1973.

*R. G. Frey*

**UTOPIA.** The word *utopia* was coined by Thomas More (1478–1535) as the name of the island described in his *Libellus vere aureus nec minus salutaris quam festivus de optimo reip[ublicae] statu, deq[ue] noua Insula Vtopia* (1516). While More wrote in Latin, he based his new word on Greek. More combined *topos* (*place* or *where*) with *u* or *ou* (*no* or *not*) to create *nowhere,* but in "Six Lines on the Island of Utopia,"

**1518 woodcut by Ambrosius Holbein from Thomas More's *Utopia*.** Although the concept of utopia has existed in many different religions and societies since ancient times, the term itself was originated by Thomas More in his early-sixteenth-century work.

part of the larger work, he suggests that the word *eutopia,* or good place, is a better descriptor. Thus, from the time of More's original coinage, the word *utopia* has been conflated with *eutopia* to mean a nonexistent good place.

The word *utopia* entered Western languages quickly—the book was translated into German in 1524, Italian in 1548, French in 1550, English in 1551, and Dutch in 1553, and the word itself often entered these languages before the book was translated. In the eighteenth century, the word *dystopia* was first used to characterize a nonexistent bad place, but the word did not become standard usage until the mid-twentieth century.

While More coined the word and invented the genre of literature that grew from the book, he was not the first to imagine the possibility of a society better than the one currently existing and to describe such a society. Examples of such imaginings can be found in ancient Sumer, classical Greek, and Latin literature, the Old Testament, Buddhism, Confucianism, and Hinduism, among other predecessors.

While it is no longer possible to see utopia as a product of the Christian West, the role of utopia in Christianity has long been an area of dispute. Eden, the millennium, and heaven all have clear utopian elements, but the extent to which they can be achieved through human action is open to dispute. The Fall and the resultant emphasis on sinful human nature has led some commentators to view utopia as anti-Christian and heretical. Human beings are simply not capable of a utopia in this life. But other commentators, like the theologian Paul Tillich (1886–1965) and the founders of Liberation Theology, have argued that utopia is central to any understanding of the social message of Christianity.

## Expressions of Utopianism

Today dreaming of or imagining better societies is usually called "utopianism," and utopianism can be expressed in a variety of ways. Utopian literature, the creation of intentional communities or communes, formerly called utopian experiments, and utopian social theory are the most commonly noted forms in which utopianism is expressed, but there are other means of expressing utopianism, such as the design of ideal cities.

*Utopian literature.* Utopian literature is most common in the English-speaking world, with particularly strong traditions in England, the United States, and New Zealand. Brazil, France, Germany, Greece, Italy, Russia, and Spanish America also have strong utopian traditions, and we now know that there are substantial utopian traditions in other European countries and in the non-Western world. The strongest non-Western utopian tradition is found in China, but such traditions exist throughout the Middle East and in India and Southeast Asia; there are also developing utopian traditions in various African countries. Even Japan, which was once thought to have no such tradition, has recently been shown by young Japanese scholars to have one.

Although early scholarship in the field treated utopias from all times and places as if they were alike, these utopian literatures differ from each other in significant ways, and national and cultural differences are now recognized. Also, as a direct result of the influence of feminist scholarship, we are now more aware of both the similarities and differences found in utopias written by men and woman, and recently such awareness has been extended to differences and similarities based on ethnicity, race, religion, and other such characteristics.

From its earliest expression to the present, a basic human utopia is found in which everyone has adequate food, shelter, and clothing gained without debilitating labor and in which people lead secure lives without fear of, in early versions, wild animals, and in later versions, other human beings. But these basic elements are expressed in different ways in different times and places and also reflect individual concerns; as a result, the range of utopias present throughout history is immense.

Much utopian literature, particularly the dystopian, has been marketed as science fiction, and one minor scholarly controversy had some arguing that utopias were a subgenre of science fiction and others arguing that historically it was the other way around. In the late twentieth and early twenty-first century, there was clearly an intellectual as well as a marketing overlap with the most prolific writers of utopias, like Ursula K. Le Guin (b. 1929) and Mack (Dallas McCord) Reynolds (1917–1983), using science fictional motifs and tropes. In *Scraps of the Untainted Sky* (2000), Tom Moylan carefully considers the relationships between utopia, dystopia, and science fiction.

Scholarship on utopian literature increased in both quantity and quality in the 1970s and 1980s with the publication of definitional essays by Lyman Tower Sargent and Darko Suvin that helped clarify the conceptual muddle; bibliographies by Arthur O. Lewis, Glenn Negley, and Sargent that transformed the understanding of the subject; and important books by Krishan Kumar, Frank E. and Fritzie P. Manuel, Tom Moylan, and Kenneth M. Roemer that rewrote the history of utopian literature. At the same time, there was a major revival of utopian writing, the most important works being Le Guin's *The Dispossessed* (1974), significantly subtitled *An Ambiguous Utopia,* and *The Left Hand of Darkness* (1969); Joanna Russ's (b. 1937) *Female Man* (1975); Marge Piercy's (b. 1936) *Woman on the Edge of Time* (1976); Samuel R. Delany's (b. 1942) *Dhalgren* (1975) and *Triton* (1976); and Margaret Atwood's (b. 1939) *The Handmaid's Tale* (1985).

A major contribution to our understanding of the changes utopias were undergoing was Moylan's development in *Demand the Impossible* (1986) of the "critical utopia." Moylan wrote:

> A central concern in the critical utopia is the awareness of the limitations of the utopian tradition, so that these texts reject utopia as a blueprint while preserving it as a dream. Furthermore, the novels dwell on the conflict between the originary world and the utopian society opposed to it so that the process of social change is more directly articulated. Finally, the novels focus on the continuing presence of difference and imperfection within the utopian society itself and thus render more recognizable and dynamic alternatives. (pp. 10–11)

Even though positive utopias were published in every year of the twentieth century, the dystopia has been the most frequently published form of utopian literature from World War I to the early twenty-first century. The dystopia uses the depiction of a usually extrapolated negative future as a means of warning the present to change its behavior. The message of the dystopia is that if the human race continues in the direction it is now heading, this is what will happen. The dystopia, thus, has a positive element in that it suggests the possibility of change. In this, the dystopia is in the tradition of the *Jeremiad*, or a work modeled on the Book of Jeremiah, in which a condemnation of contemporary behavior and a warning of retribution also holds out hope of improvement if the warning is heeded.

Although there were precursors, the dystopia came to prominence through four works: *We* (1924), by Yevgeny Zamyatin (1884–1937); *Brave New World* (1932), by Aldous Huxley (1894–1963); and *Animal Farm* (1945) and *Nineteen Eighty-Four* (1949), by George Orwell (Eric Arthur Blair; 1903–1950). They were concerned with the effects of the dominant ideologies of the twentieth century and each raised the question of the potential danger of a utopia based on one of these ideologies being imposed on some country. Such works continued to be written, albeit rarely as well, throughout the rest of the century. Later the dystopia was applied to other areas. Two works by John Brunner (1934–1995) are outstanding examples: *Stand on Zanzibar* (1968), focusing on the effects of overpopulation, and *The Sheep Look Up* (1972), focusing on the effects of pollution.

Some authors, such as Fredric Jameson and Sargent, have made a distinction between dystopia and anti-utopia. Sargent reserves the latter for works written against positive utopias or utopianism. Jameson does the same, but in doing so makes a political point by arguing that anti-utopianism has dominated the late twentieth century.

The most important twentieth-century theme of positive utopias has been feminism. The discovery of *Herland* (published serially in 1915) by Charlotte Perkins Gilman (1860–1935) with its first book publication in 1979 led to the discovery or rediscovery of many early feminist utopias, particularly *The Description of a New World, Called the Blazing World* (1666), by Margaret Cavendish, duchess of Newcastle (1623?–1674); *A Serious Proposal to the Ladies* (1694), by Mary Astell (1668–1731); and *A Description of Millenium Hall* (1762), by Sarah Scott (1723–1795).

Such feminist utopias are found throughout the history of utopian literature, but the greatest number were published from the mid-1970s through the end of the twentieth century, with the most important being those by Le Guin, Piercy, and Russ. Small feminist presses published many of these novels, and the many lesbian utopias were published almost exclusively by lesbian presses. Such lesbian utopias included *Retreat: As It Was!* (1979), by Donna J. Young; *Daughters of a Coral Dawn* (1984), by Katherine Forrest (b. 1939); and *Womanseed: A Vision* (1986), by Sunlight.

The other major theme of the late twentieth century was environmentalism. *Ecotopia* (1975), by Ernest Callenbach (b. 1929), the most influential of the environmental utopias, was initially published by a small press and then reissued by a mass-market publisher. Later, environmentalism and feminism combined in ecofeminism, and most utopias that are feminist or reflect environmentalism include the other perspective.

***Intentional communities.*** The aspect of turn-of-the-twenty-first-century utopian studies that might appear least connected to the tradition of utopianism is intentional communities, but most such communities had a clear vision of how they hoped to live, which was in many cases explicitly utopian. In most cases, the actuality of the communities had little to do with the visions. Still, the visions were there, and they attracted and continue to attract people who choose to try to live the vision, even if they regularly fail to do so.

Many intentional communities were founded in the late 1960s through the 1970s, and while most were short-lived, there are a substantial number of such communities, like Twin Oaks in Virginia and The Farm in Tennessee, that are well past their thirtieth anniversary. And there are individual communities in various countries that are past fifty or seventy-five years. The phenomenon continues to grow, with more communities planned and some founded each year, and although members now downplay the utopian aspects, they are still there.

***Utopian social theory.*** The first major theorist to use utopia as an aspect of social theory was Karl Mannheim (1893–1947). Mannheim's sociology of knowledge is concerned with the social origins of thought systems, and to understand them he contrasts ideology and utopia. Ideology characterizes dominant social groupings who unconsciously obscure the fragility of their position. Utopia characterizes subordinate social positions; it reflects the desire to escape from reality. The utopian mentality is at the base of all serious social change.

Karl R. Popper (1902–1994) objected to utopianism in his *The Open Society and Its Enemies* (1945). Popper argued that utopianism leads to violence and totalitarianism, saying, "the Utopian approach can be saved only by the Platonic belief in one absolute and unchanging ideal, together with two further assumptions, namely (a) that there are rational methods to determine once and for all what this ideal is, and (b) what the best means of its realization are" (vol. 1, p. 161). Popper's position came to dominate discussions of utopianism.

Those opposing Popper and supporting utopianism, like Ernst Bloch (1885–1977) and Frederik L. Polak (1907–1985), argued that utopianism was an essential element of all positive social theory. Polak argues that it is fundamental to the continuance of civilization, saying:

> if Western man now stops thinking and dreaming the materials of new images of the future and attempts to shut himself up in the present, out of longing for security and for fear of the future, his civilization will come to an end. He has no choice but to dream or to die, condemning the whole of Western society to die with him. (vol. 1, p. 53)

Others have argued that while some people may be willing to impose their vision on others if they have the power to do so, this is not a problem with utopianism but with people misusing power.

Karl Marx (1818–1883) and his followers argued that their version of socialism was scientific, in contrast to the socialism of the so-called utopian socialists. This position was most famously expressed by Friedrich Engels (1820–1895) in his *Socialism: Utopian and Scientific* (1882), but Marxists have always been more ambivalent about utopianism than this simple division suggests, and while many Marxists were anti-utopian, others were clearly utopian themselves.

Thus, while Bloch was a Marxist, he did not have the negative attitude to utopias of many Marxists because his philosophy stressed the end or goal of human life. He saw utopia as an aspect of present reality, saying, in his *Principle of Hope* (1955–1959):

So far does utopia extend, so vigorously does this raw material spread to all human activities, so essentially must every anthropology and science of the world contain it. *There is no realism worthy of the name if it abstracts from this strongest element in reality, as an unfinished reality.* (p. 624; emphasis in the original)

Bloch makes a key distinction between "abstract" and "concrete" utopia. "Abstract utopia" includes the wishful thinking or fanciful elements found in the utopian tradition, such as the golden ages, earthly paradises, and cockaignes that occur early in most utopian traditions but also continue throughout their histories. "Concrete utopia" anticipates and affects the future, something like Polak's idea that our images of the future are part of the creation of our actual future. But for Bloch, as a Marxist, utopia must be part of praxis, it must grow out of present reality and influence actual political activity. Utopia, for Bloch, is a mechanism that has the potential of being reached. As Oscar Wilde famously put it, "A map of the world that does not include Utopia is not worth even glancing at, for it leaves out the one country at which Humanity is always landing. And when Humanity lands there, it looks out, and, seeing a better country, sets sail. Progress is the realization of utopias (p. 27).

Bloch's approach is based on the joined concepts of "hope" and "desire," in which desire can become an active agent of change. In *The Concept of Utopia* (1990), Ruth Levitas uses Bloch's approach to develop an understanding of utopia as a politically important tool whose essence is desire.

## Postmodernism

The coming of postmodernism, with its rejection of universals, posed a problem for those utopians who see utopias as generalizable solutions. But as Moylan points out in *Demand the Impossible*, writers of utopias had begun to change their approach even as postmodernism became influential. Le Guin's subtitle, *An Ambiguous Utopia,* signaled an explicit rejection of perfection and the recognition that utopias will face problems and will change over time.

Fredric Jameson, one of the most important theorists of postmodernism, has written extensively on utopianism. Jameson, like Bloch, argues that the literary utopia is a form of praxis rather than representation. But for Jameson, utopias are not goals, as they are for Bloch, but critiques of the present that help reeducate us regarding the present.

Both positive and negative utopias continue to be published. Intentional communities continue to be founded, and while most will fail, some will last for many years, fulfilling at least some of the expectations of their members. And attempts to understand the roles played by utopianism in human thought continue. Utopias have always expressed both the hopes and fears of humanity, the highest aspirations for human life and the deep-seated fear that we may not be capable of our own aspirations.

## Non-Western Utopianism

While some well-regarded scholars argue that utopianism is a Western phenomenon and that utopias do not appear outside the West until the influence of More's *Utopia* was felt, others have argued that utopianism developed independently in non-Western cultures. Thomas More invented a literary genre, but there are texts in the West and outside it that predate More's *Utopia* that describe a nonexistent society that is identifiably better than the existing society. Probably the best-known early non-Western utopia is "The Peach Blossom Spring," a poem of T'ao Yüan Ming (also known as T'ao Ch'ien) (365–427), that describes a peaceful peasant society, but there are golden ages, earthly paradises, and other forms of utopianism found in Sumerian clay tablets and within Buddhism, Confucianism, Hinduism, Islam, and Daoism.

Once it is established that there are utopian traditions that are certainly non-Western, there are problems that confront a scholar approaching the subject at the beginning of the twenty-first century. One is the issue of what is non-Western. Scholars disagree profoundly over what constitutes non-Western and Western. Some would limit Western to Europe, North America, Australia, and New Zealand and thereby exclude the substantial Portuguese and Spanish literatures published in Central and South America, which contain many utopias. Others would include these literatures. A second problem is that there are no good bibliographies of any non-Western utopianism not written in English. A related problem is that there are debates in a number of countries, even in countries such as India, where English is an official language, over the status of works written in English, particularly those written by authors who choose to live outside the country.

In ancient China, Moist and Legalist thought had utopian elements, and the same can be said for neo-Confucianism and Daoism. In twentieth-century China, Mao Zedong (1893–1976) was clearly utopian in his desire to transform Chinese society along the lines of his vision for it, and it can be argued that Mao's Communism was both Marxist and rooted in Confucianism.

There have been a number of twentieth-century political movements with utopian dimensions. In India, Mohandas K. Gandhi (1869–1948) was a utopian and used the Hindu notion of Ramaraja (the rule of the Rama), the golden age, as a means of communicating his ideas. The vision of the Islamic republic developed by Ayatollah Ruhollah Khomeini (1900?–1989) and by the Taliban for Afghanistan were also clearly utopian and fit Popper's analysis of the dangers of utopianism.

There are oral utopian traditions among the aborigines in Australia, the first nations in Canada, the Maori in New Zealand, and the Native American Indians in the United States. The struggle against colonialism produced millennial movements with strong utopian elements, such as the Taiping Rebellion (1851–1864) in China and the Ghost Dance movement in the United States. There were dozens of such movements in South America and movements among the Maori in New Zealand, some of whose successors still exist in the early twenty-first century, such as the Maori's Ratana Church.

Also, there is a strong communitarian tradition in both Buddhism and Hinduism, and there is a traditional communitarianism among various indigenous peoples that has redeveloped since around 1980 as chosen, better ways of living, particularly among the Maori in New Zealand.

Most non-Western utopianism is post-More and clearly connected with the genre of literature he invented, and as a result are deeply influenced by the West. Since China had the strongest pre-More utopian tradition, it is not surprising that it has the strongest post-More tradition. The Chinese utopias that are best-known in the West are Li Ju-Chen's (c. 1760–c. 1830) *Flowers in the Mirror* (1828), which favors the rights of women, and Kang Youwei's (1858–1929) *Da T'ung Shu* (1935), which is concerned with world unity.

Works that most nearly fit the genre of utopian literature appear to be most common in former colonies, and aspects of Chinese utopianism fit this model. There are utopias in English in various African countries, including South Africa, where utopias are in Afrikaans, English, and indigenous languages. In addition, there are utopias (because of limited research, how many is not known) in various indigenous languages in other African countries and in India.

African utopias in English are the works most widely read in the West. They come from many different countries and have a strong dystopian flavor. But as with many contemporary Western utopias, they often hold out hope of positive change. Ali A. Mazrui (1933–), who was born in Kenya, wrote *The Trial of Christopher Okigbo* (1971), which is mostly dystopian but still holds out hope. Authors born in Nigeria include Buchi Emechta (1944–), whose *The Rape of Shavi* (1983) shows the destruction of traditional utopia by colonialism; Wole Soyinka (1934–), whose *Seasons of Anomy* (1973) is primarily dystopian but includes the possibility of a better life; and Ben Okri (1959– ), whose *Astonishing the Gods* (1995) presents the search for utopia. Bessie Head (1937–1986) was born in South Africa and lived in Botswana; her *When Rain Clouds Gather* (1969) presents a village that is both described as a utopia and is the location of an attempt to create a utopia.

The best-known Indian utopia in English is probably Salman Rushdie's (1947– ) *Grimus* (1975), which includes a society that is described in the text as "utopian" because it functions on a basis of rough equality and with no money. Other Indian utopias do not appear to have gained much of an audience outside India.

Comparative studies on Western and non-Western utopianism are only just beginning. (An early-twenty-first-century example is Zhang Longxi's "The Utopian Vision, East and West" in the journal *Utopian Studies* [2002].)

*See also* **Equality; Paradise on Earth; Society.**

**BIBLIOGRAPHY**

Al-Azmeh, Aziz. "Utopia and Islamic Political Thought." *History of Political Thought* 11 (1990): 9–19.

Bloch, Ernst. *The Principle of Hope.* 3 vols. Translated by Neville Plaice, Stephen Plaice, and Paul Knight. Cambridge, Mass.: MIT Press, 1986.

Jameson, Fredric. *The Seeds of Time.* New York: Columbia University Press, 1994.

Kumar, Krishan. *Utopia and Anti-Utopia in Modern Times.* Oxford: Blackwell, 1987.

Levitas, Ruth. *The Concept of Utopia.* Syracuse, N.Y.: Syracuse University Press, 1990.

Lewis, Arthur O. *Utopian Literature in The Pennsylvania State University Libraries: A Selected Bibliography.* University Park: Pennsylvania State University Libraries, 1984.

Mannheim, Karl. *Ideology and Utopia: An Introduction to the Sociology of Knowledge.* Translated by Louis Wirth and Edward Shils. New ed. London: Routledge, 1991.

Manuel, Frank E., and Fritzie P. Manuel. *Utopian Thought in the Western World.* Cambridge, Mass.: Harvard University Press, 1979.

Moylan, Tom. *Demand the Impossible: Science Fiction and the Utopian Imagination.* London: Methuen, 1986.

——. *Scraps of the Untainted Sky: Science Fiction, Utopia, Dystopia.* Boulder, Colo.: Westview, 2000.

Negley, Glenn. *Utopian Literature.* Lawrence: Regents Press of Kansas, 1977.

Polak, Fred[erik] L. *The Image of the Future; Enlightening the Past, Orientating the Present, Forecasting the Future.* 2 vols. Translated by Elise Boulding. New York: Oceana, 1961.

Popper, Karl R. *The Open Society and Its Enemies.* 4th rev. ed. 2 vols. London: Routledge and Kegan Paul, 1962. Originally published in 1945.

Pordzik, Ralph. *The Quest for Postcolonial Utopia: A Comparative Introduction to the Utopian Novel in the New English Literatures.* New York: Peter Lang, 2001.

Pordzik, Ralph, and Hans Ulrich Seeber, eds. *Utopie und Dystopie in den Neuen Englischen Literaturen.* Heidelberg, Germany: Universtätsverlag C. Winter, 2002.

Roemer, Kenneth M. *The Obsolete Necessity: America in Utopian Writings, 1888–1900.* Kent, Ohio: Kent State University Press, 1976.

Sargent, Lyman Tower. *British and American Utopian Literature, 1516–1985: An Annotated, Chronological Bibliography.* New York: Garland, 1988.

——. "The Three Faces of Utopianism Revisited." *Utopian Studies* 5, no. 1 (1994): 1–37.

Schaer, Roland, Gregory Claeys, and Lyman Tower Sargent, eds.

*Utopia: The Search for the Ideal Society in the Western World.* New York: New York Public Library and Oxford University Press, 2000.

Suvin, Darko. *Metamorphoses of Science Fiction: On the Poetics and History of a Literary Genre.* New Haven, Conn.: Yale University Press, 1979.

Wilde, Oscar. *The Soul of Man under Socialism.* Boston: Luce, 1910.

Zhang Longxi. "The Utopian Vision, East and West." *Utopian Studies* 13 (2002): 1–20.

*Lyman Tower Sargent*

# V

**VEDA.** *See* **Communication of Ideas: Asia and Its Influence; Hinduism.**

**VICTORIANISM.** Even seemingly unshakeable axioms are prone to reassessment by historians, and Victorianism is no exception. Even the very period of Victorianism itself stands challenged: historians no longer refer unquestioningly to the "Victorian Age" as the precise years associated with the monarch but instead concentrate on a shorter period—a "high age"—from about 1830 to 1880. Yet critics shadowed the entire period in question, and the negative connotations were fired dramatically forward soon after the period ended, notably with Lytton Strachey's (1880–1932) mocking attack *Eminent Victorians* (1918). Moralizing, prudish, repressed (and repressive), and old-fashioned (rather than traditional)—each of these notions captures what Victorianism has meant to later generations.

*North-West Passage* (1874) by John Everett Millais. Oil on canvas. A strong patriarchal influence and the importance of family were prominent values in the Victorian Age, possibly, some say, because there were so many societal obstacles for families to overcome. © THE ART ARCHIVE/TATE GALLERY LONDON/EILEEN TWEEDY

## Early Victorianism

The early Victorian years witnessed the emergence of a cluster of values and beliefs that represented the central ideas of Victorianism. These years are associated with developments in governance, economic and social life, science, and learning that capture the essential features of Victorianism. In governance, one can look to the reforms which, if not immediately democratic, changed the structure of parliament, ushering in a tradition of evolutionary change (with major Reforms Acts in 1832, 1867, 1884) and the expansion of local, middle-class political power with the Municipal Corporations Act (1835). In economic life, the hard-nosed essentials of political economy and utilitarianism reached a high point prior to the 1850s. Associated with such notable names as Jeremy Bentham (1748–1832), James Mill (1773–1836), and David Ricardo (1772–1823), and later refined and developed by luminaries such as John Stuart Mill (1806–1873), political economy helped to shape the policy conditions for the reform of the Elizabethan Poor Law (in the form of the Poor Law Amendment Act, 1834), and the ideology of self-help which, for a while, attained the status of mantra. By the time Samuel Smiles (1812–1904) penned the popularized guide to the joys of this creed (*Self Help*, 1859), the concept had already begun to be pushed to one side by a creeping state and the tendency of the working class to collectivize in the face of demands for Smilesian individualism: hence, the staggering rise of friendly societies, trade unions, the co-operative movement, and countless other examples of collective identification by the people.

## Values and Beliefs

In religion, Victorianism balanced the ancient regime Anglicanism of the Church of England with a growing pluralism through alternative Christianities, new faiths, and the toleration of unbelief. The backdrop to this was a crisis of faith for Anglicans, dating to the early Victorian years, when the Church of England was rocked by fierce debates about Tractarianism, "Romish" rituals, and the intellectual contribution of the Oxford movement. At a more prosaic level, the Religious Census of 1851 revealed a general weakening of popular interest in the established church and many dissenting faiths, whilst Roman Catholicism prospered through Irish migration. Victorianism may be equated with spiritual piety and Christian morality, but alternative and opposite forces also had some importance. Agnosticism, advocated most notably by Thomas H. Huxley (1825–1895), offered, by the 1870s, an alternative to faith in the attempt to answer profound questions about the nature of being.

Victorianism came to be associated with patriarchical social values, stressing the importance of family and an image of motherhood captured well in Alfred Lord Tennyson's (1809–1892) poem, *The Princess* (1847):

> Man for the field and woman for the hearth;
> for the sword, and for the needle she;
> Man with the head, and women with the heart;
> Man to command, and woman to obey;
> All else is confusion.

Thus, poetry, as well as prose, painting, and music, reflected hegemonic notions. Yet, the stereotype of the Victorian family perhaps assumed its importance precisely because there were so many challenges to it. In the cities, drink and crime denied many children the full influence of parental guidance, and the critics of industrialism saw in female and child labor a collection of evils that had to be addressed. But economic conditions placed women and children in this position. Poverty, drunkenness, and alcoholism were sometimes causes of prostitution. Charles Dickens's (1812–1870) portrayal of Nancy, the pathetic, doomed heroine of *Oliver Twist* (1837–1839), obliquely, and somewhat coyly, suggested how easy it was for a woman to fall prey to professional gangs. In *Mary Barton* (1848), Elizabeth Gaskell (1810–1901) captured the horror that Victorian society felt at the sight of a "fallen women" in her portrayal of the stunted relationship of the widower John Barton and his sister-in-law, the fallen woman. Social reportage also emphasized this aspect of Victorianism: Bracebridge Hemyng's (1809–1898) study of prostitution suggested that, in 1857, London had 8,600 who plied this trade.

## Anti-Victorianism

Behind the facade of staidness there was another sort of Victorianism—a kind of anti-Victorianism. Here, stifling mores were replaced by more adventurous and plural sexualities. Liaisons outside marriage, such as Dickens's longstanding affair with the actress Nelly Ternan, were common. William Gladstone's (1809–1898) self-flagellation—a habit the four-time prime minister shared with the bohemian Algernon Swinburne (1837–1909)—was his punishment for the sexual feelings (though there are no known sexual acts) aroused by his attempts to rescue London's prostitutes. Pornographic pictures and texts were readily available in the nineteenth century. Peep shows were commonplace and provided titillation to a broad spectrum of male society. As Simon Winchester's *The Surgeon of Crowthorne* (1999) demonstrates, William Chester Minor (1834–1920), the American military doctor, murderer, and prolific contributor to the *Oxford English Dictionary,* aggressively pursued a sex life that utterly contradicted the conventional image of his age. Obsessed with sex and a regular user of prostitutes—prior to his incarceration in 1872 in the new Broadmoor Criminal Lunatic Asylum for murdering a man in London—Minor harbored such a strong sense of self-loathing that he cut off his own penis. Homosexuality may have scandalized Victorian sensibilities, but it was not invisible. Literary works with a homosexual theme, such as *Teleny* (1883), were produced; Oscar Wilde's (1854–1900) trial and imprisonment reminded Victorians that homosexuality and pedophilia were part of their worlds; while the artist and aesthete Aubrey Beardsley (1872–1898) helped to create a self-image of sexual radicalism, including an unfinished pornographic novel, *Under the Hill* (1894). Not long after, in 1899, Lord Longford was recorded for posterity in *Hansard* with a telling contribution to a parliamentary debate: "Of course I have seen people recover from homosexualism. A boy at Eton assaulted my elder brother in the bath there and was later expelled for repeating the offence on another boy. Later he became a pillar of society and captained the county cricket team" (Sweet, p. 190).

**Symbolic photograph of guardian angels watching over children. British, c. 1860s.** Religion in Victorian Britain was marked by a loss of faith in the Church of England. The period saw the creation of several new religions, a branching out of Christianity, and a growing rise of agnosticism. © HULTON-DEUTSCH COLLECTION/CORBIS

## Victorianism and Progress

No other age was quite so strongly associated with a faith in the progress of technologies. Victorianism is correctly and inextricably intertwined with inventions and the rise of the machine. Steam locomotion, iron, and then steel ships, telegraphy, and many other developments receive attention from historians, for the Victorians triumphed over so many challenges of distance and power that had held up such progress in earlier times. Justifiably, Victorianism remains associated with industrialism, urbanization, transport, technologies, travel, and communication. The essential character of Victorian technological determinism was that science and the practical men could change the world through invention and implementation.

Leaps in technology were matched by developments in social thought. Prophets of progress and the enemies of industrial modernity competed for space, and both groups contributed to the sense of what Victorianism was about. From the 1830s, the critics of Victorianism grew. Modernity was feared by many and loathed by some. Tories, such as the "Young England" group (which included Benjamin Disraeli [1804–1881]) looked back to a bygone age of preindustrial harmony, where deference, social equilibrium, and a more agreeable life was once thought to exist. Disraeli's classic, *Sybil; or the Two Nations* (1845), captured these sentiments brilliantly. Another stern early critic, the Scot Thomas Carlyle (1795–1881), shared the "Young England" aversion to modernity but

looked forward, not back. He abhorred the Victorian tendency to seek mechanical solutions to human problems and sought, instead, a reinvention of an earlier morality, but in a future setting. This style of criticism connected many early nineteenth-century thinkers, such as Carlyle and Robert Owen (1771–1858), to later socialists, such as William Morris (1834–1896). By the 1880s the critique of Victorianism was powerful indeed. Unlike on the continent, where Marxism was much more influential and where anarchism and communism posed a seemingly greater challenge, most British socialism sought accommodation with capitalism and was reformist in character. The Fabian, Sidney Webb (1859–1947), represented an administrative type of socialism, based upon efficiency and organization. William Morris's utopian socialism was characterized by a more fundamental attack upon capitalism and a pursuit of an alternative moral and spiritual way of life. Socialist criticism of modernity also had echoes in the growing feminist challenge to Victorianism. Although suffragism achieved its ends beyond the Victorian period, its seeds were sprouting long before Victoria's end.

Traditional interpretations of society as a static entity were undermined as the period progressed. Charles Darwin's (1809–1882) theories of evolution and Herbert Spencer's (1820–1903) considerations upon human development were to have a startling impact, radically altering classic Victorian notions of society and how to manage it. A social science, borrowed from evolutionary theory, that downplayed contractual in favor of organic ideas of society emerged. Social Darwinism and other evolutionary theories played some part in the development of a philosophy of state interventionism, which marked later Victorian, and particularly twentieth-century, thought (though recent studies, for example, H. S. Jones's *Victorian Political Thought* [2000], sound more cautious and complicated notes). The search for perfectibility in society, which echoed nature's selection of the fittest, could be set up for *or* against the collectivization of social welfare.

## Victorianism Beyond Britain

Victorianism—in architecture, science, governance, and culture—impacted heavily upon the wider world. Britain's short-lived preeminence as an imperial power bequeathed a rather hardier cultural imprint on the world. After the globalization of the English language, the most striking effect was in the character of civic culture in the English-speaking colonies and dominions: Canada, Australia, and New Zealand. In these places, political systems, bureaucracies, and education took on a clearly Victorian character. Victorianism also affected street design and civic building programs—in India, parts of Africa, and the Far East, as well as in the Dominions. Urbanism marked the Victorian world outside of Britain, as well as within. So great was the growth in Sydney, for example, that in 1901 that city (not Liverpool or Glasgow) boasted "it now stands as the second city of the British Empire, as estimated by the annual value of its rateable property" (Briggs, p. 310).

Even when it stood at the leading edge of world culture, exercising a hegemonic power over large swaths of the globe, Victorianism had its critics. In politics, social thought, and economics, interventionism and a demand for action pushed

**Victorian-style house at Longwood, Natchez, Mississippi (1860–1862).** In the mid-to-late-nineteenth century, buildings—especially in the United States—became elaborate and complex in design and decoration, with architects drawing upon several different styles, from Italianate to Queen Anne. © G. E. KIDDER SMITH/ CORBIS

classical *laissez-faire* ideologies to one side. Sexual repressiveness was challenged; many on the left of politics rejected capitalism; and an imperial rot set in after the arduous struggles of the Boer War (1899–1902). The challenge to Victorianism often came in the shape of a wholesale anti-Victorianism from a disparate array of groups: workers, women, socialists, bohemians, and from anticolonialists beyond the metropolitan stage.

*See also* **Empire and Imperialism; Europe, Idea of; Progress, Idea of; Social Darwinism; Utilitarianism.**

BIBLIOGRAPHY

Benson, E. F. *As We Were: A Victorian Peepshow.* London: Penguin, 2001.

Best, Geoffrey. *Mid-Victorian Britain, 1851–75.* London: Fontana, 1985.

Briggs, Asa. *Victorian Cities.* Berkeley: University of California Press, 1993.

Francis, Mark, and John Morrow. *A History of English Political Thought in the Nineteenth Century.* London: Duckworth, 1994.

Harrison, John F. C. *Late Victorian Britain, 1875–1901.* London: Fontana, 1990.

Hoppen, K. Theodore. *The Mid-Victorian Generation, 1846–1886.* Oxford: Oxford University Press, 1999.

Jones, H. Stuart. *Victorian Political Thought.* Basingstoke, U.K.: Macmillan, 2000.

Marcus, Steven. *The Other Victorians: A Study of Sexuality and Pornography in Mid-Nineteenth Century England.* London: Weidenfeld and Nicolson, 1966.

Mason, Michael. *The Making of Victorian Sexuality.* Oxford: Oxford University Press, 1995.

Read, Donald. *The Age of Urban Democracy, 1868–1914.* London: Longman, 1994.

Sweet, Matthew. *Inventing the Victorians.* London: Faber and Faber, 2001.

Tomalin, Claire. *The Invisible Woman: The Story of Nellie Ternan and Charles Dickens.* London: Penguin, 1991.

Walkowitz, Judith. *City of Dreadful Delight: Narratives of Sexual Danger in Late-Victorian London.* London: Virago Press, 1992.

Wilson, A. N. *The Victorians.* London: Arrow Books, 2003.

Winchester, Simon. *The Surgeon of Crowthorne.* London: Penguin, 1999.

Zimmerman, Bonnie, ed. *Lesbian Histories and Cultures.* New York: Garland, 2000.

*Donald M. MacRaild*

**VIRTUAL REALITY.**     *Virtual reality,* a term that became popularized in the late 1980s with the advent of critical research and new technologies developed by Scott Fisher at NASA-Ames Research Center, has its roots in a broad and colorful evolution of art, technology, and communications. The creation of virtual reality is essentially concerned with the quality and experience of immersion, whether real or simulated. The idea of immersion in this sense is related to the artistic concept of "representation," in which the world is translated into visual form. Virtual reality often extends this notion of representation by engaging other senses as well, such as sound and touch, to bring about multisensory experience.

The first part of this essay is an overview of the leading pioneers in the arts and sciences who introduced new technologies, concepts, and artistic innovation that led to the contemporary definition of virtual reality. The second part focuses on artists and theorists who have chronicled new media and virtual reality and its impact on the social condition, revealing transformations in cultural norms and the psychological effects of extending our reach into virtual space.

**Historical Overview**

By 15,000 B.C.E. Cro-Magnon had evolved with a brain capable of modern intelligence. With this new intelligence, artistic renderings were installed deep in subterranean grottos in the Dordogne region of southern France, in caves such as the well-known Lascaux. This birth of drawing and painting was among the first attempts at representation, in the modern sense of the word, in which animal figures (bison, reindeer, horses) and coded shamanist scrawls and motifs were brought to life on the walls of the caves. This recreation of both the external world of nature and the inner world of magic in the immersive space and controlled atmospheric conditions of the underground cavern was an early attempt at artistic expression for the purpose of the preservation of culture. Here, in the prehistoric caves, the human concept of virtual reality began with the multisensory, totalizing experience that engaged sight, sound, smell, and touch—the first conscious virtualization of the physical world.

The Gothic Cathedral of Notre Dame in Chartres, one of the greatest of the European Gothic cathedrals, was built in central France beginning in the late twelfth century. With its magnificent rose windows and stained glass, resonant chambers,

**Prehistoric cave paintings in Lascaux Cave, Dordogne, France.** Cave paintings were one of the first known attempts to visually recreate the physical world as a means of cultural preservation. PHOTO CREDIT: ART RESOURCE, NY

vaulted ceilings, and sacred labyrinth, the sanctuary transposed the virtues of the church by transporting the individual through the experience of immersion. The cathedral served as an architectural canvas for the depiction of the scriptures, figures from the Old Testament, and the narrative of the Crucifixion, as told through the elements of light, sculpture, glass, sound, and stone. The enigmatic labyrinth inlaid on the floor of Chartres invites the viewer to navigate its complex pattern as a spiritual exercise. From the interior of the space, the great height of the cathedral evokes the ascent of heaven. The immersive and totalizing depiction of religious life invites the visitor to consider virtual reality as a mystical realization and transformation from the material to the immateriality of human existence.

German composer Richard Wagner's (1813–1883) *Gesamtkunstwerk* (total artwork), as implemented at the Festpielhaus in Bayreuth, Germany, in 1876, illuminates our understanding of the artistic impulse behind the creation of virtual worlds as it corresponds to the theatrical environment. Wagner understood the power of virtualization through music theater, and he mastered techniques of sensory immersion in order to heighten the audience experience of the "suspension of disbelief." The composer employed a powerful articulation of this age-old theatrical device to render stage action "believable," which has been used as long as humanity has employed the

**Interior of Chartres cathedral.** The design and detailed ornamentation of the High Gothic cathedral at Chartres, France, built in the early twelfth century, served to draw the visitor into the spiritual world. © GIRAUD PHILIPPE/CORBIS SYGMA

**San Francisco Opera rehearses a 1990 performance of Wagner's *Siegfried*.** When staging his compositions, Richard Wagner sought to use various theatrical devices, such as placing the orchestra out of sight, to immerse the audience completely in the world depicted in his works. © IRA NOWINSKI/CORBIS

artifice of live performance to represent, recreate, and transform reality—transcending the notion of the sole possibility of the things that "are," replacing them with what "might be." Wagner used the mechanisms of the theater, as the computer would be used in the early twenty-first century, to transport the viewer's mind, emotion, and senses to an otherworldly virtualization where reality is reconfigured. As he stated in his essay "Artwork of the Future," "the spectator transplants himself upon the stage, by means of all his visual and aural faculties." This illustrates Wagner's desire to construct a totalizing experience through the narrative of music drama, one that fully engages the viewer's consciousness. The composer's invention of such theatrical devices as darkening the house, hiding the musicians in the orchestra pit, and reintroducing Greek amphitheatrical seating to orient audience perspective directly to the stage all contributed to the powerful illusion that takes place within the frame or "interface" of the proscenium arch—the portal to the imaginary space of the theatrical stage.

In the late 1940s, MIT scientist Norbert Wiener founded the field of cybernetics (derived from the Greek word for "steersman," or "governor") to explore the sociological impact of communications between human and machine. This research is critical to an understanding of the impact of virtual reality, as Wiener opened the door to the study of human relationship to technology and the cyberborgian (cybernetic organism) nature of the symbiosis of the two. Wiener describes an increasingly technological society reliant on machines, and he explains how the nature of those interactions affects the quality of life. The design of virtual reality technologies that extend our reach, such as tele-robotic devices (the control of robots at a distance), is informed by Wiener's research in cybernetics and his concern with the nature of sending messages and the reciprocal feedback inherent in those systems.

The virtualization of reality and the simulation of human consciousness by engaging the full range of the viewer's sensory mechanisms is illustrated by cinematographer Morton Heilig's claim in the 1950s that the cinema of the future—a medium already transformed by such innovations as the panoramic perspective of Cinerama—would "no longer be a 'visual art,' but an art of consciousness . . . [a] simulation so lifelike that it gives the spectator the sensation of being *physically* in the scene" (p. 250; emphasis in original). The experience of "being there" has since been a paramount quest in the development of virtual reality. Heilig's Sensorama, for example, a nickolodeon-style arcade prototyped in the 1960s, immersed the viewer in a multisensory excursion through the

**Norbert Wiener.** Mathematician Norbert Wiener introduced the study of cybernetics, which sought to explain how information is transformed into performance by examining both machines and the human nervous system. © UPI/CORBIS-BETTMANN

streets of Brooklyn that engaged all the senses through the synchronization of media using the technology of film.

In the mid-1960s, the engineer Douglas Engelbart conducted critical research at the Augmentation Research Center at Stanford Research Institute, which resulted in the invention of the computer mouse, hypertext, and other interactive information technologies. For the first time, one could virtually navigate information space as an alternative to the linear methods of earlier forms of computing. The mouse pointer (cursor) and keyboard in conjunction with the visual display extended the intellectual reach of the individual. Engelbart believed that this intuitive and cybernetic approach to information processing would lead to the "augmentation of human intellect," by engaging the individual in new methodologies of complex problem solving, far beyond the scope of previous tools.

Computer graphics specialist Ivan Sutherland, the first scientist to bring real-time graphics simulation to the computer screen, advanced the possibilities of reality construction, claiming, "the ultimate display would, of course, be a room

**A NASA researcher wearing Virtual Interactive Environment Workstation (VIEW) apparatus.** Created in the late twentieth century, VIEW manipulated sensory input to transport a person to another reality in which they could manipulate objects. NASA/PHOTO RESEARCHERS, INC.

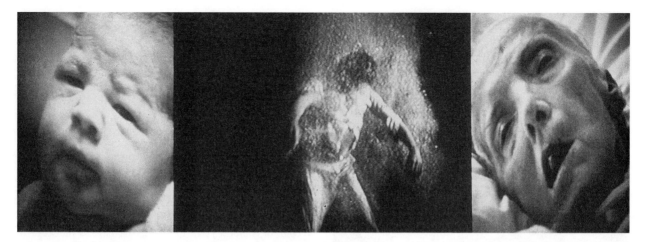

*Nantes Triptych* (1992) by Bill Viola. Video and installation artist Viola likened the memory storage of computers to that of ancient structures, such as cathedrals and mystical temples, and uses it in his art to create cultural histories. TATE GALLERY, LONDON, GREAT BRITAIN, 1992. © ART RESOURCE, NY

Science fiction cyberpunk author William Gibson. Gibson, the first person to coin the term *cyberspace,* writes novels portraying decentralized future societies where humanity is often subjugated by technology. © MATTHEW MCVAY/CORBIS

within which the computer can control the existence of matter . . . a bullet displayed in such a room would be fatal" (p. 256). At the University of Utah in 1970, Sutherland introduced the first head-mounted display (miniaturized graphics display) that enabled the superimposition of low-resolution computer graphics in the physical environment. Expressing the

spirit of Lewis Carroll's *Alice in Wonderland,* Sutherland believed in a new mathematical wonderland that transformed the abstract nature of mathematical constructions into virtual objects and imaginary worlds.

The defining development in virtual reality was carried out in the late 1980s at the NASA-Ames Research Center in northern California by the artist and scientist Scott Fisher, who sought to render virtual worlds even more closely coupled to our sensory mechanisms. Fisher oversaw the creation of the VIEW system (Virtual Interactive Environment Workstation), the first virtual reality (VR) system that integrated the head-mounted display, dataglove (sensing device worn as a glove), voice recognition, and three-dimensional (3-D) audio, which enables the listener to experience the location and movement of specific sounds more realistically than the two-dimensional stereo field of left to right. As a result of this research, Fisher established the field of telepresence, in which one could virtually transport oneself to another place, real or imaginary, experiencing remote spaces and controlling objects at a distance. According to Fisher, virtual reality's potential was now as limitless as reality itself.

In the early 1990s, Daniel Sandin, along with his colleagues Thomas DeFanti and Carolina Cruz-Neira, developed the CAVE System (Cave Automatic Virtual Environment) to project interactive, computer-generated 3-D imagery and audio into a physical space defined by multiple projection screens and a surround-sound system. The immersive nature of CAVE was intended as an allusion to Plato's Cave, evoking the shadowy presence of the representation of reality. The CAVE System also returns full circle to the earliest attempts at virtualization and multisensory experience, as practiced in the prehistoric caves of Lascaux, seventeen thousand years earlier.

## Cultural Implications

While a graduate student at MIT in 1979, the artist Michael Naimark collaborated on the *Aspen Movie Map,* the navigable

*Lustmord,* **a virtual reality interactive environment from the** *Virtual Reality: An Emerging Medium* **exhibition at the Guggen-heim Museum, 1993.** Jenny Holzer, in collaboration with Jeff Donovan, created an interactive world that told of the violent crimes perpetrated against women during the Bosnian war. © 2004 JENNY HOLZER / ARTISTS RIGHTS SOCIETY (ARS), NEW YORK

laserdisc tour through Aspen, Colorado. Using a touch screen monitor and interactive display, the viewer navigates the streets of Aspen, exploring the environment virtually by controlling the direction and speed of the video. The *Aspen Movie Map* was Naimark's first exploration into what he refers to as "surrogate travel," in which the viewer is transported virtually to another place. Naimark's research opened up new interest in virtual forms of navigation in real or imagined places, in which the possibilities for nonlinear storytelling and interactive experience might alter our perception of time and space.

The video artist Bill Viola has been concerned with the idea of "dataspace" since the 1980s as a means to record cultural history in electronic or virtual space, inspired by the "memory palaces" of Greek temples and Gothic cathedrals. Viola compared these ancient architectural vessels of knowledge to the contemporary personal computer with its capacity for storage and instant-access retrieval of information. According to Viola, the symbolic ornamentation, paintings, and stained-glass windows of the European cathedrals might serve as a model for the branching pathways and hypermediated environments of computer-controlled video works, resulting in what he refers to as "idea space"—the conceptual basis for

recent virtual reality applications that employ 3-D simulation of information space.

William Gibson coined the term *cyberspace* in his 1984 science fiction novel *Neuromancer.* By adding this term to contemporary vocabulary, Gibson gave literary meaning to the wires, hubs, networks, and computers that constitute the material manifestation of the more abstract virtual information space. Gibson foresaw a habitable, immersive terrain that would become a new environment for the staging of narratives concerned with the far-reaching possibilities of cyber activity. This reconstruction of the material world through the emerging information technologies would, in Gibson's terms, spark an age of the "posthuman," in which utopian dreams and dystopian nightmares are imagined and realized in digital form.

The computer scientist Pavel Curtis developed one of the first multiuser environments at Xerox PARC (Palo Alto Research Center) in the early 1990s, entitled LambdaMOO, and designed as a text-based virtual reality. The purpose of his research was to explore social phenomena in real-time virtual space—the forerunner of the chat room. Curtis's observation of social behavior in cyberspace is fundamental to our understanding of the

**Performance artist Laurie Anderson.** Anderson's performances frequently utilize varied forms of media such as dance, music, and computer technology. Often the pieces are interactive and audience members are invited to participate. AP/WIDE WORLD PHOTOS

sociological implications of communications in virtual reality. His research also explored the new paradigms of anonymity, the fluidity of multiple identity creation, and the extensibility of world building in digital spaces, and how they might come to transform social interaction.

Marcos Novak, a digital architect, describes his 3-D designs as "liquid architectures," digital spaces that are composed to virtually situate the viewer into complex "fourth-dimensional" environments. He has conceived of these immersive spaces as "navigable music" and "habitable cinema," with their allusion to musical and narrative forms. Novak poetically describes his research: "liquid architectures . . . is an architecture without doors and hallways, where the next room is always where I need it to be and what I need it to be" (p. 259). In Novak's renderings, architecture need no longer be experienced as a fixed or finite space, but rather engages the viewer in the interactive, fluid, and transformational properties of digital media. He has created a vocabulary and set of paradigms for future architects who will no longer work within the physical constraints of solid materials.

In 1993, *Virtual Reality: An Emerging Medium* opened at the SOHO Guggenheim Museum in New York City, one of the first exhibitions to investigate new artistic directions in virtual reality. The show featured two virtual worlds by Jenny Holzer. The first, *The Lost Ones,* was inspired by one of Samuel Beckett's short stories. The second, *Bosnia,* offered a response to the violence against women in the Bosnian war. The observer enters and discovers a vast patterned desert of striking color: bright orange earth and deep blue sky. As one travels across the landscape, one reaches villages with block huts. Each hut harbors a different voice, and each village has a different story to tell. *Bosnia* points to a form of interactive storytelling in which the viewer virtually enters into and inhabits the "narrative space," where the narrative unfolds according to viewer's interactions.

The multimedia artist Laurie Anderson created large-scale theatrical works during the 1980s that integrated dance, music, performance art, and technology. In 1995 she explored the interactive medium, creating the CD-ROM *Puppet Motel* as a nonlinear sequence of scenes and vignettes based on previous theater pieces. *Puppet Motel* is a new form of performance art that takes place on the virtual stage of the computer desktop; the audience becomes the performer, controlling the flow of time and the movement of the narrative. Anderson's experimentation with interactive multimedia can be viewed as a new form of "digital *Gesamtkunstwerk,*" in which the theatrical "fourth wall" dissolves; the fourth wall is the mechanism that traditionally separates the audience from the stage to preserve the illusion of the stage. Here the viewer enters into, inhabits, and interacts with objects in an illusionary world conceived as theater in digital space.

The artist Char Davies has explored new ways to interface with the technologies of virtual reality: the apparatus worn by an "immersant" in her work *Osmose* (1995), which includes a head-mounted display and harness, incorporates breath and movement as a means for navigating a sequence of virtual environments. The viewer uses body motion similar to the scuba diver to negotiate the floating, meditative worlds of the artwork—the contemplation of self, space, nature, and sound, has a powerful effect in the evocation of otherworldly conditions. As Davies describes her work, "The medium of 'immersive virtual space' or virtual reality . . . has intriguing potential as an arena for constructing metaphors about our existential being-in-the-world and for exploring consciousness as it is experienced subjectively, as it is felt" (p. 295). *Osmose* reveals the potential for virtual reality to transform the inner being, similar to the effects of drugs or meditation to induce mind-altering or "out-of-body" experience.

In viewing virtual reality's historical evolution and cultural impact, we see the timelessness and cyclical nature of human expression—from the dreams and representations as depicted in the prehistoric caves of Lascaux; to the totalizing experience of the *Gesamtkunstwerk*; to recent digital forms of immersive experience and altered states of consciousness. The Japanese curator Toshiharu Ito, describing *conFiguring the CAVE,* an immersive artwork created in 1997 by Jeffrey Shaw, Agnes Hegedues, Bernd Linterman, and Leslie Stück for the CAVE

System at the InterCommunication Center (ICC) in Tokyo, Japan, refers to a fourth dimension that exists between the work and the viewer, a space in which the viewer's awareness and bodily experiences can be restructured and recreated.

In describing immersive forms, "we cannot," according to Margaret Morse, "fully anticipate what it means to experience that realm until we are inside." Virtual reality is experiential and sensory—one does not simply observe the object, one is the object. One is not merely a detached observer—one enters into and becomes part of the landscape. The medium of virtual reality functions as an extension of the self, a reconfiguration of identity, intellect, dreams, and memories—ultimately blurring the boundary between self and exterior, between the real and the imaginary.

See also **Cinema; Computer Science; Landscape in the Arts; Sacred Places; Visual Order to Organizing Collections.**

BIBLIOGRAPHY

Campbell, Joseph. *The Masks of God: Primitive Mythology.* New York: Penguin Books, 1991.

Curtis, Pavel. "Mudding: Social Phenomena in Text-Based Virtual Realities." In *Multimedia: From Wagner to Virtual Reality,* edited by Randall Packer and Ken Jordan. New York: Norton, 2001.

Davies, Char. "Changing Space: Virtual Reality as an Arena of Embodied Being." In *Multimedia: From Wagner to Virtual Reality,* edited by Randall Packer and Ken Jordan. New York: Norton, 2001.

Engelbart, Douglas. "Augmenting Human Intellect: A Conceptual Framework." In *Multimedia: From Wagner to Virtual Reality,* edited by Randall Packer and Ken Jordan. New York: Norton, 2001.

Fisher, Scott. "Virtual Interface Environments." In *Multimedia: From Wagner to Virtual Reality,* edited by Randall Packer and Ken Jordan. New York: Norton, 2001.

Gibson, William. *Neuromancer.* New York: Ace Books, 1984.

Heilig, Morton. "Cinema of the Future." In *Multimedia: From Wagner to Virtual Reality,* edited by Randall Packer and Ken Jordan. New York: Norton, 2001.

Morse, Margaret. *Virtualities: Television, Media Art, and Cyberculture.* Bloomington: Indiana University Press, 1998

Novak, Marcos. "Liquid Architectures in Cyberspace." In *Multimedia: From Wagner to Virtual Reality,* edited by Randall Packer and Ken Jordan. New York: Norton, 2001.

Sandin, Daniel, Thomas DeFanti, and Carolina Cruz-Neira. "A Room with a View." In *Multimedia: From Wagner to Virtual Reality,* edited by Randall Packer and Ken Jordan. New York: Norton, 2001.

Sutherland, Ivan. "Ultimate Display." In *Multimedia: From Wagner to Virtual Reality,* edited by Randall Packer and Ken Jordan. New York: Norton, 2001.

Viola, Bill. "Will There be Condominiums in Cyberspace." In *Multimedia: From Wagner to Virtual Reality,* edited by Randall Packer and Ken Jordan. New York: Norton, 2001.

Wagner, Richard. "Artwork of the Future." In *Multimedia: From Wagner to Virtual Reality,* edited by Randall Packer and Ken Jordan. New York: Norton, 2001.

Wiener, Norbert. *Cybernetics; or, Control and Communication in the Animal and the Machine.* Boston: MIT Press, 1948.

*Randall Packer*

# VIRTUE ETHICS.

Virtue ethics is one of the three major ethical approaches in modern moral philosophy, the other two being utilitarianism and deontology. Unlike the latter two, it focuses on the virtues. In the Western tradition of philosophy, virtue ethics begins with the ethical writings of Plato and Aristotle, but in the Eastern tradition its origins are even earlier. Confucius discussed in detail what might be regarded from a Western perspective as the virtuous character traits of charity, righteousness (the virtue pertaining to public affairs), propriety, wisdom, and sincerity and subscribed to something like Aristotle's doctrine of the mean regarding virtue. Siddhartha Gautama, the Buddha, recognized such virtues—perfections of character—as patience, self-restraint, contentment, sympathy, mildness, courage, meditation, and knowledge. All the ancient ethical writers, from East and West, shared the view that there is an answer to the question "How should a human being live?" and that the answer is "virtuously."

The later Greek and Christian writers continued to emphasize the central importance of the virtues in human life, Augustine being the first Christian writer to place the theological virtues of the New Testament—faith, hope, and charity (*caritas,* or love)—beside Plato's four "cardinal" virtues—courage, temperance, justice, and wisdom. Aquinas took more from Aristotle than from Plato, in particular Aristotle's view that our emotions and appetites can, through habituation, be brought into harmony with our reason. The striking consequence of this view is that, if perfect virtue is acquired, the agent does what is right, as reason directs, without inner conflict.

In Aquinas, and in later Christian writers, discussion of the virtues ran alongside discussions of God's, or "natural," law, but the rise of natural law jurisprudence in the seventeenth century saw this increasingly replaced by discussion of rules or principles intended to identify right—and in particular, just—acts, regardless of the motive or character from which they sprang. This trend was rejected by Hume, who insisted that all right actions derive their merit only from virtuous motives and devoted most of his second *Enquiry* to a discussion of the virtues.

The real break with the virtue ethics tradition came with the emergence of the theoretical alternatives, deontology and utilitarianism, offered by Immanuel Kant and then John Stuart Mill. Although the tradition continued to some extent among Continental philosophers, it disappeared from Anglo-American moral philosophy for about a hundred years.

## The Rise of Modern Virtue Ethics

Modern virtue ethics is generally assumed to have been launched by G. E. M. Anscombe's 1958 article "Modern Moral Philosophy," in which she roundly criticized utilitarian and Kantian ethics, briefly indicated "how Plato and Aristotle talk" about ethics, and startlingly claimed that we should give up doing moral philosophy until we had "an adequate philosophy of psychology." The latter turns out to involve, particularly, "an account of what *type of characteristic* a virtue is . . . and how it relates to the actions in which it is instanced."

Fortunately, Anscombe's article did not deter moral philosophers from sticking to their subject. In the 1970s and

1980s Philippa Foot, Iris Murdoch, Alasdair MacIntyre, Bernard Williams, John McDowell, and Julia Annas followed her in criticizing contemporary moral philosophy from the perspective of their reading of the ancient Greeks (and in some cases Aquinas), in which talk about the virtues and vices naturally occurred.

They were not alone in finding the prevailing ethical literature unsatisfactory. By the 1970s, it had become respectable for moral philosophers to do applied ethics. (In the first half of the century they had concentrated almost exclusively on the methodology of ethical theory, metaethics, and the language of moral discourse.) But, despite the fact that articles on contemporary moral issues had become common, moral philosophy seemed to some almost as abstract and removed from everyday life as what had been done in the first half of the century. If "real life" was what was being discussed, why was there no mention of friendship and family relationships, of the morality of the emotions, of motives and moral character, or of moral education? Why did no one ever address the questions of what sort of people we should be and how we should live? Why was the concept of happiness, when it was employed, so unrealistically shallow? The writings of Anscombe's early followers alerted the dissatisfied to the exciting fact that all of these topics were discussed in Aristotle in connection with the topic of virtue.

By the early 1980s, a flood of books and articles had been published, enough to justify a survey article, Gregory Pence's 1984 "Recent Work on Virtues." Its title, however, was significant. The work surveyed was mostly on the virtues themselves, often on a single virtue such as courage or integrity, or on a group such as the virtues involving sympathy, or on the virtues' relation to knowledge or the emotions. Most of the writings discussed were not explicitly on what we would now call "virtue ethics," an approach that could replace the traditional deontological or utilitarian theories—though, as Pence notes, many of them made "grand claims" about this possibility. Nevertheless, they frequently contained passing and sometimes sustained criticism of the prevailing orthodoxy and illustrated, albeit perhaps in relation to only one virtue, how "a return to the virtues" avoided the problem identified.

### Virtue Ethics's Criticisms of Prevailing Orthodoxy
A constant target of this criticism of the contemporary forms of deontology and utilitarianism was their shared conception of the task of ethical theory—that it was to come up with a set (possibly one-membered in the case of act-utilitarianism) of general rules or principles that, applied to particular cases, would provide a decision procedure for determining what the right action was. The theory would reveal what was right about the actions everyone already agreed were right, by showing them to be grounded, or justified, by the rules in question. Even more importantly, it would resolve any moral disagreements about what it would be right to do in problematic situations. The virtue ethicists' attack on the idea that moral dilemmas were best resolved by finding general principles received unexpected support from Carol Gilligan's 1982 book attacking the principles-based view of moral development espoused by the educational psychologist Lawrence Kohlberg.

Closely related to the criticism of deontology and utilitarianism as obsessed with the formulation of general rules that would deliver cut-and-dried answers were trenchant objections to their use in ideal moral decision making. According to a prevailing view, a truly moral motive involved acting for the sake of duty, but in an influential 1976 paper, Michael Stocker highlighted the oddity of supposing that ideally your friend should visit you in the hospital because it was his duty rather than simply because you were his friend. Similar objections were pressed against the prevailing assumption that taking up "the moral point of view" involved being impartial—according all rational autonomous agents, or the interests of all sentient beings, equal value. The virtue ethicists stressed that impartiality or justice was but one virtue among many and that how one should act in relation to one's own children, partners, parents, friends, students, patients, and so on was a central aspect of morality that was being ignored.

Before the reemergence of virtue ethics, Anglo-American moral philosophy had accepted as gospel John Rawls's claim (in *A Theory of Justice,* 1971) that there are just two "main" or "basic" concepts in ethics, "the right" and "the good." It is a mark of the extent to which virtue ethics has prevailed that it is now widely (though by no means universally) accepted that the concept of virtue is as important as the other two. This has had a beneficial effect on the other two approaches. Now that the significance of virtue has been recognized, deontologists and utilitarians are seeking ways to incorporate it into their theories, to the extent that it has become necessary to distinguish between virtue theory—an account of virtue or the virtues within the framework of any ethical approach—and virtue ethics. There is thus revived interest in Kant's *Doctrine of Virtue* and in the new wave of character-based versions of consequentialism.

Another way in which virtue ethics has made its mark can be seen in the extent to which moral philosophers have retreated from their earlier position that a normative theory must come up with a decision procedure that will provide specific practical guidance in difficult situations. The virtue ethicists' stress on the importance of *phronesis* (practical or moral wisdom) eventually brought recognition that such wisdom is needed to apply rules or principles correctly (since we all know that the Devil can quote Scripture to his own purposes), and that they cannot be usefully applied in difficult situations by people who lack experience, insight, and moral sensitivity.

### Current Debates about Virtue Ethics
Notwithstanding this concession, the claim that virtue ethics, unlike the other two approaches, cannot provide adequate guidance on actions persists as the most common objection to it. This is reflected in what is increasingly becoming the new commonplace among moderate anti-virtue ethicists, namely that "what we need" (for a complete ethical theory) is "an ethics of virtue AND an ethics of rules."

In the earlier days of modern virtue ethics, this was a plausible objection. It was based on the premise that the only guidance virtue ethics could come up with was that you should do what the virtuous agent would do in the circumstances. It is true that the earlier virtue ethics literature offered little more. But then it was pointed out by Rosalind Hursthouse (1991) that every virtue generates a prescription (Do what is honest, Do what is charitable/benevolent) and every vice a prohibition (Do not do what is dishonest, uncharitable/malevolent). The existence of these "v-rules," expressed in the vocabulary of the virtues and vices and hence part of "an ethics of virtue," refutes (literally) the premise on which the objection was based; what plausibility, if any, is retained by the claim that an ethics of virtue needs to be supplemented by an ethics of rules or principles is now the central debate.

In some instances, the claim seems no more than a verbal flourish; the v-rules must be "supplemented" by a principle of benevolence, a principle of nonmalevolence, and so on. Why so, one might ask, but why not indeed if people think it sounds more authoritative? Many criticisms of the v-rules fall foul of an obvious tu quoque (this applies to you, too) response. Of course, the requirements of the different virtues may, at least apparently, conflict. Honesty points to telling the hurtful truth, kindness or compassion to remaining silent or even lying. But so too do the related deontologists' and rule-utilitarians' rules, rightly reflecting the fact (ignored by the old act-utilitarians) that life does present us with dilemmas whose resolution, even if correct, should leave us with a remainder of regret. Like the other two approaches, virtue ethics seeks resolutions of such conflicts in a more refined or nuanced understanding or application of the rules involved; and as with the other approaches, its proponents may disagree about the correct resolution.

Perhaps overimpressed by Alasdair MacIntyre's early work, critics of virtue ethics have commonly asserted that the v-rules are inherently culturally specific and conservative because they are developed within existing traditions and societies. Virtue ethicists are amused by the implicit assumption that what their rivals find "reasonable" or "rationally acceptable" is not shaped by modern Western culture and (predominantly) American society, and are more than willing to admit that they have no reason to suppose that their own lists of rules are complete.

However, they do point out that their lists of rules—particularly perhaps the list of vice-rules—is remarkably long in comparison with any that their rivals have produced, and grows naturally (albeit within our own culture) as people's experience of modern life contributes new terms. And they appeal to their list to rebut the charge that the guidance they offer is less specific than that provided by others. "Tell the truth," even if filled out to provide plausible answers to "All of it? Always? To anyone?" is still much less specific than what is yielded by "Do what is honest," "Do not do what is disingenuous, rude, insensitive, spiteful, hypocritical, untrustworthy, treacherous, manipulative, phony, sneaky," and so on. The issue is still hotly contested.

See also **Natural Law; Philosophy, Moral; Utilitarianism; Wealth.**

BIBLIOGRAPHY

Annas, Julia. *The Morality of Happiness.* New York: Oxford University Press, 1993.

Anscombe, G. E. M. "Modern Moral Philosophy." In *Virtue Ethics,* edited by Roger Crisp and Michael Slote. Oxford and New York: Oxford University Press, 1997. Originally published in 1958.

Crisp, Roger, and Michael Slote, eds. *Virtue Ethics.* Oxford and New York: Oxford University Press, 1997.

Foot, Philippa. *Virtues and Vices.* Oxford: Oxford University Press, 2002.

Gilligan, Carol. *In a Different Voice.* Cambridge, Mass.: Harvard University Press, 1982.

Hursthouse, Rosalind. *Dependent Rational Animals.* Chicago: Open Court, 1999.

———. *On Virtue Ethics.* Oxford: Oxford University Press, 1999.

———. "Virtue Theory and Abortion." In *Virtue Ethics,* edited by Daniel Statman. Edinburgh: Edinburgh University Press, 1997. Originally published in 1991.

MacIntyre, Alasdair. *After Virtue.* 2nd ed. Notre Dame, Ind.: University of Notre Dame Press, 1984.

Pence, Gregory E. "Recent Work on the Virtues." *American Philosophical Quarterly* 21 (1984): 281–297.

Stocker, Michael. "The Schizophrenia of Modern Ethical Theories." *Journal of Philosophy* 14 (1976): 453–466.

Swanton, Christine. *Virtue Ethics: A Pluralistic View.* Oxford: Oxford University Press, 2003.

*Rosalind Hursthouse*

**VIRTUOSO.** *See* **Genius.**

**VISUAL CULTURE.** While visual culture has certainly been around as long as culture itself, the phrase *visual culture* used to denote a specific component of culture in general, a set of visual practices, or an academic discipline is quite recent. James Elkins, one of this emerging field's leading scholars, dates the term from 1972, saying that it "was used—perhaps for the first time . . . —in Michael Baxandall's *Painting and Experience in Fifteenth Century Italy*" (p. 2). The recent provenance of the term *visual culture* is important because it indexes a historical shift in the importance of vision itself that has led to an ongoing reconceptualization of the visual and what has been called, in another neologism, *visuality.* Elkins locates the origins of visual culture as an emerging academic discipline in the cultural studies movement that started in England during the late 1950s, and sees visual culture as an American (U.S.) extension of that project (with an emphasis on the visual that did not really get off the ground until the 1990s). What is visible, how it appears, and how it affects nearly every other aspect of social life is suddenly of paramount concern.

The emergence of an idea called *visual culture* surely implies the emergence of a set of urgent problems for which the idea should enable some kind of answers. At a certain moment in the late twentieth century, a new consideration of the role of the visual, of perception, of images, and of the technologies and subjectivities that are embroiled in these relations became an urgent matter for scholars. This moment, which may be identified with what has been called from various corners and with differing emphasis as poststructuralism, the information age, media society, postindustrial society, postmodernism, postcolonialism, and/or globalization, is marked above all else by a new degree of saturation of social space by visual technologies, and, one must assume, a related shift in their social function and significance.

## The Visual Turn

While it is arguable that this visual turn is indeed the meta-event that might show the deep interrelationships and common logic of the other periodizing categories mentioned above, it is true that the conditions of possibility for the emergence of the idea of visual culture were a long time in the making. As noted, culture always and necessarily has had a visual component. However, the shift in emphasis toward an increasing importance of the visible (and its manipulation) is due principally to two related factors: the organization of economies and societies with and by images and the related hyper-development and intensification of visual technologies. Of course, this claim raises more questions than it answers. Image technologies from photography to cinema, television, and computerization are more and more deeply woven into the very fabric of reality. Such interweaving is imbricated to the point where the function of images has become inseparable from any consideration of what might be called the contemporary human condition, including the situation of other categories of analysis central to the humanities including race, class, nation, gender, and sexuality. What might be thought of as an industrialization of the visible is not, strictly speaking, a natural emergence, any more than it is natural that there be skyscrapers or music television. Rather, the visual turn is the contingent result of a matrix of historical and economic forces. In particular (and this is an argument, not a mere statement of fact), the rise of visual culture is a response to the need to efficiently organize and manage huge populations composed of disparate cultures and/or races, in multiple locations and with varying degrees of economic power in what has become the capitalist world-system. The emergence of visual culture is the historical answer to a complex set of organization questions posed at the scale of the human species.

## Visuality

Many scholars locate the emergence of visual culture in relationship to the development of visual technologies, the history of pictorial art, and the emerging recognition of the priority of the visual as the king of the senses. Most, if not all, see this new field as being connected to the streams of images and information that continuously assault spectators from all corners of their environments. No one seems to doubt that, from an experiential standpoint, that which is visible—its intensity, its demands, its possibilities, as these come to us via television, cinema, video, DVD, Internet, electronic billboard, or Mars rover—is something qualitatively new. Yet a smaller number of scholars (Arjun Appadurai, Jonathan Crary, Nicholas Mirzoeff, Sean Cubitt, and a few others) see the emergence of the visual as part of a necessary and practical reconfiguration of subjectivity. The cutting edge of visual cultural studies, however, understands that visuality and the visual technologies that mediate it are part of a larger social project in which the interiority of concrete individuals is being reconfigured. As the

British art historian Norman Bryson writes, "Between subject and the world is inserted the entire sum of discourses which make up visuality, *that cultural construct*, and make visuality different from vision, the notion of unmediated visual experience" (pp. 90–91, italics added). We should add here that visuality is constructed via the interweaving of the discourses that would capture vision and the technologies that utilize it.

Stated dramatically, the social project being undertaken by ostensibly external visual technologies and the economics thereof is not only a reorganization of social macro-structures on a planetary scale but also a total reconfiguration of the interiority of persons. This reconfiguration, which enables and indeed necessitates persons to effectively retool themselves as media for the reception and transmission of social vectors of force—to become mediators among the mediations, implies a new modality of what used to be thought of as human being. It is around these questions that the debates regarding visual culture are perhaps most interesting and fruitful. As nearly all persons, from U.S. presidents, to Hollywood directors, to international consumers, to middle-class workers, to television viewers, to war victims, to dollar-a-day sweatshop chip manufacturers are locked into an economy that passes through the visual, and as the visual is mediated by new technologies, financial institutions, and the military industrial complex, it is fair to say that humanity, if one can still call it that, has become at once more profoundly collective and more inexorably cybernetic than ever before.

## Historical Emergence of the Field of Vision as a Site of Power and Social Control

In Nicholas Mirzoeff's "The Subject of Visual Culture," an essay that serves as an introduction to his important edited volume *The Visual Culture Reader*, he writes that "By the visual subject I mean a person who is both constituted as an agent of sight and as the effect of a series of categories of visual subjectivity" (p. 10). Sketching the emergence of some of these categories, Mirzoeff traces an arc from René Descartes (1596–1650) to roughly Jean-Paul Sartre (1905–1980) and Jacques Lacan (1901–1981). This arc spans the early modern Cartesian notion of "I think, therefore I am" to what Mirzoeff calls "a new mantra of visual subjectivity: 'I am seen and I see that I am seen'" (p. 10). Notably, the modern subject who first emerges through the negation of the visual field (Descartes begins his meditations by doubting the veracity of vision itself, specifically whether it is his hand he sees before his face), and after being subject to a variety of disciplinary regimes of surveillance (in the work of Michel Foucault [1926–1984]), is later constituted in and through the visual (Lacan's "I see myself seeing myself"). The Lacanian analysis of the visual field derives a great proportion of the algebra of subjectivity from scopic relations. Marking a shift in the development and organization of a subject who was effectively located at the (0,0) Cartesian coordinate point in a visible universe of axonometric space developed by Leon Battista Alberti (1404–1472) and point perspective and formalized by Descartes, Mirzoeff astutely sites the utilitarian philosopher Jeremy Bentham's (1748–1832) prison design known as the Panopticon (1786) as emblematic of the utilization of visual surveillance for disciplinary purposes. Brilliantly analyzed by Foucault in "The Eye of Power," Bentham's prison design created a circular array of fully transparent prison cells forming a perimeter around a central hub—a guard tower of smoked glass. The genius of the panopticon was in its economy: the prisoners knew that they could always be seen by the guard in the tower wherever they were in their cells; because they could not tell whether the guard tower was occupied (guards were changed via an underground tunnel), the prisoners effectively watched themselves, that is, policed themselves. Foucault called this form of self-surveillance the "internalization of the gaze of power." While Foucault notes the efficient advance in disciplinary technology marked by the panopticon (it is much cheaper to have people police themselves than to have to continuously beat them into submission), what is at least as important here is that the visual is explicitly grasped as a medium of organization and social control, and that the visual field can be structured via architecture and therefore via design and technology.

The fact that vision and the gaze become the media for the orchestration of social control is in no way confined to technologies of surveillance. As suggested above, the organization of the visual is for many thinkers constitutive of subjectivity, of modern psychology, and therefore of conceptualization of self and other. The fact that Freudian psychoanalysis and the origins of cinema (developed by the Lumiere brothers) share 1895 as an inaugural date might therefore be viewed as more than mere coincidence. Although the majority of psychoanalytic work during the twentieth century believed itself to be embarking on a description and analysis of the deep and therefore ontological structures of human desire and the psyche, it has been argued that the psychic structures available for analysis by the new discipline of psychoanalysis are in fact instantiated and developed by visual technologies themselves (Beller, 2002). Film theory includes extensive work on cinema's modulation of the gaze and its skilled and satisfying manipulation of visual pleasure, but it is at least as likely as not that the structures of apperception capable of deriving the pleasures that cinema offers emerge in dialectical relation to cinematic technologies themselves, rather than having always already been there, lying in wait.

## Historicity of the Senses

As early as 1844, Karl Marx in his *Economic and Philosophic Manuscripts* of that year argued from a historical-materialist perspective that the senses themselves developed in dialectical relationships to society's objects. New modes of perception, sensibility, and appropriation were developed for the objects and processes of industrialization.

It is only when the objective world becomes everywhere for man in society the world of man's essential powers—human reality, and for that reason the reality of his own essential powers—that all objects become for him the objectification of himself. . . . The manner in which they become *his* depends upon the *nature of the objects* and on the nature of the *essential power* corresponding *to it*; for it is precisely the *determinateness* of this relationship which shapes the particular, *real* mode of affirmation. To the eye an object comes to be other than

it is to the ear, and the object of the eye is another object than the object of the ear. The peculiarity of each essential power is precisely its *peculiar essence,* and therefore also the peculiar mode of its objectification, of it objectively *actual* living *being.* Thus man is affirmed in the objective world not only in the act of thinking, but with *all* his senses.

On the other hand, looking at this in its subjective aspect: just as music alone awakens in man the sense of music, and just as the most beautiful music has *no* sense for the unmusical ear—is no object for it because my object can only be the confirmation of one of my essential powers and can therefore only be so for me as my essential power is present for itself as a subjective capacity, because the sense of an object for me goes only so far as *my* senses go (has only sense for a sense corresponding to that object)—for this reason the *senses* of the social man are other senses than those of the nonsocial man. . . . The *forming* of the five senses is a labor of the entire history of the world down to the present (pp. 74–75).

Marx writes here both of the historical disarticulation (separation) of the senses and of the historico-social elaboration of their capacities. If the forming of the five senses is indeed a labor of the entire history of the world down to the present, then it is also true that "the psychic structures which are then derived from this organization of the senses by the objective conditions of production" are also preeminently historical. The theorist Hal Foster, in his landmark essay "Scopic Regimes of Modernity," sketches some of the varied scopic regimes (the organization of subjects and objects by differing visual systems of representation) in early modern Europe and discusses their historical basis. His work provides concrete examples of varied scopic regimes embedded in different cultural and historical moments.

Although it may not seem like much to show that the organization and development of the senses (and therefore the structures of the psyche) are historical rather than ontologically hard-wired, this insight is of great import for an understanding of the historicity of the idea of visual culture. For the idea of visual culture emerges when and only when social production itself has entered definitively into the visual realm and the site of the visual becomes indeed the privileged realm of social production.

## Race and Photo-Graphics

It is essential here to see that the processes of industrialization and then computerization that produced the new objects and eventually machines for the development of the visual do not occur in some spatio-temporal vacuum occupied by abstract individual bodies all subjected to regimes of visuality in precisely the same manner. Rather, industrialization developed on the laboring backs of specific bodies in tandem with the entire European and American projects of colonization and imperialism. If industrialization was linked to the development of capitalism, the development of capitalism was linked to the conquest of regions formerly on the periphery of capitalism: Africa, Asia, the Americas—in short, the world. Thus one must observe that the development of the various racisms (which are themselves relatively new and certainly not transhistorical) are nothing less than a complementary technology of exploitation—a process of othering that enabled and legitimated the violence done unto populations subject to conquest, genocide, enslavement, and the twenty-first century's continued neocolonialism.

That this racism has a visual component is an understatement. It is indeed ironic that the French critic Roland Barthes (1915–1980), in his celebrated work *Camera Lucida*, locates what he considers "the essence of photography" in a discussion of a lost photograph of a slave auction. That photograph would indicate the "this-has-beenness" of the abhorrent reality of slavery, and yet Barthes displaces slavery itself in order to talk about photography. The technology, finally, is for Barthes more significant than the social conditions of its emergence. However, one might also think that photography emerges alongside the social need to graph people onto a social hierarchy vis-à-vis their appearance—that slavery haunts photography. Such a graphing via the skin, a process of capture, objectification, classification, and control, defines both slavery and photography. Photography partakes of and intensifies many of the logics of racialization and the violence that is inseparable from it. There are other works, such as Vicente Rafael's work in *White Love* on census photography in the Philippines, that would support such a line of analysis.

Many black writers have commented on the visual aspects of racism directly or indirectly. Harriet Jacobs's slave narrative, *Incidents in the Life of a Slave Girl: Written by Herself* (1870?), details Jacobs's effective incarceration hidden in the attic of a shed where, for seven years as an immobilized prisoner of plantation society and invisible to everyone, she watches her own children play just below her while being unable to tell them that she loves them, is okay or even alive. This autobiographical passage creates an extraordinary image of the violence of the black/white divide imposed by white supremacist society in which black subjects were rendered invisible in their subjectivity to white subjects. Not only did slave labor produce the wealth necessary to sustain and develop plantation society (its lands, its culture, its wealth, and its dominant subjects), but the objectification of slaves as property, as Other, by whites was essential in order that they *not see* the consequences of who and what slaveholders and other whites were for slaves.

The consciousness produced by the violence of racism and the mapping of subjects via their appearance is a topic of long-standing critique, lament, and rage. W. E. B. Du Bois (1868–1963) wrote in *The Souls of Black Folk* (1903) of "a world which yields him no true self-consciousness, but only lets him see himself through the revelation of the other world. It is a peculiar sensation, this double-consciousness, this sense of always looking at one's self through the eyes of others. . . ." In the 1950s, the author Ralph Ellison declared the American black an invisible man. And in France, the political theorist Frantz Fanon, who was born and first educated in colonial Martinique, wrote in a chapter in *Black Skin, White Masks* (1952), entitled "The Fact of Blackness," of his existential crises of being perceived as black in a French context. What emerges in Fanon's writing is not only the crisis of being perceived to be black and thus other, but the constitutive and universalist racism of France. In response to his experiences, he recalls a moment of being othered while on a train by a child who says, "Look, a negro!" Fanon writes:

I was responsible at the same time for my body, my race, for my ancestors. I subjected myself to objective examination, I discovered my blackness, my ethnic characteristics; and I was battered down by tom-toms, cannibalism, intellectual deficiency, fetishism, racial defects, slave-ships, and above all else, above all: "Sho' good eatin'."

On that day, completely dislocated, unable to be abroad with the other, the white man, who unmercifully imprisoned me, I took myself far off from my own presence, far indeed, and made myself an object. What else could it be for me but an amputation, an excision, a hemorrhage that spattered my whole body with black blood? (p. 112)

The violent structuring of the visual field along racial lines, which led to violent critique of this violence by many cultural producers and revolutionaries, remains subject to an ongoing critique by subjects who identify as or with numerous races and/or ethnicities. One of the most important aspects of the study of visual culture in the early twenty-first century is the analysis and unpacking of visuality in terms of race and the allied histories of colonization and imperialism. For the structuring of visuality is tied to the production and reproduction of representations (and erasures) of racialized subjects, and these images, whether through the stimulation of fantasy or the production of perceptions of what is ostensibly reality, in turn enable much of the ongoing violence of contemporary society.

## Gender, Sexuality, and the Image

In addition to race-based critiques of dominant visual representation and its profound connection both to dominant modalities of the visual and to socio-subjective organization, scholars—particularly film theorists—have also examined the visual field in terms of its implantation in the organization of gender and sexuality. Most famously here, perhaps, is Laura Mulvey's work "Visual Pleasure and Narrative Cinema" (1975). Undertaking an analysis of Hollywood's development of scopophilia or "pleasure in looking," Mulvey understood Hollywood narrative cinema to be developing and narrativizing a particular image of woman: "Woman . . . stands in patriarchal culture as signifier for the male other, bound by a symbolic order in which man can live out his fantasies and obsessions through linguistic command by imposing them on the silent image of woman still tied to her place as bearer of meaning, not maker of meaning" (p. 199). She further comments, "As an advanced representation system, the cinema poses questions of the ways the unconscious (formed by the dominant order) structures ways of seeing and pleasure in looking" (p. 199). Though it has already been suggested here that cinema itself may be considered to be part of the dominant order that forms the unconscious itself, this dialectic for Mulvey results in the effective evacuation of the subjectivity of woman as representation, and perhaps (this has been debated in terms of the question of female spectatorship) as a concrete individual person. Without rehearsing the entire argument, suffice it to say that Mulvey sets out to attack the film industry's "satisfaction and reinforcement of the [male] ego," and understands the film industry to be effectively maintaining if not producing and intensifying patriarchal society and its domination/exploitation of women. In writing, "It is said that analyzing pleasure, or beauty, destroys it. That is the intention of this article" (p. 200), Mulvey crystallized a central point of her analysis: the link between pleasure, the production of subjectivity, and domination in patriarchal society.

While other theorists of cinema and of the visual, including Mary Ann Doane, Judith Butler, Judith Halberstam, Kaja Silverman, Linda Williams, and many others, offer differing and sometimes conflicting analysis of the organization and function of the visual in contemporary society, nearly all agree that what takes place in cinematic, televisual, and later digital media regarding the organization of gender and sexuality is not to be understood as a collection of unique instances but rather as at once symptomatic of social life and often productive of aspects of social life. Taken as a whole, mass media exert tremendous pressure on the organization of the psyche and the patterning of social performance. The critique of mass media's function has the power to alter its reception and therefore to transform its function. The possibility of such an analysis of images, and of an understanding of their processes, has been put forward under various nomenclatures, from semiotics to visual literacy to media theory.

## Alternative Media

Many people seeking social justice share the perception that the dominant media—from the Hollywood studio system to the formation of television and later cable networks—exercised a tremendous, often racist, sexist, and anti-democratic power, leading to the emergence of a variety of visual forms of resistance. These included the Third Cinema movement of the late 1960s and following, which encouraged Third World revolutionary filmmakers and fellow travelers to work "with the camera in one hand and a rock in the other," in order to enable the decolonization of spectators. Additionally, a tremendous number of experimental film and alternative video production projects took root. In the realm of film, endeavors from the French New Wave to experimental sixteen-millimeter filmmaking (especially the work of the American filmmaker Stan Brakhage) tried to investigate the materiality of the medium and its conventions for creating the most persuasive of illusions. Filmmakers such as Yvonne Rainer and Marlene Gorris, among many others, also worked on creating a feminist film corpus. Additionally, with the rise of the video portapak and the general dissemination of inexpensive video technology in the early 1970s, a whole generation of alternative video and video art began to make inroads not only in the field of what could be represented on television, but at least as importantly into the ways in which images were perceived, processed, and understood. The artists Nam June Paik, Lynda Benglis, and Linda Montano in the 1970s and 1980s and Bill Viola in the 1990s and 2000s, among many others, created video artworks, while organizations such as New York's Downtown

Community Television Center, with Jon Alpert and Keiko Tsuno, covered topics like access to healthcare and minority experiences in a documentary style. These U.S. efforts at alternative video and video art had their counterparts in Latin America, Southeast Asia, and elsewhere.

## Advertising, Attention, and Society of the Spectacle

French situationist Guy Debord began his enduring work *Society of the Spectacle* (1967) with, "The spectacle is not a collection of images; rather, it is a social relationship between people that is mediated by images" (p. 12). While this thesis is true of the spectacle in general, it is perhaps most readily intelligible from a study of advertising. Theorists from Marshall McLuhan to Robin Andersen and Sut Jhally chart the extension and penetration of advertising into both the format of media productions—particularly television, but also with product placement, the cinema—and simultaneously into the psychology and fantasy of consumers. Up until the 1920s, advertisements in print venues were principally informational (e.g., if your dentures are falling out, we make this denture cream). By the 1950s, advertisers were not selling products but a whole way of life in which consumption itself would begin to solve life's ailments. The purpose of advertising became to produce consumers. Advertising's messages overall are designed to produce feelings of lack and inadequacy that might then be treated by the consumption of a product, or more particularly, the image of that product. In the twenty-first century, these campaigns are mounted by specialized agencies that employ PhDs in psychology and use statistical techniques and brainstorming sessions (called "the theater of the mind") to elicit unconscious associations from consumers. Advertising operates through what this author calls a "calculus of affect" in order to continuously refine the efficiency by which spectators are manipulated not by rational arguments but by emotional and visceral appeals to their unconscious and sometimes conscious fantasy. Without a doubt, many of these fantasies are shot through with variants of the racism and sexism discussed above. Since corporate media exist principally for profit and their profits come from paid advertisements, it is easy to see how, structurally at least, these very media serve first and foremost as vehicles for advertisers.

The American critic Jonathan Beller's work on visual culture and media extends the idea that mass media sell eyeballs to advertisers and elaborates "the attention theory of value." In brief, this theory is a development of Marx's labor theory of value in which the production of all value for capital has its basis in human labor. It argues that attention is the superset of labor (and thus labor is a subset of attention). Just as workers labor in the factory, spectators labor in the social mechanisms known as media, building value for capital and oftentimes disenfranchising themselves. Television functions like a deterritorialized factory for the production and reproduction of consumer-citizen-subjects. The theory proposes a cybernetic model of production in which the image is the paradigmatic interface between bodies and the social armature. The logistics of media society, its modalities of operation, its affects, and its production of history, space, time, and fantasy are fully integrated into spectatorial consciousness. Imagination itself is engaged as an engine of production: attending bodies validate media pathways and simultaneously transform themselves. Indeed, as spectators are posited as nodes on media circuits that are fundamental to the production and reproduction of the global, it becomes increasingly difficult to say where mediation ends and personhood begins. As noted above, humanity itself is increasingly cybernetic.

## Visuality, Mediation, Simulation, and Cybernetics

The integration of the machinery of media circuits, the imagination of spectators, financial markets, and the military industrial complex—all on a global scale—compose what Beller calls the world-media system. This idea of a world-media system that endeavors to fully integrate modes of perception and the requisites of social production and reproduction is connected to several critical ideas. One such idea is the German philosophers Theodor Adorno and Max Horkheimer's idea of "the culture industry," in which commercial cultural products were understood "as an after-image of the work process" and in effect designed to reconcile workers to their own powerlessness and exploitation by giving them compensatory images of satisfactions that were denied to them in life. Debord begins *Society of the Spectacle* with the idea that "The whole life of those societies in which modern conditions of production prevail presents itself as an immense accumulation of spectacles. All that was once directly lived has become mere representation" (p. 12). The political theorist Paul Virilio has shown the intimate developmental relationships between war machines and the cinematic apparatus, as well as the role of visual technologies in surveillance and the rendering of targets abstract, virtual, and therefore more easily destroyable, both practically and in terms of the conscience of the killers. Murder becomes technologized and as easy as the touch of a button. The French sociologist Jean Baudrillard has written about the connections between mass media and what he calls *simulation,* a process that creates copies without originals. Images for Baudrillard are "hyperreal," that is more real than real, and have, for him at least, effectively rendered reality impossible and consequently short circuited genuine thought. What is clear from the work of these thinkers and others whom they have inspired is that the media environment has radically altered the very fabric of reality, the character of the human sensorium, and the nature of the consciousness that might mediate between the two.

Along these lines, the French intellectual Régis Debray, in his important work *Media Manifestos* (1996), has argued that the word *communication* is a radical misconception of what transpires in the messaging process and should thus be replaced by the word *mediation,* because messages don't just travel from A to B. Rather, "sender and receiver are modified from the inside by the message they exchange, and the message itself modified by its circulation" (p. 44). Instead of looking at particular cultural products or texts, Debray's analysis is more interested in "change[s] in the system of manufacture/circulation/storage of signs" (p. 19) and charts a historical, planetary shift from what he dubs the *logosphere* to the *graphosphere* to the *videosphere*—that is, regimes of the written word, the printed word, and the image respectively. His study of "the ways and means of symbolic efficacy" (p. 7) is more interested in the

effects of mediations rather than their meanings or contents, and points toward the techno-cultural apparatuses that manage the circulation of signs as something like the unthought of human historical process. The visual, and what is now called visual culture, is the latest and most powerful development in the management and organization of human society.

## The Future of Visual Culture and Visual Studies

It seems clear that visual culture is not about to disappear but, rather, with the growing perception that visuality is one of the profound operators of our times and therefore a site of the twenty-first century's most important questions, we may expect critical approaches to visual culture to develop quite rapidly and with tremendous diversity. The American theorist Lisa Cartwright has written about medical imaging and its sociocultural implications in *Screening the Body: Tracing Medicine's Visual Culture.* The legal scholars Kimberle Williams Crenshaw and Garry Peller have written on the evidentiary character of amateur video and the way in which racist, state, and aesthetic ideologies overcode the image. Writers from Raymond Williams to Lynn Spigel have analyzed television's reorganization of social space. Linda Williams considers pornography to be of central importance. Political scientist Armand Mattelart and sociologist Manuel Castells discuss the manner in which media and information flows are linked to the movement of capital and the restructuring of imaginary and built environments. Still others (such as the philosopher Douglas Kellner) have written on the connections between commercial television, ideology, and the waging of war. The theorist and artist Lev Manovich has written on the possibilities and implications of digital cinema, and Cubitt has broached the questions of digital aesthetics with tremendous insight and erudition. The media theorist Lisa Parks has written on "satellite and cyber visualities."

Looking toward the future and toward possible forms of the institutionalization of what he pointedly calls visual studies, the art historian James Elkins suggests that visual literacy courses should include history of Western art and mass media, but also an understanding and analysis of multicultural as well as multidisciplinary image making processes, including non-Western aesthetic productions, and scientific and satellite imaging. This author's view is that visual studies will amount to little more than an accommodation to shifting conditions of domination and the intensification of global inequality unless it is also imbued with the commitment to demonstrate both the preconditions for the production of images as well as the consequences of different modes of reception of these images.

*See also* **Aesthetics; Arts; Cinema; Cultural Studies; Media, History of; Other, The, European Views of; Postmodernism; Propaganda; Third Cinema.**

BIBLIOGRAPHY

Adorno, Theodor, and Max Horkheimer. *Dialectic of Enlightenment.* Translated by John Cumming. New York: Seabury Press, 1972.

Andersen, Robin. *Consumer Culture and TV Programming.* Boulder, Colo.: Westview Press, 1995.

Appadurai, Arjun. *Modernity at Large: Cultural Dimensions of Globalization.* Minneapolis: University of Minnesota Press, 1996.

Baudrillard, Jean. *Simulacra and Simulation.* Translated by Sheila Faria Glaser. Ann Arbor: University of Michigan Press, 1994.

Barthes, Roland. *Camera Lucida: Reflections on Photography.* Translated by Richard Howard. New York: Hill and Wang, 1981.

Beller, Jonathan. *Acquiring Eyes: Philippine Visuality, Nationalism and the World-Media-System.* Manila, Philippines: Ateneo de Manila University Press, 2004.

———."Kino-Eye, Kino World: Notes on the Cinematic Mode of Production." In *The Visual Culture Reader,* 2nd ed., edited by Nicholas Mirzoeff. London: Routledge, 2002.

Benjamin, Walter. *Illuminations.* Edited by Hannah Arendt. Translated by Harry Zohn. New York: Harcourt, Brace, and World, 1968.

Berger, John. *Ways of Seeing.* London: British Broadcasting Corporation, 1972.

Boyle, Deirdre. *Subject to Change: Guerrilla Television Revisited.* New York: Oxford University Press, 1997.

Bryson, Norman. "The Gaze in the Expanded Field." In *Vision and Visuality,* edited by Hal Foster. Seattle: Bay Press, 1988.

Butler, Judith. *Bodies That Matter: On the Discursive Limits of "Sex."* New York: Routledge, 1993.

Cartwright, Lisa. *Screening the Body: Tracing Medicine's Visual Culture.* Minneapolis: University of Minnesota Press, 1995.

Castells, Manuel. *The Internet Galaxy: Reflections on the Internet, Business, and Society.* Oxford: Oxford University Press, 2001.

Crary, Jonathan. *Suspensions of Perception: Attention, Spectacle, and Modern Culture.* Cambridge, Mass.: MIT Press, 1999.

Crenshaw, Kimberle Williams, and Garry Peller. "Reel Time/Real Justice." In *Reading Rodney King/Reading Urban Uprising,* edited by Robert Gooding-Williams. New York: Routledge, 1993.

Cubitt, Sean. *Digital Aesthetics.* London: Sage, 1998.

Debord, Guy. *La société du spectacle.* Paris: Buchet-Chastel, 1967. Translated by Donald Nicholson-Smith as *The Society of the Spectacle.* New York: Zone Books, 1994.

Debray, Régis. *Media Manifestos.* Translated by Eric Rauth. London: Verso, 1996.

Doane, Mary Ann. *The Emergence of Cinematic Time: Modernity, Contingency, the Archive.* Cambridge, Mass.: Harvard University Press, 2002.

Du Bois, W. E. B. *The Souls of Black Folk.* Chicago: A. C. McClurg, 1903. Reprint, New York: Penguin Books, 1996.

Elkins, James. *Visual Studies: A Skeptical Introduction.* New York: Routledge, 2003.

Fanon, Frantz. *Black Skin, White Masks.* Translated by Charles Lam Markmann. New York: Grove Press: 1967.

Foster, Hal. "Scopic Regimes of Modernity." In his *Vision and Visuality.* Seattle: Bay Press, 1988.

Foucault, Michel. *Power/Knowledge: Selected Interviews and Other Writings 1972–77.* Translated by Colin Gordon, et al. New York: Pantheon, 1980.

Halberstam, Judith, and Ira Livingston, eds. *Posthuman Bodies.* Bloomington: Indiana University Press, 1995.

Hall, Doug, and Sally Jo Fifer, eds. *Illuminating Video: An Essential Guide to Video Art.* New York: Aperture, 1991.

Jacobs, Harriet A. *Incidents in the Life of a Slave Girl: Written by Herself.* Cambridge, Mass.: Harvard University Press, 1987.

Jhally, Sut. *The Codes of Advertising: Fetishism and the Political Economy of Meaning in the Consumer Society.* London: F. Pinter, 1987.

Lacan, Jacques. *The Four Fundamental Concepts of Psycho-analysis.* Translated by Alain Sheridan. London: Hogarth, 1977.

Manovich, Lev. *The Language of New Media.* Cambridge, Mass.: MIT Press, 2001.

Marx, Karl. *Economic and Philosophic Manuscripts of 1844.* In *The Marx-Engels Reader,* edited by Robert C. Tucker. New York: Norton, 1972.

Mattelart, Armand. *The Information Society: An Introduction.* Translated by Susan G. Taponier and James A. Cohen. London: Sage, 2003.

McLuhan, Marshall. *Understanding Media: The Extensions of Man.* New York: McGraw-Hill, 1964.

Mirzoeff, Nicholas, ed. *The Visual Culture Reader.* 2nd ed. London: Routledge, 2002.

Mitchell, W. J. T. *Picture Theory: Essays on Verbal and Visual Representation.* Chicago: University of Chicago Press, 1994.

Mulvey, Laura. "Visual Pleasure and Narrative Cinema." In *Narrative, Apparatus, Ideology: A Film Theory Reader,* edited by Philip Rosen. New York: Columbia University Press, 1986.

Rafael, Vicente L. *White Love: And Other Events in Filipino History.* Durham, N.C.: Duke University Press, 2003.

Silverman, Kaja. *The Subject of Semiotics.* New York: Oxford University Press, 1983.

Solanas, Fernando, and Octavio Getino. "Towards a Third Cinema: Notes and Experiences for the Development of a Cinema of Liberation in the Third World." In *Movies and Methods: An Anthology,* 2 vols., edited by Bill Nichols. Berkeley: University of California Press, 1976–1985.

Spigel, Lynn. *Make Room for TV: Television and the Family Ideal in Postwar America.* Chicago: University of Chicago Press, 1992.

Sturken, Marita, and Lisa Cartwright. *Practices of Looking: An Introduction to Visual Culture.* Oxford: Oxford University Press, 2001.

Virilio, Paul. *The Vision Machine.* Bloomington: Indiana University Press, 1994.

———. *War and Cinema: The Logistics of Perception.* Translated by Patrick Camiller. London: Verso, 1989.

Williams, Raymond. *Television: Technology and Cultural Form.* New York: Schocken, 1974.

*Jonathan Beller*

# VISUAL ORDER TO ORGANIZING COLLECTIONS.

A generation trained to select icons on a desktop computer is able to take a fresh approach to the visual cues within early rooms of collection. Visual cues often preceded catalogs and inventories, helping users to situate themselves in the room and to locate items of the collection. In searching out the modes of conceptualizing, mapping, and classifying of collections, we shall see that the distinctive details of ceilings, walls, cabinets, or furniture of a collection room may be functional elements organizing manuscripts or other valuable objects in the room. Scholars Alain Besson, André Masson, Eric Garberson, and Maryanne Cline Horowitz have examined visual classification schemes, especially in libraries and studies, but a plethora of extant as well as defunct rooms of collections might similarly be examined. The *Journal of the History of Collections* (founded 1989) might be the appropriate venue.

Each section of this entry features a distinctive type of iconography for rooms of collection: hunting, horticulture, cabinets of curiosity, author portraits, imperial busts, the

***Biblioteca di Cesarea di Palestina* (painting) by Baldassarre Croce.** Since ancient times, libraries, studies, and other rooms of collections have featured designs that incorporate visual cues to the organization of the items displayed within. © BIBLIOTECA APOSTOLICA VATICANA (VATICAN)

disciplines of knowledge, the circle of knowledge, secular temples, and towers of knowledge.

## Hunting for Precious Objects

Excavations in the basement of the Louvre reveal the circular fortress of the Tour de la Fauconnerie (Tower of Falconry), where medieval French kings sent birds out tower windows and stored their hunting gear. In 1367, imitating the three floors of manuscripts of the Tour de la Garde-Robe (Tower of the Vestments) of the papal palace in Avignon, King Charles V (r. 1364–1380) moved the royal collection of books to this tower, renaming it the Tour de la Librairie. Christine de Pisan in her 1405 book about wise King Charles V of France notes the orderly arrangement of his library. The reference to "hunting" for manuscripts is most evident in the frescos completed about 1345 on the four walls of the Chambre du Cerf (Room of the Deer) in the Tour de la Garde-Robe, Avignon. The frescos of hunting with birds, hunting with dogs, fowling in trees, and fishing in ponds would help a cleric to locate a handwritten animal-skin manuscript on one of the tables in the room (Horowitz, 1998, pp. 123–128). By ancient rhetorical theory, a trained student is a huntsman finding the locations of hidden knowledge, and from Petrarch onward humanists were praised as manuscript-hunters.

Isabella d'Este (1474–1539), in setting up her second suite of rooms in the ducal palace of Mantua, transformed the *scalcheria* (the room where meat, vegetables, and other delicacies were previously prepared for banquets) into a room for sorting and arranging her collection of antiquities. With good humor, she commissioned Lorenzo Leonbruno to paint on the upper walls female hunters hunting for deer; seen from below, the Amazons appear to be pointing their arrows down toward the objects in the room. Isabella d'Este—who to acquire desired antiquities wrote both the duke of Milan and Andrea

**Caesar Travelling Library constructed for Sir Julius Caesar (1558–1636).** Throughout the centuries, some collections have been mobile, allowing for their display in multiple locations. BY PERMISSION OF THE BRITISH LIBRARY, C.20.F.15–58

Mantegna on their deathbeds—with Amazonian imagery likened hunting to collecting.

The Boston Public Library in Boston, Massachusetts, opened in 1896, was noted for its large card-catalog room with a decorative frieze of the search for the Holy Grail; the published dissertation on the topic (Ferris Greenslet, *The Quest of the Holy Grail,* 1902) misses the humor of the implied analogy between the adventures within medieval legends of seeking the cup from which Jesus drank and the often time-consuming, circuitous paths between card-catalog entries and

**Studiolo of Isabella d'Este, Palazzo Ducale, Mantua, Italy.**
D'Este's elaborately detailed grotto in Corte Vecchia is one example of a cabinet of curiosity, a type of collection popular in the sixteenth and seventeenth centuries. PHOTO CREDIT: ALINARI/ART RESOURCE, NY

shelves to finding the ideal cup of knowledge (or book) for which one longs.

## Horticulture and Culture

Thirteenth-century Richard de Fournival discusses his "garden" of manuscripts in *La biblionomia*. This catalog shows the rows of his plantings: about three hundred manuscripts entered the founding collection of the Sorbonne of which forty of Fournival's have survived. The duke of Berry, most famous for his manuscript of the calendar months, utilized the insignia of vegetative "roots" to designate his manuscripts. Piero de' Medici, father of Lorenzo the Magnificent, created a *studiolo* (a study) in the Medici Palace, Via Larga, Florence. The twelve calendar months by Luca della Robbia on the ceiling are a visual cataloging system pointing out the twelve categories of Piero's classical and Christian books below, color-coded in the written catalogs of 1456 and 1464–1465 (Horowitz, 2003).

Isabella d'Este's second suite of *schaleria, studiolo,* grotto, and garden created an atmosphere of a garden of virtues, as in the Mantegna painting *Pallas Expelling the Vices from the Garden of Virtue* (1499–1502) which hung in the *studiolo* (now in the Louvre). Hovering in a cloud on the right are the three cardinal virtues; below in the distance, a pleasant landscape seen through the tree-lined archways reveals vices fleeing and new growth

growing from old roots; in the foreground on the left is the Mother of Virtue imprisoned in a tree; and in the center, vices pollute the pond. Minerva (Pallas Athene) and two goddesses enter and seek to bring about a return to a garden of virtue.

The analogy of "culture" and horti"culture" is evident in many languages. The tree catalog of the library of Saint-Lambrecht, a painted panel by Michel Boeckyn (1688–1742), utilizes the common image of a tree of knowledge, with the various branches of knowledge rising from a trunk (fig. 4, Masson, 1981). One might plant a collection of books or other valuables, many might labor in the fields of scholarship and the arts, and a society devoted to cultivating the arts might create an abundant culture. French King Francis I (r. 1515–1547) was praised by his courtiers for his cultivation of the humanist virtues, which are equally evident in his manuscript collection, in the flowery ephemeral art of his royal entries, and in the flowers and fruit ornamenting the wall paintings in the Galerie Francis I, Fontainebleau. The analogy of writing to agricultural productivity, like the analogy of collecting to hunting, also helped make these cultural activities appropriately aristocratic.

Agricultural abundance ornamenting cultural institutions was so prevalent in the eighteenth century that it barely receives comment; note especially the decoration of the rotunda library of the Radcliffe Camera, Oxford, and of the stucco ceiling at the entrance to the Ashmolean Museum, Oxford. In the mid-nineteenth century, the upper walls of the main reading room of the Bibliothèque nationale were painted with illusionistic windows revealing sky and treetops. The implication that natural vegetative growth encourages the growth of the mind was expressed in the medieval tradition of drawings of a scholar in a study with an open cupboard showing fruit. (John Clark, in *The Care of Books* [1901], asks why the fruit are there [p. 313].)

## Cabinets of Curiosity

In the sixteenth and seventeenth centuries, collectors arranged a diversity of natural and crafted objects within decorative furniture cabinets, as well as within rooms that served as cabinets of curiosity. When one enters Isabella d'Este's grotto in Corte Vecchia, one feels that one is inside an elaborate jewelry box. Ornate marquetry woodwork decorates the doors to the cabinets that once contained her valuables; the distinctive perspective pictures would remind her of the exact location of her antiquities protected in this room.

At the corner of the Hall of the Five Hundred in the Palazzo Vecchio, Florence, is the restored study of Francesco I, the work of Giorgio Vasari in 1570–1575. Under the vaulted ceiling, there are numerous paintings. A door behind the sixth painting, Alessandro Allori's *Cleopatra's Feast,* with his *Pearl-fishing* above, opens to a staircase leading to the *tesoretto,* a small treasure room with eleven cupboards, one of which leads to a further room below. In the context of Francesco I's collecting, Allori's *Cleopatra's Feast* is his *Pearl-fishing,* a playful allusion to the hunting for treasure below.

The *studiolo* in the ducal palace of Urbino plays with this genre by appearing to show the contents of cabinets in its

***Pallas Expelling the Vices from the Garden of Virtue*** **(1499–1502) by Andrea Mantegna. Oil on canvas.** Some early collectors drew a parallel between culture and horticulture, a view reflected in Mantegna's painting, in which order is restored in a garden setting. RÉUNION DES MUSÉES NATIONAUX / ART RESOURCE

elaborate marquetry. While the open door at the front of the protruding central panel of squirrel and flower bowl is not in fact a door, a door on the right side of that panel does in fact open. Duke Federigo da Montelfeltro kept treasures in two cubicles below his *studiolo*: a temple to the muses for antiquities and a chapel to God for his relics. Also, his library contained several hundred manuscripts; some of those authors are featured in the portraits on the upper walls above the marquetry of his *studiolo*.

## "Portraits" of Authors

Providing a portrait, even if fictional, of the key authors of one's set of manuscripts helped individualize the books and encouraged the illusion that those select guests invited to the room were conversing amid the authorities. The pairs of portraits on the upper walls of the duke's *studiolo* in the Palazzo Ducale, Urbino—somewhat representative as in Petrarch, Dante, and contemporary churchmen, and fictive as in Moses (right corner) and Solomon—relate to valued manuscripts in the library a floor below.

In Julius II's (r. 1503–1513) study in the Vatican, the Stanza della Segnatura, bookcases were attached to the walls under the now famous paintings *School of Athens, Parnassus, Dispute over the Sacrament,* and *Jurisprudence.* Plato, Aristotle, Homer, and others are portrayed with their books, which would have been in the room for Julius's usage. Two hundred eighteen of Julius's books were in this room, known in his lifetime as "the upper library." As André Masson pointed out, the *Dispute over the Sacrament* and the *School of Athens* were imitated later in the library of Jesuits of Valenciennes (1740–1742) to distinguish the collecting of classical works from the collecting of Christian disputations.

The frieze of over two hundred authors in the Bodleian Library, Oxford University, depicted in 1616–1618 in the three-sided gallery (now the Upper Reading Room), have numerical references in each author's portrayal to the shelf location of the author's respective books in the neighboring Duke Humphrey's Library, where the books remain chained today. The Bodleian Gallery displays the innovative wall shelves with heroes above (except for one heroine, Sappho) of the respective faculties of

**Reading Room at the Bibliothèque Nationale, Paris, France.** Decorative motifs involving vegetation as an allegory for learning were prevalent during the eighteenth century, such as the trees painted in the reading room of the Bibliothèque Nationale. © PAUL ALMASY

theology, arts, medicine, and law. First one walks between the theologians seeming to vie with each other across the room, then one peruses the classical authors of the liberal arts, and then one walks between the teachers of medicine and the teachers of law. The visual cues of the arts section lead one to the referenced manuscripts of classical and "modern" authors in Duke Humphrey's Library.

David Rogers has suggested that the frieze portrait imitates and enlivens the manuscript image of Roger Bacon. Further research might be done on the respective pictorial examples,

seeking sources for the particular image, gesture, sayings, and symbols, as in André Thevet's *Portraits des hommes illustres,* 1584, and in Théodore de Bèze's (Beza; 1519–1605) *Icones vivorum illustrium,* 1580. The author frieze, the 1604 catalog, and the 1620 catalog are alternative Renaissance innovations in the area of indexing an exclusive collection for members of Oxford University, government dignitaries, and foreigners (either university students or graduates).

An alternative type of frieze is not of authors but of dignitary patrons or users of a local library. Sixty-seven portraits of

**Portraits on walls of Federico da Montefeltro's Studiolo (study), c. 1472–1476, Palazzo Ducale, Urbino, Italy.** The use of author portraits in libraries gave the collections an air of legitimacy. Da Montefeltro's study featured several such portraits of prominent writers. SCALA/ART RESOURCE, NY

fathers of the Abbaye de Saint-Victor adorn their library in Paris (1684); the architectural construction of the frieze high above the wall bookshelves is modeled on the Ambrosiana Library in Milan, designed by Federigo Borromeo, 1603–1609 (Masson, 1972, pp. 107, 117, fig. 58).

### Imperial Busts

To collect imperial coins or busts and to organize one's objects in the categories of Suetonius's twelve emperors suggests an appearance of imperial activity. Many Renaissance collections of ancient Roman imperial coins are displayed in room two of the Archaeological Museum, Venice, and busts of the emperors are displayed in the Room of the Emperors in the Palazzo Borghese. A common pastime among Italian humanists and antiquarians was the collection of coins with heads of the twelve Caesars discussed in Suetonius's *Lives of the Caesars.* Most influential, Petrarch collected such coins of the emperors and utilized both image and inscription to corroborate

information. Furthermore, applying such numismatics to challenging church history and policy, Lorenza Valla wrote in 1440 the *Declamation Concerning the False Donation of Constantine.* Filarete, in discussing the collection in Piero de' Medici's *studiolo* of the 1450s to 1460s, mentioned intaglios of Caesar, Octavian, Vespasian, Tiberius, Hadrian, Trajan, Domitian, Nero, and Antonius Pius, as well as Faustina, and viewed them as a more accurate record than writing. Humanists learned from Pliny, *Natural History* 35.2.9–10, that portraits and busts inspired readers in ancient libraries, and some humanists and collectors, such as Piero's brother, Giovanni de' Medici (d. 1463), organized a *studiolo* by busts of emperors.

The culmination of organizing via busts of emperors is the continuing use of imperial names as the cataloging system of the Cotton collection of the British Library, a collection visually central to the new British Library. Colin C. Tite has argued that in the 1620s the Cotton House displayed busts of the twelve emperors and of Cleopatra and Faustina

**Frieze portrait of Roger Bacon at Bodleian Library, Oxford, England.** Bodleian Library features a frieze decorated with authors whose works are represented in the library. Numbers incorporated into the portraits correspond to the shelf location of the author's works. BODLEIAN LIBRARY, UNIVERSITY OF OXFORD

**Manuscript image of Roger Bacon in door of convent.** Roger Bacon's portrait on the frieze at Bodleian Library was based on this image by a French artist, although the frieze image seems to represent a younger version of Bacon. BODLEIAN LIBRARY, UNIVERSITY OF OXFORD, MS. BODL. 211, FOL. 5.

above the presses containing the books labeled by that imperial name.

Cotton's many coins gave him full examples of Roman images of the emperors. The British Library manuscript room contains the first catalog of Cotton manuscripts arranged in accordance with the emperor system, Additional MS 36682, fols. 14v–15 (approximately 1638). It places the books marked Cleopatra and Faustina after the books marked Julius and Augustus, and then continues the line of emperors; on the other hand, the Thomas Smith *Catalogue,* 1696 (reprint, 1984) lists the books marked Cleopatra and the books marked Faustina after the books of the twelve emperors. An imagined reconstruction focuses on the noncontroversial location of the presses of the first two emperors Julius and Augustus. Books and objects were arranged by size within the fourteen categories.

**Disciplines of Knowledge**

Classification of books by disciplines occurs in the Chinese, Islamic, and European traditions. Starting in the third century, the imperial library of China classified books into four disciplines: canonical and classical, historical, philosophical, and literary, and there was a corresponding color-coding scheme. Chinese encyclopedism, which began in the fourth century B.C.E., reached a culmination under Emperor Quianlong, whose reign extended from 1736 to 1795. A devotee of

arts and letters who personally painted and did calligraphy according to the great masters, Quianlong in 1772 launched a copying project for over ten thousand books and manuscripts. The project—involving 16 directors, 361 scholars, and 4,000 assistants or copyists—resulted in an extensive collection of over ten thousand books and manuscripts. Likewise, Quianlong commissioned the covers of the books in the traditional color scheme: green for classics, red for history, blue for philosophy, gray for literature. The catalog of 10,254 entries follows the four-part scheme; three original copies have survived (Schaer, pp. 350–367).

Piero de' Medici, father of Lorenzo the Magnificent, used color-coding in his catalog of books and in his book bindings in his *studiolo* in the Medici Palace, Florence. Many of these hand-illuminated works are in good condition in the Biblioteca Laurenziana, Florence. The main room designed by Michelangelo opened in 1571; the subject names still survive on the sides of the lecterns where the books were then chained. Likewise, the Latin words for "Grammar books" and "Medical books" appear on window inscriptions of the library of the cathedral chapter of Bayeux (c. 1464) and correspond in location to that indicated in the catalog of 1480.

In the Escorial Library of Philip II of Spain, designed by Juan de Herrara and constructed 1575–1792, as a great hall 212 feet by 35 feet with a barrel vault 35 feet from the floor, paintings of personifications of the liberal arts rise from above the wall bookcases. These are Philosophy, Grammar, Rhetoric, Dialectics, Arithmetic, Music, Geometry, Astrology, and Theology. The figure of Grammar thus rose above the shelves designated for grammar in the Escorial Library (fig. 31, Masson, 1972*)*. While decorating a library with muses or personifications of the liberal arts was not new, lining a rectangular room with wood bookcases was a new innovation, allowing those entering to see and grasp the unity of the open-spaced room and

**Interior view of San Lorenzo dell'Escorial library, near Madrid, Spain.** The Escorial library, built for Phillip II of Spain, introduced the concept of wall bookcases, an innovation that quickly became a standard fixture of Italian libraries and collection houses. THE ART ARCHIVE/DAGLI ORTI (A)

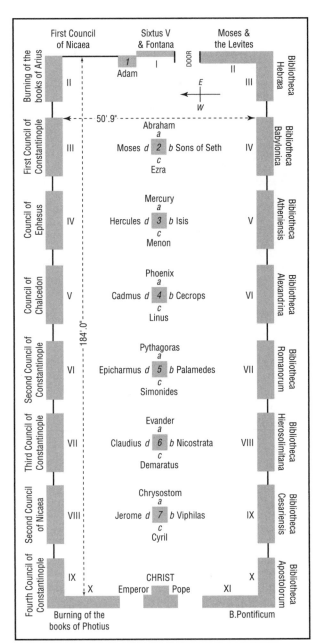

**Outline of the Salone Sistino of Pope Sixtus, Vatican Library.** The Vatican Library took a strong interest in preserving previous cultures, as is shown in this depiction of the libraries of various civilizations throughout history. ADAPTED FROM FIGURE 18 IN *THE CARE OF BOOKS* BY JOHN WILLIS CLARK, 1901.

to use the books stacked horizontally on the shelves (Frey Jose de Siguenza, *Fundacion del Monasterio de El Escorial,* 1595 (reprint, 1963), pp. 279–280). The Ambrosian Library, Milan, 1603–1609, established wall bookcases as the norm for Italy.

Until about 1700, Fearlier in Italy, upper wall and ceiling figures of muses might correlate with the matching books inspired by that muse. The books in lecterns, cases, or shelves would correlate with the appropriate decor of that classification. For example, Garberson has studied a transition library, the Austrian Biblotheca Windhagiana, built 1650–1673, which gave more decorative space to theology to match the extensive collection in that field on the shelves below. Allowing for a unified decor despite continuing purchase of books in varying fields, later libraries allowed the architectural space to designate a balanced distribution of design illustrating the overall purposes of the library. Nevertheless, in the 1764 first printing of *Descripcion del Real Monasterio de San Lorenzo del Escorial,* Andres Ximenez classified his partial list of four thousand volumes by the muses in Pellegrino Tibaldi's paintings decorating the ceiling and archway of the main floor of the library.

Through the nineteenth century, the muses remained a popular decorative scheme in libraries, as well as in opera houses, where they are often dancing in a circle. Above the

entry hall staircase of the Boston Pubic Library, Pierre-Cécile Puvis de Chavannes painted the muse of history viewing ancient ruins, as well as a new iconography for physics, represented by figures of good and bad news holding the telegraph pole.

Extensive collections required division not simply by a section of a room, but by multiple rooms. Avicenna (Ibn Sina), awed by the size of the Islamic library at Bukhara at the end of the tenth century, reported that each room was designated

**The circular botanical garden at Padua, Italy.** Founded in 1545, the famous botanical garden at the Padua medical university occupies an area of two hectares and has a circular design that was popular during the Renaissance period. © DAVID LEES/CORBIS

for a particular discipline of knowledge and contained trunks of books: poetry and Arabic philology, jurisprudence, and others. Sorting knowledge into "rooms" is a theme in the Roman Quintillian's (c. 35–c. 100) *Art of Rhetoric.* In the Institute of Research in History in the Senate House of the University of London, there is virtually a house of history with, for example, rooms for specific national histories in specific centuries. On a smaller scale, in his influential 1885 design for a history seminar room on German precedent at Johns Hopkins University, Herbert Baxter Adams planned the room to house alcoves of histories, of related disciplines such as political science and economics, and of primary sources such as laws and public documents; nearby rooms were designated for ancillary tools such as maps and statistics (Smith, p. 1159, illustration).

**Succession of Collections**

Great book collections, as well as large museums, have absorbed within them previous collections. The Vatican Library took pride in its role as a preserver of and successor to previous cultures. Sixtus V (r. 1585–1590) commemorated that tradition by commissioning fictive fresco images of some of the libraries contained within his collecting project. The graphical design shows the arrangement of images of great libraries of diverse peoples and the great council meetings that set church doctrine. Works that in private hands might cause an accusation of heresy

against their owner were safely stored in the closed cabinets five feet high on the perimeter wall and around the columns of this rectangular great hall, 184 by 57 feet.

The neo-Gothic library of the London Guild House also has visual renditions of earlier libraries. Starting with the Louvre in the late eighteenth century, great museums sought to collect works from a succession of great civilizations: the Egyptian, the Greek, the Roman, the Christian, the Italian Renaissance, the French Classical, and so forth. With changing tastes in the nineteenth century, curators added additional works of medieval art and of Northern Renaissance art.

**Circles of Knowledge**

In the Renaissance, the sphere and the circle were viewed as perfect forms. The medical school in Padua, in initiating one of the earliest and most famous botanical gardens, chose a circular arrangement. Plants from the Americas were transplanted there.

Reading rooms imitating the ancient Roman Pantheon dome became an engineering feat and architectural possibility in the mid-nineteenth century.

In 1857 Sidney Smirke worked with Anthony Panizzi to construct the reading room within the courtyard of the British Museum. Ten years later in 1867, Henri Labrouste, having

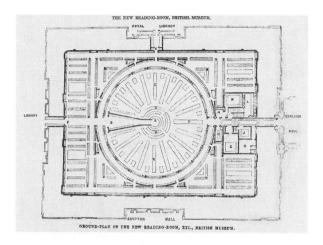

**Floor plan of the British Museum reading room (1857).** Commissioned in 1857, the main reading room at the British Museum was designed by Sidney Smirke and built in the Great Court of the museum. © CORBIS

studied the London feat and applying the analogy of culture to horticulture, which he already had applied in the tree decoration of the bibliothèque Sainte-Geneviève, created the main reading room of the Bibliothèque nationale, Richelieu.

Readers in either room were encircled by topically organized reference books; they literally might walk around the circle of knowledge. This central wheel of essential knowledge has spokes leading out to the stacks of more detailed books retrieved by librarians at the reader's request desk.

The United States imitated both great circular reading rooms in the 1886–1897 construction of the Main Reading Room of the Jefferson Building of the Library of Congress. The figures painted on the dome depict a chronological sequence of civilizations contributing to the collection: Egypt, Judea, Greece, Rome, Islam, Middle Ages, Italy, Germany, Spain, England, France, America. Statues of eight personifications of disciplines and of two great male achievers for each discipline encircle readers seeking knowledge of Philosophy, Art, History, Commerce, Religion, Science, Law, and Poetry.

## Awe-Inspiring Temples

Some of the earliest rooms of collection of Chinese Buddhist art are in Toshodaiji near Nara, Japan. In the Kondo (main hall) at Toshodaiji, 759 C.E., one sees an arrangement reminiscent of an emperor with courtiers in the rendition of a large seated Buddha with Bodhisattvas on either side. The entire complex of buildings at Toshodaiji is symmetrical, the great Buddha hall as the center with twin pagodas on either side. Museum goers may thus study ancient Chinese culture within Japanese temples.

During the Italian Renaissance, Venice was a good location for studying ancient Greek culture. La Libreria Sansoviniana in the Biblioteca Nazionale Marciana is on the second floor of a columned building across from the ducal palace and basilica of Venice. Built by architect Jacopo Sansovino in 1591, it is especially famous for its ceiling painting by Titian of

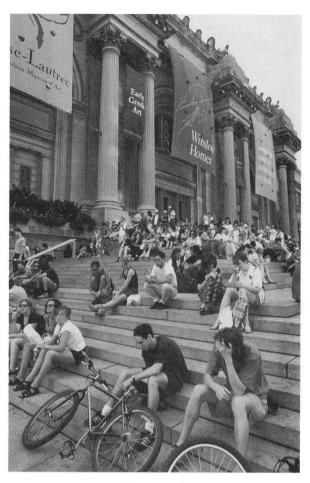

**New York's Metropolitan Museum of Art.** Some institutions that house artistic collections feature large-scale, impressive architectural components which reflect the importance of that which is housed within. © BOB KRIST/CORBIS

Wisdom. Nicola Ivanoff has elaborated on the Neoplatonic iconography of the ceiling and wall decoration of the room containing the rare manuscripts. The scheme involves personifications for virtues and for the disciplines (Ricciardi, pp. 33–44 with illustrations). Slanted desks housed the valuable possessions of Greek manuscripts collected by Cardinal Bessarion and donated to the city of Venice in 1468.

Considering this special room in the context of the path to it, one finds large caryatids by Alessandro Vittoria (1553–1555) guarding the original entrance, which leads up a winding vaulted staircase to a vestibule heavily decorated with classical sculpture donated in 1587 by the cardinal and patriarch of Aquileia, Giovanni Grimani.

In ancient Greek temple sites, as in Athens, one walked up a holy path to the hilltop temple and then stood outside the temple housing the statue of the god or goddess. To reach the collection of Greek manuscripts, one walks up a holy way and stands in a vestibule of ancient sculpture. The holy of holies in La Libreria Sansoviniana is not the effigies of gods but the Greek manuscripts.

**Bibliothèque Nationale, Paris, France.** France's new national library is a complex consisting of a garden surrounding four towers—shaped like open books—that house the institution's collections. AP/WIDE WORLD PHOTOS

Monumental staircases, grandiose like ancient Egyptian or Aztec step pyramids, became the pathway to grandiose collections, such as the Louvre, the Widener Library, the Columbia University Library, and the Metropolitan Art Museum. The winged victory goddess, which has become the insignia of Niketown, marks the turn in the grand internal staircase of the Louvre, Paris; the Chicago Art Institute imitated the design. At the end of the twentieth century, a glass pyramid entrance downward displaced the grand staircase as the main entryway to the Louvre. The crowds of diverse population line the outdoor staircase to the Metropolitan Museum of Art, New York.

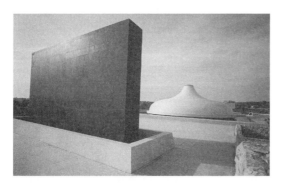

**The Shrine of the Book.** Part of the Israel Museum in Jerusalem, the Shrine of the Book contains the Dead Sea Scrolls. © DAVID RUBINGER/CORBIS

The Shrine of the Book in Jerusalem enlarges the lid of an ancient clay jar in which the Dead Sea Scrolls were found in 1947 into a monumental white dome museum housing the seven ancient scrolls in Hebrew and Aramaic. Designed by Frederick J. Kiesler and Armand P. Bartos, the white dome juxtaposes with a black wall, representing the struggle of light and darkness, good and evil, in the ancient biblical texts enclosed within.

**King's Library at the British Library.** Many institutions store collections in tower form, such as the British Library, which houses certain of its books—including those of King George III—in six-story bookcases. © IRENE RHODEN; REPRODUCED BY PERMISSION OF THE BRITISH LIBRARY

**British Museum reading room. Nineteenth-century engraving.** Constructed in the domed style of ancient Roman architecture, the reading room at the British Museum served as the main reading room for the British Library until 1997. © BETTMANN/CORBIS

## Towers of Knowledge

In the basement of the Louvre, one can still observe the walls of the tower wherein King Charles V set his library. An M. C. Escher–influenced medieval tower is featured in the scene of manuscripts burning in the film *The Name of the Rose*; therein one sees Richard de Fournival portrayed rescuing manuscripts that will later enter into the library of the Sorbonne. In the upper story tower study of Château de Montaigne, Michel de Montaigne in the 1570s, 1580s, and early 1590s utilized the book collections of his father and of his friend Étienne de La Boétie to nourish his own thoughts on numerous important social concerns of his day in his *Essais*. Imagining his mind as an infertile field and as a galloping horse, he recommends as a remedy proper

---

### VISUAL CUES TO A COLLECTION

This British Library miniature library for the traveler is related to three others extant. It has clear visual cues to its collection. Books of theology and philosophy are on the top shelf and listed in the left column, books of history are on the middle shelf and listed in the middle column, and books of poetry are on the bottom shelf and listed on the right column. The theology and philosophy books have a floral ornament on the spine and originally had blue ties, the history books have a flaming heart on the spine and red ties, and the poetry books have either a six-pointed star or a rosette on the spine and have green ties. While the history and poetry texts are primarily from ancient Greece and Rome, theology includes Old and New Testament and Christian texts, and philosophy emphasizes Stoic philosophers to Justus Lipsius.

---

sowing and careful reining (*Essais* 1.8 on idleness, "De l'oiseveté"). With self-discipline, he inscribed on the beams of his ceiling his favorite literary and philosophical sayings. After his death in 1592, Marie de Gournay worked in the book-lined tower study to prepare the 1595 posthumous edition of his essays and to track down the original sources of Montaigne's Greek and Latin classical quotes.

The newest Bibliothèque nationale, at François-Mitterrand/ Tolbiac in Paris, rises in four towers of books from the rectangular garden of trees. The Tower of Time, the Tower of Letters, the Tower of Numbers, and the Tower of Law appear to grow from the arboretum. The "Haut-de Jardin," the upper garden, serves to cultivate the general public while the "Rez-de-Jardin" encourages the deeper cultivation of the research scholar.

While the new library in Paris stores the books in towers, the new British Library in the St. Pancras Building, opened by the queen in June 1998, stores the books underground. Both great national and international collections utilize the latest technology for online reader requests as well as automated, mechanical means for book retrieval. Nevertheless, the British especially value the books extant from John Cotton's Library as well as the rest of King George III's books, which King George IV gave to the nation in 1823. These books rise in a six-story bronze and glass tower in the center of the new British Library.

*See also* **Classification of Arts and Sciences, Early Modern; Communication of Ideas; Iconography; Knowledge; Museums.**

**BIBLIOGRAPHY**
Béguin, Sylvie, ed. *Le studiolo d'Isabelle d'Este: Catalogue.* Paris: Edition des Musées Nationaux, 1975.
Besson, Alain. *Medieval Classification and Cataloguing from the Twelfth to Fifteenth Centuries.* Biggleswade, U.K.: Clover, 1980.
Chartier, Roger. *The Order of Books: Readers, Authors, and Libraries in Europe between the Fourteenth and Eighteenth Centuries.* Translated by Lydia. G. Cochrane. Stanford, Calif.: Stanford University Press, 1994.
Cheles, Luciano. *The Studiolo of Urbino: An Iconographic Investigation.* University Park: Pennsylvania State University Press, 1986.
Clark, John. *The Care of Books: An Essay on the Development of Libraries and Their Fittings, from the Earliest Times to the End of the Eighteenth Century.* Cambridge, U.K.: Cambridge University Press, 1901.
Findlen, Paula. *Possessing Nature: Museums, Collecting, and Scientific Culture in Early Modern Italy.* Berkeley: University of California Press, 1994.
Garberson, Eric. "Biblotheca Windhagiana: A Seventeenth-Century Austrian Library and Its Decoration." *Journal of the History of Collections* 5, no. 2 (1993): 109–128.
Gulik, W. R. Van et al., eds. *From Field-Case to Show-Case: Research, Acquisition, and Presentation in the Rijksmuseum voor Volkenkunde (National Museum of Ethnology) Leiden.* Amsterdam: Gieben, 1980.
Hall, Marcia, ed. *Raphael's "School of Athens."* Cambridge, U.K.: Cambridge University Press, 1997. See especially pp. 6–13.
Hobson, Anthony. *Great Libraries.* London: Weidenfeld and Nicolson, 1970.
Hooper-Greenhill, Eilean. *Museums and the Shaping of Knowledge.* London: Routledge, 1992.
Horowitz, Maryanne. "Humanist Horticulture: Twelve Agricultural Months and Twelve Categories of Books in Piero de' Medici's *Studiolo.*" *Viator: Medieval and Renaissance Studies* 34 (2003): 272–307.
———. *Seeds of Virtue and Knowledge.* Princeton, N.J.: Princeton University Press, 1998. See especially pp. 120–128 on Chambre du Cerf, Tour de la Garde-Robe, Palais des Papes, Avignon.
Hudson, Kenneth. *Museums of Influence.* Cambridge, U.K.: Cambridge University Press, 1987.
Impey, Oliver, and Arthur MacGregor, eds. *The Origins of Museums: The Cabinet of Curiosities in Sixteenth- and Seventeenth-Century Europe.* Oxford: Clarendon, 1985.
Kobayashi, Takeshi. *Nara Buddhist Art: Todai-ji.* Translated and adapted by Richard L. Gage. New York: Weatherhill, 1975.
Liebenwein, Wolfgang. *Studiolo: Die Entstehung eines Raumtyps und seine Entwicklung bis um 1600.* Berlin: Mann, 1977.
Makowiecka, Elzbieta. *The Origin and Evolution of Architectural Form of Roman Library.* Warsaw: Wydawnictwa University, 1978.
Masson, André. *Le décor des bibliothèques du Moyen Age à la Révolution.* Geneva: Droz, 1972.
———. *The Pictorial Catalogue: Mural Decoration in Libraries.* Translated by David Gerard. Oxford: Clarendon, 1981.
Pomian, Krzysztof. *Collectors and Curiosities: Paris and Venice, 1500–1800.* Translated by Elizabeth Wiles-Portier. Cambridge, U.K.: Polity, 1990.
Raggio, Olga. "The Liberal Arts Studiolo from the Ducal Palace at Gubbio." *Metropolitan Museum of Art Bulletin* 53 (spring 1996).
Ricciardi, Maria Luisa. *Biblioteche dipinte: Una storia nelle immagini.* Rome: Bulzoni, 1996.
Rogers, David. *The Bodleian Library and Its Treasures, 1320–1720.* Henley-on-Thames, U.K.: Aidan Ellis, 1991.
Schaer, Roland. *Tous les saviors du monde: Encyclopédies et bibliothèques, de Sumer au XXIe siècle.* Paris: Bibliothèque nationale/ Flammarion, 1996.
Signorelli, Luigi. *The Palazzo Vecchio and the Piazza della Signoria: Handbook and Itinerary.* Translated by Hilda M. R. Cox. Florence, Italy: Arnaud, 1952.
Smith, Bonnie G. "Gender and the Practices of Scientific History." *American Historical Review* 100 (1995): 1150–1176.
Staikos, Konstantinos Sp. *The Great Libraries from Antiquity to the Renaissance.* London: Oak Knoll Press and the British Library, 2000.
Stam, David H., ed. *International Dictionary of Library Histories.* 2 vols. Chicago: Dearborn, 2001. See especially Edwin Wolff II, "Library Buildings," and Mohamed Taher, "Islamic Libraries."
Tite, Colin G. C. *The Manuscript Library of Sir Robert Cotton.* London: The British Library, 1994.
Ventura, Leandro, Daniela Ferrari et al. *Isabella d'Este: I luoghi del collezionismo: Mantova, Palazzo ducale, appartamenti isabelliani.* Modena: Bulino, 1995.
Verheyen, Egon. *The Paintings in the* Studiolo *of Isabella d'Este at Mantua.* New York: New York University Press, 1971.

*Maryanne Cline Horowitz*

**VOLKSGEIST.** *Volksgeist* (folk or national spirit) is perhaps the best known of a family of terms referring to sets of mental, intellectual, moral, and cultural traits that define particular human groups represented as being "nations" or "peoples." Additional related words include *Volksseele* ("folk soul"), "national character," *esprit de la nation* ("spirit of the nation"), and a host of others. These terms have never had narrowly fixed meanings, either individually or in comparison with each other. Sometimes they have been used to denote irreducible, irrational spiritual forces that lie close to the foundations of perception and behavior and explain why people of one nation must differ radically from those of another. More often, they have served as platforms for arraying ranges of cultural characteristics in such a way that distinctions between nationalities can be identified, the moral and political implications of the distinctions can be developed, and the cultural similarities among people of the same nationality can be used to construct a conscious national community. Regardless of their stated intentions, writers employing these terms have tended to apply them both descriptively and judgmentally and seldom have avoided tautology. *Volksgeist* (which will stand here for the entire family) has not been a popular word among intellectuals since the middle of the twentieth century, but concepts closely related to it are far from uncommon in contemporary public discourse.

Benedict Anderson has argued that nations are "imagined communities." *Volksgeist* originated mainly in the efforts of early modern Europeans to imagine communities that corresponded either to the extensive, politically centralized territorial states emerging around them (France, for instance) or to groups of people of similar language who were not experiencing such political developments but might do so in the near future (Germans and Italians). Its relationship to actual states in the eighteenth century was quite complex. *Volksgeist* was created as much by the critics of the major nation-states as by their apologists. Charles-Louis de Secondat, baron de Montesquieu (1689–1755), one of the originators of the concept, argued that the cultural identities—the "spirits"—of peoples derived mainly from their interactions with their environments over time, which suggested that the efforts of the French state to establish cultural uniformity among the various nations of which France was composed was as illegitimate as its attempts to extend its imperial control over nations beyond its borders and to impose a single, authoritarian political hegemony over the diverse orders of French society. Johann Gottfried Herder (1744–1803), generally acknowledged as the person who first brought most of the conventional elements of *Volksgeist* together into a coherent whole, represented nations as embodiments of unique sets of cultural characteristics in explicit opposition to attempts to define nations politically.

Herder bears the reputation of being the father both of *Volksgeist* and of modern nationalism. In each case the reputation is only partly deserved, but his contribution was profound nonetheless. Herder used extended expressions such as *Geist des Volkes* rather than *Volksgeist,* but in representing peoples (*Völker*) as actual humans with individual differences, sharing cultural traits shaped by their ancestors' history and experience of a particular physical environment and mentally constructing their world through language and law inherited from earlier generations, he expressed the essence of the concept and laid the groundwork for what would later be called ethnology. Herder's presentation shows that there was more to the creation of *Volksgeist* than simply engagement with the implications of the nation-state. It was also a reaction to the

inadequacies of the model of the abstract rational individual that underpinned the Lockean interpretation of society. With regard to nationalism, Herder did not call for a unified state defined by the German *Volksgeist,* even though he argued against imposing French political and cultural hegemony on Germans. He did, however, claim that the only effective and legitimate governments were ones that developed naturally among particular nations and that reflected, in their differences from other polities, the cultures of the peoples they governed. Whether such a relationship was possible between nations defined as natural cultural entities and governments that ruled very extensive areas was, to Herder, at best questionable. He did not foresee the massive efforts of nineteenth-century nation-states to create common nationalities among their diverse citizens by such means as public education.

The word *Volksgeist* itself was coined by Georg Wilhelm Friedrich Hegel (1770–1831) to denote the separate spiritual essences of the diverse nations that characterized the present stage of human history and that would, through a dialectical process, produce the uniform "world-spirit" which spelled history's end. Hegel's formulation had some resonance later in the nineteenth century, but the most important versions of the idea followed more directly the line established by Herder. Early nineteenth-century Romantic philologists such as Jacob and Wilhelm Grimm (1785–1863, 1786–1859) focused on the centrality of language in framing the distinctive ways in which particular peoples interpret the world, on the history of languages as the key to the real history of nations, and on the study of folk tales as a means of comprehending the spiritual realities of peoples that lay hidden beneath layers of sophistication and cultural borrowing. These intellectual concerns were often bound up with political ones, as national character was commonly cited as a justification for claiming political autonomy within imperial states or asserting independence (Hungarians and Czechs in the Austrian Empire, for example, or the Irish with respect to Great Britain) or for insisting on the union of peoples of similar language (as in Germany). *Volksgeist* was also frequently connected with democratic, or at least anti-hierarchical, political tendencies. If the core of a genuine nation lay not in the power or civilization of its elite, but rather in the language and folk heritage of its common people, it followed that in some manifest way those people should participate in the political life of the national state.

Apart from its political implications, the most important consequence of the formulation of *Volksgeist* was its influence on the formulation of the concept of *culture* in the middle years of the nineteenth century. The idea that "peoples" identified by particular, but wide, arrays of traits could be taken as the fundamental units of social and historical study was basic to the establishment of ethnology as a science. The comparative ethnology of both the diffusionist and the functionalist schools was predicated on this assumption, which dominated cultural science until past the middle of the twentieth century. Comparative studies of folk culture, pioneered in Germany by Wilhelm Heinrich Riehl (1823–1897), were also strongly affected by the concept of *Volksgeist.* Such studies found echoes in many countries. Another human science that incorporated *Volksgeist* was *Völkerpsychologie* (folk psychology), which aimed at distinguishing psychological characteristics and mental operations that were common to all people from those derived from their varied cultures. The broad complex of cultural studies affected by the idea of *Volksgeist* provided discursive and conceptual frameworks to intellectuals throughout the world—to George Eliot (1819–1880), for example, and to W. E. B. DuBois (1868–1963), whose book, *The Souls of Black Folk* (1903), examines in great depth the relationship between a people, the larger political nation to which it belongs, and the distinctive forms of perception that it derives from its history and culture.

In the late nineteenth and early twentieth centuries, *Volksgeist* came to be associated with the fashion for biological racialism that swept through social thought in Europe and America, helping to produce what has been called "*völkisch*" ideology. It was this association that, perhaps more than anything else, caused the sudden decline of *Volksgeist* as a respectable term in intellectual discourse after World War II.

*See also* **Cultural History; Ethnicity and Race; Nation; Nationalism; Regions and Regionalism, Eastern Europe.**

**BIBLIOGRAPHY**
Anderson, Benedict. *Imagined Communities: Reflections on the Origin and Spread of Nationalism.* London: Verso Editions, 1983.
Berlin, Isaiah. *Vico and Herder: Two Studies in the History of Ideas.* New York: The Viking Press, 1976.
Greenfield, Liah. *Nationalism: Five Roads to Modernity.* Cambridge, Mass., and London: Harvard University Press, 1992.
Herder, Johann Gottfried. *Philosophical Writings.* Translated and edited by Michael N. Forster. Cambridge and New York: Cambridge University Press, 2002. See especially Part IV.
Smith, Woodruff D. *Politics and the Sciences of Culture in Germany, 1840–1920.* New York: Oxford University Press, 1991.

*Woodruff D. Smith*

**VOLUNTEERISM, U.S.** The meaning of volunteerism is contingent on the nature of government, particularly the extent and ways in which it enables individuals to make uncompensated donations of money and labor to some form of collective activity or shared purpose.

Over the course of the five centuries since European colonists first occupied North America, the meaning and practice of volunteerism has changed as part of the broader evolution of legal and government structures.

Volunteerism first appeared within the framework of state action in the form of donations of land, money, and labor to public purposes. Some of these are outlined in the Statute of Charitable Uses, a 1601 act of Parliament intended to regulate charitable abuses. They include assisting the poor, sick, and injured, education, caring for orphans, tax relief, ransoming captives, helping young tradesmen, and constructing public works. To these ends charitable gifts were given to municipal corporations, the church, and other public bodies. Privately funded schools, hospitals, and other institutions required the sanction of the state, either through the granting of corporate charters or court approval.

Early voluntary giving in England was strictly regulated by the state, which not only limited the purposes for which funds could be donated (a donor could not, for example, support any other religion but the Church of England), but also placed the authority with the Lord Chancellor and the chancery courts.

Eamon Duffy's studies of English religious life before the Protestant Reformation depict a rich culture of what appears to be voluntary activity (1992, 2001). But like most early volunteerism, failure to serve was punishable by fines—suggesting that it was viewed as a public obligation, much like paying taxes, rather than a genuinely voluntary act. Duffy suggests that the English Reformation ruthlessly eliminated broad-based lay participation in congregational life, centralizing sacramental and administrative functions in the hands of clergy and community leaders. Their service on vestries and other parochial boards may have been voluntary to the extent that such notables were not compelled to serve. But to the extent that it constituted one of the central functions of the aristocracy and gentry as governing classes, it could hardly be considered private in the modern sense.

Old World traditions of public volunteerism were carried to the colonies. Colonists were compelled to attend and support churches. Colonial government required all men of military age to serve in the militia. Townships levied on citizens' labor to maintain roads and other public works (McKinney, 1995).

Private volunteerism emerged from the complex politics of English Protestantism. Henry VIII's break with Rome was not intended to radically alter English religious life. But at a time when mechanical printing made the wide circulation of ideas possible, England could not be insulated from the religious ferment of the Protestant Reformation, then unfolding on the Continent. England became a battleground between religious factions, some favoring traditional Catholic conceptions of religious authority, others favoring Lutheran, Calvinist, and Anabaptist ideas that emphasized the spiritual sovereignty of believers (Dickens, 1964; Marsh, 1998).

For much of the period before 1689, the Church of England was a broad tent, permitting wide ranges of practices. This gave encouragement to a kind of spiritual volunteerism under which worshipers gravitated to preachers with whose views they sympathized, rather than being constrained by the geographical boundaries of the parishes to which the law assigned them. This practice of "gadding sermons" helped to produce the national subculture of religious individualism that gave rise first to efforts by the British state to enforce religious uniformity under the Stuarts and, ultimately, to the Puritan Revolution of 1640–1665. "Liberty of conscience" became a byword not only for religious toleration but for more encompassing conceptions of political freedom.

### Volunteerism in Colonial America

The early migrations to New England exemplify the coexistence and common roots of public and private volunteerism. The Pilgrims who settled in Plymouth in 1620 were adherents of a Protestantism that rejected the idea of a state church in favor of a church as a voluntary gathering of believers (Ahlstrom, 1972). Rejecting ecclesiastical hierarchy and the authority of the priesthood, these "separatists" established independent self-governing congregations in which members covenanted with one another to live under a common religious discipline and accept responsibility for maintaining the church and its ministry. Though an important step toward modern forms of private volunteerism, the separatists nonetheless rejected religious toleration—the existence of competing congregations—and their congregations maintained many of the characteristics of state churches.

By contrast, the settlers of the Massachusetts Bay Colony, while embracing many of the theological positions and ecclesiastical practices of their Plymouth neighbors, saw themselves as operating within the Church of England and sustained the hope that their mode of worship would set an example for the reform of the church in the old country. Because the Massachusetts Bay Colony drew on a far broader range of the spectrum of Puritan belief and practice, the first decade of settlement was fraught with intense conflict between factions on a number of issues, including the civil role of the church. Though ultimately embracing a state church model—intolerant of religious diversity and depending on taxation for its support—the Massachusetts Bay churches nonetheless regarded themselves as covenanted bodies of believers and, to this extent, embodied important characteristics of modern volunteerism.

Conflicts over theology and church polity in the 1630s resulted in the fracturing of Puritan unity. A number of Massachusetts groups, including most notably the antinomian followers of Roger Williams, were expelled from the colony. The new colony they established on Narragansett Bay (Rhode Island) permitted complete religious tolerance, requiring all churches to be supported by their members and rejecting state support. The Baptist and other congregations of Rhode Island offer the first examples of completely private volunteerism.

Ironically, the new colony's religious diversity stood in the way of any large-scale voluntarily supported enterprises. As the Massachusetts colonists moved to define and enforce religious orthodoxy, they were able to allocate public funds and to encourage private philanthropy to found Harvard College in 1636. Harvard was in no sense a private institution: most of its revenues came from government rather than from private donations; the members of its governing boards were ex officio ministers and magistrates. Nonetheless, to the extent that it solicited gifts and bequests from individuals, it did embody elements that would become basic elements of private institutions when they ultimately emerged. Colonies with religious establishments—Massachusetts, Connecticut, and Virginia—all established colleges by the first decade of the eighteenth century. In contrast, the colleges that embraced religious tolerance—Rhode Island, New York, New Jersey, and Pennsylvania—would not do so until decades later.

Even in Massachusetts, where the precursors of modern volunteerism would first take root, authorities were not entirely comfortable with the idea of voluntary activity outside the purview of the state. In 1638, when a group of Boston merchants petitioned the Massachusetts General Court requesting a charter for a private artillery company, worried legislators pondered "how dangerous it might be to erect a standing authority of military men, which might easily, in time, overthrow the civil power" (quoted in Bremer, p. 309). The Ancient and Honorable Artillery Company was allowed to organize, but was denied corporate status.

In the later years of the seventeenth century, a variety of kinds of secular volunteerism began to flourish in England (Jordan, 1959, 1960, 1962). The most important of these were mutual benefit organizations—fraternal societies like the Freemasons, friendly societies, and social clubs—membership associations that enabled participants to assist one another in times of illness and death, to share resources like books, and to provide places of entertainment and relaxation. By the first decades of the eighteenth century, variants of these types of voluntary associations began to appear in North America. As early as 1710, Boston's preeminent religious leader, Reverend Cotton Mather (1663–1728), urged readers of his pamphlet *Bonifacius* to organize neighborhood "societies" to worship privately and to identify and care for residents in need. He also encouraged people to create associations to suppress disorders, to visit the sick and needy, and to enable young artisans to help one another.

Mather's writings had a profound influence on Benjamin Franklin, who, during his apprenticeship in London in the 1730s, had an opportunity to see firsthand the potent possibilities of voluntary association. On his return to America, he helped to introduce Freemasonry (which soon became one of the most important translocal organizations in the colonies) and, later, was instrumental in organizing young men's associations (the Junto), voluntary fire companies, an academy, and a hospital (Franklin, 1993).

## Volunteerism in the Early Republic

Volunteerism, both public and private, played an important part in the American Revolution (Fischer, 1994; Bullock, 1996). Freemasonry, which embraced Enlightenment political and religious ideals, helped to consolidate the emergent revolutionary elite, while at the same time serving as a model for such radical organizations as the Sons of Liberty (Hammill, 1998). The voluntary religious activity that grew out of the Great Awakening of the 1730s and 1740s helped to create political, social, and economic networks friendly to the cause of independence. Together these facilitated a loosening of ties between volunteerism and government. Early in the revolutionary struggle, many militias—military bodies nominally subject to the authority of civil government—were persuaded to volunteer their services to fight the British. After the battles at Lexington and Concord, local militias throughout New England defied local authorities and marched to Boston to join the revolutionary forces gathering in and around the city.

The centrality of volunteerism to the success of the American Revolution helped to kindle hostility toward it once independence was achieved. When veteran officers of the Continental Army organized the Society of the Cincinnati in 1783, its enemies viewed it as a covert effort to overthrow republican institutions and replace them with a hereditary aristocracy (Burke, 1784). In *Federalist* no.10, James Madison warned of the hazards that factions—by which he meant private political groups—posed to republican institutions. In the mid-1790s, when opponents of the new Federalist regime began organizing "democratic societies"—precursors of modern party organizations—President Washington warned against "self-created societies" intended to "subvert the Power of the People, and to usurp for themselves the reins of Government; destroying afterwards the very engines which have lifted them to unjust domination" (Washington, 1948).

The U.S. Constitution established conditions that made the growth of volunteerism inevitable. By mandating majoritarian decision-making while at the same time guaranteeing individual rights of expression, worship, and assembly, the Constitution posed an unresolvable tension between political equality and individual voice. Groups that did not prevail at the ballot box would be drawn to extragovernmental instruments—the press and voluntary associations—to advance their views and to work for victory in future elections.

Citizens of the early republic found themselves compelled to use voluntary associations, despite the uneasiness that they engendered. Because Americans feared government power, states and municipalities strictly limited the range of services they provided citizens. At the same time, the dismantling of religious establishments in the decades following the Revolution made volunteerism the central organizing principle of religious life throughout the nation. Like it or not, if Americans wanted to be educated, healed, entertained, politically represented, or provided with places of worship, they had to be willing to join with like-minded private citizens to pursue these ends.

The rise of voluntary action preceded the articulation of coherent ideas about the practice. The evangelical preacher Lyman Beecher (1775–1863), one of the first Americans to attempt to understand the role of volunteerism in institutional and political life, describes his plunge into promoting voluntary activity—in connection with early temperance efforts—as impulsive rather than deliberate. Only later, when he saw how powerful voluntary activity could be, did he begin to understand that the "voluntary system" could be used to organize all sorts of enterprises, from political reform movements, through schools, colleges, and religious crusades (Beecher, 1961). In the course of building his reputation as one of the nation's most influential evangelists, Beecher made the promotion of volunteerism one of the central themes of his efforts. For Beecher and his coreligionists, uncoerced voluntary action became an important source of moral and spiritual development for individuals and communities (Bacon, 1832; Mathews, 1969).

Beecher played a particularly important role in the development of American volunteerism. Concerned about growing numbers of unchurched and uneducated citizens, Beecher came to recognize that voluntary activity, literacy, and broadly shared public values were the precondition for religious conversion. Accordingly, he and his colleagues devoted their

energies to secular reforms that could attract broad coalitions of citizens and citizen organizations such as temperance, antislavery, education, and the relief of poverty. Appealing to a broad rather than a sectarian public, Beecher not only helped teach countless numbers of Americans the skills of volunteerism, but also to overcome attitudes that had equated volunteerism with destructive factionalism.

By the time Alexis de Tocqueville visited the United States in the late 1820s, private volunteerism was well on the way to becoming one of the most distinctive expressions of American democracy. Taking note of the temperance movement, he was quick to draw comparisons between European and American styles of civic action. "The first time I heard in the United States that a hundred thousand men had bound themselves publicly to abstain from spirituous liquors," he wrote,

it appeared to me more like a joke than a serious engagement, and I did not at once perceive why these temperate citizens did not content themselves with drinking water by their own firesides. I at last understood that these hundred thousand Americans, alarmed by the progress of drunkenness around them, had made up their minds to patronize temperance. They acted in just the same way as a man of high rank who should dress very plainly in order to inspire the humbler orders with a contempt of luxury. It is probable that if these hundred thousand men had lived in France, each of them would singly have memorialized the government to watch the public houses all over the kingdom. (vol. 1, pp. 109–110)

Although he observed the importance of voluntary association as a counterpoise to the potential for majoritarian tyranny in democracies and to the hazards of overly powerful government, Tocqueville undoubtedly exaggerated the ubiquity of private volunteerism in the United States. Many states adopted laws that discouraged private philanthropy (in Mississippi, for example, it was illegal to establish charitable trusts until well into the twentieth century) and kept voluntary organizations under strict regulatory scrutiny (i.e., New York's Regents of the University of the State of New York, which oversaw the activities of all educational, charitable, cultural, and professional organizations) (Zollmann, 1924). Only in New England and the upper Midwest was private volunteerism allowed to flourish relatively unimpeded—and even there, prominent leaders like Unitarian theologian William Ellery Channing and Baptist political economist Francis Wayland wrote widely circulated critiques of voluntary associations as posing dangers to republican government (Channing, 1900; Wayland, 1838).

In the antebellum era, voluntary associations began to play crucial roles in empowering Americans who, because of gender, race, or ethnicity, were disenfranchised. By the late eighteenth century, as whites began excluding free blacks from their congregations, black religious leaders organized their own churches. Women, generally barred from full economic and political participation, carved out a "separate sphere" of civic activism, using voluntary associations to expand their traditional domestic helping and caring roles to the dependent, disabled, unchurched, and uneducated (Scott, 1991). Immigrant associations helped those newly arrived from Europe to find economic opportunities, show their political muscle, and meet their needs in times of distress.

### Volunteerism during and after the Civil War

The Civil War helped Americans to overcome whatever qualms they may have had about volunteerism. Though the war gave rise to a strong national government, it also strengthened the voluntary impulse. Armies on both sides—at least in the first years of the war—depended on volunteer soldiers. In the North, caring for the wounded and attending to the public health needs of the armed forces depended on national voluntary associations, the United States Sanitary Commission and the United States Christian Commission. These national bodies used local chapters to raise funds, produce medical supplies, and raise morale (Brockett, 1864; Frederickson, 1965).

After the war, voluntary associations flourished on an unprecedented scale (Skocpol, 2003). Fraternal and sororal organizations proliferated in countryside and city alike. Veterans' organizations with chapters in every city and village advocated for the interests of those who had served in the armed forces. The growth of cities and the increasing corruption of the political system encouraged the growth of associations advocating civil service, sanitary, and education reform. The growth of industry gave rise not only to national trade associations to advance the interests of merchants and manufacturers, but to labor organizations to defend the rights of working people. As demands for specialized expertise grew, professionals of every sort—physicians, lawyers, clergy, architects, engineers, and educators—organized membership associations to set professional standards and advance their collective legislative interests.

The rapid growth of voluntary associations among a people that, on the whole, had little experience with them led inevitably to considerable organizational disorder. Union army officer Henry M. Robert (1837–1923), assigned to posts in Washington State, California, Massachusetts, and Wisconsin, encountered what he described as "virtual parliamentary anarchy" in voluntary organizations (Doyle, 1980). This moved him to write his famous *Rules of Order*—which became the national standard for Americans swept up in the tidal wave of association building in the closing decades of the nineteenth century.

By the beginning of the twentieth century, two parallel traditions of volunteerism, one public, the other private, were firmly in place. On the public side, most municipalities depended on the voluntary energies of citizens, who served on boards and commissions and ran key municipal services (such as fire protection) on a voluntary basis. On the private side, many public services, such as social welfare and health care, had become largely dependent on voluntary donations of money and labor. But even when formally private, volunteerism sought not merely to serve members in their private capacities—it was almost always linked to government, seeking to sway public opinion on civic issues or to elicit government commitment. During the 1920s, Herbert Hoover sought to create an "associative state"

based on partnerships between voluntary associations and government agencies (Hoover, 1922; Hawley, 1977).

Volunteerism served both democratic and undemocratic purposes. Organizations like the American Protective Association and the Ku Klux Klan—both voluntary associations—sought to disempower and terrorize racial, ethnic, and religious minorities. Elite art museums, symphony orchestras, and universities sought both to enlighten the public and to shape its values in ways favorable to the interests of monied elites (DiMaggio, 1986). Professional associations often used efforts to elevate professional standards as ways of excluding Catholics and Jews (Auerbach, 1976). At the same time, voluntary associations were vehicles for national and international efforts to oppose lynching, promote economic and social justice, and advance women's suffrage (see, for example, Dray, 2002).

Inevitably, as the twentieth century advanced, hitherto voluntary activity began to be affected by professionalization. As the revenue needs of educational, health, and social welfare institutions grew, they were increasingly likely to turn to professional fundraising firms instead of depending on the efforts of volunteers (Cutlip, 1990). As medical and social work practice increasingly required higher levels of expertise, professionals and managers began to replace volunteers as key decision makers in health and welfare agencies (Starr, 1982; Perrow, 1963). By the late 1920s, the establishment training programs for volunteer trustees and directors in schools, libraries, and social agencies suggest that even volunteering itself began to require trained expertise (Hall, 2000). Inevitably, professionals pushed volunteers to the margins in most large nonprofit organizations.

### Volunteerism and the Rise and Fall of the Welfare State

As the World War II ended, American policymakers began to take the full measure of the domestic and international responsibilities the nation had taken on as leader of the free world. International leadership would require the development of capacities to manage the domestic economy, to maintain internal political stability, and to sustain military preparedness. This would require a vast expansion of government.

The realities of the U.S. federal system, with its divided and subordinated responsibilities, combined with continuing popular distrust of big government prevented the creation of a European-style centralized bureaucratic state. The American welfare/warfare state, as it emerged, concentrated revenue gathering and policy powers in the national government while allocating most of the tasks of implementing national policies to states, localities, and private sector actors (Webber and Wildavsky, 1986; Donahue, 1989).

Tax policy became one of the most important instruments of the welfare state. The universalization of income taxation and steeply progressive individual and corporate taxes provided a powerful tool for influencing the activities of citizens and citizen organizations. Although the federal government used grants and contracts to influence private sector activity, the deductibility of donations and bequests and exemption from corporate income and other forms of taxation became effective ways of encouraging transfers of funds between private sector actors. Implementing this system required a revolution in the tax treatment of charitable enterprises. Between 1947 and 1954, Congress rewrote the tax code, creating powerful incentives for charitable, educational, and religious organizations to incorporate and seek certification of charitable status from the federal government.

Depriving many voluntary membership organizations of tax exemptions that they had historically enjoyed, in combination with the establishment of federal social insurance programs, eliminated the raison d'etre for the mutual benefit organizations that comprised the majority of secular voluntary associations in the United States. By the 1960s, traditional voluntary membership associations were dying out and, as Robert Putnam has noted, volunteerism of every sort was declining (Putnam, 2000; Skocpol, 2003).

The place of voluntary membership associations was being taken by charitable tax-exempt "nonprofit organizations" that were increasingly likely to be run by professional managers and funded by a mix of donations, commercial revenues, and foundation and government grants and contracts. Though volunteers still played a role in the nonprofit sector, they were increasingly likely to be involved with start-up organizations (which, if successful, quickly became professionalized) and religious bodies. There were exceptions to this pattern: religious organizations continued to command nearly two-thirds of the volunteer labor in the nonprofit sector; self-help groups, like Alcoholics Anonymous, explicitly rejected professionalism and depended entirely on the voluntary support of their members (Wuthnow, 1994); character building organizations like the Girl Scouts and Boy Scouts also continued to depend almost entirely on volunteers.

The last decades of the twentieth century witnessed a revival of public volunteerism. The Peace Corps, established in the early 1960s, sent American volunteers to developing countries. During the War on Poverty of the late 1960s, VISTA (Volunteers in Service to America) drew volunteers to impoverished urban and rural areas within the United States. The conservative revolution, which began in earnest with the election of President Ronald Reagan in 1980, advocated voluntary community efforts as a substitute for big government programs that, conservatives argued, perpetuated a culture of poverty. Some of these efforts, like Americorps, were government-sponsored. Others, like Habitat for Humanity, enlisted private citizens to help address public problems, such as poor housing. Colleges and universities became enthusiastic promoters of student voluntarism and community service as forms of experiential learning.

Dismantling big government through devolution (shifting burdens from the national government to states and localities) and privatization (shifting government responsibilities to private sector actors) was the central project of the conservative revolution. George H. W. Bush's speeches following his nomination as Republican candidate for the presidency in 1988 were not only high-profile official endorsements of volunteerism, but also suggested a peculiar blurring of public and private conceptions of volunteerism at the end of the twentieth century. In his 1989 inaugural speech, the president declared

> I have spoken of a thousand points of light, of all the community organizations that are spread like stars throughout the Nation, doing good. We will work hand in hand, encouraging, sometimes leading, sometimes being led, rewarding. We will work on this in the White House, in the Cabinet agencies. I will go to the people and the programs that are the brighter points of light, and I will ask every member of my government to become involved. The old ideas are new again because they are not old, they are timeless: duty, sacrifice, commitment, and a patriotism that finds its expression in taking part and pitching in.

At the end of the twentieth century, the traditions of public and private volunteerism that had diverged two centuries earlier were evidently converging as institutions—government, business, and universities—promoted volunteering as ways of fulfilling their responsibilities to the public. Such institutionally sponsored efforts—which often contain coercive elements (such as being requisites for graduation or promotion)—raise questions about the voluntariness of contemporary volunteerism.

*See also* **Citizenship; Civil Society.**

**BIBLIOGRAPHY**

Ahlstrom, Sydney E. *A Religious History of the American People.* New Haven, Conn.: Yale University Press, 1972.

Auerbach, Jerold S. *Unequal Justice: Lawyers and Social Change in Modern America.* New York: Oxford University Press, 1976.

Bacon, Leonard. *The Christian Doctrine of Stewardship in Respect to Property.* New Haven, Conn.: Printed by Nathan Whiting, 1832.

Bremer, Francis J. *John Winthrop: America's Forgotten Founding Father.* New York: Oxford University Press, 2003.

Brockett, L. P. (Linus Pierpont). *The Philanthropic Results of the War in America. Collected from Official and Other Authentic Sources, by an American Citizen.* New York: Sheldon, 1864.

Bullock, Steven C. *Revolutionary Brotherhood: Freemasonry and the Transformation of the American Social Order, 1730–1840.* Chapel Hill: University of North Carolina Press.

Burke, Aedanus. *Considerations on the Society or Order of Cincinnati.* Hartford, Conn.: Reprinted by Hudson and Goodwin, 1784.

Channing, William Ellery. "Associations." In *The Works of William E. Channing, D.D.* Boston: American Unitarian Association, 1900. Originally published in 1828.

Cutlip, Scott M. *Fund Raising in the United States: Its Role in America's Philanthropy.* New Brunswick, N.J.: Transaction Publishers, 1900.

De Tocqueville, Alexis. *Democracy in America.* Translated by Henry Reeve. New York: Knopf, 1945.

Dickens, A. G. *The English Reformation.* New York: Schocken Books, 1964.

DiMaggio, Paul J. "Cultural Entrepreneurship in Nineteenth-Century Boston." In his *Nonprofit Enterprise in the Arts: Studies in Mission and Constraint.* New York: Oxford University Press, 1989.

Donahue, John D. *The Privatization Decision: Public Ends, Private Means.* New York: Basic Books, 1989.

Doyle, Don H. "Rules of Order: Henry Martyn Robert and the Popularization of American Parliamentary Law." *American Quarterly* 32, no. 3 (1980): 3–18.

Dray, Philip. *At the Hands of Persons Unknown: The Lynching of Black America.* New York: Random House, 2002.

Duffy, Eamon. *The Stripping of the Altars: Traditional Religion in England, c. 1400–c. 1580.* New Haven, Conn.: Yale University Press, 1992.

———. *The Voices of Morebath: Reformation and Rebellion in an English Village.* New Haven: Yale University Press, 2001.

Fischer, David Hackett. *Paul Revere's Ride.* New York: Oxford University Press, 1994.

Franklin, Benjamin. *Autobiography and Other Writings.* Edited by Ormond Seavey. New York: Oxford University Press, 1993.

Hall, Peter Dobkin. "Faith, Practice, and Civic Engagement: A Historical Case Study." In *Religion and Democracy,* edited by Mary Jo Bane and Brent Coffin. Cambridge, Mass.: Harvard University Press. Forthcoming.

———. "Resolving the Dilemmas of Democratic Governance: The Historical Development of Trusteeship in America, 1636–1996." In *Philanthropic Foundations: New Scholarships, New Possibilities,* edited by Ellen Condliffe. Bloomington: Indiana University Press, 1999.

Hamill, John. *Freemasonry.* London: Salamander, 1998.

Hawley, Ellis W. "Herbert Hoover, the Commerce Secretariat, and the Vision of an 'Associative State.'" In *Men and Organizations,* edited by Edwin J. Perkins. New York: G. P. Putnam, 1977.

Hoover, Herbert. *American Individualism.* Garden City, N.Y.: Doubleday, Page, 1922.

Jordan, W. K. *The Charities of London, 1480–1660: The Aspirations and the Achievements of the Urban Society.* London: Allen and Unwin, 1960.

———. *The Charities of Rural England, 1480–1660: The Aspirations and the Achievements of the Rural Society.* New York: Russell Sage Foundation, 1962.

———. *Philanthropy in England, 1480–1660 : A Study of the Changing Pattern of English Social Aspirations.* London: George Allen and Unwin, 1959.

Marsh, Christopher. *Popular Religion in Sixteenth-Century England.* New York: St. Martin's, 1998.

Mather, Cotton. *Bonifacius. An Essay upon the Good . . .* Edited by David Levin. Cambridge, Mass.: Belknap Press

of Harvard University Press, 1966. Originally published in 1710.

Mathews, Donald G. "The Great Awakening as an Organizing Process, 1780–1830: An Hypothesis." *American Quarterly* 21, no. 1 (1969): 23–43.

McKinney, Hannah J. *The Development of Local Public Services, 1650–1860: Lessons from Middletown, Connecticut.* Westport, Conn.: Greenwood Press, 1995.

Perrow, Charles. "Goals and Power Structures: A Historical Case Study." In *The Hospital in Modern Society,* edited by Eliot Friedson. New York: Free Press, 1963.

Putnam, Robert D. *Bowling Alone: The Collapse and Revival of American Community.* New York: Simon and Schuster, 2000.

Scott, Anne Firor. *Natural Allies: Women's Associations in American History.* Urbana: University of Illinois Press, 1991.

Skocpol, Theda. *Diminished Democracy: From Membership to Management in American Civic Life.* Norman: University of Oklahoma Press, 2003.

Starr, Paul. *The Social Transformation of American Medicine.* New York: Basic Books, 1982.

Washington, George. "Sixth Annual Address to Congress (1796)." In *Basic Writings of George Washington,* edited by Saxe Commins. New York: Random House, 1948.

Wayland, Francis. *The Limitations of Human Responsibility.* New York: D. Appleton, 1838.

Webber, Carolyn, and Aaron Wildavsky. A History of Taxation and Expenditure in the Western World. New York: Simon and Schuster, 1986.

Wuthnow, Robert. *"I Come Away Stronger": How Small Groups are Shaping American Religion.* Grand Rapids, Mich.: W. B. Eerdmans, 1994.

Zollmann, Carl. *American Law of Charities.* Milwaukee: The Bruce Publishing Company, 1924.

*Peter Dobkin Hall*

**VOODOO (VODUN).** *See* **Religion: Africa; Religion: African Diaspora.**

**VOTING.** *See* **Democracy.**

# W

**WAR.** How does one define a war? How can one distinguish between the war on drugs, the war on terrorism, jihad, anarchy, and wars between states? Definitions are relevant as they provide the rationale for considering a war legitimate and just and contribute to decisions about international interventions, aid, and protocol. This has become particularly important in contemporary international affairs, when the most prevalent conflicts have been nationalist and or ethnic in character and international terrorism has escalated. War has been defined in a number of ways: as "organized violence carried out by political units against each other" (Bull, p. 184); as "the legal condition which equally permits two or more hostile groups to carry on a conflict by armed force" (Wright, p. 698); and as "an act of force to compel our enemy to do our will" (Clausewitz, p. 75). These definitions encapsulate the notion of war as political, as organized violence carried out by a collective, and as ordered in that it has rules and customs of behavior. An underlying assumption is that war is a regular occurrence in the international arena and is an inevitable outcome of organized human societies.

This latter idea has been critiqued by Margaret Mead, who sees warfare as one of many inventions constructed to order our lives, in the same realm as "writing, marriage, cooking" and so on. War, like culture, takes on the veneer of an ancient tradition, something having historical depth, and has prevailed since early organized human societies. Mead suggests that war is an invented and learned activity and is not inherent to human behavior. The contending opinion emphasizes the "innateness" of human aggression, the consequences of which are sometimes violence and war. Without denying the complex interplay between genetic and environmental variables, these theories see human aggression as biologically driven. Humans fight over land, resources, and personal relationships in much the same way as other primates do, hence war in this perspective is not a social or cultural invention.

John Vasquez sees war as learned but also includes the notion that war comes out of a long-term process, is a product of interaction, is a way of making decisions, and is multicausal, and he recognizes that there are many different types of wars. Although this is a more comprehensive list of defining characteristics of war, the emphasis is on "interstate" wars and international peace and security.

## Defining States as Warring Units

Should we assume states to be the main contending parties in war? Many influential definitions of war place states as a key variable. They assume that states are rational actors made up of coherent territorial units with recognized leaders, governmental institutions, and discernable civil societies. However, in many of the major conflicts in the 1980s and 1990s, transnational activity reduced the significance of states as key actors. Post–Cold War central Africa and eastern Europe exemplify instances where intra- and interethnic conflicts within states sparked violent confrontations between states. Should these conflicts be classified as wars even though individual states did not declare war against other states? In some instances, belligerent ethnic groups within one state declared war on ethnic groups in another state, as in the Serbian Serb-Bosnian Muslim conflict in the former Yugoslavia from 1992 to 1995. In an attempt to answer the question of the types of nationalism that are most likely to cause war, Stephen Van Evera isolates four attributes: the movement's political status with respect to statehood, its relationships with its national diaspora, its stance toward other nations, and its treatment of its own minorities. Using this scheme, it might be possible to evaluate the potential of a nationalist (or ethnic) conflict to escalate into a war. Theorists such as Van Evera have attempted to shift attention from states to nationalist movements as indicators showing the potential for war.

In other cases, there was no legitimate and overarching ruling authority within the state, as in Somalia from 1992 to 1994, when political anarchy prevailed and rival clan leaders battled each other. There refugees, guerrilla groups, and targeted factions fled across borders, initiating conflicts and instability in these regions. How should these conflicts be classified? If such conflicts are considered "domestic," falling under the purview of sovereign states, then international interventions become extremely difficult. Given the regional instability that such conflicts produce, the devastation that follows, and the gross human rights violations that are committed, defining this as a national issue has many negative repercussions.

The havoc wrought by terrorists also challenges definitions of war. Highly skilled, trained, motivated, and ordered like soldiers in conventional armies, international terrorists have instigated some of our most intense wars. The U.S. invasion of Afghanistan in 2002 and Iraq in 2003 are good examples of the repercussions terrorists can invoke, in this case, the 9/11/2001 attack on the World Trade Center and the Pentagon. In pursuit of the masterminds behind the attacks, the United States believed that Osama Bin Laden (thought to be residing in Afghanistan) and Saddam Hussein (of Iraq) were key players, hence prompting the invasions. Should the citizenship of terrorists determine the belligerent state? Must we assume that all states are able to control all their citizens and

***For the Common Grave!,*** an etching by Francisco José de Goya y Lucientes from his *Disasters of War* series **(1810–1820).** The consequences of a war, whether it is considered justified or not, are often terrible, testing the humanity and mores of the participating combatants. © ARCHIVO ICONOGRAFICO

must take responsibility for their actions? How do we determine the target state when some terrorists have multiple citizenships and divided loyalties? Can we isolate a particular state as belligerent when some terrorists fight for political ideals and religious doctrines that transcend national state borders? Can we classify an attack by terrorists as an act of war? These questions challenge the assumption that states are the key units in war and challenge ideas of the causes and rules of war.

### Jus ad bellum

Can war be morally justified? Most war doctrines include two considerations: first, the conditions under which one may have recourse to war (*jus ad bellum*); second, the rules and codes by which war may be conducted (*jus in bello*.) The act of war, a license to kill, tests our adherence to morality, our acceptance of what we assume are human and civilized codes of behavior, our notion of the distinctions between the divine and the profane, our understanding of authority and legitimacy, and our sense of self- and moral consciousness. There are two main discourses dealing with *jus ad bellum*. The first makes a distinction between just and unjust wars, and the second makes distinctions between offensive and defensive wars.

St. Augustine of Hippo (354–430 C.E.) first grappled with the Christian ideal of love that prohibited killing and wounding in one's own defense but also obliged Christians to aid others, thus justifying the use of force on the aggressors. Yet Augustine did not provide a theory that isolated causes for a just war, nor did he suggest that a Christian cause was most just. Instead, he proposed that Christian ethics gave people and their leaders a capacity to know the moral limits of armed action but did not provide them with the attributes to "compare unerringly the over-all justice of regimes and nations" (Ramsey, p. 32). For Augustine, as all parties in war are engaging in wrongdoing, the warring parties cannot be divided into good versus bad, but rather Christian ethics provide guidance and the parameters for conduct in war of all parties involved.

St. Thomas Aquinas (1225–1274) expanded the idea of a just war and also initiated a shift from "voluntarism" to "rationalism" in understanding the nature of the political community, emphasizing a natural-law notion of justice (Ramsey, p. 32). According to Aquinas, a just war had three necessary requirements: declaration by a legitimate constitutional authority, a just cause, and the right intention. Francisco de Vitoria

**United States soldier during Persian Gulf War.** In 1990, Iraqi forces under the control of military dictator Saddam Hussein occupied the country of Kuwait, prompting the deployment of an international coalition of forces that repelled the invasion. © YVES DEBAY/CORBIS

(1486?–1546) and Francisco Suárez (1548–1617) added further conditions: the means of war should be proportional to the injustices being prevented or remedied by war, all peaceful means to remedy injustices should be exhausted, and the war should have a reasonable hope of success.

The recognized rules of *jus ad bellum,* as outlined by Aquinas and others, are often used to determine whether or not a war is justifiable. Some of the objections to these criteria are that they are overly subjective, leaving ample space for self-interested rationalization; that they rest on normative criteria about the nature of good and evil; that these categories were designed for evaluating the causes of war in the Middle Ages; and that in the nuclear age, with its emphasis on deterrence, they provide little guidance as to how to evaluate the "moral significance of different levels of threat and of risk " (Adeney, p. 97).

There are also those who question the very notion of war as having moral legitimation. Reinhold Niebuhr, for example, argues that "Christianity should recognize that all historic struggles are struggles between sinful men." Given this, he adds that "it is just as important to save what relative decency and justice the western world still has, against the most demonic tyranny of history" (Niebuhr, p. 35). Niebuhr recognizes that

**"Sniper's Alley" in Sarajevo, 1994.** Shortly after the disintegration of Yugoslavia in 1991, Serbians in the region began a military campaign for ethnic supremacy. During the three-year-long battle, Serb forces laid siege to the Bosnian capital of Sarajevo, causing widespread destruction in the city. © CHRIS RAINIER/CORBIS

---

### JUS AD BELLUM: UNITED NATIONS CHARTER OF 1945

Chapter 1, Article 2(4)

All Members shall refrain in their international relations from the threat or use of force against the territorial integrity or political independence of any state, or in any other manner inconsistent with the Purposes of the United Nations.

Chapter 7, Article 51

Nothing in the present Charter shall impair the inherent right of individual or collective self-defence if an armed attack occurs.

Chapter 7, Article 42

Should the Security Council consider that measures provided for in Article 41 would be inadequate . . . it may take such action by air, sea, or land forces as may be necessary to maintain or restore international peace and security. Such action may include demonstrations, blockade, and other operation by air, sea, or land forces of Members of the United Nations.

---

while war can never be morally justified, it might be the only way to safeguard liberal democratic values.

In reflecting on the morality of the Gulf War, several authors came up with different conclusions. George Weigel argues that opposing the aggression of Saddam Hussein's invasion of Kuwait was justified in both intention and execution according to the criteria set out by just-war theory. Jean Bethke Elshtain, on the other hand, argues that war cannot be justified merely by checking off the list of criteria associated with the just-war theory. Instead, she suggests that the theory begs us to pause, to think about the ramifications of war, and to show some skepticism and queasiness about war. Above all, she asks that in drawing the balance sheet for the Gulf War, we evaluate technological accuracy and military might alongside the devastation and long-term effects of war on Iraqi children and society.

The just-war mode of reasoning attempts to reconcile the requirements of national defense with the moral obligations of protecting the innocent. In the age of modern warfare, where nuclear deterrence is the most significant element in preventing wars, the ideas behind just-war theory require a lot of tweaking before it begins to make any sense at all. In evaluating the justifiability of a contemporary war, some of the rules pertaining to *jus ad bellum,* particularly the rules of proportionality and reasonable hope of success, are seriously challenged. With the capacity and probability of killing large numbers of innocent people in warfare, the tensions inherent between *jus ad bellum* and *jus in bello* become sharper.

When looking specifically at modern warfare, Bernard T. Adeney sees deterrence as an "embarrassment and a puzzle" with respect to just-war theory. In terms of the criteria laid out under *jus ad bellum,* deterrence appears to be the "only

possible means of resisting unjust aggression" (Adeney, p. 112). Yet deterrence has the inherent ability to violate the basis of *jus in bello.* The Catholic Church responded to the Gulf War in a statement that put the very idea of just war in peril. The theory of just war, they said, was "indefensible and has been abandoned. In reality—with the sole exception of a purely defensive war against acts of aggression—we can say that there are no 'just wars,' and there is no 'right' to wage war" (La civiltà cattolica, p. 118). For many pacifists, who recognize the existence of political conflict, war is an unjustifiable means of resolution.

### Jus in bello

Can war be controlled? Carl von Clausewitz says war is an act of force, and "there is no logical limit to the application" of force (Clausewitz, p. 77). However, others see war as a social activity that demands social organization and control, requiring a military that uses violence with deliberation for political objectives. As instruments of the state, the military employs violence (or uses force) in a purposeful, deliberate, and legitimate manner. Two criteria that maintain order and military discipline in war are the general value system of culture and the presupposition that the cost of war should not outweigh its benefits.

Focusing on the notion that language reflects "the moral world and gives us access to it" and that "our understanding of moral vocabulary is sufficiently common and stable so that shared judgments are possible," Michael Walzer makes an argument for moments when the rules of *jus in bello* can be overridden (Walzer, p. 52). In a "supreme emergency," determined by the "imminence of danger" and the "nature" of the threat, one might be "required to override the rights of innocent people and shatter the war convention" (Walzer, p. 259). Nazism,

---

*JUS IN BELLO*

Hague Convention IV of 1907

Governs methods and means of warfare, such as weapons that are restricted and tactical battlefield restraints.

Geneva Conventions of 1949

Concerned with the protection of victims of armed conflict—defined as the wounded, sick and/or shipwrecked, prisoners of war and civilians.

1977 Protocol I Additional to the 1949 Geneva Conventions (Article 1[4])

Armed conflicts in which peoples are fighting against colonial domination and alien occupation and against racist regimes in the exercise of their rights of national self-determination, as enshrined in the Charter of the United Nations.

1977 Protocol II Additional to the 1949 Geneva Conventions (Article 1[1])

Covers conflicts that take place in the territory of a High Contracting Party between its armed forces and dissident armed forces or other organized armed groups which, under responsible command, exercise such control over part of its territory as to enable them to carry out sustained and concerted military operations and to implement this Protocol.

---

which represented the "ultimate threat to everything decent in our lives," constituted a supreme emergency, and Walzer sees the decision by Winston Churchill to bomb German cities in 1940 as a legitimate and justifiable decision. Although the initial decision qualified as a supreme emergency, according to Walzer, the decision to continue bombing cities after 1942, when the Russians and Americans had entered the war, was not justified, and Churchill ought to have asked his army to resort to attacking legitimate military targets.

A justified war is not necessarily a just war, as we also need to be concerned about justifiable moral means of behaving in war. Most theorists argue that the ends justify or structure the means, in that if the cause is justified, the use of all necessary and appropriate means is also justified. But some see an independent standard for judging *jus in bello,* especially in prohibiting all intentional killing of innocent people. However, it is difficult to know exactly what the appropriate means are until the war ends. For example, because the U.S. military has not found the weapons of mass destruction purportedly manufactured in Iraq for use by terrorists and the Hussein regime, it is difficult to evaluate whether the destruction of property and deaths of civilians and soldiers was indeed justified in the U.S. invasion of Iraq in 2003. Justice in the waging of war (that is, the justifiability of the violence and killing that is intrinsic to warfare) is a necessary condition for *jus ad bellum* and *jus in bello.*

Contention over the parameters of *jus in bello* during the nuclear arms race invigorated the debate between realists and idealists in international relations. The characteristics of human nature lay at the basis of contention. Drawing on Thucydides (d. c. 401 B.C.E.), Niccolò Machiavelli (1469–1527), and Thomas Hobbes (1588–1679), realists start with the premise that human nature is inherently bad, self-serving, evil, and desirous of power. States in the international system also reflect these characteristics and exist in a state of anarchy where war is constant and insecurity is the norm. In this perspective deterrence is one of the ways in which states can prevent wars, in that their military capabilities act as a deterrent against possible attack. For idealists, human nature is essentially good, and bad behavior is due mainly to evil institutions that encourage people to act selfishly. For example, Mahatma Gandhi (1869–1948) maintained that the means justified the ends, and in this perspective nonviolence and *Satyagraha* (soulforce) were the appropriate ways in which to achieve equality and a just system. Idealists believe that war is an international problem that requires collective, multilateral cooperation and diplomacy.

The notion of the appropriate means necessary to fulfill desired ends became particularly pertinent in the nuclear age. Some argued that if nuclear weapons were used in an all-out war scenario, it would be a "monstrously disproportionate response to aggression on the part of any nation" (U.S. Catholic Bishops, p. 103). The bishops argued that good ends could not justify "immoral means" and urged the superpowers to invest in diplomacy, peacemaking, and disarmament.

Other theorists have argued that nuclear deterrence is necessary if we are to defend our freedom and fundamental rights, that deterrence in fact works to prevent war and destruction.

Nuclear deterrence in this perspective is necessary to prevent war and to enable peace and security. John J. Mearsheimer adds that the Cold War period was largely peaceful because of the bipolar distribution of power, the "rough equality of military power between the two polar states," and the presence of nuclear weapons that made deterrence "far more robust" (Mearsheimer, p. 9). Proponents of this view add that while we have to be judicious in the decisions to engage in war to preserve our values, we also have to develop military capabilities suited to our moral commitments. Although increasing military capacity might increase tensions, they act as a deterrent to possible attacks, but most importantly, they will be adequate means to defend our values if we are forced to do so.

International organizations that attempt to create a forum for international diplomacy and peacemaking have less significance in the realist perspective. John Gerard Ruggie argues that realism has failed to grasp the integral role of international institutions like the United Nations in promoting cooperative and multilateral ways of maintaining peace and preventing wars. Criticisms against the notion that nuclear deterrence is one of the strongest means of preventing wars are prolific. Although quite varied, many of them see world politics as socially constructed, that is, that international politics are social rather than material and that structures shape identities interests and behavior. Structures are considered "discourses" made up of shared knowledge, material resources, and practices. Here the emphasis is not on human nature but rather on the social relationships that are forged and the complex interplay between leaders, state structures, and civil society. Feminists critique the realist paradigm by questioning the "denial of female images and female-linked imperatives" in the foundational assumptions about human nature, the character of states, and the international system (Elshtain, "Just War as Politics," p. 261). Even in just-war theory, men are considered the soldiers or just Christian warriors, while women are relegated to the private sphere, the "beautiful soul" who is peaceful, frugal, and self-sacrificing. A reevaluation of war and peace from a feminist perspective energizes the debate on the causes of war and appropriate and acceptable behavior during war. The use of rape as a weapon of war, used in Italy in 1943 and in Bosnia in the early 1990s, has become part of the international human rights agenda but is also crucial to determining the parameters of *jus in bello* and to the idea that with constantly changing "means" of war, the war conventions must be open to change as well.

*See also* **Christianity; Machiavellism; Peace; Terror.**

**BIBLIOGRAPHY**

Adeney, Bernard T. *Just War, Political Realism, and Faith.* Philadelphia: American Theological Library Association; Metuchen, N.J.: Scarecrow Press, 1988.

Bull, Hedley. *The Anarchical Society.* New York: Columbia University Press, 1977.

Clausewitz, Carl von. *On War.* Edited and Translated by Michael Howard and Peter Paret. Princeton, N.J.: Princeton University Press, 1984.

Elshtain, Jean Bethke. "Just War as Politics: What the Gulf War Told Us about Contemporary American Life." In *But Was It Just? Reflections on the Morality of the Persian Gulf War,* edited by David E. Decosse. New York: Doubleday, 1992.

———, ed. *Just War Theory.* New York: New York University Press, 1992.

Johnson, James Turner. *Can Modern War Be Just?* New Haven, Conn.: Yale University Press, 1984.

———. *Just War Tradition and the Restraint of War: A Moral and Historical Inquiry.* Princeton, N.J.: Princeton University Press, 1981.

La civiltà cattolica. "Modern War and the Christian Conscience." Translated by Peter Heinegg. In *But Was It Just? Reflections on the Morality of the Persian Gulf War,* edited by David E. Decosse. New York: Doubleday, 1992.

Mead, Margaret. "Warfare Is Only an Invention—Not a Biological Necessity." *Asia* 40 (1940): 402–405.

Mearsheimer, John J. "Back to the Future: Instability in Europe after the Cold War." In *Theories of War and Peace: An international Security Reader,* edited by Michael E. Brown et al. Cambridge, Mass.: MIT Press, 1998.

Niebuhr, Reinhold. *Christianity and Power Politics.* New York: Charles Scribner's Sons, 1940.

Ramsey, Paul. *War and the Christian Conscience: How Shall Modern War Be Conducted Justly?* Durham, N.C.: Duke University Press, 1961.

Ruggie, John Gerard. "The False Premise of Realism." *International Security* 20, no. 1 (Summer 1995): 62–70.

U.S. Catholic Bishops. "The Challenge of Peace: God's Promise and Our Response: The Pastoral Letter on War and Peace." Reprinted in *Just War Theory,* edited by Jean Bethke Elshtain. New York: New York University Press, 1992.

Van Evera, Stephen. "Hypotheses on Nationalism and War." In *Theories of War and Peace: An International Security Reader,* edited by Michael E. Brown et al. Cambridge, Mass.: MIT Press, 1998.

Vasquez, John A. *The War Puzzle.* Cambridge, U.K.: Cambridge University Press, 1993.

Walzer, Michael. *Just and Unjust Wars: A Moral Argument with Historical Illustrations.* New York: Basic Books, 1977.

Weigel, George. "From Last Resort to Endgame: Morality, the Gulf War, and the Peace Process." In *But Was It Just? Reflections on the Morality of the Persian Gulf War,* edited by David E. Decosse. New York: Doubleday, 1992.

Wright, Quincy. *A Study of War.* Vol. 2. Chicago: University of Chicago Press, 1942.

*Movindri Reddy*

**WAR AND PEACE IN THE ARTS.** Depictions of violence have been part of human culture for millennia. What began as an effort of early humans to come to terms with the awe-inspiring power of weapons to kill their prey, and thus sustain human life, or ward off danger (for example, the cave paintings of Altamira, Spain) has evolved into a complex social code to help us try to make sense of total war, which industrialization and the modern nation-state made possible during the twentieth century.

**The Military Leader**

The most common image of war is that of the military leader, typically depicted on horseback or in a chariot, leading his troops into battle, and vanquishing the enemy. Before the late nineteenth and twentieth centuries, a king or an emperor had to be a skilled military leader in order to seek, obtain, and maintain political power. Thus, depictions of his military successes were an important means of demonstrating to his subjects and would-be challengers the king's legitimacy as a ruler. These images were displayed on the bas reliefs of public buildings and temples, and as statuary in public places where as many people as possible could see and admire their achievements. Such images were also created for private viewing, usually to remind the ruling elite of the king's power and legitimacy. Paintings commissioned by the king or emperor would show the leader in various idealized poses as brilliant battlefield commander or god-anointed ruler.

## The Heroic Soldier

The second most commonly depicted individual in war art is the heroic soldier. In the Western world the characteristics of the archetypal hero were defined in Homer's ninth-century epic poems about the Trojan War, the *Iliad* and the *Odyssey*. The Homeric hero, as personified by Achilles, was courageous in battle, loyal to his friends and comrades, and quick to anger. He suffered grievous loss, sometimes even death, and was curiously attracted to the thrill of battle but was equally appalled by its horrifying consequences. In the visual arts the Homeric heroes were repeatedly depicted in the red and black figures of painted Ancient Greek pottery. The image of Ajax carrying the body of Achilles is particularly poignant as it reminds the viewer that death often accompanies heroic actions on the battlefield.

More commonly the hero has been depicted as the protector of society who symbolically defeats the enemy as snake or dragon, as demonstrated by the innumerable depictions of Saint George, who was adopted as the patron saint of England in the fourteenth century. Or the hero is depicted, often on horseback, leading his troops into battle with firm conviction of the high moral purpose of the battle about to be fought, as when William the Conqueror leads his troops into the Battle of Hastings (1066) in an early piece of war propaganda, the Bayeux Tapestry.

It was sometimes acknowledged that to be a hero one had to be a little bit mad. To willingly face physical harm or death and to be able to urge one's fellows to do likewise and to lead them into battle required a sense of commitment that might appear to verge on madness. Albrecht Dürer caught this in his copper engraving *Knight, Death, and the Devil* (1513), where the steadfast knight, accompanied by his loyal dog, looks intently forward, trying to avoid the distractions of Death, who brandishes his hourglass, and of the Devil, who leers at him.

Two countertypes stand in contrast to the model of the heroic soldier: the heroic female soldier, or "warrior queen," and the antihero. Many warrior queens who led nations but not armies into battle wished to show themselves the equal of their male counterparts, at least in works of art. A coronation painting of Empress Catherine II of Russia (r. 1762–1796) shows her on horseback, in uniform, holding a sword but with armed troops almost hidden in the background; Maria Theresa of Austria also wanted to be painted on horseback but, although she brandishes a sword, she wears robes, not a military uniform, and sits side-saddle.

Actual warrior heroines like the ancient Briton, Boadicea, are depicted riding a chariot (a bronze statue by Thomas Thornycroft, 1902) or standing on a slight rise above her troops exhorting them to battle; Amazons were depicted on an equal footing with Greeks in art; Joan of Arc is often depicted wearing full armor but kneeling in prayer or standing with a battle standard, and less frequently on horseback. In India, the Rani of Jhansi, who led men into battle against the British in 1858, is depicted on horseback and brandishing a sword.

The Robin Hood of legend was the classic antihero—an aristocrat who donned the garb of ordinary peasants and took up their cause of opposing taxation and other feudal obligations while an absentee king fought in foreign wars. Courage and resistance are among the hallmarks of the antihero. John Simpson Kirkpatrick, an Australian soldier who served in the Gallipoli front (Turkey, 1915) in World War I, demonstrated his courage not by killing the enemy but by rescuing the injured, often under fire, and bringing them back to the first aid stations on the back of his donkey. The image of "Simpson and his donkey" became a potent one in photographs, posters, and, later, statues. It was used both as propaganda for Australian recruitment and as an antiwar statement of how one man turned his back on the killing and sought to save life.

## Civilian Casualties in War

Jacques Callot's series of etchings *The Miseries of War* (midseventeenth century) was the first attempt to depict the impact of war on civilians. Callot's finely detailed etchings of war-ravaged Lorraine during the Thirty Years' War (1618–1648) show pillaged farm houses, burning churches, and the raping and killing of peasants by marauding soldiers and deserters. But this is not a thoroughgoing antiwar perspective; rather, it shows what happens when legitimate authority temporarily breaks down and soldiers become an ill-disciplined rabble as a result. A good Catholic and monarchist, Callot concludes his series with the just punishment and rewards meted out by the absolute monarch according to God's will, no doubt—the wicked soldiers are hung en masse and the well-disciplined officers get their monetary rewards and promotions.

Francisco Goya (1746–1828) achieves a more consistent antiwar perspective in his graphic depiction of the horrors of guerrilla warfare in Spain under the occupation of Napoleon's troops (1808–1813). His adoption of enlightened ideas of reason and the natural rights of man meant that Goya regarded as a crime and a disaster what others had accepted previously as inevitable, namely the killing of civilians. The particular circumstances of the guerrilla war in Spain brought this aspect of war into particularly sharp focus. His series of eighty-three etchings, *The Disasters of War* (1810–1814; published posthumously because of their radical perspective and graphic depiction of atrocities), documents the horrors committed by both sides—the Spanish people fighting a foreign occupying army and the French rooting out "terrorists" in order to bring the ideals of the French Revolution to an apparently unwilling populace.

## THE WORLD WARS IN FILM

From the earliest years of moving pictures the topic of war provided exciting and attractive material. At first, directors "restaged" current events such as the Spanish-American War, the Boxer Rebellion in China, or the Boer War in South Africa in order to entertain and "inform" movie-goers. During World War I all sides rushed propaganda movies into production in order to show the enemy in the worst possible light and to bolster popular support for the war. The need of the modern military for intelligence and training required people skilled in photography, so it is ironic that many individuals who would go on to make war movies in the 1920s and 1930s (sometimes antiwar movies) got their training during World War I serving in military intelligence. One such individual was the American Lewis Milestone who went on to make the classic antiwar movie *All Quiet on the Western Front* (1930).

Important films about World War I include William Wellman's *Wings* (1927) with its spectacular and thrilling aerial combat sequences; Milestone's *All Quiet on the Western Front*, which defined the genre of the anti-war film for decades to come; Jean Renoir's *The Grand Illusion* (1937), a subtle French film about how class, race, and language divide men even more than nationality; Stanley Kubrick's *Paths of Glory* (1957), which shows how ambitious generals use war to promote their own careers at the expense of the enlisted men; Joseph Losey's *King and Country* (1964), a grim film that questions the British policy of executing soldiers for suffering mental breakdown under extreme combat stress or "shell shock"; and Peter Weir's *Gallipoli* (1981), which forces Australians to question the wisdom of fighting for the concept of "Empire" so far from home.

During World War II Hollywood threw its whole-hearted support behind the war effort and produced a large number of "combat films" designed to boost recruitment into the armed forces and morale on the home front. The formula for these movies was to take a diverse group of "typical Americans" (e.g., an Italian from New York, a Texan, a midwesterner, a Californian, a Jew, an Hispanic, and so on) and show how they overcame their differences to become a coherent fighting unit dedicated to achieving the government's war aims. Typical of this genre is *Bataan* (1943), directed by Tay Garnett, and *Guadalcanal Diary* (1943), directed by Lewis Seiler.

Only rarely toward the end of the war and occasionally afterwards did more critical and thoughtful films emerge that looked beyond the established stereotypes. John Ford's *They Were Expendable* (1945) hints at the futility of what some men were asked to do, while Sam Fuller's autobiographical film *The Big Red One* (1980) suggests that personal survival and loyalty to the platoon is what motivated men, not grandiose schemes dreamed up by politicians; Keith Gordon's *A Midnight Clear* (1992), based upon William Wharton's autobiographical novel set during the Battle of the Bulge in December 1944, suggests that fear, chaos, and incompetence determined the outcome of battle.

Hollywood continued to produce blockbuster movies about World War II well into the 1960s, until the Vietnam War began to sour the taste for celebratory war movies. *The Longest Day* (1962), directed by a committee of Andrew Marton, Ken Annakin, and Bernhard Wicki, based on the book by Cornelius Ryan about the Normandy invasion in June 1944, and *The Battle of the Bulge* (1965), also directed by Ken Annakin about the last counterattack by the Germans in December 1944, were the last gasp of this type of World War II movie.

The European and Japanese perspective on World War II was quite different, as one might expect. Societies that either had done the conquering and occupying (like Germany and Japan), or had been conquered, occupied, and then divided into resistors and collaborators (like the French, Italians, Poles, Russians, and so on) would be expected to see the war in a different light than the Americans, Britons, and Australians who had not been conquered and occupied.

*(continued on the next page)*

## THE WORLD WARS IN FILM

*(continued from previous page)*

German war films about World War II have been understandably few and far between. In the last months of the Nazi regime, enormous resources were expended in the making of "historical films" like *Kolberg* (1945), directed by Veit Harlan; these were designed to rally the German people to one last stand against the "invading" allied armies by reminding them of successful heroic last stands put up by German Baltic towns like Kolberg as Napoleon was marching toward Moscow. But generally Germans preferred to forget the war years as they rebuilt their lives and enjoyed the benefits of the post-war economic miracle. Low budget films like Bernhard Wicki's *Die Brücke* (*The Bridge*; 1959) sometimes appeared but they were rare. Wicki shows a group of conscript teenage boys forced to pointlessly defend a minor bridge against advancing American tanks as the Nazi regime crumbles. Death for all naturally ensues. Higher production values were used to make *Die Blechtrommel* (*The Tin Drum*; 1979), directed by Volcker Schlöndorff and based on the novel by Günter Grass, but the point it may have been trying to make is lost in the bravura performances of the cast. A major international success came with the submarine drama *Das Boot* (*The Boat*; 1981), directed by Wolfgang Petersen, which brilliantly shows the claustrophobic nature of submarine warfare in the Atlantic, but which completely clouds the issue of why men fought so desperately for the Nazi regime. It took an American director, Sam Peckinpah, notorious for his violent westerns, to take a German autobiographical novel about the appalling conflict on the Eastern Front and turn it into a film designed to debunk comfortable Hollywood films about World War II—*Cross of Iron* (1977). Its depiction of the brutal fighting on this front is only equaled by the Russian director Elem Klimov's *Idi i smotri* (*Come and See*; 1985).

The French were also reluctant to confront the painful issues raised by defeat, collaboration, and resistance. An early film by René Clément, *La Bataille du Rail* (1946), depicts French railway workers as resistance fighters, and thus by extension all French people as heroic, thereby glossing over the issue of collaboration or apathy. A later film by Clément, *Jeux interdits* (*Forbidden Games*; 1952), follows parentless children traumatized by the 1940 invasion of France as they retreat into parodies of Catholic death and the burial rituals, their subjects deceased farm animals.

The very few Japanese films about World War II did not appear until the late 1950s as the Japanese people, like the German people, either strove to forget the war or were prevented by the censorship laws of the occupying Americans, which forbade patriotic war films or films that were critical of the United States. Kon Ichikawa made a pair of disturbing films, *Biruma no tate-goto* (*The Harp of Burma*; 1956), about a Japanese soldier in Burma who refuses to be repatriated with his unit at the end of the war until he has made amends by dressing as a Buddhist monk, searching out the unburied corpses of the war dead and burying them himself; and *Nobi* (*Fires on the Plain*; 1962), about a soldier who is trapped in the jungle by the advancing American forces in the Philippines, in February 1945, and is forced to endure hunger and disease rather than surrender. At the same time, Masaki Kobayashi made a nine-hour trilogy, *Ningen no joken* (*The Human Condition*; 1959–62), about a young man who worked as a manager in a mine in Manchuria that uses Chinese slave labor; he is conscripted to fight in the Imperial Japanese Army in China and endures the brutality of Japanese army discipline, and then, after the Japanese army collapses, is forced to walk back to his homeland to escape the advancing Red Army. After this very promising start, Japanese treatment of war in film virtually disappears as the "economic miracle" of the 1960s preoccupies everyone's mind. So when distribution in 1990 is sought for *Blood Oath* (directed by Stephen Wallace, it is also known as *Prisoners of the Sun*), an Australian film about the

*(continued on the next page)*

## THE WORLD WARS IN FILM

*(continued from previous page)*

brutal treatment of POWs on the island of Ambon in Indonesia, few Japanese people have ever heard of these events (Japanese school textbooks carry no mention of them) and no mainstream cinemas are willing to show the film.

After having dropped out of fashion due to the traumas resulting from the Vietnam War, the World War II movie made a come-back in the late 1990s with Steven Spielberg's *Saving Private Ryan* (1998). This film cleverly combines many elements of the traditional World War II combat movie with just a hint of the criticism that had emerged previously in films like Fuller's *The Big Red One,* namely that men fight more for their immediate comrades and in order to survive, rather than for abstract, lofty ideals.

In the twentieth century the widespread use of the camera made possible the depiction of the impact of war, especially total war, on civilian populations in much greater detail: whole cities reduced to rubble by "carpet bombing" during World War II; a naked Vietnamese girl running toward the camera with her napalm wounds exposed; a room full of human skulls in Cambodia. In the early twenty-first century the small and cheap digital camera made possible the graphic depiction of the treatment of Iraqi prisoners in Abu Ghraib prison camp. Among the outright pornographic is the iconic image of a hooded and cloaked Iraqi with arms outstretched, Christlike, with wires from his extremities hooked up to some source of electricity. The camera is able to capture and reveal two extremes of war's impact—the personal and individual suffering that war causes, and the panorama of mass destruction—but the middle ground seems to be missing.

Photographic images that have become closely associated with the Holocaust are pictures of rooms full of victim's shorn hair, spectacles, shoes, empty suitcases, and boxes of gold fillings extracted from inmates' teeth—the by-products of the industrialized process of killing human beings and recycling their property. In camps like Theresienstadt, art work by inmates was sometimes officially commissioned or tolerated by the Nazis as a useful diversion. In other camps, making sketches or drawing was strictly forbidden, and inmates were severely punished if they were caught. Yet, many did make a visual record of their experience in the camps, and some returned to the topic in paintings they made after the war ended. The themes dealt with by camp artists include portraits, images of daily hardships, images of death and dying, and gallows or black humor. The art produced in the Nazi camps is extraordinary testimony to the will to survive of human beings and to the deeply felt need to document human experience.

The atomic bombing of Hiroshima and Nagasaki, Japan, by the United States in World War II also gave rise to new images of war. The image of the mushroom-shaped cloud produced by the explosion of an atomic bomb is now universally recognized. What is less well known is the art produced by the people on the ground who lived through the explosion. In 1976 the Japanese Broadcasting Corporation, NHK, collected images drawn by survivors of the atomic bomb blast. The pictures (published in *Unforgettable Fire*), all drawn by amateur artists, provide a moving and very different set of images of atomic warfare. A number of images that appear repeatedly in their work include bloodshot and bleeding eyes; people walking about naked; and people walking about with what appear to be rags or cloth draped over their bodies but which are in fact sheets of burnt skin that have peeled away. Many walked with their arms outstretched, held away from their body in order to prevent the burnt flesh from rubbing. In Japanese culture, this is the way ghosts walk. The atomic bomb victims had been transformed into living ghosts.

In spite of the camera's success in capturing the experience of war in the twentieth century, perhaps the most powerful and best-known depiction of innocent civilians in war is Pablo Picasso's mural *Guernica* (1937), inspired by the bombing of a Basque town by German fighter bombers serving with the Nationalists during the Spanish Civil War. In a complex, triangular structured painting Picasso depicts burning houses surrounding a square, a woman calling out a warning to others, a mother holding her dead baby, a woman running from the mayhem, a fallen and broken statue of a warrior, a stabbed and screaming horse. In spite of the fact that much worse atrocities against civilians were perpetrated and depicted in the second half of the twentieth century (or perhaps because of it), the power of this painting still shocks nearly seventy years after its creation.

### The Ordinary Soldier in Battle

Like civilians, the ordinary soldier was largely invisible in war art until the nineteenth century. Only when mass conscript armies of citizens took to the field after the French Revolution and the Napoleonic Wars had revolutionized the nature of warfare did artists and photographers begin to take notice. The emergence of mass circulation newspapers, the technology to cheaply reproduce sketches and photos, a reading public interested in the fate of their fathers and sons on the battlefield, and a growing liberal concern for the welfare of the ordinary soldier, were also contributing factors.

During the American Civil War, artists like Winslow Homer (1836–1910) produced a steady stream of illustrations of battles (usually not personally witnessed but reconstructed afterward) and of the life of the ordinary soldiers in their camps. Many of these camp illustrations show the boredom of soldiers with nothing to do while they wait for the next bloody battle. Photographers like Matthew Brady, Alexander Gardner, and Timothy H. O'Sullivan revolutionized the depiction of war with their images of the dead littering the battlefield, or of the execution of rebels by hanging.

World War I produced a number of gifted war artists whose visual record of the war is significant. Among these is the German graphic artist Otto Dix, who served from 1914 to 1918 and saw action on the Western Front. His most interesting work consists of a set of fifty etchings simply called *Der Krieg* (1924; The war) and some oil paintings, especially the disturbing *War Triptych* (1929–1932). Iconic images of World War I include the desolation of the landscape caused by the incessant shelling and the digging of trenches along the Western Front. In *Der Krieg* Dix shows how ordinary soldiers dealt with these appalling conditions—they became one with the earth in both death and life. In death their bodies were literally consumed by the soil and the worms (the worm-riddled *Skull*); in life they spent their lives covered in dirt and living in holes and trenches dug in the earth (*Feeding-Time in the Trench*). The only hope for life seems to be the flowers and worms that grow out of the craters and skulls of men. In the *War Triptych* Dix takes the traditional Christian image used to portray the life, death, and resurrection of Christ and applies it to the front-line soldier in the trenches.

The experience of ordinary soldiers who were captured by the enemy was largely hidden from public view during World War II and did not surface until well after their release. Cameras were forbidden, of course, and those prisoners who were caught keeping diaries or making sketches were severely punished. Nevertheless, some prisoners of war (POWs) were able to keep their diaries and sketches and publish them after the war. British soldier-artists such as Ronald Searle and Jack Chalker, captured after the fall of Singapore in 1942, were sent to work building the Thai-Burma railways as slave workers for the Imperial Japanese Army. In their art they document the brutal treatment the POWs received as many of their comrades were worked to death. They produced images that have a number of similarities to those produced by European victims of the Nazi Holocaust—emaciated, sick bodies lying on flimsy beds and brutal captors with batons and rifle butts ready to beat them. Of the 60,000 POWs who worked on the railway nearly one third died. Not surprisingly, their anger at their treatment tinges their art with racist depictions of their oppressors.

## Bringing War to an End

The formal ending of a state of war is commonly achieved by means of a surrender, armistice, or peace treaty. For the losing party there is no pleasant way to accept defeat. For the victor, there is an opportunity for propaganda, as a number of works of art demonstrate. The seventeenth-century Spanish painter Diego Velasquez was commissioned by the Spanish court to contribute to a series of victory paintings during the Thirty Years' War. His *Surrender of Breda* (1634–1635) shows Justin of Nassau handing the keys of the besieged Dutch city of Breda to the marchese Spinola in 1625 after the city had

endured a terrible ten-month siege. Both men have their hats off, as equals might greet each other, and the Spaniard has his arm on the Dutchman's shoulder in a conciliatory gesture. Given the impact of a siege on a civilian city such a gesture might seem somewhat inadequate, but it was how the Spanish wished to be seen in victory.

A less generous depiction of a surrender, but no less propagandistic, is a popular Japanese woodcut that shows the Russian surrender of the fortress of Port Arthur to the Japanese in 1905, also after a long siege. The Japanese officers stand with their hats on under the shelter of a tent that flies the Japanese flag. The Russian officers stand humiliated in the snow outside the tent with their hats off submissively, waiting to sign the surrender papers. The battle is significant because it was the first time an Asian military power had defeated one of the great powers of Europe. Thus the Europeans had to be humiliated as well as defeated.

The humiliation was returned forty years later, when the Japanese formally signed surrender documents on the deck of the U.S. battleship Missouri on 2 September 1945. The official American military photograph shows the Japanese party literally surrounded by Allied personnel as they approach the signing table. Immediately above them and to the side, dozens of American enlisted men sit on the ship's giant guns with their feet dangling over the side. They will not show any respect by standing for the Japanese delegation. Directly overhead, at the moment of the signing, 400 B-29 bombers and 1,500 naval fighters flew past, drowning out all words. The surrender was total, unconditional, and utterly humiliating.

The American painter Winslow Homer took a different approach to the end of war. In *The Veteran in a New Field* (1865), a Northern veteran has taken off his jacket and canteen and put them to one side. He has taken up a scythe and begins to harvest a field of wheat. We can imagine that, like the Roman leader Cincinnatus (b. c. 519 B.C.E.), who left his farm to assume the dictatorship of Rome and defend it from its enemies only to relinquish that power and return to his farm, this veteran has turned his back on war and taken up peaceful and productive agricultural labor. The image brings to mind the biblical verse: "And they shall beat their swords into ploughshares, and their spears into pruning hooks; nations shall not lift up sword against nation, neither shall they learn war any more" (Isaiah 2:4).

*See also* **Arts; Cinema; Gender in Art; Humanity in the Arts; Pacifism; Peace; War.**

### BIBLIOGRAPHY

Basinger, Jeanine. *The World War II Combat Film: Anatomy of a Genre.* New York: Columbia University Press, 1986.

Bohm-Duchen, Monica ed. *After Auschwitz: Responses to the Holocaust in Contemporary Art.* Sunderland: Northern Centre for Contemporary Art, 1995.

Chipp, Herschel B. *Picasso's Guernica: History, Transformations, Meaning.* Berkeley: University of California Press, 1988.

Cochrane, Peter. *Simpson and the Donkey: The Making of a Legend.* Portland, Ore.: International Specialized Book, 1992.

De Silva, Amil, and Otto von Simson, eds. *War and Peace.* Vol. 1 of *Man through His Art.* London: Educational Productions, 1963.

Doherty, Thomas Patrick. *Projections of War: Hollywood, American Culture, and World War II.* New York: Columbia University Press, 1993.

Eberle, Matthias. *World War I and the Weimar Artists: Dix, Grosz, Beckmann, Schlemmer.* New Haven, Conn.: Yale University Press. 1985.

Fox, Robert. *The Hulton Getty Picture Collection: Camera in Conflict: Armed Conflict.* Köln: Könemann Verlagsgesellschaft, 1996.

Fraser, Antonia. *The Warrior Queens.* New York: Knopf, 1989.

Gassier, Pierre. *Goya: A Witness of His Times.* Translated by Helga Harrison. Secaucus, N.J.: Chartwell. 1983.

Kelly, Andrew. *Cinema and the Great War.* New York: Routledge, 1997.

Moyes, Norman B. *Battle Eye: A History of American Combat Photography.* New York: Metro, 1996.

Schonberger, Howard et al., trans. *Unforgettable Fire: Pictures Drawn by Atomic Bomb Survivors.* Tokyo: Nippon Hoso Shupan Kyokai, 1977.

Warner, Marina. *Joan of Arc: The Image of Female Heroism.* Berkeley: University of California Press, 1999.

Welch, David. *Propaganda and the German Cinema, 1933–1945.* Oxford: Clarendon Press, 1989.

Woodford, Susan. *The Trojan War in Ancient Art.* Ithaca, N.Y.: Cornell University Press, 1993.

*David M. Hart*

**WEALTH.** Wealth has been viewed as a blessing and as a curse; as a prerequisite of virtue and an embodiment of vice; as an expression of merit and of fault. This nonexhaustive list illustrates that not only is the history of wealth a history of contention, it is also intimately bound up with moral evaluations. These differing evaluations themselves indicate a range of divergent cultural judgments. "Wealth," however, is not simply an item of moral discourse. It has a central place in political and economic vocabularies. While there is, perhaps, a core linkage with the notion of "resources," that itself is an elastic category, referring to "goods" both tangible and immaterial (such as clean air, a healthy environment, and general quality of life). Wealth with all its cultural and ethical connotations is applied descriptively to an individual (the "rich man"), to a group or class of individuals ("the wealthy"), and to a country or, as in the title of Adam Smith's famous book, to nations.

With this range of reference it is unsurprising that most of the established "great thinkers" in what is unreflectively labeled the "Western tradition," from Aristotle to St. Thomas Aquinas to Jean–Jacques Rousseau to Karl Marx to Thorstein Veblen, have had something to say on the topic. But the issues and debates are neither exclusively Western nor intellectual. Most of the great religions include in their teaching some reference to wealth, though not without manifesting the idea's contentiousness. In addition, wealth plays a ubiquitous role in social and cultural life from grave goods to potlatch ceremonies. An attempt will be made in this entry to represent this range of concern, though its major focus will be on the place of wealth in Western intellectual debates.

The entry is organized along two axes—thematic and chronological. Thematically, the discussion is organized in terms of two basic associations—wealth and virtue, and wealth and power. Each theme is explored in rough chronological order—charting the history of wealth's interactions with virtue and with power. Throughout these explorations three questions will implicitly recur: What is wealth? that is, what is supposed, in different times, with respect to virtue and power, to constitute it; Who has it? that is, what is supposed similarly about its distribution; and, closely related, Why or on what grounds does X rather than Y have that item of wealth? that is, what is supposed to justify or legitimate the distribution.

## Wealth and Virtue

Historically the association between wealth and virtue has been viewed both positively and negatively. These will be examined in turn.

***Positive.*** Aristotle (384–322 B.C.E.) identifies "liberality" as a virtue that is the mean between prodigality and illiberality. The context is money or wealth. The liberal man (the gender is not incidental) will "give with a fine end in view, and in the right way; because he will give to the right people, and the right amounts, and at the right time" (Aristotle [1976] p. 143:1120a25). When acting liberally, it is the disposition that matters, not the sum or sort of resources. Though giving is more virtuous than receiving, nonetheless, the "liberal" will accept wealth under similar constraints. The most important source of wealth is the ownership of property, especially landed property. This ownership is associated with other estimable traits such as responsibility, prudence, and steadfastness. By exercising these virtues, wealth qua landed property is sustained so that, accordingly, there are resources available with which to act liberally. Importantly, wealth thus understood imposes obligations; it does not reflect an acquisitive mentality and it is not valued for its own sake.

Although worked up theoretically by Aristotle, this link between wealth and obligation and the stress on the use made of wealth is pervasive. The early Christian theologian St. Clement of Alexandria (c. 150–between 211 and 215) does not subscribe to the asceticism prescribed by many of the church fathers but, nonetheless, instructs that wealth is to be used for charitable purposes and not retained possessively. This is echoed in the Koran, and, somewhat similarly, in Hindu teaching wealth (*artha*) needs to be cultivated but by virtuous means so that the wherewithal is possessed that goodness may be exercised. This is an attribute of many cultures. The form this often takes is of hospitality. The Israelites in the Old Testament are enjoined to give succor to the improvident, while for Kalahari bushmen, and many others, wealth exists to be shared. In these latter examples it is less that wealth calls forth individual virtue than it manifests a cultural norm of reciprocity. In both cases, however, wealth is justified as a means to further good ends.

This understanding of the importance of wealth, and its justification, has endured beyond its presence in Aristotelian theory and cultural practice. Only if one is wealthy can generosity or charity—whether by the Good Samaritan or by millionaires—be exercised and only if a society is wealthy can it support extensive welfare programs. In a just society, according to

John Rawls (1921–2002), the wealth enjoyed by the more fortunate, as a consequence of arbitrarily distributed natural talents, could be viewed as a "collective asset" to be used, once freedom has been accorded priority, to further the interests of the worse-off (p. 179). However, supporting welfare need not mean collective provision. F. A. Hayek (1899–1992) justified retaining wealth within families as an expression of freedom, which includes making responsible welfare decisions. This was also an essential means to prevent the concentration of wealth in the hands of the state.

Hayek is here making a consequentialist case for inheritance. This pays little attention to the source of wealth, but a positive case for wealth is that its possession is the deserved outcome of the virtue of industry or hard work. The Protestant ethic, as articulated by Max Weber (1864–1920) in his *Die protestantische Ethik und der Geist des Kapitalismus* (1920; *Protestant Ethic and the Spirit of Capitalism*), psychologically compelled the "elect" (those chosen for salvation by God) to seek proof of their election. This took the form of diligence and industriousness, which led to success in worldly activity, but since waste was also proscribed, and frugality prescribed, it meant that wealth was accumulated. In a historically important argument, John Locke (1632–1704) developed a version of this. He argued that God enjoined everyone to be industrious and that through mixing their labor (as he termed it) to natural resources they were entitled to the fruits of that labor as their private property. Provided they did not accrue wastefully all the resources to themselves, the inequality of holdings derived from greater industry was justified. Nonetheless, true to his own Nonconformist (Calvinist) background, Locke also held that if people lived providently without the desire for luxuries then wealth would be increased even more. Locke here broaches the negative link between wealth and virtue.

*Negative.* While Aristotle does link wealth with virtue positively, his more sustained and influential argument (in the *Politics*) is that the former can lead to a corruption of the latter. Wealth and its maintenance is properly an attribute of household management (of economics, *oikonomikē*), its purpose being to give the male head of the household the freedom to act virtuously—not only via liberality but also via participation in the affairs of the community (the polis), an activity that is natural since man is by nature a political animal. Wealth is limited to this instrumental function. However, it is liable to transgress those limits. Some exchange is permissible, when it serves to meet the naturally limited consumption needs of the household, but once it is undertaken for its own sake, and not as a means to an end of consumption, then it becomes money-making (*chrēmatistikē*). This activity can be engaged upon without limit. There is a natural limit, for example, to how much food can be consumed but not to how much money is possessed. A transgression of the proper purpose or end of activity represents a corruption, a perversion of virtue.

This moral critique of wealth has been enormously influential. One particularly potent occurrence was its linkage with the fall of the Roman republic. Originally austerely virtuous, the republic became corrupted once riches were imported from abroad ("Asia"). This wealth-induced corruption in the form

People look for a different kind of wealth and wealth acquisition and rightly so for natural wealth and wealth acquisition are different. Natural wealth acquisition is a part of household management, whereas commerce has to do with the production of goods, not in the full sense, but through their exchange. . . . The wealth that derives from this kind of wealth is without limit.

SOURCE: Aristotle, *The Politics,* trans. C. Reeve (Indianapolis: Hackett, 1998), 14, 17 [1256b27–33, 1257b16–25].

of avarice and luxury was condemned by Stoic moralists such as Seneca (4 B.C.E.?–65 C.E.) or Epictetus (c. 55–c. 135 C.E.) and was illustrated through the normatively loaded narrative of historians of Rome like Sallust (86–35 or 34 B.C.E.) and Livy (59 B.C.E.–17 C.E.). The latter, for example, opened his *History of Rome* by contrasting Rome's virtuous beginnings with the ruin that the influx of wealth or riches (*divitiae*) had wrought. The undermining of Roman virtues by the spread of wealth and luxury also became the object of satirical poets like Horace (65–8 B.C.E.) and Juvenal (c. 55 or 60–in or after 127 C.E.). Due to the importance that a "classical education" had in the pedagogy of Europe from the Renaissance onward, the "fall of Rome," and the role of wealth therein, became a clichéd commonplace.

This culturally received wisdom was abetted by the appropriation, for their own end of demonstrating the transience and superficiality of worldly goods, by Christians. The early Christians, such as Saints Ambrose (339–397), Augustine of Hippo (354–430), and John Chrysostom (c. 347–407), took up this moral critique of wealth. It was an important source of their advocacy of asceticism but it built also upon Paul's (who was himself influenced by the Stoics) pronouncement in his Epistle to Timothy that the love of money was the root of all evil. The message was reiterated by Thomas Aquinas (1225–1274) and by other Christian philosophers upon the rediscovery of Aristotle's works. It received a significant boost in the republican tradition that was reenergized by Niccolò Machiavelli (1469–1527), though here the "political" rather than the moral dimension (see below) is dominant. Much the same can be said of Jean-Jacques Rousseau (1712–1778), perhaps the last great exemplar of this tradition.

This critique was responsible for significant ripostes. David Hume (1711–1776)—followed by his fellow Scot, Adam Smith (1723–1790)—turned the tables. Hume, in his essay *Of Luxury* (1752), linked virtue with wealth, and not with ascetic poverty, and identified this linkage as the definitive characteristic of ages of refinement or commerce. He stressed both the intrinsic benefit of the pleasure that accrued from being

> The natural effort of every individual to better his own condition, when suffered to exert itself with freedom and security, is so powerful a principle, that it is alone, and without any assistance, not only capable of carrying on the society to wealth and prosperity, but of surmounting a hundred impertinent obstructions with which the folly of human laws too often incumbers its operations.
>
> SOURCE: Adam Smith, *An Inquiry into the Nature and Causes of the Wealth of Nations,* ed. R. Campbell and A. Skinner (Indianapolis: Liberty, 1976), vol. 1, p. 540.

able to enjoy goods that gratified the senses and the great instrumental benefits that came from the industry that was undertaken to obtain the wealth that permitted such goods to be enjoyed. The commercialism that Hume and others defended has not been without critics. In the twentieth century it expressed itself in the critique of consumerism. In an effective rerun of Aristotle, the acquisition of goods, the accumulation of wealth, or what C. B. Macpherson (1911–1987) labeled the legitimization of possessive individualism, has been subject to condemnation. A culture committed to consumerism is judged deleterious to the individual who, lacking a proper instrumental perspective, is at the mercy of the fads of fashion and the interests of those who benefit from the manufacture of demand. It is also bad for society because it embodies a misdirection of resources away from societally advantageous investment and entrenches the gap between wealthy and poor economies. The celebration of consumption and the desire to emulate the supposed spending power of the rich also led, in the latter decades of the twentieth century, to the development of "Green" thought, which argues that this entire emphasis on gratification is practically disastrous for the environment and symptomatic of a hubristic arrogance toward Nature. E. F. Schumacher (1911–1977), for example, advocated, in his popular essay *Small Is Beautiful* (1973), what he termed Buddhist economics as a way to halt this degradation.

## Wealth and Power

In all stratified societies (which includes virtually all societies for which records exist) the hierarchy is significantly determined by differential access to, and possession of, wealth. To be wealthy enables one to exercise economic and political power. This exercise is frequently related to the question of virtue. Hence the resources at the disposal of Aristotle's "liberal man" stemmed from what was under his control. Sociologically this man was the head of the household whose position rested upon his command of his wife and slaves as they created the "leisure" time for him to pursue intrinsically

worthwhile ends. True wealth for Aristotle consisted in a store of goods that were sufficient for life and useful for the good life. This wealth had to be secure and it was best obtained through land ownership in marked contrast to the insecure foundation of commerce and money.

This secure source of wealth sustained political independence. This association between landed wealth and political activity has been one of the most historically enduring linkages. The crux of the corruption of Rome was held to be the replacement of a commitment to the public good, which was sustained by relative equality and independence, by a devotion to private satisfaction, which followed from the emergence of the rich, who used their wealth to advance their own personal ambition. Machiavelli drew an evocative picture of this pattern as it appeared in Renaissance Italy. He depicted the gentry (*gentiluomini*) as "a pest" because they use their wealth to hire others to work for them. Crucially these hired hands, being dependent on their masters for their livelihood, could be used to support their selfish ambitions. The only way to end this corrupting dependency is to (re)establish equality through fostering a sense of civic virtue. To further this objective, Machiavelli advocated, drawing on Roman precedents, an Agrarian law that precluded the accumulation of large estates. Other republicans took a similar line. James Harrington (1611–1677) went into minute detail in his imagined constitutional republic of *Oceana* (1656). In Rousseau's legitimate polity there should be a level of equality such that no one is wealthy enough to be able to create dependents and no one poor enough to become dependent on others. With the economic structure in this way forestalling the emergence of dependency—creating differential wealth, there is more chance, he believed, that acting for the common good (or willing "the general will"), rather than out of private self-interest, will occur.

In Rousseau's republican vision political power was possessed by equal citizens, but that meant it was restricted to those who were independent. On that criterion Aristotle excluded from citizenship slaves, manual laborers, and women (also excluded by Rousseau) and, when it came to the franchise, the exclusion of the latter two categories lasted into the twentieth century. It was a received commonplace that the privilege of political citizenship (the right to vote for a representative as well as to be a representative) required sufficient wealth to ensure economic independence. It followed that those economically dependent were without a direct political voice. In the eighteenth century Edmund Burke (1729–1797) defended the restricted franchise on the grounds that only those individuals with a direct stake in the country could be entrusted with its well-being. Thanks to their economic status they were able to exhibit the crucial political virtues of "constancy, gravity, magnanimity, fortitude, fidelity and firmness" (p. 427). Burke explicitly called these masculine virtues, but their possession meant that the interests of women, as well as the bulk of the disenfranchised population, would be properly looked after. Certainly the schemes for greater equality that were fomented by the Revolution in France would be disastrous. Much of the political history of the nineteenth century concerned the continual redefinitions of what constituted economic independence (and later how women were to be accommodated).

This history, and the surrounding debates, not only saw the increasing articulation of a modern idea of democracy but also the growth of socialism. Of course, the effect of the possession of wealth on sustaining dependency was not a uniquely Western phenomenon. The *jajmani* caste system in southern India (especially) operated in such a way that the lowest caste, in exchange for the lease of land owned by members of the high caste, had to provide the latter with labor service and a portion of their crop output. The fact that the caste system was integral to the belief systems of Hindus did not make it immune to criticism. Some of these criticisms were internal (as by Dayananda Sarasvati [1824–1883] or Mahatma Gandhi [1869–1948]), but the challenges to such inequality that the Western ideas of democracy and socialism articulated were also influential.

***The socialist critique.*** The most powerful Western voice was Karl Marx (1818–1883). Marx saw the key to history in the association between wealth and power. The source of wealth for Marx lay in ownership of what he called the forces of production. These had developed over time from slaves (human labor) to land to capital. Those who owned the forces—slave owners, landlords, capitalists, or bourgeoisie—were able because of that control to rule over nonowners—slaves, serfs, the proletariat. Ownership appears to be legal title, but law for Marx is part of society's "superstructure," which is determined by the economic base. Political power, which is used to enforce legal title, also upholds the interests of the dominant economic power; in a celebrated phrase, "the executive of the modern State is but a committee for managing the common affairs of the whole bourgeoisie" (Marx and Engels, p. 475). These interests are for Marx obviously opposed to the interests of those without economic power, and history reveals a struggle between the class of the owners of wealth and the class of nonowners.

Marx devoted most attention to the contemporary struggle within capitalism. His major work, *Das Kapital* (1867; *Capital*), identified the particular form that wealth took under that mode of production. The rationale of capitalism was accumulation. For Marx, the only source for this was the "surplus value" extracted from the worker in the process of production. The exchange-value received in the form of wages by the worker for "his" labor-power is less than the exchange-value received by the capitalist for the commodity made by that power. This exploitative extraction was disguised because the level of wages appeared to be the consequence of a free contract between employer and employee. While Marx saw the initial source of the wealth in the blatant form of expropriation, forcing the landless into factories, the capitalists' ongoing accumulation of wealth was derived from this exploitation inherent to the system. However, he argued this was an unsustainable and self-defeating process that resulted in the immiserization of the workers whose labor-power was the source of accumulation. That misery, he predicted, would generate a proletarian revolution and the ushering in of a communist society. Here (though Marx was not very forthcoming) there would be equality and sufficient wealth to be shared since production would be geared to meeting needs, not accumulation.

Although Marx's predicted revolutionary trajectory did not transpire, revolutions did occur in his name. These inspired a

The greater the social wealth, the functioning capital, the extent and energy of its growth, and, therefore, also the absolute mass of the proletariat and the productiveness of its labor, the greater is the industrial reserve army. The same causes which develop the expansive power of capital, develop also the labor-power at its disposal. The relative mass of the industrial reserve army increases therefore with the potential energy of wealth. . . . This is the absolute law of capital accumulation. . . . Accumulation of wealth at one pole is, therefore, at the same time the accumulation of misery, agony of toil, slavery, ignorance, brutality, mental degradation, at the opposite pole.

SOURCE: Karl Marx, *Capital,* trans. S. Moore and S. Aveling. In *Marx Engels Reader,* 2nd ed., ed. R. Tucker (New York: Norton, 1978), 429–431.

vast literature both in lands like Russia (in the form of Leninism) and China (Maoism), where these revolutions were sited, as well as in the West, where Marx's ideas were the dominant source of criticism of capitalism. Increasingly these critiques paid less attention to Marx's economic analysis and more to his early philosophical writings, with their focus on alienation. While the issue of wealth correspondingly lost some of its salience, the association between the economic and the political was resilient. The universalizing power of capitalism, which Marx did predict, seems to have been reinforced since 1989 and the fall of the Soviet Union. One prominent expression of this has been debate on the meaning and morality of "globalization." The focus has been on the relative impotence of national governments when confronted by worldwide markets and the power of the institutions of global finance like the World Bank and the International Monetary Fund. The least powerful are the least wealthy (the most indebted), effectively the non-Western world.

***Mercantilism and its critique.*** Marx was not original in seeing historically a development between wealth and economic-political power. Adam Smith had argued that societies (though not universally and unexceptionally) went through four stages—hunting/herding, herding, farming, and commercial. In each case there was a system of subordination, which, although based on personal qualities in the first stage, in the next two rested on control of the dominant means of wealth, that is, of herds and land. He was explicit that government was instituted to protect the propertied (the owner of the herds and of the land) against those without property. The fourth commercial stage saw a difference because the impartial rule of law was established to

In order to gain and to hold the esteem of men it is not sufficient merely to possess wealth or power. The wealth or power must be put in evidence, for esteem is awarded only on evidence. And not only does the evidence of wealth serve to impress one's importance on others and to keep their sense of importance alive and alert but it is scarcely less use in building up and preserving one's self-complacency. . . . Abstention from labor is the conventional evidence of wealth and is therefore the conventional mark of social standing; and this insistence on the meritoriousness of wealth leads to a more strenuous insistence on leisure. . . . According to well-established laws of human nature, prescription presently seizes upon this conventional evidence of wealth and fixes it in men's habits of thoughts as something that is itself substantially meritorious and ennobling.

SOURCE: Thorstein Veblen, *The Theory of the Leisure Class* (New York: Dover, 1994), 42, 44–45.

provide a formal equality. In his *Wealth of Nations* (1776) he analyzes the basis of wealth in the modern world. Part of his task was to assault the then dominant understanding of the linkage between wealth and economic-political power.

According to this prevalent view (usually labeled "mercantilism"), as expressed by Thomas Mun (1571–1641), the way to increase wealth is "to sell more to strangers yearly than wee consume of theirs in value" (p. 125). Mun distinguished between natural wealth, essentially minerals and direct agricultural products, and artificial wealth, which was the manufacture of materials (clothing rather than wool or flax). He thought more profit (exports) could be earned from the latter source. To achieve this it was necessary—and this is central to the mercantilist view—to maintain a favorable balance of trade. This maintenance needed to be managed or regulated and, as such, had to be an item of policy, the ultimate objective of which was the promotion of the wealth, and thence of the power and security, of the state. Indeed, the very idea of the "state" as an impersonal entity emerged at this time.

Whether mercantilism ever constituted a coherent theoretical position, as opposed to practical responses, has been contested, but Smith gave it an identity. Smith judged the mercantilist method of acquiring and maintaining wealth/power as theoretically misconceived. For Smith the real wealth of a nation lay in the annual produce of the land and labor of the society. The way to increase this wealth is through what

he called the system of natural liberty. This entailed removing the panoply of regulations and restrictions characteristic of mercantilism, such as those on employment, like guild-sponsored apprenticeships; on the mobility of property, like entails; on consumption, like sumptuary laws; and on trade, like tariffs. Without these obstacles, a free economy would produce a growth in wealth that would benefit the entire population (the "trickle-down" effect).

Smith, although he has become by far the most famous, was not alone in reevaluating the meaning of wealth. One significant dimension had always been population. The wealthier a country, the more people it could sustain, and that in turn would provide both economic and political-cum-military clout. In the Aristotelian tradition, one of the attacks made on commerce was that it enfeebled nations because its citizens were too busily engaged in their private tasks of money-making to devote themselves to their civic responsibilities, which included fighting. For Machiavelli and his intellectual heirs, a citizen militia was the appropriate martial institution, and professional standing armies were not only a threat to civic liberty but also less effective as fighting machines. Smith rejected this. He countered that the wealthier a country was, the more resources were at its disposal to provide sophisticated weaponry and to train soldiers effectively. It was one consequence of this that population by the nineteenth century ceased to have the same value as a marker of national strength; indeed the worries were rather that industrialization was producing too many people to be provided for adequately.

### Status

The link between wealth and power can also be expressed indirectly. Thorstein Veblen (1857–1929) in his *Theory of the Leisure Class* (1899) articulated this through his notion of conspicuous consumption. He argued that to enjoy esteem it was not sufficient merely to be wealthy, others had to be made aware of that fact (it had to be conspicuous). In its purest form, consuming conspicuously is consumption of the totally useless, but (less perfectly) it is the consumption of "high maintenance" goods like white clothes in a dirty industrial environment. While there were predecessors (including Adam Smith), Veblen's analysis was free of the moralizing that often appeared in economists. The leading contemporary economist of Veblen's time, Alfred Marshall (1842–1924) in his *Principles of Economics* (1890), declared the desire for wealth as a means of display to be unwholesome. Marshall was here following his most distinguished predecessor, John Stuart Mill (1806–1873), who had declared that the subject of political economy itself was wealth, which he defined (after a critique of the mercantilist version) as "all useful or agreeable things that possess exchangeable value" (p. 15). However, he proceeded to maintain that the English needed instruction in the use of wealth and how to appreciate those objects of desire that wealth cannot purchase. Mill here implied a distinction between the pursuit of wealth (the art of "getting on" as he put it) and the worthwhileness of what is being pursued (the art of living).

This implicit distinction is made explicit and its moralism exposed by Veblen. He distinctively drew attention to the divergence between the drive to accumulate wealth, as a symbol of reward for industry, and the desire, once it has been accumulated, to look upon its possession as intrinsically worthy. Since social status is attributed to the possession of wealth, the imperative is to exhibit leisure (the nonproductive consumption of time) and dissociate thereby the actual possession of the wealth from the effort expended to attain it. Later economists have developed his ideas in their analysis of consumption in the form of the "demonstration effect" and what they call nonfunctional demand. A "Veblen effect" has been identified where, in an exact reversal of the assumed practice of the rational consumer, the demand increases when the price rises. Only the "truly" wealthy can afford to flout that rationality.

Of course, at another level there is a rationality at work—namely that of demonstrating one's wealth and impressing others by its possession. Under that guise this indirect linkage between wealth and power is a recurrent feature. One of its most striking manifestations is the practice of "potlatch." The status system of the tribes of northwest America is maintained by display, as exhibited in the hosting of great feasts. In the Nootka tribe the chief is presented with the first catch of the salmon traps, the first pickings of ripe fruit, and so on, but having received these, he then holds a feast where the gifts are communally consumed. This pattern is also characteristic of the so-called big man systems of the Pacific. Among the Kaoka of Guadalcanal, reputation is enhanced not by accumulating wealth but by giving it away. The more one can bestow upon others, the greater one's social standing. Hence every significant event such as a birth or wedding is celebrated by a feast, and the more feasts, and the more lavish the fare, that can be "afforded," the greater the prestige. The social leaders (the holders of political power) in all such systems are those whose wealth is manifest by being able to give away most.

## The Dangers of Wealth

That the possession of wealth conveys political power has long been a source of suspicion. For both Plato (428–348 or 347 B.C.E.), in *The Republic,* and Aristotle an oligarchic constitution was associated with rule by the wealthy "few." In both cases this was a negative association. The wealthy used their economic power to rule politically in their own interest, as opposed to the interests of all. In the idea of a "cycle of constitutions" propounded by Polybius (c. 200–118 B.C.E.), in his *Histories* [of Rome] (and reiterated many times over during the succeeding centuries), oligarchy represented a corrupt falling away from good rule by the few (aristocracy) but that was itself displaced in reaction to its self-serving rule by the initially virtuous rule of the many (what became called democracy).

Contemporary (liberal) democracies all have practices and policies that in some way aim to forestall any pernicious effects that might follow from concentration of wealth in a few hands. Some of these are direct. The buying of votes is universally made illegal but frequently, in addition, there are restrictions on the use of money in political campaigns. Other prescriptions are indirect, for example, wealth taxes, and other redistributive fiscal mechanisms. One of the intentions behind such policies is to enhance the possibility of the equality of opportunity. If jobs are "open to the talents," if individuals are provided with the educational resources (in particular) to enable

them to compete, then the differing amount of wealth subsequently earned is justified. However, for that differential to pass down to the next generation undiluted is, it is argued, to undermine that equality. It remains, however, one of the longest running disputes in modern political philosophy the extent to which policies designed to neutralize the inequalities associated with wealth infringe upon the value of liberty and autonomy. A libertarian thinker like Robert Nozick (1938–2002), in his *Anarchy, State, and Utopia* (1974), argues that attempts to impose a preferred distribution of assets illicitly infringe on the rights of individuals. More egalitarian writers, like Michael Walzer (b. 1937) in his *Spheres of Justice* (1983) or, from very different premises, Jürgen Habermas (b. 1929) in a range of writings, seek to keep the political or civic sphere free of the baneful effects of the economic power and reach of wealth.

## Conclusion

Wealth continues to be a subject of debate. Its distribution and effects on social and public policy and welfare are a matter of both practical and academic concern. Its generation and allocation is a central topic in economics; its justification similarly is a major issue in moral and political philosophy. These current disputes without much distortion carry with them the weight of millennia of speculation and in so doing demonstrate that the history of the idea of wealth encapsulates a wealth of ideas.

*See also* **Christianity; Communism; Economics; Power; Property; Virtue Ethics.**

### BIBLIOGRAPHY

PRIMARY SOURCES

Aristotle. *The Ethics of Aristotle: The Nicomachean Ethics.* Translated by J. Thomson. Harmondsworth, U.K.: Penguin, 1976.
———. *The Politics.* Translated by C. Reeve. Indianapolis: Hackett, 1998.
Burke, Edmund. *Speech on American Taxation.* 1774. In *Works,* vol. 2. London: George Bell, 1882.
Locke, John. *Second Treatise of Government.* 1689. Edited by P. Laslett. Cambridge, U.K.: Cambridge University Press, 1970.
Machiavelli, Niccolò. *Discourses on Livy.* 1531. Translated by L. Walker (trans. revised by B. Richardson). Harmondsworth, U.K.: Penguin, 1974.
Marx, Karl. "Preface to a Critique of Political Economy." 1857. In *Marx-Engels Reader,* 2nd ed., edited by R. Tucker. New York: Norton, 1978.
Marx, Karl, and Engels Friedrich. *Communist Manifesto.* 1848. In *Marx-Engels Reader,* 2nd ed., edited by R. Tucker. New York: Norton, 1978.
Mill, John Stuart. *Principles of Political Economy.* 1848. In *Collected Works,* vols. 2 and 3, edited by J. Robson. Toronto: University of Toronto Press, 1964.
Mun, T. *English Treasure by Forreign Trade.* 1664. Reprinted in *Early English Tracts on Commerce,* edited by John Ramsey McCulloch. Cambridge, U.K.: Economic History Society, 1952.
Rousseau, Jean-Jacques. *Social Contract.* 1765. Edited by V. Gourevitch. Cambridge, U.K.: Cambridge University Press, 1997.
Smith, Adam. *An Inquiry into the Nature and Causes of the Wealth of Nations.* 1776. Edited by R. H. Campbell and A. S. Skinner. New York: Oxford University Press, 1976.

Veblen, Thorstein. *The Theory of the Leisure Class.* 1899. New York: Dover, 1994.

SECONDARY SOURCES

Berry, Christopher. *The Idea of Luxury: A Conceptual and Historical Investigation.* Cambridge, U.K.: Cambridge University Press, 1994. Covers episodically issues and debates from the Greeks to the present day.

Coates, Alfred. *On the History of Economic Thought.* London: Routledge, 1992. A collection of previously published essays, a number of which summarize and discuss mercantilism, Smith, and nineteenth-century economists.

Hayek, F. A. *Law, Liberty, and Legislation.* 3 vols. London: Routledge, 1982.

Leibenstein, H. "Bandwagon, Snob, and Veblen Effects in the Theory of Consumers." *Quarterly Journal of Economics* 64 (1950): 183–207.

Macpherson, Crawford B. *The Political Theory of Possessive Individualism.* Oxford: Clarendon, 1962.

Price, B. B., ed. *Ancient Economic Thought.* London: Routledge, 1997. A collection of essays covering Greek, Roman, Indian, and Hebraic ideas.

Rawls, John A. *A Theory of Justice.* Oxford: Clarendon, 1972.

Sahlins, Marshall. *Stone Age Economics.* London: Tavistock, 1974. At times controversial but informative essays in anthropological economics.

Troeltsch, Ernst. *The Social Teaching of the Christian Churches.* 2 vols. Translated by Olive Wyon. New York: Macmillan, 1931. A classic work and still of value. German edition, 1911.

*Christopher J. Berry*

# WESTERNIZATION.

This entry includes three subentries:

*Africa*
*Middle East*
*Southeast Asia*

## AFRICA

As applied to non-Western societies, the term *Westernization* is almost always equated with modernization. It is important, however, to distinguish between the two, for modernization, considered as an overhauling of African societies, predates the incursion of the West on the continent. Before the Europeans, the most important agents of modernization in Africa were the Arabs, who, after their settlement in North Africa, introduced Islam into West Africa and thus set in motion a profound transformation of societies and cultures in the region. Similarly, the coastal peoples of East Africa were in touch with external civilizations long before the arrival of Europeans; the influence of the Arabs in this area has been as deep and durable as in West Africa. Internally, the Zulu leader Chaka's (1786–1828) conquests of and his creation of the Zulu nation out of diverse ethnicities over an extensive area in South Africa entailed a restructuring of their societies; the same can be said of Ashanti hegemony exercised over neighboring societies and peoples drawn into its sphere of imperial authority and cultural influ-

ence. In all these cases, what is involved is not merely a process of adjustment consequent upon conquest, but an extensive refashioning of the institutions and cultural practices of the societies affected in conformity with a new model of the world.

There is, however, a fundamental difference between these earlier processes of change and modernization as it is understood in the twenty-first century: that is, as the transition from an agrarian to an industrial-technological civilization. The origins of this process in the West and its global character constitute this civilization as a universal paradigm. It is in this sense that Westernization can be said to be synonymous with modernization in relation to the impact of the West on Africa.

The historical context of Westernization in Africa is the encounter with Europe, under the specific conditions of the Atlantic slave trade and the European colonial adventure, which was its logical extension. The forced acculturation of the black populations in the New World, already in full swing by the mid-eighteenth century, represents the first sustained assimilation of Western culture by Africans. It is significant to note the contribution that diaspora blacks were later to make to the process of Westernization in Africa, notably through their role in Christian evangelization and education.

The colonial factor was essential to the process of Westernization in Africa itself. The comprehensive reorganization of African societies in every sphere of life signaled a new dispensation that functioned as the comprehensive framework of the African experience under colonialism. The boundaries that resulted from the nineteenth century partition of Africa were determined without regard to antecedent institutions and cultures; the entities that emerged from partition represented a patchwork of administrative territories that in the twenty-first century have evolved into "modular states," each encompassing a diversity of languages and ethnicities. The colonial powers, especially the French and the Portuguese, undertook a systematic dismantling of indigenous institutions in order to establish colonial rule as the primary source of legitimacy in the territories they controlled. Moreover, they imposed new legal systems based upon European concepts of law, often at variance with indigenous legal systems and almost always with serious implications for such questions as property and inheritance.

A major effect of European colonialism was the progressive integration of Africa into the world capitalist system, within which Africa functioned primarily as a source of raw materials for Western industrial production. This required a total reorganization of African economic life, beginning with the introduction of the cash nexus and the imposition of taxation, which forced Africans into wage labor, a more intense and problematic variant of which was the migrant labor created by the mining industry in Southern Africa. Colonial economy also caused agriculture to be diverted toward the production of primary products and cash crops: cocoa, groundnut, palm oil, sisal, and so on. In the settler colonies—notably in Kenya and Rhodesia—the alienation of native land complicated the economic situation of the indigenous populations. The infrastructure undertaken by the colonial administrations was minimal, developed strictly as a function of the requirements of the new economy, which saw the rise of the colonial cities such as

Dakar, Lagos, Nairobi, and Luanda. Urbanization led to rural exodus and the displacement of large segments of the population.

It is against this background of the disaggregation of African societies and the destabilization of African life that the impact of Christianity has to be considered, for this has been the most important single factor in the process of Westernization in Africa. Western education, involving literacy and the mastery of a European language, became the condition for entry into the modern sector. For most of the colonial period, education was in the hands of the Christian missions, who sought not only to convert Africans but also to inculcate Western values. In West Africa, the assimilation of Western lifestyles was mediated by returnees from the diaspora—the West Indians, Brazilians, and Sierra Leoneans—whose education and skills enabled them to play an effective role in Christian evangelization and the nascent colonial civil service; their relatively privileged status enabled them to serve as a major reference group for indigenous Africans.

Christianity challenged traditional belief systems and promoted the diffusion of new ideas and modes of life; in particular, it sought to impose monogamy and the nuclear family as the norm. Romantic love and new conceptions of the self emerged, a development that was reinforced in the postwar period by the influence of the cinema and popular literature from the West. All over the continent throughout the colonial period, Africans were adopting new habits and acquiring new tastes derived from Western culture, often considered progressive in relation to traditional culture. This cultural revolution came to be associated with the new elite that was spawned by Christian education, an elite developed from an initial body of clerks, interpreters, and later, of teachers and lay preachers, expanding with time to include professionals, especially lawyers and doctors.

The ranks of the elite swelled with the establishment of the universities after World War II. Because they were linked at first with the metropolitan universities and staffed by Europeans, and the structure and content of the education they dispensed, they functioned essentially as outposts of Western culture, which thus proved a determining factor of modern cultural expression. This is attested by the dominance of Western-educated Africans, products of the new universities, in the genesis and evolution of a new literature written in the European languages, for which the forms and conventions of the metropolitan literatures have served as reference. Western cultural forms also provided expressive channels in other areas of aesthetic manifestation. This was most notable in music, where Western instruments such as the piano, the trumpet, and the guitar have been adopted by African artists to fashion a new musical idiom fusing indigenous and foreign modes, a creative syncretism that is forcefully demonstrated in African popular music, and that can be observed in other areas such as the visual arts.

The transformations provoked by the pressures of colonial rule in all spheres of life are sufficiently extensive and pervasive to qualify as the signs of a new modernity in Africa. In no area is the association of Westernization with modernization clearer than in the impact of science and technology on African experience and consciousness. Modern medicine has largely taken precedence over traditional methods in matters of health; ironically, the drastic reduction of infant mortality it has made possible has also complicated the demographic issues in Africa, with consequences for agriculture and social services. Although no major effort of industrialization took place during the colonial period, and there has been no significant development since, Western technology has long entered the lives of Africans through familiarity with manufactured products imported from the West.

As with other societies and cultures in the so-called Third World, the impact of Western civilization on Africa has occasioned a discontinuity in forms of life throughout the continent. This has led to a cultural dualism that often presents itself as a real dilemma in concrete, real-life situations. In other words, the African experience of modernity is fraught with tensions at every level of the communal and individual apprehension. African nationalism was predicated on the conjugation of nation-building and economic development as a means for the improvement in standards of living. Beyond these immediate objectives, it was concerned more fundamentally with the establishment of a new order informed by modern concepts of political life and behavior and by a rationality in conformity with a modern world outlook. The upheavals of the postindependence era have derived from the stresses arising from the quest for this ideal. It is thus fair to observe that the fundamental issue with which the contemporary societies of Africa are confronted is that of their full and orderly accession to modernity, that is, to a mode of collective organization based on the model of the liberal and democratic nation-state and of the industrial-technological civilization, a model that is associated with the West.

This is not to restrict Africans to a single model, nor to deny the capacity for adaptation manifested by African societies. There is an undeniable energy in the movement toward a new integration evident in the original forms of life and expression that have been evolved on the continent since the encounter with Europe. As Melville Herskovits and William Bascom have observed, "There is no African culture which has not been affected in some way by European contact, and there is none which has entirely given way before it" (p. 3).

Indeed, the significant fact about African cultural history is the convergence upon the indigenous tradition of the two external influences—the Arab-Islamic and the European-Christian—to which the continent has been exposed for well over a millennium. The values and lifestyles associated with these traditions have been assimilated and to a large extent indigenized on the continent. This observation provides a broader perspective on the phenomenon of Westernization in Africa, an observation made as early as the late nineteenth century by the great African cultural theorist Edward Wilmot Blyden and summed up in the late twentieth century by Ali Mazrui as "the triple heritage."

*See also* **Arts: Africa; Colonialism: Africa; Diasporas: African Diaspora; Religion: Africa; Religion: African Diaspora; Third World; University: Postcolonial.**

WESTERNIZATION

BIBLIOGRAPHY

Ajayi, J. F. Ade. *Christian Missions in Nigeria, 1841–1891: The Making of a New Elite.* Evanston, Ill.: Northwestern University Press, 1969.

Anderson, Benedict R. *Imagined Communities: Reflections on the Origin and Spread of Nationalism.* London: Verso Editions/ NLB, 1983.

Herskovits, Melville J., and William B. Bascom. "The Problem of Stability and Change in African Culture." In *Continuity and Change in African Cultures,* edited by Melville J. Herskovits and William B. Bascom. Chicago: University of Chicago Press, 1959.

*F. Abiola Irele*

## MIDDLE EAST

The notion of Westernization in the Middle East raises a number of interrelated issues. First, it refers to a period (nineteenth to twentieth centuries) in which Middle Eastern intellectuals engaged Western political philosophy in a self-conscious search for modernity. Albert Hourani, in his groundbreaking *Arabic Thought in the Liberal Age, 1798–1939* (1983), dates this engagement from Napoleon Bonaparte's invasion of Egypt in 1798. This defeat revealed the weaknesses of Ottoman government and sent shockwaves throughout the Ottoman Empire. How had the Europeans gained such superiority, and how could the Muslims catch up? Selim III (1761–1808), the Ottoman sultan in Istanbul, and Muhammad Ali (1769?–1849), the Ottoman governor of Egypt, enlisted European advisors to implement military and governmental reforms on the Western model (*tanzimat*). A generation of "new men," many graduates of these European-style schools, began a period of intense reflection and critique. They studied Rousseau, the Manchester textile mills, and parliamentary government for clues to European power. They also criticized traditional Islamic institutions and advocated reform of education, government, and the Arabic language.

These two avenues of reform raise a second issue: did the reform movement mark "Westernization" or a local modernity forged by traditional intellectuals? Many historians have defined Westernization narrowly as the "all-out adoption of the Western model," which they contrast to "modernization," an Islamic response to political, economic, and social pressures from the West. Modernity and Westernization cannot be separated, however. Islamic modernist thought was formulated as a specific response to the European challenge. Thinkers from Muhammad Abduh (1849–1905) to Ali Shari'ati (1933–1977) had to explain European superiority and propose specific solutions for Muslim decline. Even when Western models were not adopted, the West provided the terms of the debate: industrialization, women's rights, secular law, the bureaucratic state, and popular sovereignty. Finally, modernism itself, a self-conscious effort to organize and govern society according to rational principles, was invented in the West. Islamic modernizers embraced the centrality of reason, which led them back to a classical question: "What is the relationship of reason to revelation?"

Yet the Muslim modernizers posed the question in a new way. How could reason and religion be reconciled to reform Islam, and how could this purified Islam be applied to society? Thus, our subject is actually the reform of Islam and its new transformative role, a program formulated in engagement with the West. The relationship between the Middle East and the West occurred at a number of levels. First, the reforms on the Western model (*tanzimat*) centralized the states in Egypt and Anatolia, disciplined their populations, and laid the social foundations of modern Egyptian and Turkish nationalisms. Second, the modernizers adapted Western ideologies (liberalism, socialism, nationalism) to create cultural hybrids. Colonial industrialization was part of this process, for changes in labor and production produced new classes and new consciousness. Finally, even those intellectuals who rejected the West unwittingly adopted Western approaches to knowledge. Islamic modernizers rejected Gnostic knowledge and mysticism (Sufism), much as Western positivists tried to fit all knowledge into a rational framework. This helps to explain a central puzzle in Islamic history: the secularists and the Islamic fundamentalists (one branch of the *Salafiyya*) spring from the same intellectual root.

At first contact, Egyptians were not impressed with liberalism and the French Republic. Consider the Egyptian chronicler Abd al-Rahman al-Jabarti's reaction to the French and their political ideas:

> [Napoléon] saying "[all people] are equal in the eyes of God the Almighty," this is a lie and stupidity. How can this be when God has made some superior to others as is testified by the dwellers in the Heavens and on the Earth . . . those people are opposed to both Christians and Muslims, and do not hold fast to any religion. You see that they are materialists, who deny all God's attributes. . . . (p. 31).

Yet as Ottoman rulers adopted European institutions, a new generation of intellectuals adopted French political ideas. The Egyptian Rifa'a Rafi'a al-Tahtawi (1801–1873) tried to reconcile the republic with the *umma* (community of believers), secular law with the *shari'a* (Islamic law), the *ulema* (religious scholars) with the republican legislator. Tahtawi argued that Muslims had failed to develop theories of government; they saw the executive only as a guardian of Islamic law and spiritual guidance. However, government also gave order to society and should thus be used to promote the public welfare. Creating the just society and upholding the will of God were thus compatible if not identical projects. Drawing on the thought of al-Farabi, Ibn Sina, and the Mu'tazili school of the Middle Ages, al-Tahtawi argued that reason and philosophy were two paths to the same ultimate reality and thus must be reconcilable. Al-Tahtawi was the first to articulate the notion of an Egyptian nation, a historical community of the Muslim and Christian occupants of Egypt, and a brotherhood "over and above the brotherhood in religion." He attributed Egyptian decadence to foreign rule, specifically that of the Turkish overlords (Mamluks and later Ottomans) who ruled Egypt from the thirteenth century.

Yet Tahtawi's project failed to address a basic tension between secular and religious law. In a republic, the people are sovereign and the social contract defines the members of the

2468                                                                                      **New Dictionary of the History of Ideas** political body. The law is the expression of the general will and thus utilitarian and subject to change. In the *umma,* the community is defined in relation to God; the Muslims are those who submit to God's will, (a Muslim is "he who submits [to God]"). Since God is sovereign and the law is the expression of his will, many Muslim jurists argued that once the Koran and hadith had been elaborated into a legal code (*shar'ia*), by the fourteenth century, it was universally valid and permanent, and so "the gates of *ijtihad* [independent legal reasoning] are closed." A second question arose: if Islamic law is divine, what checks, if any, should there be on the executive? Finally, Muslim scholars feared that Western institutions might be inseparable from a secular worldview. Indeed, historians of the scientific revolution have argued that elements of Western modernity could not be conceived before the "paradigm shift," the replacement of religious worldviews by a Newtonian universe. Finally, Muslims had to answer Orientalists like Ernest Renan, who claimed that Islam was antithetical to science.

In response to all of this, Muhammad Abduh and Jamal al-Din al-Afghani (1839–1897) presented a synthesis that "rationalized" Islam and opened the door to both secularism and Islamic fundamentalism. Abduh argued that the true Islam of the Companions (*al-salaf*) of the prophet Muhammad was the tool for social modernity. Islam must be freed of antiquated scholarship; he demanded that the traditional Islamic institutions like Al-Azhar in Egypt replace rote memorization with a new *ijtihad* and teach the modern sciences. Islam must be unified into a single creed: Shiism was a "heresy" and Shiites must be brought into the fold. Abduh suggested unifying the four Sunni schools of Islamic law (Hanafi, Hanbali, Shafa'i, Maliki) into a single school. Islam was to be purified of heterodoxy and foreign elements; thus the modernizers condemned Sufism (mystical Islam), visitation of the graves of the *awliya'* (holy men), and other popular practices (amulet-writing, healing) as *shirk,* or worship of things other than God.

Abduh collapsed the divide between the secular and the religious in *The Sociological Laws of the Qur'an.* He argued that Islam and Western civilization were of the same order of knowledge and that a purified Islam held the answers to all modern social problems. Parliaments, railroads, and space travel were anticipated in the Koran and fully compatible with its message. He translated legal conceptions of the medieval period to the "modern day": *ijma'* (consensus of the jurists) was "public opinion," *shura'* (consultation, especially in the selection of the caliph) was "parliamentary democracy." Among his disciples, this synthesis split into two strands.

One strand was secular nationalism (1900–1939), and nationalists in Egypt, Lebanon, Syria, Turkey, Morocco, Algeria, Tunisia, Iraq, and Iran embraced the institutions of political liberalism under French and British "protection." Secularists dropped the project of "Islamic government" because, as they argued, the Koran contained or prefigured (or so they believed) Western institutions. Religious minorities—Copts, Druze, Maronites, Jews—welcomed the opportunity for full participation in political life. The Egyptian Qasim Amin advocated women's emancipation as a national project. However, as liberals failed to address growing labor and social

problems or bring an end to colonial rule, liberal constitutionalism lost popular support.

Other secularists turned to Marxist socialism. Lenin's *Imperialism: The Highest Stage of Capitalism* provided an economic critique of colonialism and a plan of revolutionary action. The 1952 "Arab Socialist" revolution of Jamal 'Abd al-Nasser (1918–1970) proposed social equality for all citizens through state capitalism. Nationalism in Algeria and Tunisia grew from the trade unionism of migrant labor in France (Étoile Nord-Africaine). However, the materialism of Marx was difficult to reconcile with Islam, and the Iranian Islamist intellectual Ali Shari'ati rejected Marxism as a solution to social ills.

Finally, the second group of Abduh's successors, led by Muhammad Rashid Rida (1865–1935), focused on the rationalization of Islam to create a "true Islamic state." Rida believed that Sufism (mystical Islam) had created division in the Islamic community and that westernizers undermined its moral foundation; only a strict adherence to *shari'a* and the Islam of the *salaf* would rejuvenate the *umma.* This strain of thought found various expressions in the work of Islamists such as Sayyid Qutb, the premier theoretician of the Egyptian Muslim Brotherhood, and Shii form in the work of Ayatollah Ruholla Khomeini (1900–1989), leader of the 1978–1979 Islamic Revolution in Iran. Thus, even the ideas of the contemporary Islamist radicals were formulated in dialogue with the West.

*See also* **Anticolonialism: Middle East; Empire and Imperialism: Middle East; Nationalism: Middle East.**

**BIBLIOGRAPHY**

Hourani, Albert. *Arabic Thought in the Liberal Age, 1789–1939.* Cambridge, U.K., and New York: Cambridge University Press, 1983.

Jabarti, Abd al-Rahman al-. *Napoleon in Egypt: Al-Jabarti's Chronicle of the French Occupation, 1798.* Translation by Shmuel Moreh. Princeton, N.J.: Markus Wiener, 2001.

Keddie, Nikki. *Sayyid Jamāl ad-Dīn "al-Afghānī."* Berkeley: University of California Press, 1972.

Laqueur, Walter. *A History of Zionism: From the French Revolution to the Establishment of the State of Israel.* New York: MJF Books, 1972.

Rahnema, Ali. *An Islamic Utopian: A Political Biography of Ali Shari'ati.* London: Taurus, 2000. This essay has been devoted exclusively to Islamic modernism, but there are significant parallels in the development of Zionism and the *haskala* movement.

Renan, Ernest, and Jamal al-Din Afghani. *L'Islam et la science: Avec la reponse d'Afghani.* Montpellier, France: Archange Minotaure, 2003.

Sirriyeh, Elizabeth. *Sufis and Anti-Sufis: The Defence, Rethinking and Rejection of Sufism in the Modern World.* Richmond, U.K.: Curzon, 1999.

Tibi, Bassam. *Arab Nationalism: Between Islam and the Nation-State.* 3rd ed. New York: St. Martin's, 1997.

Weismann, Itzchak. *Taste of Modernity: Sufism, Salafiyya, and Arabism in Late Ottoman Damascus.* Leiden, Netherlands: Brill, 2001.

*Ellen Amster*

## SOUTHEAST ASIA

Westernization in world history can refer to the transmission and reception of European ideas, technology, lifestyles, and institutions throughout the globe. Much of the scholarly attention has tended to concentrate on the intensity and nature of that transmission during the era of European colonialism and its attempts to transform the very consciousness of the peoples it encountered. Although the modes of transfer, the locales of interaction, and the intellectual capital are no longer the sole domain of Europe, the nature of Westernization continues to be relevant as local traditions become more integrated (or subsumed) within supposed "universal" values. Societies that are unable to cope with the blistering pace of technological change, the fluctuations of an interdependent world economy, or the insensitivity of an "international" community often find fault with "Westernization," which is associated with these uncontrollable and unfamiliar pressures on local societies. As a result, the idea of Westernization continues to be a part of twenty-first-century historical discourse, framing the ways in which scholars examine the interactions among cultures, regions, and nations.

### Approaching Westernization in Eurasian History

Contemporary ideas of what constitutes "Western culture" reflect its postcolonial origins and twentieth-century politics, just as the idea of the "West" may have had slightly different meanings between the fifteenth and nineteenth centuries. In the history of Southeast Asia, Europeans had competing ideas about the cultural values they represented and were attempting to infuse into the societies they encountered. Spanish policy in the Philippines was exceptionally different from Dutch policy in Indonesia, and the Spaniards and the Dutch certainly did not see each other as representing a single, unified, cultural domain. These motivations were often couched in religious or political agendas that many times reveal tensions between empires as much as they disclose the tensions within. Scholars gazing toward the past sometimes project "Westernization" into the histories of exploration, trade, and colonialism, despite the fact that those participating in these global exchanges probably saw and articulated their missions in slightly different ways. Caution must be employed when considering Westernization as a process because it was often much more disparate in nature than coherent. Nonetheless, using Westernization as a category of analysis can provide a useful lens into the history of global interactions with Europe.

In the history of colonialism, the term *Westernization* reveals the geographic context and self-referential perspective that would inform the ways in which peoples of Asia would be categorized and understood, though elites within these societies would also adopt the term to represent their notion of "modernity." This association can be attributed partly to the rhetoric of colonialism, which blended Europe's cultural forms with theories of human development in order to organize and tabulate the communities and societies that came under colonial authority. Colonized elites would appropriate these conceptions of modernity and apply them to their own societies, fundamentally changing their own identity in relation to the world. Within these discourses, the "East" or the "Orient" was

seen as something homogenous, unified, and fundamentally opposite to that which was European, even though the idea of a coherent "West" encountering a coherent "East" tended to overstate the complexity, nature, and composition of these societies. In addition to Asia, this process of European interaction also occurred in Africa and the Americas, producing very similar narratives of exchange, acculturation, and domination. Whatever the context, early European scholars, traders, soldiers, and missionaries viewed themselves and the people they encountered as coming from very different worlds. In some instances, Europeans would view Westernization as the process of making others more like themselves, though they probably did not consider this transformation as "Westernization" per se. Throughout history, Westernization would come to have different meanings, effects, and forms, but in essence it refers to one of many global processes that have characterized the interaction of human societies.

From a regional perspective, the history of Westernization in Southeast Asia can be seen in much the same way: It is but one of many continuing processes that have contributed to the region's character. For a millennium, Southeast Asia has benefited from its unique geographic location of being both a mainland and maritime crossroad between the Indian and Chinese cultural zones. This vital location has given it exposure to three great religions (Buddhism, Islam, and Christianity), global trade, and the movement of peoples from all over the world. Many scholars have chosen to consider the dynamics of regional change in the context of Islamization, Indianization, and Sinicization (modification under Chinese influence), to which Westernization might be compared. While these regionally specific processes may be associated with particular times in Southeast Asia's deep past, closer readings of how these exchanges occurred in specific cases reveal that all four processes continue to interact, intersect, and overlap, thereby illustrating the complexity of these ideas and their interrelatedness in the Southeast Asian context.

### The Structure of Westernization in Southeast Asian History

Most scholars have approached the structure of Westernization in Southeast Asia as a process that has developed over stages and varying intensities according to location, internal receptiveness, and the circumstances in which the encounter took place. One of the most important mechanisms contributing to the transmission of Western culture to the region was trade. In this context, trade consists of the movement, over the centuries, of peoples, goods, and ideas between the Mediterranean, Bengal, and Southeast Asian waters. With this in mind, Western interaction with Southeast Asia can be organized chronologically into four stages.

In the first stage, labeled Early Maritime Influence (1511–1670), initial contacts were made through the agency of European and Southeast Asian traders. The nature of interaction here could be described as minimal in terms of cultural penetration, but certain important technological exchanges did occur. During this period the Portuguese and the Spanish began to make headway into the region, securing the regional port of Malacca in the case of the former and Cebu in the case of the latter. The Dutch also began to initiate activity in the Southeast Asian waters, but powerful Muslim states and trading networks still continued to thrive, producing minor levels of exchange. Although Portuguese firearms would contribute to the reintegration of the Burmese kingdom in the 1550s, European influence was marginal on the Southeast Asian mainland.

By 1670, Dutch penetration of the regional trade networks intensified as they slowly began to involve themselves in internal political issues of succession and power relations. Under this second stage of Accelerated Influence (1670–1820), the main Muslim kingdoms disintegrated and regional trading networks fragmented as the Dutch (in particular) increased their influence in the island interiors. Similarly it is during this period that the Spanish increased their role in the Philippines, inserting the religious-political structures that would become the foundation of their strong presence among the local communities there. While the islands of Southeast Asia were beginning to be exposed to Western technology, religion, and economic pressures, the mainland on the other hand was left on its own, as the spices and other natural resources of the island world continued to draw Europe's attention.

By the early nineteenth century, however, the mainland was to bear the brunt of new European initiatives in the form of Full Scale Conquest (1820–1870). Because of European political maneuvering and competition, and the promise of the Chinese market, mainland Southeast Asia was conquered during this period by the British (Burma) and the French (Indochina). With the establishment of colonial governments, mainland Southeast Asian communities were slowly integrated into new economic, political, and ideological shadows of empire. For the most part, because of the limitations of military operations, coastal sections of the mainland were more intensely affected than the interior, leaving the people in the latter area and their ways of life somewhat unaffected.

With the opening of the Suez Canal, the improvements in steam technology, and the development of the telegraph, Southeast Asian societies experienced an intensification of Western influence under High Imperialism (1870–1942). Because of changing world demands for natural resources, the potential for capital from the taxing of local populations, and the influence of new theories of European cultural superiority, Europeans began to actively pursue and initiate programs designed to colonize the consciousness of ordinary Southeast Asian people. Colonial bureaucracies, churches, schools, and other institutions produced a consolidated view of the world that placed European civilization at the peak of humanity's development, self-justifying the role and influence Europeans had on indigenous peoples of Southeast Asia. New standards of language, authority, health, and knowledge were produced, professed, and dictated that fundamentally questioned the role and place of indigenous values and beliefs. Throughout the region, colonialism would change the character of Westernization by restructuring the nature of this global exchange through the reduction of local autonomy.

Yet the contribution by Southeast Asians to the shape of Westernization was not minimal in any regard. Southeast Asians adapted, modified, and reshaped colonial influences to

fit their needs and concerns—just as they had done for centuries through Indianization, Sinicization, and Islamization. Colonialism produced a particular body of knowledge and symbols that were consciously (and at times unintentionally) adopted by indigenous elites in order to improve local power and prestige. The idea of nationalism in Southeast Asia developed in just this manner, through local innovation and appropriation of ideas either introduced in schools or through the mechanics of the civil service. Southeast Asians contributed to the construction of what was Western and especially what was not—by identifying and constructing elements of "traditional" Southeast Asian culture (using Western modes of knowledge production) that might stand independent of Western influence. In the case of Thailand, the monarchy actively engaged European education, nation-building, and popular culture in order to transform itself into a modern country based on European definitions. Though not formally colonized, it initiated reforms that paralleled colonial legislation in British Burma, French Indochina, and Dutch Indonesia. In short, Westernization was as much a part of Southeast Asian regional processes as it was an encounter between cultures.

In postcolonial Southeast Asia, the nature of engagement continued in much the same way, though the colonial powers were no longer formally (except in the case of Vietnam) dictating the nature of this exchange. Southeast Asians continued to view Western technological and economic influences with interest in some cases and distrust in others. Burma withdrew into itself and limited interaction with what it viewed as the colonial "West," though it continued to adopt certain principles of European economic planning in order to craft a locally sensitive state policy called the "Burmese Way to Socialism." Because of its history of direct colonialism and the disruption of its most important cultural institutions, Burma's postcolonial history has viewed Western influences with considerable hesitation. Understandably, measures to "de-Westernize" or decolonize itself have even included changing the nation's name back to its precolonial form, Myanmar. In contrast, Thailand's autonomy throughout the age of High Imperialism has left it more culturally secure, with its institutions intact, and less wary of Western influences. While sharing a similar historical and cultural trajectory as its Western neighbor, it has chosen a completely different path from Burma, choosing to adopt Western forms and ideas at a ferocious pace while at the same time applying adjustments along the way. In short, the intensity of colonialism has affected the intensity of the response to colonialism and its cultural features.

### Shaping Westernization in Southeast Asian Studies
Scholarship has addressed the concept of Westernization in Southeast Asia indirectly through alternative themes and interests. That the early histories of Southeast Asia by colonial officials were actually the history of Westerners in Asia and their perspective on the region's culture reveals something about the idea of Westernization. As many early accounts describing this process were involved in the spreading of ideas, technology, or goods, their assessments tended to reflect their interests and their unfamiliarity with the region as a whole. One aspect of this approach was to view Southeast Asian

history within the chronological and narrative framework of the West's own history, leading to judgments proclaiming the region's political, social, and technological levels to be inherently backward. It was believed that through colonial policies, Southeast Asia under European tutelage would be emancipated from itself, joining the civilized world by emulating it. Thus, early assessments by colonial officials saw the process of Westernization as the process through which traditional cultures could be made modern.

This view was shared to some degree by Southeast Asian observers as well. The emerging class of indigenous elites who were trained in Western schools began considering the idea that European culture had something to offer and could improve their situation. These groups began to speak in European languages, adopt European modes of dress, and evaluate the world through European conceptions of it. For many scholars following World War II, Westernization became viewed in terms of nationalism and its specific role in the process of constructing the nation-state. Histories were produced that deemphasized pre-European elements and themes in favor of more "modern" narratives that embraced the structures, ideas, and values of "Western" historical writing. As a result, nationalist histories supported the idea that Westernization and the formation of the nation were inevitable and inextricably linked. Ironically, colonial and nationalist historians envisioned Westernization and its role in history in much the same way.

In response to colonial and nationalist histories, attempts were made toward writing histories that promoted "Southeast Asian" perspectives, with the emphasis placed on alternative, locally defined categories upon which new narratives of regional history could be written. Scholars began to question the role and place of European influence on the superstructure of Southeast Asian beliefs. Many began to see Westernization as a "thin and flaking glaze" over more enduring ideas and institutions that had defined the region for centuries. With this shift in perspective, Westernization was perceived as having far less of an impact in Southeast Asia than previously held before, swinging the pendulum to the other side. Studies of anticolonial movements, economic systems, nationalism, rituals, and identity deemphasized the impact of Westernization in order to accentuate Southeast Asia's cultural integrity more clearly. As a result, the reappraisal of colonialism led to a different reading of Southeast Asia's Westernization. Where the colonial period might have previously represented a significant conjuncture in the region's long history, scholars now viewed more continuity with the precolonial past and its traditions.

With changes in the world of the early twenty-first century, and most notably in postcolonial scholarship, the shape of Westernization has once again taken a more prominent place in Southeast Asian studies. The realization that many of the categories once thought "Southeast Asian" were actually colonial constructions led to important reappraisals of European and U.S. influence in the region. This shift has thus reinserted the importance of European culture back into the mix that is Southeast Asian culture. Scholarship since the late 1990s has also shown that, in the last two centuries of the colonial encounter, the distinctions between "West" and "East" were

much more ambiguous than once held; that identities of race, ethnicity, gender, and religion were openly contested; and that the nature of Westernization in relation to the idea of modernity has not only changed in terms of its receptiveness, but that it was also losing its distinctiveness as being derived from Europe. Popular culture from Japan, technological innovation from India, and cultural tourism have redefined the relationship between what is perceived as Western influence and what is not, while growing economic, political, and technological integration has moved the region much closer to its neighbors around the world.

*See also* **Anticolonialism: Southeast Asia; Colonialism: Southeast Asia; Empire and Imperialism.**

BIBLIOGRAPHY

Cooper, Frederick, and Ann Laura Stoler, eds. *Tensions of Empire: Colonial Cultures in a Bourgeois World.* Berkeley and Los Angeles: University of California Press, 1997.

Dirks, Nicholas B., ed. *Colonialism and Culture.* Ann Arbor: University of Michigan Press, 1992.

Lieberman, Victor. *Strange Parallels: Southeast Asia in Global Context, c. 800–1830,* Vol. 1: *Integration on the Mainland.* New York: Cambridge University Press, 2003.

Lieberman, Victor, ed. *Beyond Binary Histories: Re-imagining Eurasia to c. 1830.* Ann Arbor: University of Michigan Press, 1999.

Reid, Anthony. *Southeast Asia in the Age of Commerce, 1450–1680,* Vol. 1: *The Lands below the Winds.* New Haven, Conn.: Yale University Press, 1988.

———. *Southeast Asia in the Age of Commerce, 1450–1680,* Vol. 2: *Expansion and Crisis.* New Haven, Conn.: Yale University Press, 1993.

Reid, Anthony, ed. *Southeast Asia in the Early Modern Era: Trade, Power, and Belief.* Ithaca, N.Y.: Cornell University Press, 1993.

Steinberg, David Joel, ed. *In Search of Southeast Asia: A Modern History.* Rev. ed. Honolulu: University of Hawaii Press, 1987.

Tarling, Nicholas. *Southeast Asia: A Modern History.* South Melbourne, Australia: Oxford University Press, 2001.

Tarling, Nicholas, ed. *The Cambridge History of Southeast Asia,* Vol. 2: *The Nineteenth and Twentieth Centuries.* Cambridge, U.K.: Cambridge University Press, 1992.

*Maitrii Aung-Thwin*

**WILDLIFE.** Prehistory makes clear that our ancestors continuously conceptualized their relations with the myriad forms of plants and animals with whom their existence was interwoven. These ancient musings, more mythological than scientific, were the first sustained efforts to comprehend the order of nature. The noun *wildlife* has been in use no more than 125 years. But the swirl of ideas around wildlife, however inchoate, is nearly as old as the human species.

Reconstructions of the conceptual dimensions of wildlife prior to the advent of agriculture are based on carvings, paintings, burial, and other material artifacts as well as the study of contemporaneous indigenous cultures living outside the cocoon of industrial civilization. While generalization remains provisional, the Paleolithic era of hunting and gathering was marked by notions of plants and especially animals as totems and dual presences. As totems the other species taught their two-legged kin the ways of the world: survival more than anything else. As dual presences the others encouraged the notion that all creatures were shape-shifters, bound up in the ongoing cyclical process of life in relationships based on reciprocity rather than dominion. The "economy of nature" (itself a modern term) was conceptualized as sacramental, based on the myth of the eternal return.

The New Stone Age (c. 15,000–10,000 B.P.) slowly but inexorably overturned the established notion of one creation binding all creatures together. The cultivation of cereal grasses and domestication of animals led to a binary categorization of the wild and tame. The wild encompassed the plants and animals not under human control. Unwanted plants intruding upon fields became weeds. Population blooms of insects that ravaged the fields became plagues. Animals that preyed on livestock became predators.

The tame included the lands and domesticated species under the control of civilization. Domestication entails selection for characteristics that, however desirable for human purposes, would in many cases be lethal in a natural environment. Cereal grasses were valued because their seeds were retained in the head so that they could be harvested. Domesticated cattle were valued because they were docile and amenable to herding.

As permanent settlement spread, lingering memories of a time before agriculture when humans were intimately entwined with the others were expressed in sources such as the *Gilgamesh* epic and the Old Testament. Psalm 104 praises the glory of a creator god and the intricacy of the living creation. Even as the psalmist sang, there was a dawning realization that humankind was not a good steward: "I brought you into a fruitful land, to enjoy its fruit and the goodness of it; but when you entered upon it you defiled my land, and made the home I gave you an abomination" (Jeremiah 2:7).

## Changing Conceptions of Wildlife in Darwin's Century

Nineteenth-century evolutionary theory and the discovery of Paleolithic archeological materials established three fundamental ideas. First, that biophysical evolution existed on a temporal scale far beyond conventional schemes of history and culture. Second, the human species itself had a natural history that, however poorly understood, clearly linked the "Descent of Man," as Charles Darwin put it, with an ancient and continuing evolutionary stream. And third, evolutionary theory made clear that the domestication of plants and animals was little more than tinkering with natural history for human purposes, especially economic ones.

While the nineteenth century did not overturn the modern notion that humankind was the master and possessor of nature, a somewhat chastened estimate of our place in nature emerged. Henry David Thoreau (1817–1862) observed in 1838 that hunting and trapping had eliminated the mountain lion and black bear from most of New England. He challenged his coevals to reconsider the fate of a culture that was losing

connection with wild places and creatures. Near the end of the century, John Muir (1838–1914) argued for the creation of national parks as refugia for wildlife and as places to nourish the human spirit. While protective legislation dates to the early 1600s (e.g., Bermuda's protection of the cahow and the green turtle), the late nineteenth and early twentieth centuries marked the beginnings of systematic approach to the conservation of wildlife. Yellowstone (1872) was the first national park in America. Created primarily to protect unique geological features, Yellowstone's value for wildlife preservation soon became apparent. President Theodore Roosevelt's (1858–1919) and Gifford Pinchot's (1865–1946) efforts around the turn of the century were instrumental in legislative efforts to create a system of public lands that offered protection for wildlife. Progressive resource conservation found many allies, such as sport hunters, who reacted vigorously to the depredations of market hunting on wildlife. (Predators did not enjoy legislative protection until passage of the Endangered Species Act near the end of the twentieth century).

## Wildlife in the Twentieth Century

The early- to mid-twentieth century was marked by an increased scientific understanding of wildlife and an increased willingness on the part of nations to protect it. The International Union for the Protection of Nature (now the World Conservation Union) was established in 1948 and gave birth shortly thereafter to the World Wildlife Fund. These and other global organizations, such as the United Nations, and conventions, such as the Convention Concerning the Protection of World Cultural and Natural Heritage (1972), were dedicated to protecting wildlife through a variety of strategies. These included moratoriums on trade in endangered species and the creation of reserves, such as those designated as World Natural Heritage Sites.

Despite such efforts, the continuing humanization of the planet made the long-term survival prospects for wildlife increasingly uncertain. As the twentieth century ended, the biological sciences conclusively established the reality of an anthropogenic mass extinction of terrestrial flora and fauna. Estimates of human-caused extinction rates ranged from a low of one hundred to a high of one thousand times greater than natural rates. Humankind's increasing population and subsequent levels of economic demand led to rapid development of the few remaining areas, such as Amazonia, that were primary habitats for wildlife. Patterns of human settlement in developed nations, including sprawl, urbanization, and the fragmentation of habitat, increasingly impacted remnant populations of wild plants and animals. Less direct impacts on wildlife were the consequence of the increase in global temperature, predicted by the Intergovernmental Panel on Climate Change to increase by 5 to 10 degrees Fahrenheit over the twenty-first century. Given such dramatic increase, the possibility of retreat by heat sensitive species appeared doubtful.

Progress in scientific understanding was paralleled by ethical advance. The pioneering work of Thoreau and Muir was followed in the twentieth century by a variety of ecological ethics that charged humanity with obligations to conserve wild places and things, and to restore those species, such as the wolf, that had been thoughtlessly endangered. These ranged from the secular, such Aldo Leopold's (1887–1948) land ethic, *A Sand County Almanac* (1949), to the religious caring for creation movement that followed Lynn White, Jr.'s charge in a 1967 issue of *Science* magazine that Jews and Christians were to blame for ecological crisis.

Rachel Carson's *Silent Spring* (1961), which focused on the consequences for avian species of the toxic chemicals used in a war against nature, marked the point where the environmental movement became a mass phenomenon. Membership in organizations dedicated to the conservation, preservation, and restoration of wildlife soared. As public interest increased in America, legislative action, such as the passage of the Wilderness Act (1964), the National Environmental Policy Act (1969), and the Endangered Species Act (1973), followed. Such laws, and similar ones passed in other nations, are the cornerstone of wildlife protection.

### Wildlife in the New Millennium

As the twenty-first century begins, our ideas of wildlife are being transformed through the advance of the natural and human sciences. Humankind has engendered a mass extinction event and caused "the death of birth" (i.e., disrupted the processes of speciation), thus creating uncertain prospects for plants and animals, and ourselves, over the millennium. Three pivotal themes stand out.

Economically considered, the value of nature, including the plant and animal species (the total number of which are unknown to the nearest order of magnitude), has been calculated to exceed the value of the artifice of the human economy by two to one. Potential uses of great significance in medicine and agriculture alone give ample reason to work toward international solutions for the biodiversity crisis.

Humanistically considered, interdisciplinary inquiry has established a close connection between the extinction of experience and the extinction of wildlife. Cultural diversity goes hand in hand with biodiversity. The almost unchecked processes of globalization, legitimated under the banner of progress, and euphemistically termed cultural homogenization and assimilation, are rushing literally thousands of indigenous cultures, their languages, and the associated wild places and things to extinction.

Finally, humankind vitally needs the others in ways that we barely comprehend. Our natural history reveals that continual close interactions with the plants and animals are the norm. The small interval of time beginning with the Neolithic revolution and continuing to the present is a mere moment in that long history. There is increasing agreement across a variety of scientific communities that we ignore our continued need for and value of the others at great peril.

*See also* **Biology; Ecology; Environment; Nature.**

**BIBLIOGRAPHY**
Ackerman, Diane. *The Rarest of the Rare: Vanishing Animals, Timeless Worlds.* New York: Vintage Books, 1997.
Crosby, Alfred W. *Ecological Imperialism: The Biological Expansion of Europe, 900–1900.* Cambridge, U.K., and New York: Cambridge University Press, 1986.
Grumbine, Edward. *Ghost Bears: Exploring the Biodiversity Crisis.* Washington, D.C.: Island Press, 1992.
Maffi, Luisa, ed. *On Biocultural Diversity: Linking Language, Knowledge, and the Environment.* Washington, D.C., and London: Smithsonian Institution Press, 2001.
Matthiessen, Peter. *Wildlife in America.* 2nd ed. New York: Viking, 1987.
Mighetto, Lisa. *Wild Animals and American Environmental Ethics.* Tucson: University of Arizona Press, 1991.
Oelschlaeger, Max. *The Idea of Wilderness: From Prehistory to the Age of Ecology.* New Haven and London: Yale University Press, 1991.
Shepard, Paul. *The Others: How Animals Made Us Human.* Washington, D.C.: Island Press, 1995.
White, Lynn, Jr. "The Historical Roots of Our Ecological Crisis." *Science* 155 (1967): 1203–1207.

*Max Oelschlaeger*

**WISDOM, HUMAN.** Wisdom is irretrievably linked with age and experience in human societies. If wisdom comes mainly through age and experience, it also requires "sense" to achieve. It is associated with the capacity to deal with experience in a constructive manner. If someone acts in a way that seems sensible, we may use the phrase "he has sense." Sense is the internal quality that promotes the learning process.

The question of the knowledge of creative activity, of intellectuals, of originality, even if this is viewed in a more limited way as only having a better memory, has little directly to do with the notion of wisdom but it has some overlap. A wise individual is definitely someone who knows about human affairs, or at least some segment of these affairs such as midwifery (*sage femme*, wise woman in French). Equally, the three kings in the story of the magi at the birth of Christ were wise men, not only in realizing the importance of that event, but also perhaps in the way they carried out their ritual and religious roles. Wisdom, knowledge, and common sense are all interrelated in complex ways.

### Oral Cultures

Unwritten languages do not lack abstraction, as has sometimes been suggested; language use itself depends on that very process. But in purely oral cultures words do tend to be more concrete in their reference, established as they are by face-to-face interaction. There seem to be relatively few nouns for qualities such as *wisdom* (nouns in any case being more common in written languages).

In an oral culture, one acquires wisdom and more generally knowledge through the aging process. The young can hardly be wiser or more knowledgeable than the old since they have had less experience, on which wisdom is based, and have acquired less knowledge, which in any case comes from the elders. There are no books that the young can read to acquire wisdom and learning independently of their seniors, who are largely members of the same family.

The discussion of wisdom ties up with the question of whether we find "intellectuals" in oral cultures. Clearly there are not only different levels of knowledge about cultural affairs, but also differences in the ability to create that knowledge. In his work on the cosmology of the Dogon of Mali, Marcel Griaule offers his *Conversations with Ogotemmêli* (1948) as if they presented a picture of the people's worldview. It is not altogether clear how much of this account comes from the actor's mouth and how much from the interpreter and the anthropologist. But what is apparent is that Ogotemmêli was an exceptional man who was capable of shaping his own view of the world. Exceptional, but not all that rare. In nonliterate societies, in the absence of a written text to which they can refer, many elaborate their own version in areas of what is often thought to be "common knowledge."

*Bagre.* The Bagre is an association found in various groups in northern Ghana to which the majority of the inhabitants belong in order to ward off disease. It consists of a series of initiatory performances over six months at which elders repeat a recitation in two parts, the White and the Black, that comprises an account of the ceremony itself and, in the Black, a version of how the people came to have the culture they do and the problems they face as humans. The extensive Bagre recitations of the LoDagaa, which display some features of later philosophic discourse (for example, an awareness of "the problem of evil"), do not refer to anything that has been translated as "wisdom." On the other hand, "wise" as an adjective is something used in the translations.

In the Bagre, the notion of *wisdom* is closely connected with age. In the Black Bagre, the "deepest" of the two parts, a repeated phrase has been translated as "little old woman"; in the other, White Bagre, a similar phrase has been translated as "wise old woman." The shift could be an error of transcription, but it is not all that important, since the notion of aged already implies *wisdom*. While you may find foolish old men or women, generally age proclaims wisdom.

For the LoDagaa, the capacity to act in a wise manner is helped by learning from one's elders, who are more experienced in the ways of the world. But it also comes from one's knowledge of "oral literature," with having a wide range of reference to common culture, starting with proverbs, running to folk tales (mainly told to children, often with a "moral" ending, though not of the Rudyard Kipling sort), but more thoroughly with the knowledge of the Bagre recitation. Not everyone belongs to the association whose members have this "myth" repeatedly recited to them, but the majority of men are initiated and so too are women, at least as far as the lower White Bagre, as a result of which restriction they lack some ritual knowledge, though they acquire this after menopause, when they count "as men." In this recitation, especially in the Black, many matters concerning the human experience are discussed, including the problem of evil. But the role of God as Creator and as Supreme Being is also frequently referred to, especially in what has elsewhere been called the First Bagre (Goody, 1972).

In the Bagre a great deal of attention is paid to learning and to knowledge that brings wisdom. In a way, the whole of the recitation is about how humans *learned* to do what they do, who taught them, who deceived them. The knowledge comes from supernatural agencies, ultimately from the creator god,

more immediately from the beings of the wild who can deceive. It was they who instructed our ancestor(s), who in turn passed the knowledge on to us, often in the course of recitals such as the Bagre. We have to *understand* (hear) this knowledge with the aid of our *sense* (*yen*). Wisdom consists in the judicious application of knowledge and experience to actual situations; it is based on a knowledge not so much of the supernatural as of the natural world, the world of man. While there is no general quality translatable as "wisdom," the wise application of knowledge both religious and secular does seem to be recognized by the actors. And part of the knowledge on which it is based does emerge from the recitation of the Bagre, which could be seen as a kind of "schooling" process—that is, it aims to transfer knowledge to the initiates. However, it is possible for elders of either sex to be perceived as wise without actually being a member. There are other ways of becoming a sound counselor and solving disputes in the course of ordinary life.

While wisdom is a feature of human relationships, sense is also an internal quality that can manifest itself in the young. In the Bagre, God's child is said to have

had much sense
in his head (Goody, 1972, First Black Bagre, l. 1480–1481)

At one point in the recitation, he has just been told by his father, who claims possession, that a woman passing by was not his mother:

"You have no mother."
The boy
laughed softly
and asked his father,
"Have you seen anyone
who has no mother
and yet has a father?" (l. 1438–1444)

While this child has sense, mainly it is the old who are wise. When the father and mother of God's child are quarrelling about the ownership, "the wise old woman"

laughed loudly
and said
that one child
is causing two people
to quarrel. (l. 864–868)

She takes the case before God himself (a bearded old man sitting on a cow's hide), who asks them to keep calm and "resolve" the problem by asking the mother and the father to urinate down a hollow stalk. This arbitrary task hardly matches the wisdom of Solomon in similar circumstances and in fact resolves nothing. The quarrel continues, but the problem of the duality of parenthood has been made explicit. This situation seems not atypical of oral cultures.

As is shown by the various published versions of the LoDagaa recitation of the Bagre, memory is rarely verbatim, and the performers are therefore "forced to be free," obliged to fill in the gaps and in many cases wanting to make their own contribution. Changes, often creative changes, are frequent. And there is considerable difference in that creative ability, which is recognized in the recitation itself in the injunction to new initiates to learn to recite. In the recorded versions, the First Bagre, both Black and White, is considerably more sophisticated, partly because the speaker was more of an "intellectual," a person who gave more thought to the nature of things, which is how later philosophers like to think of themselves.

## Written Cultures

In written cultures, wisdom is often associated with the elders and their experience. But it is largely expressed in their writings, in the wisdom literature of the ancient world, in Proverbs and the wisdom of Solomon in the Bible, the wisdom books of ancient Egypt, of the *Baghavad Gita* in Hinduism, and of the equivalents in Buddhist writings. Once again these texts are concerned with relations between humans rather than about relations of humans with gods. There are right and wrong ways of conducting the latter, but in general wisdom is not a notable feature. Wisdom literature, however, is concerned not with the more abstract questions of the ethical philosopher, whose activities are involved with general principles, but with the immediate problems of daily life.

Priests may be knowledgeable, even wise, about the ways of the gods, but there is no special wisdom automatically attached to being a priest, although they are often expected to conduct themselves in a restrained manner. Wisdom is more likely to be seen as the result of reading the works of secular authors, especially philosophers, interested in morality and the daily conduct of human affairs.

Societies with writing were heavily divided, until very recently, into those who could read and those who could not. The latter are sometimes spoken of as belonging to an oral culture; some would rather see them as attached to an oral tradition, one that has been significantly affected by the "high culture" of the written. An oral tradition, when combined with a written culture such as the biblical, has its own characteristics. The written culture may incorporate and transform earlier oral culture and myth and produce a "folk wisdom" that enters into oral repetition. That may consist in the appropriate reference to proverbs, such as "a stitch in time," but it also produces a kind of wisdom, more often associated with the country rather than the town, that draws on a wider experience not of books but of life as it is lived in the round. The paradigmatic example of such unlettered wisdom is provided by the peasant Karataev in Leo Tolstoy's *War and Peace,* whose "wisdom" is contrasted with the anxious cleverness of the aristocratic, cosmopolitan Pierre, a great reader.

The unlettered still had a wisdom to offer in a society many of whose activities were dominated by the written text. By contrast, in mixed societies too much reading is sometimes seen as leading to the loss of wits, of "sense," of contact with the real world. The text is distanced from human affairs and may prevent the profound contact that encourages wisdom, at least folk wisdom, and that comes from an unmediated experience of human affairs.

See also **Knowledge; Life Cycle: Elders/Old Age; Oral Traditions; Philosophy.**

BIBLIOGRAPHY

Goody, Jack. *The Domestication of the Savage Mind.* Cambridge, U.K.: Cambridge University Press, 1977.

———, ed. *The Myth of the Bagre.* Oxford: Clarendon, 1972.

Griaule, Marcel. *Conversations with Ogotemmêli: An Introduction to Dogon Religious Ideas.* Oxford: Oxford University Press, 1965.

Lévi-Strauss, Claude. *The Savage Mind.* Chicago: University of Chicago Press, 1966.

*Jack Goody*

**WITCHCRAFT.** The word *witchcraft* is used in many different ways. The word *witch* is derived from Old English *wicca* (masc., "wizard") and *wicce* (fem., "witch"). The term *wiccan* ("witchcraft") referred to human acts intended to influence nature, usually through the use of power unavailable to all human beings. This use of the word *witchcraft* is synonymous with the more general word *magic*. The acts associated with witchcraft were sometimes called spells (Old English "talk, tale"). The person could conduct these acts for his or her benefit, or for others who did not have access to the necessary power. In contemporary academic work and in popular culture, however, it is still generally assumed that the influence or change resulting from the act is harmful. With these negative associations, *witchcraft* is also used for diabolism, acts performed with the assistance of the devil. Other acts, those that attempt to influence nature in a beneficial way, are usually not considered. *Witchcraft* also refers to ideas and practices believed to influence nature that emerged in the twentieth century, largely in Europe and North America, sometimes referred to as neo-paganism. This use of *witchcraft* is similar to the one derived from the Old English *wiccan.*

*Witchcraft* is the term most commonly used in the social science literature, and the practices it refers to can be found in all societies. Over the years there has been some debate about the similarities and differences between the practices of witchcraft and sorcery, and in the social sciences there are several traditions. Studies conducted in Asia tend to use the term *sorcery* for the practices referred to by *magic,* while studies in South America use *shamanism* in a similar way. Studies in Africa use both *sorcery* and *witchcraft,* and the use of both terms usually assumes that the magical acts are intended to be harmful.

In the twentieth century, there were debates about whether different terms should be applied to rituals that were conducted with and without the assistance of spirits. There were also discussions about distinguishing between practitioners whose power was innate and those who learned the knowledge and skills from existing practitioners. In the social sciences, it is generally assumed that both *witchcraft* and *sorcery* can be used interchangeably, but it is important for the scholar to explain the particular way each term is being used, as well as its relationship to local terms.

## The Social and Political History of Witchcraft in Europe

The ancient Greeks made distinctions among forms of magic, although they differ from the categories found in contemporary thought. The Greeks considered all magic to be performed with the assistance of spirit entities called *diamones* ("demons") that could be either harmful or helpful. During the Hellenistic period, a new belief emerged that developed the notion that evil spirits were led by Satan. Christians then began to divide the *diamones* into good angels and harmful demons. People involved in magic were thought to use the power of demons. During the Renaissance, this idea expanded into a full-fledged belief in diabolical witchcraft. The idea of the devil in Christianity overshadowed all other ideas concerning magic, and the fear of witchcraft took a central place in the religious imagination.

During the period of the European witch craze (1450–1700), many beliefs and practices rooted in paganism and folklore came to be associated with influences from the devil. The idea of diabolical witchcraft also came to be applied to medieval heretics, who were imagined to be involved in a pact with witches and with Satan himself. In Spain and its colonies, the Inquisition, which provided a legal forum for persecuting those identified as witches and heretics, further collapsed the concepts of magic and diabolical witchcraft. Gradually, any form of magic came to be viewed in Europe as diabolical witchcraft.

During the witch craze, patterns in accusation show that the accused generally had a low social status, already had been faulted for other transgressions, and exhibited difficult personality traits. Many were practitioners of medicine, and a disproportionately large number were women, as discussed below. Although there were no witch hunts in Europe during the eighteenth and nineteenth centuries, many colonial societies developed new versions of witchcraft laws that were used to stigmatize the religious ideas and practices of colonized peoples.

## The Functions of Witchcraft

In the 1940s and 1950s sociologists and anthropologists explored the many positive functions of witchcraft and illustrated them with detailed studies. As E. E. Evans-Pritchard (1902–1973) observed in his classic study of the belief in witches in an African society, the Azande, witchcraft can be understood as an explanation for unfortunate events. That explanation enabled people to maintain a sense of control over their lives and feel that they understood their world. Understandings about witchcraft could also help to define values and moral standards in a society.

The ideas that a society creates about witches can be seen to support norms and values in that society, and, when analyzed along with a structural model of the society, can also provide insights into the organization of the culture and society. Ideas about the negative characteristics of the witch can be a way to guide behavior, as functionalist anthropologists argued in a series of studies showing that the belief in witchcraft served as a social control mechanism. In his work on the Navajo, Clyde Kluckhorn found that the fear of becoming the victim of witchcraft encouraged them to cooperate, share resources, and minimize public displays of anger. The socially permitted form of aggression toward the witch allowed other hostilities to be displaced onto an individual, a useful outlet in situations where in-group hostilities could threaten the survival of the group or damage people's abilities to act collectively.

The central problem with studies that assumed a cohesive function for witchcraft was that, like other functional analyses, the theory could not be proved or falsified. Some sociologists and anthropologists such as Max Marwick were more interested in analyzing the social basis of witchcraft accusations and the life conditions that placed particular strain on these relationships. Against the dominant functionalist trend, Robert Murphy proposed that beliefs about witchcraft and accusations could have disruptive effects. Working with the Mundurucú in Brazil, he found that witchcraft accusations, combined with a rubber economic boom, created group divisions and family migration, which eventually supported a more dispersed settlement pattern. From her comparative analysis of African Studies, Mary Douglas (1963) came to a similar conclusion.

It has been observed that people in relatively marginal positions in society might be able to use witchcraft, or the threat of witchcraft, as a form of social power. The relatively weak could then influence people with more power or wealth to redistribute it and minimize some of the inequalities in the society. In his study of the Maka in Cameroon, Peter Geschiere shows that witchcraft can work both to promote accumulation and leveling.

## Symbolic and Ideological Aspects of Witchcraft

Largely through the influence of Claude Lévi-Strauss's structuralist approach, anthropologists have placed great emphasis on the position of witches in symbolic systems. In ethnographic studies, it has often been observed that witches are associated with the left hand and with wild or nondomestic realms, and are placed in opposition to the moral standards of a society. Actors' understandings of witchcraft are extremely important, although most anthropologists are cautious in interpreting these exegeses, placing them within more comprehensive analyses that also examine symbolic meanings more generally, as well as their relationship to the social, political, and economic processes in the society. This approach is best shown in the work of Bruce Knauft in New Guinea.

Scholarship has also explored the role of witchcraft beliefs in diverting people's attention from economic and political explanations for untoward events. This kind of argument, similar to Karl Marx's (1818–1883) understanding of ideology, claims that witchcraft as a form of explanation functions to maintain the existing sociopolitical structure of a society. According to George Bond, witchcraft explanations in Muyombe, Zambia, work to obfuscate the changing labor and property relationships among villagers. While their participation in accusations emphasizes their common membership in the community, it deemphasizes their increasingly unequal economic status.

## Witchcraft and Gender Relations

Scholarly works from many different societies and time periods have shown that witch-finding rituals, popularly called witch hunts, are used by more powerful segments of a society to persecute people who are opponents or who present a threat to established power. Christina Larner shows that in sixteenth- and seventeenth-century England the church and state entered new forms of cooperation and identification that especially targeted women as witches. Her explanation is that men identified themselves as the proper professional group to offer healing services, and women were persecuted because their healing traditions competed with this new system.

It is important to understand that the disproportionate number of women targeted by European and American witchcraft accusations should not be taken to mean that this focus is a universal. In some societies, men are more commonly accused of witchcraft and represent that society's ideal witch. Diane Ciekawy (1999) shows that among Mijikenda in Kenya witchcraft accusations are primarily directed toward men. In her analysis of the witchcraft accusation process, women collect evidence and shape ideas about culpability in the homestead, thereby wielding a great deal of power. The work of Rosalind Shaw with Temne women in Sierra Leone illustrates the ways that women are active agents in diviner consultations. She shows how women can select from diviner consultations the explanations for their problems that they most favor. These chosen explanations can resist patriarchal explanations that disadvantage them or create less favorable power relations.

## Witchcraft: Questions of Translation and Meaning

Scholars continue to debate the question of how well scholarly concepts like witchcraft convey the meanings of local terms, and how much a term like *witchcraft* can reduce the diversity and complexity of ideas and actions to which it is applied. Regarding the history of scholarship around the terms *magic, sorcery,* and *witchcraft,* we see that, although magic can be indigenously conceived as having both harmful and helpful potentials, the latter can be deemphasized by scholars who are more interested in its harmful potential. While these questions are not entirely new—both Victor Turner and Malcolm Crick encouraged anthropologists to use local terms and their specific meanings as much as possible in their work—current scholarship is more sensitive to the possibility of misrepresenting the cultures it attempts to describe. In view of the political history of witch hunts in Europe, and the ways non-Christian religious ideas and practices were demonized, it is possible to ask if a similar process continues in the structure of contemporary academic discourse.

Some scholars regard witchcraft as a discourse of power that requires knowledge about the historical and ethnographic conditions that shape understandings about it. This might entail a more careful analysis of the semantic range of terms for magic and harmful magic, with an attempt to separate local discourses from wider regional or national ones. Ciekawy (1998) does this in her analysis of the application of the Witchcraft Act in colonial and postcolonial coastal Kenya. She describes different words that Mijikenda people use for harmful magic: *utsai* is a Kimijikenda term, the kiSwahili words are *uchawi* and *ulozi,* and some people use *witchcraft.* Mijikenda employ these terms in different contexts. She concludes that, for conceptual and analytical purposes, the terms must be distinguished because *utsai* refers to a discourse on harmful magic that is

created and operates within local social and political settings largely under the control of Mijikenda who use them, while *witchcraft* is best understood as a technology of power that emerged under European colonialism, supported largely through discourses of mission Christianity and colonial law and administration.

## Witchcraft as a Discourse of Power

Jeanne Favret-Saada's study of witchcraft in the Bocage of western France examines the power of words used by people to talk about witchcraft. She distinguishes this approach to witchcraft as power from its more conventional use in anthropology as knowledge or information, pointing out that in the Bocage there is no neutral position that a person can have when it concerns such socially and politically powerful speech. She also questions the way academics have viewed witchcraft as the backward and untrue beliefs of people who do not use academic forms of reasoning. This is consistent with the general approach used to study many forms of magic offered by Arens and Karp. Rather than use the words *magic* and *witchcraft,* they advocate the use of the terms *transformational capacity* and *power.*

## The Modernity of Witchcraft

Contemporary scholarly work indicates that the study of witchcraft is as relevant today as it has been in the past. Ideas about witchcraft address new circumstances and are very much a part of people's understanding of how their lives are connected to events and processes both near and far. It is common for witchcraft discourses to relate to the countryside, town, state, and world. Few current studies see witchcraft only as a social construction; it is also understood to be a concept that meaningfully provides people with a representation of the complexity of the order in which they live, including power and inequality, individual and collective interests, and resources and their allocation. Witchcraft addresses issues of globalization and transformations within the state, and continues to explain events and the mechanics of their integration into daily life. It is also important to remember that the constructions of witchcraft can be powerful realities, and have the ability to maintain or transform social relationships.

*See also* **Anthropology; Astrology: Overview; Demonology; Evil; Gender Studies: Anthropology; Heresy and Apostasy; Magic; Miracles; Nature; Superstition; Witchcraft, African Studies of.**

### BIBLIOGRAPHY

Arens, W., and Ivan Karp. *Creativity of Power: Cosmology and Action in African Societies.* Washington, D.C.: Smithsonian Institution Press, 1989.

Bond, George. "Ancestors and Protestants: Religious Coexistence in the Social Field of a Zambian Community." *American Ethnologist* 14, no. 8 (1986): 55–72.

Boyer, Paul S., and Stephen Nissenbaum. *Salem Possessed: The Social Origins of Witchcraft.* Cambridge, Mass.: Harvard University Press, 1974.

Caro Baroja, Julio. *The World of the Witches.* Translated by O. N. V. Glendinning. Chicago: University of Chicago Press, 1964.

Ciekawy, Diane. "Witchcraft and Statecraft: Five Technologies of Power in Colonial and Postcolonial Coastal Kenya." *African Studies Review* 41, no. 3 (1998): 119–141.

———. "Women's 'Work' and the Construction of Witchcraft Accusation in Coastal Kenya." *Women's Studies International Forum* 22, no. 2 (1999): 225–235.

Cohn, Norman R. C. *Europe's Inner Demons: The Demonization of Christians in Medieval Christendom.* Chicago: University of Chicago Press, 1993.

Crick, Malcolm. *Explorations in Language and Meaning: Towards a Semantic Anthropology.* New York: Wiley, 1976.

Demos, John. *Entertaining Satan: Witchcraft and the Culture of Early New England.* New York: Oxford University Press, 1982.

Evans-Pritchard, E. E. *Witchcraft, Oracles, and Magic among the Azande.* Oxford: Clarendon, 1937.

Favret-Saada, Jeanne. *Deadly Words: Witchcraft in the Bocage.* Translated by Catherine Cullen. New York: Cambridge University Press, 1980.

Geschiere, Peter. *The Modernity of Witchcraft: Politics and the Occult in Postcolonial Africa.* Charlottesville: University Press of Virginia, 1997.

Kluckhohn, Clyde. *Navaho Witchcraft.* Boston: Beacon, 1962. Originally published in 1944.

Knauft, Bruce M. *Good Company and Violence: Sorcery and Social Action in a Lowland New Guinea Society.* Berkeley: University of California Press, 1985.

Larner, Christina. *Witchcraft and Religion: The Politics of Popular Belief.* Oxford: Blackwell, 1984.

Macfarlane, Alan. *Witchcraft in Tudor and Stuart England: A Regional and Comparative Study.* London: Routledge and Kegan Paul, 1970.

Mair, Lucy P. *Witchcraft.* New York: McGraw-Hill, 1969.

Marwick, Max. *Sorcery in Its Social Setting.* Manchester, U.K.: Manchester University Press, 1965.

Middleton, John. *Lugbara Religion: Ritual and Authority among an East African People.* London: Oxford University Press, 1960.

Murphy, Robert F. *Mundurucú Religion.* Berkeley: University of California Press, 1958.

Russell, Jeffrey B. *A History of Witchcraft: Sorcerers, Heretics, and Pagans.* London: Thames and Hudson, 1980.

Shaw, Rosalind. "Gender and the Structuring of Reality in Temne Divination: An Interactive Study." *Africa* 53, no. 3 (1985): 286–303.

Trevor-Roper, Hugh R. *The European Witch-Craze of the Sixteenth and Seventeenth Centuries, and Other Essays.* New York: Harper and Row, 1969.

Turner, Victor. *The Forest of Symbols: Aspects of Ndembu Ritual.* Ithaca, N.Y.: Cornell University Press, 1967.

*Diane Ciekawy*

# WITCHCRAFT, AFRICAN STUDIES OF.

In contemporary scholarly and popular discourse, the term *witchcraft* refers to a wide variety of ideas, practices, and institutions. Among most social science scholars of Africa, particularly anthropologists, *witchcraft* is defined as an act of magic that results in harming a person or aspects of the material world on which he or she depends. In this context, *witchcraft* and *magic* are used interchangeably; it is assumed that magic used for harm and magic used for healing, or enhancement, can be distinguished, either conceptually or in practice.

The work of anthropologists from the 1930s on made the greatest contributions to the study of social and political institutions in African societies, as well as their systems of belief and logic. Their methodological and theoretical achievements influenced many disciplines in Western scholarship, notably history and philosophy. During the past forty years, witchcraft has occupied a controversial place in African Studies scholarship. As a general term that describes the harmful use of magic, *witchcraft* is not specific with respect to the societies or peoples who use it. Witchcraft and magic exist in all societies, but, as many scholars have shown, in the history of Western thought and popular culture, and in much of contemporary European-American scholarship, witchcraft has been positioned as a backward or erroneous system of thought. In the study of African religions, it is also interesting to note that Western scholarship has given it great prominence. As noted by John Mbiti in *African Religions and Philosophies,* Western scholarship has often presented witchcraft ideas out of context and emphasized their association with harm, which has resulted in a fundamental misrepresentation of African religions.

One of the central achievements of E. E. Evans-Pritchard's (1902–1973) work was to show that witchcraft among the Azande provided explanations for everyday events and presented a theory of causality. From a contemporary critical perspective, however, it can be faulted for making the assumption that it did not have the same explanatory power as scientific modes of thought and reasoning. African philosophy has been at the forefront of critical assessment of the biases of Western scholarship and the quest to develop discourses and ways of re-representing African religious life.

The study of witchcraft now involves a broader range of scholars who have extended debates and included in their studies many new areas of interest. Some of these concern questions of representation and meaning and new questions about the ability of disciplinary concepts to address local knowledge and experience.

## Early Anthropological Contributions

Witchcraft serves many different social functions. In ethnographic studies of peoples around the world, anthropologists have detailed many of the positive social functions of witchcraft. As popularized in Evans-Pritchard's work, witchcraft can be understood as an explanation for misfortune, which might function to provide people with a sense of control over their own lives and the ability to understand forces in their world. These could be called empowering functions of witchcraft. Understandings about witchcraft can be used to define values and moral standards in a society, thus contributing to a society's definition of itself or distinction from other groups. Also, people who are in relatively weak and marginal positions in society might be able to use witchcraft, or the threat of witchcraft, as a form of power. In this way, the ideas and practices of witchcraft could work to mediate social, political, or economic inequalities.

Witchcraft also serves more overtly political functions. The complex of ideas associated with witchcraft can involve rituals that identify people responsible for practicing witchcraft. Early anthropological works on African societies noted the existence of movements against witchcraft, sometimes known as anti-witchcraft movements or witchcraft eradication movements, that borrowed from these cultural institutions. Audry Richards's important essay on a witch-finding movement in Zambia shows how the movement drew from responses to the influences of colonialism, yet also drew from rituals that are part of a common complex in central African societies.

## Politics of Witchcraft: Local and Global

Building on anthropological methods for studying the politics of witchcraft, several important works demonstrate relationships between local and global worlds in the construction of witchcraft ideas and practices. Peter Geschiere's *The Modernity of Witchcraft* shows how the many different fields of everyday experience that shape witchcraft for the Maka in Cameroon are influenced by regional, national, and global forces. In her study of legal and administrative institutions in Kenya, Diane Ciekawy (1998) shows how local religious practice is both constrained and encouraged to develop in ways that further strengthen the power of state institutions. Scholars also acknowledge the challenge of segregating local discourses concerning magical harm from wider regional or national ones, particularly when the English term *witchcraft* is used in African communities.

## Philosophical Approaches to the Study of Witchcraft

African philosophy has provided some of the most critical assessments of Western scholarly traditions. In *The Invention of Africa*, V. Y. Mudimbe shows how concepts and terms used in the study of African religion, including witchcraft, developed through colonial practices and Western prejudices about African peoples and their cultures. African philosophy has also engaged in discussion about the importance of acknowledging the role of individual philosophers in the creation of knowledge (Hallen and Sodipo; Karp and Masolo).

## Moral and Ethical Relevance

Scholars are now more interested in exploring the moral and ethical questions that witchcraft presents. Elias Bongmba is also attentive to the ways that witchcraft discourse contributes to problems within African societies. Bongmba, himself from Wimbum society, uses his experience as well as fieldwork. Drawing on notions of intersubjectivity from philosophy, he examines notions of *tfu*, used by Wimbum in Cameroon. He shows that it is part of a discourse of power that includes both helpful and harmful aspects, and concludes that it gives people an opportunity to engage in face-to-face encounters. In a similar way, Ciekawy examines Mijikenda interpretations of the magical practice of *utsai*. She argues that it is a way for people to conceptualize inequality and the exploitation of one human being by another, which makes it particularly useful for comprehending the world and considering the ethical choices available to human beings.

## Modernity

Contemporary ideas of witchcraft provide an idiom for expressing individualism, innovation, and human agency that are

much a part of modern life. During this period of rapid globalization and incorporation within the postcolonial state, ideas of witchcraft have been used by African peoples as frameworks of interpretation. As interpretive constructs, they also help to shape the political world, and they are, therefore, powerful forces that can both help to maintain or transform social and political worlds.

## Conclusions

In the study of witchcraft in African societies, the concern with systems of logic and thought that has long engaged anthropology and philosophy continues. More recently, there has been a focus on indigenous systems of knowledge and hermeneutical traditions. More contemporary scholars are interested in forms of interpretation, skepticism, and cultural critique that come from within local thought traditions. Scholarship is now, more than ever before, poised to counter the academic practice of maintaining distinctions in forms of thought from Western and African societies.

*See also* **Anthropology; Demonology; Ethnography; Eurocentrism; Magic; Neocolonialism; Philosophies: African; Religion: Africa; Subjectivism; Superstition; Witchcraft.**

**BIBLIOGRAPHY**

Austen, Ralph A. "The Moral Economy of Witchcraft: An Essay in Comparative History." In *Modernity and Its Malcontents: Ritual and Power in Postcolonial Africa,* edited by Jean Comaroff and John Comaroff, 89–110. Chicago: University of Chicago Press, 1993.

Bockie, Simon. *Death and the Invisible Powers: The World of Kongo Belief.* Bloomington: Indiana University Press, 1993.

Bond, George C. "Religion, Ideology, and Property in Northern Zambia." In *Studies in Power and Class in Africa,* edited by Irving L. Markovitz, 70–188. London: Oxford University Press, 1987.

Bongmba, Elias. *African Witchcraft and Otherness: A Philosophical and Theological Critique of Intersubjective Relations.* Charlottesville: University of Virginia Press, 2001.

Ciekawy, Diane. "Policing Religious Practice in Contemporary Coastal Kenya." *Political and Legal Anthropology Review* 20, no. 1 (1997): 62–72.

———. "*Utsai* as Ethical Discourse: A Critique of Power from Mijikenda in Coastal Kenya." In *Dialogues of Witchcraft: Anthropological and Philosophical Exchanges,* edited by George C. Bond and Diane Ciekawy, 158–189. Athens: University of Ohio Press, 1991.

———. "Witchcraft in Statecraft: Five Technologies of Power in Colonial and Postcolonial Coastal Kenya." *African Studies Review* 41, no. 3 (1998): 119–141.

de Boeck, Filip. "Beyond the Grave: History, Memory, and Death in Postcolonial Congo/Zaire." In *Memory and the Postcolony: African Anthropology and the Critique of Power,* edited by Richard Werbner, 21–57. London: Zed, 1998.

Devisch, René. *Weaving the Threads of Life: The Khita Gyn-Eco-Logical Healing Cult among the Yaka.* Chicago: University of Chicago Press, 1993.

Evans-Pritchard, E. E. *Witchcraft, Oracles, and Magic among the Azande.* Oxford: Clarendon, 1937.

Fisiy, Cyprian F., and Peter Geschiere. "Judges and Witches, or How Is the State to Deal with Witchcraft? Examples from

Southeastern Cameroon." *Cahiers d'études africaines* 118 (1990): 135–156.

Fisiy, Cyprian F., and Michael Rowlands. "Sorcery and Law in Modern Cameroon." *Culture and History* 6 (1990): 63–84.

Geschiere, Peter. "Globalization and the Power of Indeterminate Meaning: Witchcraft and Spirit Cults in Africa and East Asia." *Development and Change* 29 (1998): 811–837.

———. *The Modernity of Witchcraft: Politics and the Occult in Post-colonial Africa.* Charlottesville: University of Virginia Press, 1997.

Hallen, Barry, and J. Olubi Sodipo. *Knowledge, Belief, and Witchcraft: Analytic Experiments in African Philosophy.* London: Ethnographica, 1986.

Heald, Suzanne. "Witches and Thieves: Deviant Motivations in Gisu Society." *Man* 21, no. 1 (1986): 65–78.

Jackson, Michael. *Allegories of the Wilderness: Ethics and Ambiguity in Kuranko Narratives.* Bloomington: Indiana University Press, 1982.

Karp, Ivan, and D. A. Masolo. "Introduction." In their *African Philosophy as Cultural Inquiry,* 1–18. Bloomington: Indiana University Press, 2000.

Lévi-Strauss, Claude. *The Savage Mind.* London: Weidenfeld and Nicolson, 1966.

Marwick, Max. "Another Modern Anti-Witchcraft Movement in East Central Africa." *Africa* 20, no. 2 (1950): 100–112.

Marwick, Max. *Sorcery and Its Social Setting: A Study of the Northern Rhodesian Cewa.* Manchester, U.K.: Manchester University Press, 1965.

Mbiti, John S. *African Religions and Philosophy.* New York: Doubleday, 1970.

Meyer, Birgit. *Translating the Devil: Religion and Modernity among the Ewe in Ghana.* Trenton, N.J.: Africa World Press, 1999.

Mudimbe, V. Y. *The Idea of Africa.* Bloomington: Indiana University Press, 1994.

Niehaus, Isak. *Witchcraft, Power, and Politics: Exploring the Occult in the South African Lowveld.* Sterling, Va.: Pluto, 2001.

Piot, Charles. *Remotely Global: Village Modernity in West Africa.* Chicago: University of Chicago Press, 1999.

Richards, Audry. "A Modern Movement of Witch-Finders." *Africa* 8, no. 4 (1935): 448–461.

Shaw, Rosalind. *Memories of the Slave Trade: Ritual and the Historical Imagination in Sierra Leone.* Chicago: University of Chicago Press, 2002.

*Diane Ciekawy*

**WOMANISM.** The term *womanist* first appeared in Alice Walker's *In Search of Our Mothers' Gardens: Womanist Prose* (1983), in which the author attributed the word's origin to

the black folk expression of mothers to female children, 'You acting womanish,' i.e. like a woman . . . usually referring to outrageous, audacious, courageous, or *willful* behavior. Wanting to know more and in greater depth than is considered 'good' for one . . . [A womanist is also] a woman who loves other women sexually and/or nonsexually. Appreciates and prefers women's culture . . . and women's strength . . . committed to survival and wholeness of entire people, male and female. Not a separatist . . . Womanist is to feminist as purple is to lavender. (pp. xi–xii)

Although Walker states that a womanist is a black feminist or feminist of color, she insists that a black feminist as womanist talks back to feminism, brings new demands and different perspectives to feminism, and compels the expansion of feminist horizons in theory and practice.

The introduction of "womanism" in the feminist lexicon in the early 1980s marks a historic moment in feminist engagement in the United States. The late 1970s and the 1980s witnessed an internal insurgency in feminism led by women of color who participated in fighting vigorously against sexual politics of the previous decade only to be confronted by the feminist politics of exclusion a decade later. Excluded from and alienated by feminist theorizing and thinking, women of color insisted that feminism must account for different subjectivities and locations in its analysis of women, thus bringing into focus the issue of difference, particularly with regard to race and class.

If feminism were not able to fully account for the experiences of black women, it would be necessary, then, to find other terminologies that could carry the weight of those experiences. It is in this regard that Alice Walker's "womanism" intervenes to make an important contribution. As Walker noted in the *New York Times Magazine* in 1984, "I don't choose womanism because it is 'better' than feminism . . . I choose it because I prefer the sound, the feel, the fit of it; because I cherish the spirit of the women (like Sojourner) the word calls to mind, and because I share the old ethnic-American habit of offering society a new word when the old word it is using fails to describe behavior and change that only a new word can help it more fully see" (p. 94). In other words, feminism needed a new word that would capture its complexity and fullness. Despite Walker's claims to the contrary, she suggests in her definitions of womanism (e.g., "womanist is to feminism as purple is to lavender") that the womanist/black woman is stronger and superior to the feminist/white woman.

Walker's construction of womanism and the different meanings she invests in it is an attempt to situate the black woman in history and culture and at the same time rescue her from the negative and inaccurate stereotypes that mask her in American society. First, Walker inscribes the black woman as a knowing/thinking subject who is always in pursuit of knowledge, "wanting to know more and in greater depth than is considered 'good' for one," thus, interrogating the epistemological exclusions she endures in intellectual life in general and feminist scholarship in particular. Second, she highlights the black woman's agency, strength, capability, and independence. Opposed to the gender separatism that bedevils feminism, womanism presents an alternative for black women by framing their survival in the context of the survival of their community where the fate of women and that of men are inextricably linked. As Patricia Hill Collins aptly notes, "many black women view feminism as a movement that at best, is exclusively for women, and, at worst, dedicated to attacking or eliminating men . . . Womanism seemingly supplies a way for black women to address gender-oppression without attacking black men" (p. 11).

In 1993 the word *womanism* with the meanings Alice Walker bestowed on it was added to *The American Heritage*

*Dictionary.* The concept has had a profound influence in the formulation of theories and analytical frameworks in women/gender studies, religious studies, black studies, and literary studies. Because of the linking of black women and spirituality in Walker's project, many African-American female theologians have incorporated womanist perspectives in their work. Drawing on African-American history in general and the black church in particular, black womanist theologians interrogate the subordination of women and assume a leadership role in reconstructing knowledge about women. Prominent black womanist theologians and scholars of religion—such as Cheryl Townsend Gilkes, Katie Geneva Cannon, Delores S. Williams, Emilie Maureen Townes, and Marcia Y. Riggs—bring womanist perspectives to bear on their black church, canon formation, social equality, black women's club movement of the nineteenth century, race, gender, class, and social justice. The impact of womanism goes beyond the United States to Africa where many women scholars and literary critics (Chikwenye Okonjo Ogunyemi, Tuzyline Jita Allan, and Mary Modupe Kolawole, in particular) have embraced it as an analytical tool.

Alice Walker's womanism has also generated debates and controversies. Prominent among those who challenge the terminology's appropriateness for framing and explaining the lives of women of African descent is Clenora Hudson-Weems, who proposes an alternative terminology—*Africana womanism*—that is different from Black feminism, African feminism, and Walker's womanism. Many of the debates and controversies about womanism focus on the differences and tension between womanism and black feminism. Patricia Hill Collins offers an excellent critique of both womanism and black feminism. Hill Collins notes that the debate about whether to label black women's standpoint womanist or black feminist is indicative of the diversity among black women. According to Hill Collins, "Walker's definition thus manages to invoke three important yet contradictory philosophies that frame black social and political thought, namely, black nationalism via her claims of black women's moral and epistemological superiority via suffering under racial and gender oppression, pluralism via cultural integrity provided by the metaphor of the garden, and integration/assimilation via her claims that black women are 'traditionally universalist'" (p. 11). While weaving the separatism and black moral superiority of the black nationalist philosophy, the pluralism of the black empowerment variant, and the interrogation of white feminism, womanism seeks to give a voice, a standpoint to black women but fails to adequately take into account the heterogeneity of women of African descent with their different histories and realities.

*See also* **Feminism: Africa and African Diaspora; Philosophies: African; Women's History: Africa.**

**BIBLIOGRAPHY**

Allan, Tuzyline Jita. *Womanist and Feminist Aesthetic Comparative Review.* Athens: Ohio University Press, 1995.
Cannon, Katie Geneva. *Black Womanist Ethics.* Atlanta: Scholars Press, 1988.
Collins, Patricia Hill. "What's in a Name? Womanism, Black Feminism, and Beyond." *The Black Scholar* 26, no. 1 (1996): 9–17.
Gilkes, Cheryl Townsend. *"If It Wasn't for Women": Black Women's Experience and Womanist Culture in Church and Community.* Maryknoll, N.Y.: Orbis Books, 2001.
Hudson-Weems, Clenora. "African Womanism." In *Sisterhood, Feminisms, and Power: From Africa to the Diaspora,* edited by Obioma Nnaemeka. Trenton, N.J.: Africa World Press, 1998.
———. *African Womanism: Reclaiming Ourselves.* Detroit: Bedford Press, 1993.
Kolawole, Mary Ebun Modupe. *Womanism and African Consciousness.* Trenton, N.J.: Africa World Press, 1997.
Ogunyemi, Chikwenye Okonjo. "Womanism: The Dynamics of the Contemporary Black Female Novel in English." *Signs: Journal of Women in Culture and Society* 11, no. 1 (1985): 63–80.
Riggs, Marcia Y. *Awake, Arise, and Act: A Womanist Call for Black Liberation.* Cleveland, Ohio: Pilgrim Press, 1994.
Sanders, Cheryl J., ed. *Living the Intersection: Womanism and Afrocentrism in Theology.* Minneapolis, Minn.: Fortress Press, 1995.
Townes, Emilie Maureen. *Womanist Justice, Womanist Hope.* Atlanta, Ga.: Scholars Press, 1993.
Townes, Emilie Maureen, ed. *Embracing the Spirit: Womanist Perspectives on Hope, Salvation, and Transformation.* Maryknoll, N.Y.: Orbis Books, 1997.
Townes, Emilie Maureen, ed. *A Troubling in My Soul: Womanist Perspectives on Evil and Suffering.* Maryknoll, N.Y.: Orbis Books, 1993.
Walker, Alice. "The Black Woman's Story." *New York Times Sunday Magazine,* February 12, 1984, p. 94.
———. *In Search of Our Mothers' Gardens: Womanist Prose.* San Diego, Calif.: Harcourt Brace Jovanovich, 1983.
Williams, Delores S. *Sisters in the Wilderness: The Challenge of Womanist God-Talk.* Maryknoll, N.Y.: Orbis Books, 1993.
Williams, Sherley Ann. "Some Implications of Womanist Theory." In *Reading Black, Reading Feminist: A Critical Anthology,* edited by Henry Louis Gates, Jr., 68–75. New York: Meridian, 1990.

*Obioma Nnaemeka*

# WOMEN AND FEMININITY IN U.S. POPULAR CULTURE.

Before the women's movement and deconstruction, the term *femininity* was understood as the opposite of the more obvious *masculinity.* Femininity represented those traits, characteristics, behaviors, or thought patterns not associated with a given society's expectations of men. Until the cultural upheaval of the late 1960s in the United States and elsewhere, the sweetly patient "angel of the house" persisted as the womanly ideal. Women learned to be feminine "in the image that suited the masculine desires" (quoted in Costa, p. 222), an image that included deference, respect, and obedience to males. In compensation, the woman held the passive power of the dispossessed. Submissive, soft-voiced, empathic, and maternal, the feminine woman would be willing to subordinate her own needs in order to better please others.

Femininity as a principle or "exquisite esthetic," as Susan Brownmiller puts it in *Femininity* (1984), "pleases men because it makes them appear more masculine by contrast . . . conferring an extra portion of unearned gender distinction on men, an unchallenged space in which to breathe freely and feel stronger, wiser, more competent, is femininity's special gift" (p. 16). This gift, however, costs the giver. Girls and young women learn they must adhere to standards of comportment, physical presentation, and appearance according to the demands and currency of their respective cultures and classes or face disapproval, even social failure, ostracism, rejection.

In a postbinary world, however, definitions of femininity as well as masculinity have blurred. Definitions of femininity are no longer standardized and are therefore seemingly open, writes Maggie Mulqueen in *On Our Own Terms*. They arise "*only* from the culture, not from theory. . . . In reality, though, the cultural prescriptions about femininity (and masculinity) are very narrow and influential" (p. 13). These influential prescriptions consist of social expectations and the pressure to conform, particularly in adolescence. A girl's sexual awakening and turbulent maturation eventually steer her toward pleasing boys and winning admiration, envy, and acceptance from her peers.

## Beauty and Class

In addition, the reigning elements of femininity and their effect on women resonate according to one's class and race, criteria that can locate a woman along the continuum of behavior and attractiveness. Class is a fluid or changeable category; race is generally not, though beauty treatments can "standardize" ethnic features like hair color and texture (see below) or influence acceptable limits of body size.

Related to class are the awareness of and access to proper nutrition as well as the availability of leisure time for exercise, factors associated with the maintenance of lean body mass. The proportion of lean mass to body fat contributes to the impression of overall girth and therefore health. Few men, young or old, strive to be gaunt, and fewer men than women are dissatisfied with their bodies even if they are somewhat overweight. Instead, they value size especially if the bulk is muscle rather than fat. Men's "perceptions serve to keep them satisfied with their bodies, whereas women's serve to keep them dissatisfied," writes Sarah Grogan (pp. 144–145). American women of any age, however, find thinness the only tolerable size, despite evidence that men prefer somewhat rounder female bodies than women think they do.

Preferred body size and proportion reflect class-related tastes or expectations. Researchers have suggested that different social classes have distinct ideas of attractiveness, and magazines gear to these readers. The fleshiness of magazine models varies according to the social class of the targeted audience, be it male or female. Magazines for upwardly mobile homemakers have trim but not skinny models. Family-oriented magazines present more modest images typical of pleasant-looking housewives. So-called pulp magazines feature curvier bodies: "the lower the social class ranking of the magazine the bigger the chest and hip measurements of the models," observes Nora Scott Kinzer (p. 165). Magazine models are rarely if ever overweight; in fact, compared with their counterparts from the 1950s, they generally weigh less and have smaller measurements.

## Viewing and Being Seen

Because she frequently feels on display, a woman monitors her physical appearance in mirrors, in store windows, and in the eyes and expressions of people who see her. Self-criticism originates not only in the woman herself but also from the internalized voice of male culture and the parents who teach her how to dress and present herself. John Berger's *Ways of Seeing* (1972) articulates the concepts of viewer and viewed by noting that the observer is generally male and the object observed, female. Though intended as an assessment of the subject in Western European painting, Berger's remarks apply equally to contemporary representations of women in the media: "Women watch themselves being looked at. . . . The surveyor of woman in herself is male: the surveyed female" (p. 47).

Women internalize femininity's burden of self-monitoring along with this same male gaze as they compare themselves, usually unfavorably, with the ideal face and body that they imagine the male conjures up in his mind's eye. In her article "The Persistence of Vision," Donna Haraway rejects the power that the male gaze assumes as it "mythically inscribes all the marked [e.g., female] bodies, that makes the unmarked category claim the power to see and not be seen, to represent while escaping representation. This gaze signifies the unmarked positions of Man and White" (quoted in Conboy, Medina, and Stanbury, p. 282). White males, the cliché goes, see a generic human being when they view themselves in the mirror; everyone else sees the markings of gender, race, or both.

## Femininity, Attractiveness, and Science

Scientifically measurable differences in male and female prenatal hormone levels and in brain development, among other areas, have rekindled questions of the origins of, tendencies toward, and social reinforcements of masculinity and femininity as well as gender identity. Because the data lend themselves to different conclusions as to whether or not physical attractiveness has a scientific basis beyond its aesthetic component, studies from social theorists could lead to one set of interpretations; studies by sociobiologists and evolutionary psychologists to quite another.

Genetic survival, or maximizing the number of genes passed on in successive generations, is consistent with the latter's viewpoint regarding physical attractiveness. Sociobiologists and evolutionary psychologists would associate good looks with reproductive fitness and health. Traits like waist-to-hip ratio (WHR) and signs of overall health (luster of hair, vigor) attract attention from the opposite sex presumably because they indicate reproductive vigor. This paradigm, though, does not explain popular culture's preference for thin women rather than voluptuous or even overweight bodies with the optimal WHR; nor the preference for larger breasts, despite the irrelevance of breast size to milk production.

Moreover, while a wide pelvis should indicate a desirable mate for childbearing capacity, such was not the case in the last quarter of the twentieth century. Since the exaggerated thinness of the English model Twiggy, the ideal female figure of international supermodels resembles more the body of a twelve-year-old boy with long, slim limbs and small hips—androgynous rather than womanly. This preferred body type, however, seems unconnected to carrying and suckling an infant. The trend for a flat torso and stomach has replaced the breast as the focus of the female body. So prevalent are breast implants that one no longer can assume that a generous bra size is natural. A flat, well-muscled abdomen, on the other hand, indicates controlled food intake and a fitness routine. One anthropologist terms it "a modern-day virginity symbol" that suggests "a woman who has never borne children and thus has all of her years of fertility in front of her" (quoted in Bellafante, p. 9).

The American author Kim Chernin has discussed the relationship of female slimness to the power of the mother over infant sons, a power which a more robust-sized woman would recall unconsciously in men and which would threaten them. In fact, potential mothers are expected to be physically smaller and more delicate than men—thinner and less well-muscled than their protectors—but at the same time tall enough and long enough of bone to indicate good childhood nutrition and thus reproductive vitality. Today, particularly in puritanical America, slimness suggests self-control and mastery of sensuality in a society when fattening food is readily available and sex as much a sport as an erotic or intimate experience. Yet historically, a well-padded body was considered ideal as it indicated health and prosperity in centuries when starvation and illness were a constant threat.

Sociobiologists and evolutionary psychologists would identify reproduction as the main source of aggression and display in males and females. Despite social variations in these areas, reproductive rivalry, assertive courtship behaviors, and conflicts seem universal among males as they compete for potential mates. Feminine behavior appears to confer a further advantage in public by not threatening strangers. Women displaying such qualities as compliance, warmth, receptivity, and responsiveness can disarm interpersonal tension. The Norwegian social scientist Tore Bjerke notes that "the woman who looks and acts the most feminine (stereotypically speaking) is least likely to provoke an aggressive response after intruding on others" (Van der Dennen, p. 118).

Social constructionists could argue, however, that these trends become exaggerated by class, race, status, and any given society's standards of a pleasing physical appearance—what one could label an attractiveness quotient. This quotient differs for males and females according to their biological imperatives: for men, the need to inseminate as much as possible; for women, the need to choose the male who promises the greatest stability and capacity to provide materially for offspring.

## Bionic Beauty and Distorted Views of the Self

In a culture saturated with idealized and retouched photos of models, comparisons of "ideal" and ordinary bodies seem inescapable, whether by others or by oneself. The American sociologist Leon Festinger's Social Comparison Theory of self-evaluation based on external models "would predict that people might use images projected by the media as standards for comparison" (Grogan, p. 100). Constant bombardment with an unattainable ideal of "models' bodies (slim and carefully arranged in the most flattering poses) would be expected to lead to unfavorable evaluation of the body of the perceiver" (Grogan, pp. 100–101). Some women do indeed report greater

dissatisfaction with their own appearance than before exposure, others "no change," and some even report increased satisfaction. Grogan cites another study that correlates exposure and more negative body image to pre-test attitudes about the body. Clearly, studies of women exposed to media images have yielded mixed results.

In any case, such comparisons increase a young woman's sense that her appearance is substandard and urgently in need of repair. Forgotten is the reality that hair and makeup artists spend hours preparing models for these photos. Even then, the images can be airbrushed and pasted together. One actress (Julia Roberts) found magazine photos of herself to be a composite of different shots. Another (Kate Winslet) was displeased to find that her thighs had been slimmed in a picture airbrushed without her permission.

In their real lives, not even models or media stars resemble their carefully staged professional photos. How, then, can any woman without such resources escape disappointment with her appearance? Media images are partly to blame for the wounding and deflation so many feel in our narcissistic culture. Psychologists "argue that a failure to match the ideal leads to self-criticism, guilt and lowered self-worth"; this effect is stronger for women than for men because of more frequent exposure to photographs and the "cultural pressures on women to conform to an idealized body shape are more powerful and more widespread than those on men," says Grogan (p. 100).

In addition to this psychological need to repair perceived flaws, consumerism creates appetites for products that respond to the newly-awakened need to improve one's appearance. If not born beautiful, one can own the paraphernalia of beauty. Thus marketing in tandem with industry and the media motivate women to try to remedy their disappointment in their looks. Sandra Lee Bartky refers to this in *Femininity and Domination* as the "fashion-beauty complex" (p. 42), parallel to the "military-industrial complex" in that both are "major articulation[s] of capitalist patriarchy . . . a vast system of corporations—some of which manufacture products, others services and still others information, images, and ideologies" (p. 39). The fashion-beauty complex, argues Bartky, has replaced the family as the regulator of femininity.

The American feminist Naomi Wolf addresses the conflict between social and biological requirements for attractiveness in *The Beauty Myth*. The Professional Beauty Qualification, or PBQ as she terms it, reflects the demands of a capitalist economy and the exploitation of sex and fantasy as incentives to consume and as criteria for hiring in the job market. The connection between publicity and success, status, sex appeal, and the admiration of others has long directed print and other forms of media.

Real-life achievements, based on talent, discipline, frustration, and hard work as much as on luck, seem disconnected from these images. Competency does not always help to secure or keep employment, according to widely publicized lawsuits of wrongful job termination for reasons other than weak performance. Some women have been fired because they were neither pretty enough nor slim enough to sell products in department stores, to read the news as television anchors, to work as flight attendants, or even to sing in the opera—an art form traditionally dependent on talent rather than appearance. The internationally respected soprano Deborah Voigt was dropped from a scheduled production of Richard Strauss's *Ariadne auf Naxos* because her weight strained both the costume and her credibility in the role. "Tenorissimo" Luciano Pavarotti, in contrast, was not fired for his enormous body. Rather, he chose to retire because he no longer could move on stage.

Of particular concern is the early-twenty-first century phenomenon of "makeover" programs (*What Not to Wear, How Do I Look, Date Patrol, Style Court,* and *Extreme Makeover*). The last is the most serious challenge to women's (and men's) health and well-being, fostering the fantasy that with enough money and cosmetic surgery or other procedures, anyone can have Hollywood-style glamour and, in fact, should. The program features multiple surgical procedures over a period of many hours and with good results. No information emerges about how the potential candidate's health history, suitability for extreme surgery, or physical condition are evaluated before selection is made. Minimal attention is spent on pain or complications of recovery. Television programs on stomach stapling (gastric bypass surgery) provide more information on the potential dangers of this last-chance solution to morbid obesity. Indeed, either way the patient is at serious risk. The problems with silicone breast implants are better publicized, but still women of all ages continue to desire large breasts that change the proportions of their bodies. Younger and younger adolescents ask for cosmetic surgery, a phenomenon that should not surprise a society with ever-growing numbers of young women suffering from eating disorders and body dysmorphic disorder.

"How healthy is the Surgical Age?" asks Wolf (p. 229), citing deaths caused by smoking, fasting, and other extreme methods of weight control and cosmetic surgery known as "body sculpting." She correctly aligns such practices with an intense stress that, she suggests, can contribute to mental instability. "Narcissists feel that what happens to their bodies does not happen to them" (p. 230). In other words, paying attention to various body parts or facial features contributes to a fragmented and fragmenting view of the self, a distorted sense of the body as abnormal or diseased. "The Surgical Age's definition of female 'health' is not healthy" (p. 231).

Wolf's Surgical Age goes hand-in-hand with "body dysmorphic disorder" (formerly "dysmorphophobia"), a somatoform disorder described in the *Diagnostic and Statistical Manual (DSM-IV)* (number 300.7 in the *International Classification of Diseases*). Intense preoccupation with minor flaws, real or imagined, in facial or body features can lead to excessive, almost compulsive grooming rituals to try to undo or control one's "deformity." Symptoms range from both avoiding and seeking out one's reflection in mirrors or windows to "significant distress or impairment in social, occupational, or other areas of functioning . . . [and] may be underrecognized in settings in which cosmetic procedures are performed" (*DSM-IV*, p. 467). Short of calling the Surgical Age pathological, this statement infers that genuine psychological disorders may be masked in a society that promotes an exaggerated level of self-scrutiny.

A woman who chooses to submit to multiple plastic surgeries over a period of years in order to achieve a "Barbie-doll" look for her face and body may be determined to enjoy the attention, success, and glamorous social life she thinks beauty will bring. There may be a relationship between good looks and social success, in that attractiveness increases self-confidence, an appealing trait that draws people's attention. Self-confidence can be learned, however, and does not result from physical appearance alone.

## Beauty and Race

Variations of the elements of female attractiveness have entered the beauty discourse through the popular media over the last decades. Audiences are exposed to a more inclusive standard of good looks represented by models, actresses, or contestants in international beauty pageants from various ethnic origins. Young women of color have seen more fashion icons, celebrities, and video artists of their own ethnic backgrounds in mainstream media, particularly in rap and hip-hop culture and, in some North American cities, in soap operas and talk-shows on Spanish-language television. Some of these figures—Lil' Kim, Foxy Brown, Queen Latifah—present images of beauty and sexuality different from the dominant culture's version of attractiveness or "vanilla" sex appeal. Others, like Tyra Banks, Salma Hayek, and Halle Berry, blend anglicized and ethnic features. These contrasting aesthetics bespeak an ongoing conflict between the preference for the silky blond hair and light skin or skin darkened only with a tan and of traditional Western culture with the "exotic" appearance of women of color. A mixed message underlies these images: on the one hand, a superficial acceptance of a broader range of beauty and sexual desirability; on the other, a limit to the degree of identifiable ethnicity that impinges upon the Anglo norm. Thus, in order to be considered beautiful, the faces and bodies of multiracial women must display only minor departures from the standard white Western European look.

This fusion of facial features has long been the subject of psychological studies of female appearance. German researchers at the Universities of Regensburg and Rostock have tested various theories of female facial attractiveness, including the "attractiveness is averageness" hypothesis; the "facial symmetry" hypothesis; and the theory of "multidimensional beauty perception," which suggests that faces combining childlike characteristics with more mature features are judged most attractive. Their results partially confirm the averageness hypothesis: computer-generated composite faces are considered most beautiful, but only if the features to be morphed are not unattractive to begin with.

The question of hair resonates in particular for women of color. Madame C. J. Walker (1867–1919), born into slavery, invented and marketed her hair-straightening method in the early twentieth century. Ironically, African-American women have seen curls, Afros, corn rows, and dreadlocks appropriated by white women while they themselves still turn to chemical treatments, hot irons, hair weaving, and extensions to recreate the impossible and unforgiving image of the "good hair" of the dominant culture.

The very concept of "good hair" represents another battle in the beauty wars. Kasey West, in an article about hair and identity titled "Nappy Hair: A Marker of Identity and Difference" (for the Web site *Beauty Worlds*), writes:

A return to African-based hairstyling practices by many black women in the 1960s . . . marked an assertion of national identity and heritage in the face of oppressive Western ideals of beauty and continuing disenfranchisement. Although the popular Afro was achieved by blowing hair out to straighten the curls, it was representative as an expression of beauty ideals centered on an African identity. In other words, hairstyling became a political statement of connection to the black community. . . . [B]lack hairstyles retained a cultural and political significance.

Noting the "political complexities of African-American hair and beauty culture," West quotes the sociologist Ingrid Banks, who interviewed more than fifty black girls and women between 1996 and 1998 for her book *Hair Matters* (2000) and who concluded that "hair shapes black women's ideas about race, gender, class, sexuality, images of beauty and power."

Other African-American women writers address the issue in fiction and nonfiction. Toni Morrison's novel *The Bluest Eye* exposes these conflicts through the young heroine's poignant resentment and despair as she realizes she never will attain her dream of waking up blond and blue-eyed. bell hooks' article "Selling Hot Pussy" continues the examination of bodies and race. Black women still find themselves represented as savage, primitive sex machines and are objectified and dehumanized by this image. The "black female body gains attention only when it is synonymous with accessibility, availability, when it is sexually deviant" (in Conboy, Medina, and Stanbury, p. 117; see also Gilman). In this context, beauty and racism conflate to doubly oppress women, whatever their background.

Some American women of color, Latinas among them, trace their ethnic heritage to cultures whose ideal female body differs noticeably from the bony fashion icons of today's dominant white culture. A Mexican-American woman prized by her relatives for her rounded womanly body might be judged overweight in fitness-conscious California, for example. African-American culture embraces as beautiful a range of body sizes and shapes that would fall in the "full-figured" category in fashion advertising, despite the fact that models of color featured in the edgy, glamorous photos of high fashion publications possess the characteristic tall and ultraslim body. Kathryn Zerbe notes, "In comparison to white girls, fewer African-American girls report trying to lose weight. In cultures where plumpness is valued, eating disorders are rare" (p. 160). Additionally, curvy hips and ample bust lines, the hallmarks of a female figure, can fuel racist views of hypersexuality in people of color. In *Face Value: The Politics of Beauty* (1984), by Robin Tolmach Lakoff and Raquel Scherr, Scherr recalls her adolescence filled with taunts for resembling her Mexican-Indian mother rather than

her white father. At first outraged, later she agreed with a friend's remark that "discrimination based on beauty is more prevalent than discrimination based on race" (p. 7).

At the other extreme is the very thin African-American model Gerren Taylor, who was twelve years old in April 2003 when the *Los Angeles Times* profiled her nascent modeling career: Taylor had the prepubescent and scrawny silhouette that dominates the catwalk and fashion shoots and becomes the standard to which girls and women aspire. "The debate over the sexualization of girls at younger and younger ages waxes and wanes; Gerren's mother understands that sexuality is a part of fashion and believes she can protect her child from exploitation," writes Booth Moore (p. E9).

Immigrant women of color cannot escape their adopted culture's view of body size. In order to be appealing and noticed, American women "are supposed to be thin—and if they are not, the culture assumes they are unhappy, dissatisfied, lazy, slovenly, and ugly" (Zerbe, p. 159). Zerbe cites a study of African immigrants to Great Britain. Those "who have resided in Britain for only four years will have adopted the British viewpoint with respect to size and shape. These immigrants tend to desire a smaller physique than their African peers," who "in general enjoy their fuller figures" (p. 101). Zerbe offers examples suggesting that as immigrant women acculturate in a society that places a high value on thinness, they are likely to adopt "the more stringent eating attitudes of the prevailing culture" (p. 101).

## Beyond Questions of Science

The body, writes the American feminist Susan Bordo, is a "culturally mediated form" (in Conboy, Medina, and Stanbury, p. 103), in that its appearance reflects the discourse of its society and the state of women's power or lack thereof in that society. Beyond aesthetics, the ideal appearance and female body exist in relation to the bondage of dependency, racism, and social roles. The body, in other words, is territory conquered by masculine spectatorship, the site of a struggle over ownership of resources.

Women's beauty rituals comprise part of this cultural mediation. Rituals are the repeated acts of grooming beyond basic hygiene that serve to embellish according to the tastes and standards she has internalized from her peer group, magazines, and other media. Rituals can be as innocent as preteen makeup parties, as painful as piercing or tattoos, and as life-threatening as eating disorders for weight control. Some girls choose rituals to feel good about what is asked of them; some to bind the anxiety they feel as they dodge threats to their still-formulating sense of self; and some to overcome perceived shortcomings of which they are constantly reminded by advertising.

Successful advertising seeks to address a consumer's pleasure-seeking tendencies before the reality principal dampens her impulse to buy. Along with products, companies sell fantasies of pleasure, excitement, or well-being that will arise from the act of buying and using advertised items. Scenes of arousal need not include a partner. Pampering oneself with soothing lotions satisfies the need for attention without the risks involved in a relationship. Contemporary television and print commercials feature women experiencing what looks like self-stimulation and sexual arousal from shampoo and soap use in the shower.

In addition to bath and skin treatments, creamy foods like yogurts are advertised as sensual indulgences enjoyed by oneself. But for women, eating is already overdetermined. Intentionally or not, advertising can contribute to "emotionally induced compensatory eating," says Suzanne Z. Grunert (quoted in Costa, p. 68), and thus heighten the dilemma between the immediate comfort of eating and the potential for weight gain. Perhaps in compensation, shades of lipstick, eye shadow, and nail polish often are named after food. Instead of ingesting chocolate or cinnamon, one can wear them.

Ads for beauty and grooming aids fuel self-consciousness and vulnerability by making women aware of flaws they did not know they had. They stimulate an often-panicky desire to improve and, not surprisingly, create markets for products that promise to remedy imperfections from acne to wrinkles. Magazine articles, infomercials, and niche-marketed television programs bombard young women with images and messages they ignore at their own peril. Well-socialized girls change their hairstyles and adopt fashion trends in part to conform to the standards of their peer groups—actions that indicate how well they understand and respond to peer influences as seen in their shopping patterns. Product boycotts or grassroots truth-in-advertising campaigns fight to expose the "marketization" of cultural expression, but cannot fully counteract the impact of advertising and mass marketing and their by-product, peer pressure.

Women at times can resist the expectation of prettiness by refusing to dress for the pleasure of the beholder. In renouncing what Bartky calls "institutionalized heterosexuality," lesbians, for example, can disengage from the "panoptical male connoisseur" who "resides within the consciousness of most women" (p. 72). Some remove themselves from the beauty game altogether and thus dislocate and interrupt the male gaze whether external or internalized. Comfort, serious athleticism, modesty, indifference to attention-seeking, and rejection of so-called female vanity lead others to free themselves from adornment. Young adolescents often respond to their own ambivalence about their developing bodies by dressing in shapeless t-shirts and baggy pants. This camouflage enables them to feel they can escape the judgmental stares of peers as well as surprised looks from family members unused to their daughters' emerging secondary sex characteristics.

Lesbian dressing evolved through the last decades of the twentieth century from a hard-core butch style to the appearance known as "lipstick lesbianism" and a greater repertory of looks, writes Barbara Creed in a 1999 essay titled "Lesbian Bodies." From the 1970s, when "the true lesbian" was expected to "reject all forms of clothing that might associate her image with that of the heterosexual woman and ultimately with patriarchal capitalism," to the "butch-femme renaissance of the 1980s," to the so-called heterosexual lesbians of 1990s queer culture, lesbians have renounced the "lesbian uniform" as well as "the patriarchal stereotypes of feminine dress and appearance" (pp. 122–123). In so doing they reveal the sacrifice required of women who conform to feminine attractiveness.

The cult of beauty in women represents an attempt to counteract an externally imposed sense of inadequacy. Feelings of failure arise from "a context where body image is subjective and socially determined. . . . A person's body image is not determined by the actual shape and size of that body, but by that person's subjective evaluation of what it means to have that kind of body within their particular culture," writes Grogan (p. 166). For women of any race, class, or gender identification, femininity becomes an investment of resources and discipline in order to gain fleeting attention "and some admiration but little real respect and rarely any social power" (Bartky, p. 73). Late-twentieth-century studies cited in Grogan (pp. 180–192) suggest that positive body image is linked to self-esteem and a sense of personal control over one's environment, both of which are problematic for women in a capitalist patriarchy. As long as societies teach women to evaluate themselves principally in terms of their femininity and attractiveness, self-assurance will belong more often to those who successfully conform to the cultural ideal. If instead girls and young women learn to appreciate their bodies as healthy, well-functioning instruments that enable them to lead productive lives, they will be closer to changing the conditions that relegate them to objectification.

*See also* **Body, The; Feminism; Gender; Men and Masculinity; Motherhood and Maternity.**

## BIBLIOGRAPHY

Bartky, Sandra Lee. *Femininity and Domination: Studies in the Phenomenology of Oppression.* New York: Routledge, 1990.
Bellafante, Ginia. "At Gender's Last Frontier." *New York Times,* June 8, 2003, section 9, p. 9.
Bordo, Susan. *The Male Body: A New Look at Men in Public and in Private.* New York: Farrar, Straus and Giroux, 1999.
Brownmiller, Susan. *Femininity.* New York: Linden Press/Simon and Schuster, 1984.
Chernin, Kim. *The Obsession: Reflections on the Tyranny of Slenderness.* New York: Harper and Row, 1981.
Conboy, Katie, Nadia Medina, and Sarah Stanbury, eds. *Writing on the Body: Female Embodiment and Feminist Theory.* New York: Columbia University Press, 1997.
Costa, Janeen Arnold, ed. *Gender Issues and Consumer Behavior.* Thousand Oaks, Calif.: Sage, 1994.
Creed, Barbara. "Lesbian Bodies: Tribades, Tomboys, and Tarts." In *Feminist Theory and the Body,* edited by Janet Price and Margrit Shildrick. New York: Routledge, 1999.
Frost, Liz. *Young Women and the Body: A Feminist Sociology.* Houndsmills, U.K.: Palgrave, 2001.
Gilman, Sander. *Difference and Pathology: Stereotypes of Sexuality, Race, and Madness.* Ithaca, N.Y.: Cornell University Press, 1985.
Grogan, Sarah. *Body Image: Understanding Body Dissatisfaction in Men, Women, and Children.* London: Routledge, 1999.
Halprin, Sara. *Look at My Ugly Face: Myths and Musings on Beauty and Other Perilous Obsessions with Women's Appearance.* New York: Viking, 1995.
Kinzer, Nora Scott. *Put Down and Ripped Off: The American Woman and the Beauty Cult.* New York: Crowell, 1977.

Lakoff, Robin Tolmach, and Raquel Scherr. *Face Value: The Politics of Beauty.* Boston: Routledge and Kegan Paul, 1984.

Lippa, Richard. *Gender, Nature, and Nurture.* Mahwah, N.J.: Erlbaum, 2002.

Malson, Helen. *The Thin Woman: Feminism, Post-structuralism, and the Social Psychology of Anorexia Nervosa.* New York: Routledge, 1998.

Moore, Booth. "Beyond Her Years." *Los Angeles Times,* April 30, 2003, pp. E1, E9.

Mulqueen, Maggie. *On Our Own Terms: Redefining Competence and Femininity.* Albany: State University of New York Press, 1992.

Price, Janet, and Margrit Shildrick, eds. *Feminist Theory and the Body.* Edinburgh, U.K.: Edinburgh University Press, 1999.

Van der Dennen, J. M. G., ed. *The Nature of the Sexes: The Sociobiology of Sex Differences and the "Battle of the Sexes."* Groningen, The Netherlands: Origin Press, 1992.

West, Kasey. "Nappy Hair: A Marker of Identity and Difference." Available at http://www.beautyworlds.com/beautynappyhair.htm.

Zerbe, Kathryn. *The Body Betrayed: Women, Eating Disorders, and Treatment.* Washington, D.C.: American Psychiatric Press, 1993.

*Susan Grayson*

# WOMEN'S HISTORY.

This entry includes two subentries:

*Africa*
*Asia*

## AFRICA

Since 1970 the history of African women has developed into a vital and steadily expanding area of research and study, motivated, as with other areas of women's history, by the development of the international feminist movement. African women's history also paralleled the expansion of African history following World War II, as scholars inside and outside of Africa began to focus on historical transformations on the African continent.

Before the 1970s there was little available research on African women's history per se, though information on women in Africa was found in anthropological and ethnographic studies. This focus has continued in the preponderance of research on African women appearing in development studies. The first publications in the 1970s dealt with women and economic change and with women as political activists. By the mid-1980s there were a number of important extended studies, but only in the 1990s did a substantial number of monographs on specific topics begin to appear, although the bulk of new research is still found in journal and anthology articles.

Earlier historical eras were initially neglected, in part as a result of the difficulty in obtaining historical sources that dealt with women before the nineteenth century. Written materials on earlier eras, especially from an African woman's perspective, were scarce because many African communities were decentralized and nonliterate. Topics that have archival source materials included elite women such as Queen Nzinga, a seventeenth-century ruler in what became Angola, and market women along the West African coast who interacted with European traders. Eva, a seventeenth-century African woman who settled in the early Dutch community on the Cape in South Africa and married a European colonist, is also found in archival documentation. Egypt was exceptionally strong in sources concerning women in earlier centuries.

Source availability influenced the large number of studies on slave women in the nineteenth century, which is an important issue but did not represent the experience of most women. Slaves within Africa were more likely to be women, a reflection of their productive and reproductive contributions to their communities. Scholars have retrieved information on other aspects of the lives of women in the nineteenth century, as exemplified in research that detailed women's work in Lesotho, elite women in Buganda, women's vulnerability in Central Africa, Swahili women's spirit possession cults, Asante queen mothers' political influence, religious Muslim women in West Africa, and numerous other specific areas of women's activity.

Reexamining familiar issues from a woman's perspective has altered African history more generally. For example, many of the initial studies of women's work during the colonial period showed how they had lost power and economic autonomy with the arrival of cash crops and their exclusion from the global marketplace, in contrast to men, who were more likely to benefit from these economic changes. The emphasis on the formal sector of the economy in African labor history eclipsed women's actual economic activity, which centered on agricultural work. Studying women's economic contributions meant paying attention to rural agricultural work as well as the urban efforts of market vendors, both sectors previously neglected in African labor history. Female agricultural innovations were described as essential to community survival. Women's changing position in arenas formerly seen as only male has been shown in research on mining compounds in Zambia, railway communities in Nigeria, and other urban studies.

Research on women's involvement in political activism changed previously accepted ideas of women's passivity in the face of such changes. In some areas, such as southern Nigeria in the 1920s, women drew on precolonial practices to express their displeasure with the colonial powers. New information about the leadership role of illiterate Muslim women in Dar es Salaam in the nationalist movement of the 1950s fundamentally changed the view that the Tanzanian anticolonial movement was led solely by men who were products of Christian mission education. Research on more recent years has found a proliferation of African women's organizations concerned with bringing peace to conflict-ridden areas, ending female genital cutting or mutilation (erroneously called female circumcision), and training women to get involved in national politics. Women's studies programs have been established at most African universities.

Scholars of women and religion have investigated female spiritual power in local religions and the role of women in developing local churches that were often offshoots of larger denominations. Research in the 1990s also included a focus on women and missions, with researchers demonstrating that the introduction of European ideas about marriage and family simultaneously brought new oppressions and new opportunities for women. Research on women and Islam has also grown, with new information on women and Koranic education in West Africa and on Muslim women's involvement in nationalist struggles in North Africa.

The earliest publications tended to be descriptive as scholars worked to prove that African women had made an impact on their societies. More recent studies have provided much more nuanced descriptions of the complexities of women's lives, of the changes over time, and of local and outsider ideologies about women in Africa. Helen Bradford's reanalysis of the role of the adolescent girl Nongqawuse in the Xhosa cattle killing of the 1850s has demonstrated that taking women's testimony seriously and focusing on women's experience and expression of history can fundamentally change the explanation of an event. She convincingly suggests that issues of changing sexuality and possibly abuse or incest were of central importance in understanding people's motivations, and conventional reliance on broader economic and political reasons for the upheaval is not completely satisfactory.

Among the issues continuing to appear in writings on African women's history are those of representation (who is writing this history and for what audience), sources and methodology, and periodization, as well as the usual areas of productive work, family life, and public activities such as politics and religion. Tiyambe Zeleza has described the enduring marginalization of African women's history, as the information that has been recovered is omitted from textbooks or included in very limited ways. The absence of African women historians is frequently commented on, as there are regrettably few who publish regularly. The history of women in precolonial Africa continues to be a weak point, while the history of the colonial era (from around 1880 to the 1960s for most of the continent) has shifted from examining the impact of colonialism on women (assessed as mostly negative) to investigating African communities and history from their own perspectives. This approach includes an emphasis on African women's agency and efforts to present African women's own voices. A notable effort in this regard is the Women Writing Africa Project sponsored by Feminist Press, which presents extensive materials written and recorded by African women. A single volume on English-speaking southern Africa has been published and the editors, Tuzyline Jita Allan and Abena Busia, plan several more regional collections. New research reexamines territory already covered and opens new topics while incorporating the voices of African women as both subjects and scholars, indicating the direction African women's history will take in the near future.

*See also* **Feminism: Africa and African Diaspora; Women's Studies.**

## BIBLIOGRAPHY

Badran, Margot. *Feminists, Islam, and Nation: Gender and the Making of Modern Egypt.* Princeton, N.J.: Princeton University Press, 1995.

Berger, Iris, and E. Frances White. *Women in Sub-Saharan Africa: Restoring Women to History.* Bloomington: Indiana University Press, 1999.

Bradford, Helen. "Women, Gender, and Colonialism: Rethinking the History of the British Cape Colony and its Frontier Zones, c. 1806–70." *Journal of African History* 37 (1996): 351–370.

Charrad, Mounira M. *States and Women's Rights: The Making of Postcolonial Tunisia, Algeria, and Morocco.* Berkeley: University of California Press, 2001.

Daymond, M. J., et al. *Women Writing Africa: The Southern Region.* New York: Feminist Press, 2003.

Hodgson, Dorothy L., and Sheryl A. McCurdy, eds. *"Wicked" Women and the Reconfiguration of Gender in Africa.* Portsmouth, N.H.: Heinemann, 2001.

Tripp, Aili Mari, ed. *Sub-Saharan Africa.* Vol. 6 of *The Greenwood Encyclopedia of Women's Issues Worldwide,* edited by Lynn Walter. Westport, Conn.: Greenwood, 2003.

Zeleza, Tiyambe. "Gender Biases in African Historiography." In *Engendering African Social Sciences,* edited by Ayesha M. Imam, Amina Mama, and Fatou Sow, 81–116. Dakar, Senegal: CODESRIA Book Series, 1997.

*Kathleen Sheldon*

## ASIA

The prominent roles occupied by women in the legends and myths of that complex and diverse part of the world called Asia suggest that "histories" of women in Asia have existed for a very long time. That these legends have been shaped, written, and sometimes performed by men operating in androcentric cultural contexts does not negate the impression of power and consequence their narratives convey. From Japan's sun goddess, the original ancestress of the imperial line, to Korean shamans, to the powerful and transgressive women of South and Southeast Asian myth, or China's Hua Mulan, the stories of these legendary women suggest that women in early Asian societies did "make history." Perhaps only in China does the written record present, dynasty after dynasty, legendary women whose experience is embedded in the historicity of China's changing social, political, and economic institutions.

In various parts of Asia, these myths generated questions about matriarchal societies that were reinforced by the nineteenth-century work of Friedrich Engels (1820–1895) and Garrett A. Morgan (1877–1963). This theoretical framework may have encouraged one of Japan's first historians of women, Takamure Itsue (1894–1964), to do research on family registers; that research, parts of which have been reinforced by twentieth-century scholarship, strongly suggests that families in eighth-century Japan were predominantly matrilineal. For other women in Asia, myths and legends provided models for resistance and revolution in the twentieth century (China and Vietnam) and left some, like Hiratsuka Raicho (1886–1971), wondering why and how women had lost the power and authority they once had in Japanese history.

## The Confucian Pattern

Few intellectual traditions have had a greater impact on women in Asia than Confucianism, in part because Confucian traditions were central not only to China but also to other parts of Asia (Japan, Korea, and Southeast Asia) influenced by Chinese culture. The study of women in these cultures has dismantled basic assumptions about Confucianism: its universality, monolithic nature, and immutability. The study of women has shown many different Confucianisms and has made it clear that the continuity of these traditions is the result of accommodation to social change, not stasis.

Scholars of Chinese women's history have, in recent years, moved far beyond an earlier scholarship that focused on Confucianism's role in conceptualizing and rationalizing a patriarchal, patrilineal family in which women were marginalized, victimized, and seemingly left with little opportunity to develop or exercise a sense of their own agency. Overcoming and supplanting this view has come only through the continuing research of historians who, reading against the grain of the Confucian record, have provided a much more complex picture of women's lives and of Chinese culture. Margery Wolf's work on women in Taiwan represents a rare early glimpse of women developing strategies to increase their power in the family; Susan Mann, Patricia Ebrey, and Dorothy Ko have since demonstrated, in a number of different settings, how important women were as contributors to "Chinese civilization" and how effectively they circumvented the institutional barriers ranged against them.

Elsewhere in Asia, Confucian patterns had less continuity as well as less influence. In the Japanese case, Confucian ideas about the family and statecraft were heavily moderated by existing cultural patterns, even in the two periods when Confucianism is thought to have had greatest influence—the eighth and ninth centuries when the Japanese state was being organized, and the seventeenth and eighteenth centuries of the Tokugawa period. Korea, although thoroughly conversant with Confucianism, was really not dominated by these ideas until well after the fourteenth century, and Southeast Asia, particularly Vietnam, encountered the greatest levels of Confucian influence between the fourteenth and sixteenth centuries. Recent scholarship makes it clear how difficult it is to walk the tightrope between establishing a history of women in Asia that speaks to their strengths *and* acknowledges the reality of the constraints they faced. Although historians continue to investigate stereotypical symbols of women's oppression in Asia (sati, footbinding), they do so with a heightened sense of the possibility that Western scholarship "orientalizes" women when it fails to present them as active participants in their own culture, able to find nuanced and effective ways to challenge those constraints.

## The Modern Period

There has always been a women's version of the Western civilizing narrative in Asia; in many times and places, Western colonizers sought to use the "oppression of women" in Asian cultures as a rationale for their self-proclaimed civilizing mission. The treatment of women, they often said, was the standard by which civilizations could be judged, and on that basis it was clear that Asia "needed civilizing." The history of women in Asia has convincingly demonstrated that the "Western impact" on Asia not only complicated women's ability to improve their lives but also generated an anticolonial, nationalist engagement that did not aid, but typically subverted, feminist agendas.

Growing recognition of the intellectual significance of feminism since the late nineteenth century has been coupled with the assumption that feminism's natural competitors—nationalism and socialism—have eclipsed feminism's impact in the modern period. Women have been critical to the development of nationalism and socialism in China, India, Korea, and Southeast Asia: as symbols of "tradition," workers, educators, and soldiers. Women were asked to postpone their agendas in China's great twentieth-century revolution, where leaders pursued a "backward to revolution" strategy, and in India, where connections with nationalism and anti-imperialist movements were complicated by geography, ethnicity, caste, class, and religious diversity. While South Asia may present the greatest challenges for historians of women, it is also true that, in the 1990s, scholars there such as Kumkum Sangari and Sudesh Vaid pointedly demonstrated how much a feminist standpoint adds to our understanding of nationalism, colonialism, and anticolonial movements. Independence may have brought an improvement in the legal status of women, but the partition that created the new states of India and Pakistan ushered in a long period of conflict in which large numbers of women were abducted, raped, and/or killed as part of a continuing political, ethnic, and religious struggle. Until 1990, women were an invisible part of historical analysis of this conflict; since then, historians of women, such as Urvashi Butalia in South Asia, have made clear how important women and gender are to any understanding of these conflicts.

*See also* **Feminism; Gender; Women's History: Africa; Women's Studies.**

### BIBLIOGRAPHY

Ebrey, Patricia Buckley. *The Inner Quarters: Marriage and the Lives of Chinese Women in the Sung Period.* Berkeley and Los Angeles: University of California Press, 1993.

Johnson, Kay Ann. *Women, the Family, and Peasant Revolution in China.* Chicago: University of Chicago Press, 1983.

Ko, Dorothy. *Teachers of the Inner Chambers: Women and Culture in Seventeenth-Century China.* Stanford, Calif.: Stanford University Press, 1994.

Ko, Dorothy, JaHyun Kim Haboush, and Joan R. Piggott, eds. *Women and Confucian Cultures in Premodern China, Korea, and Japan.* Berkeley, Los Angeles, and London: University of California Press, 2003.

Mann, Susan. *Precious Records: Women in China's Long Eighteenth Century.* Stanford, Calif.: Stanford University Press, 1997.

Mann, Susan, and Yu-Yin Cheng, eds. *Under Confucian Eyes. Writings on Gender in Chinese History.* Berkeley, Los Angeles, and London: University of California Press, 2001.

Mohanty, Chandra Talpade. *Feminism without Borders.* Durham and London: Duke University Press, 2003.

Ramusack, Barbara N., and Sharon Sievers. *Women in Asia.* Bloomington: Indiana University Press, 1999.

Ray, Sangeeta. *En-Gendering India: Woman and Nation in Colonial and Postcolonial Narratives.* Durham, N.C.: Duke University Press, 2000.

Sangari, Kumkum, and Sudesh Vaid. *Recasting Women: Essays in Indian Colonial History*. New Brunswick, N.J.: Rutgers University Press, 1990.

Sarkar, Tanika, and Urvashi Butalia, eds. *Women and Right-Wing Movements*. London: Zed Books, 1995.

Sekiguchi, Hiroko. "The Patriarchal Family Paradigm in Eighth-Century Japan." In *Women and Confucian Cultures,* edited by Dorothy Ko, JaHyun Kim Haboush, and Joan R. Piggott. Berkeley, Los Angeles, and London: University of California Press, 2003.

Sievers, Sharon. *Flowers in Salt: The Beginnings of Feminist Consciousness in Modern Japan*. Stanford, Calif.: Stanford University Press, 1983.

Stacey, Judith. *Patriarchy and Socialist Revolution in China*. Berkeley and Los Angeles: University of California Press, 1983.

Tonomura, Hitomi, Ann Walthall, and Wakita Haruko, eds. *Women and Class in Japanese History*. Ann Arbor: Center for Japanese Studies, University of Michigan, 1999.

Wolf, Margery. *Women and the Family in Rural Taiwan*. Stanford, Calif.: Stanford University Press, 1972.

*Sharon Sievers*

# WOMEN'S STUDIES.

**WOMEN'S STUDIES.** In its short history (from the late 1960s in the United States) women's studies has moved around the world as an idea, a concept, a practice, and finally a field or *Fach* (German for specialty or field). As late as 1982 in Germany *Frauenstudium* was not considered a *Fach* and therefore could not be studied in the university but only in special or summer courses. By the early twentieth century women's studies was recognized in higher education from India to Indonesia, from the United States to Uganda, China to Canada, Austria to Australia, England to Egypt, South Africa to South Korea.

## Definitions

Women's studies is the study of women and gender in every field. Its basic premise is that traditional education is based on a study of men—usually upper-class, Caucasian, educated men—while other groups of men and all different groups of women are erroneously subsumed under the category "mankind." Early on courses drew especially on history, literature, and sociology, but they quickly expanded to the other humanities (philosophy, religious studies, comparative literature, art, music) and the social sciences (anthropology, political science, economics, psychology, geography). Science and technology have been slower to embrace women's studies, but biology, math, technology, computer science, chemistry, physics, and medicine have all begun to examine their assumptions for sexist bias, and courses in "gender and physics," "women geologists," or "sexism and science" are de rigueur in most programs.

Over the years the term itself and the naming of the enterprise have been contested and changing. The first name was "female studies," but "women's studies" quickly found more adherents. The name "women's studies" has been criticized for its ambiguous apostrophe (the study of or by women?), for its (supposed) assumption that all women can be studied together, and for its "hegemonic narrowness" that does not take into account transgendered or lesbian identities. Some programs have changed their names to "gender studies," "women and gender studies," or "feminist studies." And of course in the exporting of "women's studies" around the world, various languages are unable to translate "gender" or "women's studies" in satisfactory ways. It is safe to say, however, that all permutations share some commonalities—that women matter and that their own assessment of their experiences is the starting point for description and analysis; that the history of women's subordination is differently experienced but commonly shared; that the elimination of that subordination is a common goal. The concept of gender as a social construction that reflects and determines differences in power and opportunity is employed as the primary analytic category.

## Origins

Women's studies, as a concept and a site of learning, really began with the second wave of the women's movement in the late 1960s. But generations of work and information gathering preceded that time, particularly in the nineteenth-century penchant for writing stories of "great women" and gathering them in collections of "women worthies." A later, more democratic strain of the study of women was begun by the historian Mary Beard, who in her 1946 volume *Woman as Force in History* took a different tack. If one looks at "long history," one finds not "great women" only but everyday women, not women as victims but women who influenced their worlds, women who had agency, even within the confines of a limited sphere, within the private realm. Simone de Beauvoir wrote of women as "other" in *The Second Sex* (1953), while Betty Friedan analyzed "the problem that has no name," the malaise and victimization of middle-class women, in *The Feminine Mystique* (1963), and Helen Hacker compared women's position to that of minorities (1951). Yet all these important precursors did not initiate women's studies.

It took a combination of the civil rights movement, the New Left, the peace movement (especially the protests against the war in Vietnam), and the various open university movements in the 1960s to help women coalesce and organize themselves into the women's liberation movement. Many more women were attending colleges and universities, many women were participating in the radical youth movements of the 1960s, and many women students and faculty were leaders in the civil rights and antiwar movements. It was thus almost inevitable that women would begin to question their role in those movements if they always had to make the coffee, do the typing, and be available as sex objects. Stokely Carmichael of the Student Non-Violent Coordinating Committee (SNCC) famously said, "The only position of women in the movement is prone," infuriating many young women. The second wave of the women's movement began with hundreds of small consciousness-raising (CR) groups in many cities and towns; as women collectively started to understand and then study their situation, they initiated courses and classes on women's history, literature, and culture, first on a community, ad hoc basis but quickly moving to the college classroom. There were hundreds of women's studies courses offered at colleges and universities in the United States in the late 1960s, and by 1970 formal women's studies programs were launched, first at San Diego State University in

California and then at Cornell University in New York. Every year after that saw an increase, from 276 programs in 1976 to 680 in 1999. Most of these programs offered minors, certificates, concentrations, or majors. A *Campus Trends* report for the American Council on Education in 1984 found that women's studies courses were offered at a majority of four-year colleges and universities and at 25 percent of community colleges; there are more now. Women's studies at the beginning of the twenty-first century enrolled the largest number of students of any interdisciplinary field. The Department of Education estimates that 12 percent of all undergraduate students in the United States have received credit for a women's studies course. But the growth in formal programs does not tell the whole story; many more students enroll in separate courses than choose to major or minor in the field.

## Growth and Institutionalization

Because American educational institutions, especially newer, less-traditional ones, are very flexible in curricular change, women's studies grew and expanded in the United States more quickly than anywhere else. But very soon there were women's studies programs in Japan, Australia, New Zealand, Finland, Sweden, India, South Korea, Taiwan, and the Philippines. By the 1980s there were programs in all countries in Western Europe, plus Thailand, South Africa, China, the Caribbean, and Uganda. Finally, after the change from communism in Eastern Europe, programs were instituted in Slovakia, the Czech Republic, Russia, Ukraine, and others, in addition to Malaysia, Vietnam, and other African nations. Two series of international conferences gave impetus to the growth of women's studies, both within universities and in community-based organizations worldwide. The International Interdisciplinary Congress on Women began in Haifa, Israel, in 1981 and has met every three years since—in the Netherlands (1984), in Ireland (1987), in New York (1990), in Costa Rica (1993), in Australia (1996), in Norway (1999), in Uganda (2002), and in South Korea (2005). Two to three thousand delegates, mostly women, both academics and community organizers, attend to present their work. Each conference draws especially on that continent's practitioners. Thus the Costa Rica conference brought together many indigenous women from Central America as well as Latin American delegates. Languages that year were Spanish, English, and a variety of Indio languages. That this congress continues to meet, without governmental or formal organizational support, is testimony to the personal importance to women all over the world of global scholarship on women.

The United Nations has sponsored four international conferences as a part of its "Decade for Women," in Mexico City (1975), Copenhagen (1980), Nairobi (1985), and Beijing (1995). The nongovernmental organizations (NGO) forums held in conjunction with each conference brought together thousands of activists and women's studies groups from all over the world, thus reminding those from the developed world of the connections between education and broader social justice issues.

## Research and Publication

Scholarly journals in women's studies were begun in the United States early on (1972 for *Feminist Studies;* 1975 for *Signs: A Journal of Women in Culture and Society;* but not until 1988 for the *National Women's Studies Association Journal*), and soon there were journals published around the world. In 1999 an informal International Network of Women's Studies Journals (now the Feminist Journals Network) was formed, meeting first in Tromso, Norway, then in Halifax, Canada, in 2001 and in Kampala, Uganda, in 2002. Thirty editors from twenty-seven journals in twenty-one countries were represented in the membership in the early twenty-first century. Joint publishing projects, including a book series by Zed Press, reprinting of articles from journals in the "economic south" (developing nations) by journals in the "economic north" (industrialized nations, mostly in the north but including Australia), a Web site, and a listserv to make members aware of current issues are all part of their work.

Ellen Messer-Davidow surveyed the number of books and scholarly monographs available in English between 1980 and 1998 and estimated that 10,200 feminist books were published during that period. As she says, the print knowledge is so voluminous that scholars cannot keep track, much less read it all. And the topics are superabundant: "everything and anything is gendered, . . . gendering is narrated, quantified, or modeled, . . . and 'gender' as an analytical category is interrogated" (Messer-Davidow, p. 167).

## Theories and Assumptions

Even though some practitioners of women's studies disavow any attempt to theorize universally about women or women's studies, most others will subscribe to a discussion of the following kinds of theories. Women's studies course material depends largely on various feminist theories, although these assumptions may not always be made explicit. Most feminist theories can be divided into two basic kinds, based on the answer to the question: How important is the physiological or biological difference between males and females? Put another way: What should one make of the sex-gender difference? Should this difference be noted and positively valued for its unique perspective? Or should it be downplayed in a system that recognizes the common humanity of men and women and attempts to unite women with institutions from which they have historically been excluded? These two basic strains of feminist theory have been variously called equality feminism and difference feminism, minimizer feminism and maximizer feminism, or individualist feminism and relational feminism. In each case, the first term includes those who seek to deemphasize difference and press for the integration of women into masculine institutions, usually emphasizing the individual; the second term includes those who seek to stress and value difference, to transform or abandon masculine systems, often emphasizing the relational qualities of women, especially in regard to children and extended families.

The term *sex-gender* is used here to refer to the biological and social difference between males and females. In the early days, the two words were used separately and distinctly. *Sex* meant the physiological difference between male and female, while *gender* meant the social overlay of education and socialization, constructed differently in different eras and societies. The two terms have become conflated in everyday speech, and

## GERDA LERNER

Gerda Lerner could be called "the mother of us all," that phrase used by Gertrude Stein in her opera about Susan B. Anthony. An American historian by training, Gerda Lerner's biography exhibits the uniqueness of her life and work. Born and educated through secondary school in Austria, she came to the United States as a part of the Jewish exodus after the 1938 *Anschluss* that brought Nazi power to Austria, first as a part of a nearly phony marriage that enabled her to gain a visa. As a young wife and mother in Los Angeles and then in New York through the war years and the early days of the Cold War, Lerner organized for such groups as the Congress of American Women. Her (second) husband, Carl Lerner, was a screenwriter, editor, and filmmaker. Both were involved in various leftist activities for years. After the war she began writing fiction and taking courses at the New School for Social Research in New York in 1948. Gerda Lerner quickly earned first her B.A. at the New School

and then her M.A. and Ph.D. at Columbia University, using her biography of the Grimké sisters of South Carolina as her Ph.D. dissertation. As a "returning student" in the years before that was a recognized category, Lerner had to persuade the authorities at Columbia to let her study women's history, not an acceptable field in the early 1960s. Beginning the women's studies program at Sarah Lawrence College (and one of the first graduate programs in women's history), Lerner proceeded to teach, write, and lecture around the country, penning several classic volumes in women's studies: *Black Women in White America* (1972), *The Majority Finds Its Past* (1979), and her two-volume magnum opus, *The Creation of Patriarchy* (1986) and *The Creation of Feminist Consciousness* (1993). In 1982, after the death of her husband, she moved to the University of Wisconsin to found the Ph.D. program in women's history. Her autobiography of her early years, *Fireweed: A Political Autobiography*, was published in 2002.

many use *gender* where *sex* would have been used earlier. For many theorists, both terms are constructed—that is, the particular culture gives its own meaning to sex and gender. Additionally, we now have much more research and experience with transgendered individuals, such that the binary of male-female is problematic at best. Any particular "sex-gender system" is of course an artifact of a particular historical time and place. Still, the two major types continue to be a useful way of understanding the various forms of the theories that underlie women's studies.

Each one of the two major types of feminist theories includes several subtypes, from conservative to radical, from positions that imply few changes in the status quo to ones in which the whole society is altered by the shift in women's status and conceptualization. It is useful to envision the positions—minimizers and maximizers of difference—on two lines that move from the more conservative to the more radical, from right to left. The most conservative feminist position on both continua is that view of women that offers a rationale for the present structure of society. The most radical position offers a call for a future society totally transformed either by the extreme of making males and females no longer different physiologically (for example, by the abolition of female reproductive capacities) or, for the maximizers, the extreme of totally separating the two sexes—physically, geographically, and socially. Beyond the conservative feminist pole, one finds reactionary positions: for the maximizers,

various sociobiologist positions; for the minimizers, the position that fails to recognize that human rights may be an issue. This latter view is based on an unstated assumption that might be expressed thus: "We are all alike; we all stand in the position of white privileged males; we all have equal rights."

***The minimizers.*** Along the "minimizers" continuum, one moves first from the "human rights" position to "women's rights," the stance of various reformist groups and theorists that advocate granting equal rights to women in all areas by working within existing political systems. This nineteenth-century egalitarian position of the first women's rights activists, such as Elizabeth Cady Stanton and Susan B. Anthony, is also known as liberal feminism. It is the point of view of John Stuart Mill in his important work *The Subjection of Women* (1869) and that of Mary Wollstonecraft in *A Vindication of the Rights of Woman* (1792). The stance is found most conspicuously in the early twenty-first century in views of the U.S. National Organization for Women (NOW).

Next along the continuum are various types of socialist feminists: those who advocate the primacy of socialist revolution, those who advocate wages for housework and other solutions to equate being a housewife (or a househusband) with working outside the home, and others who attempt to make new syntheses of feminist questions and socialist or Marxist answers that begin with an economic analysis. Historically the socialist position on women is stated most dogmatically by Friedrich

Women have been left out of history not because of the evil conspiracies of men in general or male historians in particular, but because we have considered history only in male-centered terms. We have missed women and their activities, because we have asked questions of history which are inappropriate to women. To rectify this and to light up areas of historical darkness we must, for a time, focus on a *woman-centered* inquiry, considering the possibility of the existence of a female culture *within* the general culture shared by men and women. History must include an account of the female experience over time and should include the development of feminist consciousness as an essential aspect of women's past. This is the primary task of women's history. The central question it raises is: What would history be like if it were seen through the eyes of women and ordered by values they define?

What is needed is a new universal history, a holistic history which will be a synthesis of traditional history and women's history. It will be based on close comparative study of given periods in which the historical experiences of men are compared with those of women, their interactions being as much the subject of study as their differences and tensions. Only after a series of such detailed studies has been done and their concepts have entered into the general culture can we hope to find the parameters by which to define the new universal history. But this much can be said already: Only a history based on the recognition that women have always been essential to the making of history and that *men and women* are the measure of significance, will be truly a universal history.

SOURCE: Gerda Lerner, *The Majority Finds Its Past*, pp. 178, 180.

---

Engels in *The Origin of the Family, Private Property, and the State* (1884), but many other theorists have used economics and class as a starting point. This approach is illustrated by Sheila Rowbotham's influential *Women, Resistance, and Revolution* (1972); Juliet Mitchell's four interlocking female structures (production, the reproduction of children, sexuality, and the socialization of children) in *Woman's Estate* (1971); and Zillah Eisenstein's grid pattern for understanding sex and class in concert in *Capitalist Patriarchy and the Case for Socialist Feminism* (1979). What has come to be called "state feminism" in Europe, especially in the Nordic countries, fits into this position. A women's or equality minister is a part of the government, and socialist solutions to women's traditional inequality are made a part of the law.

The next position on the minimizer continuum is one that advocates the sharing of traditional gender characteristics. In order to remedy the psychosocial tyranny that oppresses both men and women, exclusive female parenting that produced "momism" (as well as the fear and hatred of women) must be ended, these feminists argue. This gender difference is a cultural product, not an inherent biological distinction. The psychologists Nancy Chodorow, in *The Reproduction of Mothering* (1978), and Dorothy Dinnerstein, in *The Mermaid and the Minotaur* (1976), both weigh in with this view, although in different ways. Charlotte Perkins Gilman's *Women and Economics* (1898) is an early work with this perspective. Traditional masculine (and valued) characteristics had been mistakenly monopolized by one sex, she believed, while the "feminine" virtues also needed to be shared.

Those who want to abolish gender distinctions completely, creating a gender-free (but not sexless) society, are next on the continuum. Males and females are more similar to each other than either is to any other species, these theorists claim. The anthropologist Gayle Rubin proposed this view in her influential article "The Traffic in Women: Notes on the Political Economy of Sex" (1975). Simone de Beauvoir's renowned *Le deuxième sexe* (1949; *The Second Sex,* 1953) can be read as arguing this point as well. Her goal is for women to become the independent, "transcendent" human beings that men have always had the choice of becoming. Ursula Le Guin's fictional *The Left Hand of Darkness* (1977) posits an androgynous society in which people belong to a particular sex for only a few days a month; for most of the time they function androgynously in both physical and psychological ways.

The extreme pole of the minimizer position is represented by those intensely controversial thinkers who want to abolish not only gender and sex roles but also female reproduction (including conception, pregnancy, and birth) or at least their exclusive ownership by women. Gilman wrote one of the first explorations of such a society. Her fictional *Herland* (1915) envisioned a female-only culture where women conceive by parthenogenesis (without male sperm). In the more recent past, both theorists, such as Shulamith Firestone in *The Dialectic of Sex* (1970), and feminist science-fiction writers, such as Marge Piercy in *Woman on the Edge of Time* (1976), have advocated the abolition of exclusive female reproduction. Many believe that reproductive technology, with its artificial fertilization and implantation of a fertilized egg, is close to making this a reality. The film *Junior* (1994), in which Arnold Schwarzenegger's character becomes pregnant, explores this fantasy in a humorous manner.

***The maximizers.*** All feminists on the maximizer continuum are interested in seeking out, recognizing, and valuing sex-gender difference, especially as it relates to women. Women's specific talents and unique ways of contributing plead for their having a larger role in society. A bumper sticker reading "A Woman's Place is in the House—and in the Senate" uses this maximizer or difference argument, as does one that says "Clean Up Politics—Elect Women."

One notes first the historical "separate spheres" position—that women and men inhabit different physical places in society (private and public) and have different roles, virtues, aptitudes, sensibilities, and "ways of knowing." The nineteenth century saw the first clear use of the separate-spheres philosophy to help ameliorate women's position, in such thinkers as Catharine Beecher and Frances Willard. Later Jane Addams, in *Newer Ideals of Peace* (1907), enunciated the "municipal housekeeping" argument for giving women the vote: women should manage the household, but if they were to do this well, they must be concerned with clean water, pure milk, garbage disposal, and safe streets and parks for their children. They must therefore participate in municipal government by voting and standing for office. People promoting separate spheres in the twenty-first century include conservative women on the New Right and fundamentalist Christians.

The next group on the continuum wants to glorify the "feminine," wherever it may be found, often in writings of male poets. Sometimes identified as postmodern feminists, many of these thinkers are French or influenced by Jacques

Derrida, Jacques Lacan, and other French deconstructionists. Opposed to binary oppositions such as male-female, these feminists wish to assert multiple modes of being and gender. Hélène Cixous, Luce Irigaray, and Julia Kristeva are important writers here, as are Jane Gallop, Joan Scott, and Teresa de Lauretis in the United States and Toril Moi and Gayatri Spivak internationally. Additionally these thinkers would be opposed to the very idea of the two continua, since they often assert that neither "woman" nor "man" can be defined.

Cultural feminists and maternalists occupy a middle position on the maximizer continuum. Cultural feminists celebrate women's spirituality, art, music, and writing, especially in women's bookstores, cafés, theater groups, galleries, holiday centers, and support groups. Both the feminist art movement and the women's music movement, with its annual festivals, have been important in articulating these viewpoints. The maternalists cherish motherhood as the source of woman's difference and superiority. Both practical groups—lesbian parenting, natural and home-birth groups, and the women's health movement—and theorists such as Adrienne Rich in *Of Woman Born: Motherhood as Experience and Institution* (1976) and Sara Ruddick in *Maternal Thinking* (1989) are connected to the maternalist position.

The "woman-as-force" position rejects "woman-as-victim" stances and argues that because of women's close connection to nature—historically, biologically, mythologically, and psychologically—women can save humanity from the destructive path that men have begun. The historian Mary Beard enunciated the woman-as-force position in 1946, while Carol Gilligan's argument that young women take different ethical stances than young men, articulated in her *In a Different Voice* (1982), has influenced psychological and learning theories on gender differences. Another important work in this vein is Mary Field Belenky and her colleagues' *Women's Ways of Knowing* (1986).

Ecofeminism is an important subcategory of the woman-as-force position; the views of various theorists, such as Ynestra King, Susan Griffin, and Karen Warren, have been influential. The Indian nuclear physicist Vandana Shiva's work, especially *Staying Alive: Women, Ecology, and Development* (1988), explores ecofeminism on the global stage and makes connections with postcolonial and development concerns.

The female supremacists occupy the most radical position on the maximizer continuum. Either lesbian or celibate, these most extreme of the separatists advocate a complete partition of the sexes, believing that only with their own institutions can women find freedom. How far separatism is taken depends on the individual, but some advocates call for separate geographical areas for women, attempting self-sufficiency in various communal living situations. Most influential in this argument are Mary Daly, in *Gyn/Ecology: The Metaethics of Radical Feminism* (1978) and *Websters' First New Intergalactic Wickedary of the English Language* (1987); Sonia Johnson, in *Wildfire: Igniting the She/Volution* (1989); Marilyn Frye, in *Some Reflections on Separatism and Power* (1981); and various science-fiction proposals, such as Joanna Russ's *The Female Man* (1975). It should be noted, however, that lesbians are found in all categories of feminism.

### Problems with the model; or, mediating the dichotomy.
The dichotomy of equality-difference or minimizers-maximizers is difficult to maintain and often false, asserts the German critic Gisela Bock, since dichotomies are often hierarchies in disguise. Arguing strongly on the side of difference can lead to the dangerous "difference dilemma" because it can confirm women's inferiority. Yet strong arguments from the equality stance produce the "equality dilemma," in which gender differences are completely erased and everyone is presumed to be the same.

The most fruitful way to deal with the two kinds of arguments is to mediate between them, as some contemporary thinkers have done. There is a suggestive link made by African-American and multicultural feminists who argue the need for forms of socialism (a minimizer strategy) while identifying and celebrating the unique assets supplied to the struggle by strong women of color (a maximizer strategy). "The Combahee River Collective Statement," in *Home Girls* (1983), edited by Barbara Smith, and *This Bridge Called My Back: Writings by Radical Women of Color* (1983), edited by Cherríe Moraga and Gloria Anzaldúa, are essential works in this vein. Likewise the historian Gerda Lerner's conceptualization of "woman as majority" in *The Majority Finds Its Past* (1979) connects maximizer arguments about women's different strengths and special institutions with the minimizer insistence on the necessity of abolishing the sex-gender system and sharing gender.

Other creative thinkers have written of "difference in unity" or "equality in difference." Virginia Woolf, in *Three Guineas* (1938), proposes that women need to belong to a society of outsiders who have the same goals as men but must work in their own way on the borders of the patriarchal system, both inside and outside. In a spoof on the religious vows of monks and nuns, she says that women who belong to this society must take vows of poverty, chastity (of the brain), derision of honors, and freedom from the "unreal loyalties" of nation, class, sex, family, or religion. Members of the Society of Outsiders would agree to earn their own livings "expertly," not engage in any profession that promotes war, and criticize the institutions of education and religion. Only in this way can women help prevent war. Contemporary thinkers, especially Latinas and other bicultural women, such as Gloria Anzaldúa in *Borderlands: The New Mestiza = La Frontera* (1987), or African-American women, such as bell hooks in *Feminist Theory: From Margin to Center* (1984), also explore this "border" position. So-called Third or Developing World feminists (also known as postcolonial feminists) clearly mediate the two strands of theory, with their call for support for nationalist struggles ("all issues are women's issues" and "if it's appropriate technology, it's appropriate for women") and their recognition of women's continuing "double day" work (housework, child care, and productive or economic activities) at every level of society around the world.

## Controversies
As "the most powerful force affecting women in higher education today," according to Mariam Chamberlain of the Ford Foundation, women's studies stands at the cusp of several controversies. Many of the criticisms of the early days (the standard retort from men in power was "When are we going to have men's studies?") have disappeared into internal controversies among practitioners: Should women's studies attempt to integrate into the regular curriculum or remain an autonomous outsider? Should women's studies opt for discourse theory, forsaking political action on which women's studies was built? Can you teach what you have not experienced? Can a white woman teach multiculturalism? Should people give priority to transgendered and other sexual concerns over against the concerns of postcolonial and developing nations?

The dangers of identity politics and the threatening allegation of essentialism have fractured the unity of women's studies programs. But disciplinary identities can be as dangerous, such that the feminist literary critic or the feminist sociologist hearkens back to her disciplinary language and methodology, even as she is opposed to those disciplines' contents. What often happens now in women's studies programs is that the senior faculty continue their disciplinary identity, leaving the junior faculty to be the "identity reps" of Chicana, Asian, or African-American ethnicity and prey to the charge of essentialism.

Another difficulty is the ubiquitous presentism that is now everywhere in women's studies. Although women's history was one of the earliest and strongest supporters of women's studies, women's and gender history have moved largely into their own field, with dedicated journals and conferences. Few sessions on history are to be found now at National Women's Studies Association conferences or at the International Interdisciplinary Congress on Women. Both the history of the discipline and women's history itself therefore stand to be marginalized or ghettoized from women's studies. Worse, the disciplines have so embraced women's studies that "translation" is now necessary in moving a course from women's studies to, say, literature or sociology.

There is often a conflict between those faculty who "privilege gender or gender and sexuality, as analytical frameworks, and those who also incorporate race, colonialism, and class," say Laura Donaldson, Anne Donadey, and Jael Silliman, in their article in Robyn Wiegman's edited collection, *Women's Studies on its Own* (Donaldson, Donadey, and Silliman, p. 439). And often in the United States, globalization is little more than "a Cold War production of knowledge," which compares other areas to the United States to their detriment, continuing a dangerous U.S.-centrism.

Still, with all the fragmentation, the "center holds." Women's studies as a concept and a practice is here to stay. It has been so institutionalized, there is so much new knowledge and new scholarship, there have been so many hearts and minds changed through this study that the various splits and positions can only help to proliferate the ideas.

*See also* **Equality: Gender Equality; Feminism; Gender; Human Rights: Women's Rights; Structuralism and Poststructuralism; Women's History.**

**BIBLIOGRAPHY**

Belenky, Mary Field, Blythe McVicker Clinchy, Nancy Rule Goldberger, and Jill Mattuck Tarule. *Women's Ways of Knowing: The Development of Self, Voice, and Mind.* New York: Basic Books, 1986.

Bird, Elizabeth. "Women's Studies in European Higher Education." *European Journal of Women's Studies* 3, no. 3 (1996): 151–165.

Bock, Gisela. "Challenging Dichotomies: Perspectives on Women's History." In *Writing Women's History: International Perspectives,* edited by Karen Offen, Ruth Roach Pierson, and Jane Rendall, 1–24. Bloomington: Indiana University Press, 1991.

Boxer, Marilyn Jacoby. *When Women Ask the Questions: Creating Women's Studies in America.* Baltimore, Md.: Johns Hopkins University Press, 1998.

Donaldson, Laura E., Anne Donadey, and Jael Silliman. "Subversive Couplings: On Anti-Racism and Postcolonialism in Graduate Women's Studies." In *Women's Studies on Its Own,* edited by Robyn Wiegman, 438–456. Durham, N.C.: Duke University Press, 2002.

Frye, Marilyn. *Some Reflections on Separatism and Power.* East Lansing, Mich.: Tea Rose, 1981.

Grewal, Inderpal, and Caren Kaplan, eds. *Scattered Hegemonies: Postmodernity and Transnational Feminist Practices.* Minneapolis: University of Minnesota Press, 1994.

Hacker, Helen. "Women as a Minority Group." *Social Forces* 30 (1951): 60–69.

hooks, bell. *Feminist Theory: From Margin to Center.* 2nd ed. Cambridge, Mass.: South End Press, 2000.

———. *Teaching to Transgress: Education as the Practice of Freedom.* New York: Routledge, 1994.

Howe, Florence, ed. *The Politics of Women's Studies: Testimony from Thirty Founding Mothers.* New York: Feminist Press, 2000.

Lerner, Gerda. *Fireweed: A Political Autobiography.* Philadelphia: Temple University Press, 2002.

———. *The Majority Finds Its Past.* New York: Oxford University Press, 1979.

Lerner, Gerda, ed. *Black Women in White America: A Documentary History.* New York: Pantheon, 1972.

Messer-Davidow, Ellen. *Disciplining Feminism: From Social Activism to Academic Discourse.* Durham, N.C., and London: Duke University Press, 2002.

Minnich, Elizabeth Kamarck. *Transforming Knowledge.* Philadelphia: Temple University Press, 1990.

Moraga, Cherríe, and Gloria Anzaldúa. *This Bridge Called My Back: Writings by Radical Women of Color.* Latham, N.Y.: Kitchen Table/Women of Color Press, 1983.

O'Barr, Jean Fox. *Feminism in Action: Building Institutions and Community through Women's Studies.* Chapel Hill: University of North Carolina Press, 1984.

Offen, Karen. "Defining Feminism: A Comparative Historical Approach." *Signs* 17 (Fall 1988): 119–157.

Scott, Joan Wallach. *Gender and the Politics of History.* Rev. ed. New York: Columbia University Press, 1999.

Shiva, Vandana. *Staying Alive: Women, Ecology, and Development.* London: Zed Books, 1988.

Smith, Barbara. *The Truth That Never Hurts: Writings on Race, Gender, and Freedom.* New Brunswick, N.J.: Rutgers University Press, 1998.

Smith, Barbara, ed. *Home Girls.* Latham, N.Y.: Kitchen Table/Women of Color Press, 1983.

Tong, Rosemarie. *Feminist Thought: A More Comprehensive Introduction.* 2nd ed. Boulder, Colo.: Westview, 1998.

Warren, Karen J. *Ecofeminism: Women, Culture, Nature.* Bloomington: Indiana University Press, 1997.

Woolf, Virginia. *Three Guineas.* New York: Harcourt, Brace, and World, 1966.

*Margaret H. McFadden*

**WORK.** Work as a unitary experience, set off in time and place from the rest of life, is a concept bound in the culture of wage labor (see especially Thompson, 1967, on disciplined promptness and time regulation accompanying factory work). Only when effort—physical and mental—is turned into a commodity sold to an employer who then monitors and controls it can we discern an abstract concept of "work." Other concepts stand outside of that context, such as "a work" being a finished product of a craftsperson or artist, or work divided into concrete activities of particular people—warrior, farmer, smith, and so on. The situation where productive activities blend into the overall flow of daily life especially challenges our commonsense notion of work. In the recent past of the Dobe Ju/'hoansi of Botswana, women, men, and children sporadically gathered plant foods and hunted small animals, interspersed with visiting, eating, and relaxing. Hunting large animals, performed by men, stood out from the rest of life because meat was desired and was the basis for much social interchange. But although the ethnographer Richard Lee could designate specific activities as "work" in his own cultural terms, and count the hours and minutes spent in them (surprisingly little time was needed to produce quite satisfactory subsistence), no clear concept equivalent to abstract work emerged from the Ju/'hoansi themselves.

Many cultures do distinguish activities requiring disciplined effort and focus to produce a concrete result, however. Among farmer-fishermen living by Lake Titicaca, Benjamin Orlove found that the general word *work* (Spanish *trabajo* or Quechua *llank'ay*) was used only in conjunction with a specific activity. This demanded concentrated effort, often physical but sometimes mental, and produced a tangible product, so that fishing was "work" while repairing nets while sitting, chatting, and relaxing was not. The richest study of work embedded in culture is Bronislaw Malinowski's ethnographic classic, *Coral Gardens and Their Magic* (1935), which focuses on the rituals of birth, growth, and death and the magical control over chance that envelop South Pacific farming and fishing. Although there is a long tradition of considering labor to be the defining human characteristic (e.g., Karl Marx, discussed below), when looking across cultures we see instead a pattern of alternation between disciplined routine and vibrant, expressive release. Both qualities, then, must be part of our understanding of humanity.

Another methodological concern in studying work is that upper-class intellectuals have produced most of the texts. There are two serious problems with writing a history of the idea of work based solely on these authors, who may or may not have personally experienced or carefully observed nonintellectual labor. First, they represent the interests, perspectives, and biases of their social origin and position. Second, they often take the articulate words of intellectuals to be the sole or characteristic voice of their era or place. But these authoritative sources do not necessarily represent the full range of ideas within a complex and unequal society, even if they do influence the notions of others. Thus in a society dominated by men, we often hear little about women's ideas of work; in a society of landowners, artisans, and slaves, we often hear little from the latter two groups. How are we to rectify this? We should locate and listen to working people's voices as directly as possible, through novels and diaries (e.g., Levi), or at least such voices mediated by careful and sympathetic observers (e.g., Mintz; Nash). And we should be imaginative in uncovering evidence about the conceptual lives of nonintellectuals, paying attention to folklore, jokes, inscriptions on products, and so on.

## Pre-Capitalist Civilizations: The Incas, India, and Classical Greece and Rome

Getting beyond the articulate voices of intellectuals is especially a problem for understanding civilizations before the era of widespread printing and literacy. However, cross-cultural comparison allows us to highlight similarities and differences. This article compares concepts of work from three widely separated world regions: the Inca empire of the Andes before the Spanish conquest, the Indian subcontinent (South Asia) before British colonialism, and the Greek and Roman world before the Christian era. In the Andes, archaeological evidence

from the epoch before the Incas shows that large public works (walls, temples, canals) were constructed by multiple communities each working on its own small, essentially equivalent segment. There was no division of labor by task, but rather by community. Similarly, in the Inca period, people paid the principal taxes to the state not in the form of money or goods but as collective labor service, as communities or segments of communities (e.g., all young men of an area would serve as imperial message runners). Conceptually, this labor service took the form of reciprocity between unequal social ranks, from village to regional lord to emperor; for example, harvesting the lands of the emperor and his official religion, the cult of the sun, was reciprocated by extensive gifts of cloth and corn beer. In the late empire, however, what had started as a system of independent agricultural communities giving tribute to the state was radically transformed with new forms of labor that were disarticulated from the local community, and turned into permanent labor forces at the service of the Inca aristocracy.

In South Asia, we see a similar pattern of unequal reciprocity. Under the *jajmani* system, local caste groups owed a variety of work services and products to each other, from tanning to weaving to conducting rituals. Indeed, it is plausibly speculated that castes originated as hereditary occupations. At the level of ideas, work was not thought of as a unitary subject performed by a free (if socially grounded) individual; instead, group productive roles existed, marked by highly unequal but also reciprocal qualities of ritual purity, such as the work of tanners—conceived as polluting—which interlocked with the putatively pure work of Brahmin priests. Clearly, this was an ideology that explains and endorses inequality, though it also allowed space for change (as local castes maneuvered for changed work roles with improved ritual rank) and resistance (as groups dropped out of the system by conversion to egalitarian religions like Buddhism or Islam).

We notice a pattern in these precapitalist class societies in which the idea of work was differentiated into concrete products or tasks associated with specific collective groups, in turn synthesized into a functioning economy through unequal exchanges, mystified as mutual and reciprocal in nature. Though group membership was envisioned in various ways, cultural, linguistic, religious, and so forth, it was often the case that groups consisted of or were identified with a specific kind of work, and that such work carried denigrating or exalting qualities.

With this in mind, we can better situate Greek and Roman ideas about work, which constitute in part the roots of the Western intellectual tradition. The early Greek oral traditions of Homer and Hesiod idealize the work of the farmer, as do early Roman stories about Cincinnatus, the patriotic farmer-general. These "farmers," however, were owners of large estates and masters of extensive households in which women, slaves, and other subordinates labored, so these ideals highlight not hard work in general but the hands-on management of rural production. By contrast, classical Greek thought turned against work, especially for others (self-sufficient farming was still esteemed). The ideal in Plato (c. 428–348 or 347 B.C.E.) and Aristotle (384–322 B.C.E.) was the man free of necessity, with leisure to engage in politics and contemplation.

There was particular disdain for merchants, who made money by trade rather than production from the land, and for artisans, who crafted goods with their hands. The productive and reproductive work of women was largely ignored. The classic Roman authors, such as Cicero (106–43 B.C.E.), held roughly the same views. This constitutes a characteristic inversion of the social reality surrounding such authors: they lived in commercially vibrant cities whose wealth came from extensive long-distance trade in farm and handcraft products. The idle rich, with time for political and natural theory, drew income from this economy, while distinguishing themselves by denigrating its key actors: slaves, foreigners, and craftsmen.

Unlike the Inca and South Asian examples cited above, in the Greco-Roman case there seems to be no specific mandate to reciprocity (however unequal) between direct laborers and intellectual elites. Perhaps this difference is the result of the greater division of labor and differentiation of roles in the rich commercial Mediterranean, creating more conceptual separation between urban authors and direct producers. The brief glimpses we have of the idea-worlds of artisans differ significantly from the famous classical writers; numerous inscriptions on pottery express pride and status in well-made handcrafts. Also, there were in Rome collegia, large clubs of craftsmen, with a rich mythological and ceremonial life. Though inarticulate in the sense of bequeathing to us extended texts, these represent alternative views of work from the famous disdain of Plato or Aristotle.

### European Ideas from the Late Roman Era to the Industrial Revolution

Early Christianity turned away from Roman and Greek elite arrogance toward work. Jesus and the Apostles were peasant-craftsmen, and though early Christianity spread among wealthier urban populaces, there was in its communalism little room for denigration of merchants, slaves, and workers. St. Paul, a tentmaker, used the expression, "my fellow workers." St. Augustine (354–430) extolled work as a means of moral perfection and saw it as an expression of human genius, thereby glorifying God. This line of thought found practical expression in Christian monasticism, which prized hard, focused work—forest clearing, agriculture, manuscript illumination, and so forth. Monks did not value labor in itself, but insofar as it offered dedication and discipline to God, and supported the more important role of prayer. The church viewed non-monastic human work as being in the image of God's work, a generally favorable attitude to labor that would continue in Catholic thought to the present.

The medieval concept of "estates," much like the castes of India, organized society by collective work functions, duties, and rights—nobility, church, and peasantry/laborers—but relegated the direct producers of society to the lowest order. However, towns were different. They had merchants and moneylenders, the antecedents of capitalism, and also the craft guilds. Guilds embodied an ideal of gradually accumulated knowledge and dexterity, culminating in personal mastery of the entire production process, including control of the materials, tools, and markets for finished goods. This concept of control and mastery was manifested in group rules and rituals that marked guild members off from nonmembers.

The rise of Protestantism, in conjunction with growing commercialization in cities, transformed Western ideas about work. Martin Luther's (1483–1546) concepts reflected medieval social orders, in which everyone worked according to the trade in which they were born. However, he rejected the Catholic doctrine of higher and lower "callings" in favor of a singular, individualistic notion of "calling," a strong incentive to action. More importantly, John Calvin (1509–1564) forged a radically new vision of work. He saw success in life as a sign of God's predestined favor to the person. In a curious, but profound way, this doctrine that denied free will ended up strongly motivating labor and profit-making, since the individual cherished hard work and success as signs of heavenly election. Consistent with its roots in rising commercial centers, Calvinism also considered trade, profits, and finance as of equal value with direct production. This represents a distinct break with a long previous tradition of disdain for money-making in favor of farming.

Surveying this history, the great German sociologist Max Weber (1864–1920) argued that Protestantism stimulated the rise of European capitalism during the sixteenth to eighteenth centuries, but significant criticisms have emerged. First, Weber overstated the asceticism of early capitalists and underestimated the role of consumption as a stimulus to work and economic growth. Second, mercantile capitalism arose first in Catholic regions of northern Italy and southern Germany. Weber focused on a somewhat later period in its development. Likewise, a distinctive east Asian form of capitalism has taken hold in the twentieth century in a world region without deep Christian traditions (Japan, China, and Korea). It is debatably linked to Confucian and other east Asian worldviews that emphasize group orientation and profound feelings of duty (as opposed to Western individualism). Weber did, however, seem to catch a broadly applicable aspect of the thinking of rising capitalists, their breaking with agrarian traditionalism concerned with protecting inherited class privileges and old-fashioned luxuries. For intellectual history more generally, his work pioneered the exploration of ideas as causes and not just reflections of social change.

The concept that labor was the singular source of value in goods, the ultimate basis of wealth, now emerged in a context of rising landowner-capitalists dedicated to transforming traditional means of production. Unlike in later eras when this "labor theory of value" would serve to highlight conflict between workers and capitalists, the early version emphasized the new landlord's role, taking private property out of the shared state of nature by adding the specific element of organized effort. This also conformed to the European expropriation of world resources after Columbus—putting the assumed "state of nature" to work, including human populations in the slave trade, land in the plantation colonies, and silver and gold in the mines of the Americas. John Locke's (1632–1704) *Two Treatises on Government* epitomize this line of argument. It offered a truly radical turn of thought by finding value in secular human action rather than, as in the Middle Ages, from fixed social rank combined with God's awesome majesty. Instead, the image of God became like that of man: God the maker. This fascination with making was the inspiration of eighteenth-century French and British Enlightenment attention to mechanisms of all kinds, natural and artificial. Denis Diderot (1713–1784), the son of a prosperous knifemaker, included the mechanical arts in his encyclopedia of natural and philosophical knowledge and insisted on the worth of artisans and artisanry. With these ideas, and with the concurrent rise of global trade, putting out manufacturing of cloth, improved agriculture, and the like, we have set the stage for modern wage labor and capitalism.

## The Capitalist Era

Beginning in the late eighteenth century, new theories of work under capitalism emerged.

*Smith and Ricardo.* In 1776 the United States declared independence and Adam Smith (1723–1790) published *The Wealth of Nations.* Within the history of ideas, this is the year best suited to mark the full birth of capitalism, though as we saw above, the change had been long coming; and it was still to be a few decades before artificially powered factories began to diffuse outward from northern England and Scotland. Smith's view of work must be understood within his wider understanding of markets, since he saw markets as leading to the division of labor in detail, breaking production into a series of discrete operations, performed repetitively and with a focused perfection by different kinds and grades of workers. This concept, which was to become pervasive in capitalist practice, is exactly the opposite of the medieval notion of the unity of all stages of work in a craft. Smith was ambivalent about his vision of the trajectory of work, however, since he feared that this division of labor would dull the mind of the worker. (This worry is characteristic of Smith, who both forecast the power of markets and capitalism and explored moral sentiments that bind otherwise materialistic and competitive people.)

Smith accepted the labor theory of value, but it was propounded most emphatically by David Ricardo (1772–1823) around 1810. In the mid-nineteenth century, it was adopted by Karl Marx (1818–1883) and has been a mainstay of orthodox Marxism since then. The labor theory of value holds that as people make and reshape the raw materials of nature and transform them into objects of use ("use value"), their market values ("exchange value") come from the physical and mental effort in that work. It is, in part, a theory of price, but more widely it is a theory of the commonality in the values that each individual idiosyncratically attributes to objects. Clearly, a labor theory of value exalts work as a fundamental theme of human life. In Ricardo's hand, it highlighted the producing classes, capital and labor together, against the dead hand of rent-collecting landlords—in other words, it announced the birth of capitalism out of feudalism. In Marx's subsequent version, however, it valued workers against capitalists, the direct producers against the surplus-collecting owners of tools and resources ("means of production"), which are the congealed results of labors past. To Marx, this announced the future birth of communism out of capitalism. Neoclassical economists of the late nineteenth and twentieth centuries avoided the question of intersubjective value and transfer of value between classes altogether, narrowing their concern to how prices are set in particular markets. Other radical perspectives have looked to nonlabor theories of value,

especially energy and other ecological-physical value sources. Flawed as it may be, however, the labor theory of value captures something of the relationship of past work (capital) to present work (laborers), which is both an existential necessity and the basis for unequal and exploitative power relations.

*Karl Marx.* Marx offered a comprehensive, radical theory of work. In his labor-based worldview, human activity is central to making and transforming all aspects of life, including the concepts we use to understand it. It is important that we recognize that this is not a purely economic perspective, which is often assumed about Marx, but a much wider emphasis on the practice of life rather than the play of unworldly ideas. Likewise, his view of labor is wider than physical effort in factories, though Marx himself focused on this (then new) feature of capitalism. Rather, the term *labor* captures the full range of human capacities, as much mental and creative as physical and forceful.

This understood, we turn to alienation, Marx's central concern about work. At times we labor for ourselves, and though the product may be outside our bodies (e.g., my cleaned desk), we are not highly alienated from it. It is part of our being. At other times, we labor directly for others (e.g., a garden I plant for my wife), rendering a product that someone else will possess, use, and enjoy. But though the product is separated from us, it becomes part of a social bond, a nonalienated relation to another human being. However, under the condition of commodity production (making a good for anonymous sale), and even more importantly in wage labor under capitalism (working on a good that is owned by someone else, in a manner controlled by someone else), the result of our labors has no connection or relation to us. It is alienated. To take, for example, the division of labor in a bank, we will see that one worker will collect data, another sum it up, and a third give it a credit score, based on research by a fourth, fifth, and so on. No one worker has an organic relationship to the owner of the labor (the bank), the final product of labor (the mortgage), or the person who receives the product (the potential homeowner). Alienation is, in Marx, a matter of objective relationships, but it has subjective, felt implications—a sense that the product or the customer or the firm does not matter, that the individual has no control or commitment to work, that the whole goal of labor is vague or even unimaginable.

Within this broad framework, Marx launched a critical analysis of work under capitalism. If capitalists want to profit, labor has to render enough value to cover two funds. One is to pay workers enough to live, that is, to "reproduce" labor power. The other is for capitalists to hold the "surplus value." Marx thus saw unequal reward for work at the heart of capitalism; assuming the labor theory of value, work activity produces all the value, but the workers receive only part of it. The rest is captured by the owners of past labor, the means of production. If total value can be conceptually divided into the necessary payment to workers and surplus value, then capitalists who seek constantly to add to their invested capital (to "accumulate capital") have two basic strategies. One is to increase the total length of the working day, so that workers are paid for ten hours, say, enough to survive, but have to work

WORK

for two hours beyond that. Marx called this absolute surplus value. The other is to make the workers' efforts during a given period of time more productive. More could be paid to workers, possibly, but the total product would increase even more quickly, rendering yet more surplus value. Obtaining this "relative surplus value" is, according to Marx, the main logic governing work under capitalism: not that work becomes more and more brutal, though sometimes it does, but that it becomes more and more dominated by the efficiency of production, especially via technology, the dead labor of the past used to speed up the live labor of the present.

Marx thus foresaw the ultimate polarization of capital and labor, leading to a revolution by the workers. Capital would accumulate more and more means of production, pushing relative surplus value ever more extremely, and workers would have more and more in common, as each would experience the same alienated and fractured labor. Both classes would become clearer in self-definition and self-understanding, and more openly in struggle between them, until a fundamental historical transformation (a "revolution") would usher in a new state of communism. Marx failed to think clearly about this future, being always focused on the immediate task of criticism and hostile to utopias, but he hints at a life of holistic, undivided labor, producing goods that were directly shared or exchanged in webs of immediate social relations. This recital indicates two major flaws in Marx's thought. Neither workers nor capitalists have become clearly defined and self-recognized classes across national or ethnic lines, though capitalists have come closer than Marx's preferred workers. And actual communism formed a series of dystopias, dedicated to the mass production of commodities in alienating factories with worker's labor unions and other self-expressions (e.g., religion) severely controlled or repressed by domineering political-economic masters: the worst of capitalism without the leavening of democracy and civil liberties. However, no worker, student, or activist in the modern world can ignore Marx's analysis of work, whether one seeks to defend or to transform capitalism.

## Non-Marxist and Neo-Marxist Views of Work under Capitalism

Marx looked to the future, embracing the development of work under capitalism as the necessary stage before communism. Other critics looked backward, drawing on (sometimes quite unrealistic) visions of medieval craft guilds or the mutualistic cooperation of the village community. Utopian socialists in the early nineteenth century, such as Charles Fourier (1772–1837) and the Scottish industrialist-turned-radical Robert Owen (1771–1858), sought the productivity of capitalism without alienation and inequality through communal mass production and the equal exchange of products between specialized craftspeople. The late-nineteenth-century artist, designer, and philosopher William Morris put forth an ideal of craft mastery against the division of labor and of creativity rooted in knowledge of the past. The gadfly economist Thorstein Veblen (1857–1929) explored related ideals about productive creativity and disciplined work, but instead of archaic crafts guilds, he envisioned as social carriers the combined figures of industrial engineers and workers. He turned a critical gaze against financiers, the accumulators and manipulators of money, who he regarded as the parasites (the "leisure class") of otherwise productive capitalism.

Émile Durkheim (1858–1917), a French sociologist-anthropologist who worked at the beginning of the twentieth century, offered perhaps the most perceptive defense of work under capitalism in *The Division of Labor in Society*. In traditional societies, people did pretty much the same work, so they bonded with each other from their sameness ("mechanical solidarity"). But with the advance of the detailed division of labor, people no longer do the same work. Instead, their mutual interdependence creates a new, "organic" solidarity—unity from difference. This denied Marx's postulate of ultimately polarized classes. Durkheim's work is especially important in that he recognizes and confronts some of capitalism's most troubling developments, such as division and inequality (he was, we should note, a vigorous reformer who favored socialism). But his solution represents a mystical hope. Why should the division of labor result in solidarity and not worsening alienation and increasing fractionation of work?

The troubling qualities of contemporary, alienating work sparked two important mid- to late-twentieth-century statements affirming its underlying value. Catholic social teaching, as expressed in Pope John Paul II's *Laborem exercens* (*On Human Work*), views work as a distinguishing feature of humankind. Through work, people come to understand their role in and obligation to a society, and to humanity as a whole. Likewise, work is a crucial source of self-respect and identity. This both establishes ideals of what work can be and provides a basis for critical evaluation of work in capitalism and socialism, where people become the objects rather than the subjects of work. *Laborem exercens* values labor over capital, though it accepts a subordinated role for capitalism. Hannah Arendt also sees work as crucial to the human condition, but she distinguishes between labor and work in an interesting fashion. Labor is the instrumental use of the body to make things that will be consumed and will not last long; work is the use of the mind and the hands to create things that will endure, the world of art and artifacts that surround and enrich human lives. She criticizes contemporary economics for blurring these two categories, for sacrificing the enduring monuments of work in favor of impermanent, mass-produced consumer goods. Insightful as this temporal perspective is, it seems biased toward artists and intellectuals and dismisses the creativity and necessity of daily chores, particularly those associated with women.

In 1974 Harry Braverman refocused the debate over work around the perspective of Marx. He argued that capitalists do not just buy labor power but seek to control the performance of work itself. Work may be considered to have two components, mental and physical (often called manual). To capture control over work is to take its mental side, the skills, knowledge, and initiative, away from the worker and put it in the hands of the employer. This is done through observation and redesign of physical motions (time-motion engineering), by building work skills into technologies and production layouts, and by bureaucratically controlled reward systems. Debate has raged over his reading of work history; for example, some

WORK

technologies remove existing skills but introduce new skills. Nor are workers ever completely deskilled; even highly controlled and designed workplaces require subtle tricks and informal group cooperation. But after Braverman, we can no longer view new technology or management reform as simply neutral, as always means of greater efficiency and saving of effort; the forces behind such changes bear critical scrutiny.

In summary, writers of the last two centuries have viewed capitalist work with great ambivalence. From Smith, through Marx, to Arendt and Braverman, there is a sense that capitalism provides us a bounty of goods, but at the cost of controlled, subdivided, unchallenging, and unimaginative labors that do not tap the richness of human creative capacity. Ethnographers of workplaces generally agree with these views, but note that workers often find a sense of play and accomplishment in their jobs. Some bit of humanity peeks through.

## The Social Sciences and Work: Key Ideas

Feminism has contributed the social sciences' most important insight about work: that is, work often performed by males, wage work or work outside the household, has been assumed to be the only kind of work, while work often performed by women, such as childcare or gardening, is left invisible or dismissed as mere chores and hobbies (this can be extended to activities of many men, such as tinkering with cars). To think of women's labor as work means to think not only of producing objects but also reproducing (renewing) the conditions of daily life. It means widening our ideas about what work is, for example in Arlie Hochschild's studies of emotional and nurturing care as work. And it challenges everyday language, such as "going out to work" and identifying a person by their paid occupation.

We thus need to keep open minds about what sorts of activities constitute work. The world of work is more diverse than stereotypical images of factories or heavy physical labor. Bureaucrats, for example, engage in "thought-work," the partly rationalized mass production of mental and verbal operations required to classify and regulate other people. Work thus involves tremendously varied experiences and ideas about those experiences, even within wage labor. Different workplaces and occupations have their own subcultural norms and symbols; the so-called "informal" workplace organization of friendship, collaboration, and factionalism often differs from the official organizational chart of power and authority. Participant-observation in workplaces has shown that informal organization surrounding minutely differentiated tasks and pay rates interdigitates with inequalities brought from the wider world, including gender, race, and ethnic background. Workplace friction, then, both reflects and exacerbates wider societal conflicts. The concept of "segmentation" aims to summarize such patterns of inequality of work and employment conditions. It highlights, in particular, the differences between jobs with specific entry requirements (e.g., educational credentials), relative stability, ascending careers, generous fringe benefits, and so on, and jobs that come and go, with few entry requirements, little future, low pay, and poor or no benefits. Working people holding the latter jobs are much more vulnerable to recurrent unemployment, giving rise to patterns of persistent rural and inner-city poverty that we perceive as "social problems."

Social scientists have also debated whether and how work has changed in recent history. Three key phases emerge from this literature. In Taylorism, named after management consultant Frederick Taylor (most active in the 1890s), management controls virtually every motion of workers through a combination of minute subdivision of tasks, detailed instructions, and monetary incentives for rapid and efficient performance. In Fordism, named after automobile manufacturer Henry Ford (most active in the 1910s and 1920s), relatively high rates of pay joined high-speed, high-pressure jobs; its broader social effect was a high-production, high-consumption, joint corporate/labor union economy characteristic of privileged segments of the Western economy from the 1940s to the 1970s. Post-Fordism, also termed flexible production, or Japanese-style management, has emerged since the 1980s. This is a contradictory concept. On the one hand, hierarchies of control are supposedly flattened and cooperative groups promoted. On the other hand, unions are dismissed as old-fashioned, even attacked and broken, workers are treated as "flexible," that is, easy to hire and fire, and corporate culture and human relations are deftly manipulated by management.

A debate has emerged in the literature about post-Fordism over whether, with computers and other advanced technologies, the tedious, Taylorist and Fordist jobs of the past will disappear. The social theorist André Gorz argues that the immense productive capacity of the modern economy makes possible vastly reduced effort, a life of leisure, self-cultivation, or voluntary and avocational work. In abstract terms, Gorz's argument makes sense and is an appealing ideal. Yet in post-Fordist conditions, the demands of work (both in terms of sheer time spent at work and people's tendency to take work "home" via computer, cell phone, etc.) have actually increased (Schor). This debate poses the question of whether the modernist image of labor as factory work and analyses, such as Marx's, that apply to it, are relevant to contemporary (flexible or postmodern) capitalism. Contemporary capitalism involves corporate and governmental entities of enormous size, complexly distributed working processes, rapidity of movement and information transfer, and finely tuned systems of psychological control. Some authors feel that this constitutes a networked capitalism characterized by loose, relaxed relationships, flexibility, and constant change. Others portray systems of power in which external surveillance becomes included as part of the individual's own watchful self. There is a strange mixture of giddy futurism and hopeless surrender in postmodern perspectives. Though often presented as arguments against Marx, these visions extend his notion of alienated labor to the point where the commoditization of the person as worker and consumer has completely colonized the self. The main difference is that they abandon his hope of a revolutionary break with alienation. Yet we should question whether such corporate forms really have eliminated all competing notions of human creativity and self-directed discipline. Likewise, the predicted end of the factory is incorrect and Western-centric; the mind-numbing mass production of everyday goods has shifted to newly developing countries such as China, South Korea, Malaysia, Mexico, Brazil, and others. Though not simply replicas of the past, such places do in their own way re-create the "dark Satanic mills" of William Blake's early industrial Britain.

*See also* **Capitalism; Economics; Marxism; Poverty; Wealth.**

BIBLIOGRAPHY

Applebaum, Herbert A. *The Concept of Work: Ancient, Medieval, and Modern.* Albany: State University of New York Press, 1992. An excellent survey of the history of Western ideas about work, on which I have drawn substantially.

———, ed. *Work in Market and Industrial Societies.* Albany: State University of New York Press, 1984. A continuation of the previous entry.

———, ed. *Work in Non-Market and Transitional Societies.* Albany: State University of New York Press, 1984. A valuable anthology about work across cultures.

Arendt, Hannah. *The Human Condition.* Chicago: University of Chicago Press, 1958.

Braverman, Harry. *Labor and Monopoly Capital: The Degradation of Work in the Twentieth Century.* New York: Monthly Review Press, 1974.

Cornfield, Daniel B., and Randy Hodson, eds. *Worlds of Work: Building an International Sociology of Work.* New York: Kluwer Academic/Plenum Publishers, 2002. A comprehensive survey of the social sciences of work in diverse nations.

Durkheim, Émile. *The Division of Labor in Society.* New York: Free Press, 1964.

Gordon, David M., Richard Edwards, and Michael Reich. *Segmented Work, Divided Workers: The Historical Transformation of Labor in the United States.* Cambridge, U.K., and New York: Cambridge University Press, 1982. An excellent source on segmentation and changing concepts of industrial work.

Gorz, André. *Paths to Paradise: On the Liberation from Work.* Translated by Malcolm Imrie. Boston: South End Press, 1985.

Hochschild, Arlie Russell. *The Managed Heart: Commercialization of Human Feeling.* Berkeley: University of California Press, 1983.

John Paul II. *On Human Work: Encyclical Laborem exercens.* Washington, D.C.: Office of Publishing Services, United States Catholic Conference, 1981.

Joyce, Patrick, ed. *The Historical Meanings of Work.* Cambridge, U.K., and New York: Cambridge University Press, 1987. A valuable collection, emphasizing concepts of work beyond those of articulate intellectuals.

Lee, Richard B. *The !Kung San: Men, Women, and Work in a Foraging Society.* Cambridge, U.K., and New York: Cambridge University Press, 1979.

Levi, Primo. *The Monkey's Wrench.* Translated by William Weaver. New York: Summit Books, 1986.

Malinowski, Bronislaw. *Coral Gardens and Their Magic.* 2 vols. Bloomington: Indiana University Press, 1965.

Marx, Karl, and Friedrich Engels. *The Marx-Engels Reader.* Edited by Robert C. Tucker. New York: Norton, 1972.

Mintz, Sidney W. *Worker in the Cane: A Puerto Rican Life History.* New Haven, Conn.: Yale University Press, 1960.

Nash, June. *I Spent My Life in the Mines: The Story of Juan Rojas, Bolivian Tin Miner.* New York: Columbia University Press, 1992.

Orlove, Benjamin S. *Lines in the Water: Nature and Culture at Lake Titicaca.* Berkeley: University of California Press, 2002.

Schor, Juliet B. *The Overworked American: The Unexpected Decline of Leisure.* New York: Basic Books, 1991.

Smith, Adam. *An Inquiry into the Nature and Causes of the Wealth of Nations.* Edited by Edwin Cannan. New York: Modern Library, 1994.

Thompson, E. P., "Time, Work Discipline, and Industrial Capitalism." *Past and Present* 38 (1967): 56–97.

———. *William Morris: Romantic to Revolutionary.* New York: Pantheon Books, 1977. A representative figure of the nineteenth-century romantic critique of industrial work. Originally published in 1955.

Veblen, Thorstein. *The Instinct of Workmanship, and the State of the Industrial Arts.* New York: A. M. Kelley, 1964.

Weber, Max. *The Protestant Ethic and the Spirit of Capitalism.* Translated by Talcott Parson. New York: Charles Scribner's Sons, 1958.

*Josiah McC. Heyman*

# WORLD SYSTEMS THEORY, LATIN AMERICA.

The term *world systems analysis* was coined in 1974 by Immanuel Wallerstein to refer to a broad set of ideas about the global political economy, and especially the relationship between Latin America and the dominant economies of Europe and the United States, which were then gaining currency. The phrase *world system* is explored in detail in Wallerstein's famous book *The Modern World-System: Capitalist Agriculture and the Origins of the European World Economy in the Sixteenth Century* (1976). The form of critical inquiry advanced in this legendary study was then used in varying ways around the globe by such other scholars as Samir Amin of Senegal, Giovanni Arrighi of Italy, and André Gunder Frank of Germany, all of whom collaborated with Wallerstein on a notable book published through Monthly Review Press in 1982 entitled *Dynamics of Global Crisis*.

Landmark theories often emerge when the concrete events of history demand a new politics, and with it a new explanatory framework. Such was the case with world systems theory, and the preceding dependency theory of the 1960s and 1970s. As anthropologist Eric Wolf would later write, these intellectual movements tried to synthesize theoretically informed history with historically informed theory in response to the pressing problem, expressed most acutely during the political upheavals of 1968, "to discover history, a history that would account for the ways in which the social system of the modern world came into being," since "only in this way could we come to comprehend the forces that impel societies and cultures here and now" (p. ix). As this statement—and Wolf's own political activism in the United States during the 1960s—makes clear, world systems theory and its antecedent movements were not merely intellectual exercises; the scholars involved in them were also activists, many of whom risked their lives and suffered political repression, imprisonment, and exile in their efforts to transform the unequal system they abhorred.

## The Age of Decolonization and the Failings of Modernization Theory

The period after World War II marked the epoch when the age of colonialism finally crashed, as one national liberation movement after another in Asia and Africa won legal independence (from Asian nations such as India in 1947, China in 1949, and Vietnam in 1974 to African countries such as Egypt in 1951, Ghana in 1957, Nigeria in 1960, Guinea-Bisseau in

1974, and Angola in 1975, among many others). Above all, there was also the historic defeat of U.S.-enforced neocolonialism in Latin America by the Cuban Revolution of 1 January 1959—an event that had a tremendous impact on the entire hemisphere at a time when corporate capitalism reigned almost unchallenged in the Americas.

But as Western modernization replaced Western colonialism in former colonies, scholars and activists alike realized that the struggle was far from over, as it became increasingly apparent throughout the "Third World" (as it came to be called in the late 1950s and early 1960s) that Western modernization meant one thing to Western countries and quite another to non-Western countries. One and the same economic project, in the act of producing "modern nations" around the globe, generated unprecedented wealth for the West and abject poverty for the majority of citizens in non-Western countries.

World systems theory was developed by scholars on the left in response to the failures of modernization theory, which had predicted growing prosperity and development in the Third World, rather than the immiserization that befell so many new nations. Few could disagree on the facts about the stark inequalities that divided the former colonial powers from their former colonies, given the grim statistics on such social indicators as infant mortality, average life span, access to health care, and level of literacy. But explanations diverged sharply. Western apologists for mainstream modernization theory, such as W. W. Rostow in *The Stages of Economic Growth: A Non-Communist Manifesto* (1960), made a straightforward three-fold argument about the "universal" superiority of capitalist modernization. First, they maintained that the main countries comprising the West had modern economies, while most other nations simply had traditional economies characterized by low levels of industrialization, a small middle class, and hardly any advanced technology. Second, they argued that Western nations had a citizenry who possessed a modern psychology and modern cultures, which together were linked to an understanding of the need for hard work, a habit of punctuality, and a commitment to save money for investment. Conversely, the citizens of non-Western nations supposedly lacked this modern attitude and worldview to varying degrees and their economies suffered accordingly. Third, the Western apologist contended that the countries in the West were governed by modern institutions, such as parliamentary democracy, a multiparty system, an independent judiciary, and excellent public education systems. On the other hand, the "traditional societies" from outside the West were governed instead by "premodern" institutions, often with dictatorial leaders or paternalistic regimes, and no real commitment to public literacy. So, the answer, the modernization theorists maintained, was simple: the rest of the world should learn to behave like the West and to adapt its system of corporate capitalism.

By the late 1950s and early 1960s, however, something else was becoming clear, namely, the precise opposite of what modernization theorists had predicted was in fact occurring. Moreover, this development process often happened in ways that were devastating for the majority of the populations in every Latin American nation, whether it was more or less "modern." As Western capital modernized Latin American economies— from the copper mines of Chile, the oil fields of Venezuela, and the agribusinesses of Central America to the bauxite production of Jamaica—they became more contradictory and imbalanced on the national level to the degree that they were modernized by the West. Far from creating a large middle class, for example, corporate capitalism did exactly the opposite. Moreover, it soon became well documented that U.S. multinational corporations in fact preferred to do business with repressive military dictatorships and other premodern, as well as antidemocratic, political formations, in order to support a modernization that generated huge profits for the West, even as it led to very modest infrastructural gains for the host nation. In addition, it was not lost on the popular classes themselves that modernization theory was inaccurate on another count as well, that is, the relation of hard work and high productivity to remuneration. In Latin America, the members of the labor force who worked hardest within corporate capitalism were paid the least.

At this point, the issue simply was no longer one of explaining social injustice as a consequence of European-American–based modernization—these injustices had become patently, even painfully, clear to the Third World intelligentsia and progressive intellectuals in the West—but rather one of disclosing why and how the two phenomena, social injustice and capitalist modernization, were deeply interrelated. Were they incidentally connected through the misapplication of capitalist modernization by corrupt local leaders? Or were they linked through the coercive designs of imperial political policies emanating squarely from the West?

To an increasing number of critics, neither of these types of explanation were sufficient, since they did not begin with a structural economic analysis of what Karl Marx, almost a century earlier, had named the "uneven development" of modern capitalism. What was needed was a theory that began, not with individual examples of corruption or inefficiency, but with the inherent structural logic of corporate capitalism that, based as it is on an unequal "international division of labor," is unfairly organized by its very nature at the site of production, not just as a result of distribution. In an outpouring of intellectual energy beginning in the late 1950s, a new cohort of intellectuals, many from Third World countries themselves, began to develop such a theory.

## Precursors to World Systems Theory

In developing his theory, Wallerstein built upon the nineteenth-century critiques by Marx of capitalism's structural contradictions and those by the subsequent school of dependency theory that first emerged in the 1950s and 1960s throughout the Americas about the "development of underdevelopment." The latter school of thought, devoted to analyzing the structural logic of monopoly capitalism, was put forth first by such scholars as Paul Baran, Harry Magdoff, and Paul Sweezy of *Monthly Review,* then developed in interrelated books throughout Latin America by Fernando Henrique Cardoso, Theotonio dos Santos, Jaime Wheelock Román, Fidel Castro, and Orlando Núñez Soto, among several others. World systems theory also owes an intellectual and political debt to the anticolonial critiques from the Caribbean of C. L. R. James or Frantz Fanon; the celebrated *Annales* school of material history from France exemplified by Fernand Braudel, Marc Bloch, or Georges Duby; and the radical historical analysis in England of Christopher Hill, E. P. Thompson, or E. J. Hobsbawm.

***Anticolonialism.*** In 1952, Frantz Fanon of the Caribbean island of Martinique launched a stirring anticolonial analysis of the ideologically charged ethnocentrism hidden behind European efforts at "modernization" in Africa, entitled *Peau noire, masques blancs* (*Black Skin, White Masks,* 1967). (This work was also very much in the tradition of C. L. R. James's *sui generis* anticolonial study *The Black Jacobins* [1939] about revolutionary movements in Haiti and the Dominican Republic.)

***Development of underdevelopment.*** In 1957, Paul Baran published a watershed study entitled *The Political Economy of Growth,* which became one of the most popular books about political economy in the history of Latin America. (A Spanish edition of this study had gone through more than twenty different editions, since being published by the National Autonomous University of Mexico.) In it, Baran demonstrated how Western development via modernization unavoidably produced underdevelopment in Latin America, and that it was necessarily based on "uneven development" owing to its peculiar structural logic. Indeed, without major structural adjustments, Western modernization would continually lead to the development of underdevelopment in Latin America and the Third World. Far from being the solution to poverty in Latin America, Western modernization was a primary cause of it. As the formative "core" of a hemispheric system, capital in the United States (and Europe) would thus continue to siphon crucial resources from "peripheral" Latin American countries through hyper-profits generated by the international division of labor.

***Latin American dependency theorists.*** Baran's book helped to galvanize the position of an entire generation of Latin American intellectuals. They answered the call to document his abstract claims about the deforming effects of Western modernization for the Americas through concrete studies of specific instances of the effects of corporate capitalism, with a series of studies that were extensive, provocative, and often brilliant. One particularly well-known example is Brazilian scholar Fernando Henrique Cardoso's (with Enzo Faletto) *Dependencia y desarrollo en América Latina* (1969). The context of its publication reveals the increasingly fierce battle between left and right that shaped twentieth-century Latin American politics: it was authored in Chile (on the eve of the Salvadore Allende years) where Cardoso was then in exile, because of a U.S.-backed military coup in Brazil during 1964. The latter opened the way to what Western capital would celebrate as an "economic miracle" (an annual growth rate of 10% for a decade). Yet, as one Brazilian leader of the period admitted: "In my country, the economy is doing fine, but the people aren't."

Cardoso's study, based on what he terms an "*análisis global*" (global analysis), provides a structural analysis of this contradictory process. In 1950 there were at least five large nations from Latin America that, according to the standards of modernization theory, were virtually guaranteed success as modern nations who would be major players on the world economic stage: Argentina, Brazil, Chile, Columbia, and Mexico. Each of them possessed the following: (1) sufficient internal markets to propel growth; (2) a formidable industrial base; (3) abundant reserves of raw materials; (4) powerful stimuli to grow nationally; and (5) satisfactory formations of domestic capital. Yet despite their enormous structural promise and hardworking labor forces, these five countries ended up being trapped by the West in a type of *desarrollo dependiente* (dependent development) that caused a profound depression of the living standards and welfare of the vast majority of their citizenry. The result was a disadvantageous interdependency with a Western-led modernization that did not make them modern nations by the standards of the West, even as the West itself profited handsomely from this foreign labor force and the region's raw materials.

An even more extreme case of underdevelopment as a consequence of Western modernization occurred in the seven largely rural countries of Central America, which were far less prepared to succeed in the world system than were the five Latin American nations singled out by Cardoso. Few have encapsulated better in a short aphorism than did Nicaraguan author Sergio Ramírez, how the economy of a Third World region is deformed by capitalist-based underdevelopment simply to serve the consumer patterns of the West. As Ramírez noted, people in Central America figured out fairly soon what their assigned role in the world system would be: cheap desserts for the West, such as coffee, sugar, and fruit. It was another Nicaraguan intellectual and guerrilla leader, Jaime Wheelock Román, who documented extensively and explicated deftly the historical process whereby Central America's fate would be determined by the international division of labor of corporate capitalism. The latter set of relationships rigidly presupposes the preparation of raw materials on the periphery of the world system and the production of finished industrial goods primarily in the core area. Written in the 1970s, Román's *Nicaragua: Imperialismo y Dictadura* was an underground classic during the insurrection against Nicaragua's de facto leader Antonio Somoza Debayle and a guiding text for revolutionary policies by the Sandinistas after their victory over Somoza in 1979.

Even more so than Cardoso, Wheelock Román's book exemplifies the increasingly high stakes in which Latin American dependency and world systems theorists worked as an underground labor leader during a period of intense political depression. Despite these dangers, he produced one of the most important books on dependency theory ever to come out of Central America. Román carefully traces how the Nicaraguan *economía agroexportadora* based on coffee (and to a lesser extent on bananas, sugar, and cotton) was set up to provide cheap goods for the West, and produced low prices for European-American consumers through the systematic maltreatment of underfed, underpaid, and terrorized workers denied basic human rights. Moreover, the unquestioned accompaniment to this success story of corporate capitalism and its modernization project in Nicaragua was the brutal, U.S.-backed dictatorship of the Somoza family (r. 1934–1979), two of whose members even graduated from West Point. This regime insured that labor discontent in Nicaragua would not be allowed to upset the project of modernization in Central America.

The author whose career epitomizes the mix of politics and scholarship that characterized Caribbean dependency theory is Fidel Castro, who produced a monumental tour de force of dependency theory, *The World Economic and Social Crisis,* together with two teams of researchers at the University of Havana. This analytical report, presented in 1983 by Cuban president Castro to the Seventh Summit Conference of Non-Aligned Countries, compiled evidence from a massive number of nonpartisan scholarly sources to document a world division of labor that is structurally enforced at every stage of development by the forces of corporate capital and the Western militaries that back them. Criticizing the claim by modernization theorists that Third World countries were gradually industrializing and could someday rise to the level of the industrialized West, Castro and his coauthors emphasized that "in spite of some affirmations to the effect that world industry is producing a so-called restructuring . . . the really impressive thing is that 69.2% of the world's industrial work force is found in the Third World and it generates less than 9% of the world industrial production" (p. 127).

This global division of labor was the main target of Castro's critique: his book calls for a rejection of the effort to "divide the world into an industrialized area with advanced technology and a primary-commodity-producing area" (p. 67). As examples, he pointed to mining, where "the underdeveloped countries contribute 25.6% of the mining of metals, they produce only 4.1% of the metal manufacture in the world" (p. 123), and textiles, where the manufacture of yarn—"high-labor and low capital intensive" in the Third World increased from "19% in 1950 to almost 40%," while weaving "which is more capital-intensive and require high automation and concentration, is still controlled by developed countries, and based there" (p. 67). Textiles were then returned back to the Third World to be made into garments, because this industry still demands a high degree of hand labor. But critically, the most important phase of all—the manufacturing and sale of textile machinery—"requires advanced technology and a complex design, on which the future of the entire sector largely reveals the power relationship in the textile sector." Third World industries produced less than 5 percent of such machinery, and saw few possibilities for increasing their share. It is from this control of the making of machinery, according to Castro and other dependency theorists, that the so-called captive trade system arises, turning international trade into a caricature of itself (pp. 67–68).

It is this control of the machines that make all other machines, that is, the export of machines, but not the technology that reproduces these machines, that is the guiding thread of all Western modernization policy. This is a key locus of power and a primary way of maintaining Western hegemony in the world system.

## Wallerstein and World Systems Theory

Inspired by dependency theorists, Wallerstein developed the concept of world systems analysis in the 1970s as a response to the methodological impasse, or *Methodenstreit,* within the social sciences over how to explain the existence of stark inequities among three different worlds within the modern global economic order: those of societies in the core (the West and Japan), those on the semiperiphery (Eastern Europe and much of Asia), and those on the periphery (most of Africa, Latin America, along with the Middle East, except for Israel, plus some parts of Asia). Wallerstein opposed, on the one hand, what he deemed the "universalizers" in mainstream economics, sociology, and political science, who defend Western modernization theory as an international standard, and, on the other, the "particularizers" in anthropology, history, art history, and other disciplines in the humanities, for whom all economic developments are merely relative to the peculiar regions in which they occur. The latter assertion amounts to a fetishism, or universalization, of relative difference. According to Wallerstein,

> Both groups . . . tend to share one premise in common: the unit of analysis was politico-cultural structure . . . whether the term they used for this unit was the state, or the people, or the nation. . . . This book makes a radically different assumption. It assumes that the unit of analysis is an economic entity, the one that is measured by the existence of an effective division of labor, and that the relationship of such economic boundaries to political and cultural boundaries is variable. . . . Once we assume that the unit of analysis is such a "world-system" and not the "state" or the "nation" or the "people," then much changes in the outcome of the analysis. Most specifically we shift from concern with the attributive characteristics of states to concern with the relational characteristics of states. We shift from seeing classes (and status-groups) as groups within a state to seeing them as groups within a world-economy. (pp. xi–xii)

A critical example of this approach, with its emphasis on underlying economic causes for political and cultural events, was his analysis of the advent of modern society, a process that for Wallerstein begins with the novel emergence of mercantile capitalism in late fifteenth-century Europe, which ultimately produced for the first time an entire world system. Wallerstein divided his analysis of the "determining elements" of the modern world system into four major epochs: the formation of the European world economy from 1450 to 1640; the consolidation of the system between 1640 and 1815; the technological transformation of industrialization from 1815 to 1917; and the "consolidation of this capitalist world-economy from 1917 to the present, and the particular revolutionary tensions this consolidation has provoked" (pp. 10–11).

The breadth of vision and sense of political urgency that underlay this new theoretical approach is evident in the introduction to *Dynamics of Global Crisis,* a manifesto on behalf of world systems theory that included a joint statement by coauthors Wallerstein, Amin, Gunder Frank, and Arrighi in which the following shared premises were declared:

1. We believe that there is a social whole that may be called a capitalist world economy . . . [that emerged] in the sixteenth century, and that is expanded historically from its European origins. . . .

2. We believe that we cannot make an intelligent analysis of the various states taken separately without placing their so-called internal life in the context of the world division of labor, located in the world-economy. . . .

3. We believe that, throughout the history of this capitalist world-economy, there has been increasing organization of oppressed groups within the world-system and increasing opposition to its continuance. . . .

4. After World War II, the United States was the hegemonic power, having commanding power in the economic, political, and military arenas, and able to impose relative order on the world system—a fact which correlated with the world's unprecedented economic system. . . .

5. We do not believe that the struggle between capitalist and socialist forces can be reduced to, or even symbolized by, a struggle between the United States and the USSR, however much the propaganda machines of both assert otherwise. . . .

These premises laid out, it remains only to indicate our prejudices and our visions. We are all on the left. That is, we all believe in the desirability and possibility of a world that is politically democratic and socially and economically egalitarian. We do not think the capitalist world-economy has done very well on any of these accounts. We believe that capitalism, as a historical system, will come to an end. (pp. 9–10)

## Developments and Critiques of World Systems Theory since 1980

World systems theory was enormously influential throughout the world for several decades, although its influence was more profound in Third World regions such as Latin America, and in Europe, than in the United States. Even in the United States, however, major works such as Eric Wolf's study of *Peasant Wars of the Twentieth Century* (1969) or Sidney Mintz's magisterial study of the relationship between slavery and capitalism, Europe, and the Caribbean, *Sweetness and Power: The Place of Sugar in Modern History* (1985), took their inspiration directly from world systems theory.

There were always critics on the right, of course, and over time other criticisms arose, and intellectual trends that began as part of world systems theory gradually moved away from it. Conservative development theory gained new ground among politicians and development experts in the 1980s with the popularity of neoliberal reforms; within academic circles, postmodernism has both been influenced by world systems theory, and profoundly suspicious of it. The current emphasis on transnationalism clearly looks back to Wallerstein's insistence that in the face of a global economy, nation-states and local cultures cannot be analyzed in isolation from one another; at the same time, however, a distaste for "master narratives" marked the death knell for the mono-causal insistence on looking for

a single underlying structure with vast explanatory reach. Yet, as postcolonial theorists have shown, a multicausal conception of master narrative, such as colonialism, avoids the problem of any single overarching explanation that homogenizes history.

Thus by 1996, statements such as those made by York Bradshaw and Michael Wallace, two sociologists from the United States, in their book *Global Inequalities,* that despite its historical importance "world-systems analysis" is simply "out of touch with current realities," have become commonplace. Two of their criticisms are especially revealing. First, they say that "just as modernization theory places too much blame on poor countries for their own underdevelopment, [so] world-system theory errs in the other extreme: It places almost total blame for Third World poverty on core countries" (p. 51). This point has been taken up by many activists in Third World countries, who see their own leaders and educated elites using criticism of the First World to evade responsibility for their own failures. Political positions, such as cultural policies, and artistic production are all marked by a "relative autonomy" from the world system that must be acknowledged before much needed local self-criticism is possible and democratic accountability can occur.

Second, Bradshaw and Wallace observe that sometimes "world-system theory had exaggerated the harmful effects" of multinational corporations. They and others point to the relative success story of China and the four "Little Dragons" in Asia (South Korea, Taiwan, Singapore, and Hong Kong) on the advanced semiperiphery of the world system as an instance of how "underdevelopment" is less in evidence as a result of Western-style modernization. This point is related to one made by intellectuals from within the world systems tradition, who in the late 1980s and 1990s began to move from a simple view of world history in which European domination was the single, central fact to a more complex vision of history. New studies of the past looked at the emergence of previous core-and-periphery systems, before the rise of Europe, in which the core might be found in Asian empires, or in the Middle East. In a similar vein, studies of the contemporary world have emphasized a multicentric vision, in which Japanese capitalist expansion in Southeast Asia, Australian neocolonial influence in the Pacific, and the rise of India's technology centers create multiple centers of economic power, while still perpetuating an underlying capitalist system in which the drive for profit overrides all other motives, and drastic inequality is continually reproduced and exacerbated.

Indeed, critics who dismiss world systems theory as irrelevant may be both losing sight of its most critical insights and overlooking current political trends. The much-vaunted neoliberal reforms of the 1990s, modernization theory's successors, seem to have produced a series of economic crises; overall, most Latin Americans lost considerable economic ground during that dismal decade. Enlarging the definition of the core to include the bourgeosie of Third World nations, and the periphery to include the disenfranchised poor of First World nations such as Britain or the United States, is entirely in keeping with the original vision of unequal development; nor has the brunt of poverty and political repression ceased to fall on the world's nonwhite population, whether they live in Paris, London, or the Caribbean. Furthermore, presidents elected in some Latin American nations in the early 2000s, including Lula da Silva of Brazil and Hugo Chávez of Venezuela, as well as the rise of powerful new popular movements such as the indigenous movements of Ecuador and Bolivia, or the landless movement of Brazil, and the international antiglobalization movement, may indicate a new wave of political activism on behalf of the poor, which in turn may produce a new intellectual movement that will take off where world systems theory left off.

The underlying global inequalities that motivated world systems theory are still evident: in the early twenty-first century 5 percent of the population (the percentage of the population that resides in the United States) continues to control more than half of the world's resources. Unlike modernization theory, world systems theory not only highlights this grave situation, but also gives compelling reasons for how the world could be more justly organized otherwise.

*See also* **Anticolonialism: Latin America; International Order; Marxism: Latin America; Third World.**

**BIBLIOGRAPHY**

Amin, Samir, Giovanni Arrighi, Andre Gunder Frank, and Immanuel Wallerstein. *Dynamics of Global Crisis.* New York: Monthly Review Press, 1982.

Baran, Paul A. *The Political Economy of Growth.* New York: Monthly Review Press, 1957.

Bradshaw, York W., and Michael Wallace. *Global Inequalities.* Thousand Oaks, Calif.: Pine Forge Press, 1996.

Cardoso, Fernando Henrique, and Enzo Faletto. *Dependencia y desarrollo en America Latina.* Mexico City: Siglo Veintiuno Editores, 1969.

Castro, Fidel. *The World Economic and Social Crisis.* Havana, Cuba: Public Office of the Council of State, 1983.

Fanon, Frantz. *Peau noire, masques blanc.* Paris: Éditions du Seuil, 1952.

Frank, André Gunder. *Capitalismo y subdesarrollo en América Latina.* Mexico City: Sigloveintiuno, 1987.

———. *Capitalism and Underdevelopment in Latin America: Historical Studies of Chile and Brazil.* New York: Monthly Review Press, 1967.

González Casanova, Pablo. *Imperialismo y Liberación en América Latina.* Mexico City: Oceano, 1968.

James, C. L. R. *The Black Jacobins.* New York: Dial Press, 1938.

King, Anthony D., ed. *Culture, Globalization, and the World-System: Contemporary Conditions for the Representation of Identity.* Binghamton: State University of New York, 1991.

Kitching, Gavin. *Development and Underdevelopment in Historical Perspective: Populism, Nationalism, and Industrialization.* New York and London: Methuen, 1982.

Magdoff, Harry. *The Age of Imperialism: The Economics of U.S. Foreign Policy.* New York: Monthly Review Press, 1969.

Marini, Ruy Mauro. *Subdesarrollo y revolución.* Mexico City: Siglo Veialiuno Editores, 1969.

Núñez Soto, Orlando, and Roger Burbach. *Democracia y Revolución en las Américas.* Mexico City: Editorial Nuestro Tiempo, 1987.

Ramirez, Sergio. *Estás en Nicaragua.* Barcelona: Muchnik, 1985.

Rodney, Walter. *How Europe Underdeveloped Africa.* London: Bogle-L'Ouverture Publications, 1972.

Wallerstein, Immanuel. *The Modern World-System: Capitalist Agriculture and the Origins of the European World Economy in the Sixteenth Century.* New York: Academic Press, 1976.

Wolf, Eric R. *Europe and the People without History.* Berkeley: University of California Press, 1982.

*David Craven*

# YZ

**YIN AND YANG.** In Chinese cosmology, yin and yang are two opposite but complementary principles that regulate the functioning of the cosmos. Their repeated alternation provides the energy necessary for the cosmos to sustain itself, and their continuous joining and separation is at the origin of the rise and the disappearance of the entities and phenomena that exist within the world of the "ten thousand things" (*wanwu*).

According to a celebrated statement, which is found in one of the appendixes to the *Book of Changes* (*Yijing*), "one yin and one yang, this is the Dao." This sentence refers to the Dao that first determines itself as the One (or Oneness) and then through the One gives birth to the two complementary principles. As each of these stages generates the next one, yin and yang are ultimately contained within the Dao itself. At the same time, the phrase "one yin and one yang, this is the Dao" refers to the continuous alternation of yin and yang within the cosmos. When one of the two principles prevails, the other yields, but once one of them has reached the height of its development, it begins to recede; in that very moment, the other principle begins its ascent. This mode of operation is especially visible in the time cycles of the day (alternation of daytime and nighttime) and of the year (alternation of the four seasons).

The origins of these notions are impossible to ascertain. Scholars generally deem that the terms *yin* and *yang* originally denoted the shaded and sunny sides of a hill and later began to be used in an abstract sense as cosmological categories. The earliest extant text that contains a list of items arranged according to their yin and yang qualities is a manuscript found in Mawangdui entitled *Designations* (*Cheng*), likely dating from the third century B.C.E. Examples of yang and yin items, respectively, mentioned in this text include heaven and earth; above and below; day and night; summer and winter; spring and autumn; man and woman; father and child; elder brother and younger brother; ruler and minister; soldiers and laborers; speech and silence; giving and receiving; action and nonaction.

Between the third and the second centuries B.C.E., the notion of yin and yang became one of the main pillars of correlative cosmology, a feature of which is the coordination of several preexistent patterns of emblems, including, besides yin and yang, the five agents (*wuxing*) and the eight trigrams and sixty-four hexagrams of the *Book of Changes*. Each of these patterns represents a particular way of explicating the features and functioning of the cosmos. In the system of correlative cosmology, for instance, yin is related to the agents Metal (west/autumn) and Water (north/winter), while yang is related to Wood (east/spring) and Fire (south/summer), and the balance between them is represented by the central agent Soil. The association with the five agents is likely at the origin of the view that yin and yang are further subdivided into two states each: "minor yang" (Wood), "great yang" (Fire), "minor yin" (Metal), and "great yin" (Water).

The relations among the different cosmological configurations that intervene between the Dao and the "ten thousand things" are illustrated in the well-known *Diagram of the Great Ultimate* (*Taiji tu*), which was discussed at length by both Daoist and Neo-Confucian authors. This chart depicts on top the Absolute (*wuji*) as an empty circle. Below it is another circle that represents the Great Ultimate (*taiji*) as harboring the Two, or yin and yang, shown as two semicircles that mirror each other. Each of them is made of black (yin) and white (yang) lines that enclose each other to depict yin containing yang and yang containing yin. The empty circle within these lines corresponds to the empty circle on top; this alludes to the notion that yin and yang are the "function" or "operation" (*yong*) of Emptiness, which in turn is their "substance" or "core" (*ti*). Following this are the five agents, which constitute a further stage in the progressive differentiation of Oneness into multiplicity. The lines that connect them to each other show the sequence in which they are generated, namely Wood, Fire, Soil, Metal, and Water. In this cosmological configuration, the Great Ultimate is represented by the central Soil (which is said to have a "male" and a "female" aspect) and reappears as the small empty circle below, which represents the conjunction of Water and Fire ("great yin" and "great yang") and of Wood and Metal ("minor yang" and "minor yin"). The circle below the five agents represents heaven and earth or the active and passive principles that respectively give birth to and support the existence of the "ten thousand things," represented by the circle at the base of the diagram.

The notions of yin and yang have deeply affected Chinese culture as a whole. Representations of these notions are found in religion, art, and several other contexts; as part of the system of correlative cosmology, moreover, yin and yang have played a central role in traditional sciences and techniques, such as divination, medicine, and alchemy. Beyond this, the search for the balance and harmony of yin and yang has had, and continues to have, a pervasive influence on the everyday lives of Chinese people.

*See also* **Chinese Thought; Cosmology: Asia; Medicine: China.**

He asked: What is the Dao?

I replied: The Dao is Ancestral Pneuma prior to Heaven that generates the creatures. If you want to look at it, you do not see it, if you want to listen to it, you do not hear it, if you want to grasp it, you do not get it. It envelops and enwraps Heaven and Earth and gives life and nourishment to the ten thousand things. It is so great that there is nothing outside it, so small that there is nothing inside it. Confucians call it Great Ultimate, Daoists call it Golden Elixir, and Buddhists call it Complete Awareness. Fundamentally it has no name, but forced to give it a name it is called the Dao. If it is determined, one is in error, and if it is discussed, one loses it. It has no body and no image, it is not form and not emptiness, it is not Being and not Non-being. If it is attributed the images of form and emptiness, of Being and Non-being, it is not the Dao. [That is, if one uses the notions of form and emptiness, Being and Non-being in relation to the Dao, then one is not talking about the Dao, because the Dao is beyond these notions.]

He asked: If the Dao is without body and without image and if it is the One inchoate pneuma, why then does the *Book of Changes* say: "One yin and one yang, this is the Dao"?

I replied: "One yin and one yang, this is the Dao" are words used to express the function (or operation) of the Dao. "Without body and without image" are words used to express the substance (or core) of the Dao. When the Great Ultimate has not yet divided itself [into yin and yang], the Dao envelops yin and yang. After the Great One has divided itself, it is yin and yang that give life to the Dao. If yin and yang were not there, the pneuma of the Dao would not be visible. It is only in the alternation of yin and yang that the pneuma of the Dao can grow and maintain itself for innumerable eons without being damaged. In the state prior to Heaven [this pneuma], it is the Dao; in the state posterior to Heaven, it is yin and yang. The Dao is the foundation of yin and yang; yin and yang are the outgrowth of the Dao. This is what is meant when one says that the Great Ultimate divides itself and becomes yin and yang and that yin and yang joined to each other form the Great Ultimate. It is One but they are Two, they are Two but it is One.

SOURCE: Liu Yiming (1734–1821), *Xiuzhen biannan* [Discussions on the cultivation of reality], translated by Fabrizio Pregadio.

**BIBLIOGRAPHY**

Graham, A. C. *Yin-Yang and the Nature of Correlative Thinking.* Singapore: Institute of East Asian Philosophies, National University of Singapore, 1986.

Granet, Marcel. *La pensée chinoise.* Paris: La Renaissance du Livre, 1934.

*Fabrizio Pregadio*

**YOGA.** The word *yoga* comes from a Sanskrit verbal root meaning "to yoke, harness" and in general refers to one or another of the many psycho-physical techniques in Indian religions designed to obtain discipline and control over the body and mind. In its classical contexts, yoga could refer to any one of a whole variety of such self-disciplinary practices. In India, yoga transcended sectarian boundaries. There are, for example, both Hindu and Buddhist forms of yoga and within each of these religious traditions many different kinds of spiritual methods and practices are designated by this term. None of these "yogic" methods is solely physical. All entail some form of mental discipline, which can be labeled meditation; in In-

dian religions yoga and meditation almost always went hand in hand. The physical practices of yoga were usually seen at best to be only preliminary to the more spiritual forms of yoga that utilize various kinds of meditation techniques.

It is possible that yoga goes back to the earliest period of Indian history. Figurines and seals found at sites of the Indus Valley civilization, dating back to the second millennium B.C.E., have sometimes been interpreted to indicate the practice of yoga there. In particular, one seal depicts what appears to be a deity sitting in a posture typical of later yoga. In the earliest Sanskrit texts of the Vedic period (c. 1500–1200 B.C.E.) there are references to ascetics and ecstatics called *munis* ("silent sages") who are depicted with long hair, are said to be "girdled by the wind" (meaning, possibly, naked), and are described as having some of the superhuman powers later associated with advanced yoga practice. The Atharva Veda mentions a group called the *vratyas* who practice asceticism (they are said to be able to stand for a year) and assume other physical postures as part of their disciplinary regimen. They also seemed to have practiced some kind of breath control and envisioned correlations between their bodies and the cosmos.

Also already in the Vedic texts we encounter the theory and practice of *tapas* or "ascetic heat" which, when obtained by the practitioner through various methods of physical and mental asceticism, was said to impart similar powers and spiritual purity. *Tapas* was in later texts to come to the forefront of the essential disciplinary practices that were involved in yoga.

By the time of the later texts of the Vedic period, the Upanishads of the third or fourth centuries B.C.E., the word and conceptualizations of *yoga* are encountered frequently. In these texts, yoga means primarily the control of the mind and the senses. The senses are likened to horses which must be "yoked" or "disciplined" by the yogin (yogi) whose "mind is constantly held firm" and whose "senses are under control like the good horses of a charioteer. . . . They consider yoga to be the firm restraint of the senses. Then one becomes undistracted" (Katha Upanishad 3.6; 6.11). In these texts some of the physical practices of yoga are also described. The practitioner is advised to retreat to a pleasant place in the wilderness where he should assume a particular physical posture (or *asana*) and "breathe through his nostrils with diminished breath" (the practice of breath-control called in later yogic texts by the name of *pranayama*). Yoga is defined in one such Upanishad as "the unity [another possible translation of the word "yoga"] of the breath, mind, and senses, and the relinquishment of all conditions of existence" (Maitri Upanishad 6.25). As the yogin progresses in his practice his body and mind are said to change: "Lightness, healthiness, freedom from desires, clearness of countenance and pleasantness of speech, sweetness of odor and scanty exertions— these, they say, are the first stage in the progress of yoga" (Shvetashvatara Upanishad 2.13). The final stage of the practice, the goal of yoga, is also depicted in the Upanishads—and will become standard in later yogic texts. It is nothing less that the state of deathlessness or eternal life, often imagined in a body of light that never degenerates or grows old.

Yoga was systematized in different ways in two foundational texts dating to around the turn of the Common Era. In the first of these classical treatises, the Bhagavad Gita or "Song of the Lord," yoga is used to describe three apparently distinct but practically interrelated "paths" or spiritual methods. The first of these is called *jnana yoga* or the "yoga of wisdom." This path consists of deep contemplation on the nature of reality and recognizing the difference between the phenomenal world of change and the unchanging self. Through such meditation, the yogin penetrates the illusory nature of appearances and realizes the ultimate unity of all things and beings. As the Gita is also a theistic (or pantheistic) text, *jnana yoga* also entails recognizing God or Krishna in all things.

The second kind of yoga in this syncretistic work is *karma yoga,* the yoga of action. This method is one of "doing one's duty" as it is laid out by the strictures of caste and stage of life (and not renouncing action in the world as seemed to be required by the earlier Upanishadic treatises). Such worldly activity must, however, be performed in a "yogic" and self-disciplined way. While one cannot avoid action, the yogin should act not out of desire for the fruits of action but rather in a desireless and self-sacrificial way. Renouncing the ends or goals, the practitioner of *karma yoga* was to perform

desireless action dedicated to God. The third yoga outlined in the Bhagavad Gita was termed *bhakti,* "devotion," and was nothing other than the "yoking" or "union" of the self and God. It is depicted as the easiest of the three methods but also the most efficacious.

The other text of this period to synthesize yoga was the Yoga Sutra of Patanjali. Patanjali defines yoga as the "cessation of the turnings of thought," that is, the purification and becalming of the mind and the correlative attainment of higher states of consciousness. Yoga for Patanjali involves eight "limbs" or parts (*ashtanga*), each one leading to the next and culminating in release from suffering and rebirth.

The first two limbs provide the ethical foundation thought to be necessary for any further progress in yoga. The first consists of the five "moral restraints" (*yamas*): nonviolence, truthfulness, not stealing, chastity, and the avoidance of greed. The second limb, the internal "observances" (*niyamas*), provides a second set of five virtues the practitioner should perfect. These are mental and physical purity, contentment, *tapas* or the practice of austerities and asceticism, the study of sacred texts, and devotion to the "Lord" (God or the guru).

The third part of Patanjali's eightfold path consists of the physical postures or *asanas*. When the yogin has disciplined his or her moral life, the next step is to discipline the physical body. The later traditions of yoga have greatly expanded this dimension of the yogic path. The physical practices are sometimes referred to as *hatha yoga* (the "yoga of exertion") and are conceived of in terms of a rigorous program of physical exercise and digestive constraint thought to be preparatory to the more advanced and subtle forms of yoga. Some texts claim there are 840,000 yogic physical postures; a standard list gives 84 including, most famously, the "lotus position" (*padma asana*). Such postures are designed to make the practitioner's body supple and healthy and help in the general training of self-discipline. Patanjali, however, devotes a mere three verses to the purely physical dimension of yoga, saying only that one should take a position that is "steady and comfortable," for then one is ready to pursue the true goal of yoga, the state of mind wherein one is "unconstrained by opposing dualities."

More subtle than the physical body is the breath, and it is the "restraining of the breath" (*pranayama*) that forms the fourth limb of the practice. Here again, later yogic texts go into much greater detail about the various practices of breath awareness and control, including methods for retention of the breath over long periods of time. The breath is regarded as the fundamental life force in yoga, and control and manipulation of it is essential for rejuvenating and immortalizing the body. Its power is such that some texts warn about the dangers entailed in the *pranayama* practices and, as always, insist that the yogin should only practice under the watchful guidance of a master. Patanjali has little to say about it, restricting his observations to the fact that it basically refers to the control of inhalation, exhalation, and retention of breath and that it has as its purpose the making of a "mind fit for concentration."

The next stage of Patanjali's system is named the "withdrawal of the senses" (*pratyahara*) by which is meant the kind of "yoking" of the sense organs that was likened to the reining in of horses. Another very common image for this portion of the yogic training is that of a tortoise who withdraws its limbs into its shell. So too should the yogin disengage the sense organs from the objects of senses and, by means of such detachment, gain mastery over them. The ability to turn away from the distractions of the object of senses and to increasingly turn attention to the mind itself in a concentrated fashion is, of course, crucial for the meditative pursuits that describe the highest and most subtle forms of yoga.

The sixth, seventh, and eighth limbs of Patanjali's yogic system are progressively higher states of meditative ability and attainment. The sixth is called "concentration" (*dharana*), defined as the ability to "bind thought in one place" for long periods of time; it is the essence of what is sometimes known as "one-pointedness" of mind. The mastery of concentration leads the yogin to the next the stage of the path, which is called "meditation" per se (*dhyana*), the unwavering attention of the concentrated mind on the meditative object. The culmination of yoga is the attainment of the eighth limb, pure contemplation accompanied by ecstasy or, otherwise described, the trance-like state of pure "enstasis," which is termed *samadhi*. The end of the yogic path is defined by Patanjali as "meditation that illumines the object alone, as if the subject were devoid of intrinsic form." The "yogin yoked in *samadhi*" is, according to a later text in this tradition, completed liberated—free from the "pairs of opposites" or all duality, not bound by the forces of karma, unconquerable, "without inhalation and exhalation," invulnerable to all weapons, and immortal (Hatha Yoga Pradipika 4.108ff.).

Indeed, much of the third chapter of Patanjali's classic text is given over to the extraordinary powers (the "accomplishments" or *siddhi*s) that are claimed to come along with advanced practice of yoga. These include the ability to know the past and future, the languages of animals, one's previous lives, the thoughts of others, and so on. It is, in fact, said that the perfected yogin becomes omniscient. He or she also attains the power to become invisible, gets the "strength of an elephant," and wins the capability to grow larger or smaller at will. In later texts, abilities such as these are summarized as the eight "great powers" (*mahasiddhi*s): miniaturization, magnification, levitation, extension, irresistible will, mastery, lordship over the universe, and fulfillment of all desires.

The yoga systematized in Patanjali's Yoga Sutras is sometimes referred to as "classical" or "royal" yoga (*raja yoga*), especially in contrast to the *hatha yoga*, which is envisioned as preparatory to the higher spiritual practices of Patanjali's later limbs. It also came to be the charter text of the school of Hindu philosophy (*darshana*) called "Yoga," which in turn was closely related to the dualistic philosophical school known as "Samkhya" (the main difference being the atheistic quality of the latter, although the "Lord" of the Yoga Sutras is more of a Divine Yogin than a creator god). In these philosophical traditions, the purpose of yoga was understood to be the "distinction" or "discrimination" between material nature and the eternal spirit. The spirit or pure consciousness (*purusha*) is to be "isolated" from both matter and from ordinary awareness

and its afflicted mental experiences. When the *purusha* becomes thus disentangled, its pure nature can shine forth and the yogin becomes liberated.

The term *yoga*, as has already been shown, can be applied to a variety of practices and disciplines. Another important use of the term is in the phrase *mantra yoga*, the "yoga of sacred, efficacious sound." Here yoga refers to the concentration on and repetition of sacred sounds, utterances, syllables, or prayers composed from the Sanskrit language and thought to have inherent transformative power. Such mantras are transmitted from teacher to pupil in an initiatory setting, and it is indeed thought to be primarily the power of the guru that gives the mantra its efficacy. The most famous of such mantras is the sound "*om*" (sometimes written as "*aum*" to emphasize the three verbal parts of the utterance) which is regarded as the aural essence of the universe itself. While the texts do claim that *mantra yoga* will also lead to liberation, it is usually said to be suitable mainly for the practitioner of inferior intellectual capabilities.

Yoga also plays a major role in both Hindu and Buddhist "tantric" or esoteric traditions, which arose around the middle of the first millennium C.E. In Buddhism, tantric practice is divided into four classes, each one regarded higher than the other: action tantras, performance tantras, yoga tantras, and highest yoga tantras. In all forms of tantra, the goal is to transmute the physical body into a body of light, a "rainbow body," through the manipulation of the subtle energies, channels, and power centers (*cakra*s) of the mystical inner body. This is done through the practices known as *guru yoga*, the "yoking" of oneself to a tutelary deity or *yidam*, and the carrying out of a series of visualizations in which one assumes the being of that deity and meditates in that way. There is also a form of "Taoist yoga" in China that bears comparison to the Indian yogas.

Yoga has entered the West mostly as physical exercise and often not as the holistic worldview it was in its original contexts. Increasingly, however, Westerners are aware of the ethical and meditative dimensions to yoga and these elements are finding their way into the practice of yoga outside of India.

*See also* **Asceticism: Hindu and Buddhist Asceticism; Buddhism; Hinduism; Meditation, Eastern.**

BIBLIOGRAPHY

Akers, Brian Dana, trans. *The Hatha Yoga Pradipika*. Woodstock, N.Y.: YogaVidya.com, 2002.

Eliade, Mircea. *Yoga: Immortality and Freedom*. 2nd ed. Princeton University Press, 1969.

Feuerstein, Georg. *The Philosophy of Classical Yoga*. Rochester, Vt.: Inner Traditions, 1996.

———. *The Shambhala Encyclopedia of Yoga*. Boston: Shambhala Press, 2000.

Hume, Robert Ernst, trans. *The Thirteen Principal Upanishads*. 2nd ed. London: Oxford University Press, 1975.

Miller, Barbara Stoler. *Yoga: Discipline of Freedom*. New York: Bantam Books, 1998.

Varenne, Jean. *Yoga and the Hindu Tradition*. Chicago: University of Chicago Press, 1976.

*Brian Smith*

**ZEN.** One of the most important scholars of Zen Buddhism, Daisetz Suzuki, cogently explained the origins of Zen Buddhism in 1959:

> Zen is one of the products of the Chinese mind after its contact with Indian thought, which was introduced into China in the first century C.E. through the medium of Buddhist teachings. There were some aspects of Buddhism in the form in which it came to China that the people of the Middle Kingdom did not quite cherish: for instance, its advocacy of a homeless life, its transcendentalism or world-fleeing and life-denying tendency, and so on. At the same time, its profound philosophy, its subtle dialectics and penetrating analyses and speculations, stirred Chinese thinkers, especially Taoists. (p. 3)

For several centuries in China, it was thought that Buddhism was a form of Daoism returning from India along the Silk Roads. Bernard Faure relates: "At the end of his life Laozi, in the guise of the Buddha, was said to have departed to the west to convert the barbarians. To punish them for their initial lack of faith, he condemned them to celibacy" (p. 39). Conversely, the Buddhists claimed that Laozi and Confucius were sent to China to pave the way for Buddhism. In any event, many forms of Buddhism arrived in China from India.

Between the sixth and tenth centuries, Buddhism reached its apex in China with the appearance of four schools: *Tiantai* (Celestial Platform), *Huayan* (Flower Garland), *Jingtu* (Pure Land), and *Chan* (Meditation). The Sanskrit word *dhyana* is transcribed as *Chan* in Chinese and *Zen* in Japanese, meaning "collectiveness of mind or meditative absorption in which all dualistic distinctions like *I/you, subject/object,* and *true/false* are eliminated" (Schuhmacher and Woerner, p. 441). Chan is a melding of Dhyana Buddhism with its emphasis on the stillness of meditation toward enlightenment or awakening (*wu,* satori) and Daoism with its emphasis on nonaction (*wuwei*) as the way of the water. Bodhidharma (470–543), the twenty-eighth patriarch after Shakyamuni Buddha, arrived from India at the Shaolin temple in China, where he practiced seated meditation (*zuochan, zazen*) for nine years in front of a wall. This meditation aimed to clear the mind of daily desires while allowing the sitter to connect his or her true nature with the universe through the achieving of *śūnyata* (*kong, ku,* emptiness). Ninian Smart states that Bodhidharma, the first patriarch, is reputed to have summarized his teaching as follows: "A special transmission outside the scriptures; No basis in words or writing; Direct pointing to the mind of people; Insight into one's nature and attainment of Buddhahood" (p. 126).

The sixth patriarch, Huineng (638–713), refined Bodhidharma's teachings by emphasizing master-student relationships in monasteries and meditation upon what later would become "public documents" (*gongan,* koan) or unsolvable riddles. One day Huineng encountered two monks arguing about a flag waving in the breeze. One monk said that the flag was inanimate and that only the wind made it flutter. The other monk said there was no flapping at all because only the wind moved. Huineng intervened. He said that neither the flag nor the wind moved, only their minds.

Huineng debated with Shenxiu (606–706) regarding immediate or gradual enlightenment. He relates:

> "Good friends, in the Dharma there is no sudden or gradual, but among people some are keen and others dull. The deluded commend the gradual method; the enlightened practice the sudden teaching. To understand the original mind of yourself is to see into your own original nature. Once enlightened, there is from the outset no distinction between these two methods; those who are not enlightened will for long kalpas be caught in the cycle of transmigration" (Yampolsky, p. 137).

Shenxiu's northern school of gradual enlightenment soon gave way to Huineng's southern school of immediate enlightenment. Willard Oxtoby observes that Huineng's school "became known for freedom of expression and respect for the natural. Similar characteristics are associated with Daoism" (p. 270). At this time, China was ripe for Chan Buddhism. Kenneth Ch'en writes: "For over one hundred and thirty years, from 625 to 755, the T'ang Dynasty had enjoyed tranquility, security, and prosperity without any internal rebellion or external invasion to mar the orderly march of events. During this era all phases of Chinese culture, religion, art, and literature enjoyed a long period of free growth and development" (p. 360).

In the ninth century, the *Caodong zong* (Caodong school) and *Linji zong* (Linji school) sects of Chan Buddhism carried on the rivalry of gradual and sudden enlightenment. Caodong favored gradual, silent enlightenment through seated meditation. The gradual stillness of mind is like "the bird hatching the egg" (Oxtoby, p. 272). Linji favored immediate awakening through the practice of shouting, beating, and paradoxical sayings that were later compiled as *gongan.* Unanticipated shouting and blows between master and pupil could result in enlightenment. Similarly, reflection on riddles could end in a sudden awakening, like "the blossoming of a lotus or the sun emerging from behind the clouds" (Oxtoby, p. 272). The Linji master might answer a student's query "Who is the Buddha?" with the quip "three pounds of flax." Alternatively, the master might propose the riddle "What is the sound of one hand clapping?" The purpose was to encourage the student to abandon all logic and reasoning while searching for peace in the quietude of meditation.

During the Southern Song dynasty of the twelfth century, the interaction of Chinese and Japanese monks stimulated the migration to Japan of Linji (Rinzai Zen) and Caodong (Soto Zen). Eisai (1141–1215) brought Rinzai and Dogen (1200–1253) brought Soto. The Kamakura period (1185–1333) was a watershed for Zen Buddhism. Rinzai's emphasis on the controlled discipline of seated meditation and the contemplation of koan became popular among the ruling samurai clans at Kamakura. Soto's more exclusive focus on seated meditation appealed to the peasantry. Zen's influence in the arts included painting, literature, and calligraphy and carried on well into the modern era. Zen and the sword, Zen and archery, Zen and tea were intimately connected to samurai culture.

The juxtaposition of Zen's humanity and samurai warfare is difficult for Westerners to understand. At Shaolin, the Chan monks practiced martial arts (*gongfu*) to keep themselves physically fit while defeating their worst enemy: their own desire. In a world of suffering, desire is the root of misery. To do away with desire is to clear a way to the "extinction" of suffering (nirvana). In Japan the samurai were intimately linked to Zen. If Buddhism is the pure negation of the will as the extinguishing of desire, then Bushido (the warrior's way) is the pure will as the negation of the negation or the annihilation of nirvana. The juxtaposition of Zen and the warrior spirit is the essence of samurai culture. This alluring paradox is one reason that Suzuki's style of Rinzai Zen became popular in the Western world after World War II.

*See also* **Buddhism; Religion: East and Southeast Asia.**

BIBLIOGRAPHY

Ch'en, Kenneth K. S. *Buddhism in China: A Historical Survey.* Princeton, N.J.: Princeton University Press, 1964.

Faure, Bernard. *Buddhism.* Translated by Sean Konecky. New York: Konecky and Konecky, 1998.

Oxtoby, Willard G., ed. *World Religions: Eastern Traditions.* 2nd ed. Don Mills, Ontario, and New York: Oxford University Press, 2002.

Schuhmacher, Stephan, and Gert Woerner, eds. *The Encyclopedia of Eastern Philosophy and Religion: Buddhism, Hinduism, Taoism, Zen.* Boston: Shambhala, 1989.

Smart, Ninian. *The World's Religions.* 2nd ed. Cambridge, U.K., and New York: Cambridge University Press, 1998.

Suzuki, Daisetz T. *Zen and Japanese Culture.* Princeton, N.J.: Princeton University Press, 1959.

Yampolsky, Philip, trans. *The Platform Sutra of the Sixth Patriarch.* New York: Columbia University Press, 1967.

*Jay Goulding*

**ZIONISM.** The historians of nationalism have reached a consensus that modern nationalism began as a secular movement, but almost all its varieties were affected by an undertow of older religious sentiments and loyalties. In many of the nationalisms (for example, in the battles between Greeks and Turks in the second decade of the nineteenth century or in the quarrel between Catholics and Protestants in Northern Ireland) the religious dimension of the quarreling nationalisms was clear and avowed. In the case of Zionism the reverse seemed to be true. When modern Zionism appeared in the nineteenth century, it defined itself in secular terms. It did not come into the world to bring about the age of the messiah that had been foretold in many of the classic texts of the Jewish religion. Zionism offered to answer two major problems that faced contemporary Jews. They were victims of large-scale persecution, most overtly in Eastern Europe, and the Jewish intelligentsia were being all too attracted to the promise of equality in society—which was apparently only being offered to those who were willing to abandon their separateness and assimilate into the non-Jewish majority. The modern Zionist movement suggested that a Jewish national home would help solve the problems of persecution and assimilation (the Zionists really meant that they wanted a state of their own). Jews would have a homeland that would always gladly receive them, and Jews who were conflicted about their identity would be able to deal with this question in the safe and nurturing environment of a Jewish community in which they were an autonomous majority.

The question of religion did, inevitably, arise at the very beginning of modern Zionism. In the 1830s two rabbis from Central Europe, Yehudah Hai Alkalai and Zvi Hirsch Kalischer, each proposed that with nationalism burgeoning all around them—the Greeks had just won their revolt against the Turks, and other European nationalities were arising to fight for their independence—it was time for the Jews, who could trace their national existence back to biblical times, to assert their own unique identity. Surely, so Alkalai and Kalischer argued, as the oldest of all nationalities, the Jews had the right and even the duty to lead the contemporary parade of nations who were asserting their rebirths. But Alkalai and Kalischer, both of whom were not only rabbis learned in the Talmud but scholars of the Kabbalah (Jewish esoteric mystical teaching), were very careful to deny that they were announcing the beginning of a messianic movement. They held fast to the inherited doctrine that the messiah could come not as the result of human action, but as a free gift from God. The nationalism that Alkalai and Kalischer were suggesting might have some connection to messianic hopes: kabbalistic teaching had allowed that "stirrings down below" might act to remind heaven of the longing of the Jewish people for the messiah, but no political program could be built on this hope. In the nineteenth century peoples were defining themselves by their history and group identity; the Jews should therefore cease to think of themselves as a persecuted minority and begin to assert themselves as a people among the peoples of the earth.

Thus, it is inaccurate to label even the "religious Zionists" as the ancestors of contemporary Zionist messianism. This element in present-day Zionism descends from two sources; the first is the confusion that existed in the minds and hearts of some of the most seemingly secular of the Zionist leaders and thinkers. For example, Chaim Weizmann (1874–1952), the long-time leader of the World Zionist Organization and the first president of Israel, made no secret of the total secularity of his way of life. Nonetheless, at every crucial moment in the debate over the rights of Zionists to a Jewish national home and, ultimately, to a state in the Holy Land, Weizmann invoked sacred Scripture. He kept saying that "the Bible is our charter." The Zionist contemporary who was second only to Weizmann, David Ben Gurion (1886–1973), the first prime minister of Israel and the man who led the country to win its independence, was an even more avowed secularist than Weizmann. After years of studying his work, the author of this entry reached the conclusion that he was best defined by a paradox: there is no God, but he chose the Jewish people and gave them the land of Israel. So, at the time of Israel's astounding victory in June 1967, when it conquered the large territories all the way to the Jordan River and the Suez Canal, the pervasive mood in Israel and among the Jewish people as a whole was that a miracle had happened. Never mind whether it was God or the inherent "spirit of the Jewish people" that had performed the miracle. Most Jews were sure that they were living in a version of messianic times; they were free to carve out their own destiny, at least in much of the land that was now under their control.

The second source of the new messianism was in a change in the theology of the Orthodox Zionists. In the first years of the twentieth century a young and universally respected rabbinic scholar and Kabbalist, Rabbi Abraham Isaac Kook (1865–1935), arrived in Jaffa to assume the post of chief rabbi of its growing Jewish community. Kook insisted that the Jews were indeed living in messianic times. He asserted that the new Zionist movement, despite its pronounced bias against religion, was despite itself an instrument of God's hands. Modern Zionism was reviving the sacred language, Hebrew. Kook insisted that the religious character of the tongue of the Bible was so deeply ingrained that the revival of Hebrew would inevitably act to bring contemporary Zionists closer to their roots. The secular Zionists, so Kook continued, might think that they were engaged in regaining the soil of the Holy Land for a contemporary Jewish state, but this soil was inherently holy; the labor to regain it and to dwell in it would soon transform the self-avowed secular people who were devoting their lives to this task. When World War I broke out in 1914, Rabbi Kook interpreted this enormous bloodletting as the war of Gog and Magog, the ultimate destructive war that had been foretold as the last preamble to the messianic age. The gentile world was destroying itself, and the moral credit of its achievements was now worthless. So it went after each major turning point in the course of the Zionist revival. Kook saw every event as part of the immediate drama of messianism.

Kook was clearly a holy man, but his teaching contained a unexploded bomb. If the Jewish people were living in the immediate preamble to the messianic age, as he maintained, then what was to be done with the disappointments and the blockages that would occur on the path to redemption? Kook died in 1935, so these questions were left to a lesser figure, his son, Rabbi Zvi Yehudah Kook (1891–1981), to contemplate. He ultimately succeeded his father as the head of the Mercaz Harav ("the rabbi's center"), the Yeshiva, the School of Tamudic Learning and Theological Thought, which the father had established. This school taught its students not only the conventional studies in Talmudic literature that were the staples of the other yeshivot. At this unique school the students were taught to enter the army and to prepare themselves to be elite combat troops. These young people were imbued by Zvi Yehudah Kook with an activist faith that it was their privilege and duty to help bring the messiah soon, in their own day—and Zvi Yehudah Kook never gave up the dream that all of the land that the Jews had possessed in biblical times, including especially the West Bank, would and must be returned to the Jewish people. The enormous and heady victories of the Six-Day War in 1967 were hailed in this religious circle as proof of their ideology. Yes, the messianic miracle had occurred, and

the whole of the land of biblical Israel must now be possessed and never returned. Jewish settlement on the West Bank was a religious commandment, and those who opposed such settlements or hindered them or threatened to make them impossible were never to be forgiven. The most extreme thinking among this element was expressed by some younger people, especially among the rabbis who ministered to the new communities in the West Bank. Several of them were accused of encouraging Yigal Amir, the assassin who murdered Israel's prime minister, Yitzhak Rabin, in 1995. Rabin's "sin" was that he had signed the agreement that Israel and the Palestinians had made secretly in Oslo in 1992. On behalf of Israel, Rabin had agreed to allow the Palestinians ultimately to establish a state of their own on the West Bank. He was therefore regarded by the hard-line believers in the "undivided land of Israel" as leaning toward religious and national treason.

At the start of the twenty-first century the shock of this murder had not abated because the activist minority—probably 20 percent of Israel's population—made no secret that it would engage in civil, and some even in armed, disobedience against any Israeli government that intends to allow the Palestinians a state of their own on most, or almost all, of the West Bank. This embitterment had the most profound effect on the question of the very nature of the Zionist enterprise. When modern Zionism was created, there was an existing consensus among all its factions that the highest authority within the Zionist movement would be the civil government of the national home that was being established. To be sure, from the very beginning a certain amount of respect was extended to the religious elements within the Jewish community. There was no question that the kitchens of the Israeli army would be kosher everywhere and that the Orthodox rabbinate would be given the ultimate authority on such matters as marriage and divorce among Jews. Through the years some elements in Israel have chafed under these controls, but the majority have made peace with the amount of religious coloration that exists in Israel's public life, but these issues were essentially peripheral. They did not involve religious judgments on the foreign policy of Israel or the questions of relations with the Arab world. In the aftermath of the Six-Day War of June 1967, the newly awakened messianic believers reframed their Zionist aims as politically maximalist. The new messianists proposed to enact their program in the name of God's will.

More recently, in the first years of the twenty-first century, modern Zionism is under attack from two other perspectives. The ultraright Zionists are ever more forthright in insisting that if the messiah does not come soon, they will at least solve the problem of keeping a Jewish state Jewish even as it controls a population that, between the Mediterranean and the Jordan River, is already half Arab, either by denying the Arabs full political rights or by creating the conditions for the large-scale "transfer" of Arabs from the land of Israel. Such thinking used to be anathema to the Israeli mainstream, but it has become more thinkable as the armed conflict between Jews and Palestinians has become ever more embittered. By the end of 2003, there were well over two thousand dead among the Palestinians, but there had been nearly a thousand casualties among the Israelis since the outbreak of the "second intifada" in 2000. These deaths occurred in guerrilla warfare, including suicide bombings by the Palestinians, and in reprisals by the Israelis. In the current struggle, Israel's moderates have diminished after each suicide bombing, and no new moderates have appeared among the Palestinians. It seems ever less likely that Israelis and Palestinians will find a way to put their hurts behind them and make peace across the table. They will need strong leadership and pressure from the United States and from some of the rest of the international community.

By April 2004 Sharon made the first step toward accepting a notion that no one had ever expected he would accept: the demographic balance in "the undivided land of Israel" was shifting toward an Arab majority. He, therefore, proposed that the Israelis begin by evacuating all 7500 settlers from the Gaza Strip and leaving that to Arab rule. Despite opposition from his own Likud party, Sharon insisted ever more openly that demography commands Israel to cease ruling an unwilling and hostile Arab majority. Sharon's policies make an Arab state living beside Israel an inevitabilty, but one that will take much military and political turmoil to work.

On the side of the Palestinians and their sympathizers, especially in the Arab world, there is equally strong awareness that demographic trends are producing an Arab majority in the supposedly "undivided land of Israel." The basic Arab policy seems to have moved in the direction of waiting out the next few years and then demanding that only one state should exist in this land but that this state should be ruled by the principle of "one man, one vote." This notion is often dressed up as the realization of the great democratic dream, a binational state of Jews and Arabs, in which Jews can be assured that a growing Arab majority will not treat them harshly. Most of those who argue this view, however, do not manage to hide their indifference, or even glee, at the thought that the Zionist venture would then be over. The Jewish state would be gone; it would be replaced by a state with an Arab majority. All the claims that the Jews have made concerning their need and their right for a state of their own in which they could make their own destiny by their own rights would end in failure. These Jewish notions seemed plausible—so the argument goes—only late in the nineteenth century and early in the twentieth when nationalism and even colonialism still had some credit in the world.

But modern Zionism will not die so easily and certainly not in the pages of left-wing journals in the Western world or in the pronouncements by Islamic nationalists in their own media in the Arab world. The Jews who founded Zionism and their followers who began to come to Palestine more than a century ago to establish the modern Zionist presence did not suffer and die so that, as Chaim Weizmann once said, they might become "Hebrew nationals in a Palestinian State." Zionists will not allow the state of Israel to pack up and leave but are determined to stay put despite the bitter quarrels. Devotion to Israel's survival as a Jewish state does, and will, force it to fight. By the same token, the Palestinians are not going to leave. The Arab states in the Middle East have no desire to absorb any substantial number of Palestinian Arabs, and the world as a whole, especially the West, is not overly hospitable to those who would enter it as part of a new mass migration.

These considerations already existed many decades ago when it became clear that Jews and Palestinian Arabs were, despite themselves, having to find ways of living in some tolerable peace. The reigning suggestion was defined in 1937 by the Peel Commission, the highest-level investigation into the conflict in the Holy Land that the British authorities ever empowered. This body knew very well that there was no happy answer to the conflict between Jews and Arabs, but they ruled that the least obnoxious and most likely mode of making some tolerable peace would be the partition of the land between Jews and Arabs. Ten years later in 1947, the nascent United Nations reiterated the conclusions of the Peel Commission and voted to divide the land between a Jewish and an Arab state. On neither of these two occasions was the recommended solution enacted peacefully because the bulk of the Palestinians and their Arab confederates refused to recognize the legitimacy of giving the Jews even one ell of the land of Palestine for a state of their own.

The most interesting new development lies not in Palestinian and Arab opinion, but in a substantial shift among many political liberals who had traditionally supported the Zionist vision and program. This change in opinion began in some circles in 1967 when parts of the liberal intelligentsia shifted allegiance during and after the Six-Day War. They found reason to be annoyed with the Jews for concentrating on so parochial a purpose as the survival of the Jewish state and not on such wider concerns as America's misdeeds in the Vietnam War and, more immediately, on the pains and needs of the Palestinians. By 1967 the memory of the Holocaust, the murder of six million defenseless Jews in Europe, had begun to fade, and the Jewish people as a whole were becoming for many in the liberal left an annoying reminder of past deaths and past guilts. Israel was now a going concern—an increasingly powerful one—and thus the Palestinians became the new "victims" of choice. The undertow of this change in political faction was an increasing impatience with the unique demands that the Zionist state was making for special consideration for the Jewish people.

Why, indeed, should the Jews need a state of their own? The main charge that the Arab states have kept raising against the state of Israel is that it is a "rabbinic theocracy" but no one has challenged almost all of the Arab states to not conduct themselves as "Muslim theocracies" with scant concern for the right of minorities. On the contrary, left-liberal doctrine insisted that Jewish nationalism should disappear even as most other nationalisms in the world have an unquestioned right to continue. The most interesting part of this phenomenon is that some of its theories are being advanced by Jews. The older assimilationist doctrines, which stated that the Jews should meld into the majority among whom they lived, are being applied even to the Zionist community in the Middle East: it should accept and gladly welcome absorption among the many million of Arabs in the region.

In the early twenty-first century it is being argued by various spokesmen of the liberal left—many Arabs and some

Jews—that the Zionist state should be dismantled. Let one state be established in which the inevitable Arab majority could supposedly be trusted to treat the Jewish minority fairly according to democratic principles. Anyone who knows the history of the region and has any reasonable assessment of the present tensions knows that this vision is a pipe dream. It is advanced by people who might wring their hands when a supposed democracy of Jews and Arabs in one state does not live up to its promises, but then these thinkers will have lost interest in the problem. Of all the visions that are being held out to the warring Israelis and Palestinians, the one-state solution is by far the least likely because neither side to the conflict can trust the other to rein in its maximalists.

The most sober assessment has to be that the problems will continue and that the conflict will not be easily resolved, but modern Zionism and its creation, the state of Israel, are here to stay. Its future is not guaranteed by the coming of the messiah soon, but Israel is not ultimately threatened even by the intifada and the suicide bombers. It exists and will continue to exist by the will of its own people. Jews will not surrender their claim to a home of their own to which those who need to come may come freely, nor their claim to a national center of their own in which Jewish energies may continue to define what the long past of this people means in the present and what it can be understood to mean in the future.

*See also* **Judaism; Miracles; Nation; Nationalism.**

BIBLIOGRAPHY

Antonius, George. *The Arab Awakening: The Story of the Arab National Movement.* New York: Capricorn, 1965.

Cleveland, William L. *A History of the Modern Middle East.* Boulder, Colo.: Westview, 1994.

Elon, Amos. *The Israelis: Founders and Sons.* New York: Penguin, 1983.

Ezrahi, Yaron. *Rubber Bullets: Power and Conscience in Modern Israel.* New York: Farrar, Straus and Giroux, 1997.

Hertzberg, Arthur. *The Fate of Zionism: A Secular Future for Israel and Palestine.* San Francisco: HarperSanFrancisco, 2003.

———. *The Zionist Idea: A Historical Analysis and Reader.* New York: Atheneum, 1972

Khalidi, Walid, ed. *From Haven to Conquest: Readings in Zionism and the Palestine Problem until 1948.* Washington, D.C.: Institute for Palestine Studies, 1987.

Laqueur, Walter, and Barry M. Rubin, eds. *The Israel-Arab Reader: A Documentary History of the Middle East Conflict.* 5th ed. New York: Penguin, 1995.

Lustick, Ian. *Arabs in the Jewish State: Israel's Control of a National Minority.* Austin: University of Texas Press, 1980.

Morris, Benny. *The Birth of the Palestinian Refugee Problem, 1947–1949.* Cambridge, U.K.: Cambridge University Press, 1987.

Ravitzky, Aviezer. *Messianism, Zionism, and Jewish Radicalism.* Chicago: University of Chicago Press, 1996.

Said, Edward. *The Question of Palestine.* New York: Vintage, 1992.

Shipler, David. *Arab and Jew: Wounded Spirits in a Promised Land.* New York: Times Books, 1986.

Shlaim, Avi. *Collusion across the Jordan: King Abdullah, the Zionist Movement, and the Partition of Palestine.* New York: Columbia University Press, 1988.

*Arthur Hertzberg*

# LIST OF CONTRIBUTORS

JANET L. ABU-LUGHOD
Department of Sociology, Graduate Faculty, New School
University
*City, The: The Islamic and Byzantine City*

PIUS ADESANMI
Department of Comparative Literature, Pennsylvania
State University
*Literature: African Literature*

AUSTIN METUMARA AHANOTU
Department of History, California State University,
Stanislaus
*Religion and the State: Africa*

EVERETT HELMUT AKAM
Department of Political Science, Casper College
*Pluralism*

SOLA AKINRINADE
Department of History, Obafemi Awolowo University,
Nigeria
*Migration: Africa*
*Oral Traditions: Overview*

ROBERT ALBRO
John W. Kluge Center, Library of Congress
*Populism: Latin America*

ROBERTO ALEJANDRO
Department of Political Science, University of
Massachusetts, Amherst
*Justice: Justice in American Thought*

BARRY ALLEN
Department of Philosophy, McMaster University
*Knowledge*

GARLAND E. ALLEN
Department of Biology, Washington University in St.
Louis
*Eugenics*
*Genetics: Contemporary*
*Life*

DWIGHT D. ALLMAN
Department of Political Science, Baylor University
*Political, The*

ELLEN AMSTER
Department of History, University of Wisconsin—
Milwaukee
*Westernization: Middle East*

DIANE APOSTOLOS-CAPPADONA
Center for Muslim-Christian Understanding,
Georgetown University
*Humanity in the Arts*
*Landscape in the Arts*
*Nude, The*

THEODORE ARABATZIS
Department of Philosophy and History of Science,
University of Athens
*Experiment*

ARTHUR AUGHEY
School of Economics and Politics, University of Ulster,
U.K.
*Conservatism*

MAITRII AUNG-THWIN
Department of History, National University of Singapore
*Anticolonialism: Southeast Asia*
*Colonialism: Southeast Asia*
*Westernization: Southeast Asia*

ANTHONY F. AVENI
Department of Physics and Astronomy, Colgate
University
*Astronomy, Pre-Columbian and Latin American*

ANITA AVRAMIDES
St. Hilda's College, Oxford
*Philosophy of Mind: Overview*

LAWRENCE A. BABB
Department of Anthropology and Sociology, Amherst
College
*Jainism*

SOULEYMANE BACHIR DIAGNE
Department of Philosophy, Northwestern University
*Philosophies: African*

PETER BAEHR
Department of Politics and Sociology, Lingnan
University, Hong Kong
*Totalitarianism*

ELLEN T. BAIRD
Department of Art History, University of Illinois at Chicago
*City, The: Latin America*

THOMAS BALDWIN
Department of Philosophy, University of York, U.K.
*Analytical Philosophy*

ASOKA BANDARAGE
Women's Studies Program, Mount Holyoke College
*Family Planning*

AHMED S. BANGURA
Department of Modern and Classical Languages, University of San Francisco
*Orientalism: African and Black Orientalism*

MOSHE BARASCH
Hebrew University (Emeritus)
*Gesture*

E. J. W. BARBER
Linguistics and Archaeology, Occidental College
*Language, Linguistics, and Literacy*
*Textiles and Fiber Arts as Catalysts for Ideas*

STEPHEN BARNES
Department of Philosophy, Northwest Vista College
*Populism: United States*
*Philosophies: American*
*Pragmatism*

MARLEEN S. BARR
Hadassah Brandeis Feminist Research Institute, Brandeis University
*Science Fiction*

CLYDE W. BARROW
University of Massachusetts, Dartmouth
*State, The: Overview*

J. ROBERT BARTH
Department of English, Boston College
*Imagination*

EDWINA BARVOSA-CARTER
Department of Chicano/a Studies, University of California at Santa Barbara
*Identity, Multiple: Overview*

MICHAEL BAUR
Philosophy Department, Fordham University
*Idealism*

TIMOTHY BAYCROFT
Department of History, University of Sheffield, U.K.
*Nationalism: Overview*

MARC BECKER
Division of Social Science, Truman State University
*Anticolonialism: Latin America*
*Authoritarianism: Latin America*
*Dictatorship in Latin America*
*Extirpation*
*Republicanism: Latin America*

JASON DAVID BeDUHN
Northern Arizona University
*Manichaeism*

WILLIAM H. BEEZLEY
Department of History, University of Arizona
*Religion and the State: Latin America*

SHULAMITH BEHR
Courtauld Institute of Art
*Expressionism*

RONALD BEINER
Department of Political Science, University of Toronto
*Citizenship: Overview*

JONATHAN BELLER
Department of English and Humanities, Pratt Institute
*Third Cinema*
*Visual Culture*

BERNADETTE BENSAUDE-VINCENT
Département de Philosophie, Université de Paris X
*Chemistry*

JANET E. BENSON
Department of Sociology, Anthropology, and Social Work, Kansas State University
*Communication of Ideas: Southeast Asia and Its Influence*

DIRK BERG-SCHLOSSER
Institute of Political Science, Philipps-University, Marburg, Germany
*Authoritarianism: Overview*

ALAN E. BERNSTEIN
Department of History, University of Arizona
*Heaven and Hell*

MARK H. BERNSTEIN
Department of Philosophy, University of Texas at San Antonio
*Fatalism*

CHRISTOPHER J. BERRY
Department of Politics, University of Glasgow
*Poverty*
*Wealth*

BRENDA L. BETHMAN
Texas A&M University
*Jouissance*

RICHARD BETT
Department of Philosophy, Johns Hopkins University
*Epistemology: Ancient*

ELIZABETH BISHOP
University of Texas at Austin
*Nationalism: Cultural Nationalism*

KALMAN P. BLAND
Department of Religion, Duke University
*Judaism: Modern Judaism*

JACK S. BLOCKER JR.
Department of History, Huron University College,
University of Western Ontario
*Temperance*

WILLARD BOHN
Department of Foreign Languages, Illinois State
University
*Dada*
*Surrealism*

ELIAS K. BONGMBA
Religious Studies, Rice University
*Communitarianism in African Thought*
*Religion: Africa*
*Religion: African Diaspora*

MICHAEL BONNER
Department of Near Eastern Studies, University of
Michigan
*Jihad*

SUSAN BORDO
Department of English, University of Kentucky
*Body, The*

JONATHAN BOYARIN
Independent Scholar, New York, N.Y.
*Identity, Multiple: Jewish Multiple Identity*

JOEL T. BRASLOW
Departments of Psychiatry and History, University of
California, Los Angeles
VISN-22 Mental Illness Research, Education and
Clinical Center, Veterans Administration
*Psychology and Psychiatry*

SONJA BRENTJES
Institute for the Study of Muslim Civilizations, Aga
Khan University
*Islamic Science*

JOHN BREUILLY
Department of Government, London School of
Economics
*Nation*

GWEN W. BREWER
Department of English, California State University,
Northridge
*Classicism*

ANNE F. BROADBRIDGE
Department of History, University of Massachusetts
*Monarchy: Islamic Monarchy*

CHARLOTTE R. BROWN
Department of Philosophy, Illinois Wesleyan University
*Moral Sense*

LAURIE M. BROWN
Department of Physics and Astronomy, Northwestern
University
*Quantum*

VERN L. BULLOUGH
State University of New York (Emeritus)
*Gender: Overview*
*Love, Western Notions of*
*Sexuality: Sexual Orientation*

MARTIN J. BURKE
Department of History, Lehman College and the
Graduate Center, City University of New York
*Social History, U.S.*

PETER BURKE
Emmanuel College, University of Cambridge
*Context*
*Everyday Life*

WILLIAM E. BURNS
Department of History, Morgan State University
*Astrology: Overview*
*Superstition*

W. F. BYNUM
Wellcome Trust Centre for the History of Medicine,
University College London
*Health and Disease*

JOANNE CACCIATORE-GARARD
M.I.S.S. Foundation
*Death*

GIUSEPPE CAGLIOTI
Dipartimento Ingegneria Nucleare, Politecnico di Milano
*Ambiguity*

MARTHA M. CAMPBELL
School of Public Health, University of California,
Berkeley
*Population*

ARTHUR CAPLAN
Department of Medical Ethics, University of
Pennsylvania
*Bioethics*

MICHAEL C. CARHART
University of Nevada
*Enlightenment*

JEAN-CLAUDE CARRON
University of California, Los Angeles
*Rhetoric: Overview*

TERRELL CARVER
Department of Politics, University of Bristol, U.K.
*Historical and Dialectical Materialism*

STEVEN CASSEDY
Department of Literature, University of California, San
Diego
*Nihilism*
*Orthopraxy: Western Orthopraxy*
*Regions and Regionalism, Eastern Europe*

SUNDIATA KEITA CHA-JUA
Afro-American Studies and Research Program, University
of Illinois at Urbana-Champaign
*African-American Ideas*

WELLINGTON K. K. CHAN
Occidental College
*Empire and Imperialism: Asia*

JOHN CHARVET
Department of Government, London School of
Economics
*Liberalism*

CHUNG-YING CHENG
University of Hawai'i at Manoa
*Consciousness: Chinese Thought*

FREDRIC L. CHEYETTE
Department of History, Amherst College
*Feudalism, European*

LAURA CHRISMAN
Department of English, University of York, U.K.
*Postcolonial Studies*

DIANE CIEKAWY
Department of Sociology and Anthropology, Ohio
University
*Magic*
*Witchcraft*
*Witchcraft, African Studies of*

ALBRECHT CLASSEN
Department of German Studies, University of Arizona
*Other, The, European Views of*

DISKIN CLAY
Department of Classical Studies, Duke University
*Dialogue and Dialectics: Socratic*

H. FLORIS COHEN
University of Twente
*Scientific Revolution*

JEAN COMAROFF
Department of Anthropology, University of Chicago
*Ethnography*

BETH A. CONKLIN
Vanderbilt University
*Cannibalism*

R.W. CONNELL
Faculty of Education and Social Work, University of
Sydney
*Men and Masculinity*

COSTAS M. CONSTANTINOU
School of Politics, Philosophy and International
Relations, University of Keele
*Treaty*

DAVID COOK
Rice University
*Millenarianism: Islamic*

MIRIAM COOKE
Department of Asian and African Languages and
Literature, Duke University
*Feminism: Islamic Feminism*

DAVID D. COREY
Department of Political Science, Baylor University
*Sophists, The*

DRUCILLA CORNELL
Department of Political Science, Rutgers University
*Universalism*

JORGE F. CORONADO
Department of Spanish and Portugese, Northwestern
University
*Indigenismo*

SARAH COVINGTON
Department of History, Queens College
*Etiquette*
*Untouchability: Menstrual Taboos*

CLIFTON CRAIS
Department of History, Emory University
*Resistance and Accommodation*

DAVID CRAVEN
Department of Art and Art History, University of New Mexico
*Modernism: Latin America*
*World Systems Theory, Latin America*

JON CRUZ
University of California, Santa Barbara
*Interpretation*

SEAN CUBITT
Screen and Media Studies, University of Waikato, New Zealand
*Cinema*
*Media, History of*

KAREN MARY DAVALOS
Loyola Marymount University
*Mestizaje*

CATHY N. DAVIDSON
Department of English, Duke University
*Interdisciplinarity*

NATALIE ZEMON DAVIS
Department of History, Princeton University
*Gift, The*

ROSA DE JORIO
Department of Sociology, Anthropology, and Criminal Justice, University of North Florida
*Kinship*

ALYSSA DEFRAIN
Independent Scholar, Omaha, Neb.
*Death*

JOHN DEFRAIN
Department of Family and Consumer Sciences, University of Nebraska
*Death*

ADELAIDA R. DEL CASTILLO
Department of Chicana and Chicano Studies, San Diego State University
*Citizenship: Cultural Citizenship*

RICHARD DELGADO
University of Pittsburgh School of Law
*Critical Race Theory*

ROBERT DELIÈGE
Institut Orientaliste, Université de Louvain-la-Neuve, Belgium
*Untouchability: Taboos*

JERRY DENNERLINE
Departments of History and Asian Languages and Civilizations, Amherst College
*Confucianism*

WALTER B. DENNY
Department of Art History, University of Massachusetts, Amherst
*Paradise on Earth*

HEATHER DEVERE
School of Social Sciences, Auckland University of Technology
*Friendship*

PETER DICKENS
Faculty of Social and Political Sciences, University of Cambridge
Department of Sociology, University of Essex
*Social Darwinism*

ROBERT W. DIMAND
Department of Economics, Brock University
*Game Theory*

LEONARD DINNERSTEIN
Department of History, University of Arizona
*Assimilation*

PETER DINZELBACHER
University of Vienna, Austria
*Asceticism: Western Asceticism*

MAMADOU DIOUF
Department of History, University of Michigan
*Intelligentsia*
*Modernity: Africa*

FRANCESCA DI POPPA
Department of History and Philosophy of Science, University of Pittsburgh
*Dualism*
*Materialism in Eighteenth-Century European Thought*
*Monism*

THOMAS DIXON
Department of History, Lancaster University, U.K.
*Agnosticism*
*Altruism*
*Natural Theology*

ALLEN DOUGLAS
Department of History, Indiana University, Bloomington
*Orientalism: Overview*

DOUGLAS C. DOW
School of Social Sciences, University of Texas at Dallas
*Punishment*

DONNALEE DOX
Department of Performance Studies, Texas A&M
University
*Dance*

JOHN DUCKITT
Department of Psychology, University of Auckland, New
Zealand
*Prejudice*

STEPHEN DUNCOMBE
Gallatin School, New York University
*Resistance*

TIM DUVALL
Department of Government and Politics, St. John's
University
*Epicureanism*
*Happiness and Pleasure in European Thought*
*Immortality and the Afterlife*
*Political Science*

MARK DYRESON
Departments of Kinesiology and History, Pennsylvania
State University
*Sport*

SAMUEL Y. EDGERTON
Department of Art, Williams College
*Perspective*

JEFFREY EDWARDS
University of Stony Brook, State University of New York
*Philosophy, Moral: Modern*

JOHN EHRENBERG
Department of Political Science, Long Island University,
Brooklyn, New York
*Civil Society: Europe and the United States*

DALE F. EICKELMAN
Department of Anthropology, Dartmouth College
*Tribalism, Middle East*

JAMAL J. ELIAS
Department of Religion, Amherst College
*Mysticism: Islamic Mysticism in Asia*

NNAMDI ELLEH
College of Design, Architecture, Art and Planning,
University of Cincinnati, Ohio
*Architecture: Africa*

ELISABETH ELLIS
Department of Political Science, Texas A&M University
*Common Sense*
*Modernity: Overview*

STEPHEN ELLIS
Department of Philosophy, University of Oklahoma
*Rational Choice*

BENJAMIN A. ELMAN
Department of East Asian Studies, Princeton University
*Education: China*
*Examination Systems, China*

STANLEY L. ENGERMAN
Departments of Economics and History, University of
Rochester
*Slavery*

MARC MICHAEL EPSTEIN
Department of Religion and Jewish Studies Program,
Vassar College
*Dream*

GEORGE ESENWEIN
Department of History, University of Florida
*Anarchism*
*Socialism*

G. R. EVANS
Faculty of History, University of Cambridge
*Christianity: Overview*

DICKSON EYOH
African Studies Program, New College, University of
Toronto
*Modernization*

STEPHEN M. FABIAN
Writing Program, Princeton University
*Ancestor Worship*
*Calendar*

TOYIN FALOLA
Department of History, University of Texas at Austin
*Nationalism: Africa*
*Neocolonialism*

PAUL FARBER
Department of History, Oregon State University
*Natural History*

JOHN E. FARLEY
Department of Sociology and Criminal Justice Studies,
Southern Illinois University at Edwardsville
*Minority*

MARGARET E. FARRAR
Department of Political Science, Augustana College
*City, The: The City as Political Center*

RICHARD K. FENN
Princeton Theological Seminary
*Time: Traditional and Utilitarian*

DAVID E. W. FENNER
Department of Philosophy, University of North Florida
*Taste*

JAMES W. FERNANDEZ
Department of Anthropology, University of Chicago
*Trope*

DAVID FIDELER
Editor, Alexandria, A Journal of Cosmology, Philosophy, Myth, and Culture
*Pythagoreanism*

LES W. FIELD
Department of Anthropology, University of New Mexico
*Native Policy*

AUTUMN FIESTER
Department of Medical Ethics, University of Pennsylvania
*Bioethics*

GIOVANNI FILORAMO
Department of History, University of Turin Italy
*Gnosticism*

JANE FLAX
Department of Political Science, Howard University
*Equality: Gender Equality*
*Essentialism*

TYLER FLEMING
University of Texas at Austin
*Nationalism: Africa*

BENEDETTO FONTANA
Department of Political Science, Baruch College, City University of New York
*Democracy*
*Hegemony*

CYNTHIA E. FOOR
Department of Anthropology, Western Michigan University
*Family: Family in Anthropology since 1980*

CARLA FRECCERO
Literature Department, University of California, Santa Cruz
*Fetishism: Fetishism in Literature and Cultural Studies*

R. G. FREY
Department of Philosophy, Bowling Green State University
*Utilitarianism*

ALMA M. GARCIA
Department of Anthropology and Sociology, Santa Clara University
*Feminism: Third World U.S. Movement*

EUGENE GARVER
Department of Philosophy, St. John's University, Minnesota
*Reason, Practical and Theoretical*

STEPHEN GAUKROGER
Department of Philosophy, University of Sydney, Australia
*Cartesianism*

PAULA E. GEYH
Department of English, Yeshiva University
*Postmodernism*

ANAT GILBOA
Queen's University, Kingston, Canada
*Gender in Art*

CHRISTOPHER GILL
Department of Classics and Ancient History, University of Exeter, United Kingdom
*Stoicism*

NATHAN GLAZER
Department of Sociology, Harvard University
*Diversity*

THOMAS F. GLICK
Boston University
*Communication of Ideas: Middle East and Abroad*

DAVID J. GOA
Provincial Museum of Alberta
*Images, Icons, and Idols*

DAVID THEO GOLDBERG
University of California Humanities Research Institute, University of California, Irvine
*Ethnocentrism*
*Interdisciplinarity*

DEENA J. GONZÁLEZ
Department of Chicana/o Studies, Loyola Marymount University
*Internal Colonialism*

GLORIA GONZÁLEZ-LÓPEZ
Department of Sociology, University of Texas at Austin
*Machismo*

JOSHUA GOODE
Department of History, Occidental College
*Race and Racism: Europe*

HOWARD L. GOODMAN
*Mysticism: Chinese Mysticism*
*Time: China*

JACK GOODY
St. John's College, Cambridge, U.K.
*Communication of Ideas: Orality and the Advent of Writing*
*Wisdom, Human*

LEWIS R. GORDON
Department of Philosophy, Temple University
*Humanism: Africa*

JAY GOULDING
Department of Sociology, York University, Toronto, Canada
*Barbarism and Civilization*
*Globalization: Asia*
*Religion: East and Southeast Asia*
*Society*
*Zen*

DAVID GRAEBER
Department of Anthropology, Yale University
*Alienation*

DANIEL W. GRAHAM
Department of Philosophy, Brigham Young University
*Change*

I. GRATTAN-GUINNESS
Middlesex University at Enfield
*Algebras*
*Logic and Philosophy of Mathematics, Modern*
*Mathematics*

JEREMY GRAY
Centre for the History of the Mathematical Sciences, Open University
*Geometry*

SUSAN GRAYSON
Department of Spanish and French Literary Studies, Occidental College
*Women and Femininity in U.S. Popular Culture*

SEAN GREENBERG
Department of Philosophy, Johns Hopkins University
*Rationalism*

FREDERICK GREGORY
Department of History, University of Florida
*Naturphilosophie*

PAUL F. GRENDLER
Department of History, University of Toronto (Emeritus)
*Education: Europe*
*University: Overview*

ROGER GRIFFIN
Department of History, Oxford Brookes University
*Fascism*

JEFF D. GRISCHOW
Department of History, Wilfrid Laurier University
*Capitalism: Africa*

ULRICH GROETSCH
Department of History, Rutgers University
*Pietism*

JEAN GRONDIN
Département de Philosophie, Université de Montréal
*Hermeneutics*

LAWRENCE GROSSBERG
Department of Communication Studies, University of North Carolina at Chapel Hill
*Cultural Studies*

ANDREW GROSSMAN
Independent Scholar, Springfield, N.J.
*Gay Studies*

SEBASTIAN GÜNTHER
Department of Near and Middle Eastern Civilizations, University of Toronto
*Education: Islamic Education*

MATTHEW C. GUTMANN
Department of Anthropology, Brown University
*Machismo*

PAUL GUYER
Department of Philosophy, University of Pennsylvania
*Kantianism*

ALAN HÁJEK
Humanities and Social Sciences 101-40, California Institute of Technology
*Probability*

PETER DOBKIN HALL
John F. Kennedy School of Government, Harvard University
*Volunteerism, U.S.*

THOMAS D. HALL
Department of Sociology, DePauw University
*Borders, Borderlands, and Frontiers, Global*

ELTIGANI ABDELGADIR HAMID
Graduate School of Islamic and Social Sciences
*Islam: Africa*

JOHN T. HAMILTON
Department of Comparative Literature, Harvard University
*Poetry and Poetics*

M. ŞÜKRÜ HANIOĞLU
Department of Near Eastern Studies, Princeton
University
*Pan-Turkism*

BETTY J. HARRIS
Anthropology and Women's Studies, University of
Oklahoma
*Apartheid*

GLEN ANTHONY HARRIS
History Department, University of North Carolina at
Wilmington
*Ethnohistory, U.S.*

DAVID M. HART
Online Library of Liberty, Liberty Fund, Inc.
*War and Peace in the Arts*

SEAN HAWKINS
Department of History, University of Toronto
*Social Capital*

MATTHEW HEATON
Department of History, University of Texas at Austin
*Neocolonialism*

JAMES P. HELFERS
College of Liberal Arts, Grand Canyon University
*Travel from Europe and the Middle East*

FRED HENDRICKS
Department of Sociology, Rhodes University, South
Africa
*Ethnicity and Race: Africa*
*Multiculturalism, Africa*

ARTHUR HERTZBERG
Department of Religion, Dartmouth College (Emeritus)
Bronfman Visiting Professor of the Humanities, New
York University
*Anti-Semitism: Overview*
*Zionism*

WENDY S. HESFORD
Department of English, The Ohio State University
*Autobiography*

NORRISS HETHERINGTON
Office for the History of Science and Technology,
University of California, Berkeley
*Cosmology: Cosmology and Astronomy*

PAUL HEYER
Department of Communication Studies, Wilfrid Laurier
University, Waterloo, Ontario, Canada
*Communication of Ideas: The Americas and Their Influence*
*Communication of Ideas: Europe and Its Influence*

JOSIAH McC. HEYMAN
Department of Sociology and Anthropology, University
of Texas at El Paso
*Scarcity and Abundance, Latin America*
*Work*

MARC A. HIGHT
Department of Philosophy, Hampden-Sydney College
*Classification of Arts and Sciences, Early Modern*

T. J. HOCHSTRASSER
Department of International History, London School of
Economics and Political Science
*Natural Law*

DIRK HOERDER
Department of History, University of Bremen
*Migration: Migration in World History*
*Migration: United States*

VALERIE HOLLIDAY
Louisiana State University, Baton Rouge
*Genius*

CRISTOPHER HOLLINGSWORTH
Department of English, University of South Alabama
*Metaphor*

TED HONDERICH
University College London
*Determinism*

CLAIRE HOOKER
Public Health Sciences, University of Toronto
*Hygiene*

M. B. HOOKER
Faculty of Law, The Australian National University
*Islam: Southeast Asia*

ELLIS HOROWITZ
Department of Computer Science, University of
Southern California
*Computer Science*

MARYANNE CLINE HOROWITZ
Department of History, Occidental College
*Humanity: European Thought*
*Renaissance*
*Visual Order to Organizing Collections*

JANET HOSKINS
Department of Anthropology, University of Southern
California
*Matriarchy*

KEVIN JAMES HOUK
Modern History and Literature, Drew University
*Cosmopolitanism*

COLUM HOURIHANE
Princeton University
*Iconography*

MICHAEL HUGHES
Edgewood College
*Philosophy, Moral: Modern*

WILLIAM HUGHES
School of English and Creative Studies, Bath Spa
University College
*Genre*

JONATHAN P. HUNT
Department of English, Santa Clara University
*Naturalism*

VALERAE M. HURLEY
Department of History, Monmouth University
*Radicals/Radicalism*

ROSALIND HURSTHOUSE
Department of Philosophy, University of Auckland, New
Zealand
*Virtue Ethics*

AÍDA HURTADO
Department of Psychology, University of California,
Santa Cruz
*Feminism: Chicana Feminisms*

PATRICK H. HUTTON
Department of History, University of Vermont
*Memory*
*Presentism*

PABLO L.E. IDAHOSA
African Studies, Social Science, York University,
Toronto, Canada
*Socialisms, African*

MOSHE IDEL
Institute of Jewish Studies, The Hebrew University Mt.
Scopus
*Judaism: Judaism to 1800*
*Mysticism: Kabbalah*

F. ABIOLA IRELE
Department of Romance Languages and Literatures,
Harvard University
*Westernization: Africa*

GERALD N. IZENBERG
Department of History, Washington University
*Romanticism in Literature and Politics*

ANNAMARIE JAGOSE
University of Auckland, New Zealand
*Queer Theory*

JAMES JANKOWSKI
University of Colorado (Emeritus)
*Ethnicity and Race: Islamic Views*
*Nationalism: Middle East*
*Pan-Arabism*

MICHEL JANSSEN
Program in History of Science and Technology,
University of Minnesota
*Relativity*

CHEN JIAN
Corcoran Department of History, University of Virginia
*Maoism*

ROBERT N. JOHNSON
Department of Philosophy, University of Missouri
*Obligation*
*Relativism*

THOMAS PYKE JOHNSON
Mugar Library, Boston University
History Department, University of Massachusetts, Boston
*Environmental History*

WILLIAM M. JOHNSTON
Department of Church History, Yarra Theological Union
at the Melbourne College of Divinity
*Monasticism*

DAVID JORAVSKY
Department of History, Northwestern University
*Lysenkoism*

SARA JORDAN
Texas A&M University
*Bureaucracy*

MATTHEW KADANE
History and Literature, Harvard University
*Deism*

ANN M. KAKALIOURAS
Department of Anthropology, Appalachian State
University
*Ethnicity and Race: Anthropology*

NORIKO KAMACHI
Department of Social Sciences, University of Michigan,
Dearborn
*Pan-Asianism*

RACHANA KAMTEKAR
Department of Philosophy, University of Michigan
*Character*

OUSMANE KANE
School of International and Public Affairs, Columbia
University
*Sufism*

ANDRZEJ KARCZ
University of Kansas
*Formalism*

NIKKI R. KEDDIE
Department of History, University of California, Los
Angeles
*Secularization and Secularism*

DONALD R. KELLEY
Department of History, Rutgers University
*Cultural History*
*Eclecticism*
*Historicism*
*History, Idea of*
*Ideas, History of*
*Linguistic Turn*
*Periodization*
*Prehistory, Rise of*

DOUGLAS KELLNER
Graduate School of Education and Information Studies,
University of California, Los Angeles
*Critical Theory*

HENRY ANSGAR KELLY
Center for Medieval and Renaissance Studies, University
of California, Los Angeles
*Tragedy and Comedy*

JEFFREY T. KENNEY
Department of Religious Studies, DePauw University
*Fundamentalism*
*Pan-Islamism*

MAXIM KHOMIAKOV
Department of Philosophy, Ural State University
*Hierarchy and Order*

MARGARET L. KING
Department of History, Brooklyn College and the
Graduate Center, City University of New York
*Childhood and Child Rearing*

ROBERT M. KINGDON
Department of History, University of Wisconsin—
Madison
*Reformation*

REBECCA KINGSTON
Department of Political Science, University of Toronto
*Citizenship: Overview*

GYULA KLIMA
Department of Philosophy, Fordham University
*Form, Metaphysical, in Ancient and Medieval Thought*

GEORGE KLOSKO
Department of Politics, University of Virginia
*State of Nature*

RAYMOND KNAPP
Department of Musicology, University of California, Los
Angeles
*Absolute Music*
*Nationalism: Nationalism in Music, Europe and the United
States*

ALEXANDRA KOGL
Department of Political Science, University of Northern
Iowa
*Equality: Overview*

HELGE KRAGH
History of Science Department, University of Aarhus,
Denmark
*Science: Overview*

MARK KRAMER
Cold War Studies Institute, Harvard University
*Genocide*
*Nuclear Age*

ROSALIND KRAUSS
Department of Art History and Archaeology, Columbia
University
*Avant-Garde: Militancy*

JILL KRAYE
Warburg Institute
*Philosophy, Moral: Medieval and Renaissance*

THERESA A. KULBAGA
Department of English, The Ohio State University
*Autobiography*

KRISHAN KUMAR
Department of Sociology, University of Virginia
*Revolution*

MARION LEATHERS KUNTZ
Department of Modern and Classical Languages, Georgia
State University
*Prophecy*

DAVID KUNZLE
Department of Art History, University of California, Los
Angeles
*Protest, Political*

CHARLES KURZMAN
Department of Sociology, University of North Carolina
*Reform: Islamic Reform*

PETER LAMARQUE
Department of Philosophy, University of York, U.K.
*Aesthetics: Europe and the Americas*

JERUSHA T. LAMPTEY
Independent Scholar, Herndon, Va.
*Mysticism: Mysticism in African Thought*

MELISSA LANE
Faculty of History, Cambridge University
*Social Contract*

MARK LARRIMORE
Eugene Lang College and Graduate Department of
Philosophy, New School University
*Evil*
*Theodicy*

NEIL LARSEN
Programs in Comparative Literature and Critical Theory,
University of California, Davis
*Third World Literature*

MANFRED D. LAUBICHLER
School of Life Sciences, Arizona State University
*Development*

ROBERT LAUNAY
Department of Anthropology, Northwestern University
*Person, Idea of the*
*Polytheism*
*Ritual: Religion*
*Sacred and Profane*
*Structuralism and Poststructuralism: Anthropology*
*Totems*

JOHN CHRISTIAN LAURSEN
Department of Political Science, University of California,
Riverside
*Censorship*
*Skepticism*
*Toleration*

BABATUNDE LAWAL
Department of Art History, School of the Arts, Virginia
Commonwealth University
*Arts: Africa*

PATRICK LE GALÈS
CEVIPOF/CNRS/Sciences Po, Paris
*City, The: The City as Cultural Center*

LUIS LEAL
Department of Chicano Studies, University of California,
Santa Barbara
*Aztlán*

YANN LEBEAU
Centre for Higher Education Research and Information,
The Open University, U.K.
*University: Postcolonial*

MICHAEL LeBUFFE
Department of Philosophy, Texas A&M University
*Metaphysics: Renaissance to the Present*

ARTHUR M. LESLEY
Hebrew Language and Literature, Baltimore Hebrew
University
*Ghetto*

MICHAEL LEVENSON
Department of English, University of Virginia
*Modernism: Overview*

HEATHER LEVI
Department of Sociology and Anthropology, Lake Forest
College
*Practices*
*Reflexivity*

ALAN MITCHELL LEVINE
Department of Government, American University
*America*

DAVID LEVINE
Ontario Institute for Studies in Education/University of
Toronto
*Marriage and Fertility, European Views*

FREDERICK LIERS
Department of Comparative Literature, University of
California, Los Angeles
*Biography*
*Cycles*

IVAN LIGHT
Department of Sociology, University of California, Los
Angeles
*Cultural Capital*

SONYA LIPSETT-RIVERA
Department of History, Carleton University
*Honor*

C. SCOTT LITTLETON
Department of Anthropology, Occidental College
*Anthropology*
*Demonology*
*Sacred Places*
*Syncretism*

HAIMING LIU
Ethnic and Women's Studies Department, California
State Polytechnic University, Pomona
*Asian-American Ideas (Cultural Migration)*
*Race and Racism: Reception of Asians to the United States*

CHARLES H. LOHR
Theological Faculty, University of Freiburg
*Aristotelianism*

RUTH LORAND
Department of Philosophy, University of Haifa
*Beauty and Ugliness*

BEN LOWE
   Department of History, Dorothy F. Schmidt College of
   Arts and Letters, Florida Atlantic University
   *Peace*

JOSEPH A. LOYA
   Department of Theology and Religious Studies,
   Villanova University
   *Ecumenism*

MARTIN LYNN
   School of History, Queen's University, Belfast
   *Empire and Imperialism: Europe*

PETER MACHAMER
   Department of History and Philosophy of Science,
   University of Pittsburgh
   *Dualism*
   *Materialism in Eighteenth-Century European Thought*
   *Monism*

REYNALDO F. MACÍAS
   César E. Chávez Department of Chicana and Chicano
   Studies, University of California, Los Angeles
   *Bilingualism and Multilingualism*

COLIN MACKERRAS
   Department of International Business and Asian Studies,
   Griffith University
   *Eurocentrism*

CATHARINE MACKINNON
   Faculty of Law, University of Michigan
   *Sexual Harassment*

DOUGLAS MACLEAN
   Department of Philosophy, University of North
   Carolina, Chapel Hill
   *Environmental Ethics*

DONALD M. MACRAILD
   Victoria University of Wellington, New Zealand
   *Victorianism*

GREGORY H. MADDOX
   Department of History, Texas Southern University
   *Black Consciousness*
   *Oral Traditions: Telling, Sharing*

DANIEL A. MADIGAN
   Institute for Religions and Cultures, Pontifical Gregorian
   University, Rome
   *Sacred Texts: Koran*

JESS MAGHAN
   Forum for Comparative Correction
   *Hate*

ZINE MAGUBANE
   Department of Sociology, University of Illinois at
   Urbana-Champaign
   *Black Atlantic*

PARAMANONDA MAHANTA
   Department of Physics, Dibrugarh University
   *Futurology*

JANE MAIENSCHEIN
   Department of Philosophy, Arizona State University
   *Development*

VICTOR H. MAIR
   Department of Asian and Middle Eastern Studies,
   University of Pennsylvania
   *Diffusion, Cultural*
   *Language and Linguistics*

W. O. MALOBA
   Department of History, University of Delaware
   *Anticolonialism: Africa*

FEDWA MALTI-DOUGLAS
   Departments of Gender Studies and Comparative
   Literature, Indiana University, Bloomington
   *Orientalism: Overview*
   *Sexuality: Islamic Views*

AMINA MAMA
   African Gender Institute, University of Cape Town
   *Feminism: Africa and African Diaspora*

JOHN MARENBON
   Faculty of Philosophy, University of Cambridge
   *Language, Philosophy of: Ancient and Medieval*
   *Logic*
   *Metaphysics: Ancient and Medieval*

MICHAEL MARTIN
   Department of Philosophy, Boston University
   *Atheism*

PHILIP L. MARTIN
   Department of Agricultural and Resource Economics,
   University of California, Davis
   *Human Capital*

ALBERTO A. MARTÍNEZ
   Program in History and Philosophy of Science,
   California Institute of Technology
   *Field Theories*

MARTIN E. MARTY
   Fairfax M. Cone Distinguished Service Professor
   Emeritus, University of Chicago
   *Religion and the State: United States*

MICHELLE MASKIELL
Department of History, Montana State University
*Education: India*

D. A. MASOLO
Department of Philosophy, University of Louisville
*Humanity: African Thought*
*Sage Philosophy*
*Sociability in African Thought*

CYRUS MASROORI
Department of Political Science, California State
University, San Marcos
*Religion and the State: Middle East*

MARC MATERA
Department of History, Rutgers University
*Pan-Africanism*

FRANZ MAYR
Department of Philosophy, University of Portland,
Portland, Oregon
*Continental Philosophy*

AMA MAZAMA
Department of African American Studies, Temple
University
*Afrocentricity*

JOHN MUKUM MBAKU
Department of Economics, Weber State University
*Corruption in Developed and Developing Countries*

ELIZABETH MCCARTNEY
Center for Seventeenth- and Eighteenth-Century Studies,
University of California, Los Angeles
*Ritual: Public Ritual*

RUSSELL T. MCCUTCHEON
Department of Religious Studies, University of Alabama
*Religion: Overview*

BONNIE MCDOUGALL
School of Literatures, Languages, and Cultures,
University of Edinburgh
*Privacy*

MARGARET H. MCFADDEN
Interdisciplinary Studies, Appalachian State University
*Women's Studies*

RICHARD MCGREGOR
Vanderbilt University
*Mysticism: Islamic Mysticism*

ROBERT P. MCINTOSH
Department of Biological Science, University of Notre
Dame
*Ecology*

ALYSON MCLAMORE
Department of Music, California Polytechnic State
University, San Luis Obispo
*Motif: Motif in Music*
*Musical Performance and Audiences*

ALLAN MEGILL
Corcoran Department of History, University of Virginia
*Marxism: Overview*

MAURICE MEISNER
Department of History, University of Wisconsin—
Madison
*Marxism: Asia*

YITZHAK Y. MELAMED
Department of Philosophy, Yale University
*Hegelianism*

KIDANE MENGISTEAB
Department of African and African American Studies,
Pennsylvania State University
*Globalization: Africa*
*Globalization: General*

RAMDAS MENON
*Demography*

MELISSA MCBAY MERRITT
Department of Philosophy, Georgia State University
*Epistemology: Early Modern*

THOMAS J. MERTZ
Department of History, University of Wisconsin—
Madison
*Antifeminism*

GUY C. Z. MHONE
Graduate School of Public and Development
Management, University of the Witwatersrand
*Neoliberalism*
*Privatization*

HEIKKI MIKKELI
Renvall Institute for Area and Cultural Studies,
University of Helsinki
*Europe, Idea of*

ANN MILES
Department of Anthropology, Western Michigan
University
*Family: Family in Anthropology since 1980*
*Life Cycle: Adolescence*

JEFFREY MILLER
Department of Political Science, State University of New
York, New Paltz
*Happiness and Pleasure in European Thought*

MARA MILLER
Independent Scholar, Philadelphia, Penn.
*Aesthetics: Asia*
*Garden*

TYRUS MILLER
Department of Literature, University of California, Santa Cruz
*Avant-Garde: Overview*

THEODORE R. MITCHELL
History Department, Occidental College
*Education: North America*

ALOIS MLAMBO
Department of Historical and Heritage Studies, University of Pretoria, South Africa
*Peasants and Peasantry*

KENNETH MONDSCHEIN
Fordham University
*Love, Western Notions of*
*Meme*

JAMES A. MONTMARQUET
Department of Languages, Literature, and Philosophy, Tennessee State University
*Good*

DAVID K. MOORE
Department of Political Science, University of Northern Iowa
*Equality: Overview*

IRENE VASQUEZ MORRIS
Department of Social Sciences and Department of Chicano/a Studies, California State University, Dominguez Hills
*Chicano Movement*

ROSALIND C. MORRIS
Institute for Research on Women and Gender, Department of Anthropology, Columbia University
*Fetishism: Overview*
*Gender Studies: Anthropology*

PAUL K. MOSER
Department of Philosophy, Loyola University of Chicago
*Foundationalism*

JOHN MOWITT
Department of Cultural Studies and Comparative Literature, University of Minnesota
*Text/Textuality*

MPALIVE-HANGSON MSISKA
School of English and Humanities, Birkbeck College, University of London
*Realism, Africa*

JAMES MULDOON
John Carter Brown Library
*Empire and Imperialism: Overview*
*International Order*

PAT MUNDAY
Department of Technical Communication, Montana Tech
*Science, History of*

D. E. MUNGELLO
Department of History, Baylor University
*Christianity: Asia*

H. ADLAI MURDOCH
Department of French, University of Illinois at Urbana-Champaign
*Creolization, Caribbean*
*Negritude*

ANDREW R. MURPHY
Christ College, Valparaiso University
*Corruption*

THOMAS F. MURPHY III
ABC-CLIO
*Public Sphere*

ALEXANDER MURRAY
University College, Oxford
*Suicide*

WINSTON P. NAGAN
School of Law, University of Florida
*Law*

L. E. NAVIA
Department of Social Sciences, New York Institute of Technology
*Cynicism*

IAN NEATH
Department of Psychological Sciences, Purdue University
*Learning and Memory, Contemporary Views*

CARY J. NEDERMAN
Texas A&M University
*Capitalism: Overview*
*Class*
*Human Rights: Overview*
*Humanism: Europe and the Middle East*
*Individualism*
*Monarchy: Overview*
*Organicism*
*Religion and the State: Europe*
*Republicanism: Republic*
*Sovereignty*

# LIST OF CONTRIBUTORS

CARYN E. NEUMANN
Department of History, The Ohio State University
*Loyalties, Dual*

JACOB NEUSNER
Institute of Advanced Theology, Bard College
*Dialogue and Dialectics: Talmudic*

PAUL NEWMAN
Independent Scholar, St Austell, U.K.
*Literary History*
*Terror*

THOMAS NICKLES
Department of Philosophy, University of Nevada, Reno
*Empiricism*
*Falsifiability*
*Positivism*

ALLEEN PACE NILSEN
Department of English, Arizona State University
*Humor*

DON L. F. NILSEN
Department of English, Arizona State University
*Humor*

EMMANUEL NNADOZIE
Department of Economics, Truman State University
*Economics*

OBIOMA NNAEMEKA
Departments of French and Women's Studies, Indiana University, Indianapolis
*Womanism*

TARA E. NUMMEDAL
Department of History, Brown University
*Alchemy: Europe and the Middle East*

JOHN NUNLEY
Arts of Africa, Oceania, and the Americas, Saint Louis Art Museum
*Masks*

FRANCIS B. NYAMNJOH
Department of Sociology, University of Botswana
*Third World*

EBENEZER OBADARE
Department of Social Policy, London School of Economics and Political Science
*Civil Society: Responses in Africa and the Middle East*

MAX OELSCHLAEGER
Department of Humanities, Northern Arizona University
*Nature*
*Wildlife*

ROBERT OLBY
Department of the History and Philosophy of Science, University of Pittsburgh
*Genetics: History of*

MICHAEL R. OLNECK
Departments of Educational Policy Studies and Sociology, University of Wisconsin—Madison
*Americanization, U.S.*

EBERE ONWUDIWE
Center for African Studies, Central State University
*Afropessimism*

THOMAS M. OSBORNE JR.
Center for Thomistic Studies, University of St. Thomas (Houston, Tex.)
*Free Will, Determinism, and Predestination*

KWADWO OSEI-NYAME JR.
Africa Department, School of Oriental and African Studies, University of London
*Authenticity: Africa*

MARGARET J. OSLER
Department of History, University of Calgary
*Mechanical Philosophy*

KRISTEN LEE OVER
Department of English, Northeastern Illinois University
*Motif: Motif in Literature*

RANDALL PACKER
Department of Computer Science, Audio Technology, and Physics, American University
*Virtual Reality*

DAVID W. PANKENIER
Department of Modern Languages and Literature, Lehigh University
*Astrology: China*

ANTHONY PAREL
Department of Political Science, University of Calgary
*Civil Disobedience*
*Nonviolence*

JANE L. PARPART
Department of History, Dalhousie University
*Dependency*

KEVIN PASSMORE
Department of History, Cardiff University
*National History*

MANOLIS PATINIOTIS
Department of History and Philosophy of Science, University of Athens
*Newtonianism*

**New Dictionary of the History of Ideas**

HARRY W. PAUL
Department of History, University of Florida
*Medicine: Europe and the United States*

VINCENT P. PECORA
Departments of English and Comparative Literature,
University of California, Los Angeles
*Literature: Overview*

PETER N. PEREGRINE
Department of Anthropology, Lawrence University
*Trade*

CHARMAINE PEREIRA
Centre for Research and Documentation
*State, The: The Postcolonial State*

LAUREN F. PFISTER (FÈI LÈRÉN)
Department of Religion and Philosophy, Hong Kong
Baptist University
*Justice: Justice in East Asian Thought*

JAMES PHELAN
Department of English, Ohio State University
*Narrative*

YURI PINES
Department of East Asian Studies, Hebrew University of
Jerusalem
*Legalism, Ancient China*
*Mohism*

KATHRYN PISARO
Department of Music, California Institute of the Arts
*Composition, Musical*

MALCOLM POTTS
School of Public Health, University of California,
Berkeley
*Population*

JOHN POWERS
Centre for Asian Societies and Histories, Australian
National University
*Communication of Ideas: Asia and Its Influence*
*Consciousness: Indian Thought*
*Humanity: Asian Thought*
*Sacred Texts: Asia*

PAUL R. POWERS
Department of Religious Studies, Lewis and Clark
College
*Death and Afterlife, Islamic Understanding of*

FABRIZIO PREGADIO
Department of Religious Studies, Stanford University
*Alchemy: China*
*Daoism*
*Yin and Yang*

STATHIS PSILLOS
Department of Philosophy and History of Science,
University of Athens
*Causality*

NING QIANG
Department of the History of Art, University of
Michigan
*Heaven and Hell (Asian Focus)*

JUAN GÓMEZ QUIÑONES
Department of History, University of California, Los
Angeles
*Chicano Movement*

ALBERT RABIL JR.
State University of New York, College at Old Westbury
(Emeritus)
*Humanism: Renaissance*

SUSAN ELIZABETH RAMIREZ
Department of History, Texas Christian University
*Colonialism: Latin America*
*Empire and Imperialism: Americas*
*Pre-Columbian Civilization*
*Religion: Latin America*

DAVID RANDALL
Department of History, Rutgers University
*Puritanism*

AMIT RAY
Department of Language and Literature, Rochester
Institute of Technology
*New Criticism*

MOVINDRI REDDY
Occidental College
*War*

TIM REES
Department of History, University of Exeter
*Communism: Europe*

STEVEN P. REMY
Department of History, City University of New
York—Brooklyn College
*Generation*

MATTHIAS RIEDL
Department of Political Science, Friedrich-Alexander-
University Erlangen-Nuremberg
*Eschatology*
*Mysticism: Christian Mysticism*

MARY RIZZO
Department of American Studies, University of
Minnesota
*Consumerism*

JESSICA M. ROA
Department of Psychology, University of California,
Santa Cruz
*Feminism: Chicana Feminisms*

KEVIN C. ROBBINS
Department of History, Indiana University–Purdue
University, Indianapolis
*Philanthropy*

MARY NOOTER ROBERTS
UCLA Fowler Museum of Cultural History
*Aesthetics: Africa*

THIERRY JEAN ROBOUAM
Faculty of Comparative Culture, Sophia University,
Tokyo
*Japanese Philosophy, Japanese Thought*

JONATHAN ROSE
Graduate Program in Modern History and Literature,
Drew University
*Reading*

PHILIPP W. ROSEMANN
Department of Philosophy, University of Dallas
*Scholasticism*

LELAND M. ROTH
Department of Art History, School of Architecture and
Allied Arts, University of Oregon
*Architecture: Overview*
*Architecture: Asia*

GILBERT ROZMAN
Department of Sociology, Princeton University
*Modernization Theory*

JAMES H. RUBIN
Department of Art, Stony Brook, State Univerity of New
York
*Impressionism*
*Realism*

ERIKA RUMMEL
Emmanuel College, University of Toronto
*Reform: Europe and the United States*

MICHAEL RUSE
Department of Philosophy, Florida State University
*Consilience*
*Creationism*

MICHAEL RYAN
English Department, Northeastern University
*Structuralism and Poststructuralism: Overview*

NAOKI SAKAI
Department of Comparative Literature and Department
of Asian Studies, Cornell University
*Translation*

STEVEN B. SAMPLE
University of Southern California
*Leadership*

LYMAN TOWER SARGENT
Department of Political Science, University of
Missouri—St. Louis
*Utopia*

HENRY M. SAYRE
Department of Art, Oregon State University
*Arts: Overview*

BEN-AMI SCHARFSTEIN
Department of Philosophy, Tel Aviv University
*Machiavellism*

RICHARD SCHEINES
Department of Philosophy, Carnegie Mellon University
*Causation*

FREDERICK F. SCHMITT
Department of Philosophy, Indiana University
*Truth*

RICHARD SCHMITT
Department of Philosophy, Brown University
*Power*

WHIT SCHONBEIN
Department of Philosophy, Mount Holyoke College
*Representation: Mental Representation*

SILVAN S. SCHWEBER
Department of Physics, Brandeis University
*Field Theories*

JOHN T. SCOTT
Department of Political Science, University of California,
Davis
*General Will*

JOHN R. SEARLE
Department of Philosophy, University of California,
Berkeley
*Intentionality*

KENNETH SEESKIN
Department of Philosophy, Northwestern University
*Autonomy*

ROBERT A. SEGAL
Department of Religious Studies, Lancaster University
*Myth*

JENNIFER L. SHAW
Department of Art and Art History, Sonoma State University
*Symbolism*

MIRI SHEFER
Department of Middle Eastern and African History, Tel Aviv University
*Medicine: Islamic Medicine*

KATHLEEN SHELDON
Center for the Study of Women, University of California, Los Angeles
*Women's History: Africa*

YU SHEN
Department of History, Indiana University Southeast
*Chinese Warlordism*

WILLIAM E. SHEPARD
University of Canterbury, Christchurch, New Zealand
*Religion: Middle East*

TAKASHI SHOGIMEN
Department of History, University of Otago, Dunedin, New Zealand
*Constitutionalism*
*Heresy and Apostasy*
*Liberty*

SHARON SIEVERS
Department of History, California State University, Long Beach
*Women's History: Asia*

SOEK-FANG SIM
International Studies, Macalester College
*Authoritarianism: East Asia*

DEAN KEITH SIMONTON
Department of Psychology, University of California, Davis
*Creativity in the Arts and Sciences*

KIMBERLY SIMS
Trinity College
*Platonism*

MAINA CHAWLA SINGH
College of Vocational Studies, University of Delhi, India
*Feminism: Overview*
*Motherhood and Maternity*

DAVID W. SISK
Computing and Information Technology, Macalester College
*Dystopia*

GIULIA SISSA
Department of Classics, University of California at Los Angeles
*Hedonism in European Thought*

NATHAN SIVIN
Department of the History and Sociology of Science, University of Pennsylvania
*Medicine: China*
*Science: East Asia*

ESTHER M. SKELLEY
School of Public and International Affairs, University of Georgia
*Communism: Latin America*

DIANE SKOSS
Koryu Books
*Bushido*

PETER SLUGLETT
Department of History, University of Utah, Salt Lake City
*Anticolonialism: Middle East*

ROBERT SMID
Independent Scholar, Brookline, Mass,
*Cosmology: Asia*
*Orthopraxy: Asia*

BRIAN SMITH
Department of Religious Studies, University of California, Riverside
*Asceticism: Hindu and Buddhist Asceticism*
*Buddhism*
*Hinduism*
*Meditation, Eastern*
*Time: India*
*Yoga*

CHARLES D. SMITH
Department of Near Eastern Studies, University of Arizona
*Empire and Imperialism: Middle East*

JUSTIN E. H. SMITH
Department of Philosophy, Concordia University, Montreal, Quebec, Canada
*Philosophy, History of*

WOODRUFF D. SMITH
Department of History, University of Massachusetts Boston
*Volksgeist*

VASSILIKI BETTY SMOCOVITIS
Departments of Zoology and History, University of Florida
*(continued on the next page)*

(continued from page 2537)
  *Biology*
  *Evolution*

HOLLY SNYDER
  John Nicholas Brown Center for the Study of American Civilization, Brown University
  *Diasporas: Jewish Diaspora*

SAMANTHA SOLIMEO
  Department of Anthropology, University of Iowa
  *Life Cycle: Elders/Old Age*

ROBERT C. SOLOMON
  Department of Philosophy, University of Texas at Austin
  *Emotions*
  *Existentialism*
  *Phenomenology*
  *Philosophy: Historical Overview and Recent Developments*

CHRISTOPHER SOUTHGATE
  Department of Classics and Theology, University of Exeter
  *Religion and Science*

JULIAN SPALDING
  Writer and Broadcaster, Edinburgh, Scotland
  *Museums*

RUSSELL SPEARS
  School of Psychology, Cardiff University
  *Identity: Personal and Social Identity*

D. A. SPELLBERG
  Department of History and Middle Eastern Studies, University of Texas at Austin
  *Gender: Gender in the Middle East*

KAYLEE SPENCER-AHRENS
  Department of Art and Art History, University of Texas at Austin
  *Periodization of the Arts*

HORTENSE J. SPILLERS
  Department of English, Cornell University
  *Literary Criticism*

GAYATRI CHAKRAVORTY SPIVAK
  Department of English, Columbia University
  *Postcolonial Theory and Literature*

SARAH LINSLEY STARKS
  Neuropsychiatric Institute Health Services Research Center, University of California, Los Angeles
  *Psychology and Psychiatry*

RANDOLPH STARN
  Department of History and Italian Studies, University of California, Berkeley
  *Crisis*

WARD STAVIG
  Department of History, University of South Florida
  *Millenarianism: Latin America and Native North America*

MICHAEL ST. CLAIR
  Department of Psychology, Emmanuel College
  *Millenarianism: Overview*

JEAN STEFANCIC
  University of Pittsburgh School of Law
  *Critical Race Theory*

JAMES P. STERBA
  Department of Philosophy, University of Notre Dame
  *Justice: Overview*

MATTHIAS STEUP
  Department of Philosophy, St. Cloud State University
  *Epistemology: Modern*

DEVIN J. STEWART
  Department of Middle Eastern and South Asian Studies, Emory University
  *Islam: Shii*
  *Law, Islamic*

NORMAN A. STILLMAN
  University of Oklahoma
  *Anti-Semitism: Islamic Anti-Semitism*

M. W. F. STONE
  Department of Philosophy, Katholieke Universiteit, Leuven, Belgium
  *Casuistry*
  *Philosophy: Relations to Other Intellectual Realms*
  *Philosophy and Religion in Western Thought*
  *Philosophy of Religion*

GREGORY W. STREICH
  Department of Political Science, Central Missouri State University
  *Authority*
  *Equality: Racial Equality*

DAVID J. STUMP
  Department of Philosophy, University of San Francisco
  *Fallacy, Logical*
  *Paradigm*
  *Pseudoscience*

BLAIR SULLIVAN
  Center for Medieval and Renaissance Studies, University of California at Los Angeles
(continued on the next page)

*(continued from page 2538)*
*Harmony*
*Musicology*

CHRIS SWOYER
Department of Philosophy, University of Oklahoma
*Rational Choice*
*Subjectivism*

HIDEKI TAKEMURA
Teacher Education Center, Keio University
*Education: Japan*

CHRISTOPHER S. TAYLOR
Department of Religious Studies, Drew University
*Islam: Sunni*

LOU TAYLOR
School of Historical and Critical Studies, University of
Brighton
*Dress*

RICHARD C. TAYLOR
Department of Philosophy, Marquette University
*Philosophies: Islamic*

UDO THIEL
Department of Philosophy, School of Humanities,
Australian National University
*Identity: Identity of Persons*

PETER THIELKE
Department of Philosophy, Pomona College
*Hegelianism*

NORMAN J. W. THROWER
Department of Geography, University of California, Los
Angeles
*Geography*
*Maps and The Ideas They Express*

ALAIN TOUWAIDE
Department of Botany, National Museum of Natural
History, Smithsonian Institution
*Environment*

NANCY TUANA
Department of Philosophy, Pennsylvania State University
*Philosophies: Feminist, Twentieth-Century*

AVIEZER TUCKER
Australian National University
*Consciousness: Overview*
*Objectivity*

THOMAS TURINO
School of Music, University of Illinois at Urbana-
Champaign
*Music, Anthropology of*

KARIN TYBJERG
Department of History and Philosophy of Science,
University of Cambridge
*Greek Science*

ARISTOTLE TYMPAS
Department of History and Philosophy of Science,
National and Capodistrian University of Athens
*Calculation and Computation*
*Technology*

LAURA UBA
Department of Asian American Studies, California State
University, Northridge
*Identity, Multiple: Asian-Americans*

MONICA UDVARDY
Department of Anthropology, University of Kentucky
*Body, The*

CASSANDRA RACHEL VENEY
Dept. of African and African American Studies and
Women's Studies, The Pennsylvania State University
*Abolitionism*
*Segregation*

ANDREW VINCENT
Department of Politics, Sheffield University
*Patriotism*

HANS VON RAUTENFELD
Department of Philosophy, University of South Carolina
*Representation: Political Representation*

MATTHEW F. VON UNWERTH
Abraham A. Brill Library, New York Psychoanalytic
Institute
*Psychoanalysis*

ELINA VUOLA
Institute of Development Studies, University of Helsinki
*Liberation Theology*

CHAOHUA WANG
Department of Asian Languages and Cultures, University
of California, Los Angeles
*Modernity: East Asia*

Q. EDWARD WANG
Department of History, Rowan University
*Causation in East Asian and Southeast Asian Philosophy*
*Education: Asia, Traditional and Modern*
*Occidentalism*

JOHN WARD
School of Philosophical and Historical Inquiry,
University of Sydney
*Rhetoric: Ancient and Medieval*

**New Dictionary of the History of Ideas**

# LIST OF CONTRIBUTORS

EARLE H. WAUGH
University of Alberta, Edmonton, Alberta, Canada
*Orthodoxy*

JEFFREY WEEKS
Faculty of Humanities and Social Science, South Bank University
*Sexuality: Overview*

NADINE WEIDMAN
Department of History of Science, Harvard University
*Behaviorism*
*Phrenology*

PATRICK WEIL
CNRS (National Center for Scientific Research), University of Paris
*Citizenship: Naturalization*

JERRY WEINBERGER
Michigan State University
*Progress, Idea of*

GABRIEL P. WEISBERG
Department of Art History, University of Minnesota, Minneapolis
*Naturalism in Art and Literature*

G. J. WEISEL
Department of Physics, Penn State Altoona
*Physics*

MARY J. WEISMANTEL
Department of Anthropology, Northwestern University
*Family: Modernist Anthropological Theory*
*Life Cycle: Overview*

DAVID WELCH
School of History, Centre for the Study of Propaganda, University of Kent, Canterbury
*Propaganda*

STEPHEN WELDON
University of Oklahoma
*Humanism: Secular Humanism in the United States*

LEIF WENAR
Department of Philosophy, University of Sheffield
*Property*

MICHAEL WERNER
Department of History, University of Chicago
*Marxism: Latin America*

MARGARET WERRY
Department of Theatre Arts and Dance, University of Minnesota
*Cultural Revivals*
*Theater and Performance*

HYLTON WHITE
Department of Anthropology, University of Chicago
*Tradition*

NORMAN E. WHITTEN JR.
Department of Anthropology, University of Illinois at Urbana-Champaign
*Animism*
*Religion: Indigenous Peoples' View, South America*

HOWARD J. WIARDA
Department of International Affairs, University of Georgia
*Communism: Latin America*
*Empire and Imperialism: United States*

MEREDITH WILLIAMS
Department of Philosophy, Johns Hopkins University
*Language, Philosophy of: Modern*

HOWARD WINANT
Department of Sociology, University of California, Santa Barbara
*Discrimination*
*Race and Racism: Overview*

KWASI WIREDU
Department of Philosophy, University of South Florida
*Personhood in African Thought*
*Philosophy, Moral: Africa*

LAURA R. WOLIVER
Department of Political Science, University of South Carolina
*Political Protest, U.S.*

WILLIAM A. WOOD
Department of History and Political Science, Point Loma Nazarene University
*Nomadism*

KENNETH L. WOODWARD
Independent Scholar, New York, N.Y.
*Miracles*

DANIEL WOOLF
University of Alberta
*Historiography*

CHRISTINE MIN WOTIPKA
International Institute, University of California, Los Angeles
*Human Rights: Women's Rights*

LINNEA WREN
Gustavus Adolphus College
*Periodization of the Arts*

DOMINIK WUJASTYK
Wellcome Trust Centre for the History of Medicine,
University College London
*Medicine: India*

JOHN A. XANTHOPOULOS
Department of Education, University of Montana—
Western
*Education: Global Education*

GENZO YAMAMOTO
Department of History, Wheaton College
*Education: Japan*
*Race and Racism: Asia*
*Shinto*

XINZHONG YAO
Department of Theology and Religious Studies,
University of Wales
*Chinese Thought*

RICHARD YEO
Centre for Public Culture and Ideas, Griffith University,
Brisbane, Australia
*Encyclopedism*

CHARLES M. YOUNG
Department of Philosophy, Claremont Graduate
University
*Philosophy, Moral: Ancient*

NIGEL YOUNG
Department of Sociology and Anthropology, Colgate
University
*Pacifism*

JIYUAN YU
Department of Philosophy, State University of New York
at Buffalo
*Humanism: Chinese Conception of*

PAUL TIYAMBE ZELEZA
Departments of History and African and African
American Studies, Pennsylvania State University
*Africa, Idea of*
*Colonialism: Africa*
*Communication of Ideas: Africa and Its Influence*
*Democracy, Africa*
*Diasporas: African Diaspora*
*History, Economic*

ELEANOR ZELLIOT
Carleton College
*Untouchability: Overview*

CARL ZIMMER
Independent Scholar, Guilford, Conn.
*Mind*

MICHAEL J. ZIMMERMAN
Department of Philosophy, University of North Carolina
at Greensboro
*Responsibility*

ROBERT ZIOMKOWSKI
Independent Scholar, Ithaca, N.Y.
*Microcosm and Macrocosm*
*Neoplatonism*

SHERIFA ZUHUR
Strategic Studies Institute, U.S. Army War College
*Honor, Middle Eastern Notions of*
*Intercession in Middle Eastern Society*

STEPHEN ZUNES
Department of Politics, University of San Francisco
*Terrorism, Middle East*

JACK ZUPKO
Department of Philosophy, Emory University
*Philosophy of Mind: Ancient and Medieval*

# INDEX

*Page references include both a volume number and a page number. For example, 3:1282–1283 refers to pages 1282–1283 in volume 3. Page numbers in **boldface** indicate the main article on the subject. Page numbers in italics refer to illustrations, tables, and figures.*

## A

AA. *See* Alcoholics Anonymous

Abacha, Mariam, 2:812

Abacha, Sani, 2:557, 5:2256

Abacus, 1:257

Abani, Chris, 3:1310

'Abbas (descendant of Muhammad), 3:1146, 4:1494

Abbas, Ferhat, 1:89

'Abbas al-Jawhari, al-, 3:1157

Abbasid caliphate, 1:xliii, 2:642, 3:1251, 4:1455, 1494, 1495
    Baghdad founding and, 1:349
    Islamic philosophy and, 4:1770
    Sunni Islam and, 5:2067

Abbott, C. C., 5:1888–1889, 1890

ABC machine (Atansoff-Berry Computer), 1:258, 2:429

'Abd al-Jalil al-Sijzi, 3:1156

'Abd-al-Karim Qasim, 1:90

'Abdallah al-Marwazi, 3:1157

'Abd Allah Baydawi, 2:720

'Abd al-Malik, 5:2155

'Abd-al-Mumin, 3:1145

'Abd al-Qadir, 1:88, 89, 5:2028

'Abd al-Qahir al-Baghadi, 3:1158

'Abd al-Rahman al-Sa'di. *See* Sa'di, 'Abd-al-Rahman al-

'Abd al-Rahman al-Sufi, 3:1156

'Abd al-Wahhab. *See* Muhammad Ibn 'Abd al-Wahhab

'Abduh, Muhammad, 2:644, 3:1253, 5:2028, 6:2468, 2469

Abdul Aziz, Ottoman sultan, 4:1711

Abdülhamid, II, Ottoman sultan, 3:1277, 4:1711, 1713

'Abdulmajid I, Ottoman sultan, 2:644

Abel, Niels Henrik, 1:46, 4:1381

Abel, Richard, 1:331

Abelard, Peter, 3:1239, 1312, 4:1434, 1630, 1695–1696, 5:2110, 6:2338
    Heloise's love letters and, 3:1318

moral philosophy and, 4:1790
    philosophy of religion and, 4:1780

Abeokuta Women's Union, 2:811

Aberdeen Philosophical Society ("Wise Club"), 1:381

Abiko, Kyutaro, 5:2000

Abiogenesis, 3:1282–1283

Abiola, Moshood, 2:389

Abolitionism, 1:1–4, 26, 227, 2:699
    African nationalism and, 4:1583
    civil disobedience and, 1:353
    justice and, 3:1181, 1183
    protests and, 5:1836–1837
    slavery and, 5:2214–2215

Aboriginal societies
    Australia and, 2:517, 518, 677, 3:1321, 6:2349–2350, 2408
    cultural revivals and, 2:517, 518
    Dreamtime and, 2:594–595
    environment and, 2:677
    native policy and, 4:1594–1598
    totemism and, 6:2349–2350
    *See also* Maori; Pacific Islanders

Abortion
    family planning and, 1:313, 2:789, 794, 5:1846, 1849
    feminism and, 2:805, 808–809, 4:1767
    legalization of, 4:1846
    motherhood and, 4:1511
    political protest and, 5:1836, 1837
    as privacy right, 5:1901
    sex-selective, 1:313, 2:792–793

Abraham (biblical), 3:1302, 5:1931, 6:2368

Abraham, Karl, 5:1952

Abraham, Otto, 4:1526

Abraham, William, 5:2018

Abrahams, Peter, 3:1309

Abrams, Henri, 2:670

Abrams, M. H., 3:1293–1294, 5:1830, 2138–2139

Abri, Muhammad, 1:104

Absolute acceleration, 5:2039

Absolute idealism, 4:1503

Absolute music, 1:4–6, 4:1592–1594

Absolute Spirit (Hegelian concept). *See* Spirit

Absolute surplus value, 6:2501

*Absolute Weapon, The: Atomic Power and World Order* (Brodie, ed.), 4:1646

Absolutism. *See* Totalitarianism

Abstract art, 4:1467

Abstract Expressionism, 4:1654, *1737*
    as Dada derivative, 2:531

Absurd, 2:470, 531, 764

Abu 'Abd al-Rahman Sulami, 4:1550

Abu al-'Abbas al-Fadi al-Nayrizi, 3:1157

Abu al-Hassan al-Ash'ari. *See* Ash'ari, Abu al-Hassan al-

Abu al-Wafa' al-Buzajani, 3:1157, 1158

Abubakar dan Atiku, 1:lxv

Abu Bakr (first caliph), 3:1145, 1148, 1151, 4:1494, 5:2081

Abu Bakr Kalabadhi, 4:1550

Abu Bakr Muhammad ibn Zakariya ar-Rhazi (Rhazes). *See* Rhazi, Abu Bakr Muhammad ibn Zakariya ar-

Abu Bishr Matta, 3:1240, 1313, 4:1771

Abu Dawud, 3:1252

Abu Gharaib prison (Iraq), 6:2458

Abu Hamid Muhammad al-Ghazali. *See* Ghazali, Abu Hamid Muhammad al-

Abu Hanifah, 3:1157, 1251

Abu Hayyan al-Tawhidi, 3:1157

Abu Ja'far Muhammad ibn Musa al-Khwarizmi. *See* Khwarizmi, al-

Aesthetics *(continued)*
    Africa and, **1:6–8**, 143–148, 4:1622, **5:**2018
    Asia and, **1:9–13**
    beauty and, 1:198–203
    classicism and, 1:362–365
    classification and, 1:367, 368
    communism and, 2:419
    Dada and, 2:529
    dance and, 2:532–534
    Europe and the Americas and, **1:13–19**, 4:1469–1472
    feminist philosophy and, 4:1768
    iconography and, 3:1069–1077
    Kantianism and, 3:1193
    literature and, 3:1306
    music and, 4:1537, 1538
    "The Nude" and, 4:1649
    organicism and, 1:200–201, 4:1673
    periodization and, 4:1736
    poetics and, 3:1306, 5:1830–1831
    postmodernism and, 5:1869
    taste and, 3:1306, 6:2291–2294
*Aesthetics* (Croce), 5:1830
"Aesthetics of Hunger" (Glauber), 6:2321
*Aesthetics of Music, The* (Scroton), 1:17
*Aesthtica* (Baumgarten), 1:367
*Aeterni Patris* (encyclical), 1:135
Aethelred of Rievaulx, 2:844–845
'Affan. *See* 'Uthman ibn 'Affan
*Affecting Presence, The: An Essay in Humanistic Anthropology* (Armstrong), 4:1525
*Affections* (Hippocratic text), 4:1399
Affective fallacy, 5:1833
Affinity, 2:781–782
Affirmative action, 2:590, 591–592, 707–708, 5:1895
Afghani, al-. *See* Sayyid Jamal al-Din al-Afghani
Afghanistan
    historiography and, 1:lxxiv
    Islamic fundamentalism and, 2:808, 3:1253, 5:2072, 2082, 6:2302, 2408
    Islamic state and, 5:2082
    Pan-Turkism and, 4:1714
    terrorism and, 6:2301
    U.S. war in, 2:664, 6:2302–2303, 2449
    women's movements and, 2:808
*Afghan Nomads* (photograph), 4:*1642*
Afkhami, Mahnaz, 2:819

Africa
    abolitionism and, 1:4
    aesthetics and, 1:6–8, 143–148, 4:1622, 5:2018
    ancestor worship and, 1:70–71
    anticolonialism and, 1:80–83, 265–266, 373–374, 2:714, 5:2104, 2107, 6:2503–2504
    architecture and, 1:124–128
    arts and, 1:6–8, 143–148, 4:1762–1763
    Atlantic slave trade and, 1:370, 2:497, 4:1444, 1447, 1451, 6:2466
    authenticity and, 1:170–172
    bilingualism and, 1:210
    biography and, 1:219
    *Black Atlantic* and, **1:226–228**
    black theology and, 3:1271
    body concepts and, 1:231
    brain drain and, 4:1445–1446
    capitalism and, 1:265–267, 370, 371, 4:1585
    Christianity and, 1:325, 3:1143, 1145, 4:1583, 1584
    civil society and, 1:358–359
    colonialism and. *See under* Colonialism
    colonial withdrawal from, 2:660
    communication of ideas and, 2:385–391
    communism and, 1:107, 5:2235–2236
    communitarianism and, 2:424–427
    cosmology and, 3:1022, 4:1559, 1762, 5:1846, 2051
    dance and, 4:1763
    democracy and, 2:556–560
    dependency theory and, 1:266, 369–370, 371, 2:564, 565, 566
    development economics and, 2:618, 620, 621–622
    economic historiography and, 3:1003
    economics and, 2:617
    education and, 4:1518–1519
    ethnicity and race and, 2:713–716, 4:1583, 1585
    Eurocentrism and, 2:737–740
    European settlers in, 4:1444
    family planning and, 2:792
    fascism and, 2:796, 797, 799
    female circumcision and, 2:808
    feminism and. *See under* Feminism

    gender studies and, 2:558, 810, 813–814
    globalization and, 1:267, **3:938–940**, 948, 949, 1163, 4:1585, 1586
    historiography and, lxiv–lxvii, 1:lxv, 369–370
    HIV/AIDS and, 1:113, 2:792, 4:1706
    humanism and, 3:1021–1024
    humanity beliefs and, 3:1035–1038
    imperialism and, 1:369–370, 2:656, 658, 659, 662. *See also* Colonialism, Africa and
    Islam and, 1:265, 3:1142–1145, 4:1584
    Islamic Arab conquests and, 3:1167, 6:2466, 2467
    Islamic historiography and, 1:xliii, 349
    Islamic racism and, 2:721
    liberation movements and. *See* Africa, anticolonialism and
    literature and, 3:1307–1311, 4:1468
    Machiavellism and, 4:1325
    magic and, 4:1330
    masks and, 4:1371, *1371,* 1372
    menstrual taboos and, 6:2398
    migration and, 2:662, 4:1443–1446, 1447, 1519
    miracles and, 4:1463
    modernity and, 4:1475–1479, 6:2467
    moral philosophy and, 4:1786–1788
    motherhood and, 4:1507, 1508, 1510
    multiculturalism and, 4:1518–1519
    musical anthropology and, 4:1526
    musical performance and, 4:1531
    mysticism and, 4:1559–1560
    nationalism and, 1:19–25, 81–83, 374, 4:1444, 1582–1586, 6:2469
    nationalist historiography and, 1:369–370, 373–374
    negritude and, 4:1621–1623
    neocolonialism and, 4:1623, 1624, 1625
    nomadism and, 4:1641
    nudity and, 4:1653–1654
    obligation and, 4:1679

Alzheimer's disease, **3**:906, 1289, **4**:1420

Amabile, Teresa, **2**:496

Amadi, Elechi, **3**:1309

Amadiume, Ifi, **1**:373, **2**:558, 813, **5**:1864

Amaterasu (goddess), **3**:942

Amateur media, **4**:1396

*Amazing Stories* (pulp science fiction), **5**:2189

Amazon region, **2**:654

Amazon River, **2**:755

Amazons (mythical), **4**:1384, **6**:2455

*Ambassadors, The* (Holbein), **1**:364

Ambedkar, B. R., **5**:1992, **6**:2395, 2396, 2397

Ambiguity, **1**:53–55

    fallacies of, **2**:776

Ambrose of Milan, St., **2**:401, **4**:1352, 1790, **5**:1871, **6**:2461

Ambrosiana Library (Milan), **6**:2434

Amendola, Giovanni, **6**:2342, 2346

America, **1**:55–60

    aesthetics and, **1**:13–19

    assimilation and, **1**:60–62, 160

    colonialism and, **1**:375–377

    communication of ideas and, **2**:391–395

    empire and imperialism and, **1**:375–377, **2**:653–654

    Enlightenment and, **1**:58, **3**:1028, **5**:2084–2085

    exploration and, **1**:325, **6**:2369

    historiography and, **1**:lvii–viii, lxxv–lxxvi, lxxix

    machismo and, **4**:1328–1330

    mapmaking and, **4**:1344

    migration and, **4**:1450–1452

    missionizing of, **1**:325

    nationalism and, **1**:lvi, lvii–viii

    philosophies and, **4**:1763–1766

    pre-Columbian civilization and, **1**:351–352, 375, **5**:1886–1887

    travel narratives and, **6**:2370

    *See also* Latin America; New World; North America; *specific countries by name*

*America* (Baudrillard), **1**:59

*America Is in the Heart* (Bulason), **5**:2000

American Academy of Arts and Sciences, **5**:1890

American Anthropological Association, **3**:1197

*American Antiquarian* (journal), **5**:1890

American Antiquarian Society, **5**:1890

American Association for the Advancement of Science, **5**:1890

American Association of Anthropology, **5**:1863

American Birth Control League, **4**:1509

American Civil Liberties Union (ACLU), **2**:490, 491, **5**:2197, 2208

American Civil War. *See* Civil War, American

American Colonization Society, **1**:4, **4**:1702

American Ethnological Society, **5**:1890

American Folk-Lore Society, **5**:1890

American Geographical Society, **5**:1890

American Historical Association, **1**:lx, lxiv, **2**:515, **5**:2088

*American Historical Review*, **1**:lx, **5**:2088

American Humanist Association, **3**:1034

American Indian Ethnohistoric Conference, **2**:729

American Indian Movement (AIM), **2**:820, **4**:1450

*American Indian Thought: Philosophical Essays* (Waters), **4**:1764

American Institute of Biological Sciences, **1**:225

Americanization, U.S., **1**:60–63

    assimilation and, **1**:160–162

    diversity and, **2**:590–593

    dual loyalties and, **3**:1320–1321

    education and, **2**:648–649

    naturalization and, **1**:339–341

*American Journal of Archaeology*, **5**:1890

*American Kinship: A Cultural Account* (Schneider), **3**:1197

American Law Institute, **5**:2208

*American Men of Science*, **5**:2187

*American Naturalist* (journal), **5**:1890

American Philosophical Society, **5**:1890

American Political Science Association (APSA), **5**:1840, 1844

*American Political Science Review* (APSR), **5**:1840, 1844

American Protective Association, **6**:2446

American Psychiatric Association (APA), **3**:869, 873, **5**:1959, 2208

American Revolution, **1**:57, **2**:647, 685, **5**:2113, 2116–2117

    democracy and, **2**:553–554, 555

    Enlightenment and, **2**:673

    Europe and, **2**:741

    generation and, **3**:894

    historiography and, **1**:lvi, lvii, lviii

    liberty and, **3**:1276

    loyalty and, **3**:1321

    modernity and, **3**:1175

    political protest and, **5**:1836, 1837

    propaganda and, **5**:1916

    radical liberalism and, **5**:2002

    regime change and, **5**:1836

    volunteerism and, **6**:2444

American Scientific Affiliation, **2**:490

American Society for Environmental History, **2**:682

American Society for Ethnohistory, **2**:729

American University of Beirut, **2**:644

American University of Cairo, **3**:875

*American Voter, The* (survey), **3**:894

*Amerika Is Devouring Its Children* (Belloli), **5**:*1946*

Amerindians. *See* Native Americans

Amery, Jean, **3**:1174

Amery, Leo, **2**:659

Ames, William, **1**:271

Amici, Giovanni Battista, **1**:223

Amicitia, **2**:845

Amin, al-, **3**:1155

Amin, Idi, **5**:2072, 2237

Amin, Qusim, **2**:644

Amin, Samir, **1**:266, 372, **2**:558, 564, 565, **3**:1023, **4**:1624, **5**:1864, **6**:2503, 2506–2507

Amina, queen of Zazzu, **2**:810

Amino acids, **3**:900, 1283

Amir, Yigal, **6**:2515

'Amiri, al-, **4**:1771

Amish, **2**:464

Ammonius, **4**:1629, 1770, 1773

Ammon oracle, **5**:1933

Amnesty International, **2**:636, **3**:911

Amniocentesis, **3**:888

    sex-selective abortion and, **2**:792

Amo, Wilhelm, **3**:1023

*Amoco Cadiz* (oil tanker), **2**:678

Amoda, Olu, **2**:596

Amonius Saccas, **5**:1825

Amoretti, Maria Pellegrina, **6**:2390

Amos (biblical), **5**:1930

Ampère, André-Marie, **1**:303, **2**:831, **4**:1381, **5**:1815, 1817

Amphiboly, **2**:776

*Ampitheatrum sapientiae aeternae solis verae* (Khunrath), **1**:43

Amputation, **4**:1407

Amtower, Laurel, **5**:2013

Ancient Greece *(continued)*
    equality and, 2:695
    Eurocentrism and, 2:738, 740
    evil and, 2:745, 746
    evolution and, 2:750–751
    female communities and, 1:312
    female demons and, 2:563
    fiber arts, 6:*2309*
    form and, 2:834–835
    friendship and, 2:844, 845
    gardens and, 3:857, 859, 860–861
    gender in art and, 3:877
    genre and, 3:913–914
    geography and, 3:918, 919
    geometry and, 2:485, 3:923–924,
        955–956, 4:1378
    god of terror and, 6:2300
    good and, 3:952, 953, 954
    harmony and, 3:960–962, 963
    health and disease and, 3:966, 967
    heaven and hell and, 3:970, 971
    hegemony and, 3:977–978, 980
    hierarchy and order and,
        3:987–988
    historiography and, 1:xxxvii, xliv,
        xlvi, 3:1005, 1030
    homosexuality and, 3:866–867
    humanism and, 3:1026–1027
    hygiene and, 3:1064–1065
    language and, 3:1238
    liberty and, 3:1266, 1272
    life cycle and, 3:1283
    literature and, 3:1298, 1303
    love and, 3:1317
    magic and, 6:2477
    male heroic images and,
        4:1422–1423
    male warrior-heroes and, 4:1422
    maps and, 4:1342
    mathematics and, 4:1378
    medicine and, 2:677–678, 3:957,
        967, 4:1398–1400, 1401
    memory and, 4:1418
    metaphysics and, 4:1434
    microcosmic theory and, 4:1440
    migration and, 4:1447
    miracles and, 4:1463
    monarchy and, 4:1493
    museums and, 4:1520
    musical performance and, 4:1530,
        *1531*
    myth and, 1:xxxvii, 2:593–594,
        3:955, 1299, 1317, 4:1384,
        1418, 1422
    peace and, 4:1724
    Persian war with, 3:977

    perspective and, 4:1746
    philanthropy and, 4:1758
    poetics and, 3:1298, 5:1829
    political representation and,
        5:2093
    privacy and, 5:1901
    prophecy and, 5:1933, 1934
    racial standards and, 5:1994
    radical nationalism and, 5:2003
    Renaissance humanism and,
        3:1030
    revolution and, 5:2113
    rhetoric and, 5:2122, 2123, 2126
    Roman domination of, 2:631–632
    sacred places and, 5:2152–2153
    scientific tradition of,
        5:2192–2193
    sculptured human images and,
        3:*1044,* 1045, 1048, 1049,
        1051, 1052
    slavery and, 5:2215
    sport and, 5:2247, 2248
    suicide and, 5:2270, 2271
    syncretism and, 5:2288
    taste and, 6:2291
    toleration and, 6:2337
    university precedents in, 6:2387,
        *2387,* 2388
    virtue ethics and, 3:1042, 6:2421,
        2422
    work and, 6:2498–2499
    writing and, 1:315, 3:1236, *1236,*
        1237
    *See also* Athens; Greek drama;
        Greek philosophy; Greek science;
        Hellenism
Ancient India. *See* Hinduism; India
Ancient Rome
    anti-Semitism and, 1:98–99
    architecture and, 1:114, 116–117,
        126
    astrology and, 1:162
    authoritarianism and, 1:172
    calendar and, 1:260
    censorship and, 1:291
    childhood and, 1:313
    Chinese trade contacts with, 3:943
    Christianity and, 1:324, 2:709,
        5:1871
    Christianization of, 1:325, 6:2337
    citizenship and, 1:336
    city and, 1:350
    civil society and, 1:355, 356
    class and, 1:359
    classicism and, 1:362–363, 364

    clothing and, 6:2313
    constitutionalism and, 2:458
    Cynicism and, 526
    democracy and, 2:552–553
    divine right and, 4:1492
    dreams and, 2:593–594
    eclecticism and, 2:611
    education and, 1:315, 2:631–632
    empire conception of, 2:651, 652
    Epicureanism and, 2:685–687,
        4:1389
    equality and, 2:695
    everyday life study of, 2:743
    friendship and, 2:844, 845
    gender in art and, 3:877
    genre and, 3:913, 914
    Germany and, 2:653
    gestures and, 3:928, *930,* 933
    heaven and hell beliefs and, 3:971
    historiography and,
        1:xxxvii–xxxviii, xli, xliv, xlvi,
        xlviii, 3:1005–1006, 1030
    homosexuality and, 3:867
    human rights and, 3:1015
    international order and,
        3:1132–1133
    Italian Fascism and, 2:798, 6:2346
    Jewish diasporas and, 2:584
    justice and, 3:1187
    landscape art and, 3:1207
    law and. *See* Roman law
    liberty and, 3:1272
    literature and, 3:1303
    love and, 3:1317
    mapmaking and, 4:1342
    marriage age and, 4:1353
    mathematics and, 4:1379
    medicine and, 4:1398, 1399
    memory and, 4:1418
    migration and, 4:1447
    patriotism and, 4:1722
    peace and, 4:1724
    philanthropy and, 4:1758–1759
    poetics and, 5:1829
    political representation and,
        5:2093
    Pompeii courtyard garden from,
        3:*859*
    property transfer and, 4:1352
    prophecy and, 5:1933–1934, 1935
    racial standards and, 5:1994
    religion and, 5:2076, 2084
    Renaissance imperial bust collec-
        tions and, 6:2434–2435
    republicanism and, 5:2099–2101

Arts *(continued)*
  incongruity and, **3**:1062
  intellectual property and, **5**:1928
  Jews and, **3**:1176
  landscape and, **3**:1205–1223
  Mexican Mural Movement and, **4**:1469, 1470, 1472
  modernism and, **4**:1465–1472
  myth-ritualist theory and, **4**:1564
  naturalism and, **4**:1466, 1604–1607, **5**:2014–2016
  Nazism and, **2**:800
  overview of, **1:136–143,** **5**:2276–2277
  paradise depictions in the, **4**:1719, *1719,* 1720–1721
  periodization of, **4**:1732–1740
  perspective and, **4**:1746–1754
  political protest and, **5**:1937–1949
  postmodernism and, **5**:1869–1871
  realism and, **5**:2015
  surrealism and, **5**:2276–2277
  taste and, **6**:2291–2294
  war and peace depictions in the, **6**:2454–2459
  *See also* Art history; Visual culture; *specific art forms by name*
Arts and crafts movement, **2**:597
Aryans (people), **2**:626, 639, 721
  Hindu castes and, **6**:2395
  Hinduism and, **3**:991–992, 993
Aryan theory, **2**:706, 718, 719, 721, 741, 795, 799, 800
Asad, Talal, **5**:2024, 2138, 2266, **6**:2335
Asada Akira, **4**:1484–1485
Asanga, **4**:1503
Asante (people), **3**:1022
Asante, Molefi, **1**:21, 30–32, **4**:1679
Asceticism, **1:149–158,** 243
  Hindu and Buddhist, **1:149–154,** **3**:1161–1162
  hygiene and, **3**:1066
  Iranian Sufism and, **4**:1550–1551
  monasticism and, **4**:1497
  mysticism and, **4**:1548, 1550
  poverty idealization and, **5**:1871, 1873
  tantraism and, **3**:997
  Western, **1:154–158,** **6**:2460
  yoga and, **6**:2510–2512
Asclepius, **4**:1399, **5**:1933
Ascott, Roy, **4**:1392
Asdiwal, myth of, **4**:1566

Ash'ari, Abu al-Hassan al-, **3**:1143, 1158, **4**:1770, **5**:2068
Ash'arites, **2**:842, **3**:1143–1144, 1147, **4**:1502, 1773, 1774
Ashbee, Henry Spencer, **3**:1072
Ashcroft, Bill, **4**:1586, **5**:1864
*Ashramas* (Hindu theory), **6**:2333
Ashton, Dore, **4**:1469
Ashvaghosha, **1**:243, **3**:971
Ashwood, Amy. *See* Garvey, Amy Ashwood
Asia
  aesthetics and, **1**:9–13
  African diaspora and, **2**:580
  ancestor worship and, **1**:70–71
  anticolonial resistence and, **5**:2104
  architecture and, **1**:128–132
  Christianity and, **1**:326–327
  communication of ideas and, **2**:395–398, 646
  cosmology and, **2**:480–485, 524, **5**:1972, **6**:2329, 2330–2331, 2333, 2509–2510
  development economics and, **2**:618, 620, 621–622
  dreams in art of, **2**:594
  economic historiography and, **3**:1002, 1005
  education and, **2**:625–627
  empires and, **2**:654–655, 658, 659
  Enlightenment and, **2**:738
  Eurocentrism and, **2**:737–740
  gardens and, **3**:861, 862, 865
  globalization and, **2**:809, **3**:941–946, 949, 1166
  heaven and hell concepts and, **3**:970–971, 972, 973–974
  historiography (twentieth-century) and, **1**:lxvii–lxxiv
  humanity beliefs and, **3**:1038–1041
  Islamic mysticism and, **4**:1550–1552
  landscape art and, **3**:1211–1213, *1214,* 1215, 1217, *1218,* 1220, *1220,* 1222, 1223
  liberation movements and, **6**:2503
  Manichaeism and, **4**:1335
  Maoism and, **4**:1340
  Marxism and, **4**:1364–1367
  Marxist environmental determinism and, **2**:738
  masks and, **4**:1373
  meditation and, **4**:1413–1415

  migration and, **1**:158–160, **4**:1444, 1451–1452
  miracle beliefs and, **4**:1463, 1464–1465
  "missing women" phenomenon and, **2**:792–793
  nationalism and, **1**:81–83, **2**:656
  Occidentalism and, **5**:1989–1992
  Orientalism and, **5**:1989–1992
  orthopraxy and, **4**:1684–1691, **5**:1880
  Pan-Asianism and, **4**:1709–1710
  peasantry and, **4**:1728, 1729, 1730
  philosophy and, **4**:1778
  population and, **5**:1846
  postcolonialism and, **5**:1857, 1865
  racism and, **5**:1989–1992
  sacred texts and, **5**:2160–2163
  slavery and, **5**:2216
  as Third World, **6**:2325–2326, 2327
  Third World literature and, **6**:2327–2328
  women's history and, **6**:2482, 2489–2490
  women's movements and, **2**:807–808
  women's studies and, **6**:2492
  yin and yang and, **3**:862, 941, **6**:2509–2510
  *See also* Southeast Asia; *specific countries and regions by name*
Asian-American ideas (cultural migration), **1:158–160,** 219
Asian-Americans
  critical race theory and, **2**:503, 505
  diversity and, **2**:590
  feminism and, **2**:807, 820, 821, **3**:1265
  migration and, **1**:159
  multiple identity and, **3**:1094–1097
  racism and, **2**:706, 708
  U.S. reception of, **5**:1999–2001
  World War II and, **5**:2000–2001
Asian Exclusion League, **5**:2000
Asikpassazade (Asiki), **1**:xliv
Asing, Norman, **5**:1999
Asley, William, **3**:1002
*As Nature Made Him* (Colapinto), **3**:872
Aśoka, Mauryan king of India, **1**:242, **2**:397, **6**:2337
*Aspects of the Novel* (Forster), **4**:1569

Brazil *(continued)*
  cinema and, 1:333
  dictatorship and, 2:798
  fascism and, 2:796, 797–798, 799,
    800
  historiography and, 1:lviii
  liberation theology and, 3:1270
  Marxism and, 44
  military regime and, 1:174
  motherhood and, 1:312
  New Social Movements and,
    5:1851
  populism and, 5:1850
  Portuguese colonialism and, 1:376
  republicanism and, 5:2096
  segregation and, 5:2198
  slavery and, 5:2215
  women's movements and, 2:807
Brazilian Integralist Action (AIB),
  2:797–798, 799, 800
Breast-feeding, 1:312, 314, 2:789
Breccia, Alberto, 5:1949
Breccia, Enrique, 5:1949
Brecht, Bertolt, 3:1300, 4:1467
Breckenridge, Carol, 5:1863
Breeding. *See* Eugenics
Brelwi, Ahmad, 5:2028
Bremond, Claude, 4:1570
Brennan, Geoffrey, 2:479
Brennan, Timothy, 5:1857
Brenner, Robert, 1:264, 361
Brenner, Sydney, 3:900
Brentano, Clemens, 5:2138, 2142
Brentano, Franz, 2:441, 4:1757, 1794
  consciousness and, 2:468, 469
  intentionality and, 3:1122, 1123
Bresson, Robert, 4:1514
Brethren of Purity (Islamic text),
  4:1441, 1772
Breton, André, 2:529, 531, 4:1468,
  5:1958
Bretton Woods Institutions. *See* International Monetary Fund; World Bank
Breuer, Josef, 5:1952
Breuilly, John, 4:1582
Brévié, Jules, 4:1678
Brew, Kwesi, 3:1309
Breward, Christopher, 2:596–597
Brewer, Marilynn, 3:1088
Brezhnev, Leonid, 2:420
"Briar Patch, The" (Warren), 3:1294
Bribery, 2:477, 3:937
*Bridge, The* (film), 6:2457
*Bridge Called My Back, The: Writings by
  Radical Women of Color* (Moraga and
  Anzaldúa, eds.), 6:2496

Bridges, Calvin, 3:898, 899
Bridget of Sweden, St., 2:594, 4:1694
*Bridgewater Treatises,* 4:1611, 1613
*Brief über den Humanismus* (Heidegger), 2:469
"Brigitte study" (Germany), 4:1426
Briggs, Cyril V., 1:28
Brigham, Carl C., 2:733
Brigham, John, 5:1892
Bright, John, 4:1480
Brightman, Edgar S., 4:1765
Brik, Osip, 2:837
Brink, André, 3:1309
Brioist, Pascal, 5:2090
Brissot, Jacques-Pierre, 1:3
Britain. *See* Great Britain
*Britannia* (Camden), 1:xlv
British Anti-Slavery Society, 1:3
British Association for the Advancement of Science, 2:612
British Broadcasting Corporation
  (BBC), 5:1919
British deism, 2:547–548
British Ecological Society, 2:615
British Empire. *See* Great Britain, empire
British Library, 2:2441, 4:1520, 1522,
  6:2434–2435, *2440*
  visual cues to collection of, 6:2440
British Mass Observation (project),
  1:331
British Museum, 2:670, 4:1522,
  6:2437–2438
  circular reading room, 6:*2440*
  Egyptian Exhibit, 4:1520, *1520*
"British Rule in India, The" (Marx),
  2:738
British Union of Fascists, 2:799, 800
British Vegetation Committee, 2:613
British Women's Temperance Association, 6:2298
Brittan, Samuel, 3:949
Briusov, Valeri, 5:2280
Broca, Paul, 4:1459, 1807, 1809
Brochtorff Circle (Malta excavation),
  1:114
Brock, Peter, 4:1726
Brocka, Lino, 6:2322, 2323
Brockman, John, 2:851
Brodie, Bernard, 4:1646
Broederbond (Afrikaner secret society),
  1:106
Broglie, Louis de, 5:1978
*Broken People* (journal), 6:2396
Bromyard, John, 4:1725

Brontë, Charlotte, 2:508
Brontë, Emily, 3:908
Brönte family, 2:394
Bronze Age, 5:1888, 6:2312, 2314
Brooke, John Hedley, 4:1613
Brookes, Edgar H., 5:2199
Brooklyn Botanical Garden, 3:862
Brooks, Cleanth, 5:1831
  New Criticism and, 4:1630, 1631
Brooks, Rodney, 2:851
Brooks, Romaine, 5:2285
Brophy, Philip, 1:334
Brosses, Charles de, 2:822, 823, 825,
  826
  totemism and, 2:822, 6:2349
Brotherston, Gordon, 5:1860, 1861
Broude, Norma, 3:881
Brouwer, L. E. J., 3:1315, 1316
Brown, Donald L., 5:1900
Brown, James, 5:1839
Brown, Lancelot ("Capability"), 3:857
Brown, Lawrence A., 2:588
Brown, Louise, 4:1510
Brown, Peter, 4:1654
Brown, Robert, 1:223
Brown, Wendy, 2:699
Browne, Janet, 5:2185
Browne, Thomas, 5:2274
Brownian motion, 5:1975
Browning, Robert, 3:1300
Brownlow, Kevin, 1:331
Brownmiller, Susan, 6:2482–2483
*Brown v. Board of Education* (1954,
  U.S.), 2:502, 649, 706, 707
"*Brown v. Board of Education* and the
  Interest Convergence Dilemma"
  (Bell), 2:502
*Brücke, Der* (film), 6:2457
Brücke, Ernst, 3:1282
Brücke artists, 2:770
Brucker, J. J. (Johann Jakob), 2:611,
  612, 3:1082, 4:1628
Bruckner, Anton, 1:6
Brueghel, Pieter, the Elder, 2:595,
  3:*1208*, 1209–1210, 1211, 5:1944
Brugmann, Karl, 3:1225
Bruin, Joris. *See* Braun, Georg
Brumberg, Stephan, 1:62
Brumfiel, Elizabeth, 5:1887,
  6:2355–2356
Brunelleschi, Filippo, 4:1748, *1749*
Bruner, Edward M., 4:1525
Bruner, Jerome, 2:466, 3:1087, 1226,
  4:1717
Brunetière, Ferdinand, 5:2287

*Dictionary of the history of ideas* (Wiene, ed.), 3:1083

*Dictionnaire historique et critique* (Bayle), 1:xlviii, 2:670, 6:2319

*Dictionnaire philosophique* (Voltaire), 3:1306, 4:1375

*Dictionnaire universal* (Furetière), 2:670

*Didascalicon* (Hugh of St. Victor), 2:669

Diderot, Denis, 1:57, 101, 138–140, 169, 2:402, 549, 553, 611, 671, 674, 3:975, 1028, 1299, 4:1374, 1375, 1502, 1632, 5:2002

    art criticism and, 1:367

    fetishism and, 2:822

    general will and, 2:891, 3:891

    human nature and, 3:1042

    materialism and, 4:1376

    motif and, 4:1513, 1516

    museums and, 4:1522

    progress and, 5:1913

    religion and, 4:1797

    technology and, 6:2500

    *See also* Encyclopédie

Didron, Adolphe-Napoléon, 3:1072

Diego, Juan, 2:773

Diels, Hermann, 5:2169

*Dies irae* (chant), 4:*1516*

Dietary restrictions (religious). *See* Food prohibitions

Dieterlen, Germaine, 2:424

Dietrich of Freiberg, 4:1630

"Différance, La" (Derrida), 4:1587, 5:2262–2263, 2266

Difference

    cultural, 2:455, 3:1266

    cultural citizenship and, 1:338–339

    cultural revivals and, 2:518

    feminism and, 1:95–96, 2:474, 807, 3:1266–1267, 4:1767, 6:2495, 2496

    gender and, 3:871–873, 1266–1267

    liberalism and, 3:1266–1267

    liberty and, 3:1275

    queer theory and, 5:1983–1984

    *See also* Diversity; Identity

*Difference between Fichte's and Schelling's System of Philosophy, The* (Hegel), 3:1080

Difference engine (Babbitt calculating machine), 1:256, 2:*430*

*Differences* (journal), 5:1981

*Différend, Le* (Lyotard), 2:510, 5:2263

Differential geometry, 3:925–926

Differential radicalization, 2:503

Differentials, 4:1379

*Different War, A* (Lippard), 5:1945

Diffusion, cultural, 1:380, 2:587–588, 3:1285

*Digambaras* Jainism, 3:1161, 1162

Diggers, 5:2116

Digital technology

    architecture and, 6:2420

    computer science and, 1:257, 2:429, 432–433

    films and, 1:330, 334

Dignity. *See* Human rights

*Digression on the Ancients and the Moderns* (Fontenelle), 5:1913

Dijk, Teun van, 3:1229–1230

Dike, Kenneth Onwuka, 1:lxvi, 4:1667

*Dilbert* (comic strip), 3:1256

Dillon, John, 4:1628

Dilthey, Wilhelm, 1:lxii, lxxvi, 2:606, 3:893, 1129, 1138, 1139, 4:1755, 5:2087

    continental philosophy and, 2:468

    hermeneutics and, 2:471, 3:982, 983, 984, 985, 986

    linguistic turn and, 3:1291

Dimensions theory, 4:1382

Diminishing margical product, 2:619

Diminishing returns, law of, 2:618

*Dinner Party, The* (Chicago installation), 3:881

Dinnerstein, Dorothy, 1:236, 6:2494

Diodorus Siculus, 3:858

Diogenes Laertius, 1:219, 2:574, 611, 686, 4:1779, 5:2211, 2271

Diogenes of Sinope, 2:487, 526

Diome, Fatou, 3:1310

Diomedes, 6:2360

Dionisio Gallo, 5:1936

Dionysian cults, 4:1373

Dionysius Exigus, 1:xli

Dionysius of Halicarnassus, 1:xxxvii, 3:1005–1006, 5:2126

Dionysius the Areopagite. *See* Pseudo-Dionysius

Dionysodorus, 5:2241, 2242

Diop, Birago, 3:1308

Diop, Cheikh Anta, 1:21, 170, 369, 2:389, 3:1023, 4:1477, 1705, 1761

Diop, David, 3:1308

Diop, Ousmane Socé, 4:1477–1478

Diophantus of Alexandria, 1:44, 3:1156

*Dioptrics* (Descartes), 5:1811

Dior, Christian, 2:603

Dioscorides, 2:677–678

Dipanagoro, 1:93

Diphtheria, 4:1408

Diplomacy

    cosmopolitanism and, 2:488

    treaty-making and, 20–82

Dirac, Paul Adrien Maurice, 2:832, 833, 5:1978, 1979–1980

Direct Action Network, 5:2005

Directed Acyclic Graphs (DAGS), 1:286

Directed evolution, 2:754

Dirichlet, J. P. G., 4:1381

Dirks, Nicholas B., 5:1882

Dirlik, Arif, 4:1663

Disabled persons, 2:590

*Disasters of War* (Goya), 5:1939, 6:*2450*, 2455

*Discipliens* (Varro), 2:669

*Discipline and Punish: The Birth of the Prison* (Foucault), 4:1587, 5:1970, 2265

*Discobolus* (Myron), 1:53, *54*

*Discources* (Machiavelli), 1:xlv, 2:525

*Discourse of Free-thinking* (Collins), 4:1377

*Discourse on Colonialism* (Césaire), 5:1864

*Discourse on Inequality* (Rousseau), 3:891

*Discourse on Method* (Descartes), 1:269, 2:606

"Discourse on Music" (Xunzi), 1:10

*Discourse on the First Ten Books of Livy* (Machiavelli), 3:1273

*Discourse on the Origin of Inequality* (Rousseau), 5:2258

*Discourse on the Pure Good* (Islamic text), 4:1771

*Discourse on the Sciences and Arts* (Rousseau), 2:475, 3:891

*Discourses on Art* (Reynolds), 2:496

*Discourses on Livy* (Machiavelli), 1:336, 3:1032, 5:2100

Discourse studies, 3:1229–1230

*Discoverers, The* (Boorstin), 5:2183

Discrimination, 2:588–590

    Asian-American migration and, 1:159

    critical race theory and, 2:501–507

    feminist philosophy and, 4:1767

    gender and. *See* Sexism

    Indian postindependence ban on, 5:1992

Interactive technology, 6:2417, 2420

*Inter caetera* (1493 papal bull), 3:1134, 1135, 6:2374

Intercession in Middle Eastern society, **3:1125–1126**

InterCommunication Center (Tokyo), 6:2421

Interdisciplinarity, 1:214, **3:1126–1131**
  environmental history and, 2:683–684
  history of ideas and, 3:1082, 1083
  iconography and, 3:1070, 1072, 1076
  interpretation and, 3:1139–1141
  narrative and, 4:1570–1571
  philosophy and, 4:1779–1783
  postcolonial studies and, 5:1863

*Interesting Narrative of the Life of Olaudah Equaino, The, or, Gustavus Vassa, the African* (Equiano), 2:388

Intergovernmental Panel on Climate Change, 6:2473

Intergroup emotion theory (IET), 3:1088

Internal colonialism, **3:1131–1132**

International African Friends of Abyssinia, 4:1703

*International African Opinion* (journal), 4:1703

International African Service Bureau, 4:1703

International agreement. *See* Treaty

International Association for Cultural Studies, 2:520

International Biological Program (IBP), 2:614

International Chamber of Commerce, 2:478

International Conference on Population and Development (ICPD), 2:790–791

International Congress of Americanists, 2:587

International Congress of Mathematics, 4:1402

International Convention on the Elimination of All Forms of Racial Discrimination (CERD), 3:1249

International Court of Arbitration, 3:1135

International Covenant on Civil and Political Rights, 3:1246

International Criminal Court (ICC), 3:911, 1137, 1247–1248

International Criminal Tribunal for Rwanda, 3:1247–1248

International Criminal Tribunal for the Former Yugoslavia (ICTY), 3:1247–1248

International Decade for Women. *See* Decade for Women

International Encyclopedia of Unified Science, 2:672

International families, 2:786–787

International Federation of Gynecology and Obstetrics, 4:1510

International Geographical Union (IGU), 3:920

International Geophysical Year (IGY), 4:1350

International Interdisciplinary Congress on Women, 6:2492, 2497

Internationalization, globalization vs., 3:941

International law, 3:1244, 1245–1249
  intellectual property and, 5:1928
  privacy rights and, 5:1902–1903

International Map of the World (IMW), 3:919, 4:1350, *1351*

International Meridian Conference (1884), 4:1348

International modernism, 4:1469–1472

International Monetary Fund (IMF), 2:558, 699, 3:947, 5:2005, 2245, 2253, 6:2463
  African capitalism and, 1:265

International Network of Women's Studies Journals, 6:2492

International order, **3:1132–1137**
  genocide and, 3:909–911
  peace and, 4:1724–1727
  sovereignty and, 3:1246–1247
  treaty and, 6:2372–2376
  war and, 6:2449–2454

International Planned Parenthood, 2:789

International Society for Chinese Philosophy (ISCP), 3:943

International Trade Union Committee of Negro Workers, 4:1703

International Union for the Protection of Nature, 6:2473

International Women's Year (1975), 3:1019, 5:1921

Internet, 2:672, 4:1420
  censorship and, 1:294
  formation of, 1:259, 2:431–432
  intellectual property law and, 5:1928
  memes and, 4:1417
  pragmatism web site, 5:1886
  propaganda and, 5:1921–1922

  as protest vehicle, 5:1839
  rhetoric and, 5:2125

Internment camps, 5:2001, 6:2345, 2346

Internment memoirs, 1:185

Interpol, 2:478

Interpretation, **3:1137–1142**
  hermeneutics and, 3:982–986
  historical presentism and, 5:1897–1898
  poetics and, 5:1830–1831
  translation and, 6:2366–2367

*Interpretation* (Aristotle), 3:1303

*Interpretation of Dreams, The* (Freud), 3:1296, 4:1408, 1565, 5:1952

Interracial marriage, 1:161

Inter-Religio (Buddhism), 2:624

Inter-University Consortium for Political and Social Research, 5:2225

*Interventions* (journal), 5:1864

*In the Chinks of the World Machine: Feminism and Science Fiction* (Lefanu), 5:2190

*In the Name of Eugenics: Genetics and the Uses of Human Heredity* (Kevles), 5:2186

*Into Darkness Peering: Race and Color in the Fantastic* (Leonard), 5:2190

Intonation, 3:961

Intrinsic ethical value, 2:680

Intrinsic good, 3:952

*Introductio ad philosophiam audicam* (Thomasius), 2:611

*Introduction à la Renaissance* (Michelet), 5:2087

*Introduction á l'histoire de l'Asie* (Cahun), 4:1713

*Introduction aux études historiques* (Langlois), 1:lxiv

*Introduction to Stoic Philosophy* (Lipsius), 2:611

*Introduction to the Study of Experimental Medicine, An* (Bernard), 4:1407, 1603

*Introduction to the Study of Language* (Bloomfield), 3:1226

Introspection, 2:443

Intuitionism, 4:1793–1794

*Inventing Eastern Europe: The Map of Civilization on the Mind of the Enlightenment* (Wolff), 5:2032

Inventio, rhetoric and, 5:2123, 2126

*Invention of Africa, The* (Mudimbe), 1:21, 5:2016, 2170, 6:2480

*Invention of Art, The* (Shiner), 1:143

*Invention of Tradition, The* (Hobsbawm and Ranger), 2:516, 4:1420–1421

Islam *(continued)*

education and. *See* Islamic education

ethnicity and race and, **2:**720–721

Eurocentrism and, **2:**737, 738, 739

family planning and, **2:**789

feminism and. *See under* Feminism

founding date of, **1:**349

free will vs. determinism and, **2:**841–842, **5:**2068

fundamentalism and, **1:**lxxv, 291, **2:**778–779, 848–849, **3:**1168–1169, **5:**2070, 2082, **6:**2469. *See also* Islamism

gardens and, **3:**859, **4:**1721

gender and, **3:**874–876

geographical lore and, **3:**918–919

geometry and, **3:**924–925

heaven and hell and, **3:**972

Hegira and, **1:**xlii, 349, **3:**1167

heresy and, **3:**982

Hinduism and, **3:**991, 993

historiography and, **1:**xlii–xliv, lxxiv, lxxv, **3:**1175

honor and, **3:**1008, 1009, 1011, 1012, **5:**2006

humanism in North Africa and, **3:**1022

humanism in tenth century and, **3:**1027

images and, **3:**1098, 1099, 1100, 1101–1102

imagination and, **3:**1103

immortality and, **2:**546, **3:**1108

imperialism and, **5:**2072

India and, **2:**626, 639, 644, **3:**991, **4:**1712

Indian historiography and, **1:**l–li

individualism and, **3:**1114

Indonesian matriarchy and, **4:**1388

intelligentsia and, **3:**1121

intercession and, **3:**1125–1126

international order and, **3:**1133

Iranian revolution and, **2:**663, 818–819, 847–848, **4:**1455, 1496

Jewish diasporas and, **2:**584, 585, **5:**2069

jihad and, **3:**1166–1169

Koran and law in, **5:**2166

language and, **3:**1240

Latin America and, **5:**2078

law and. *See* Law, Islamic

liberty and, **3:**1276–1277

literature and, **3:**1305

male circumcision and, **3:**1011

Manichaeism and, **4:**1335

mapmaking and, **4:**1343

marriage and, **1:**314

mathematics and, **4:**1379, **5:**1809

Mecca and, **5:**2157–2159

medicine and. *See under* Islamic science

medieval logic and, **3:**1313

medieval metaphysics and, **4:**1434, 1502

medieval moral philosophy and, **4:**1790–1791

microcosmic theory and, **4:**1441

Middle East nationalism and, **4:**1592

Middle East state loyalties and, **2:**663

migration and, **4:**1447

millenarianism and, **4:**1454–1455

miracles and, **4:**1464

modernity and, **6:**2468–2469

monarchy and, **4:**1492, 1494–1496

as monotheistic, **5:**1844

moral philosophy and, **4:**1790–1791

Muhammad succession controversy and, **5:**2067–2068

mysticism and, **3:**1149, 1154, **4:**1549–1552, 1559, 1774–1775, **5:**2068

non-Muslim treatment by, **3:**1168

nonviolence and, **4:**1644, 1645

North African historiography and, **1:**lxiv–lxv

"The Nude" and, **4:**1653

Orientalism and, **4:**1674, 1675, 1677, 1678, 1679, 1680, **5:**2032

orthodoxy and, **4:**1681–1682

orthopraxy and, **4:**1687

Pan-Arabism and, **4:**1709

Pan-Islamism and, **4:**1711–1712

paradise and, **4:**1718–1719, 1720–1721

peace and, **4:**1726

philanthropy and, **1:**350, **4:**1758, 1760

philosophy and, **4:**1770–1775, 1795

pilgrimage and, **6:**2368, 2370

political practice and, **5:**1839

poverty and, **5:**1872

power and, **5:**1880

property inheritance and, **1:**314, **5:**1925

prophecy and, **5:**1932

reform and, **5:**2028–2029

religion–state relationship and, **5:**2080–2082

ritual and, **5:**2132

sacred places and, **5:**2153–2155. *See also* Mecca

sacred text of. *See* Koran

science and. *See* Islamic science

secularism and, **2:**663, **5:**2072, 2081, 2196, **6:**2469

sexuality and, **5:**2206

Shii, **3:**1145–1148. *See also* Shii

social intercession and, **3:**1125–1126

Southeast Asia and, **3:**1149–1150

spiritual friendship and, **2:**844

Sufism and, **4:**1502, **5:**2269–2270. *See also* Sufism

Sunni, **3:**1150–1154, 1156. *See also* Sunni

superstition and, **5:**2273

syncretism in, **5:**2288

temperance and, **6:**2297

Temple Mount and, **5:**2153–2155

terrorism and, **6:**2301–2302, 2303

toleration and, **6:**2337, 2340

totalitarianism and, **6:**2343–2344, 2348

travel and, **6:**2368, 2370

tribalism and, **6:**2377

universities and, **6:**2388

U.S. neocolonialism and, **2:**664

utopias and, **6:**2408

wealth and, **6:**2460

Westernization and, **5:**2072, **6:**2468–2469

women's education and, **2:**644

women's history and, **1:**lxxv

women's movements and, **2:**808

women's status and, **2:**809, 819, **3:**874–876, 1011–1012, *1012,* **4:**1682, **5:**1925

*See also* Muhammad

*Islam and the West African Novel: The Politics of Representation* (Bangura), **4:**1678

*Islam: A Very Short Introduction* (Ruthven), **4:**1687

Islamic Development Bank, **5:**2073

Manifest destiny, **3:**1183

"Manifesto for Cyborgs, A" (Haraway), **3:**888

*Manifesto of Surrealism,* **5:**2276

*Manila in the Claws of Light* (film), **6:**2323

Manipulation, **5:**1877

*Maniyadanabon* (Sin), **1:**lxx

Manlius, **1:**162

*Man Machine* (La Mettrie), **1:**270

Mann, Michael, **6:**2348

Mann, Susan, **6:**2490

Mann, Thomas, **3:**868, **4:**1468, **5:**1958, 1997

Manners. *See* Etiquette

Mannheim, Bruce, **4:**1525

Mannheim, Karl, **3:**1201, **4:**1657
    generation and, **3:**893, 894, 895
    historicism and, **3:**1000–1001
    interpretation and, **3:**1139, 1140, 1141
    situated knowledge and, **2:**466
    utopian social theory and, **6:**2406

Manning, Sam, **4:**1703

Mannoni, Octave, **2:**827

Manovich, Lev, **1:**334, **6:**2428

Mansel, Henry Longueville, **1:**27, 35

Mansfield, Harvey C., Jr., **2:**455

Mansfield, Katherine, **2:**845

Mansour, Jihad, **5:**1948

Mansur, al-, **3:**1155

*Man's World?, A* (Pease and Pringle, eds.), **4:**1427

Mantegna, Andrea, **4:**1736, **6:**2430, *2432*

Mantic way (China), **4:**1543

Manuel, Frank E. and Fritzie, **6:**2405

Manutius, Aldus, **2:**401, **3:**1030

*Man with a Movie Camera, The* (Vertov), **5:**2023

Mao Dun, **4:**1482

Maoism, **4:1335–1341,** 1365–1366
    atrocities and, **3:**909, **6:**2345
    dress and, **2:**598
    education and, **2:**629
    historiography and, **1:**lxvii–lxviii
    ideology of, **4:**1336–1488, 1365–1366
    Legalism and, **3:**1261
    Marxism and, **4:**1361, 1365–1366
    modernity and, **4:**1484
    post-Mao policies and, **4:**1340, 1366

totalitarianism and, **6:**2343, 2344, 2346, 2347, 2348
    wealth and, **6:**2463

Maori (people), **6:**2398, 2408
    cultural revival and, **2:**517
    dress and, **2:**597–598, **2:***598*
    postcolonial studies and, **5:**1864
    Treaty of Waitangi and, **6:**2374–2376

Mao Tse-tung. *See* Mao Zedong

Mao Zedong, **1:**69, 81, **2:**598, **3:**894, 998, 1119, 1121, 1261, **4:**1665, **5:**1948, 1991, 2120, **6:**2407
    aesthetics and, **1:**10–11
    background and career of, **4:**1337
    death of, **4:**1340
    historiography and, **1:**lxvii–lxviii
    Marxism and, **4:**1360, 1361, 1365
    political ideology of, **4:**1335–1337
    religion and, **5:**2061
    Third World and, **6:**2325
    totalitarianism and, **6:**2343, 2345, 2346, 2347, 2348
    Yan'an period and, **4:**1337–1338
    *See also* Maoism

Mapplethorpe, Robert, **3:**881

Maps, **4:1341–1352**
    Africa and, **1:**22–23
    America and, **1:**56
    computers and, **4:**1351
    geography and, **3:**918–919, 920
    geological, **4:**1348, *1349,* 1350
    mathematics and, **4:**1379
    topolographical, **4:**1350

*Maqamat, The* (al-Hariri), **2:**642

Marable, Manning, **1:**26

Maran, René, **3:**1309, **4:**1622

Maravall, José Antonio, **4:**1395

Marc, Franz, **2:**770

Marcel, Gabriel-Honoré, **2:**470, 473, 761

Marcellinus, Ammianus, **1:**xxxviii

March, Reginald, **5:**1944

Marching bands, **4:**1532, *1532*

March on Washington (1963), **2:**707

*March to War of the Pope* (Cranach), **5:***1937*

Marcion, **3:**950

Marc Jacobs International, **2:**603

Marco Polo. *See* Polo, Marco

Marcos, Ferdinand, **1:**173

Marcus, George, **3:**1140, **5:**2024, 2266

Marcus Aurelius, emperor of Rome, **1:**117, **2:**943

Marcuse, Herbert, **1:**361, **4:**1362, **5:**1880, 2004, **6:**2343
    continental philosophy and, **2:**473
    Frankfurt School and, **2:**508, 509

Marduk (god), **1:**xxxvi

*Mare liberum* (Grotius), **3:**1135

Marett, Robert Ranulph, **1:**72, **4:**1331

Marey, Étienne-Jules, **1:**334

*Margaret Mead and Samoa: The Making and Unmaking of an Anthropological Myth* (Freeman), **3:**1286

*Margarita philosophica* (Reisch), **2:**669, *671*

Marghinani, al-, **3:**1253

Margiela, Martin, **2:**603, 604

Marginalization, **5:**1984

Marginal utility, **2:**618

Margolin, Jean-Louis, **3:**910

Maria Lionza cult, **5:**2055

*Marianismo. See* Virgin Mary

Marias, Julius, **3:**893

Mariátegui, José Carlos, **3:**1112, 1113, **5:**2173

Maria Theresa, empress of Austria, **4:**1696, **6:**2455

Marie, countess of Champagne, **3:**1318

Marie, Michel, **6:**2307

Marie Antoinette, queen of France, **3:**880, **5:**2103

Marie de France, **3:**1318

Marignan, Albert, **3:**1072

Marinella, Lucretia, **3:**1031, 1042

*Mariners, Renegades, and Castaways* (James), **4:**1368

*Mariner's Mirrour* (atlas), **4:**1345

Marinetti, Filippo Tommaso, **4:**1467

Maritain, Jacques, **1:**51, **2:**761

Mark, Gospel According to, **4:**1453, **5:**1880, 1932

*Markandeya Purana* (Hindu text), **3:**970–971

Marketing, **2:**463–464, **4:**1395. *See also* Advertising

Market system. *See* Capitalism

Mark I computer, **1:**258, **2:**429, *431*

Marks, Laura U., **1:**334

Marks, Shula, **5:**1864

"Marlboro Man" (advertising campaign), **4:**1425, *1425*

Marley, Bob, **4:**1527

Marlowe, Christopher, **3:**1299

Maronite Christians, **2:**662, **5:**2073, **6:**2301

Maroons, **2:**498

Marquard, Odo, **5:**2212

*Raft of the Medusa, The* (Géricault),
  5:1944
Rageb, F. Jamil, 3:1157
Ragionalism, 4:1504
Raglan, Lord, 4:1564, 1566, 1567
Ragore, Rabindranath, 4:1710
Rahe, Paul, 5:2098
Rahner, Karl, 1:325
Rahula, 1:243
Rai, Shirin, 5:2256
Railton, Peter, 6:2401
Rainer, Yvonne, 6:2427
Rajan, Rajaswari Sunder, 5:1864
*Rajavaliya* (Indian text), 1:l
*Rajtarangini* (Kalhana), 1:xlix
Raleigh, Walter, 2:731
Ram, Kanshi, 6:2396–2397
Rama (avatar), 3:992, 993, 4:1464
Rama I, king of Siam, 1:lxxi
Rama IV, king of Siam, 1:lxxi
Rama, Angel, 3:1112–1113
Ramakrishna, Sri, 2:488
Ramaraja, 6:2408
Ramayana (epic), 1:lxxix
*Ramayana* (Hindu text), 2:395, 396,
  411, 563, 3:993, 994, 4:1326, 5:1991
Rameau, Jean-Philippe, 1:268, 3:963
Ramée, Pierre de la. *See* Ramus, Petrus
Ramírez, Serio, 6:2505
Ramos, Alcida Rita, 4:1597
Ramram Basu, 1:l
Ramsay, William, 1:304
Ramses VI, king of Egypt, 3:*1235*
Ramsey, Frank Plumpton, 1:276,
  5:1910, 1911, 6:2382–2383
Ramus, Petrus (Pierre de La Ramée),
  2:611, 3:1030, 4:1431, 5:2124,
  2210
Ramussio, Giovanni, 6:2371
Rand, Ayn, 1:69, 170, 3:955, 1117
RAND Corporation, 3:853, 855
Randolph, A. Philip, 5:2199
Randomness theory, 5:1911
Ranger, Terence, 2:516, 4:1420–1421,
  1581, 1583, 1585–1586, 1588,
  6:2359
Rani Jhansi, 6:2455
Rank, Otto, 4:1565, 1566, 1567,
  5:1957
Ranke, Leopold von, 4:1575, 1576,
  5:2187
  historiography and, 1:xlv, lvii,
    lix–lx, lxi, lxii, lxiii, lxvii, lxxviii,
    3:1006, 1007
  trope and, 6:2379

Ransom, John Crowe, 3:1293, 1295,
  4:1630, 1631
· Ransome-Kuti, Funmilayo, 2:811
Ranson, Paul, 5:2282
Ranters, 4:1456
Rao, Sehagiri, 2:624
Rape as war weapon, 6:2454
Rape of Europa (legend), 2:741
*Rape of Europa* (Vos), 2:*741*
*Rape of Shavi, The* (Emechta), 6:2408
Raphael, 1:364, 4:1736, 5:2009, *2009*
Rap music, 3:895
Rapoport, Arnold, 3:855
Rapp, Rayna, 3:888, 5:1884
Rappaport, Joanne, 4:1596
Rappaport, Roy, 5:2135
*Rasalil* (Islamic text), 4:1441
Rashid, Harun al-, 2:405
Rashid al-Din, 1:xliii
Rask, Rasmus, 3:1225
Raskin, Victor, 3:1064
Rasnake, Roger, 4:1595
*Rasselas* (Johnson), 6:2319
*Rassenhygiene* (eugenics movement),
  2:732
Rastafarianism, 4:1702
Rational choice, 5:2006–2008
  class and, 1:361
  economics and, 1:263
  game theory and, 3:855
  moral sense and, 4:1505, 1506
  utilitarianism and, 6:2401–2403
Rational expection economics, 2:619
Rationalism, 2:425, 4:1614, 1615,
  1694, 5:2008–2012
  antirational Counter-Enlighten-
    ment and, 2:673, 674
  Dada and, 2:529
  emotions and, 2:649, 650–651
  empiricism and, 2:665–666, 668
  Enlightenment and, 2:673, 674,
    5:1987, 2011
  environmental ethics and, 2:681
  epistemology and, 2:687–689
  idealism and, 3:1078
  Islam and, 3:1144
  Kantianism and, 3:1193, 6:2385
  modernity and, 4:1476
  moral sense and, 4:1504, 1505,
    1506, 1787, 1792
  universalism and, 6:2385
Ratsiraka, Didier, 5:2237
Ratti-Menton, Benoît Ulysse de, 1:104
Ratzel, Friedrich, 3:919, 5:1889

Rauschenberg, Robert, 1:190, 2:531
Rauschenbusch, Walter, 4:1690
Raven, Charles, 4:1613
Ravenholt, Reimert, 5:1847
Ravidas, 6:2395
*Raw and the Cooked, The* (Lévi-Strauss),
  5:2265
Rawlings, Jerry, 2:557
Rawls, John, 2:425, 555, 593, 698,
  3:1194, 5:2220–2221
  authority and, 1:182
  autonomy and, 1:187
  citizenship and, 1:337
  civil disobedience and, 1:354, 355
  equality and, 2:702
  good and, 3:954, 1180, 6:2401
  happiness and, 3:960
  liberalism and, 3:1265–1266
  liberty and, 3:1276
  moral philosophy and, 4:1794
  state of nature and, 5:2257, 2258
  universalism and, 6:2385, 2386
  utilitarianism and, 6:2401, 2402
  virtue ethics and, 6:2422
  wealth inequality and, 5:1876,
    6:2461
  welfare liberal justice and,
    3:1178–1179, 1180, 1181,
    1184–1186, 1187, 4:1794
Ray, John, 1:221, 4:1611
Ray, Man, 1:*233*
Ray, Satyajit, 1:335
Ray, Supryia M., 3:914
Rayleigh, Lord (John William Strutt),
  1:304
Raymond, Henry, 2:393
Raymond, Janice, 2:845
Rayner, Rosalie, 1:207
Raz, Joseph, 3:1276
*Raza cósmica, La* (Vasconcelos),
  4:1428
*Raza de bronce* (Arguedas), 3:1112
Raza Unida Party, 1:306
Razi, Abu Bakr Muhammad ibn Za-
  kariya al-, 1:42, 4:1400, 1413, 1495,
  1772
Razi, Fakhr al-, 4:1774
Read, Herbert, 1:69, 2:508, 3:1046,
  1047, 1059, 1060
Reader-response theory, 5:1832–1833
Reading, 5:2012–2014
  cognitive function and, 4:1459
  interdisciplinarity and, 3:1129
  modernism, 4:1467
  privacy and, 5:1900

*Scepsis Scientifica* (Glanvill), **5:**2212

*Sceptical Chymist, The* (Boyle), **5:**2212

Schacter, Daniel, **3:**1258

Schäfer, Dietrich, **2:**514

Schaff, Adam, **2:**473

Schaffer, Simon, **2:**767, **5:**2185

Schall von Bell, Adam, **6:**2331

Schapiro, Meyer, **3:**1074, 1111, **4:**1734, **5:**2016

Schapiro, Miriam, **4:**1739

Schechner, Richard, **6:**2317, 2318

Schechter, Zalman, **4:**1558

Scheele, Karl Wilhelm, **1:**301, **5:**2184

Scheffler, Samuel, **4:**1662, **6:**2401

*Scheherezade* (Rimsky-Korsakov), **4:**1594

Scheibler, Christoph, **1:**135

Scheines, Richard, **1:**286–287, 288

Scheler, Max, **2:**467, **4:**1756, 1794

Schell, Jonathan, **4:**1648

Schelling, Caroline, **5:**2140

Schelling, Friedrich Wilhelm Joseph von, **1:**lvii, 15, **3:**1105, 1193, **4:**1673, **5:**2138

   evil and, **2:**745

   evolution and, **2:**751

   Hegelianism and, **3:**976

   idealism and, **3:**1080, 1081, **4:**1503

   Kabbalah and, **4:**1558

   Naturphilosophie and, **3:**1105, **4:**1620–1621, 1621, **5:**1815, 2072

   prehistory study and, **5:**1888

Schelling, Thomas, **3:**854, **4:**1646, 1648

Scheman, Naomi, **4:**1768

Schenker, Heinrich, **1:**5, **4:**1516

Schenley Wine Company, **2:**816

Scheper-Hughes, Nancy, **1:**312, **5:**2024

Scherer, Suzanne, **2:**596

Schermerhorn, Richard A., **4:**1462

Scherr, Raquel, **6:**2486

Scheub, Harold, **2:**387

Schick, Irvin Cemil, **4:**1692

Schickard, Wilhelm, **1:**255

Schiller, Johann Christoph Friedrich von, **1:**15, 204, 364, **3:**1194, 1306, **4:**1593, 1736, **5:**1830, 1885

Schimper, Andreas Franz Wilhelm, **2:**613

Schizophrenia, **3:**905

Schlafly, Phyllis, **1:**97

Schlegel, Alice, **3:**1286

Schlegel, August Wilhelm, **5:**2138

Schlegel, Dorothea, **5:**2140

Schlegel, Friedrich von, **3:**1000, **4:**1673, **5:**1832, 2138, 2141, 2142

Schleicher, August, **1:**76

Schleiden, Matthias, **1:**223, **3:**968, **5:**2185

Schleiermacher, Friedrich, **1:**325, **2:**708, **3:**983, 1291, 1292, **4:**1804, **5:**1821, 2138, 2141, 2142

   hermeneutics and, **2:**471, **3:**1138, **5:**1832–1833

Schleitheim Articles (1527), **5:**2031

Schlesinger, Arthur M., Jr., **5:**1827

Schlick, Morris, **1:**275, **5:**1854

Schlöndorff, Volcker, **6:**2457

Schlözer, August, **1:**liv, lvii

Schlözer, Ludwig von, **1:**293

Schmidt, James, **2:**676

Schmidt, Johann Lorenz, **1:**293

Schmidt, Wilhelm, **1:**79, **2:**587

Schmidt-Rottluff, Karl, **2:**770

Schmitt, Carl, **2:**802, **5:**1834, **6:**2342

Schmitter, Philippe, **1:**176

Schmitz, David F., **1:**180

Schmoller, Gustav, **3:**1000

Schneider, Carl D., **5:**1905

Schneider, David, **2:**781, 785, 787, **3:**1196, 1197, **4:**1384

Schneier, Bruce, **5:**1904

Schnitzler, Arthur, **2:**441

Schoeman, Ferdinand, **5:**1905

Schoenberg, Arnold, **1:**6, **2:**428, **3:**1176, **4:**1467, **5:**1871

Schoenhals, Michael, **6:**2346

Scholasticism, **3:**1299, **4:**1442, 1632, **5:**2174–2176, 2258

   architecture and, **1:**118

   Aristotelianism and, **1:**134

   casuistry and, **1:**270, 271

   causality and, **1:**272

   critics of, **2:**685

   education and, **2:**632

   free will vs. predestination and, **2:**842

   human rights and, **3:**1015, 1016

   imagination and, **3:**1103, 1105

   intentionality and, **3:**1122

   Islamic humanism and, **3:**1022

   liberty and, **3:**1274

   metaphysics and, **4:**1434, 1435

   monarchy and, **4:**1493

   moral philosophy and, **4:**1790

   philosophy and religion and, **4:**1796

Scholem, Gershon, **4:**1558

Scholes, Robert, **5:**2190

Scholte, Bob, **5:**2024

Schönerer, Georg Ritter von, **5:**1996

*School ad Society, The* (Dewey), **1:**309

   absolute music and, **1:**5

Schooling. *See* Education

School of Ancient Meaning (Japan), **3:**1165

*School of Athens, The* (Raphael fresco), **5:**2009, *2009*

*School of Athens, The* (Stanza), **4:**1774

"School of Evidentiary Research" (China), **1:**lv

Schopenhauer, Arthur, **1:**169, **3:**962, 1194, 1201, **4:**1776, 1797

   aesthetics and, **1:**15

   atheism and, **4:**1797, 1804

   casuality and, **1:**274–275

   continental philosophy and, **2:**467

   Eastern philosophy and, **4:**1778

   feminist critique of, **2:**474

   humor and, **3:**1062

   symbolism and, **5:**2280, 2282

   theodicy and, **2:**748, **6:**2320

Schöpflin, George, **5:**2034

Schor, Naomi, **2:**827

Schotter, Andrew, **3:**855

Schröder, Ernst, **3:**1314

Schrödinger, Edwin, **2:**832, **5:**1975, 1978, 1979

Schrödinger equation, **5:**1979

Schubert, Franz, **4:**1593

Schultz, Theodore, **2:**620, **3:**1013

Schulze, Gottlob Ernst (Aenesidemus), **5:**2211

Schumacher, E. F., **5:**1876, **6:**2462

Schumacher, John N., **1:**lxxiii

Schumpeter, Joseph, **2:**555, 616, 619

Schuré, Édouard, **5:**2283

Schurz, Carl, **5:**2003

Schüssler Fiorenza, Elizabeth, **3:**1271

Schutz, Alfred, **2:**744

Schuyler, George, **1:**29

Schwann, Theodor, **1:**223, **3:**968, **5:**2185

Schwartz, Benjamin, **4:**1476

Schwarzenegger, Arnold, **6:**2494

Schwarzkopf, Norman, **4:**1564

Schwerin, Karl, **2:**728

Schwinger, Julian, **2:**833, **5:**1980

Schwitters, Kurt, **2:**529

Science, **5:**2176–2182

   antifeminism and, **1:**96

   behaviorism and, **1:**207

   bioethics and, **1:**213, 214

*Structural Transformation of the Public Sphere* (Habermas), 2:676, 5:1901

*Structure of Scientific Revolutions, The* (Kuhn), 2:613, 778, 4:1715, 1717, 5:1853, 2177, 2183

*Structures élémentaires de la parenté, Les* (Lévi-Strauss), 2:781

Struensee, Johann Friedrich, 1:294

*Strukturwandel der Öffentlichkeit* (Habermas), 2:676, 5:1901, 1964–1965

Strutt, John William. *See* Rayleigh, Lord

Strzygowski, Josef, 3:1072

Stubbs, William, 1:lxiii, 2:830

Stuck, Franz von, 5:2285

Stück, Leslie, 6:2420–2421

Student activists, Chicano movement, 1:191

Student Nonviolent Coordinating Committee (SNCC), 1:29, 2:707, 6:2491

Student protests, 3:894, 1295, 5:*1836*, 2104, 6:2491

Students against Destructive Decisions, 6:2298

Students for a Democratic Society (SDS), 5:2004

*Studia z metryki polskiej* (Siedlecki), 2:838

*Studies in Iconology* (Panofsky), 3:1075

*Studies in Muslim Apocalyptic* (Cook), 4:1455

*Studies in Themes and Motifs in Literature* (series), 4:1515

*Studies on Hysteria* (Freud and Breuer), 5:1952

*Studio of the Painter, The: A Real Allegory* (Courbet), 1:189, 5:2015

Studites, Theodore, 3:1100

*Study of History, A* (Toynbee), 1:lxxvi, 2:525

*Study of Writing, A* (Gelb), 3:1230

Stumpf, Carl, 4:1526

Sturm, Circe, 4:1596

Sturm, J. C., 2:611

Sturm Gallery (Berlin), 2:770

Sturm und Drang, 5:1821

Sturtevant, Alfred Henry, 3:898

Sturtevant, William, 2:729

*Styles of Scientific Thinking in the European Tradition* (Crombie), 5:2177

Suárez, Francisco, 1:134, 270, 3:1016, 1134, 4:1435, 1608, 5:2260, 2273, 6:2451

Suavi, Ali, 4:1714

Subaltern studies, 1:lxxix
  essentialism critique by, 2:712
  Eurocentrism and, 2:740
  gender studies and, 3:887
  hegemony and, 3:979, 980
  Latin America and, 5:1863
  postcolonial theory and, 5:1859, 1863

Subatomic particles, 1:297, 2:831–832, 834

*Subjection of Women, The* (Mill), 3:1180, 6:2493

Subjectivism, 5:2267–2269
  beauty and, 1:202
  good and, 3:952–953
  objectvity and, 4:1657, 1658
  probability and, 5:1910–1911
  self-consciousness and, 2:443–444
  taste and, 6:2291, 2293–2294
  visual culture and, 6:2424

"Subject of Visual Culture, The" (Mirzoeff), 6:2424

Sublime, 6:2300
  beauty vs., 1:201–202
  classification and, 1:367
  landscape art and, 3:1206, 1207–1208, 1220, 1222
  poetics and, 5:1830

Substantivism, 6:2354

Suburban Psycho-Realism (painting style), 5:2015

"Succession of Forest Trees, The" (Thoreau), 2:612

*Sucesos de las Islas Filipinas* (Morga), 1:lxxiii

Sudan, 1:lxiv, 3:911, 5:2072
  communism and, 5:2236
  Islamic law and, 3:1253
  Islamic state and, 5:2082
  terrorism and, 6:2302

Sudbury, Julia, 2:814

Suetonius, 1:218, 3:1030, 6:2434

Suez Canal, 2:661, 662, 6:2471

Suez Crisis (1956), 2:660, 4:1705

Suffering
  Brahmanism and, 2:450
  Christian persecution and, 6:2338
  evil and, 2:744, 746, 748–749
  theodicy and, 6:2320, 2321

Sufficient Reason, Principle of (Leibniz), 4:1437

Suffrage
  democracy and rise of, 2:554
  inequality and, 2:697, 705, 707
  justice and, 3:1181

Latin American republicanism and, 5:2096
  socialism and, 5:2229
  wealth and, 6:2462
  women and, 2:554, 697, 805, 3:1181, 4:1467

Sufi brotherhood, 2:845, 3:1155
  Africa and, 3:1143, 1144, 1145

Sufism, 2:639, 3:1022, 4:1673, 5:2068, 2269–2270, 6:2297, 2370
  beliefs and practices of, 4:1551–1552, 5:2069
  brotherhoods and, 2:844, 4:1549
  dream paintings and, 2:595
  heaven and hell concept and, 3:972
  Islamic philosophy and, 4:1774–1775
  liberty and, 3:1277
  Manichaeism and, 4:1335
  monism and, 4:1502
  mysticism and, 4:1549, 1550–1552
  origins of, 4:1550–1551
  Southeast Asia and, 3:1149
  Sunni Islam and, 3:1154
  Westernization and, 6:2469

Sufyani, 4:1455

Sugarman, Jane, 4:1527

Suharto, 1:lxxiii

Suhrawardi, 4:1774, 1775

Suicide, 5:2270–2272

*Suicide* (Durkheim), 5:2147, 2271

Suicide bombings, 6:2301, 2303, 2516

*Suicide of Lucretia* (Reni painting), 5:*2271*

Sui dynasty, 2:626, 645

Suka, 1:xlix

Sukhavati (heaven), 3:973

Sulak Sivaraka, 2:624

*Sulalat'us-Salatin* (Malay history), 1:lxxii

Sulami. *See* Abu 'Abd al-Rahman Sulami

Süleyman I (the Magnificent), Ottoman sultan, 4:1455, 1495

Suleyman Chelebi, 3:1126

Sulfa drugs, 4:1408

Sullivan, Harry Stack, 5:1957

Sullivan, Lawrence, 5:2063, 2064, 2065

Sullivan, Michael, 1:10, 3:1222

Sultanate, 4:1495–1496

# For Reference

**Not to be taken from this room**